D1598396

ARTIFICIAL INTELLIGENCE METHODS AND APPLICATIONS

Advanced Series on Artificial Intelligence – Vol. 1

Artificial Intelligence Methods and Applications

Edited by

Nikolaos G. Bourbakis

SUNY – Binghamton
T J Watson School of Applied Science
Department of Electrical and Computer Engineering
New York, USA

Published by

World Scientific Publishing Co. Pte. Ltd.
P O Box 128, Farrer Road, Singapore 9128
USA office: Suite 1B, 1060 Main Street, River Edge, NJ 07661
UK office: 73 Lynton Mead, Totteridge, London N20 8DH

Library of Congress Cataloging-in-Publication data is available.

ARTIFICIAL INTELLIGENCE METHODS AND APPLICATIONS

ISBN 981-02-1057-4

Printed in Singapore by Utopia Press.

INTRODUCTION TO ADVANCED SERIES ON ARTIFICIAL INTELLIGENCE

NIKOLAOS G. BOURBAKIS

A BRIEF INTRODUCTION OF AI

What is Artificial Intelligence (AI)?

The concept of Artificial Intelligence is not as new as it seems to be. It has its roots in Aristotle's time (Greece, 1607 BC): "It would be nice for humans to have intelligent machines to serve them". Only very recently, in the last fifty years, researchers attempted to provide formal definitions for the determination of AI. Here, we provide a few of them:

> "AI is the field of science and engineering concerned with the computational understanding of what is commonly called intelligent behavior, and with the creation of artifacts that exhibit such behavior." [S.C. Shapiro]
>
> "AI is a software that programs use to solve symbolic rather than numeric problems." [Rauch–Hindin]
>
> "AI is the study of how to make computers do things at which, at the present, people are better." [E. Rich]
>
> "AI is the study of intelligence using the ideas and methods of computation." [Brady–Bobrow–Davis]
>
> "AI is the study of intelligent behavior." [Genesereth–Nilsson]
>
> "An AI system is a system which attempts to imitate natural intelligence." [Bench–Capon]
>
> "AI is the science which studies the behavior of intelligent systems.*" [N. Bourbakis]

* Intelligent systems (or machines) are the systems designed and programmed to operate in a way analogous (not necessarily the same) to some human actions, such as sensing, searching, solving problems, learning rules, patterns and concepts, reasoning, extracting and acquiring knowledge in various forms, deciding under uncertainty, developing planning strategies, understanding and interpreting of events, etc.

Which are the Main Subfields of AI?

The AI field can be divided into three major subfields as shown in the following diagram: (i) Perception Systems (PS), (ii) Language Systems (LS) and

(iii) Knowledge Engineering (KE).

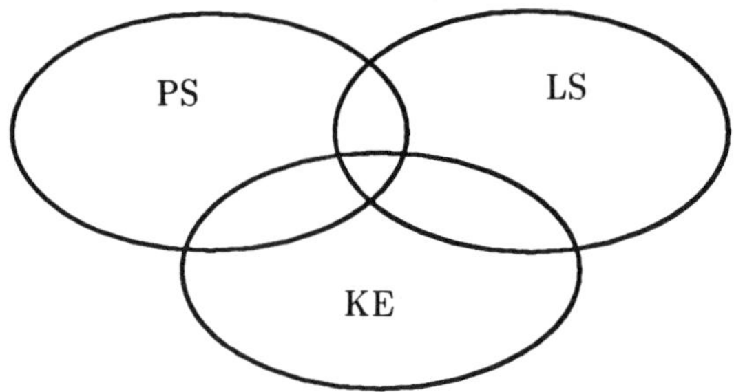

The PS subfield includes sensing systems such as vision, speech, sound, signal, touching. The LS subfield includes AI languages and parsers, natural languages, NL interfaces, machine translation, computational linguistics, AI programming languages, OO programming. The KE subfield includes expert systems, knowledge-bases, knowledge-based systems, rule-based systems, etc.

AI Processes

There is a variety of methods and techniques that can be used and classified as AI processes (mechanisms). Some of them are: searching, solving problems, reasoning, planning, synthesis, recognition, acquisition, explaining, learning, understanding, interpreting, etc.

Where is AI in the Application Domain?

Artificial Intelligence (AI) offers not only a new prospective and a new methodology (frame) for the solution or explanation of complex scientific and application oriented "problems", by making machines behave with intelligence, but also attempts to improve the computational power and abilities of these machines beyond the conventional levels. Moreover, the technological side of AI has been well established by demonstrating a significant variety of commercial applications, such as medical diagnosis systems, investment planning, finance analysis, manufacturing, VLSI chip design/analysis, databases accessing, robotics, education, natural language systems, computer vision systems, simulation, etc.

Availability of AI

The decreasing prices of AI software/hardware and the availability of AI languages and environments for conventional computers and engineering workstations make AI accessible to a large number of corporate and technical people. At the same time, the development of a great variety of AI application tools provide professionals, scientists and application experts the capability of building knowledge-based systems, expert systems, perception systems and natural language (native) interfaces for their applications (i.e. from small databases to complex multimedia systems).

FOREWORD TO THE SERIES

Why Another Series of AI Books

Artificial Intelligence is one of the exponentially growing fields of research with a great variety of applications, especially in the engineering domain. Research groups and individuals have developed various AI methods and techniques by providing several solutions to a variety of important engineering problems and to increasing demands for efficient manipulation of new and old forms of knowledge. Since the few existing series of AI research books are not adequate to cover completely the evolution of the AI field, the series proposed here will respond and contribute to increasing demands by providing high quality work from experts in AI theoretical issues, AI tools development and evaluation, and AI applications.

Aims and the Scope of the Series

The main aim and scope of the series are: the challenge of AI issues, such as evaluation of AI methodologies and tools; natural languages ambiguities, image interpretations, knowledge conversion, etc.; a recent update of AI methods and applications; the promotion of high quality new ideas, techniques and methodologies in the AI field; and the presentation of AI tools in an effort to fill the gap between AI theory and AI applications.

Benefits for the Reader

The first two books of this series are the introductory volumes that address a number of AI issues. The subsequent volumes will focus more on various AI topics providing the state-of-the-art in a selected AI topic. Some of the benefits for readers will be:

- Covering of AI topics and addressing their importance in the application domain.

- Providing a quick updating on the AI field and many AI applications.
- Addressing new AI problems and suggesting approaches for them. Providing ideas for the development of AI tools.
- An excellent set of AI methodologies and tools.
- A fruitful ground of references from the AI field.
- An overview of the existing AI techniques and tools.
- New ideas and techniques for AI problems and engineering applications.

The Main Audience of the Series

The main audience of the series will be: researchers in the AI field; professionals from industries related with AI; university professors working on AI topics; graduate students (especially at the Ph.D. level); AI professionals working with the Government; individuals that want to learn more about AI and AI tools.

PROLOGUE

This book is the first volume of a series in advances in AI. Its aim is to respond quickly to engineering demands by providing classical and recent AI methods and techniques related with theoretical aspects, such as logic, solving search problems, genetic algorithms and learning schemes, reasoning and planning strategies, etc., AI languages and architectures. Moreover, it also includes significant applications in a variety of areas, such as parallel processing, vision, speech, OCR, signal undersatnding and VLSI.

This particular book, entitled *Artificial Intelligence Methods and Applications*, combines collectively the efforts of 43 specialists in various AI subfields by covering theoretical and application issues. It features algorithms, languages and architectures which represent the state-of-the-art in several AI subregions.

It is organized into seven main sections: The first section deals with Horn logic. In particular, it presents methods for reasoning about Horn logic theories including personal suggestions for some AI issues. Section 2 deals with searching methods. It comprises two chapters. The first chapter covers several approaches of using optimization methods to solve search problems, with emphasis on the satisfiability (SAT) problem. The second chapter discusses an application of genetic algorithms to the permutation problem where the standard approaches to intermixing genes leads to longer search chains. Section 3 deals with learning. The first chapter presents a logical framework to induce concept descriptions from a given set of examples and counter examples in the presence of background knowledge described by a set of Horn classes. The second chapter discusses the application of genetic algorithms to a symbolic learning task, supervised concept learning from examples. The third chapter presents a software system (PM), which automates the software reuse process, extracting procedural knowledge from software systems using inductive learning. The fourth section deals with planning strategies and contains two chapters. Its first chapter discusses a new paradigm for constructing a partially ordered plan network, referred to as "resource-oriented parallel planning" (RPP), where goal-states are grouped into a collection of goal states subsets associated with a particular resource. The second chapter deals with a methodology for path planning in a 3-D environment. A knowledge based system is used to incorporate efficiently the robot model and the workspace representation for planning collision free paths of the multilinked walking robots. Section 5 deals with AI languages in four chapters. The first chapter presents a parser generator for advanced applications, such as developing a knowledge based shell, and describes the parsing technology on which it is based. The second chapter discusses the potential use of object-oriented programming (OOP) in developing natural language processing (NLP) systems. It presents TARO, an interactive OO tool, implemented in KSL, for building natural language processing systems. The third chapter discusses technical issues of spoken language translation and describes one of the first experimental systems developed so far. The fourth chapter evaluates the execution efficiency of AI related problems written in various languages and run in different system architectures. The sixth section deals with AI architectures and comprises five chapters. The first chapter provides a generalized analysis and synthesis of intelligent systems by using a Petri-net representation structure. The second chapter discusses the past, present and future evolution of the AI programming languages and AI architectures by covering a great variety of them. The third chapter proposes a dataflow algorithmic translation and dataflow architectures for implementing parallel machine learning computations with applications in robotics. The fourth chapter presents an evaluation of a variety of semantic network architectures. The fifth chapter provides a quick survey on artificial neural and neuromorphic models with emphasis on the Athena and Hermes systems. The seventh section deals with AI applications. It consists of five chapters. The first chapter presents the specifications for the development of a knowledge-based image understanding system by using graph models. The second chapter describes the architecture of a reading machine to achieve a high rate of correct interpretations of text. The reading machine is used for recognition of character and postal addresses. The third chapter studies the feasibility of using machine learning techniques to support the development of speech understanding systems. The fourth chapter presents the results of a study of recognizing a variety of signal modulations in a radio spectrum. The fifth chapter describes a knowledge-based environment for integrated circuits testing. The environment employs knowledge base technology to achieve its operational requirements. It also provides the implementation and applications of testing VLSI circuits.

This book can be used by: AI professionals as an excellent set of AI methodologies and tools; graduate students as a complementary AI text with numerous techniques and examples; and researchers in AI as a quick reference on recent achievements in the AI field.

CONTRIBUTORS

- S. Aletan, *Louisiana Tech, LA*
- W. Arden, *Telos Corp., NJ*
- N. Bourbakis, *SUNY, Binghamton, NY*
- B. Buckles, *Tulane Univ., LA*
- J. Carter, *Drexel Univ., PA*
- G. Castrodale, *Duke Univ., NC*
- Y. P. Chien, *Purdue Univ. at Indianapolis, IN*
- K. Chung, *Soongsil Univ., Seoul, Korea*
- P. Cullen, *SUNY, Buffalo, NY*
- A. Dollas, *Duke Univ., NC*
- K. De Jong, *George Mason Univ., VA*
- J. Delgado-Frias, *SUNY, Binghamton, NY*
- J. Goshtasbi, *Pennsylvania State Univ., PA*
- T. Gowrishankar, *Univ. of Illinois at Chicago, IL*
- J. Gu, *Univ. of Calgary, Canada*
- S. Herath, *Southwest Texas State Univ., TX*
- J. Herath, *Drexel Univ., PA*
- T. Ho, *SUNY, Buffalo, NY*
- R. Hughes, *E-Systems Inc., VA*
- M. Ibrahim, *EDS Corp., AI Div., MI*
- J. Kipps, *Univ. of California at Irvine, CA*
- H. Kitano, *Carnegie Mellon Univ., PA*
- E. Kounalis, *Univ. of Rouen, France*
- C. Koutsougeras, *Tulane Univ., LA*
- S. Lam, *SUNY, Buffalo, NY*
- S. Lee, *Univ. of Southern California, Los Angeles and JPL, Caltech, CA*
- M. Loos, *E-Systems Inc., VA*
- W. Mahood, *E-Systems Inc., VA*
- J. Maletic, *Wayne State Univ., MI*
- P. Marquis, *CRIN-CRNS and INRIA, Univ. of Nancy II, France*
- D. McNeill, *E-Systems Inc., VA*
- F. Petry, *Tulane Univ., LA*
- R. Reynolds, *Wayne State Univ., MI*
- M. Rusinowitch, *Univ. of Rouen, France*
- P. Sheu, *Rutgers Univ., NJ*

- W. Spears, *NRL, Washington, DC*
- S. Srihari, *SUNY, Buffalo, NY*
- S. Twohig, *Louisiana Tech, LA*
- G. Triantafyllos, *IBM Glendale, NY*
- S. Vassiliadis, *IBM Glendale, NY*
- J. Whelchel, *E-Systems Inc., VA*
- Q. Xue, *Purdue Univ. at Indianapolis, IN*
- E. Zannoni, *Wayne State Univ., MI*

CONTENTS

SECTION 1: **LOGIC**

SECTION 2: **SEARCHING**

Chapter 2: ON OPTIMIZING A SEARCH PROBLEM
by J. Gu

Chapter 3: APPLICATION OF GENETIC ALGORITHMS TO PERMUTATION PROBLEMS
by F. E. Petry and B. P. Buckles

SECTION 3: **LEARNING**

Chapter 8: PATH PLANNING FOR A MULTI-LINKED WALKING ROBOT IN A 3-D ENVIRONMENT
by Q. Xue, P. C. Y. Sheu and Y.-P. Chien

SECTION 5: **AI LANGUAGES**

Chapter 9: ADVANCED PARSING TECHNOLOGY FOR KNOWLEDGE-BASED SHELLS
by J. R. Kipps

Chapter 15: PERFORMANCE ANALYSIS OF AN ASYNCHRONOUS DATAFLOW COMPUTING MACHINE FOR PARALLEL MACHINE LEARNING
by J. Carter, S. Herath and J. Herath

Chapter 16: ARCHITECTURAL SCHEMES FOR SEMANTIC NETWORKS
by J. G. Delgado-Frias, S. Vassiliadis, J. Goshtasbi and G. Triantafyllos

SECTION 1

LOGIC

CHAPTER 1

FUNDAMENTAL METHODS FOR HORN LOGIC AND ARTIFICIAL INTELLIGENCE APPLICATIONS

Emmanuel KOUNALIS
Laboratoire d'Informatique de Rouen
Université de Rouen
B.P. 118 - Place Emile Blondel
76134 Mont-Saint-Aignant, FRANCE

Pierre MARQUIS
CRIN-CNRS and INRIA-Lorraine
Université de Nancy II
B.P. 239 - Campus Scientifique
54506 Vandœuvre-lès-Nancy Cedex, FRANCE

ABSTRACT. Universally-quantified Horn theories, *i.e.*, sets of formulas of the form $\forall x_1, ..., x_n$ (P $\Rightarrow$ L), occur frequently in many Artificial Intelligence problems including Automated Theorem Proving, Expert Systems, Machine Learning, Program Synthesis, Planning, Diagnosis ... This paper presents rewrite methods for reasoning about Horn theories, including personal suggestions to approach some of the issues which have been recently addressed in AI.

The presentation is partly informal, and aimed at practice; we unfold this material through the medium of examples each of which illustrates not only its expressive power but also its flexibility in manipulation.

This paper is not intended to be complete, nor does it claim that rewrite methods are superior to any other methods. However, it hoped that, despite these limitations, this material may be used both in defining and in reasoning about Artificial Intelligence systems.

1 INTRODUCTION

1.1 The Scope and Motivation of this Chapter

Most Artificial Intelligence programs are quite complex objects and mastering their complexity is a major research goal. Progress in that domain relies both on experience and theory. Recently, interest has been concentrated on developing formal methods and tools for the systematic construction of sound AI programs. This is due in part to the growing realization that AI programs are often wrong, that debugging is often a large part of their cost, and that the cost of developing AI software can be a large part of the overall cost of developing a complex AI system. A comprehensive study of the problems that exist in AI programs requires a precise formalization so that detailed analyses can be carried out and satisfactory solutions can be obtained.

Most of the formal AI studies that are underway at present use *Mathematical Logic* as their framework. A logic-based study is primarily concerned with representing in the realm of mathematical logic the real-word entities that comprise its subject matter. The representation should facilitate the discovery of mathematical relationships in the form of formulas. Any such interpretation increases our understanding of, and systematizes our knowledge about, the subject domain. But a more immediate reason for representing entities derives from the fact that it usually leads to significant pratical advances.

The revelance of logic to AI should be clear. First, logic is at the heart of reasoning, and reasoning is at the heart of intelligence. Second, the wide variety of systems of logic offers an equally wide variety of formats for representing information (together with built-in inferences mechanisms). Thus the expressive power of various logics has become one of the central aspects of the field of knowledge representation: *Temporal Logic* has been used to reason about actions and plans, *Modal Logic* has been applied to knowledge and action, *Fuzzy Logic* has been used to expert systems and to perform approximate reasoning, *Non-monotonic Logic* is the basis for default reasoning, ...

Horn Logic, a restriction of first-order logic, has provided a most useful logical basis for many AI applications including Expert Systems, Logic Programming (which is, strictly speaking, just a restricted form of Automated Theorem Proving), Program Specification, Planning, Program Synthesis, ... A (universal) *Horn theory* is just a set of formulas over some language A(F, P, X) built out of a set F of function symbols, of a set P of predicate symbols, and of a countably infinite set X of variables. Each such a formula is of the form $P \Rightarrow L$ where the *head* (conclusion) L is an atom and the *body* (condition) P is a conjunction of atoms. We often consider Horn theories in which the conclusion is an equation, *i.e.*, L is of the form $t = s$ where t and s are terms in A(F, P, X). The motivations for using Horn logic for AI problems stem from at least three reasons:

a) Horn logic is a simple implicative formalism, and many AI problems have a natural implicative form for given statements and a single positive statement or an implication as the consequence that supposedly "follows" from the given statements.

b) Horn logic is computability powerful: Every partial recursive function can be computed by a Horn program,

c) Horn logic contains a number of methods and techniques which are established in a rigorous mathematical framework.

Now the ability to *reason* about Horn theories and *compute* with them is important in many Artificial Intelligence problems. As in any other logical theory, reasoning about Horn theories may involve deciding if a Horn formula "follows" as a consequence of a given set of Horn formulas or if a Horn formula is true in a given model, or what values of the variables satisfy a given Horn formula ... When a Horn theory is regarded as a set of "oriented" formulas (that is, as a conditional rewrite system), it may be used to compute, *i.e.*, to reduce expressions to normal (canonical) form.

A Horn logic-based study of an AI problem is mainly concerned with first representing in the language of Horn logic the objects that comprise its subject matter, and second discovering of their relationships in the form of Horn formulas. When Horn logic is used in this manner, Horn formulas *state properties* that hold between objects. Consider for example the following set H of Horn formulas for left-cancellative monoids:

1. $x.1 = x$
2. $1.x = x$
3. $x.(y.z) = (x.y).z$
4. $x.y = x.z \Rightarrow y = z$

We might wish to know if another Horn formula:

$$x.(1.(y.(1.z))) = (1.x).((1.w).s) \Rightarrow y.z = w.s$$

is a consequence of H, that is, is true in all left-cancellative monoids. This is a typical example of "reasoning" about Horn theories. It is well-known that such a Horn formula $P \Rightarrow t = s$ can be shown to "follow" as a consequence of a given Horn theory H by using the inferences rules for Horn logic with equality, *e.g.*, the *cut* rule, the *substitution* rule, and the rule of *replacement* equal from equals, provided that the variables in P are treated as constants. If the Horn formula is positive unit (*i.e.*, a Horn formula with empty body, *e.g.*, an equation) these inferences rules are *sound* (*i.e.*, applying them for deducing new Horn formulas always yield Horn formulas that are true in *all* (first-order) models of a given Horn theory H) and *complete* (*i.e.*, every positive unit Horn formula which is true in *all* models of a given Horn theory H can be deduced using these rules). These two properties imply that, for the class of (first-order) models satisfying a given set of Horn formulas, the *model theoretic* notion of a positive unit Horn formula being a consequence of a given set of Horn formulas coincides with the *proof theoretic* notion of a positive unit Horn formula being derivable from a given set of Horn formulas by the inferences rules of Horn logic. This set of inferences rules was shown to be sound and complete with respect to positive unit Horn formulas in (Padawitz, 1988). However this set of rules is not complete with respect to general Horn formulas. Using the technique of Skolemization it is possible to derive also Horn formulas with this inference system. For a complete and sound set of inferences rules for Horn logic without using Skolemization, see (Selman, 1971). Note that, a complete set of inference rules for equational logic has already been given by (Birkhoff, 1935).

Horn formulas may also be viewed as *definitions*. The use of Horn formulas as definitions is well known in Computer Science and Artificial Intelligence since programs written in (first-order) LISP-like functional (applicative) languages, and in PROLOG-like logic programming languages are clearly of this nature. When Horn formulas are definitions, they may be used to *compute*. For example, consider the following recursive program H (Horn formulas) which defines the greatest common divisor (gcd) of two natural numbers:

1. gcd(x, x) = x
2. 0 < x = true ∧ x < y = true ⇒ gcd(x, y) = gcd(y - x, x)
3. 0 < y = true ∧ y < x = true ⇒ gcd(x, y) = gcd(x - y, y)
4. x < y = false ⇒ succ(x) < succ(y) = false
5. x < y = true ⇒ succ(x) < succ(y) = true
6. x < 0 = false
7. 0 < succ(x) = true
8. x - 0 = x
9. 0 - x = 0
10. succ(x) - succ(y) = x - y

We can use those definitions to *compute*, say:

gcd(succ(succ(0)), succ(succ(succ(succ(0)))))

into normal form **succ(succ(0))**. However, reasoning about Horn formulas considered as definitions requires more than just first-order reasoning: Some kind of *induction* is necessary. For instance, it is well know that < is a total ordering on the natural numbers, or that gcd satisfies the commutativity law, but proving these theorems requires using induction schemata, for example, on the structure of natural numbers. The reason for this lies in that every set of Horn formulas actually defines a (isomorphic class of) model, called the *standard model*, which gives the meaning of the symbols involved in the formulas. Thus, the previous Horn formulas are valid for all natural numbers, which constitute a standard model of H. This is a typical example of asking whether a Horn formula is true in a specific model, which is the distinguished (standard) interpretation, we have in mind, when we write down this set of Horn formulas. And of course, for all main applications in AI, the attention is often focused on those formulas which are true in a standard model. Unfortunately, there is no a simple proof theory which captures the semantic notion of the standard model. According to Gödel's incompleteness theorem for arithmetic there does not exist a complete system for the set of all first-order formulas that are true in the standard model of natural numbers. To overcome this problem, one uses formula schemata to formulate induction axioms which are used to prove formulas for validity in the standard model. However, no (recursively axiomatizable) set of induction schemata is strong enough to constitute a complete theory the model of which is the standard model.

We attempt here to give a clear undertanding of the the various semantics one can associate with Horn theories and the methods available for reasoning about them and computing with them. We show that these reasoning abilities are also important in many AI applications including Automated Theorem Proving, Machine Learning, Program Synthesis, and Diagnosis.

A/ Automated Theorem Proving

"Automated Theorem Proving" is the activity in which computers are programmed to prove, or help prove, which formulas of some logical system are either theorems or not. Theorem-proving programs are usually forms from first-order logic or its restriction, Horn logic. In the case of Horn logic the general problem of Automated Theorem Proving may be decomposed in three activities, which are formulated as follows:

a) Verify whether a given Horn theory H is *satisfiable* (*i.e.*, verify whether H admits a model),

b) Decide whether a Horn formula C is a *deductive theorem* of a given Horn theory H (*i.e.*, whether C is true in all first-order models of a H),

c) Check whether or not a Horn formula is an *inductive theorem* of a given Horn theory H (*i.e.*, check whether C is true in all Herbrand models or in the least Herbrand – initial – model of H).

For a simple example, consider the following set H of Horn formulas, we want to check for satisfiability, *i.e.*, to verify if H has a model:

1. 0 < succ(x)
2. x < y ⇒ succ(x) < succ(y)
3. x < 0 ⇒

In general, to verify whether H has a model we use theorem-proving techniques. The most widely used techniques are the resolution-based inference rules, where a set of Horn formulas is unsatisfiable if and only if the empty clause is derivable from the set of formulas by resolution. Now, by applying successively the (unconstrained) resolution rule to our example, an infinite set of formulas is generated. However, if we use the maximal atom strategy presented in these notes, there is no resolvent between the formulas, because *x < y is smaller than x < succ(y))* with respect to some ordering on the Herbrand Universe of the Horn theory under consideration. Therefore, any prover which uses the maximal atom strategy will simply stop and report "satisfiable".

Matters get more complicated when the equality relation appears in a Horn theory. Part of this complication is due to the difficulties resulting from simply axiomatizing it. Dealing effectively with the equality relation is notoriously difficult. Simply adding equality axioms almost invariably leads to unacceptable inefficiencies. Consider, for example, the following set of Horn formulas which defines the *inf_or_equal* predicate on the set of integers, where **0**, **pred**, and **succ** represent the zero, predecessor and successor functions respectively:

1. x = x
2. succ(pred(x**))** = x
3. pred(succ(x**))** = x
4. inf(0, 0) = **true**
5. inf(0, p(0)) = **true**
6. inf(0, x) = **true** ⇒ **inf(0, succ(x))** = **true**
7. inf(0, x) = **false** ⇒ **inf(0, succ(x))** = **false**
8. inf(succ(x), y) = **inf(x, pred(y))**
9. inf(pred(x), y) = **inf(x, succ(y))**
10. true = **false** ⇒

Suppose we want to check H for satisfiability. To verify satisfiability of Horn theories (as any other first-order theory) with equality, the inference rule of *paramodulation* is used. However, using the paramodulation rule to our example without any restriction, an infinite set of formulas is generated. Now, if we use the set INF of inferences rules presented in these notes, we shall stop after deriving two new formulas (see Section 4.1) and report "satisfiable".

We provide here a complete set of inferences rules for Horn logic which are mainly based on rewrite concepts. This set severely restricts applications of resolution with paramodulation by incorporating an ordering on (atoms) and terms. Inferences are limited in the following ways:

a) Paramodulation into variables is avoided, and

b) The axioms of equality are not needed (except x = x), and

c) Resolution and paramodulation inferences always involves the maximal atoms of the parent formulas, where the maximality notion is defined relatively to a complete simplification ordering on the Herbrand Universe.

Consider now the following Horn theory H of positive integers with addition, and the even, and odd predicates:

1. 0 + x = x
2. succ(x) + y = **succ(x + y)**
3. x + **0** = x
4. x + **succ(y)** = **succ(x + y)**
5. even(0) = **true**

6. even(succ(0)) = false
7. even(succ(succ(x))) = even(x)
8. even(x) = true ⇒ odd(x) = false
9. even(x) = false ⇒ odd(x) = true

Suppose we want to determine (decide) whether the conjectures, say:

10. odd(succ(0)) = true
11. even(succ(succ(succ(0))) = false
12. odd(succ(succ(succ(0)))) = even(succ(succ(succ(0)))))

are deductive theorems of H (*i.e.*, whether they are true in all first-order models of H).

One way of deciding this consists in "compiling" H into a set of rewrite rules R (*i.e.*, formulas of the form $P \Rightarrow t \rightarrow s$) and using R to reduce expressions to canonical form. There have been many attempts to design procedures to compile an *equational theory* (*i.e.*, a set of equations (positive unit Horn formulas)) into a *canonical rewrite system* (*i.e.*, is a set of rewrite rules which repeatedly replace subterms of a given term with equal terms until the simplest possible term is obtained, regardless of the nondeterministic choices made). The extension to Horn theories is difficult. We provide here a set, called CINF, of inferences rules that allows us to compile Horn theories into canonical sets of formulas. CINF offers flexibility and large applicability, since:

a) It allows non-orientable equations in the conclusions of formulas, and

b) The pre-conditions of a Horn formula need not be smaller than the rule itself nor to be lower in a hierarchy of symbol.

c) It allows extra variables in the conditions of Horn formulas.

Finally, the ability to prove theorems whose proof usually requires *induction* is very important in many Computer Science and Artificial Intelligence applications including Program Verification, High-level Programming Languages, Machine Learning ... Consider, for example, the following conjectures of the even-odd definition stated above:

13. $x + y = y + x$
14. $(x + y) + z = x + (y + z)$
15. even(x + x) = true
16. odd(x + x) = false

It can be seen that for all non-negative integer values of x, y, and z these conjectures are consequences of the given Horn theory H. In other words these formulae are valid in Peano arithmetic. This suggest to prove them using mathematical induction, *i.e.*, using applications of Peano's induction schemata. To accomplish the task classical theorem proving provides explicit induction or inductionless induction which tries to get rid of induction steps by switching to consistency proofs. However, one of the hardest problems in using either approaches is to find induction schemata which describe suitably the infinitely many premises needed for the proof or (disproof) of the theorem. Further, both methods have many limitations either on the theorems to be proved or on the underlying theory. For instance, explicit induction is unable to provide us automatically with suitable induction schemata, and cannot disprove false conjectures. On the other hand, the inductionless induction technique often fails where explicit induction succeeds. Morever, there does not exist any realistic inductionless induction for Horn theories.

We show in these notes how to prove (or disprove) automatically inductive theorems in Horn theories, and how the method applies to handle simple fragments of arithmetic This method has a large effective applicativity since:

a) It does not restrict itself to equational theories: General formulas can be proved (or refuted) to be inductive theorems in theories axiomatized by a set of Horn formulas,

b) It does not use completion-based methods, conditional simplification is the only inference rule, and

c) It find automatically induction schemata which describe suitably the infinitely many premises needed for the proof (or disproof) of the theorem.

B/ Learning

"Learning" is a broad term covering a wide range of processes including the acquisition of new declarative knowledge, the organization of new knowledge into general, effective representations, and the discovery of new facts and theories through observation and experimentation. A central process in many kind of learning is the process of *generalization* or *concept learning* from a set of training instances (a set of examples and counterexamples) in presence of some background knowledge described by a Horn theory.

For example, consider the problem of learning a concept about heights of arches built out of blocks. The following Horn theory H describes the background knowledge about arches:

1. higherthan(x, y) $\Rightarrow$ higherthan(plus1(x), y)
2. higherthan(plus1(b), b)

where **higherthan(x,y)** means that arch x is higher than arch y, **plus1(x)** designs the arch obtained by pushing a block on the top of the arch x, and **b** is a constant symbol which designes the empty arch. Thus, **higherthan(x, y) $\Rightarrow$ higherthan(plus1(x), y)** expresses the rule: If arch x is higher than arch y, then the arch which obtained by pushing a block on the top of x will be higher than y. On the other hand, the positive unit formula **higherthan(plus1(b), b)** expresses the fact that the arch with one block on the top of the empty arch is higher than the empty arch. If we now consider the examples:

higherthan(plus1(b), b)
higherthan(plus1(plus1(b)), b)

higherthan(plus1(plus1(b)), plus1(b))
higherthan(plus1(plus1(plus1(b))), b)
higherthan(plus1(plus1(plus1(b))), plus1(plus1(b))) ...

and the counter examples:

higherthan(b, b)
higherthan(b, plus1(b))
higherthan(b, plus1(plus1(b)))
higherthan(b, plus1(plus1(plus1(b))))
higherthan(plus1(b), plus1(plus1(b)))
higherthan(plus1(b), plus1(plus1(plus1(b)))) ...

then the examples and the counter examples can be generalized, by a variable binding mechanism, *i.e.*, by substituing variables for terms, to get the formula:

G' ≡ **higherthan(x, y) / higherthan(z, z)** ∨ **higherthan(b, plus1(z))**

By using the methods presented in this paper we get a new formula G ≡ **higherthan(plus1(z), b)** from G'. G is the desired concept description (G is a generalization) since it is *"consistent"* with the given set of training instances (examples and counterexamples) and the background knowledge. In other words,

a) G matches every example and no counter example, and
b) Geliminates some models of H, and
c) G is true in the least Herbrand model of H.

Thus, G expresses the concept: "Any arch with at least one block is higher than the empty arch".

We show here how to induce general concept descriptions from a set of training instances (a set examples and counterexamples) in presence of some background knowledge described by a Horn theory.

C/ Program Synthesis

"Program synthesis" is the derivation of a program from a given specification. For example, consider the specification S_{double}:

1. **double(x)** = x + x

of a function to *double a nonnegative integer* and suppose we are given the following facts D (domain knowledge) about addition:

2. x + 0 = x
3. x + **succ(y)** = **succ(x + y)**

4. succ(x) + y = succ(x + y)

A *correct recursive program* R for doubling nonnegative integers may be the following:

5. double(0) → 0
6. double(succ(x)) → succ(succ(double(x)))

This system R is a *correct recursive program* in the sense that:

a) It does not use addition for doubling,

b) It terminates, *i.e.*, no infinite derivation are possible,

c) It is correct with respect to the specification S_{double} and the domain knowledge D, *i.e.*, it preserves the standard model of $S_{double} \cup D$.

In general all synthesized programs should meet these requirements. The rationale for these requirements is that *computation* is the transformation (simplification) of a ground term to its normal form.

The methods, we propose here are used to develop a new automatic method of deriving (conditional) equational provably correct computer programs which meet the requirements pointed out above. Domain knowledge and specifications are given as sets of (conditional) equations and *purely (algebraic) simplification* is the engine used to generate target programs. In general, our approach regards program synthesis as a transformational task that combines features of deduction and induction within a single framework. We shall show application of our method to the derivation of primitive recursive programs computing on domains such as integers, lists ...

D/ Diagnosis

“Diagnosing” a system consists of inferring its real state from its observed behaviour. As far as logic-based diagnosis is concerned, two main approaches have been proposed. On one hand, the consistency-based approach consists of explaining the discrepancy between the observed behaviour of a system and its expected one, derived from its description. This approach is essentially *deductive* in the sense that the “abnormal” parts of the resulting possible states of a system can be derived by deduction from what is known. On the other hand, the *abductive* approach to diagnostic consists of explaining directly the observed behaviour of a system by formulating hypothetical states that support what is observed given what is already known.

For example, consider the circuit CIRC as described below, where the components are inverters. The following description SD of the system CIRC represents the correct model of the components, their types, the connexions of CIRC, the negation laws and the independence of the logical values:

$$SD = \{\forall x\ ((\mathbf{inv}(x) \wedge \mathbf{ok}(x)) \Rightarrow (\mathbf{out}(x) = \mathbf{not}(\mathbf{in}(x)))),\ \mathbf{inv}(c1),\ \mathbf{inv}(c2),\ \mathbf{out}(c1) = \mathbf{in}(c2),\ \mathbf{not}(O) = 1,\ \mathbf{not}(1) = 0,\ \neg(0 = 1)\}.$$

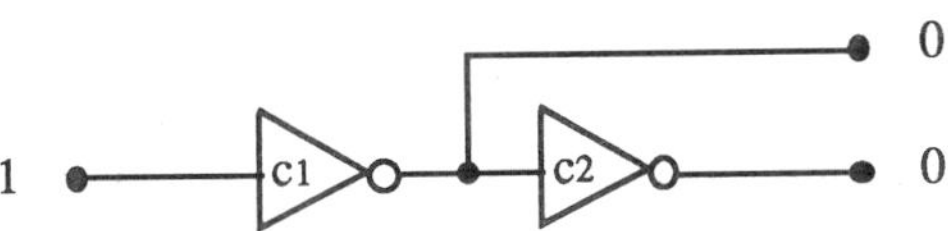

The observations OBS of CIRC are I ∪ O with I = {**in(c1) = 1**} and O = {**out(c1) = 0, out(c2) = 0**}.

We shall show here how our complete set of inference rules can be used to compute consistency-based diagnoses and abductive diagnoses. For the axiomatization of the two-inverters circuit described above, it allows us to derive one consistency-based diagnosis, namely **(ok(c1)** ∧ ¬**ok(c2))** and one abductive diagnosis for the output **out(c1) = 0**, namely **ok(c1)**.

1.2 The Character of Rewrite Methods

In this section, we discuss the demanding criteria we would like a set of methods to meet in order to allow us to describe succintly and to manipulate a wide variety of AI problems which use Horn logic as a framework.

A useful set of methods and tools for reasoning about Horn systems as of anything else, must have a high level of articulacy implying not only richness in expression but also flexibility in manipulation. It should be possible to reason about existing systems, to be used to describe new ones and to argue in a formal way about them.

Apart from articulacy, the presented set of rewrite methods for reasoning about Horn systems are based on a small well-defined collection of concepts which justifies the manipulations of them. This is very important since understanding them and assessing them is only possible if they can be seen a logical growth from a very small number of assumptions and concepts.

For example, the notion of first-order terms often used for representing data objects, programs, and computations is the most primitive layer on the top of which any other tool may be constructed. The use of appropriate operations on terms, *e.g.*, replacement, allows us to design powerful algorithms for matching or unifying two terms. Matching and unification are two of the most important mechanisms in AI.

On the other side, rewrite systems have been widely used for computation in formula manipulation and equational-logic systems. They also provide a paradigm of computation that combines the clean syntax and semantics of both PROLOG-like logic programming and (first-order) LISP-like functional (applicative) programming in a uniform matter. The whole theory of rewrite systems is based on the abstract diagrammatic properties of a binary relation, called *reduction*, and the operation of replacement of terms.

We finally want to consider some sociological points about using Horn logic and the presented methods for reasoning about it. It seems to be common in AI that the introduction of new formal methods is always met with some scepticism. It may be said that "no open problems have been solved", and that "the use of this additional machinery is unjustified". This was the case for logic programming. It was introduced in an article by Kowalski in 1974 and for a long time not much happened. But now, 17 years latter, several hundred papers on it have been published. Of course, the first task of any method must be to re-express exist results; but the real success comes with new results. This is not to deny the possibility of a technique which is genuiely unsuitable, trivial, wrong, over-complex, or over-sophisticated. We believe that rewriting methods have proved themselves in regards of such criticisms, since they applied succesfully on a wide class of problems going from high-level programming languages to hardware verification.

1.3 Some History and Relations to Other Approaches

Rewrite methods do not, in our view, compete with other approaches to reason about AI problems. Rather, they complement other approaches for those who like logical style, by providing simplicity in manipulation and generality and efficiency in application.

Automated Theorem Proving has become a field by itself when J.A. Robinson (Robinson, 1965) invented the resolution principle, which combines several rules of first-order logic with a single and compact one. The *resolution* rule of inference is an extension of the standard *modus ponens* rule in logic, which permits the derivation of P from Γ and $\Gamma \Rightarrow$ P. Resolution simply states that if C is the formula (L, $\Gamma \Rightarrow$ P) and D is the formula ($\Delta \Rightarrow$ L') such that L and L' are unifiable with mgu σ, then ($\Gamma\sigma$, $\Delta\sigma \Rightarrow P\sigma$) is a resolvent of C and D. Thus, a set of Horn clauses is unsatisfiable if and only if the empty clause is derivable from the set of clauses by resolution and resolution is *refutation complete*. About twenty years ago (see (Chang and Lee, 1973) for references) some efficient and general-purpose theorem proving systems based on resolution in first-order logic without equality were developed and used to prove theorems which have not previously been proved automatically.

Morever, the special relation of equality is so common in (first-order) theories that a special treatement is given in mechanical theorem proving procedures. It is well known that any first-order theory with equality is expressible as a first-order theory in which the equality symbol is uninterpreted, since the axioms of equality, including functional reflexivity, are themselves (Horn) formulas. Thus, resolution, or any other variation of resolution which is refutation complete for first-order theories, could be used to verify satisfiability of first-order theories with equality, but the cost of treating equality axioms like any other formula is prohibitively high. For this reason, special inference rules have been devised for reasoning about equality, for example, *paramodulation* (Wos and Robinson, 1969). Paramodulation improves the resolution procedure by performing term replacement steps instead of sequences of resolutions with equational axioms.

Paramodulation is an equality inference rule that perform substitution directly. The paramodulant rule states that if C is a formula ($\Gamma \Rightarrow s = t$), and D be another formula ($\Delta, L \Rightarrow P$) such that a subtem s', occurring at n in the atom L, is unifiable with s with mgu σ, then ($\Gamma\sigma, \Delta\sigma, L[n \leftarrow t] \Rightarrow P\sigma$) is a paramodulant of C into D at n. Resolution plus paramodulation is complete provided the functional reflexive axioms (axioms such as f(x,y) = f(x,y)) are included (see (Wos and Robinson, 1969) for details).

Since that time, many work has been focused on the so-called "functional reflexive problem", that is, the problem of proving that resolution and paramodulation is complete without functional reflexive axioms (see, for instance, (Brand, 1975), (Brown, 1975), (Lankford, 1975)). The reason for this lies in that paramodulation is a very weak inference rule because it produces mountains of irrelevant formulas which rapidly clog the search space. In (Brand, 1975) an indirect proof of this problem (as a corollary of the completeness of modification method) was given. A direct proof was given in (Peterson, 1983). A generalization of this proof was suggested by (Hsiang and Rusinowitch, 1986) and (Rusinowitch, 1989). At the core of the method is the notion of *complete simplification ordering* on Herbrand Universe. Intuitively, this type of well-founded ordering takes into account the syntactic structure of terms when comparing them. The E-interpretations, *i.e.*, the Herbrand interpretations which preserve the equality axioms, can be built (transfinite) inductively with respect to these orderings. The collection of these E-interpretations forms a (transfinite) E-semantic tree. These ideas have been served as a basis on developing completeness of theorem proving strategies involving equality by minimizing the amount of paramodulation, while maximizing the amount of simplification, without threatening completeness using rewrite methods. For several further restrictions of paramodulation for the full first-order case, see (Rusinowitch, 1989). This work was the first treating the completeness of theorem proving strategies in presence of simplification rules. Further work on this area was announced by (Kapur and Zhang, 1988) and by (Bachmair and Ganzinger, 1990a). Based on the work by (Hsiang and Rusinowitch, 1986), (Kounalis and Rusinowitch, 1987 and 88) (see also (Kounalis and Rusinowitch, 1991a)) have proposed a complete set of inference rules for Horn logic with, in addition, specific strategies for simplification.

In 1970, Knuth-Bendix working independently of Robinson and Wos, developed a very efficient procedure, so-called *completion* procedure, for deriving useful consequences from sets of equations (positive unit formulas). Their procedure is still based on paramodulation, but since it also used *demodulation (simplification)* (Wos *et al.*, 1967) and subsumption removal, most of the derived equations were discarded. The main idea they promote was the concept of *complete sets of reductions* (*canonical rewrite systems*). They showed that canonical rewrite systems may be used to decide if an equation "follows" as a deductive consequence of a given equational theory (*i.e.*, the *validity problem* in the given theory - in other words, the truth of an equation in the class of all models of the given theory): To determine if two terms are equal, the rules are repeatedly applied to both terms until unextendible terms (normal forms or canonical forms) are obtained. If the normal forms are identical, then, and only then, the two terms are equal in all models of the given set of equations. However the extension of Knuth-Bendix procedure to Horn theories was difficult. Some progress had been reported in (Remy, 1982), (Plaisted 1985), (Kaplan, 1987), (Ganzinger, 1987). (Bachmair *et al.*, 1987) and (Hsiang and Rusinowitch, 1987) have proved that an extended version of the Knuth and Bendix algorithm uses a refutationally complete set of inference rules (for equational logic) to generate all the consequences of the initial set of equations. (Kounalis and Rusinowitch, 1987) have shown how to design a completion procedure for Horn formulas starting from a refutationally complete set of inference rules for Horn logic (note that Horn formulas, with both equality and non-equality atoms can be expressed as a conditional theory with equality atoms only. This can be done by representing every non-equality atom A with the equation A = T, where T is a new constant). This was the first attempt to obtain canonical systems for non-trivial Horn theories that can be used to decide the validity problem. Recent work on conditional (Horn) theories are in (Dershowitz and Okada, 1990), (Kounalis and Rusinowitch, 1990a), (Bertling, 1990), (Dershowitz, 1990), (Bachmair and Ganzinger, 1990b), (Ganzinger, 1991), (Kounalis and Rusinowitch, 1991b), etc.

One of the most powerful ways of proving properties of numbers, data structures, or programs is *proof by induction*. To accomplish the task, classical theorem proving provides *explicit induction* (more or less heuristic) to solve the problem (see (Burstall, 1969), (Manna, 1970), (Boyer and Moore, 1979), (Kapur *et al.*, 1987)). (Musser, 1980) first suggested using completion to prove theorems in the standard model of an equational theory; such proofs normally requires structural induction. This approach, so-called *inductionless-induction* (since it tries to get rid of induction) has further extended by (Huet and Hullot, 1982), (Dershowitz, 1982 and 87), (Jouannaud and Kounalis, 1986 and 89), (Fribourg, 1986), (Bachmair, 1988), (Reddy, 1990) ... However, one of the hardest problems in using either approaches is to find induction schemata which describe suitably the infinitely many premises needed for the proof or (disproof) of the theorem. In (Kounalis and Rusinowitch, 1990a and 90b), a new proof system for mechanizing induction has been proposed. This method combines the full power of induction and inductionless induction.

The formal foundations of the learning from examples paradigm are given in the papers by Plotkin (Plotkin, 1970 and 71), (Huet, 1976), Mitchell (Mitchell, 1978), Vere (Vere, 1980), Greiner and Genesereth (Greiner and Genesereth, 1983), Michalski (Michalski, 1983 and 86), Lassez and Marriott (Lassez and Marriott, 1987), Buntine (Buntine, 1988), ... Greiner and Genesereth (Greiner and Genesereth, 1983) attempt to give a semantic definition of what is a "new" fact in a theory. Plotkin (Plotkin, 1970 and 71) studies θ–subsumption as a proof theoretical mecanism for generalizations. Buntine (Buntine, 1988) suggests generalized θ–subsumption as a model to study generalizations with Horn logic. Lassez and Marriott (Lassez and Marriott, 1987) give algorithms to decide whether a formula is a generalization and how to transform an implicit generalization into an equivalent explicit (disjunctive) one, provided that no relations between the function symbols which appear in the examples and counterexamples are allowed (*i.e.*, without background knowledge). Michalski (Michalski, 1983 and 86) describes a theory and a methodology to learn concepts from examples and counterexamples. Vere (Vere, 1980) gives an algorithm to generate nested implicit generalizations from examples and counterexamples. Mitchell (Mitchell, 1978) uses finite sets of maximal and minimal terms to represent all possible generalizations of a set of examples and counterexamples. All these papers open up important new issues in learning. Rewrite methods are well-suitable for getting decision learning procedures, in particular if we want to incorporate "new" facts into an existing Horn theory. A first approach is used in Kounalis (Kounalis, 1990b), (Kounalis and Rusinowitch, 1990c and 90d).

Much work in program synthesis relies stronly on using deductive methods (in particular, resolution-based theorem proving) to derive executable programs from formal specifications (Green, 1969). Since mid-eigthies various approaches to the automated synthesis of (first-order) functional and logic programs have been proposed: Burstall-Darlington (Burstall and Darlington, 1977), Manna-Waldinger (Manna and Waldinger, 1979 and 80), Darlington (Darlington, 1981), Hogger (Hogger, 1981), Smith (Smith, 1982). They are all based on the direct application of transformation or rewrite rules to the program specification. More recently, inductive-based methods have also been used to accomplish this task (see Smith (Smith, 1980), Shapiro (Shapiro, 1983)). The use of pure rewrite methods to derive executable programs are first proposed by (Dershowitz, 1985) and improved in (Dershowitz, 1987) and (Reddy, 1989). In this approach directed equations (rules) are used both as a specification language and as a target programming language within a synthesis system. The Knuth-Bendix completion procedure has been proposed as the deductive engine to generate the target program. However, when the target program contains equations that are only true in the standard model of the given specification, inductionless-induction methods may be used to derive provably correct computer programs. It was however unfortunate that such methods work only for equational programs. Morever, the use of Knuth-Bendix completion procedure limited the applicativity of the method. Thus a new method has been proposed (see (Kounalis, 1990a)) to develop conditional provably correct computer programs which meet the requirements pointed out above. Domain knowledge and specifications are given as sets of conditional equations (Horn formulas) and purely (algebraic) simplification is the engine used to generate target programs.

Consistency-based diagnosis and abductive diagnosis have been intensively studied (see, for instance, (Reiter, 1987) (De Kleer, 1987) (De Kleer *et al.*, 1990) (Raiman, 1989) (Raiman, 1990) for the former and (Pople, 1973) (Reggia *et al.*, 1985) (Cox and Pietrzykowski, 1987) (Console and Torasso, 1990) for the latter). Furthermore, comparisons between these approaches have also been thoroughly investigated (see, for instance, (Nau and Reggia, 1986) (Poole, 1988) (Poole, 1989)). The introduction of rewrite methods to provide a formal basis and computational methods for supporting both consistency-based diagnosis and abductive diagnosis was suggested in (El Ayeb *et al.*, 1990). In particular, it was shown that a complete set of inference rules for Horn logic can be used to derive consistency-based and abductive diagnoses.

1.4 Layout of the Chapter

In Chapter 2, we present the necessary background material for Horn theories. In particular, we describe the framework in which we are interested, as well as the fundamental notions about Horn proof systems.

In Chapter 3, we first present the basic notions of rewrite systems and the way they may be used in order to reason about Horn theories. Then, we show how these concepts may be used to provide a complete set of inference rules for Horn logic. Finally, we give a set of inferences rules to obtain canonical systems for Horn theories.

In Chapter 4, we outline some Artificial Intelligence problems whose solutions are based on the methods presented in Chapter 3. In particular we show how to prove (or disprove) deductive or inductive theorems, how to learn concepts from a set of examples and counterexamples, how to synthesize recursive functions from their specifications, and how to perform logic-based diagnostic reasoning.

2 HORN LOGIC

The part of predicate logic in which Horn formulas are the only admitted formulas can be considered as a separate formal system and called *Horn Logic*. In this logic Horn formulas $P \Rightarrow L$ with variables $x_1, \ldots, x_n$ are treated as if they were sentences $\forall x_1, \ldots, x_n\ (P \Rightarrow L)$ where $\forall$ is the universal quantifier. Horn formulas occur frequently in Mathematics, and Computer Science. In what follows, we first survey the various syntactic notions of Horn logic, and then consider their associated model theory. For a survey of Horn logic, see (Lloyd, 1984). A more detailed study of Horn logic is given in (Padawitz, 1988). A nice introduction to subsumption lattice of first-order terms is given in (Huet, 1980).

2.1 The Subsumption Lattice of First-OrderTerms

We briefly survey properties of the set T(F, X) of first-order terms, ordered by substitution.

A/ Terms and Replacements

Terms are often used to represent data objects, programs, and computations. They constitute also the most primitive layer on the top of which any other tool may be constructed.

Let T(F, X) be the set of (first-order) *terms* built out of *function* symbols taken from a *signature* $F \equiv F_0 \cup F_1 \cup F_2 \cup \ldots$ and *variables* from a set X. A (first-order) term t in T(F, X) may be viewed as a finite ordered tree, the leaves of which are labeled with variables (from X) or *constants* (from F_0) and the internal nodes of which are labeled with function symbols (from $F_1 \cup F_2 \cup ...$) of positive arity, with outdegree equal to the arity of the label. For readability purposes, we use parentheses and write terms in polish infix notation. For instance, if $F \equiv \{0, s, +\}$, then we write $(x + 0) + s(y)$ instead of ++x0sy. However, in some examples, the layout of terms will be adapted to the underlying signature where parenthesized polish prefix notation may occur as well. Variable-free terms are called *ground* (or *closed*). The term $(x + 0) + s(y)$ is non-ground, whereas $(0 + 0) + s(0)$ is ground. The set $T(F, \emptyset)$ of ground terms will be denoted by $T(F)$. From now on, we will always make the assumption that there is at least one constant in the signature. Thus, the set $T(F)$ (also called the *Herbrand Universe*) is non-empty.

We now formalize the notion of *occurrence* of a *subterm* in a term: A term s is said to be a subterm of a term $t \equiv f(t_1, ..., t_n)$ if either s is t, or else s is a subterm of some term t_i, $1 \leq i \leq n$. By a *proper* subterm of t, we mean a subterm of that is distinct from t. For example, $(x + 0)$ is a proper subterm of $(x + 0) + s(y)$. From now on, we use sequences of positive integers, called *positions*, to refer to the subterms in a given term. Let N* be the set of sequences of positive integers, ε the empty sequence in N*, and . the concatenation operation on sequences. We shall call the members of N* positions and denote them u, v. We say that a position u is *below* position v or (v is *above* u) if and only if $u \equiv v.v'$, for some v'. If v' is non-empty, then u is said to be *strictly below* v. Further, two positions are said to be *disjoint* if neither one is below to other. For instance, 1.1.1 is strictly below 1.1 (or 1.1 is strictly above 1.1.1) and disjoint to the position 1.2.1. For the sake of economy in writing, we shall usually omit occurrences of the concatenation operator, thus, for example, 1.2.1 rending as 121. A sequence of positive integers u is a position in a term $t \equiv f(t_1, ..., t_n)$ if and only if either u is ε, or $u \equiv iv$, for some $1 \leq i \leq n$, ,where v is a position in t_i. If u is a position in $t \equiv f(t_1,...,t_n)$, then the *subterm t/u at position u* is defined to be t if $u \equiv \varepsilon$, and t_i/v if $u \equiv iv$, for some $1 \leq i \leq n$. For convenience, we sometimes use the notation t[s] to express that the term t contains as subterm the term s whenever its position t is not important. For example, if $u \equiv 11$ in the term $t \equiv (x + 0) + s(y)$, then the subterm t/11 at position 11 is x.

Reasoning about Horn formulas requires replacing subterms by other terms. The replacement of the subterm t/p by a term s is a term $t[u \leftarrow s]$, defined to be s if $u \equiv \varepsilon$, and $f(t_1, ..., t_{i-1}, t_i[v \leftarrow s], t_{i+1}, ..., t_n)$ if $u \equiv iv$. For example, if $u \equiv 1$ in the term $t \equiv (x + 0) + s(y)$ and $s \equiv s(x + x)$, then $t[u \leftarrow s] \equiv s(x + x) + s(y)$.

To fix notations, the letters r, t, s will denote arbitrary terms, the letters f, g, h, and a, b, c are used for function symbols, u and v will denote positions, and the letters x, y, and z are used to denote variables.

B/ Substitutions, Matching and Unification.

The operations of *matching* and *unification* are fundamental in Artificial Intelligence. They are based on the notion of substitution which is a special kind of replacement operation:

A *substitution* is uniquely defined by a mapping from variables to terms, and written out as $\{x_1 \leftarrow s_1, \ldots, x_k \leftarrow s_k\}$ when there are only finitely many variables x_i not mapped to themselves. Each element $x_i \leftarrow s_i$ is called a *binding* for x_i. Formally, a substitution σ is a function from X to T(F, X), extended to a function from T(F, X) to itself (also denoted σ and for which we use postfix notation) in such a way that $f(t_1, \ldots, t_n)\sigma \equiv f(t_1\sigma, \ldots, t_n\sigma)$, for each f (of arity n) in F and for all terms t_i in T(F, X). Lower Greek letters will be used to denote substitutions. The composition of two substitutions σ and τ is denoted by $\sigma\tau$. For example, if $\sigma \equiv \{x \leftarrow s(y), y \leftarrow z\}$ and $\tau \equiv \{x \leftarrow 0, y \leftarrow 0, z \leftarrow y\}$, then $\sigma\tau \equiv \{x \leftarrow s(0), z \leftarrow y\}$. That is $\sigma\tau$ is just the composition of two functions; thus, if $x\sigma \equiv s$ for some variable x, then $x\sigma\tau \equiv s\tau$. We say that substitution σ is *at least as general* as substitution ρ (with respect to a subset X' of X) if there exists a substitution τ such that $\sigma\tau \equiv \rho$ (when σ and ρ are restricted to X'). Substitutions are used to define the operations of matching and unification:

A term t *matches* a term s if $s\sigma \equiv t$ for some substitution σ. In that case we write $s \leq\!< t$ and also say that t is an *instance* of s or that s subsumes t. The relation $\leq\!<$ is a *quasi-ordering* (*i.e.*, a reflexive and transitive binary relation) on terms, called *term subsumption.* For example, $x + y \leq\!< z + z$, and $x + y \leq\!< g(z) + y$. On the other hand, $s \equiv z + z_1$ and $t \equiv x + y$ are equally general, since s and t are instances of each other. In general we say that s is a *variant* of t if and only if s and t are instances of each other. This relation is evidently symmetric. Two terms are *variants* of each other if and only if they can be obtained from each other by suitable renaming of variables. Further, two terms s and t are said to be *unifiable* if and only if there is a substitution σ, called a *unifier*, such that $s\sigma$ and $t\sigma$ are identical. A *most general unifier* of s and t is a unifier σ, such that for evey unifier τ there exists a substitution τ' with $\sigma\tau' \equiv \tau$. For example, if $s \equiv s(x) + y$ and $t \equiv z + 0$, then s and t are unifiable, since $\sigma \equiv \{x \leftarrow 0, z \leftarrow s(0), y \leftarrow 0\}$ is a unifier. A most general unifier is $\tau \equiv \{z \leftarrow s(x), y \leftarrow 0\}$. The most general unifier of two terms s and t may be found by the unification algorithm of (Robinson, 1965).

2.2 Atoms and Horn Formulas

In this section we shall attempt to give a fairly comprehensive survey of the syntactic and semantics constructs of Horn logic. In particular we discuss the various semantics one can associate with Horn formulas, and then consider their corresponding proof theories (if any).

A/ Atoms and Equations

Given a sequence of terms $t_1 \ldots t_n$ and a *predicate* symbol p, the expression $\alpha \equiv p(t_1, \ldots, t_n)$ is said to be an *atom* (over F). p, q, ... will be used to denote predicate symbols, and P, Q, L will be reserved for atoms or conjunctions of atoms. If p is the *equality* predicate and thus $\alpha \equiv p(t_1, t_2)$ for some t_1, t_2 in T(F, X), then $p(t_1, t_2)$ is an *equation*, written as $t_1 = t_2$. If $t_1 \equiv t_2$, then $t_1 = t_2$ is *reflexive*. In other words, the difference between the formula $t_1 = t_2$ and the structural identity of two terms t_1, t_2 denoted by $t_1 \equiv t_2$ is the following: = is a predicate *symbol*, while ≡ *means* equality.

The part of predicate logic in which equations, *i.e.*, formulas of the form $\forall x_1, \ldots, x_n\ (s = t)$, are the only admitted formulas can also be construed as a separate formal system and called *Equational Logic*. Tarski has endeavored to equationally axiomatize the foundations of mathematics. The standard survey on equational logic is given in (Tarki, 1968). For an algebraic-based overview of equational logic, see (Taylor, 1979). A fairly comprehensive treatement of first-order equations in the framework of traditional abstract algebra is given in (Huet and Oppen, 1980).

To illustrate the discussion above, let F ≡ {null, cons, append}. Then the following set of equations (an *equational theory*) defines the function **append**:

1. append(null, x) = x
2. append(cons(x, y), z) = cons(x, append (y, z)

We can use this definition to compute, say, **append(cons(A, cons(B, null)), cons(C, null))** into **cons(A, cons(B, cons(C, null)))**. This example shows us that reasoning about equations and computing with them is actually closely related.

Finally, the notions of *instance*, *unifier*, and *ground* extend from terms to atoms as if predicate symbols were function symbols.

B/ Horn Formulas and Theories

Let A(P, F, X) be the set of first-order atoms built out of predicate symbols taken from a set P, function symbols taken from a set F and variables from X. A *Horn formula* $C \equiv P \Rightarrow L$ over A(P, F, X) consists of an atom L, the *conclusion* (or *head*) of C, and a conjunction P of atoms, the *premise* (or *body*, or *conditions*) of C. If L is an equation, then C is a *conditional equation*. If P is empty, then the (positive-unit formula) is said to be a (unconditional) equation, and C is identified with L. If $C \equiv P \Rightarrow t = s$ is a Horn formula, the term t will be called the *left-hand side*; s is *the right-hand side*. For example, **even(x) = true ⇒ odd(x) = false** is a Horn formula, **odd(x) = false** is its head (conclusion), and **even(x) = true** is its body (condition), **odd(x)** is the left-hand side; **false** is the right-hand side. A *Horn theory* is just a set of Horn formulas.

Horn theories, with both equality and non-equality atoms, can be expressed as conditional equations with equality atoms only. This can be done by representing every non-equality atom A with the equation A = T, where T is a new constant. Thus, in what follows we shall mainly deal with Horn theories each element of which is:

– Either an (unconditional) equation $s = t$,
– Or an expression of the form $s_1 = t_1 \wedge \ldots \wedge s_n = t_n \Rightarrow s = t$,
– Or an expression of the form $s_1 = t_1 \wedge \ldots \wedge s_n = t_n \Rightarrow$,
– Or the empty clause $\Rightarrow$,

where $s_1, t_1, \ldots, s_n, t_n, s, t$ are either terms over F or a new constant T, not in F. Thus, from now on, $P \Rightarrow s = t$ will denote arbitrary Horn formulas. Horn theories are important in Computer Science and Artificial Intelligence. They may be used to specify abstract data types, to express functional-like programs, to express logic programs with equations, to perform automated reasoning, and to model the background knowledge of many programs used in various Expert Systems, Learning Systems, Program Synthesis Systems, etc.

C/ Models and Theorems of Horn Theories

As we already have pointed out reasoning about Horn theories may involve deciding if a Horn formula "follows" as consequence of a given set of Horn formulas (axioms) or if a Horn formula is true in a given model. In other words, reasoning about Horn theories consists of solving the *validity problem* which can be stated as follows: Given a class of models MOD of a Horn theory H and a Horn formula $C \equiv P \Rightarrow s = t$, decide whether C is *valid* (*true*) in every element of MOD. It is well known that many AI problems can be formulated as instances of this scheme. Note that if MOD = {A} and C is a ground equation, then the validity problem is called the *word problem* for A.

To set the machinery in resolving the validity problem, it is useful to start with a clear understaning of the various semantics (models) one can associate with Horn theories. In general, the models of Horn theories are *structures*, that is, sets (domains) with functions and relations on their elements. For example, consider the following set H of Horn formulas over the signature $F \equiv \{$®, **e**, **c**$\}$:

1. x ® e = x
2. e ® x = x
3. (x ® y) ® z = x ® (y ® z)
4. c ® x = c ® y ⇒ x = y

What *models* (underlying semantics) one can associated with H ? There are at least three kinds of models (more precise definitions are given below):

a) The class of all *(first-order) models* of H, denoted by FOM(H),

b) The class of all *term-generated models (Herbrand models)* of H, denoted by TGM(H),

c) The (isomorphic) class of *initial models (least Herbrand model)* of H, denoted by INM(H).

AI community have given a number of reasons for preferring one or the other of a), b), and c). In general, for many purposes, not all models are of equal interest. For applications like Program Verification, Machine Learning, Program Synthesis, Negation in Logic Programming, ... our attention is focused on those models that are *generated* from the signature itself, in which every element of the underlying domain is the denotation of some term built out of F, *i.e.*, we are interested in models b) and c). To illustrate the previous discussion, consider the following structures M1, M2, and M3:

– Let M1 be the set of non-zero invertible square matrices M_+ under multiplication. It is easy to see that M_+ is a model of H (*i.e.*, every Horn formula in H is true in M_+), by interpreting the binary symbol ® as $*_{M+}$, the constant symbol **e** as the unit square matrice. The model M1 belongs to FOM(H).

– Let M2 be the set of non-zero natural numbers N_+ under multiplication. Try to grasp intuitively that N_+ is a model of H, by interpreting the binary symbol ® as $*_{N+}$, the constant symbol **e** as the number 1. Further, the model M2 belongs to TGM(H)

– Let M3 be the set of natural numbers N under addition. It is also easy to see that N is a model of H, by interpreting the binary symbol ® as $+_N$, the constant symbol **e** as the number 0 and **c** as the number 1. The model M3 belongs to INM(H).

Thus, one has to deal with three notions of validity in Horn theories. For instance, the *validitity problem in the class of all (first-order) models* of a Horn theory H is stated as follows: Is a Horn formula C ≡ P ⇒ L valid (true) in every model in FOM(H) ? If so, we write FOM(H) ⊨ C and speak about C being a *deductive consequence* of H. For example, the equation **x** ® (**c** ® (**c** ® **e**))) = (**x** ® **c**) ® **c** is valid in FOM(H). Similarly, the Horn formula **c** ® (**x** ® (**c** ® **e**))) = (**c** ® (**y** ® (**x** ® **c**))) ⇒ **x** ® **c** = (**y** ® **x**) ® **c** is valid in FOM(H). Our primary interest in classifying the class of models of Horn theories lies in being able to restrict the notion of validity to the class of term-generated models or initial models of a given Horn theory since these models capture in a nice way what we have in mind when we use Horn formulas as definitions. Thus, the *validitity problem in the class of term-generated models* (resp. *initial models*) of a Horn theory H is stated as follows: Is a Horn formula C ≡ P ⇒ L valid (true) in every model in TGM(H) (resp. INM(H)) ? If so, we write TGM ⊨ C (resp. INM(H) ⊨ C) and speak about C being an *inductive consequence* of H. For example, the equation **x** ® **y** = **y** ® **x** is valid in TGM(H). Similarly, the Horn formula **y** ® **x** = **z** ® **x** ⇒ **y** = **z** is valid in TGM(H). Further, either formula **x** ® **y** = **y** ® **x**, **y** ® **x** = **z** ® **x** ⇒ **y** = **z** is valid in INM(H). In general, every equation which is valid in the class of term-generated models of a Horn theory H is also valid in the class of initial models of H, and vice-versa. However, there exist Horn formulas L ⇒ P with L ≠ ∅ which hold in INM(H) but are not valid in the class of term generated model of H. On the other hand, neither of these formulas is valid in FOM(H), even though every ground instance of them is. In other words, for a given Horn theory H, the validitity problem of an equation in TGM(H) or in INM(H) is the same as the validity problem in FOM(H) of all its ground instances, and this capture the notion of standard model mentioned above. Note that we restrict ourselves to first-order Horn theories: We do not treat Horn theories that model non-terminating computations since for such theories sophisticated semantics (continuous models) have to be considered.

Let us now give the formal definitions related to the above discussion. Given a set of function symbols F and a set of predicate symbols P, a *(F, P)-(first-order) structure*

M consists of a *carrier set*, a function for each function symbol in F and a relation for each predicate symbol in P. The equality symbol is always interpreted by the equality on the carrier set. Since we have assumed the existence of at least a constant symbol in F, carrier sets are non-empty. Next, a (F, P)-(first-order) structure M is *term-generated* if each element of its carrier set is the interpretation of a ground term over F. Finally, a (F, P)-(first-order) structure M is *initial* if for each other first-order structure M' there exists a unique homomorphism from M to M'. In fact, a first-order theory admits initial models if and only if it is a universally quantified Horn theory (Makowsky, 1985).

Further, a structure M *satisfies* a Horn formula $C \equiv P \Rightarrow L$ (or C is *valid* (*true*) in M) if for all assignments σ of values in M to variables in C such that $P\sigma$ is true, then $L\sigma$ is true. If L is the equation t = s, then $t\sigma$ and $s\sigma$ represent the same element of M. Thus a (first-order, resp. term-generated, initial) structure M is a (*first-order*, resp. *term-generated, initial*) *model* of a given set H of Horn formulas if every Horn formula C in H is valid (true) in M. Finally, a Horn formula C is a *deductive* (resp. *inductive*) *consequence* of a given Horn theory if C is valid in every first-order (resp. term-generated, initial) model of H.

Having answered the various semantics one can associate to Horn theories, our next step consists on determining their associated syntactic characterizations. In other words, we would like to be able to answer the following question: What is the proof-theoretic characterization of validity in FOM(H), TGM(H), and INM(H) ? For example, as we asserted above, the equation **x ® (c ® (c ® e))) = (x ® c) ® c** is valid in FOM(H). Here is a proof: **x ® (c ® (c ® e))) = x ® (c ® c) = (x ® c) ® c**. To make some progress on it we have to agree on the set of inferences rules to reason about Horn theories like the one stated above. The set of inferences rules are the following (see (Padawitz, 1988)):

– *Substitution rule*: Let $P \Rightarrow L$ be a Horn formula and σ be a substitution. Then $P \Rightarrow L$ implies $P\sigma \Rightarrow L\sigma$.

– *Cut rule*: Let L, L' be atoms and P, P' be conjunctions of atoms. Then $L' \wedge P \Rightarrow L$ and $P' \Rightarrow L'$ imply $P \wedge P' \Rightarrow L'$.

Let $\vdash$ denote the corresponding inference relation. The set AX of *equality formulas* consists of all Horn formulas of the form:

– $x = x$ (reflexivity)

– $x = y \Rightarrow y = x$ (symmetry)

– $x = y \wedge y = z \Rightarrow x = z$ (transitivity)

– $x_1 = y_1 \wedge x_2 = y_2 \wedge \ldots \wedge x_n = y_n \Rightarrow f(x_1, x_2, \ldots, x_n) = f(y_1, y_2, \ldots, y_n)$, $f \in F$

– $x_1 = y_1 \wedge x_2 = y_2 \wedge \ldots \wedge x_n = y_n \Rightarrow p(x_1, x_2, \ldots, x_n) = p(y_1, y_2, \ldots, y_n)$, $p \in P$

(context application, or functional reflexivity).

We are now ready to give equivalent syntactical characterizations of the semantic notions of the validity problem in a given Horn theory:

Theorem (Padawitz, 1988). Let H be a Horn theory, and $C \equiv P \Rightarrow L$ be a Horn formula. Then:

– FOM(H) $\models$ C if and only if H $\cup$ AX $\cup$ Pξ $\vdash$ Lξ, where ξ is a substitution which replace new constants (Skolem) for each variable in C.

– TGM(H) $\models$ C if and only if for all ground substitution instances Cσ we have H $\cup$ AX $\cup$ Pσ $\vdash$ Lσ.

– INM (H) $\models$ C if and only if for all ground substitution instances Cσ we have H $\cup$ AX $\vdash$ Pσ implies H $\cup$ AX $\vdash$ Lσ.

The first statement of the theorem tells us that a Horn formula P $\Rightarrow$ L is true in the class of first-order models of a given Horn theory H if and only if its Skolem version can be obtained from the Horn formulas in H by applications of the cut rule, by substitutions, and by replacing equals by equals. In that case we also say that C is a *deductive theorem* of H. For example, **x ® (c ® (c ® e))) = (x ® c) ® c** and **c ® (x ® (c ® e))) = (c ® (y ® (x ® c))) ⇒ x ® c = (y ® x) ® c** are deductive theorems of H. Whenever H is a recursive set of Horn formulas, this gives us a semi-decision procedure for the validity problem in the class of all first-order models. Thus, deductive theorems can be proved by refutation, *i.e.*, by deriving a contradiction from $\neg$C $\wedge$ H. Usually, $\neg$C is transformed into a universal sentence U by introducing *Skolem functions*. This means that the signature has to be extended. Most theorem-proving techniques relies on Herbrand theorem which states that U $\wedge$ H is unsatisfiable if and only if it has no Herbrand model (with respect to the extended signature).

The second statement of the above theorem shows that the validity problem in term-generated models is the same as the validity problem in first-order models as far as the ground instances of the Horn formulas are concerned: A Horn formula P $\Rightarrow$ L is true in the class of first-order models of a given Horn theory H if and only if every ground instance of it can be obtained from the Horn formulas in H by applications of the cut rule, by substitutions, and by replacing equals by equals. In that case we also say that C is a *inductive theorem* of H. For example, the formulas **x ® y = y ® x** and **y ® x = z ® x ⇒ y = z** are inductive theorems of the above theory. Unfortunately, there is no simple proof system associated with the semantic notion of term-generated models. In general structural induction on ground substitutions is needed to show validity in term generated models, but no induction schema will be strong enough to solve the validity problem in term-generated models. The situation is similar, even worst, with the third statement of the theorem. The inductive proof methods may also be used to prove and disprove theorems in the initial model of Horn theories. However, this does not help in the case where a general Horn formula is not valid in the class of term generated models of H. To illustrate the above discussion, consider the formulas **x ® y = y ® x**, **y ® x = z ® x ⇒ y = z**: Either formula is true in the initial model, but its proof relies on double induction arguments. However, an automatic proof of **x ® y = y ® x** is given Section 4.1.

3 REWRITING METHODS FOR HORN LOGIC

Rewriting methods which have been used succesfully in equational logic have turned out to be among the more elegant approaches to reason about Horn theories. We outline here the basic relation concepts and show how to use them in order to reason about Horn theories.

3.1 Overview of Rewriting Concepts

The central idea of using rewriting is to impose directionality on the use of the formulas. The whole enterprise is based on binary relations on terms that possess several fundamental properties.

A/ Binary Relations on Terms

In what follows, we will mainly be dealing with a binary relation on terms, denoted by $\rightarrow$. Our motivation in studing properties of any arrow-like binary relation $\rightarrow$ on T(F, X) stems from problems arising in Horn theories. The standard work on rewriting is (Huet and Oppen, 1980). A recent survey of rewriting is in (Dershowitz and Jouannaud, 1991).

Given a arrow-like binary relation $\rightarrow$ over a set of terms T(F, X) , $\rightarrow^*$ denotes its reflexive-transitive closure (also called *derivability*, or *reachability*) , $\leftarrow$ its inverse, $\leftrightarrow$ its symmetric closure, $\rightarrow^+$ its irreflexive-transitive closure and $\leftrightarrow^*$ its reflexive-symmetric-transitive closure (*i.e.*, $\leftrightarrow^*$ is the smallest equivalence relation containing $\rightarrow$, also called *convertibility*). For example, if a, b, c are terms in T(F, X) and $\rightarrow = \{(a, b), (b, c)\}$, then $\leftarrow = \{(b, a), (c, b)\}$, $\rightarrow^+ = \{(a, b), (b, c), (a, c)\}$, $\rightarrow^* = \{(a, b), (b, c), (a, c), (a, a), (b, b), (c, c)\}$, $\leftrightarrow = \{(a, b), (b, c), (b, a), (c, b)\}$, and $\leftrightarrow^* = \{(a, b), (b, c), (b, a), (c, b), (a, c), (c, a), (a, a), (b, b), (c, c)\}$. For readability purposes we shall use the notation $t \rightarrow s$ instead of $(s, t) \in \rightarrow$. A term t in T(F, X) is *irreducible* in $\rightarrow$ (or $\rightarrow$–*irreducible*) if there is no s such that $t \rightarrow s$. In the above example, term c is $\rightarrow$–irreducible. An irreducible term t is called a *normal form* of s for $\rightarrow$ (or t is $\rightarrow$–*normal form* of s) if $s \rightarrow^* t$ and this is denoted by $s \rightarrow^! t$. In the above example, term c is a $\rightarrow$–*normal form* of term a, since $a \rightarrow^! c$.

An arrow-like binary relation $\rightarrow$ over a set of terms T(F, X) is *compatible* if $t \rightarrow s$ implies $c[t] \rightarrow c[s]$, for all terms t, s, and context c[ ]. $\rightarrow$ is *stable* if $t \rightarrow s$ implies $t\sigma \rightarrow s\sigma$, for all terms t, s and substitutions σ. An arrow-like binary relation $\rightarrow$ over a set of terms T(F, X) is *monotonic* if it satisfies both properties. Suppose we are interested in the reflexive-symmetric-transitive closure $\leftrightarrow^*$ of a binary relation $\rightarrow$. The following notions are the basis that permit us to recognize if $t \leftrightarrow^* s$ when using only $\rightarrow^*$.

We say that the binary relation $\rightarrow$ over a set of terms T(F, X) is *terminating* if there is no infinite sequence $t_1 \rightarrow t_2 \rightarrow \ldots \rightarrow t_n \rightarrow \ldots$ This definition appears in various places in the literature under several names, including *noetherian, finitely terminating*, and *uniformly terminating*. The importance of terminating relations lies in the possibility of inductive proofs in which the hypothesis is assumed to hold for all elements t such that s $\rightarrow^+$ t when proving it for arbitrary s. In the above example $\rightarrow$ is terminating, since a $\rightarrow$ b $\rightarrow$ c, b $\rightarrow$ c, and term c is $\rightarrow$-irreducible. If $\rightarrow$ is terminating, then any element in T(F, X) has at least a $\rightarrow$–normal form in T(F, X). We say that two terms s and t are *joinable*, denoted by s $\downarrow$ t, if there exists r such that s $\rightarrow^*$ r $\leftarrow^*$ t. For example, terms a and c are joinable. The binary relation $\rightarrow$ is *confluent* if s $\leftarrow^*$ r $\rightarrow^*$ t implies that s and t are joinable. In other words $\rightarrow$ is confluent if any two terms with a common ancestor have a common descendent. In the above example $\rightarrow$ is confluent. When $\rightarrow$ is a confluent relation on the set of ground terms T(F), we say that $\rightarrow$ is *ground confluent.* If $\rightarrow$ is confluent (resp. ground confluent), then the $\rightarrow$–normal form of any element, if it exists, is unique. If $\rightarrow$ is confluent , then the following "Church-Rosser" property holds: For all t and s in T(F, X), t $\leftrightarrow^*$ s if and only if t $\downarrow$ s. In other words, $\rightarrow$ is Church-Rosser, if any two convertible terms have a common descendent. A relation $\rightarrow$ is *canonical* (or *convergent*) (resp. *ground canonical (convergent)*) if it is terminating and confluent (resp. ground confluent). In canonical relations, terms have unique normal forms.

B/ Rewrite Systems

We shall develop here one of the main paradigm for reasoning about Horn theories and computing with them, by interpreting Horn theories as rewrite systems. Horn formulas as rewrite rules are used to compute by rewriting repeatedly, until, perhaps, a normal form is reached.

A *(conditional) rewrite system* R over a set of terms T(F, X) is a set of directed (conditional) equations (Horn formulas), called *(conditional) rewrite rules*, each of the form ($s_1 = t_1 \wedge \ldots \wedge s_n = t_n \Rightarrow l \rightarrow r$) where s_i, t_i, l and r are terms over T(F, X). We will abbreviate conditions by writing, instead, P $\Rightarrow$ l $\rightarrow$ r. If R is a set of rewrite rules, the D(R) denotes the maximun depth of the left-hand sides of the concusions of the rules in R. Rewrite rules in R are used to replace repeatedly subterms of a given term (or formula) with equal terms (or formulas) until the simplest term (or formula) possible is obtained. This simplest term is what we call a *normal form.* For example, if R is the following rewrite system :

1. $\mathbf{gcd(x,\ x) \rightarrow x}$
2. $\mathbf{0 < x = true \wedge x < y = true \Rightarrow gcd(x,\ y) = gcd(y - x,\ x)}$
3. $\mathbf{0 < y = true \wedge y < x = true \Rightarrow gcd(x,\ y) = gcd(x - y,\ y)}$
4. $\mathbf{x < y = false \Rightarrow succ(x) < succ(y) \rightarrow false}$
5. $\mathbf{x < y = true \Rightarrow succ(x) < succ(y) \rightarrow true}$
6. $\mathbf{x < 0 \rightarrow false}$
7. $\mathbf{0 < succ(x) \rightarrow true}$
8. $\mathbf{x - 0 \rightarrow x}$

9. 0 - x → 0
10. succ(x) - succ(y) → x - y

and t is the term **gcd(succ(succ(succ(succ(0)))), succ(succ(0)))**, then the term s ≡ **succ(succ(0))** is a normal form of t. Term **succ(succ(0))** is the final result of an unextensible sequence of rule applications from R. Thus when Horn theories are compiled into rewrite systems they may be used to compute: A *computation* is the transformation (simplification) of a term to its normal form. As we may notice in the above computation a normal form (if any) of a term is reached by replacing an instance of the left-hand side l by the corresponding instance of the right-hand side r, provided that the corresponding instance of the condition P holds.

If R is a (conditional) rewrite system, the corresponding rewrite relation $\rightarrow^R$ is the smallest monotonic relation generated by R. In other words, if R is a set of conditional rules and t is a term or a formula, then $t \rightarrow^R s$, *i.e.*, t *rewrites* (*reduces*) to s in T(F, X), if $t/u \equiv l\sigma$, $R \models P\sigma$ and $s \equiv t[u \leftarrow r\sigma]$, for some rule $P \Rightarrow l \rightarrow r$, position u, and substitution σ, where rewrite rules in R are regarded as Horn formulas. In practice, one is usually interested in terminating rewrite systems in which $\rightarrow^R$ is decidable.

A (strict) *partial* ordering relation > (*i.e.*, transitive and irreflexive) over a set of terms T(F, X) is is *well-founded* if it admits no infinite descending sequences of elements $t_1 > t_2 > t_3 > \ldots$ of T(F, X). To prove that a rewrite system R terminates one has to show that the ordering $\rightarrow^{+R}$ is well-founded. A *reduction ordering* > on T(F, X) is any well-founded monotonic. A rewrite system R terminates if and only if it is containing in some reduction ordering. Most orderings are simplification orderings: A *simplification ordering* is a reduction ordering > which satisfies the following *subterm property*: $s[t] \geq t$, for all terms s and t. The ordering described below is sufficient for the purpose of our study. For a detailed study of further orderings and termination in general we refer to (Dershowitz, 1985).

If > is a partial ordering on T(F, X), then the multiset ordering $>_M$ is the smallest transitive relation such that $X \cup \{x\} >_M X \cup \{y_1, \ldots, y_n\}$, whenever $n \geq 0$ and $x > y_i$, for $1 \leq i \leq n$. According to this ordering an element of a multiset can be replaced by any finite number of elements that are smaller with respect to >. The following ordering, based on the multiset ordering, exploit the structure of terms:

Let $>_p$ be an ordering, called *precedence*, on the set of the function symbols F. The corresponding *recursive path ordering* > (Dershowitz, 1985) is recursively defined by:

– $s = f(s_1, \ldots, s_m) > t = g(t_1, \ldots, t_n)$ iff either $s_i \geq t$, for some i, $1 \leq i \leq n$
– Or $f >_p g$, and $s > t_j$, for all j, $1 \leq j \leq n$,
– Or $f = g$, and $\{s_1, \ldots, s_m\} >_M \{t_1, \ldots, t_n\}$.

Thus, if $>_p$ is a well-founded precedence ordering on the function symbols, then any recursive path ordering is a simplification ordering (Dershowitz, 1985). This provides us with a method to prove termination of rewrite systems. From now on, we assume given a reduction ordering > on T(F, X). A reduction ordering can be extended to atoms by comparing the multiset of their members with the multiset extension of > (see (Dershowitz and Manna, 1979)). Formulas are compared by using the multiset extension of this last ordering to the multiset of their atomic subformulas. Since there is no ambiguity, all these extensions will also be denoted by >. An equation $s = t$ will be written $s \rightarrow t$ if $s\sigma > t\sigma$ for all ground substutions σ; in that case we say that the equation $s = t$ is *orientable.*

If R is a rewrite system, then R is said to have the *confluence* property, if whenever a term t can be rewritten to two distinct terms t_1 and t_2, both t_1 and t_2 can be rewritten to some term s. Confluence is equivalent to the Church-Rosser property. Confluence of a rewrite system is a property that ensures that no term has more than one normal form. A *canonical* (*convergent*) rewrite system is one with both the confluence and the termination properties. For a convergent rewrite system R, an equation $s = t$ holds in the theory defined by R iff the normal forms of s and t are identical. The Knuth-Bendix completion method (Knuth and Bendix, 1970) was designed to generate convergent rewrite systems for a given set of unconditional equations. The basic idea of this method consists of that confluence of finite terminating systems can be effectively tested by checking equality of normal forms of a finite set of pairs of terms, called *critical pairs*, formed by overlapping left-hand sides of the rules. In next section we propose an extension of Knuth-Bendix method to conditional theories.

3.2 Rewriting for Horn Logic

We show here how the previous concepts can be applied to Horn logic. In particular, we develop a set of inference rules which is refutationally complete for Horn logic with equality, based on term orderings. We then show how to compile a Horn theory into a canonical rewrite system.

A/ A Complete Set of Inference Rules for Horn Logic

We present a set of inference rules which is refutationally complete for Horn logic with equality. Our set of inference rules, denoted by INF, is given in (Kounalis and Rusinowitch, 1987, 88 and 91a). Our theorem-proving strategy relies on a well-founded complexity measure on terms in order to select the more complex subformula where to perfom inferences. The complexity of terms is obtained by an ordering which has to meet stability properties. Such an ordering will be called a *complete simplification ordering* which is a simplification ordering that is total on ground terms:

Let A(P, F, X) be the set of first-order atoms built out of predicate symbols taken from a signature P, function symbols taken from F and variables from X. A complete simplification ordering < on $A(P, F, X) \cup T(F, X)$ is an ordering with the following properties:

(1) < is well-founded,

(2) < is total on $A(P, F, X) \cup T(F, X)$,

(3) For every $u, v \in A(P, F, X) \cup T(F, X)$ and every substitution σ, $u < v$ implies $u\sigma < v\sigma$,

(4) For every $u \in A(P, F, X) \cup T(F, X)$ and every $s, t \in T(F, X)$, $t < s$ implies $u[p \leftarrow t] < u[p \leftarrow s]$,

(5) For every $u \in A(P, F, X)$ and every $s, t, a, b \in T(F, X)$ with $t \leq s$ and $b \leq a$:

– if s is a strict subterm of u, then $s < u$,
– if s is a subterm of u and u is not an equality, then $(s = t) < u$,
– if s is a strict subterm of a or b, then $(s = t) < (a = b)$,

(6) For every ground atom u and every ground terms a, b, c such that $(a = c) < u < (a = b)$, $a > b$ and $a > c$, then there is a ground term t such that u is equal to the atom $(a = t)$.

Examples of complete simplifications ordering are given in (Peterson, 1983) (Hsiang and Rusinowitch, 1986). Let Γ and Δ denote any sequence of atoms:

Resolution
Let C be the Horn formula $(L, \Gamma \Rightarrow P)$ and D be the Horn formula $(\Delta \Rightarrow L')$ such that L and L' are unifiable with mgu σ and:

(1) For every $A \in \Gamma \cup \{P\}$, $L\sigma \nleq A\sigma$ and for every $A \in \Delta$, $L'\sigma \nleq A\sigma$

(2) If L is an equality literal and D is $x = x$ then $(\Gamma\sigma, \Delta\sigma \Rightarrow P\sigma)$ is a *resolvent* of C and D.

Left Paramodulation
Let C be a Horn formula $(\Gamma \Rightarrow s = t)$. Let D be another Horn formula $(\Delta, L \Rightarrow P)$ such that a non-variable subtem s', occurring at n in the atom L, is unifiable with s with mgu σ. We suppose that $s\sigma \nleq t\sigma$ and:

(1) For every $A \in \Gamma$, $(s = t)\sigma \nleq A\sigma$ and for every $A \in \Delta \cup \{P\}$, $L\sigma \nleq A\sigma$

(2) If L is an equation, s' occurs in the largest member of L, then $(\Gamma\sigma, \Delta\sigma, L[n \leftarrow t] \Rightarrow P\sigma)$ is a *paramodulant* of C into D at n.

Right Paramodulation
Let C be a Horn formula $(\Gamma \Rightarrow s = t)$. Let D be another Horn formula $(\Delta \Rightarrow L)$ such that a non-variable subtem s', occurring at n in the atom L, is unifiable with s with mgu σ. We suppose that $s\sigma \nleq t\sigma$ and:

(1) For every $A \in \Gamma$, $(s = t)\sigma \nleq A\sigma$ and for every $A \in \Delta$, $L\sigma \nleq A\sigma$

(2) If L is an equation, s' occurs in the largest member of L, then $(\Gamma\sigma, \Delta\sigma \Rightarrow L[n \leftarrow t])$ is a *paramodulant* of C into D at n.

In the following, by paramodulation we mean either left paramodulation or right paramodulation. Let us emphasize here that the functional reflexive axioms are not needed, and that paramodulation is never performed into variables: These two conditions ensures efficiency of the inference system. Let us consider the clause $\mathbf{s(a) = s(b) \Rightarrow a = b}$. We are not allowed to use $\mathbf{a = b}$ for paramodulation, since it is smaller than the conditional part (negative atoms). The intuitive reason of such a restriction is that we want to reduce the problem of checking an equality to less complex subproblems. On the contrary our paramodulation rule favours the use of **s(a) = s(b)** since it decreases the "size" of problems.

Now we present a set of deletion rules which are fundamental for efficiency. Moreover, for many satisfiable systems, the deletion inference rules prevent the generation of infinitely many new clauses.

Proper subsumption

The Horn formula C *properly subsumes* the Horn formula D if C subsumes D and D does not subsume C. Any Horn formula of S which is properly subsumed by another formula in S can be deleted.

Simplification

If the unit equation $s = t$ is in S, $D[s\sigma]$ is a Horn formula of S which contains an instance $s\sigma$ of s, $s\sigma > t\sigma$, and there is an atom A in $D[s\sigma]$ such that $A > s\sigma = t\sigma$, then the Horn formula $D[t\sigma]$ is a *simplification* of $D[s\sigma]$ by $s = t$. The simplification rule states that one may replace a Horn formula in S by the same one after it has been simplified.

Tautology deletion

Tautologies can be deleted.

Clausal simplification

If the unit atom L is in S, then we can replace any Horn formula in S which contains a negated instance of L by the same Horn formula where this instance has been deleted.

In order to get a refutationally complete strategy, we need some *fairness assumptions* to ensure that no crucial inference will be postponed forever. Given an initial set of Horn formulas H, the derivation $H_0 \rightarrow H_1 \rightarrow \ldots \rightarrow H_i$ where each H_j is obtained from H_{j-1} by one inference step, is *fair* if, for every j, $S \in \cap_{(k \geq j)} RP(H_k)$ implies that S is subsumed by a clause in $\cup_{(k \geq 0)} H_k$, where RP(S) denotes the whole set of resolvents and paramodulants which can be inferred (in one step) from a set of Horn formulas S. From now on we suppose that INF is submitted to a scheduler which let only fair derivations be generated. We say that a formula is normalized by H when it is fully simplified by the unit oriented equations available in H. We also suppose that before adding a new formula, it is always immediately normalized and checked whether it is subsumed by a formula in H.

Theorem (Kounalis-Rusinowitch, 1988 and 91a). The set INF is refutationally complete for Horn logic (with equality). To be more precise, any fair derivation of an unsatisfiable set of Horn formulas containing $x = x$ yields the empty formula.

As we may notice above, the main feature of this system is that any inference step always involves the maximal atoms of the parent Horn formulas, where the maximality notion is defined relatively to a complete simplification ordering on Herbrand Universe.

B/ Canonical Systems for Horn Theories

Our problem here consists in "compiling" a Horn theory into a canonical rewrite system. It has been proved in (Bachmair *et al.*, 1987) and (Hsiang and Rusinowitch, 1987) that an extended version of the Knuth and Bendix algorithm uses a refutationally complete set of inference rules (for equational logic) to generate all the consequences of the initial set of equations. The completion procedure can be interpreted as an attempt to *saturate* a set of equations by inference rules, in hope to derive a finite set which has no non-trivial consequences. This nice feature is generalized naturally to Horn formulas using the proposed methods (see also (Kounalis and Rusinowitch, 1990a)): Starting from a set of Horn formulas, and based on a refutationally complete system of inference rules, we iterate a set of rules, called CINF (see below), on the initial set. If the procedure halts, the resulting set of Horn formulas provides a very efficient way to solve the validity problem in the Horn theory under consideration by what can be called "conditional normalization", which is a combination of backward chaining (trying to check pre-conditions before using a rule for simplification) and forward chaining (using a rule for simplification). Horn formula heads are used as simplifiers, whose pre-conditions are gathered within the negative atoms. Formally:

Let H be a set of Horn formulas. Let A be a term or a formula, and u a position of a. Then $A[u \leftarrow s\sigma] \rightarrow_H B[u \leftarrow t\sigma]$ if σ is a substitution and there is a formula $P \Rightarrow s = t$ in H such that $s\sigma > t\sigma$, $H \models P$ and $(s = t)\sigma > P\sigma$.

Thus, a term (a formula) A is reducible with respect to H, if there is a term B such that $A \rightarrow_H B$. Otherwise A is said to be irreducible. A Horn theory H is *canonical* (or H can be compiled into a *canonical* set of rewrite rules) if for all terms t, s in T(F), $H \models t = s$ implies there exists r such that $t \rightarrow^*_H r$ and $s \rightarrow^*_H r$.

Canonical systems of Horn theories have the property that two terms are equal if and only if they simplify to identical ones. In this section, we provide a method, called *saturation*, to obtain canonical systems for Horn theories which may be used to decide the validity property in the class of all first-order models of a given theory H. Our method is still based on a total simplification ordering < and the inference rule of *superposition*: The only inferences which are allowed are those obtained either by paramodulating maximal members of conclusions into maximal members of conclusions, or by paramodulating maximal members of conclusions into maximal members of conditions (maximal refers here to the ordering <). Formally, let H be a set of Horn formulas, then we define the sets SP(H) and CN(H) as follows:

$SP(H) = \{(P \wedge P' \Rightarrow l[s] = r)\sigma : \exists (P \Rightarrow l[s'] = r) \in H, \exists (P' \Rightarrow t = s) \in H$ such that s' is not a variable and $s'\sigma \equiv t\sigma$ and $l\sigma > P\sigma, r\sigma$ and $t\sigma > P'\sigma, s\sigma\}$,

$CN(H) = \{(P \wedge P' \wedge l[s] = r \Rightarrow L)\sigma : \exists (P \wedge l[s'] = r \Rightarrow L) \in H$ and

$(P' \Rightarrow t = s) \in H$ such that s' is not a variable and $s'\sigma \equiv t\sigma$ and $l\sigma > P\sigma, r\sigma, L\sigma$ and $t\sigma > P'\sigma, s\sigma\}$.

The relation $\supseteq$ defined on Horn formulas denotes the inclusion on their sets of atoms. We are now ready to present a set of inferences rules, call it CINF, wich may be used to derive canonical systems for Horn theories:

Deduce $H \vdash H \cup C$ if $C \in SP(H)$
Narrow $H \vdash H \cup C$ if $C \in CN(H)$
Delete $H \cup \{P \Rightarrow r = r\} \vdash H$
Trivial $H \cup \{P \wedge P' \Rightarrow P\} \vdash H$
Subsume $H \cup \{C, D\} \vdash H \cup \{C\}$ if $D \supseteq C\sigma$
Reflect $H \cup \{P \wedge s = t \Rightarrow l = r\} \vdash H \cup \{P \wedge s = t \Rightarrow l = r, (P \Rightarrow l = r)\sigma\}$ if $s\sigma \equiv t\sigma$ and $(s = t)\sigma > P\sigma$ and $(s = t)\sigma > (l = r)\sigma$

C-simplify $H \cup \{P[s\sigma]\} \vdash H \cup \{P[t\sigma]\}$ if $P[s\sigma] \rightarrow_H P[t\sigma]$ and $(s= t)\sigma < P[s\sigma]$
S1 $H \cup \{P \wedge s = t \Rightarrow L[s]\} \vdash H \cup \{P \wedge s = t \Rightarrow L[t]\}$ if $s > t$
S2 $H \cup \{P[s] \wedge s = t \Rightarrow L\} \vdash H \cup \{P[t] \wedge s = t \Rightarrow L\}$ if $s > t$

The Knuth-Bendix method has been designed to derive canonical systems from equational theories. This procedure halts with success when all possible deductions are trivial. Applying the previous set CINF of inferences rules to Horn theories we can generalize the Knuth-Bendix result:

Theorem (Kounalis-Rusinowitch, 1990a). If there is an application of CINF which allows to derive from a Horn theory H a finite rewrite system R, then R is canonical for H.

This technique to get canonical systems for Horn logic does fail neither in presence of *non-reductive* Horn formulas (*i.e.*, rules in which at least one of the conditions is bigger than the conclusion) nor in presence of non-orientable equations. Morever, purely negative Horn formulas are allowed too. A Horn formula can be used as a rewrite rule only if the matching substitution can make it a reductive rule, *i.e.*, a rule in which all conditions are smaller than the conclusion. When a Horn clause has no reductive instance, it is considered as a non operational rule which means that it may be used during the completion process to generate new consequences, but it can be dropped when the completion is achieved. This results generalizes and extends previous result (*e.g.*, (Remy, 1982), (Remy and Zhang, 1985), (Kaplan, 1987), (Ganzinger, 1987), (Kounalis and Rusinowitch, 1988). As a simple example consider the following Horn theory:

1. x < y true ⇒ x < succ(x) = true
2. pred(x) < x = true

3. succ(pred(x)) = true

By using the precedence **pred** > **succ** > **true** we can easily verify that no inference step would add a non-trivial consequence. Thus the following rewrite system R is canonical for the above Horn theory:

1. x < y true ⇒ x < succ(x) → true
2. pred(x) < x → true
3. succ(pred(x)) → true

4 APPLICATIONS

We show here how to apply the previous material for solving AI problems. In particular, we show applications to Automated Theorem Proving, Machine Learning, Program Synthesis, and Diagnosis.

4.1 Automated Theorem Proving

There is an increasing need for programs that reason to assist AI researchers in Theorem Proving. We point out here how the methods presented in Section 3.3 allows us to show:

1) How to prove satisfiability of a set of Horn formulas,
2) How to prove (or disprove) deductive theorems,
3) How to prove (or disprove) inductive theorems.

Note that there is a qualitative difference between *checking satisfiability* and *proving (or disproving) deductive theorems*. Checking satisfiability is based on a theorem prover which is deemed to be "complete" if it can detect any theory which is unsatisfiable. In other words if it can prove *any provable conjecture (theorem)*. Proving (or disproving) deductive theorems is based on a compilation-like process, so-called *completion*, whose goal is to find "canonical" rewrite systems that can later be used to prove (or disprove) *any conjecture* for deductive validity in a given theory effectively.

A/ Checking for Satisfiability

Although elegant, the basic resolution-paramodulation procedure usually produces intermediate formulas, at an overwhelming rate. Thus, restricted forms of resolution and paramodulation that would also permit eventual detection of any valid formula (the completeness property) are further investigated. Our complete set INF of inference rules for Horn logic, which minimizes the amount of paramodulation, while maximizing the amount of simplification, without threatining completeness, allows, thus, to tackle the following theorem-proving problem:

> **Input:** A Horn theory H with(out) equality
> **Determine:** Is H satisfiable ?

Let us show on two examples how the complete set INF of inference rules for Horn logic stated in the previous chapter allows us to verify whether a set of Horn formulas is satisfiable:

Example 1. Consider the following Horn formulas:

1. P(0)
2. P(x) $\Rightarrow$ P(f(x))

we want to verify for satisfiability. The main feature of our set of inferences rules INF consists in that any inference step always involves maximal literals of the parent formulas, where the maximality notion is defined relatively to a complete simplification ordering on Herbrand Universe. In other words, resolution and paramodulation need only to be performed on maximal atoms. On the other hand, when using an equality in a formula to paramodulate, only the larger of the two terms in the equality needs to be considered for paramodulation.

Now, if we use the maximal literal strategy INF, there is no resolvent between the two formulas, because P(x) < P(f(x)) in any complete simplification ordering. Therefore whatever ordering is used, the prover will always simply stop and report "satisfiable". Note that, if we apply unrestricted resolution, an infinite set of formulas is generated: P(f(0)), P(f(f(0))), ..., P(f^n(0)), ...

Example 2. Consider now the following set of Horn formulas which defines the *inf_or_equal* predicate on the set of integers, where **0**, **pred**, and **succ** represent the zero, predecessor, and successor functions respectively:

1. x = x
2. succ(pred(x)) = x
3. pred(succ(x)) = x
4. inf(0, 0) = true
5. inf(0, pred(0)) = true
6. inf(0, x) = true $\Rightarrow$ inf(0, succ(x)) = true
7. inf(0, x) = false $\Rightarrow$ inf(0, succ(x)) = false
8. inf(succ(x), y) = inf(x, pred(y))
9. inf(pred(x), y) = inf(x, succ(y))
10. true = false $\Rightarrow$

When the set INF of inferences rules is applied to 1. ... 10. with the lexicographic RPO and the following precedence: **inf > pred > succ > 0 > true > false**, we shall stop after deriving the new formulas:

11. inf(0, p(x)) = true ⇒ inf(0, x) = true by paramodulation of 2. and 6.
12. inf(0, s(x)) = false ⇒ inf(0, x) = false by paramodulation of 3. and 7.

Therefore, the above set of Horn formulas is satisfiable. Note that if we apply unrestricted resolution, an infinite set of formulas is generated.

B/ Proving (or Disproving) Deductive Theorems

Demodulation (or simplification, or rewriting) has been recognized as a powerful technique to increase efficiency of theorem-provers. For a given set of unconditional equations, the completion procedure of Knuth and Bendix was introduced as a means of generating canonical rewrite systems (a set of rules) that can be used to decide the *validity problem* in the given theory (*i.e.*, the truth of an equation in the class of all models of the given theory).The completion procedure can be interpreted as an attempt to *saturate* a set of equations by inference rules, in hope to derive a finite set which has no non-trivial consequences. This nice feature is generalized naturally to Horn theories by using the set of inferences rules CINF, which allows us to deal with the following problem:

Input: A Horn theory H with(out) equality, and a Horn formula C.
Determine: Whether C is a deductive theorem of H ?

A method to solve the previous problem consists in compiling the Horn theory into a canonical rewrite system. The set of inferences rules CINF may be used to derive such systems. Let us illustrate the solution of the previous problem on two simple examples:

Example 1. Consider the following recursive program which states the parity of a non-negative integer:

1. 0 + x = x
2. succ(x) + y = succ(x + y)
3. x + 0 = x
4. x + succ(y) = succ(x + y)
5. even(0) = true
6. even(succ(0)) = false
7. even(succ(succ(x))) = even(x)
8. even(x) = true ⇒ odd(x) = false
9. even(x) = false ⇒ odd(x) = true

and the conjectures C:

10. odd(0 + succ(0)) = true
11. odd(x) = true ⇒ odd(succ(succ(x))) = true
12. odd(succ(succ(succ(0)))) = even(succ(succ(succ(0))))

We want to verify whether the conjectures C are deductive theorems of H. By using the set of inferences rules CINF the following canonical rewrite system R can be produced:

1. 0 + x → x
2. succ(x) + y → succ(x + y)
3. x + 0 → x
4. x + succ(y) → succ(x + y)
5. even(0) → true
6. even(succ(0)) → false
7. even(succ(succ(x))) → even(x)
8. even(x) = true ⇒ odd(x) → false
9. even(x) = false ⇒ odd(x) → true

Now R may be used to determine whether C are theorems of H. The proof can proceed as follows (the number of a rule which is used in a proof step appears as subscript):

10. odd(0 + succ(0)) $\rightarrow_4$ **odd(succ(0 + 0))** $\rightarrow_1$ **odd(succ(0))** $\rightarrow_8$ **true**

The proof of the implicative theorem **odd(x) = true ⇒ odd(succ(succ(x))) = true** can be done as follows: By the deduction theorem it is equivalent to add to H the formula **14. odd(c) = true**, where **c** is a new constant, and to prove **15. odd(succ(succ(c))) = true**. This can be achieved by simplification, as above.

To verify whether the equation **12.** is an deductive theorem of H we simplify both sides of **odd(succ(succ(succ(0)))) = even(succ(succ(succ(0)))**. However, the left-hand side rewrites to **false** and the right-hand side rewrites to **true**. Therefore, **12.** is not a deductive theorem of H.

Example 2. Consider now the following recursive program which defines the minimun of a list of integers. We assume the following precedence: **min > < > cons > nil > succ > 0 >true > false**:

1. true = false ⇒
2. succ(x) = 0 ⇒
3. succ(x) = succ(y) ⇒ x = y

4. $0 < succ(x) = true$
5. $x < 0 = false$
6. $succ(x) < succ(y) = x < y$
7. $min(cons(x, nil)) = x$
8. $x < min(l) = true \Rightarrow min(cons(x, l)) = x$
9. $x < min(l) = false \Rightarrow min(cons(x, l)) = min(l)$

If we apply the completion procedure CINF, then by superposing 7. and 9. we get the following interesting consequence:

11. $x < min(nil) = false \Rightarrow x = min(l)$

By superposing 8 and 9 we get:

12. $x < min(l) = false \wedge x < min(l) = true \Rightarrow x = min(l)$

By self simplification, we can obtain the following formula which is subsumed by 1.:

$x < min(l) = false \wedge false = true \Rightarrow x = min(l)$

No new consequence can be deduced. This implies that the following system R is canonical:

1. $true = false \Rightarrow$
2. $succ(x) = 0 \Rightarrow$
3. $succ(x) = succ(y) \Rightarrow x = y$
4. $0 < succ(x) \rightarrow true$
5. $x < 0 \rightarrow false$
6. $succ(x) < succ(y) \rightarrow x < y$
7. $min(cons(x, nil)) \rightarrow x$
8. $x < min(l) = true \Rightarrow min(cons(x, l)) \rightarrow x$
9. $x < min(l) = false \Rightarrow min(cons(x, l)) \rightarrow min(l)$
10. $min(l) = x \Rightarrow min(cons(x, l)) \rightarrow x$

Thus R may be used used to decide the validity problem in the above theory of lists.

C/ Proving (or Disproving) Inductive Theorems

One of the most powerful ways of proving properties of numbers, data structures, or programs is proof by induction. And one of the most powerful ways of defining AI programs or data structures is by inductive definition, also referred to as a recursive definition. Automatic proofs by induction is important in many Computer Science and AI applications. Thus, the induction problem on Horn theories can be stated as follows:

> **Input:** A Horn theory H with(out) equality, and a Horn formula C.
> **Determine:** Is C an inductive theorem of H ?

Let us show on two two examples how to prove (or disprove) inductive theorems. However, for space limitations, we restrict ourselves to conjectures which are (first-order) equations. The reason is that the proof of general Horn formulas uses more sophisticated simplification relations (*e.g.*, case simplification ...). For a full treatement of these theorems, see (Kounalis and Rusinowitch, 1990b), and (Bouhoula, Kounalis and Rusinowitch, 1991).

Example 1. Consider the following conjectures of the program above which states the parity of a non-negative integer:

16. x + y = y + x
17. (x + y) + z = x + (y + z)
18. even(x + x) = true
19. odd(x + x) = false

It can be seen that for all non-negative integer values of x, y, and z these conjectures are consequences of the given Horn theory. In other words these formulae are valid in Peano arithmetic. This suggest to prove them using mathematical induction, *i.e.*, using applications of Peano's induction schemata.

The first step of our method consists of supplying a well-founded ordering on ground terms. Using a well-founded ordering to orient Horn formulas ensures that the system of rules terminates. For instance, the system R stated above:

1. $0 + x \rightarrow x$
2. $succ(x) + y \rightarrow succ(x + y)$
3. $x + 0 \rightarrow x$
4. $x + succ(y) \rightarrow succ(x + y)$
5. $even(0) \rightarrow true$
6. $even(succ(0)) \rightarrow false$
7. $even(succ(succ(x))) \rightarrow even(x)$
8. $even(x) = true \Rightarrow odd(x) \rightarrow false$
9. $even(x) = false \Rightarrow odd(x) \rightarrow true$

The second step of our method consists of computing the *structural schemata* for the terminating system R: A finite set of terms which, in essence, is a finite description of the standard model of the system R (*cf.* definition below). The set

S(R0) = {0, succ(z)} constitutes a suitable set of structural schemata for R. In general the *structural schemata S(R) for R* is a finite set of R-irreducible terms such that:

a) For any R-irreducible ground term s, there exists a term t in S(R) and a substitution σ such that $t\sigma = s$.

b) Every non-ground (sub)term in S(R) has at least one R0-irreducible ground instance,

c) Every non-ground term in S(R) is of depth equal to D(R) and with variables only at depth D(R).

Requirements a) and c) of the above definition are crucial in proving theorems whereas requirement b) is fundamental in disproving conjectures, provided that R is canonical: If some term t which is obtained by replacing its variables by elements of S(R) is R-irreducible, then the requirement b) allows for constructing a ground instance of t which is also R0-irreducible. Note that the construction of structural schemata S(R) for a set of unconditional rules R is decidable and can be performed in a relatively efficient way. The algorithm is based on pumping lemmas in tree languages and uses complex combinational properties on terms (see (Kounalis, 1990c)). In (Kounalis and Rusinowitch, 1990a) we have given a method to derive structural schemata in the conditional case, provided that a set of free constructors (function symbols) is available.

Having computed the structural schemata S(R) of a set R our next step consists of fixing the variables in C which should be replaced by the elements of S(R). Thus, the next step consists of replacing the variables in the conjecture to be proved **x + y = y + x** with the elements of the structural schemata S(R) of R, to get the formulas:

A. 0 + 0 = 0 + 0
B. 0 + succ(z) = succ(z) + 0
C. succ(z) + succ(w) = succ(w) + succ(z)

The last step of our inductive method consists of simplifying (rewriting) these formulas using the rules of the terminating system R.

The simplification strategy may use rules from R, previously proved conjectures, and instances of the conjecture itself as long as they are smaller (with respect to a well-founded (noetherian) relation that contains the rewriting relation) than the currently examinated conjecture.

This last point captures the notion of *induction hypothesis* in the proof by induction paradigm (see for details (Kounalis and Rusinowitch, 1990a and 90b)). Thus the first two conjectures, namely A and B, are trivials. The left-hand side of the last one can be simplified as follows:

$$\mathbf{succ(z) + succ(w)} \rightarrow_2 \mathbf{succ(z + succ(w))} \rightarrow_4 \mathbf{succ(succ(z + w))}$$

The right- hand side can also be simplified as follows:

succ(w) + succ(z) $\rightarrow_2$ **succ(w + succ(z))** $\rightarrow_4$ **succ(succ(w + z))** $=_A$ **succ(succ(z + w))**

Here the axiom **x + y = y + x** is applied after the first simplification step and therefore its application is smaller *with respect to a well-founded relation* than the initial conjecture: **succ(z) + succ(w) = succ(w) + succ(z)**. We therefore have that both sides of the formulas A, B, and C are reduced to identity and therefore **x + y = y + x** is an inductive theorem of H.

However, most of the time several rounds are needed before getting the proof of a conjecture. At each round the obtained formulas are in fact intermediate lemmas needed for the proof of the initial conjecture. Therefore new instantiations by using the elements of the structural schemata for the variables of the new conjectures are necessary. Further, there is no hierarchy between the intermediate lemmas to be proved, and therefore no difficulty for the management of inductive hypothesis: Every intermediate lemma will be set into the initial set of conjectures. However, if the initial set of Horn formulas is a ground canonical set of (unconditional) rewrite rules, then we shall disproof, in finite time, any equation which is not an inductive theorem of the given theory. This is probably the most amazing feature of our proof system. The whole enterprise for this point is based on the definition of structural schemata. In (Bouhoula, Kounalis and Rusinowitch, 1991) we give a full treatement of the proof by induction paradigm with computer experiments. Similarly we may prove the conjectures 17, 18, 19.

Example 2. Consider now the following program which defines the predicate *less than* on natural numbers:

1. x < y = false ⇒ succ(x) < succ(y) → false
2. x < y = true ⇒ succ(x) < succ(y) → true
3. x < 0 = false
4. 0 < succ(x) = true

and let us show that < is an irreflexive ordering on the set N of natural numbers. To see it we must verify that the following theorem is true in N:

5. x < x = false

The set S(R0) = {0, succ(z)} constitutes a suitable set of structural schemata for R. By substituting terms in S(R) for the variables of the formula 5., we get:

A. 0 < succ(0) = true
B. succ(z) < succ(succ(z)) = true

The first conjecture is trivial. Let us verify the second one: The left-hand side **succ(z) < succ(succ(z))** can be simplified to **true**, by using rule 2. provided that the condition **z < succ(z) = true** of the rule is verified. However, this condition is valid since, by induction hypothesis, we assumed that instances of **x1 < succ(x1) = true** are valid provided they are smaller than the currently examined conjecture, *i.e.*, the conjecture **succ(z) < succ(succ(z)) = true.**

4.2 Learning

"Learning" is a broad term covering a wide range of processes including the acquisition of new declarative knowledge, the organization of new knowledge into general, effective representations, and the discovery of new facts and theories through observation and experimentation. One process central to many kind of learning is the process of *generalization* or *concept learning*; that is, characterizing a class of specific observations by abstracting the important features common to members of that class. The problem of generalizing, in a formal way, from a set of training instances has ben studied by many researchers over the last two decades (*e.g.*, (Plotkin, 1970 and 71), (Vere, 1980), (Mitchell, 1978), (Buntine, 1988), (Kounalis and Rusinowitch, 1990c and 90d), (Michalski, 1983), (Kounalis, 1990), (Lassez and Marriot, 1987), (Kodratoff, 1988), (Lassez, Maher and Marriot, 1991), ... In many cases, the process of generalizing from a set of training instances should be performed in presence of some background knowledge described by a Horn theory. In this context the generalization problem may be stated as follows:

> **Input:** A language in which to describe concepts, a Horn theory H (over the language) describing the background knowledge, and a set EX of examples and a set CE of counterexamples of some "target concept" (concept to be learned).
> **Determine:** A concept description G that is consistent with the background knowledge H and the presented training instances EX ∪ CE.

Here a concept description G is considered to be *consistent* with a set of training instances (examples and counterexamples) and the background knowledge if and only if:

a) It matches every example and no counter example in the set EX ∪ CE, and

b) It eliminates some models of H, and

c) It is true in the standard model (least Herbrand model) of H.

In our view, these requirements capture the essence of incorporating a *new* fact into an existing theory (see (Greiner and Genesereth, 1983)). Let us illustrate the solution of concept learning problem on two simple examples:

Example 1. Consider the problem of learning a concept about the heights of arches built out of blocks. The following Horn theory H describes the background knowledge about arches of blocks:

1. higherthan(x, y) ⇒ higherthan(plus1(x), y)

2. higherthan(plus1(b), b),

where **higherthan(x, y)** denotes the situation where arch x is higher than arch y, **plus1(x)** designs the arch which is obtained by pushing a block on the top of the arch x, and **b** is a constant symbol which designes the empty arch. Thus, **higherthan(x, y) ⇒ higherthan(plus1(x), y)** expresses the rule: If arch x is higher than arch y, then the arch which obtained by pushing a block on the top of x will be higher y. On the other hand, the unit clause **higherthan(plus1(b), b)** expresses the fact that the arch with one block on the top of the empty arch is higher than the empty arch.

Consider now the examples EX:

higherthan(plus1(b), b)
higherthan(plus1(plus1(b)), b)
higherthan(plus1(plus1(b)), plus1(b))
higherthan(plus1(plus1(plus1(b))), b)
higherthan(plus1(plus1(plus1(b))), plus1(plus1(b))) ...

and the counter examples CE:

higherthan(b, b)
higherthan(b, plus1(b))
higherthan(b, plus1(plus1(b)))
higherthan(b, plus1(plus1(plus1(b))))
higherthan(plus1(b), plus1(plus1(b)))
higherthan(plus1(b), plus1(plus1(plus1(b)))) ...

What is the concept description which matches every example and no counter example in the set EX ∪ CE, eliminates some models of H, and is true in the least Herbrand model of H ?

The first step of our method consists of checking whether H is a saturated set of formulas. By using the the saturation test presented in Section 3, we may easily see that H is saturated. Thus, H is interpreted as the following canonical set R of rewrite rules:

1. higherthan(x, y) = T ⇒ higherthan (plus1(x), y) → T
2. higherthan(plus1(b), b) → T

The second step consists of finding candidate formulas which eventually describe the concept to be learned. The formulas we shall consider here are of the form G' ≡ **P / P1** ∨ ...∨ **Pn**, where **P** is a generalization of the set of examples, and **P1**, ..., **Pn** are atoms (generalizations) of the set of counterexamples. That is, we are dealing with formulas involving vectors of atoms which are *anti-instances* of vectors of atoms describing sets of examples and counterexamples. The reason for considering such a kind of formulas is based on the well-known scenario of the learning from examples paradigm: Given a set of examples and counterexamples of a concept, the learner tries to induce a general concept description that induces all examples and none of the counterexamples. In this kind of situation, examples force generalization whereas counterexamples prevent overgeneralizations (the induced concept should never be so general to include any counterexample). This most typical form of learning leads us to think that the generalization process is incremental: The learner first must form its formulas using atoms from the complete *lattice* of atoms (with an added least element modulo variable renaming) which is defined using the anti-instance relation on atoms (see (Plotkin, 1970 and 1971)). He must then verify whether these formulas describe new facts with respect to the existing theory (which describes the background knowledge). If a formula is not new with respect to a given theory, then, in order to change it (either by forgetting something - *i.e.*, further generalizing the examples - or by completing the description - *i.e.*, further specializing the counterexamples) we shift to other elements of the complete lattice of atoms. We think that this process capture the essence of basic generalization constructions based on the *variable binding* mechanism and the *dropping condition rule* (see (Michalski, 1983)).

Here, the examples and the counter examples can be generalized to get the formula:

G' ≡ **higherthan(x, y)** / **higherthan(z, z)** ∨ **higherthan(b, plus1(z))**

Having listed the kind of formulas we are interested in, (*i.e.*, the kind of formulas we want to check for concept description with respect to a Horn theory), our next step consists of verifying whether G' provides a concept to learn. To check it we must first get rid of the instances of **higherthan(x, y)** which are instances either of **higherthan(z, z)** or of **higherthan(b, plus1(y))**. The following labeled tree may be used to accomplish the task (for the construction of such trees, see (Kounalis, 1985)):

higherthan(x, y)

higherthan(b, y) higherthan(plus1(x1), y)

higherthan(b, b) higherthan(b, plus1(y1)) higherthan(plus1(x1), b) higherthan(plus1(x1), plus1(y1))

Now the atoms **higherthan(b, b)**, **higherthan(b, plus(y1))** are instances of **higherthan(z, z)** and **higherthan(b, plus1(y))** respectively. Thus, the atoms **higherthan(b, b)** and **higherthan(b, plus1(y1))** cannot be part of the concept description. Since, in our learning from examples process, we assume the existence of background knowledge described by a set of Horn formulas, it must be verified whether each of the remaining leaf labels are true in the least Herbrand model of H. This is achieved by computing an answer set A(R) for R, *i.e.*, a finite set of substitutions, which, in essence, is a finite description of all ground substitutions which need to be considered for checking whether an atom is valid is the least Herbrand model. For our purposes, the set A(R) = {b, plus1(x)} is a suitable answer set for H. In general, the set of terms A(R) = {t | t is any term in T(F, X), t is of depth no greater than D(R) with variables only at depth D(R)} is said to be an *answer set* for a Horn theory R.

Having computed an answer set A(R) for R, our fourth step consists of replacing terms in A(R) for the variables of **higherthan(plus1(x1), b)** and **higherthan(plus1(x1), plus1(y1))** to get:

higherthan(plus1(b), b)
higherthan(plus1(plus1(x)), b)
higherthan(plus1(b), plus1(b))
higherthan(plus1(b), plus1(plus1(y1)))
higherthan(plus1(x1), plus1(b))
higherthan(plus1(plus1(x1), plus1(plus1(y1)))

Having constructed the instances **higherthan(plus1(b), b)** and **higherthan(plus1(plus1(x)), b)** of **higherthan(plus1(x1), h)** our last step consists of simplyfing these formulas using H and the rule **higherthan(plus1(x1), b)** $\to$ **T** to verify conditions. Now, **higherthan(plus1(b), b)** $\to$ **T** by using the first rule in R. **higherthan(plus1(plus1(x)), b)** $\to$ **T** by using the second rule provided that the premise **higherthan(plus1(x), b)** is equal to **T**. Now by applying **higherthan(plus1(x1), b)** $\to$ **T** we get the result. Thus, **higherthan(plus1(x1), b)** is valid in the least Herbrand model of H. On the other hand, **higherthan(plus1(x1), plus1(y1))** is not valid in the least Herbrand model of H since the ground instance **higherthan(plus1(b), plus1(b))** of it cannot be rewritten to T by using R.

Thus, G ≡ **higherthan(plus1(x1), b)** is a generalization and the concept to be learned is the following: "Any arch with at least one block is higher than the empty arch".

Example 2. Consider the universe of *natural numbers* with the well-known functions **number**, **even**, **double**, **succ**, **0**, **true**, and **false**. Assume that the background knowledge of natural numbers is described by the following set of Horn formulas H:

1. **number(x)** $\Rightarrow$ **even(double(x)))**
2. **number(0)**
3. **number(double(x))**
4. **number(succ(x))**
5. **even(0)**

Consider now the examples EX:

even(0)
even(double(0))
even(double(succ(0)))

even(double(double(succ(0))) ...

and the counterexamples CE:

even(succ(0))
even(succ(succ(0)))

In order to discover the concept induced by the previous sets of examples and counterexamples our first step consists of travelling in the lattice of terms which contains all anti-instances of the set of examples and counterexamples under consideration. For instance, consider the sentence:

G' ≡ **even(x)** / **even(succ(y))**

The term **even(x)** is an anti-instance (a generalization) of the previous examples and the term **even(succ(y))** is an anti-instance of the counterexamples. Having computed sentences G', our next step consists of verifying whether G' is a generalization with respect to H, *i.e.*, whether G' provides a concept to be learned. To check it we must first get rid of the instances of **even(x)** which are instances of **even(succ(x)**. The following labeled tree may be used to accomplish the task:

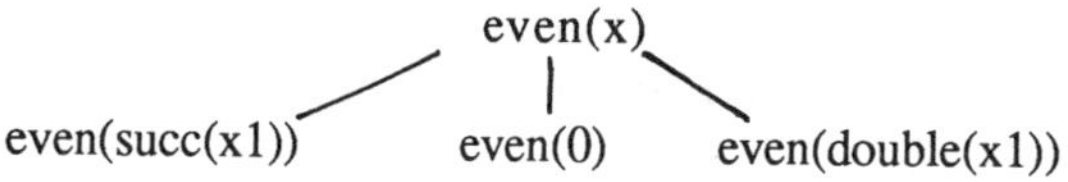

```
                        even(x)
                 /         |        \
even(succ(x1))          even(0)       even(double(x1))
```

The term **even(succ(x1))** is an instance of a counterexample. To see whether the terms **even(0)**, **even(double(x1))** provide a concept to be learned we have to compute the answer set A(R) of the previous set of rules: A(R) = {0, double(x) succ(y))}. Consider now:

even(double(0))
even(double(double(x1)))
even(double(succ(x1)))

By using simplification as above we get that **even(double(x1))** is true in the least Herbrand model of H and thus the concept to be learned is: "Any natural number which is either zero or the double of some number is even".

4.3 Program Synthesis

As we already have pointed out, "Program Synthesis" is the derivation of a program from a given specification. Various approaches to the automated synthesis of (first-order) functional and logic programs have been proposed. The early work in program synthesis relied stronly on using deductive methods (in particular, resolution-based theorem proving) to derive executable programs from formal specifications (Green, 1969). In mid-eigthies, program synthesis and theorem proving tended to go separate ways: (Burstall and Darlington, 1977), (Manna and Waldinger, 1979 and 80), (Darlington, 1981), (Hogger, 1981), (Smith, 1982) have proposed the direct application of transformation or rewrite rules to the program specification. More recently, inductive-based methods have also been used to accomplish this task (see (Smith, 1980) , (Shapiro, 1983)).

Newer approaches that employ both deductive and inductive methods to derive, in automatic way, executable programs have been proposed by Dershowitz (Dershowitz, 1985a and 85b) and recently improved by (Reddy, 1989) and (Dershowitz and Pinchover, 1990). In these approaches directed equations (rules) are used both as a specification language and as a target programming language within a synthesis system. The Knuth-Bendix completion procedure (Knuth and Bendix, 1970) has been proposed as the deductive engine to generate the target program. However, when the target program contains equations that are only true in the standard model of the given specification, the well-known inductionless-induction methods (see (Musser, 1980), (Huet and Hullot, 1990), (Jouannaud and Kounalis, 1986), (Bachmair, 88), (Kounalis and Rusinowitch, 1990 and 90a), (Reddy, 1990)) may be used to derive provably correct computer programs. More recently, (Kounalis, 1990a) has proposed a simplification-based approach to generate the target programs from Horn specifications. This approach unifies and generalizes the previous ones by treating not only equational theories by general Horn theories and by using only one inference rule: *Simplification*. In this context, the program synthesis problem can be stated as follows:

Input: A Horn theory D describing the domain knowledge and a Horn formula S_f describing the specification of a function f.
Determine: A synthesized program R which is a correct recursive definition of the function f.

A *correct recursive program* is a set of rewrite rules R such that:

a) It does not use specification symbols,

b) It terminates, *i.e.*, no infinite derivation are possible,

c) It is correct with respect to the given specification S_f and the domain knowledge D, in the sense that any two ground terms that are equal according to S_f and D are also equal according to the target system R. In other words, the correctness of R with respect to $S_f \cup D$ preserves the set of ground equivalence classes of $S_f \cup D$: The standard model of $S_f \cup D$ remains invariant.

In general all synthesized programs should meet these requirements since they allow us to compute, in an efficient way, by replacing instances of a left-hand side with the corresponding right-hand side. Input terms are therefore repeatedly rewritten (simplified) according to the rules of the target program. When and if no rule applies, the resultant *normal form* is considered the *value* of the initial term. The rationale for these requirements is that *computation* is the transformation (simplification) of a ground term to its normal form.

The methods we propose here (see also (Kounalis, 1990a)), are used to develop a new automatic method of deriving (conditional) equational provably correct computer programs which meet the requirements pointed out above. Domain knowledge and specifications are given as sets of (conditional) equations and *purely (algebraic) simplification* is the engine used to generate target programs. In general, our approach regards program synthesis as a transformational task that combines features of deduction and induction within a single framework. We shall show application of our method to the derivation of primitive recursive programs computing on domains such as integers, lists.

Let us show how to generate a correct target program R from a set of rules $R0 = S_f \cup D$, where S_f is the program specification and D is supposed to contain the definitions (in terms of "primitive" functions), together with any properties required for them. Thus, S_f defines some new functions without modifying the standard model of D. This is crucial for the identification of what should be preserved by the program synthesis process: The target program R should "meet" the specification S_f and should "preserve" the set of ground equivalence classes of D. Without discussing the technical details of the proposed method let us describe it on two simple examples:

Example 1. Consider the specification S_-:

1. x - y = x + op(y)

of a function to *subtract* integers and suppose we are given the following facts D (domain knowledge) about addition and inverse:

2. x + 0 = x
3. x + succ(y) = succ(x + y)
4. x + pred(y) = pred(x + y)
5. op(0) = 0
6. op(succ(x)) = pred(op(x))
7. op(pred(x)) = succ(op(x))

Assume that we wish to generate a recursive correct program for subtracting integers, *i.e.*, a program R which:

a) uses only the function - and the "primitive" function symbols (*e.g.*, **succ**, **pred**, **0**)

b) is correct with respect to the specification S_- and the domain knowledge D.

The first step of our method consists of supplying a well-founded ordering on terms. Using a well-founded ordering to orient equations ensures that the system of rules *terminates* (*i.e.*, for no input term is an infinite sequence of rewrites possible). The ordering must reduce any term composed of the function we wish to synthesize (*e.g.*, the function -) and primitive symbols to a term which consists wholly of primitives. Such an ordering ensures that "specification" symbols (*e.g.*, **+** and **op**) are greater than the "synthesized" functions (*e.g.*, the function **-**), which in turn are greater than the "primitive" function symbols (*e.g.*, **succ, pred, 0**). Now the following system R0 is a terminating one:

1. x + op(y) → x - y
2. x + 0 → x
3. x + succ(y) → succ(x + y)
4. x + pred(y) → pred(x + y)
5. op(0) → 0
6. op(succ(x)) → pred(op(x))
7. op(pred(x)) → succ(op(x))

The second step of our method consists of computing the *structural schemata* for the terminating system R0 (see Section 4.1). The set S(R0) = {0, succ(z), pred(z)} constitutes a suitable set of structural schemata for R0. The requirements a), b), c) of the definition of structural schemata are crucial in the program synthesis process: If some term t which is obtained by replacing its variables by elements of S(R0) is R0-irreducible, then the supplied domain knowledge is not sufficient to get a correct target program. More important, such a program does not exist for the given set R0 of rules.

Having computed the structural schemata S(R0) of a set R0 of rules of the problem definition D and program specification S_f, our next step consists of fixing the variables in S_f which should be replaced by the elements of S(R0). Thus, the next step consists of replacing the *inductive* variables in the specification formula:

x - y = x + op(y)

with the elements of the structural schemata S(R0) of R0, to get the formulas (*patterns*):

8. x - 0 = x + op(0)
9. x - succ(z) = x + op(succ(z))
10. x - pred(z) = x + op(pred(z))

In general, if R0 = $S_f \cup$ D is a set of rules and t is a term, then an *inductive variable* of t is a variable whose position in some subterm of t corresponds to a function symbol in a left-hand side of a rule in R0. Thus, the set of inductive variables of a conditional equation C is the union of the inductive variables of the terms in C.

The last step of our program synthesis method consists of simplifying these formulas using the rules of the terminating system R0 in order to get the desired target program:

8. x - 0 = x + op(0) $\rightarrow_5$ **x + 0** $\rightarrow_2$ **0**

9. $x - succ(z) = x + op(succ(z)) \rightarrow_6 x + pred(op(z)) \rightarrow_4 pred(x + op(z)) \rightarrow_1 pred(x - z)$
10. $x - pred(z) = x + op(pred(z)) \rightarrow_7 x + succ(op(z)) \rightarrow_3 succ(x + op(z)) \rightarrow_1 succ(x - z)$

We therefore generate the following correct recursive target program for subtracting integers:

1. $x - 0 \rightarrow 0$
2. $x - succ(z) \rightarrow pred(x - z)$
3. $x - pred(z) \rightarrow succ(x - z)$

The rules 1, 2, 3 constitute the desired correct target program since they satisfy the requirements stated above. For the correcteness proof, see (Kounalis, 90a). Note that if the Knuth-Bendix method is used here, then an infinite sequence of rules will be generated.

Example 2. Consider now the specification S_{halve}:

1. $halve(x) = x / succ(succ(0))$

of a function for *halving* a nonnegative integer and suppose we are given the following terminating set D of rules (domain knowledge) about integer *division*:

2. $x < y = true \Rightarrow x / y \rightarrow 0$
3. $x < y = false \Rightarrow x / y \rightarrow (x - y / y) + succ(0)$
4. $x < y = false \Rightarrow succ(x) < succ(y) \rightarrow false$
5. $x < y = true \Rightarrow succ(x) < succ(y) \rightarrow true$
6. $x < 0 \rightarrow false$
7. $0 < succ(x) \rightarrow true$
8. $x - 0 \rightarrow x$
9. $0 - x \rightarrow 0$
10. $succ(x) - succ(y) \rightarrow x - y$
11. $x + 0 \rightarrow x$
12. $x + succ(y) \rightarrow succ(x + y)$

Assume that we wish to generate a recursive correct program for halving nonnegative integers. The set {0, succ(0), succ(succ(z))) constitutes the structural schemata for R0 = $S_{halve} \cup$ D. Now by replacing the variable x in the specification formula:

$halve(x) = x / succ(succ(0))$

with elements from the set {0, succ(0), succ(succ(z))} we get the formulas:

13. halve(0) = 0 / succ(succ(0))
14. halve(succ(0)) = succ(0) / succ(succ(0))
15. halve(succ(succ(z))) = succ(succ(z)) / succ(succ(0))

Our last step now consists of using rules from R0 to simplify these formulas:

13. halve(0) = 0 / succ(succ(0)) $\rightarrow_2$ **0**
14. halve(succ(0)) = succ(0) / succ(succ(0)) $\rightarrow_2$ **0**
15. halve(succ(succ(z))) = succ(succ(z)) / succ(succ(0))

The term **succ(succ(z)) / succ(succ(0))** can be simplified to **succ(succ(z)) – succ(succ(0)) / succ(succ(0)) + succ(0)** provided that the premise **succ(succ(z)) < succ(succ(0)) = false** is valid. However, **succ(succ(z)) < succ(succ(0))** → **succ(z) < succ(0)** → **z < 0** → **false**. In general, preconditions are not valid in the whole class of models of the specification under consideration, but they are valid only in the initial model of R0. In this case some kind of induction is necessary. What is interesting here is that the proposed method may also be used to verify the premises for validity in the initial model .

Now the term **succ(succ(z)) - succ(succ(0)) / succ(succ(0)) + succ(0)** can be simplified to **z - 0 / succ(succ(0)) + succ(0)**, by using twice rule 10., which in turn is simplified to **z / succ(succ(0)) + succ(0)** by using rule 8. Thus, the term **z / succ(succ(0)) + succ(0)** is simplified to **halve(z) + succ(0)**, by applying the specification rule (*i.e.*, the rule **x / succ(succ(0))** → **halve(x)**). Finally, the term **halve(z) + succ(0)** can be simplified to **succ(halve(z))** by first using rule 12. and next rule 11. Thus, **halve(succ(succ(z)))** → **succ(halve(z))** and the finally target program for halving nonnegative integers is:

1. halve(0) → **0**
2. halve(succ(0))) → **0**
3. halve(succ(succ(z))) → **succ(halve(z))**

This is a very efficient program for halving nonnegative integers (compare it to the initial set of rules R0). A similar program has been generated by (Dershowitz and Pinchover, 1990) by using auxiliary function definitions and heuristic devises.

4.4 Diagnosis

"Diagnostic" is an important application for AI research. Intuitively, diagnosing a system consists of inferring its real state from its observed behaviour. Such an informal definition is sufficiently general to apply to a wide class of diagnostic problems, for instance, medical diagnostic, where the state of a system is a set (possibly empty) of diseases and its behaviour is a set of observed symptoms, as well as device diagnostic, where the state of a system is a set of abnormal components and its behaviour is given by the set of its outputs. Thus, a diagnosis problem can be stated as follows:

> **Input:** A description of a system and of its observed behaviour.
> **Determine:** All possible states of the system that accounts for its observed behaviour.

As far as logic-based diagnosis is concerned, two main approaches have been pointed out so far. On one hand, the consistency-based approach consists of explaining the discrepancy between the observed behaviour of a system and its expected one, derived from the system description. This approach is essentially deductive in the sense that the abnormal parts of the resulting possible states of a system can be derived by deduction from what is known. Consistency-based diagnosis, pioneered by R. Reiter and J. De Kleer, is the cornerstone of a number of recent researches, like circumscription-based diagnosis, and numerous systems. On the other hand, the abductive approach to diagnostic consists of explaining directly the observed behaviour of a system by formulating hypothetical states that support what is observed given what is already known. The role of abduction for diagnosis is also well-known in the AI community for quite a long time.

Consistency-based diagnosis and abductive diagnosis have been intensively studied (see, for instance, (Reiter, 1987) (De Kleer, 1987) (De Kleer *et al.*, 1990) (Raiman, 198) (Raiman, 1990) for the former and (Pople, 1973) (Reggia *et al.*, 1985) (Cox and Pietrzykowski, 1987) (Console and Torasso, 1990) for the latter). Furthermore, comparisons between these approaches have also been thoroughly investigated (see, for instance, (Nau and Reggia, 1986) (Poole, 1988) (Poole, 1989)). Subsequently, it is not our purpose to compare here these approaches, nor to describe exhaustively their variants. We only aim at presenting their principles in a formal frame, then proposing some computational methods for supporting them. More precisely, the objective of the following discussion is to show how the materials described in Section 1 to 3 apply as a formal basis for both the consistency-based and the abductive approaches to diagnosis.

Let us start this discussion by providing several definitions and illustrating them on a very simple example:

A *system* is a triple S = <COMPONENTS, SD, OBS> where:

1. COMPONENTS is the *finite set of components* of S described by constant symbols c1, ..., cn of F ;

2. SD, the *system description*, is a set of Horn formulas representing the given knowledge about S (*e.g.* the system connexions, the types of its components and the descriptions of the models of these components) ;

3. OBS, the *observations*, is a set of Horn formulas corresponding to the inputs (I) and the outputs (O) of S.

We distinguish a unary predicate, usually denoted **ok**, for representing the states of the components. The argument of such a predicate belongs necessarily to COMPONENTS. **ok(c)** is interpreted as "the component c is normal".

Let us consider, for instance, the circuit CIRC as described below, where COMPONENTS = {c1, c2}.

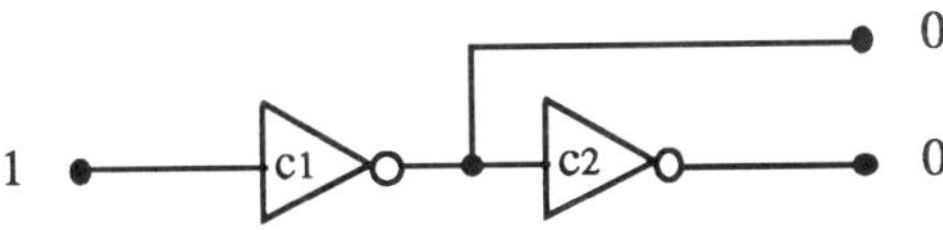

The following description SD of the system CIRC represents the correct model of the components, their types, the connexions of CIRC, the negation laws and the independance of the logical values:

$$\begin{aligned} SD = \{ & \forall x\ (\mathbf{inv(x)} \wedge \mathbf{ok(x)}) \Rightarrow (\mathbf{out(x)} = \mathbf{not(in(x))}), \\ & \mathbf{inv(c1)},\ \mathbf{inv(c2)}, \mathbf{out(c1)} = \mathbf{in(c2)}, \\ & \mathbf{not(O)} = \mathbf{1},\ \mathbf{not(1)} = \mathbf{0},\ \neg(\mathbf{0} = \mathbf{1})\}. \end{aligned}$$

The observations OBS of CIRC are I $\cup$ O with I = {**in(c1)** = **1**} and O = {**out(c1)** = **0**, **out(c2)** = **0**}.

A *diagnosis* Δ of a system S is a conjunction of literals the predicate of which is ok (*ok–literals*). The set of components which occur in Δ is denoted $\mathcal{C}(\Delta)$. The set of positive ok–literals in Δ is denoted Δ^+ and the set of negative ok–literals in Δ is denoted Δ^-. Any formula built solely on the ok–predicate is referred to as an ok–*formula*.

A first logic-based diagnostic approach is the consistency-based one. By definition, $\Delta = \Delta^+ \cup \Delta^-$ is a *consistency–based diagnosis* of a system S if:

– Δ is a complete diagnosis of S: The state of each element of COMPONENT is described in Δ, and

– SD $\cup$ OBS $\cup$ {Δ} is a satisfiable set, and

– No complete diagnosis Δ' of S such that Δ'^+ is strictly included in Δ^+ satisfies the previous property.

As shown in (De Kleer *et al.*, 1990) (El Ayeb *et al.*, 1990), consistency-based diagnoses can be characterized by means of the notions of *implicants* / *implicates*, where, intuitively, a prime implicate of a first-order formula is a most general clause which follows from that formula and a prime implicate of a formula is a most specific (existentially quantified) conjunction of literals which implies that formula. Clearly, prime implicants and implicates are dual concepts in the sense that every prime implicant of a formula is the negation of a prime implicate of the negation of that formula.

Another central logic-based approach for diagnostic relies on abduction. By definition, Δ is an *abductive diagnosis* of a system S for a non-empty subset CO of O if:

– Δ, SD, I $\models$ CO and

– SD ∪ I ∪ {Δ} is a satisfiable set ;

– No abductive diagnosis Δ' of S for CO is strictly included in Δ.

As shown in (El Ayeb *et al.*, 1990), abductive diagnoses can be computed as the prime implicants of the formula ((SD ∧ I) ⇒ CO) which are built solely on the ok predicate and which are consistent with SD ∪ I.

The interest of the set of inference rules described in Section 3.3 according to the diagnostic problem relies on the fact that it can be used to derive all the prime implicates built solely out of the ok predicate (ok-prime implicates), given an ordering on atoms such that any ok-literal is strictly smaller than any literal with another predicate symbol (El Ayeb *et al.*, 1990). To be more specific, the procedure which consists of applying to a given set of clauses S the resolution and paramodulations rules each time it is possible to do so and removing properly subsumed clauses and tautologies leads to derive, among other, all the ok-prime implicates of S and, in particular, the empty clause if S is unsatisfiable. It is worth noting here that the prime implicates / implicants of first-order formulas do not always exist in general (see (Marquis, 1991a and 91b) for details). However, this is not the case for the ok-prime implicates / implicants. It is equally interesting to note that resolution strategies with ordering and paramodulation do not allow to derive prime implicant / implicate in general. Finally, the termination of the procedure described above is ensured for some simplification orderings when S is a set of ground clauses. Since the equality predicate is allowed, this situation does not reduce to the mere propositional logic. In the standard approaches, the only termination case to be mentioned is the propositional one.

For the axiomatization of the two-inverters circuit described above, our strategy allows us to derive one consistency-based diagnosis, namely **(ok(c1) ∧ ¬ok(c2))** and one abductive diagnosis for CO = {**out(c1) = 0**}, namely **ok(c1)**.

5 BIBLIOGRAPHY

Bachmair, L. (1988). "Proof by Consistency in Equational Theories", Proc. *3th IEEE Symposium on Logic in Computer Science (LICS)*, Edinburgh.

Bachmair, L. and Dershowitz, N. (1991). "Equational Inference, Canonical Proofs, and Proofs Ordering", *JACM* (to appear).

Bachmair, L., Dershowitz, N. and Plaisted, D. (1987). "Completion without Failure", Proc. *Colloquium on Resolution of Equations in Algebraic Structures*, Lakeway, Texas.

Bachmair, L. and Ganzinger, H. (1990a). "Completion of First-Order Clauses with Equality", Proc. *2nd CTRS*, Montréal.

Bachmair, L. and Ganzinger, H. (1990b). "On Restriction of Ordered Paramodulation with Simplification", Proc. *10th CADE*.

Bertling, H. (1990). "Knuth-Bendix Completion of Horn Clause Programs for Restricted Linear Resolution and Paramodulation", Proc. *2nd CTRS*, Montréal.

Birkhoff, G. (1935). "On the Structure of Abstract Algebras", Proc. *Cambridge Philosophical Society* 31, pp. 433-545.

Bouhoula, A., Kounalis, E. and Rusinowitch, M. (1991). "A Mechanization of Inductive Reasoning", (submitted).

Boyer, R.S. and Moore, J.S. (1979). *A Computational Logic*, Academic Press, New York.

Brand, (1975). "Proving Theorems with the Modification Methods", *SIAM Journal of Computing* 4, pp. 412-430.

Brown, T.C. Jr (1975). A Structured Design-Method for Specialized Proof Procedures, Ph.D. Thesis, California Institute of Technology, Pasadena (CA).

Buntine, W. (1988). "Generalized Subsumption and its Applications to Induction and Redundancy", *Artificial Intelligence* 36 pp. 149-176.

Burstall, R.M. (1969). "Proving Properties of Programs by Structural Induction", *Computer Journal* 12 (1), pp. 41-48.

Burstall. R. and Darlington. J. (1977). "A Transformation System for Developing Recursive Programs", *JACM* 24 (1).

Chang, C.L. and Lee, R.C.T. (1971). *Symbolic Logic and Mechanical Theorem Proving*, Academic Press, New York.

Console, L. and Torasso, P. (1990). "Integrating Models of Correct Behavior into Abductive Diagnosis", Proc. *9th European Conference on Artificial Intelligence (ECAI)*, Stockholm, pp. 160-166.

Cox, P.T. and Pietrzykowski, T. (1987). "General Diagnosis by Abductive Inference", Proc. *Symposium on Logic Programming*, San Francisco, California, pp. 183-189.

Darlington, J. (1981). "An Experimental Program Transformation and Synthesis System", *Artificial Intelligence* 16 (1).

De Kleer, J. (1987). "Diagnosing Multiple Faults", *Artificial Intelligence* 32, pp. 97–130.

De Kleer, J., Mackworth, A.K. and Reiter, R. (1990). "Characterizing Diagnoses", Proc. *International Workshop on Expert Systems in Engineering*, Vienna, LNAI 462, Springer-Verlag, pp. 1-15.

Dershowitz, N. (1982 and 1987). "Applications of the Knuth-Bendix Completion Procedure", Proc. *Séminaire d'Informatique Théorique*, Paris, pp. 95-111. Revised version in 1987.

Dershowitz, N. (1985). "Computing with rewrite systems", *Information and Control* 65 (2/3), pp. 122-157.

Dershowitz, N. (1985). "Synthesis by Completion", Proc. *9th International Joint Conference on Artificial Intelligence (IJCAI)*, Los Angeles (USA).

Dershowitz, N. (1987). "Termination of Rewriting", *Journal of Symbolic Computation* 3 (1&2).

Dershowitz, N. (1990). "Canonical Sets of Horn Clauses", Proc. *2nd CTRS*, Montréal, pp. 267-278.

Dershowitz, N. and Jouannaud, J.P. (1991). "Rewrite Systems", in J. Van Leeuwen (ed.), *Handbook of Theoretical Computer Science*, North-Holland, pp. 243-320.

Dershowitz, N. and Okada, M. (1990). "A Rationale for Conditional Equational Programming", *Theoretical Computer Science* 75, pp. 111-138.

Dershowitz, N. and Manna, Z. (1979). "Proving Termination with Multiset Orderings", *CACM* 22 (8), pp. 465-476.

Dershowitz, N. and Pinchover, E. (1990). "Inductive synthesis of equational programs", Proc. *8th National Conference on Artificial Intelligence (AAAI-90)*, Boston (USA).

El Ayeb, B., Marquis, P. and Rusinowitch, M. (1990). "A New Diagnosis Approach by Deduction and Abduction", Proc. *International Workshop on Expert Systems in Engineering*, Vienna, LNAI 462, Springer-Verlag, pp. 32-46.

Fribourg, L. (1986). "A Strong Restriction of the Inductive Completion Procedure", Proc. *13th ICALP*, Rennes.

Ganzinger, H. (1987). "Ground Term Confluence in Parametric Conditional Equational Specifications", Proc. *4th Symposium on Theoretical Aspects of Computer Science*, Passau, RFA.

Ganzinger, H. (1991). "A Completion Procedure of Conditional Equations", *Journal of Symbolic Computation.*, Mars 1991.

Green, C.C. (1969). "Application of Theorem-Proving to Problem Solving", Proc. *1st International Joint Conference on Artificial Intelligence (IJCAI)*, Washington (DC), pp. 219-239.

Greiner, R. and Genesereth, M. (1983). "What's New ? A Semantic Definition of Novelty", Proc. *International Joint Conference on Artificial Intelligence (IJCAI)*, pp. 450-454, Karslruhe.

Hogger, C.L. (1982). "Derivation of Logic Programs", *JACM* 28 (2).

Hopcroft J. and Ullman, J. (1979). *Introduction to Automata Theory, Languages and Computation*, Addison - Wesley, Reading.

Hsiang, J. and Rusinowitch, M. (1986). "A New Method for Establishing Refutational Completeness in Theorem Proving", Proc. *8th CADE*, Oxford, LNCS 230, Springer-Verlag, pp. 141-152.

Hsiang, J. and Rusinowitch, M. (1987). "On Word Problems in Equational Theories", Proc. *14th International Colloquium on Automata, Languages and Programming*, Karlsruhe, RFA, LNCS 267, Springer-Verlag, pp. 57-71.

Huet, G. (1976). Résolution d'équations dans des langages d'ordre 1, 2, ..., ω, Thèse d'Etat, Université de Paris 7.

Huet, G. (1980). "Confluent Reductions: Abstract Properties and Applications to Term Rewriting Systems", *JACM* 27 (4), pp. 797-821.

Huet, G. and Hullot, J.M. (1982). "Proofs by Induction in Equational Theories with Constructors", *Journal of Computer System Sciences* 25 (2).

Huet, G. and Oppen, D.C. (1980). "Equations and Rewrite Rules: A Survey", in R.V. Book (ed.), *Formal Language Theory: Perspectives and Open Problems*, Academic Press.

Jouanaud, J.P. and Kounalis, E. (1986 and 1989). "Automatic Proofs by Induction in Equational Theories without Constructors", Proc. *1st IEEE Symposium on Logic in Computer Science*. Full paper in Information and Control 82 (1989), pp. 1-33.

Waldmann, B. (1986). "Reductive Conditional Term Rewriting Systems", Rapport de DEA, CRIN, Nancy

Kaplan, S. (1987). "Simplifying Conditional Term Rewriting Systems: Unification, termination, Confluence", *Journal of Symbolic Computation* 4, pp. 295-334.

Kapur, D., Narendran, P. and Zhang, H. (1987). "On Sufficient Completeness and Related Properties of Term Rewriting Systems", *Acta Informatica* 24, pp. 395-415.

Kapur, D. and Zhang, H. (1988). "Mechanizing Induction for Equational Specifications", Proc. *9th CADE*, Argone (USA), LNCS 310, Springer-Verlag.

Knuth, D. and Bendix, P. (1970). "Simple Word Problems in Universal Algebras", In *Computational Problems in Abstract Algebra*, pp. 263-297.

Kodratoff, Y. (1988). *Introduction to Machine Learning*, Pitman.

Kounalis, E. (1985). "Completeness in Data Type Specifications", Proc. *European Conference in Computer Algebra (EUROCAL)*, Linz (Austria), LNCS 204, Springer-Verlag, pp. 348-362.

Kounalis, E. (1990a). A Calculus of Systems with Equality, Mémoire d'Habilitation à Diriger des Recherches en Informatique, Université de Nancy I.

Kounalis, E. (1990b). "Learning from Examples and Counterexamples with Equational Background Knowledge", Proc. *2nd IEEE International Conference on Tools for Artificial Intelligence*, Herndon, VA, (USA), pp. 254-260.

Kounalis, E. (1990c). "Pumping Lemmas for Tree Languages Generated by Rewrite Systems", Proc. *15th Conference on Mathematical Foundations of Computer Science (MFCS 90)*, Banska Bystrica, LNCS 452, Springer-Verlag, pp. 369-378.

Kounalis, E. (1990d). "Testing for Inductive-(Co)-Reducibility in Rewrite Systems", Proc. *15th Colloquium on Trees in Algebra and Programming (CAAP 90)*, Copenhagen, LNCS 431, Springer-Verlag, pp 221-238.

Kounalis, E. and Rusinowitch, M. (1987). "Operational Semantics of Horn Clauses", *1st CTRS*, Paris.

Kounalis, E. and Rusinowitch, M. (1988). "On the Word Problem in Horn Theories", Proc. *9th CADE*, Argone (USA), LNCS 310, Springer-Verlag, pp. 347-357.

Kounalis, E. and Rusinowitch, M. (1990a). "A Mechanization of Conditional Reasoning", Proc. *1st International Symposium on Mathematics and Artificial Intelligence*, Fort Lauderdale (Florida).

Kounalis, E. and Rusinowitch, M. (1990b). "Mechanizing Inductive Reasoning", Proc. *8th National Conference on Artificial Intelligence (AAAI-90)*, Boston(USA), pp. 240-245. Also in the Bulletin of the European Association of Theoretical Computer Science (EATCS), n° 41, June 1990, pp. 216-226.

Kounalis, E. and Rusinowitch, M. (1990c). "Discovering New Facts in First-Order Knowledge-Based Theories", Proc. *4th International Symposium on Knowledge Engineering*, Barcelona, pp. 186-199.

Kounalis, E. and Rusinowitch, M. (1990d). "A Logical Basis for Learning in Robots' Worlds", Proc. *5th International Conference on Applications of Artificial Intelligence In Engineering*, Boston (USA), vol. 2, Manufacture and Planning, pp. 275-288.

Kounalis, E. and Rusinowitch, M. (1991a). "On Word Problems in Horn Theories", *Journal of Symbolic Computation.*, Mars 1991.

Kounalis, E. and Rusinowitch, M. (1991b). "Studies on the Ground Convergent Property of Conditional Theories", Proc. *2nd International Conference on Algerbraic Merthodology of Software Technolog,* Iowa City (USA), May 1991.

Lankford, D.S. (1975). "Canonical Inference", Technical Report ATP-32, University of Texas at Austin.

Lassez, J.L. and Mariott, K. (1987). "Explicit Representation of Term Defined by Counterexamples", *Journal of Automated Reasoning* 3, pp. 301-317.

Lassez, J.L., Maher, M. and Marriott, K. (1991). "Elimination of Negation in Term Algebras", Proc. *16th Conference on Mathematical Foundations of Computer Science (MFCS 91)*, Poland.

Lloyd, W. (1984). *Foundations of Logic Programming*, Springer-Verlag.

Loveland, D.W. (1978). *Automated Theorem Proving. A Logical Basis*, North-Holland.

Maher, M. (1988). "Complete Axiomatizations of the Algebras, Rational and Infinite Trees", Proc. *3rd IEEE Symposium on Logic in Computer Science*, pp. 348-357.

Manna, Z. (1970). "Fixed Point Induction of Programs", in *CACM*.

Manna, Z. and Waldinger, R. (1980). "A Deductive Approach to Program Synthesis", *ACM Transactions on Programming Languages* 2 (1).

Marquis, P. (1991a). Contribution à l'étude des méthodes de construction d'hypothèses en intelligence artificielle, Thèse d'Université, Université de Nancy 1.

Marquis, P. (1991b). "Extending Abduction from Propositional to First-Order Logic", Proc. *Fundamentals of Artificial Intelligence Research* (FAIR), Bratislava, LNAI 535, Springer-Verlag.

Michalski, R.S. (1983). "A Theory and Methodology of Inductive Learning", *Artificial Intelligence* 20 (1983) , pp. 111-161.

Michalski, R.S. (1984 and 86). *Machine Learning: An Artificial Intelligence Approach*, vol. 1 & 2, Springer-Verlag.

Mitchell, T.M. (1978). Version Spaces: An Approach to Concept Learning, Ph.D. Thesis, STAN-CS-78-711, Stanford University.

Musser, D.R. (1980). "On Proving Inductive Properties of Abstract Data Types", Proc. *7th POPL Conference*, Las Vegas.

Nau, D.S. and Reggia, J.A. (1986). "Relationships between Deductive and Abductive Inference in Knowledge-Based Diagnostic Problem Solving", Proc. *1st International Workshop on Expert Database Systems*, San Diego, California, pp. 549-558.

Padawitz, P. (1988). *Computing in Horn Clause Theories*, Springer-Verlag.

Peterson, G.E. (1983). "A Technique for Establishing Completeness Results in Theorem Proving with Equality", *SIAM Journal of Computing* 12 (1), pp. 82-100.

Plaisted, D. (1985). "Semantic Confluence Tests and Completion methods", *Information and Control* 65 (2/3), pp. 182-215.

Plotkin, G.D. (1970). "A Note on Inductive Generalization", in *Machine Intelligence* 5, pp. 153-163.

Plotkin, G.D. (1971). "A Further Note on Inductive Generalization", in *Machine Intelligence* 6, pp. 101-124.

Poole, D. (1988). "Representing Knowledge for Logic-Based Diagnosis", Proc. *Fifth Generation Computer Systems Conference*, Tokyo, pp. 1282-1290.

Poole, D. (1989). "Normality and Faults in Logic-Based Diagnosis", Proc. *11th International Joint Conference on Artificial Intelligence (IJCAI)*, Detroit, Michigan, pp. 1304-1310.

Pople, H.E. Jr (1973). "On the Mechanization of Abductive Logic", Proc. *3rd International Joint Conference on Artificial Intelligence (IJCAI)*, Stanford, California, pp. 147-152.

Przymusinski, T. (1987). "On the Declarative Semantics of Stratified Deductive Databases and Logic Programs".

Raiman, O. (1989). "Diagnosis as a Trial: The Alibi Principle", Proc. *IBM Workshop on Model-Based Diagnosis*, Paris, pp. 1-10.

Raiman, O. (1990). "A Circumscribed Diagnosis Engine", Proc. *International Workshop on Expert Systems in Engineering*, Vienna, LNAI 462, Springer-Verlag, pp. 90-101.

Reddy, U. (1989). "Rewriting Techniques for Program Synthesis", Proc. *3rd International Conference on Rewriting Techniques and Applications*, Chapell Hill (USA), LNCS 355, Springer-Verlag.

Reddy, U. (1990). "Term Rewriting Induction", Proc. *10th CADE.*

Reggia, J.A., Nau, D.S. and Wang, P.Y. (1985). "A Formal Model of Diagnostic Inference", *Information Sciences* 37, pp. 227-285.

Reiter, R. (1987). "A Theory of Diagnosis from First-Principles", *Artificial Intelligence* 32, pp. 57-95.

Rémy, J.L. (1982). Etude des Systèmes de Réécriture Conditionnels et Application aux Types Abstraits Algébriques, Thèse d'Etat, Institut National Polytechnique de Lorraine.

Rémy, J.L. and Zhang, H. (1985). "Contextual Rewriting", Proc. *Rewriting Techniques and Applications*, LNCS 202, Springer-Verlag, pp. 46-62.

Robinson, J.A. (1965). "A Machine-Oriented Logic Based on the Resolution Principle", *JACM 12*, pp. 23-41.

Rusinowitch, M. (1989). *Démonstration automatique - Techniques de réécriture*, InterEditions.

Rusinowitch, M. (1990). "Theorem Proving with Resolution and Superposition", *Journal of Symbolic Computation* 11, pp. 21-49.

Selman, A. (1971). "Completeness of Calculi for Axiomatically Defined Classes of Algebra", *Algebra Universalis* 2, pp. 20-32.

Shapiro, E. (1983). *Algorithmic Program Debugging*, MIT Press, Cambridge.

Smith, D. (1980). "A Survey of Synthesis of LISP Programs from Examples", Proc. *International Workshop on Program Construction*, Bonas.

Smith, D. (1982). "Derived Preconditions and their Uses in Program Synthesis", Proc. *6th CADE*, New York.

Tarski, A. (1968). "Equational Logic and Equational Theories of Algebras", In K. Schutte (ed.), *Contribution to Mathematical Logic*, North-Holland.

Taylor, (1979). "Equational Logic", in G. Grätzer (ed.), *Universal Algebra*, pp. 378-400.

Vere, S.A. (1980). "Multilevel Counterfactuals for Generalization of Relational Concepts and Productions", *Artificial Intelligence* 14, pp. 139-164.

Wos, L.T., Robinson, G.A., Carso, D.F. and Shalla, L. (1967). "The Concept of Demodulation in Theorem Proving", *JACM* 14(4).

Wos, L.T. and Robinson, G.A. (1969). "Paramodulation and Theorem Proving in First-Order Theories with Equality", in *Machine Intelligence* 4, Elsevier, pp. 135-150.

SECTION 2

SEARCHING

CHAPTER 2

On Optimizing a Search Problem[1]

Jun Gu
Dept. Electrical Engineering, University of Calgary
Calgary, Canada T2N 1N4
gu@enel.UCalgary.CA

ABSTRACT

Many search techniques have been developed during the past several decades. In this article, we discuss approaches of using optimization methods to solve search problems. Due to its theoretical significance and practical applicability, we have used the satisfiability (SAT) problem as a nontrivial case study. Many efficient optimization algorithms have been developed to solve the SAT problem. Tested through years of real program execution, it has been shown that such algorithms are capable of solving hard, large-scale and practical satisfiability problems with satisfactory performance. We have found that many search problems, such as constraint satisfaction problems (CSP), can be solved by optimization methods.

Keywords: Artificial intelligence (AI), continuous optimization, local search, satisfiability (SAT) problem, very large-scale satisfiability (VLSS) problem.

1 Introduction

Search problems are ubiquitous in AI. Almost every AI program depends on a search procedure to perform its prescribed functions. For every interesting problem encountered there might be numerous alternatives to consider. In character recognition, a program searches through numerous character models in the dictionary to find a model character that matches the input character pattern. In machine learning, many potential hypotheses must be considered before a good one is chosen. In scheduling problems, a search among possible schedules of the objects must be performed and a feasible schedule that meets the given timing and/or resource constraints is then selected. In theorem proving, clauses must be found by searching axioms and assertions which together resolve to give the empty clause. This requires a search of literals which unify and then a search to find resolvable clauses. In playing a game, one usually tries to think of a best-possible move among many alternative choices.

[1]The material present in this chapter is a summary of technical report [17] and several subsequent publications. This research was supported in part by 1988 and 1989 ACM/IEEE academic scholarship awards, and is presently supported in part by a Strategic Grant.

A search problem is typically defined in terms of a space consisting of a set of states and a set of operators that map from one state to other states. A solution to the search problem is a sequence of operators that map an initial state to a goal state. Search spaces are usually represented as a graph or a search tree structure, and a search is finding a path from some start node to a goal node. So far many search techniques have been developed [45, 47, 48, 69]. Some recent surveys of search techniques can be found in [38, 39].

Search is one of the most interesting problems in AI that exhibits the frustrating property. Consider an airline scheduling problem. Given a set of timing options each with its corresponding capacity restrictions and a number of airplanes each with a specific combination of timings, we want to find out a sequence of airplanes that meets the capacity restrictions. If, for example, 10 airplanes have to be scheduled, then there are $10! = 3{,}628{,}800$ possible scheduling sequences. This number determines the search or computing time: the hay-stack that hides the needle. With one more airplane, this stack becomes 11 times bigger, with another, 12 times, etc. This is to say, the number of possibilities grows faster and faster where the number of airplanes only grows one by one. The computing time for this problem is hard to control: it grows *exponentially*, due to *combinatorial explosion*.

Search is a general mechanism for intelligence, what limits its applicability is the efficiency with which it can be performed. Thus, the *central issue* in search is efficiency. Two important measures of efficiency are the amount of time and the amount of memory required to find the solution.

In this chapter, we discuss search problem-solving techniques with an emphasis on describing approaches of using optimization methods to solve search problems. Due to its theoretical significance and its practical applicability, we have selected the satisfiability (SAT) problem as a nontrivial case study. Tested through years of real program execution, we have found that search algorithms developed based on practical optimization techniques are capable of solving hard, very large-scale and practical satisfiability problems with satisfactory performance.

To start, in the next section, we will briefly review some traditional search techniques.

2 Basic Search Techniques

Search is characteristic of almost all AI problems and has a long and distinguished history in AI. Many problem-solving techniques can be viewed as search techniques.

Brute-force search methods. This is a blind search that uses no knowledge about the problem other than the problem space itself. Alternatives in the space are explored mechanically until a goal is found, a time limit has been reached, or failure occurs. At the worst case, it may be necessary to explore the whole search space before finding a solution. Examples of blind searches include depth-first search, breadth-first search, depth-first iterative deepening search [35], uniform-cost search, backward chaining, and bidirectional search [49]. The problem with all brute-force search algorithms is that their time complexities grow exponentially with problem size. The sizes of problems that can be solved by these techniques is quite limited.

Heuristic Search. When some knowledge information is available about the goals, the problem states, or the problem in general, it may be possible to guide the search process and eliminate a number of implausible paths. Surprisingly, a small amount of knowledge often has a fairly dramatic effect on the efficiency of a search algorithm. Heristic search methods include, for examples, general best-first, hill-climbing, branch-and-bound, A^* [28], iterative deepening A^* [35], and optimal AND-OR heuristic search. The heuristic algorithms do not defeat exponential complexity, but merely delay its effect.

Abstraction. The basic idea of abstraction is that, given a complex problem, one should at first ignore the low-level details of the problem and concentrate on the essential features, and then take into account the details later. Techniques in this category include a single level of abstraction [50, 55] and multiple hierarchical levels of abstraction. In order to reduce the problem complexity, we need to extract more knowledge. Subgoaling, macro-operators [36] and abstract problem spaces [37] are some examples of the kinds of knowledge that might be useful. A drawback of using these techniques is that we almost always sacrifice solution optimality.

Two-Player Games. Chess games usually have a well-structured, finite problem domain with perfect information. The skill of playing games has long been regarded as a distinctive mark of human intelligence which makes it an ideal place of studying certain aspects of AI. Search techniques in this area include minimax search [44, 57], alpha-beta pruning [27], node ordering, quiescence, iterative deepening [60], and special-purpose hardware [2, 9].

Constraint-Satisfaction Problems (CSP). CSPs are an important class of problems in AI and operations research. Many practical problems can be formulated as CSPs, i.e., finding a set of consistent assignments to a set of variables subject to a set of constraints. Methods of solving CSPs include waltz filtering [68], lookahead processor [13, 26, 53], network consistency [41, 7], brute-force backtracking, intelligent backtracking [11, 51, 52], local search [17, 19, 63, 65], quantitative approach [22, 31], and special-purpose hardware architectures [23, 24, 42].

As an alternative approach, in this chapter, we describe some of our past work in using practical optimization techniques to solve search problems. For most search problems we have solved, in terms of computing time and space, such techniques achieve many orders of magnitude of performance improvement.

3 Optimization for a Search Problem

3.1 The Optimization Problem

Optimization has been an important unifying theme that cuts across many areas in science, engineering, management, agriculture, industry, and medicine. The concept of optimization is well rooted as a principle underlying the analysis of many complex decision problems. It offers a certain degree of philosophical elegance that is hard to dispute, and it often offers an indispensable degree of operational simplicity.

In spite of its wide applications, there is a common philosophical background underlying the principle of optimization. When one approaches a complex decision problem, involving the selection of values of a number of interrelated variables, one should focus on a single objective (or a few objectives) designed to qualify performance and measure the quality of the decision. The *core* of the optimization process is to minimize (or maximize) the objective subject to the constraints imposed upon the values of the decision variables by the problem. Traditionally we use the term *object function* to denote such an objective.

Computers are efficient at performing repetitive operations. Most present algorithms designed for optimization are iterative in nature. Typically, in seeking a vector that solves the optimization problem, an initial vector $\mathbf{x}_0$ is selected and the algorithm generates an improved vector $\mathbf{x}_1$. The process is repeated and an even better solution $\mathbf{x}_2$ is found. Continuing in this fashion, a sequence of ever-improving points $\mathbf{x}_0$, $\mathbf{x}_1$, ..., $\mathbf{x}_k$, ..., is found that approaches a solution point $\mathbf{x}^*$. For the linear programming problem, the generated sequence reaches the solution point exactly after a finite number of steps. For nonlinear programming problems, the sequence does not necessarily reach the solution point, but converges towards it. That is, the process is terminated at some point sufficiently close to the solution point.

Two aspects of the theory of the iterative algorithms are global convergence and local convergence rate. *Global convergence* concerns, starting from an initial point, whether the sequence of points will converge to the final solution point. *Local convergence rate* is the rate at which the generated sequence of points converges to the solution.

In the rest of this paper, a quantity $f(n)$ is said to be $O(g(n))$ if $\lim_{n\to\infty} f(n)/g(n) \geq 0$. A quantity $h(n)$ is said to be $o(g(n))$ if $\lim_{n\to\infty} h(n)/g(n) = 0$.

3.2 Local Optimization

Local search, or local optimization, is one of the primitive forms of continuous optimization in a discrete problem space. It was one of the early techniques proposed during the mid-sixties to cope with the overwhelming computational intractability of NP-hard combinatorial optimization problems. Unlike continuous optimization techniques, local search has often been used in AI research and it has established a strong link between AI and the operations research area.

Given a minimization (maximization) problem with object function f and feasible region F', a typical local search algorithm requires that, with each solution point $x_i \in F'$, there is associated a predefined *neighborhood* $N(x_i) \subset F'$. (Note that in the areas of artificial intelligence and operations research, a point x_i in a local search framework is called a *solution point* even if it is not a *final* solution point of the given problem.) Given a current solution point $x_i \in F'$, the set $N(x_i)$ is searched for a point x_{i+1} with $f(x_{i+1}) < f(x_i)$ ($f(x_{i+1}) > f(x_i)$). If such a point exists, it becomes the new current solution point, and the process is iterated. Otherwise, x_i is retained as a *local optimum* with respect to $N(x_i)$. Then, a set of feasible solution points is generated, and each of them is "locally" improved within its neighborhood. To apply local search to a particular problem, one need only to specify the neighborhood and the randomized procedure for obtaining a feasible starting solution.

Local search is very efficient in several aspects. First, at the beginning of the search, using a full assignment of all variables in the search space, it reduces an exponential growth search space to a much smaller one. Secondly, it searches for improvement within its local neighborhood using a testing for improvement and, if there is any improvement, takes an action for improvement. Since the object function has a polynomial number of input numbers, both "testing" and "action" are relatively efficient and often perform very well for a search problem. A major weakness of local search is that the algorithm has a tendency to get stuck at a locally optimum configuration (i.e., a local minima).

Many search techniques, such as statistical optimization [5, 56], simulated annealing [34], stochastic evolution [54], conflict minimization [43, 61, 65], and genetic algorithms [15], are either local search or variations of local search.

Local search is one among a very few successful techniques for combinatorial optimization. We have used local search techniques and solved many hard, constraint-based satisfaction problems and constraint-based optimization problems. For most search problems we have solved, compared to the prior art in the area, local search can easily achieve at least five to ten orders of magnitude of performance improvement (in terms of computing time and space). For example, we have used local search to solve the n-queen problem. It dramatically outperforms the standard backtracking approaches, allowing one to solve million queen problems [62, 64], while a standard backtracking approach handles only approximately 97 queens [66].

3.3 Optimizing a Search Problem

Most optimization models can be classified in terms of the variables' behavior. If the variables are allowed to take on real values that satisfy the constraints, the optimization model is said to be *continuous*. If the variables are allowed to take on only discrete values, the optimization model is called *integer* or *discrete*. Finally, when there are some integer variables and some continuous variables in the problem, the optimization model is said to be *mixed*. In general, problems with discrete integer variables fall into the domain of *combinatorial analysis* which, in most cases, is closely linked with the search problem model.

Informally, from a philosophical point of view, we can conjecture that search problems with discrete variables are in general significantly more difficult to solve than those with continuous variables which are often used in the continuous optimization. Therefore, it is advantageous to use continuous optimization approaches to solve a search problem. Here I can only give a few intuitive points. For a detailed consideration, see: Jun Gu, *The Philosophy of Computation*.

1. **Search Bandwidth.** We define informally the search bandwidth of a solution point as the number of directly connected neighboring solution points. It gives the maximum number of choices we can make if search proceeds at that solution point. Assume that we have a 3-dimensional search space, then the search bandwidth of each discrete solution point is six since each solution point has only six directly connected neighboring solution points. Apparently, the search bandwidth of each continuous solution point is infinite.

2. **Local Effect.** The set of discrete search paths in a search space forms a *mesh* structure with nodes representing the solution points. Assume that in a particular region of the search space there are many local minima points. Most discrete search paths in the region would be trapped, the mesh would be broken, and the search would proceed with difficulty. This situation can be improved with continuous variables. A set of an infinite number of continuous search paths forms a complete terrain *surface* in the search space which could lead the search to a successful solution point.

3. **Best-Neighbor Heuristic.** A local search algorithm proceed by taking *any* solution point that decreases the object function as the next solution point. There are many neighboring solution points. A local search does not take into account its neighbors' relative performance to the object function. An effective heuristic is to select *the best neighbor point* that yields the minimum value to the object function, and take this *best neighbor's direction* as the descent direction of the object function [17, 19, 18]. Such a best-neighbor heuristic can only be implemented by using continuous optimization techniques. There are many mathematical tools available for this purpose.

At this point, a direct question that may be raised is: how does one use continuous optimization techniques to solve a discrete search problem ? There are many answers to this question: First, we can directly supply discrete values to the continuous variables as constraints to the given problem. Second, we can express discrete values as a cost function, so they are automatically added to an object function.

Third, most discrete values can be given as a separate instance of a function with the special interpretation of its values. Fourth, we can use a mixed optimization model.

The philosophy underlying the "mixed" model is simple, we discuss it using an analogy. In a telecommunication system, we are not able to transmit a speech signal directly. Using a modulator, before its transmission, we put the speech signal on a high frequency signal called "carrier." The carrier signal carries the speech signal to a receiver. At the receiver end, the carrier accomplishes its duty, a demodulator separates the speech signal from the carrier. In a mixed model, similarly, we simply put a discrete search problem into a search space with continuous variables. The problem is then solved by the continuous optimization techniques. Eventually, the results of continuous variables are decoded back to their discrete counterparts which are the solution of the original search problem.

In the next section, we will describe the satisfiability (SAT) problem. In the rest of the chapter, it will be used as a case study to illustrate our ideas and approaches.

4 The Satisfiability (SAT) Problem

One goal of the satisfiability (SAT) problem [3, 12] is to determine whether there exists a truth assignment to a set of variables (x_1, x_2, ...,x_m) that makes the following Boolean formula satisfiable:

$$c_1 \wedge c_2 \wedge \cdots \wedge c_n, \tag{1}$$

where $\wedge$ is a logical *and* connector and c_1, c_2, ..., c_n are n distinct clauses. Each clause consists of only literals combined by a logical *or* ($\vee$) connector (a literal is a variable or a single negation of a variable). The satisfiability problem is fundamental in solving many practical problems in logic programming, inference, machine learning, and constraint satisfaction. Theoretically, the satisfiability problem is a *core* of a large family of computationally intractable problems.

Many algorithms and approaches have been developed to solve the satisfiability problem. One straightforward way to solve the SAT problem is to enumerate all possible truth assignments to see if one satisfies the formula. This is unacceptable since it suffers from an exponential growth of computing time. Subject to certain restrictions, Davis and Putnam gave a procedure that was shown to solve the SAT problem in average-case polynomial time [6, 14]. These restrictions substantially limit the applications of the algorithm. Among many techniques proposed, such as term-rewriting [8, 30], production system [59], multi-valued logic [58], resolution and its variations [33, 45, 69], resolution is the most widely used method. Unfortunately, a resolution-based approach is not able to handle even moderately sized inference problems.

Recent work using local search in solving very large-scale constraint satisfaction problems (CSP) has inspired this research [16, 18, 61, 63, 65]. Since 1985, we have investigated several search approaches to solve hard, very large-scale and practical satisfiability problems [17, 18]. We have found that some efficient methods are local search and optimization approach [17, 18, 22, 31]. Several software tools based on local search ideas have been built. More detailed technical reports have been written.

In the next section, we will give a primitive local search algorithm for the SAT problem.

5 A Discrete Local Search Algorithm for the Satisfiability Problem

Many discrete local search algorithms have been developed for the satisfiability problem. In this section, we will describe a primitive local search algorithm for the satisfiability problem. For details of other algorithms, please see references [17, 18]. Following Section 4, in the following discussion, let:

- c_i be the i_{th} clause,
- x_j be the j_{th} variable,
- $\vec{\mathbf{x}}$ be a vector of m variables,
- $|c_i|$ be the number of literals in clause c_i, and
- l be the average number of literals in each clause: $\frac{\sum_{i=0}^{n} |c_i|}{n}$,

where $i = 1, ..., n$ and $j = 1, ..., m$.

A basic local search algorithm for the satisfiability problem is given in Figure 1. The algorithm consists of an initialization stage and a search stage. Several operations, *get_a_SAT_instance*(), *select_an_initial_point*(), *compute_conflicts*(), *test_swap*(), *perform_swap*(), and *local_handler*() are needed. We will see their operation in the following discussion of the algorithm.

Initialization

Initially, the $SAT1.0$ algorithm requires a practical or a randomly generated SAT problem instance. At the beginning of search, procedure *get_a_SAT_instance*() produces a random instance of the satisfiability problem with n distinct clauses, m variables, and on average l literals per clause. Procedure *select_an_initial_point*() randomly selects an initial starting point: $\vec{\mathbf{x}}_0$. An initial starting point is an initial random truth assignment to the SAT problem.

The object function $conflicts$ in the $SAT1.0$ algorithm returns the number of "conflicting" clauses that have a *false* truth value. Based on such a formulation of

```
procedure SAT1.0 ()
begin
    /* initialization */
    get_a_SAT_instance();
    x⃗_0 := select_an_initial_point();
    conflicts := compute_conflicts(x⃗_0);

    /* search */
    k := 0;
    while conflicts ≠ 0 do
    begin
        for each variable i := 1 to m do
            /* if swap(x_i, x̄_i) reduces conflicts */
            if test_swap(x_i, x̄_i) then
            begin
                x⃗_{k+1} := perform_swap(x_i, x̄_i);
                conflicts := compute_conflicts(x⃗_{k+1});
            end;
        if local then local_handler();
        k := k + 1;
    end;
end;
```

Figure 1: **SAT1.0:** A Local Search Algorithm for the Satisfiability (SAT) Problem.

```
procedure Local_Handler ()
begin
    randomly choose some variable x_t's;
    x⃗_{k+1} := perform_swap(x_i's, x̄_i's);
    conflicts := compute_conflicts(x⃗_{k+1});
end;
```

Figure 2: A Simple Local Handler.

the object function, the original SAT problem becomes a minimization problem to the object function [17, 18].

Search

The search process is an iterative local optimization process. During the k_{th} iteration, for each variable x_i in vector $\vec{\mathbf{x}}$, we cyclically search through its neighborhood to select a solution point that minimizes the object function. That is, during a single search step, a literal x_i is considered for its contribution to the total conflicts. The test to see if a swap of the truth value of x_i with $\overline{x_i}$ will reduce the total number of conflicts in the clauses is performed by function *test_swap*(x_i,$\overline{x_i}$). Function *test_swap*(x_i,$\overline{x_i}$) returns *true* if the swap operation would reduce the total number of conflicts in the clauses; otherwise, it returns *false*. The actual swap operation is performed by procedure *perform_swap*(x_i,$\overline{x_i}$), which produces a new solution point, i.e., $\vec{\mathbf{x}}_{k+1}$. Procedure *compute_conflicts*() updates the total number of conflicts in the clauses.

Termination

In practice, before $conflicts$ reduces to zero, the algorithm could be stuck at a locally optimum point. To solve this problem, in the $SAT1.0$ algorithm (see Figure 2), a simple local handler that can negate up to m variables is added to improve its convergence performance. The basic idea is that of generating a 'random exchange' in some current solution points, when the search was stuck on a local minima, accepting a modified point as a new current solution not only if the value of the cost function is better but also if it is worse.

In the $SAT1.0$ algorithm, due to excessive floating point computation and poorer convergence, the probability given by a Boltzmann-like law as used in simulated annealing was not taken as a decision for accepting a random change in the *local_handler*(). Instead, in this local handler, a definite selection of a new search state is taken. The local handler, in fact, has effectively improved the convergent performance of the $SAT1.0$ algorithm.

As observed by many previous researchers, local optima produced by local search have a certain average quality; they are related to the quality of the initial starting points. The use of a random initial starting point is an *unbiased* decision that enables one to sample the set of local optima widely, producing an optimized feasible starting point. In the local handler, the use of some random exchanges has the same effect of reassigning the initial feasible starting point which is a fairly general technique applied to tackle the pathological effect of worst-case instance [47]. The early success of this strategy has been renowned as Lin's important contribution to the solution of the traveling salesman problem (TSP) [40, 47].

In most combinatorial optimization problems, such as the TSP, it is effective to use a completely random starting point [40, 47]. In practical algorithm design, however, the effectiveness of the idea must be justified by additional running time. In the local handler used in $SAT1.0$ algorithm, generating a completely random starting point requires $O(m)$ time, while selecting a few variables to swap takes only a constant portion of time. So we have used a swap more frequently than would a completely random starting point.

Running Time

The running time of the $SAT1.0$ algorithm can be estimated as follows: Procedure *get_a_SAT_instance*() and function *compute_conflicts*() each take $O(nl)$ time since they go through n clauses and examine, on average, l literals per clause. Procedure *select_an_initial_point*() takes $O(m)$ time to produce an initial solution point. Accordingly, the total time for initialization is $O(nl)$.

The running time of the *while* loop equals the number of *while* loops executed (k) multiplied by the running time of the *for* loop. In the worst case, *perform_swap()* takes $O(m)$ time, *test_swap()*, *compute_conflicts*(), *local_handler*() each will take $O(nl)$ time. Combining $O(m)$ time cyclic scan of m variables, the running time of the *for* loop is $O(m(nl)))$.

Summarizing the above, the time complexity of $SAT1.0$ is:

$$O(nl) + O(knml) = O(knml). \tag{2}$$

In Equation (2), the number of iterations, k, is determined by the nature of the problem instance and is therefore nondeterministic. As is common with any probabilistic local search algorithm [4], $SAT1.0$ does not guarantee the worst case running time for a particular instance of execution, although it exhibits satisfactory performance and robust behavior. Hence, an unsuccessful attempt may occur and the algorithm will call the local handler. *In practice*, local search has been very effective for many difficult combinatorial optimization problems. It is often, in fact, the best available approach [32, 46].

In the next section, we give an average-time analysis of the $SAT1$ algorithm.

6 Average Time Analysis

The $SAT1$ algorithm described in the last section gives a general local search framework for the satisfiability problem. Many versions of the $SAT1$ algorithm were developed [17]. In this section, we will give some average time complexities of three primitive versions of the $SAT1$ algorithm, the $SAT1.1$ algorithm, $SAT1.2$ algorithm, and $SAT1.3$ algorithm. Practical and powerful $SAT1$ algorithms have been described elsewhere.

Generally, the *hardness* of the SAT problem increases when l decreases or n/m increases. That is, fewer literals in each clause and a larger number of clauses reduce the probability that all clauses are jointly satisfiable. Presently, a major effort in the research area is aimed at designing efficient algorithms to solve problems with small l and a large number of clauses. This is important in practice, since for large l, most vectors in $\{0,1\}^m$ will be the solutions of the problem, and thus, a random exhaustive search can efficiently solve the problem [14].

The $SAT1.1$ algorithm, an aggressive local search algorithm, the $SAT1.2$ algorithm, a local search algorithm with monotonic conflict minimization, and the $SAT1.3$ algorithm, a version of the aggressive strategy, are shown in Figure 3, Figure 4, and Figure 5, respectively.

Given a CNF (conjunctive normal form) formula F of m variables and a vector $v \in \{0,1\}^m$, let $f(v)$ be the number of clauses in F that have the value 0, then the SAT problem becomes a minimization problem with object function $f(v)$. The feasible search region is $\{0,1\}^m$ and for each vector (point) $v \in \{0,1\}^m$, the neighborhood $N(v)$ is defined to be

$$N(v) = \{v' | H(v, v') \leq c\},$$

where $H(v, v')$ denotes the Hamming distance between the vectors v and v' and c is a positive constant that denotes the number of different bits between the vectors v and v'. Let $c = 1$, v_i denote the ith bit of vector v, and $\bar{v}_i$ denote the negation of v_i. Then $N(v)$ can be searched by examining vectors $(v_1, \ldots, \bar{v}_i, \ldots, v_m)$ for $1 \leq i \leq m$. In the $SAT1.1$, $SAT1.2$, and $SAT1.3$ algorithms, the vector $(v_1, \ldots, \bar{v}_i, \ldots, v_m)$ is produced by procedure *perform_swap*$(v_i, \bar{v}_i)$, the value of $f(v)$ is called the number of *conflicts* and is calculated by procedure *compute_conflicts*(v).

Given a CNF formula, initially, the $SAT1.1$, $SAT1.2$, and $SAT1.3$ algorithms randomly choose a vector v from $\{0,1\}^m$ and compute $f(v)$. Next if $f(v) > 0$, these algorithms search $N(v)$ to see whether there exists a vector $v' \in N(v)$ such that $f(v') < f(v)$. If such a v' exists, then take this v' as a new vector v and continue the search until $f(v) = 0$. In practice, before $f(v)$ is reduced to zero, the algorithms tend

```
procedure SAT1.1 ()
begin
    /* initialization */
    get_a_SAT_instance();
    v := select_an_initial_point();
    conflicts := compute_conflicts(v);

    /* search */
    k := 0;
    while conflicts ≠ 0 do
    begin
        for each variable i := 1 to m do
            /* if swap(v_i, v̄_i) reduces conflicts */
            if test_swap(v_i, v̄_i) then
            begin
                v' := perform_swap(v_i, v̄_i);
                conflicts := compute_conflicts(v');
            end;
        if conflicts ≠ 0 then local_handler();
        k := k + 1;
    end;
end;
```

Figure 3: **SAT1.1:** An Aggressive Local Search Algorithm for the Satisfiability Problem.

```
procedure SAT1.2 ()
begin
    /* initialization */
    get_a_SAT_instance();
    v := select_an_initial_point();
    conflicts' := compute_conflicts(v);

    /* search */
    k := 0;
    while conflicts' ≠ 0 do
    begin
        conflicts := conflicts';
        for each variable i := 1 to m do
            /* if swap(v_i,v̄_i) does not increase conflicts */
            if test_swap(v_i,v̄_i) then
            begin
                v' := perform_swap(v_i,v̄_i);
                conflicts' := compute_conflicts(v');
            end;
        if conflicts' = conflicts then local_handler();
        k := k + 1;
    end;
end;
```

Figure 4: **SAT1.2:** A Local Search Algorithm with Monotonic Conflict Minimization.

```
procedure SAT1.3 ()
begin
    /* initialization */
    get_a_SAT_instance();
    v := select_an_initial_point();
    conflicts := compute_conflicts(v);

    /* search */
    k := 0;
    while conflicts ≠ 0 do
    begin
        for each variable i := 1 to m do
            /* if swap(v_i, v̄_i) reduces conflicts */
            if test_swap(v_i, v̄_i) then
            begin
                v' := perform_swap(v_i, v̄_i);
                conflicts := compute_conflicts(v');
            end;
        if conflicts ≠ 0 then local_handler();
        k := k + 1;
    end;
end;

procedure Local_Handler ()
begin
    for each variable i := 1 to m do
    begin
        v' := perform_swap(v_i, v̄_i);
        conflicts' := compute_conflicts(v');
        if conflicts' = conflicts then v := v';
    end;

    randomly choose some variable x_t's;
    x⃗_{k+1} := perform_swap(x_i's, x̄_i's);
    conflicts := compute_conflicts(x⃗_{k+1});
end;
```

Figure 5: **SAT1.3:** A Local Search Algorithm for the Satisfiability Problem.

to get stuck at a local optimum point. A simple local handler that can negate up to m variables is added to overcome this problem.

The $SAT1.1$, $SAT1.2$, and $SAT1.3$ algorithms use different criteria to judge whether they have been stuck at a locally optimum point. In the $SAT1.1$ and $SAT1.3$ algorithms, after one iteration cycle (i.e., $N(v)$ has been searched m times), if $f(v) \neq 0$ then the local handler is called. In the $SAT1.2$ algorithm, if there is no vector $v' \in N(v)$ such that $f(v') < f(v)$ then the local handler is called.

The running time of the $SAT1.1$ algorithm can be estimated as follows: The initialization portion takes $O(nl)$ time. The running time of the search portion equals the number of times the *while* loop is executed, say k_1, multiplied by the running time of the internal loop. The running time of the internal loop is clearly $O(nml)$. Summarizing the above, the running time of $SAT1.1$ algorithm is $O(k_1nml)$.

The running time of the $SAT1.2$ algorithm can be estimated as follows: The initialization portion takes $O(nl)$ time. The running time of the search portion equals the number of *while* iterations multiplied by the running time of each iteration. The running time of each *while* iteration is clearly $O(nml)$. The analysis of the number of the *while* loop iteration executed is more complicated. We define a search phase of the $SAT1.2$ algorithm as the computation of the algorithm from getting a random vector $v \in \{0,1\}^m$ until a solution is found or we get stuck at a local minimum point. If the $SAT1.2$ algorithm is stuck at a locally optimum point, it gets a new random vector and starts a new search phase. In each execution of the *while* loop, if the $SAT1.2$ algorithm is not stuck at a local optimum point, then the object function $f(v)$ will be reduced by at least one. Since $f(v)$ is at most n, the $SAT1.2$ algorithm will find a solution if it has never been stuck at a local optimum point for n executions of the *while* loop. Therefore, each search phase of the $SAT1.2$ algorithm takes $O(n^2ml)$ time. Thus, the running time of the search portion of the $SAT1.2$ algorithm is $O(k_2n^2ml)$, where k_2 is the number of times the search phase was executed. To summarize, the running time of the $SAT1.2$ algorithm is $O(k_2n^2ml)$.

The running time of the $SAT1.3$ algorithm can be estimated similarly as that of the $SAT1.1$ algorithm: The initialization portion takes $O(nl)$ time. The running time of the search portion equals the number of times the *while* loop is executed, say k_3, multiplied by the running time of the internal loop. The running time of the internal loop is clearly $O(nml)$. Thus, the running time of $SAT1.1$ algorithm is $O(k_3nml)$.

The theoretical analysis of the average time complexities is lengthy and complicated. Here we give some preliminary results. More formal versions have been submitted for publication [20, 21]. A summary of a few important lemmas and theorems is attached in Appendix A.

The $SAT1.1$, $SAT1.2$, and $SAT1.3$ algorithms are efficient for a much wider range of l. The average time complexity of $SAT1.1$ algorithm is estimated as follows: The run time of the $SAT1.1$ algorithm is $O(k_1nml)$, where k_1 is the number of times that the algorithm is stuck at a local optimum point. We have proved that during each phase of the search, the probability that algorithm $SAT1.1$ is stuck at a local optimum point is at most

$$1 - \{1 - [1 - (1 - \frac{l}{2^l m})^n]^l\}^m,$$

where n is the number of clauses, m is the number of variables, and l is the average number of literals in each clause of a randomly generated CNF formula. From this, the average time complexity of the $SAT1.1$ algorithm is $O(m^{O(1)}n)$ for $l \geq \log m - \log\log m$ and $n/m = O(2^l/l)$ (see Appendix A).

The run time of the $SAT1.2$ algorithm is $O(k_2 n^2 ml)$, where k_2 is the number of times that the algorithm is stuck at a locally optimum point. We have proved that during each phase of the search, the probability that the $SAT1.2$ algorithm is stuck at a local optimum point is at most

$$1 - \prod_{i=1}^{n}\{1 - [1 - (1 - \frac{l}{2^l m})^n]^i\}.$$

From this, the average time complexity of the $SAT1.2$ algorithm is $O(m^{O(1)}n)$ for $l \geq 3$ and $n/m = O(2^l/l)$ (see Appendix A).

For $l \geq \log m - \log\log m - c$ and $n/m \leq 2^{l-1}/l$, where $c \geq 0$ is any constant, we show that $SAT1.1$ exhibits a polynomial average time complexity of $O(m^{O(1)}n)$. For $l \geq 3$ and $n/m = O(2^l/l)$, we show that $SAT1.2$ exhibits a polynomial average time complexity of $O(m^{O(1)}n^2)$. For $l = o(m)$, while both $SAT1.1$ and $SAT1.2$ have the polynomial average time complexity, the well-known Davis-Putnam algorithm demonstrates a superpolynomial average running time ($O(n^{O(m/l)})$) [14]. Thus $SAT1.1$ and $SAT1.2$ algorithms have significantly improved over the Davis-Putnam algorithm.

For $l < \log m - \log\log m - c$ or $n/m >> 2^l/l$, the running time of the $SAT1.1$ algorithm goes to superpolynomial. The running time of the $SAT1.2$ algorithm is superpolynomial for $n/m >> 2^l/l$. Of courses, these two algorithms give no answer if the given formula is not satisfiable.

The search strategy used in the $SAT1$ algorithms have been independently shown to be efficient for the SAT problem by other researchers.

The above theoretical results are the most conservative, "safer" bounds for the $SAT1.1$ and $SAT1.2$ algorithms. In practice, these algorithms are much more efficient than was shown in the above theoretical bounds. The $SAT1.3$ algorithm is one version of the $SAT1.1$ algorithm. The average run time of $SAT1.3$ is $O(nml \log m)$ when $l \geq 3$ and $n/m = O(2^l/l)$ (see Appendix A).

Starting from the next section, we will describe the approaches of using continuous optimization techniques to solve the satisfiability problem.

7 *UniSAT*: A *Universal SAT* Problem Model

In the following discussion, we consider n-component vectors $\vec{\mathbf{x}} = (x_1, x_2, ..., x_n)$ as points in a vector space. We denote such an *n-dimensional Euclidean space* as E^n. A real-valued function f defined on a subset of E^n is said to be *continuous* at $\vec{\mathbf{x}}$ if $f(\vec{\mathbf{x}}_k) \to f(\vec{\mathbf{x}})$. A set of real-valued functions $f_1, f_2, ..., f_m$ on E^n can be regarded as a single vector function $\mathbf{f} = (f_1, f_2, ..., f_m)$. This function assigns a vector $\mathbf{f}(\vec{\mathbf{x}}) = (f_1(\vec{\mathbf{x}}), f_2(\vec{\mathbf{x}}), ..., f_m(\vec{\mathbf{x}}))$ in E^m to every vector $\mathbf{x} \in E^n$. Such a real-valued function is said to be *continuous* if each of its component functions is continuous. Also in the following discussion, let $\vec{\mathbf{x}}_0$ be an initial point and $\vec{\mathbf{x}}^*$ be a solution point in E^m.

The discrete variables in a search space have lower search bandwidth and contain limited heuristic information. Since only discrete values are allowed, the representation and specification of a solution point must be restricted and qualitative and the search process must be highly constrained and cumbersome. We have learned some weaknesses of formulating the SAT problem using the discrete variables. In the following unconstrained nonlinear formulation of the SAT problem, we extend the set of discrete variables, $\vec{\mathbf{x}} \in L = \{x_i = \pm 1, \text{ for } i = 1, 2, \ldots, m\}$, into the set of continuous variables: $\vec{\mathbf{x}} \in E^m$. By using continuous variables, each solution point, $\vec{\mathbf{x}}$, and the object function, $f(\vec{\mathbf{x}})$, can be characterized quantitatively. If we encode solution constraints of a given SAT problem into its object function appropriately, a direct correspondence between the solutions of the SAT problem and the global minimum points of the object function can be established. Consequently, the SAT problem can be transformed into a continuous optimization problem. In this case, the search space E^m, defined as a feasible set in mathematical programming, corresponds to a completely unconstrained, nonlinear optimization problem.

There is a variety of ways to select the formats of an object function [17, 18, 19]. To simplify the discussion, in this chapter, we give *UniSAT*7 and *UniSAT*8 models which are the simplest among all the *UniSAT* models. The foundation underlying the *UniSAT*7 and *UniSAT*8 models can be traced down to the well-known *De Morgan Laws*. The "universal" *De Morgan Laws* were developed that translate each clause in a discrete domain into an object function in a continuous domain.

The *UniSAT*7 Problem Model [17, 18, 19]: Given n distinct clauses and m variables, the satisfiability problem is transformed into an unconstrained nonlinear programming problem:

$$\min_{\vec{\mathbf{x}} \in \mathbf{E}^m} f(\vec{\mathbf{x}}), \tag{3}$$

where

$$f(\vec{\mathbf{x}}) = \sum_{i=1}^{n} \prod_{j=1}^{m} t_{ij}(x_j) \tag{4}$$

and

$$t_{ij}(x_j) = \begin{cases} (x_j - T)^{2p} & \text{if literal } x_j \text{ is in clause } c_i \\ (x_j + F)^{2p} & \text{if literal } \bar{x}_j \text{ is in clause } c_i \\ 1 & \text{if no literal of } x_j \text{ in clause } c_i \end{cases} \tag{5}$$

where T and F are constants and p is a positive integer.

The *UniSAT*8 Problem Model [17, 18, 19]: Given n distinct clauses and m variables, the satisfiability problem is transformed into an unconstrained nonlinear programming problem:

$$\min_{\vec{\mathbf{x}} \in \mathbf{E}^m} f(\vec{\mathbf{x}}), \tag{6}$$

where

$$f(\vec{\mathbf{x}}) = \sum_{i=1}^{n} \prod_{j=1}^{m} t_{ij}(x_j) \tag{7}$$

and

$$t_{ij}(x_j) = \begin{cases} (x_j - T)^{2p+1} & \text{if literal } x_j \text{ is in clause } c_i \\ (x_j + F)^{2p+1} & \text{if literal } \bar{x}_j \text{ is in clause } c_i \\ 1 & \text{if no literal of } x_j \text{ in clause } c_i \end{cases} \tag{8}$$

where T and F are constants and p is a positive integer.

In *UniSAT*7 model, discrete solution constraints to restrict solution space are coded explicitly in the object function. Since $f(\vec{\mathbf{x}})$ takes the minimum value 0 if and only if $\vec{\mathbf{x}}$ is a solution point of the SAT problem, the *UniSAT*7 model gives a direct correspondence between the global minimum points of the object function and the solutions of the original SAT problem. Such an object function contains heuristic information and guides the search process. The object function we have used consists of simple square and multiple operations, so it is fairly easy to compute.

8 A Quantitative Local Search Algorithm for the Satisfiability Problem

A quantitative local search algorithm for the satisfiability problem, the *SAT*6.0 algorithm, is given in Figure 6 [17, 18, 19]. To start, procedure *obtain_a_SAT_instance*() initializes a SAT instance or reads in a practical SAT problem instance. An object function, f, or a set of object functions, $\mathbf{f}$, is formulated that represents the given SAT problem. The SAT problem thus becomes a minimization problem to the object function(s).

To begin, an initial solution point is chosen and the corresponding value of the object function is evaluated. The search process is an iterative minimization process to the object function. Depending on the optimization strategy, during a single search

```
procedure SAT6.0 ()
begin
    /* initialization */
    get_a_SAT_instance();
    x⃗_0 := select_an_initial_solution();
    f(x⃗_0) := evaluate_object_function();

    /* search */
    k := 0;
    while  not(solution_found()) do
        for some x_i(k)s ∈ x⃗_k
        begin
            if test_min(f(x_i(k)s)) then
            begin
                x⃗_k+1 := perform_min(f(x_i(k)s));
                f(x⃗_k+1) := evaluate_object_function();
            end
            if close_to_solution() then approximate();
        end;
        if local then local_handler();
        k := k + 1;
    end;
end;
```

Figure 6: **SAT6.0:** A Quantitative Local Search Algorithm for the Satisfiability Problem.

phase, the object function(s) can be minimized in one dimension or in multiple (up to m) dimensions. The test to see if the object function can be minimized is performed by the function *test_min*(). If this is true, the minimization operation is performed by the procedure *perform_min*(), followed by the operation *evaluate_object_function*() that updates the object function. The algorithm terminates when a solution of the SAT problem is found. In practice, during the search, the algorithm could be stuck at a locally optimum point. To improve the convergent performance of the algorithm, a local handler may be added.

Algorithms $SAT6.1$, $SAT6.2$, $SAT6.3$ and $SAT6.4$ are special cases of the $SAT6$ algorithm family. They handle 1-dimensional or m-dimensional optimization problems of arbitrary object function f or $\mathbf{f}$ representing the given SAT problem. Many continuous optimization methods can be used to solve the $UniSAT$ problems. Depending on optimization strategies, some twenty families of such SAT algorithms were developed and tested, which include, for example, the discrete local search methods ($SAT1$ family), the steepest descent methods ($SAT7$ family), modified steepest descent methods ($SAT8$ family), newton methods ($SAT10$ family), quasi-newton methods ($SAT11$ family), descent methods ($SAT14$ family), conjugate direction methods ($SAT16$ family), Boolean difference method ($SAT20$ family), and other techniques [17]. Among hundreds of SAT algorithms developed, some SAT algorithms run in $O(knl)$ time and take $O(nl)$ space [17, 22].

Many continuous optimization methods can be used to solve the $UniSAT$ problems. In the $SAT14$ algorithm family, we investigated a variety of coordinate descent methods within different search frameworks. Among all descent techniques, the coordinate descent methods have the simplest structure (also, with poorer convergence properties). In the $SAT14.1$ algorithm, we used a coordinate descent local search algorithm to solve a weighted $UniSAT7$ problem [17, 18, 19, 22]. During an iterating minimization phase, for a cyclic coordinate descent method, we examine each variable dimension cyclically and search by minimizing the object function in turn with respect to x_1, then x_2, then x_3 and so on, and holding all other variables constant when optimizing with respect to variable x_i. The process is then repeated starting with x_1 again. It turns out that $SAT14.1$ has significantly improved the global convergence performance and local convergence rate of the discrete local search algorithms.

One goal of the satisfiability problem is to determine *whether* there exists a truth assignment to the variables that makes the given CNF satisfiable. That is, we may have to search for all solutions or prove the unsatisfiability. We combined a coordinate descent SAT algorithm with an intelligent backtracking framework and implemented a $SAT14.2$ algorithm [17, 18, 31]. Since $UniSAT7$ is universal and fairly simple, the $SAT14.2$ algorithm performs fairly efficient as well.

In the next section, we will give some experimental results of two representative SAT algorithms.

```
procedure SAT6.1 ()
begin
    /* initialization */
    get_a_SAT_instance();
    x⃗0 := select_an_initial_point();
    f(x⃗0) := evaluate_object_function();

    /* search */
    k := 0;
    repeat
    while  not(solution_found()) do
        for each x_i(k) ∈ x⃗k (i = 1, 2, ..., m)
        begin
            if test_min(f(x_i(k))) then
            begin
                x⃗k+1 := perform_min(f(x_i(k)));
                f(x_i(k+1)) := evaluate_object_function();
            end
            if close_to_solution() then approximate();
        end;
        if local then local_handler();
        k := k + 1;
    end;
end;
```

Figure 7: **SAT6.1:** A 1-Dimensional Quantitative Local Search Algorithm for the Satisfiability Problem (f).

```
procedure SAT6.2 ()
begin
    /* initialization */
    get_a_SAT_instance();
    x⃗_{k=0} := select_an_initial_point();
    f(x⃗_0) := evaluate_object_function();

    /* search */
    k := 0;
    repeat
    while  not(solution_found()) do
        for vector x⃗_k
        begin
            if test_min(f(x⃗_k)) then
            begin
                x⃗_{k+1} := perform_min(f(x⃗_k));
                f(x⃗_{k+1}) := evaluate_object_function();
            end
            if close_to_solution() then approximate();
        end;
        if local then local_handler();
        k := k + 1;
    end;
end;
```

Figure 8: **SAT6.2:** An m-dimensional Quantitative Local Search Algorithm for the Satisfiability Problem (f).

```
procedure SAT6.3 ()
begin
    /* initialization */
    get_a_SAT_instance();
    x⃗_0 := select_an_initial_point();
    f(x⃗_0) := evaluate_object_function();

    /* search */
    k := 0;
    while not(solution_found()) do
        for each x_i(k) ∈ x⃗_k (i = 1, 2, ..., m)
        begin
            if test_min(f(x_i(k))) then
            begin
                x⃗_k+1 := perform_min(f(x_i(k)));
                f(x_i(k+1)) := evaluate_object_function();
            end
            if close_to_solution() then approximate();
        end;
        if local then local_handler();
        k := k + 1;
    end;
end;
```

Figure 9: **SAT6.3:** A 1-Dimensional Quantitative Local Search Algorithm for the Satisfiability Problem (**f**).

```
procedure SAT6.4 ()
begin
    /* initialization */
    get_a_SAT_instance();
    x⃗0 := select_an_initial_point();
    f(x⃗0) := evaluate_object_function();

    /* search */
    k := 0;
    while  not(solution_found()) do
        for vector x⃗k
        begin
            if test_min(f(x⃗k)) then
            begin
                x⃗k+1 := perform_min(f(x⃗k));
                f(x⃗k+1) := evaluate_object_function();
            end
            if close_to_solution() then approximate();
        end;
        if local then local_handler();
        k := k + 1;
    end;
end;
```

Figure 10: **SAT6.4:** An m-dimensional Quantitative Local Search Algorithm for the Satisfiability Problem (**f**).

9 Experimental Results

The experimental results indicate practical performance of the SAT algorithms. There is a variety of heuristics and optimization approaches available, any introduction of a few of them would refine a SAT algorithm and possibly produce a new and better algorithm. So it is fairly difficult to compare relative performance among many SAT algorithms.

Instead of showing the best performance, for many families of SAT algorithms we have developed, we give some practical performance evaluation of two typical SAT algorithms: the $SAT1.1$ algorithm, a simple discrete local search algorithm, and the $SAT14.2$ algorithm, a coordinate descent algorithm with backtracking. Compared to more powerful SAT algorithms we have developed, the performance figures of the two algorithms are certainly not so great. They represent, however, the two most primitive SAT algorithms in discrete domain and continuous domain. Both algorithms were coded simply without applying any heuristics or additional optimization techniques. So they might be used as a *yardstick* for performance comparison among the most primitive SAT algorithms.

9.1 Performance of the $SAT1$ algorithm

The initial problem instances were generated based on a model used by the previous researchers. A random conjunctive normal form formula consists of n independently generated random clauses. In each clause, a variable occurs with probability $1/m$. A literal of the variable occurs negatively with probability 1/2 and positively with probability 1/2. Contrary to the previous instance model used in [29], we do not allow for null clauses or any single literal clause, since those clauses can be trivially removed. The problem instances generated from our model, therefore, are harder than those of the previous models. Due to limited memory space on a $NeXT$ workstation computer, in order to experiment with large-scale SAT problems, the $SAT1$ algorithm was implemented in C in a space-efficient manner. The statistics of real execution time and the probabilistic behavior of the algorithm are reported as follows.

The real performance of the $SAT1$ algorithm running on a $NeXT$ workstation is illustrated in Table 1 and Table 2. The number of clauses (n), the number of variables (m), and the average number of literals per clause (l) are give in the first three columns. Column 4 (*Global*) indicates the number of times that the algorithm succeeds in finding a solution, i.e., a global minimum point. Column 5 (*Local*) indicates the number of times that the algorithm was stuck at a local minimum point.

Real execution time of the $SAT1$ algorithm From these results we can observe that, in terms of global convergence and convergent rate, the $SAT1$ algorithm exhibits good convergent properties for certain classes of the CNF. While a traditional

Table 1: Real Execution Performance of a Version of the $SAT1$ Algorithm on a NeXT Workstation (Time Units: seconds)

Problems (n,m,l)			Ten Trials		Execution Time			Iterations (k)		
Clauses	Variables	Literals	Global	Local	Min	Mean	Max	Min	Mean	Max
100	100	3	10	0	0.000	0.006	0.016	1	1.400	2
200	100	3	10	0	0.000	0.025	0.047	1	2.700	5
300	100	3	10	0	0.062	0.125	0.235	5	8.700	17
400	100	3	10	0	0.235	1.608	5.203	12	85.40	277
1000	1000	3	10	0	0.109	0.131	0.155	2	2.700	3
1500	1000	3	10	0	0.203	0.283	0.361	3	3.900	5
2000	1000	3	10	0	0.406	0.564	0.844	4	5.700	8
2500	1000	3	10	0	0.751	1.054	2.383	6	8.200	18
3000	1000	3	10	0	1.172	2.276	3.954	8	15.00	26
3500	1000	3	10	0	3.252	17.57	39.12	19	99.00	222
1000	1000	4	10	0	0.030	0.087	0.124	1	1.600	2
2000	1000	4	10	0	0.249	0.270	0.327	2	2.200	3
3000	1000	4	10	0	0.422	0.609	0.827	2	3.200	4
4000	1000	4	10	0	1.078	1.186	1.578	4	4.400	6
5000	1000	4	10	0	1.421	2.404	3.484	4	7.200	10
6000	1000	4	10	0	3.297	5.570	12.92	8	13.80	32
7000	1000	4	10	0	9.687	13.45	20.19	20	28.29	43
8000	1000	4	10	0	20.73	78.56	176.6	38	144.8	327
10000	1000	5	10	0	4.218	6.137	9.312	5	6.800	10
11000	1000	5	10	0	4.703	8.004	12.17	5	8.000	12
12000	1000	5	10	0	7.765	14.30	25.61	7	12.60	23
13000	1000	5	10	0	10.65	20.33	40.61	9	16.40	33
14000	1000	5	10	0	19.65	44.50	67.67	14	32.70	50
15000	1000	5	10	0	50.48	127.9	253.6	34	87.00	174
10000	400	6	10	0	11.65	24.78	39.09	10	21.70	34
10000	500	6	10	0	4.437	8.676	18.11	3	4.500	8
10000	600	6	10	0	2.889	5.017	9.110	3	4.500	8
10000	700	6	10	0	2.641	4.066	6.812	3	3.800	6
10000	800	6	10	0	2.531	3.620	6.437	3	3.600	6
10000	900	6	10	0	2.219	2.695	4.407	2	2.700	4
10000	1000	6	10	0	2.124	2.376	2.671	2	2.400	3
20000	1000	7	10	0	4.871	6.758	10.65	2	2.500	4
30000	2000	7	10	0	8.358	9.539	12.18	2	2.300	3
40000	3000	7	10	0	11.14	13.02	16.45	2	2.200	3
50000	4000	7	10	0	14.88	17.18	20.05	2	2.100	3
60000	5000	7	10	0	18.43	20.81	22.89	2	2.000	2
10000	1000	10	10	0	0.156	0.271	0.437	1	1.000	1
20000	2000	10	10	0	0.467	0.761	1.047	1	1.000	1
30000	3000	10	10	0	0.753	1.450	2.783	1	1.000	1
40000	4000	10	10	0	1.549	2.248	3.887	1	1.000	1
50000	5000	10	10	0	2.482	3.157	4.250	1	1.000	1

Table 2: Real Execution Performance of a Version of the $SAT1$ Algorithm on a NeXT Workstation (Time Units: seconds)

Problems (n,m,l)			Ten Trials		Execution Time			Iterations (k)		
Clauses	Variables	Literals	Global	Local	Min	Mean	Max	Min	Mean	Max
100	100	3	10	0	0.000	0.003	0.015	1	1.200	2
200	100	3	10	0	0.000	0.043	0.078	1	3.700	7
300	100	3	10	0	0.047	0.139	0.234	3	7.200	11
400	100	3	10	0	0.155	3.663	10.25	6	130.1	363
1000	1000	3	10	0	0.046	0.121	0.202	1	2.100	3
1500	1000	3	10	0	0.171	0.292	0.391	2	3.100	4
2000	1000	3	10	0	0.372	0.626	1.015	3	4.700	7
2500	1000	3	10	0	0.823	1.208	1.781	5	7.000	10
3000	1000	3	10	0	1.644	3.062	4.956	8	14.10	22
3500	1000	3	10	0	6.672	11.65	20.04	25	45.00	75
1000	1000	4	10	0	0.015	0.070	0.140	1	1.400	2
2000	1000	4	10	0	0.248	0.291	0.501	2	2.100	3
3000	1000	4	10	0	0.391	0.645	1.281	2	2.800	5
4000	1000	4	10	0	0.981	1.268	1.715	3	3.800	5
5000	1000	4	10	0	1.736	2.824	4.215	4	6.200	9
6000	1000	4	10	0	4.483	6.213	8.726	8	10.70	15
7000	1000	4	10	0	10.93	14.59	23.19	16	20.79	32
8000	1000	4	10	0	50.56	186.7	513.3	63	230.4	634
10000	1000	5	10	0	7.251	7.542	8.939	6	6.100	7
11000	1000	5	10	0	9.812	13.16	16.05	7	9.200	11
12000	1000	5	10	0	15.79	18.44	24.24	10	11.40	15
13000	1000	5	10	0	19.59	28.14	38.51	11	15.50	21
14000	1000	5	10	0	32.04	57.86	89.88	16	28.90	45
15000	1000	5	10	0	66.56	98.99	152.6	37	45.70	70
10000	400	6	10	0	9.313	22.88	41.29	6	14.00	25
10000	500	6	10	0	5.697	7.942	12.64	4	5.200	8
10000	600	6	10	0	3.895	5.699	10.72	3	4.000	7
10000	700	6	10	0	2.439	4.007	5.717	2	3.000	4
10000	800	6	10	0	2.126	3.928	5.681	2	3.000	4
10000	900	6	10	0	2.124	2.766	3.987	2	2.300	3
10000	1000	6	10	0	2.031	2.723	3.889	2	2.300	3
20000	1000	7	10	0	5.265	5.945	9.047	2	2.100	3
30000	2000	7	10	0	2.562	8.247	9.622	1	1.900	2
40000	3000	7	10	0	3.761	10.14	12.81	1	1.800	2
50000	4000	7	10	0	5.205	12.52	16.97	1	1.700	2
60000	5000	7	10	0	17.52	19.61	21.12	2	2.000	2
10000	1000	10	10	0	0.108	0.299	0.500	1	1.000	1
20000	2000	10	10	0	0.500	0.798	1.124	1	1.000	1
30000	3000	10	10	0	1.122	1.649	2.664	1	1.000	1
40000	4000	10	10	0	1.828	3.208	4.514	1	1.000	1
50000	5000	10	10	0	1.919	2.803	3.492	1	1.000	1

Table 3: Computing Performance of the $SAT14.2$ Algorithm on a SUN SPARC-1 for Practical CSP Problems (Time unit: seconds)

Problems (n,m,l)			Backtracks			Execution Times		
Clauses	Variables	Literals	Min	Mean	Max	Min	Mean	Max
84	16	2.19	0	3.1	6	0.000	0.015	0.030
170	25	2.18	0	0.0	0	0.010	0.016	0.020
302	36	2.16	0	8.8	38	0.020	0.077	0.230
490	49	2.14	0	3.3	21	0.050	0.081	0.180
744	64	2.13	0	3.2	18	0.090	9.130	0.280
1074	81	2.12	0	4.7	19	0.130	0.199	0.340
1490	100	2.11	0	32.9	113	0.220	0.677	1.730
2002	121	2.10	0	72.2	240	0.340	1.734	4.970
2620	144	2.09	0	25.4	56	0.490	1.081	1.860
3354	169	2.09	0	11.6	53	0.680	1.023	2.220
4214	196	2.08	0	77.9	243	0.940	3.783	9.570
5210	225	2.08	0	35.1	175	1.180	2.784	9.360
6352	256	2.07	0	76.4	269	1.580	5.724	16.80
7650	289	2.07	0	46.6	255	2.130	5.377	21.09
9114	324	2.06	0	9.8	28	2.580	3.351	4.840
10754	361	2.06	0	26.5	76	3.230	5.450	9.820
12580	400	0.26	0	42.2	141	3.900	7.999	16.99
24850	625	2.05	0	47.4	260	9.720	19.62	66.13
43270	900	2.04	0	11.1	45	21.35	25.52	35.52
103560	1600	2.03	0	27.7	131	68.14	87.67	157.5
111602	1681	2.03	0	8.6	59	73.2	81.04	118.2

resolution-based algorithm is not able to handle even moderately sized inference problems, the $SAT1$ algorithm is capable of solving large-scale inference problems.

The probabilistic behavior of the $SAT1$ algorithm. The $SAT1$ algorithm uses a probabilistic local handler. Tables 1 and 2 show its probabilistic behavior, the number of iterations required in finding a solution. The tables indicate that the algorithm succeeds for most SAT problem instances. For most SAT problem instances listed in the table, only a few *while* loops might be required. For numerous *practical* problem instances we have encountered, $SAT1$'s performance seems fairly robust.

9.2 Performance of the $SAT14.2$ algorithm

For the $SAT14.2$ algorithm, instead of taking randomly generated SAT problem instance, we used practical SAT problem instances generated from the real CSP problems. We have run our algorithms for years and have found that, in fact, they are able to solve hard and practical SAT problem instances, for example, one with $n = 111602, m = 1681$ and $l = 2.03$.

10 Conclusion

Bearing various mathematical forms, *search* is essentially a philosophical problem. Mathematically, it is important to determine the time and space complexities before investing too much programming effort. The most important *guideline* to designing a search strategy is to judge its philosophy and simplicity. A good search algorithm must be philosophically solid and correct. An efficient search algorithm must be natural and simple.

Generally, optimization methods are an effective and practical way to solve the search problems. To apply optimization techniques to solve a search problem, two steps are essential: First, one must map a search problem into an appropriate optimization framework. This is the most non-trivial step and often determines the efficiency of the resulting search algorithm. Second, once a mapping model is found, one can use some existing optimization technique to solve the problem. We have used optimization methods and solved many hard and practical search problems, often with excellent performance.

Korf [38] classified the classical search problems into three general types: constraint-satisfaction problems (e.g., the n-queen problem), path-finding problems (e.g., the traveling salesman problem), and two-player games (e.g., chess). We may unify all three areas of search problems into a single theory of heuristic search: all of them can be formulated as the minimization problem. Generally, we can prove that all these three search problems can be polynomially transformed to the satisfiability problem which, as discussed in this chapter, can be formulated as a minimization problem in terms of the optimization theory. Informally, we can see that, in constraint-satisfaction problems, we minimize some object function (*conflicts*) and produce a "conflict-free" solution; in path-finding problems, we minimize some constraints and performance objectives (e.g., the route length in TSP) and find a route with minimum length; in two-player games, we minimize the risk of failure as well as the opponent's chance of success, both could be expressed directly by some object functions.

We have developed, in fact, a systematic procedure to transform a CSP into a SAT problem which deals uniformly with binary constraints as well as high order, k-ary constraints ($k \geq 2$) [22, 31]. Basically, for a CSP with Boolean variables, there is a direct correspondence between a CSP and a SAT problem. The SAT problem can be viewed as a CSP in which all variables are Boolean and all constraints are represented explicitly in the "negative form." For a CSP with multiple variable values, two simple transformations, variable transformation and constraint transformation, convert the CSP to the SAT problem. In our quantitative approach, once a CSP is transformed into a SAT, any conventional optimization algorithm can be used to find the extreme points of the SAT which correspond to the solutions of the original CSP. We have used this approach to experiment with numerous randomly generated CSP instances and practical CSP instances [22, 31].

The area of optimization is a rich land of well-developed theory and techniques. To apply optimization methods to solve the search problems seems a natural and promising way to handle the search problems. Not only the end results of such an endeavor have a major scientific impact, but in the process it will push optimization technology to its limit.

Acknowledgements

Xiao Wang, Rok Sosič, Qian Ping Gu, Xiaofei Huang, Kent Smith, Richard Fujimoto and Vipin Kumar have provided interesting discussions and comments. Qian Ping Gu and Idan Shoham have carefully read the entire manuscript. Vipin Kumar and Xiaotie Deng have provided some recent papers.

The original idea to solve the SAT problem was inspired in design automation research to develop fast computer architectures for which I received financial support from the IEEE and ACM.

APPENDIX A: The Average Time Complexities of Several $SAT1$ Algorithms

The formal theoretical work for the SAT algorithms was performed during the past several years. The original work is lengthy and complicated. In this section, we give the basic results for a few simple SAT algorithms. More complete materials can be obtained from the author or from [18, 20, 21].

A.1 Preliminaries

To base our analysis of the average time complexity of the $SAT1$ algorithms, we first give some definitions.

Let $X = \{x_1, \bar{x_1}, x_2, \bar{x_2}, ..., x_m, \bar{x_m}\}$. A randomly generated CNF formula from the set X of literals is a CNF formula with independently generated clauses. In each clause, each literal q is randomly chosen from X with $\Pr[q = x_i] = 1/(2m)$ and $\Pr[q = \bar{x_i}] = 1/(2m)$ $(1 \le i \le m)$.

Let F denote a randomly generated CNF formula from X with n clauses and on average l literals in each clause and let c_i denote a clause of F.

For a vector $v \in \{0,1\}^m$, let v_k denote the kth bit of v. For $v \in \{0,1\}^m$, let $f(v)$, $c_i(v)$, and $q(v)$ denote the values of formula F, clause c_i, and literal q, respectively. For example, for v with $v_k = 1$, $x_k(v) = 1$ and $\bar{x_k}(v) = 0$. If no confusion arises, we will also use c_i to denote the set of literals appearing in clause c_i.

For a *CNF* formula F and a vector $v \in \{0,1\}^m$, let

$$C_0(v) = \{c_i | c_i \text{ is a clause of } F \text{ and } c_i(v) = 0\}$$

and

$$C_1(v) = \{c_j | c_j \text{ is a clause of } F \text{ and } c_j(v) = 1\}.$$

For any set S, we will use $|S|$ to denote the number of elements in S. Clearly, $|C_0(v)| + |C_1(v)| = n$ and the object function $f(v)$ equals $|C_0(v)|$.

For a *CNF* formula F and vector $v \in \{0,1\}^m$, let $X_0(v)$ be the set of literals that appear in clauses which have value 0, i.e.,

$$X_0(v) = \bigcup_{c_i \in C_0(v)} c_i.$$

Clearly, for any literal $q \in X_0(v)$, $q(v) = 0$.

We shall use $\log x$ and $\ln x$ to express $\log_2 x$ and $\log_e x$, respectively.

The following proposition will also be used in our analysis:

For $h_1, h_2 > 1$ and for t a positive integer, let $L(t, h_1, h_2) = \min\{r|$ In r independent Bernoulli trials with probability at least $1/h_1$ of success, the probability of at least t successes is at least $1 - 1/h_2.\}$.

Proposition 1 *[1, 10, 25, 67] For $t \geq 1$ and $h_1, h_2 > 1$,*

$$L(t, h_1, h_2) \leq 2h_1(t + \ln h_2).$$

A.2 The Average Time Complexity of the $SAT1.1$ Algorithm

We first analyze the average time complexity of the $SAT1.1$ algorithms for the randomly generated CNF formulae with n clauses, m variables, and on average l literals in each clause. As we have estimated, the time complexity of the $SAT1.1$ algorithm is $O(k_1 nml)$, where k_1 is the number of times that the *while* loop of $SAT1.1$ algorithm is executed. To get the average time complexity of the $SAT1.1$ algorithm, we need to find the average value of k_1.

From a detailed analysis, we can show that the following lemma holds:

Lemma 2 *In one execution of the while loop in the $SAT1$ algorithms, the probability that for a given clause $c_i \in C_0(v)$, the value of c_i is changed into 1 meanwhile the values of all clauses in $C_1(v)$ remain unchanged is at least*

$$1 - [1 - (1 - \frac{l}{2^l m})^n]^l.$$

From Lemma 2, we have the following lemma:

Lemma 3 *for a given CNF formula F and a vector $v \in \{0,1\}^m$, in one execution of the while loop of the $SAT1.1$ algorithm, the probability that $f(v)$ is reduced to 0 is at least*

$$\{1 - [1 - (1 - \frac{l}{2^l m})^n]^l\}^m.$$

We now prove the average time complexity of the $SAT1.1$ algorithm.

Theorem 4 *The average time complexity of the $SAT1.1$ algorithm is $O(m^{O(1)}n)$ for $l \geq logm - \log\log m - c$ and $\frac{n}{m} \leq \frac{2^{l-1}}{l}$, where $c > 0$ is any constant.*

Proof: Let p denote the probability that $f(v)$ is reduced to 0 in one execution of the *while* loop of the $SAT1.1$ algorithm. Then from Lemma 3

$$p \ \geq \ \{1 - [1 - (1 - \frac{l}{2^l m})^n]^l\}^m. \tag{9}$$

From (9) and a detailed calculation, we have that for $l \geq \log m - \log\log m - c$ and $\frac{n}{m} \leq \frac{2^{l-1}}{l}$

$$p \geq \frac{1}{m^{O(1)}}.$$

From this and Proposition 1 (taking $h_1 = 1/p$, $t = 1$ and $h_2 = e^m$), we have that

$$\Pr[k_1 = m^{O(1)}] \geq 1 - e^{-m}.$$

Thus, the theorem holds. □

Remark: *In practice, for a vector $v \in \{0,1\}^m$, the average value of $f(v)$, i.e., $|C_0(v)|$ is approximately $n/2^l$, and thus, the $SAT1.1$ algorithm is more efficient than was shown in Theorem 4.*

A.3 The Average Time Complexity of the $SAT1.2$ Algorithm

We now analyze, for randomly generated CNF formulae with n clauses, m variables, and on average l literals in each clause, the average time complexity of the $SAT1.2$ algorithm.

As we have estimated, the time complexity of the $SAT1.2$ algorithm is $O(k_2 n^2 ml)$, where k_2 is the number of search phases executed in the $SAT1.2$ algorithm. To get the average time complexity of the $SAT1.2$ algorithm, we need to find the average value of k_2. To do this, we first give, in each iteration of the *while* loop of the $SAT1.2$, the probability that $conflicts' = conflicts$.

Lemma 5 *For a vector $v \in \{0,1\}^m$ with $f(v) = 0$, the probability of $conflicts' = conflicts$ in one execution of the while loop is at most*

$$[1 - (1 - \frac{l}{2^l m})^n]^{|X_0(v)|}.$$

Proof: The lemma follows from the definitions of $X_0(v)$ and $C_0(v)$, and Lemma 2. □

Lemma 5 gives the probability that $SAT1.2$ is stuck at a local minimum point in one execution of the while loop. On the other hand, for any $v \in \{0,1\}^m$, clearly the $SAT1.2$ algorithm will find a solution if it has never been stuck at a local optimum point for n executions of the *while* loop. Thus, we can get the probability that the $SAT1.2$ algorithm finds a solution in one search phase and then get the average value of k_2 from Lemma 5.

For $v \in \{0,1\}^m$, let $|X_0(v)|$ be denoted by $L_{f(v)}$. That is, for $v \in \{0,1\}^m$ with $f(v) = i$, $|X_0(v)|$ is denoted by L_i $(1 \le i \le n)$. Then we have the following lemma.

Lemma 6 *The probability that the $SAT1.2$ algorithm finds a solution in one search phase is at least*

$$\prod_{i=1}^{n}\{1-[1-(1-\frac{l}{2^l m})^n]^{L_i}\}.$$

We now calculate the average time complexity of the $SAT1.2$ algorithm.

Theorem 7 *The average time complexity of the $SAT1.2$ algorithm is $O(m^{O(1)}n^2)$ for $l \ge 3$ and $\frac{n}{m} = O(\frac{2^l}{l})$.*

Proof: Clearly, $k_2 \le k_1$. Thus, we only calculate the average value of k_2 for small l, i.e., $l = O(\log m)$.

Let p be the probability that the $SAT1.2$ algorithm finds a solution in one search phase. Then by Lemma 6, we have

$$p \ge \prod_{i=1}^{n}\{1-[1-(1-\frac{l}{2^l m})^n]^{L_i}\}. \tag{10}$$

For a vector $v \in \{0,1\}^m$ with $f(v) = i$ (i.e., $|C_0(v)| = i$), L_i (i.e., $|X_0(v)|$) is approximately $i \times l$ when i and l are small. Clearly $L_i \ge 1$ for $i \ge 1$ and it is easy to see that for $l \ge 3$ and sufficiently large m, $L_i \ge c\log m$ for $i > c\log m$, where $c > 0$ is any constant. Thus, from $\{1-[1-(1-\frac{l}{2^l m})^n]^i\}$ is monotonically increasing in i, we have, for $1 \le i \le c\log m$,

$$\{1-[1-(1-\frac{l}{2^l m})^n]^{L_i}\} \;\ge\; (1-\frac{l}{2^l m})^n$$

and for $i > c\log m$,

$$\{1-[1-(1-\frac{l}{2^l m})^n]^{L_i}\} \;\ge\; \{1-[1-(1-\frac{l}{2^l m})^n]^{c\log m}\}.$$

Therefore, by (10), we have

$$\begin{aligned} p &\ge \prod_{i=1}^{n}\{1-[1-(1-\frac{l}{2^l m})^n]^{L_i}\} \\ &\ge \prod_{i=1}^{c\log m}(1-\frac{l}{2^l m})^n \times \prod_{i=c\log m+1}^{n}\{1-[1-(1-\frac{l}{2^l m})^n]^{c\log m}\} \\ &= (1-\frac{l}{2^l m})^{n\times c\log m} \times \{1-[1-(1-\frac{l}{2^l m})^n]^{c\log m}\}^{n-c\log m}. \end{aligned} \tag{11}$$

From (11) and a detailed calculation, we have that

$$p \geq \frac{1}{m^{O(1)}}.$$

From this and Proposition 1 (taking $h_1 = 1/p$, $t = 1$ and $h_2 = e^m$), we have that

$$\Pr[k_2 = m^{O(1)}] \geq 1 - e^{-m}.$$

Thus, the theorem holds. □

A.4 The Average Time Complexity of the $SAT1.3$ Algorithm

Finally we analyze, for randomly generated CNF formulae with n clauses, m variables, and on average l literals in each clause, the average time complexity of the $SAT1.3$ algorithm, which is a version of the $SAT1.1$ algorithm.

By a similar analysis for the $SAT1.1$ algorithm, we can find that the running time of the $SAT1.3$ algorithm is $O(k_3nml)$, where k_3 is the average number of times the *while* loop is executed. We will call k_3 to be the average iteration times of the $SAT1.3$ algorithm. To get the average run time of the $SAT1.3$ algorithm, we need to derive the average number of iterations k_3.

Lemma 8 *For a CNF formula F and $v \in \{0,1\}^n$, let f_0 be the average value of $|C_0(v)|$ and f_i be the average number of clauses that have a $false$ truth value, after the ith iteration. Then*

$$f_0 = \frac{n}{2^l}$$

and

$$f_i = \lceil f_{i-1} \times [1 - (1 - \frac{l}{2^l m})^n]^l \rceil + \lceil n \times \frac{l}{2^l m} \rceil.$$

Proof: The lemma follows from Lemma 2. □

Theorem 9 *For $l \geq 3$ and $\frac{n}{m} = O(\frac{2^l}{l})$, $k_3 = O(\log m)$.*

Proof: Clearly, the average iteration times

$$k_3 \leq i + \lceil \frac{1}{\{1 - [1 - (1 - \frac{l}{2^l m})^n]^l\}^{f_i}} \rceil. \tag{12}$$

From Lemma 8, we have that

$$\begin{aligned} f_i &\leq \lceil f_{i-1} \times [1-(1-\frac{l}{2^l m})^n]^l \rceil + \lceil n \times \frac{l}{2^l m} \rceil \\ &\leq f_{i-1} \times [1-(1-\frac{1}{2^l m})^n]^l + \lceil n \times \frac{l}{2^l m} \rceil + 1. \end{aligned} \tag{13}$$

Let

$$a = [1-(1-\frac{l}{2^l m})^n]^l$$

and

$$b = \lceil n \times \frac{l}{2^l m} \rceil + 1.$$

Then from (13) and $f_0 = \frac{n}{2^l}$, we have

$$\begin{aligned} f_i &\leq f_{i-1} \times a + b \\ &\leq \frac{n}{2^l} \times a^i + (a^{i-1} + a^{i-2} + \ldots + a + 1) \times b \\ &= \frac{n}{2^l} \times a^i + \frac{1-a^i}{1-a} \times b \\ &\leq \frac{n}{2^l} \times a^i + \frac{b}{1-a}. \end{aligned}$$

From this, we have that for $i \geq -\frac{\log n - l}{\log a}$,

$$f_i \leq \frac{b}{1-a} + 1.$$

Therefore, from (12), we have

$$k_3 \leq \lceil -\frac{\log n - l}{\log a} \rceil + \lceil \frac{1}{(1-a)^{\frac{b}{1-a}+1}} \rceil. \tag{14}$$

For $l \geq 3$ and $\frac{n}{m} = O(\frac{2^l}{l})$,

$$\begin{aligned} a &= [1-(1-\frac{l}{2^l m})^n]^l \\ &\leq \tfrac{1}{c} \end{aligned}$$

for some constant $c > 1$ and

$$\begin{aligned} b &= \lceil n \times \frac{l}{2^l m} \rceil + 1 \\ &= O(1). \end{aligned}$$

Therefore, from (14) and $\log n = \log m + l + c' - logl$, where c' is a constant, we have

$$k_3 = O(\log m).$$

□

From Theorem 9, the average run time of the $SAT1.3$ algorithm is $O(nml \log m)$, for $l \geq 3$ and $\frac{n}{m} = O(\frac{2^l}{l})$.

Remark: Given l, m and n, formula (14) can be used to predict the average run time of the $SAT1.3$ algorithm to find a solution of F. The iteration times given by formula (14) are very close to the experimental results.

References

[1] H. Chernoff. A measure of asymptotic efficiency for tests of a hypotheses based on the sum of observations. *Ann. Math. Stat.*, 23:493–509, 1952.

[2] J.H. Condon and K. Thompson. Belle chess hardware. *Advances in Computer Chess, 3*, Pergamon Press, 1982.

[3] S.A. Cook. The complexity of theorem-proving procedures. In *Proceedings of the Third ACM Symposium on Theory of Computing*, pages 151–158, 1971.

[4] T.H. Cormen, C.E. Leiserson, and R.L. Rivest. *Introduction to Algorithms.* MIT Press, Cambridge, 1990.

[5] V. Cĕrny. A thermodynamical approach to the travelling salesman problem: An efficient simulation algorithm. Technical report, Institute of Physics and Biophysics, Comenius University, Bratislava, 1982.

[6] M. Davis and H. Putnam. A computing procedure for quantification theory. *J. of ACM*, pages 201–215, 1960.

[7] R. Dechter and J. Pearl. Network-based heuristics for constraint-satisfaction problems. *Artificial Intelligence*, 34:1–38, 1988.

[8] N. Dershowitz, J. Hsiang, N. Josephson, and D. Plaisted. Associative-commutative rewriting. In *Proceedings of IJCAI*, pages 940–944, 1983.

[9] C. Ebeling. *All the Right Moves.* The MIT Press, Cambridge, 1987.

[10] P. Erdös and I. Spencer. *Probabilistic Method in Combinatorics.* Academic Press, New York, 1974.

[11] E. C. Freuder. A sufficient condition for backtrack-free search. *J. ACM*, 29(1):24–32, Jan. 1982.

[12] M.R. Garey and D.S. Johnson. *Computers and Intractability: A Guide to the Theory of NP-Completeness.* W.H. Freeman and Company, New York, 1979.

[13] J. Gaschnig. *Performance Measurements and Analysis of Certain Search Algorithms.* PhD thesis, Carnegie-Mellon University, Dept. of Computer Science, May 1979.

[14] A. Goldberg, P. W. Purdom, and C. A. Brown. Average time analysis of simplified davis-putnam procedures. *Information Processing Letters*, 15(2):72–75, 6 Sept. 1982.

[15] D.E. Goldberg. *Genetic Algorithms in Search, Optimization, and Machine Learning.* Addison-Wesley, Reading, 1989.

[16] J. Gu. Parallel algorithms and architectures for very fast search. Technical Report UCCS-TR-88-005, Jul. 1988.

[17] J. Gu. How to solve Very Large-Scale Satisfiability (VLSS) problems. 1988 (Present in part in, J. Gu, Benchmarking SAT Algorithms, Technical Report UCECE-TR-90-002, Oct. 1990).

[18] J. Gu. *Constraint-Based Search: Algorithms and Architectures.* Cambridge University Press, New York, 1992.

[19] J. Gu. Efficient local search for very large-scale satisfiability problem. *SIGART Bulletin*, 3(1):8–12, Jan. 1992, ACM Press.

[20] J. Gu and Q.P. Gu. Average time complexities of several local search algorithms for the satisfiability problem. Submitted for publication. Nov. 1991.

[21] J. Gu and Q.P. Gu. Average time complexities of several quantitative local search algorithms for the satisfiability problem. Submitted for publication. Nov. 1991.

[22] J. Gu and X. Huang. Implementation and performance of the SAT14 algorithm. Submitted for publication. Feb. 1991.

[23] J. Gu and W. Wang. DRA VLSI Architectures. Mar. 1986. (Present in part in: J. Gu, W. Wang and T. C. Henderson, A Parallel Architecture for Discrete Relaxation Algorithm, in *IEEE Trans. on Pattern Analysis and Machine Intelligence*, PAMI-9(6): 816-831, Nov. 1987).

[24] J. Gu and W. Wang. A novel discrete relaxation architecture. *IEEE Trans. on Pattern Analysis and Machine Intelligence*, PAMI-14, 1992.

[25] Q. P. Gu and A. Maruoka. Learning monotone boolean functions by uniformly distributed examples. Accepted in SIAM J. on Computing, to appear in 1992.

[26] R. M. Haralick and G. Elliot. Increasing tree search efficiency for constraint satisfaction problems. *Artificial Intelligence*, 14:263–313, 1980.

[27] T.P. Hart and D.J. Edwards. The alpha-beta heuristic. MIT AI Project Memo, MIT, 1963.

[28] T.P. Hart, N.J. Nilsson, and B. Raphael. A formal basis for the heuristic determination of minimum cost paths. *IEEE Trans. on Systems, Man, and Cybernetics*, SMC-4(2):100–107, 1968.

[29] J.N. Hooker. Resolution vs. cutting plane solution of inference problems: Some computational experience. *Operations Research Letter*, 7(1):1–7, 1988.

[30] J. Hsiang. Refutational theorem proving using term-rewriting systems. *Artificial Intelligence*, pages 255–300, 1985.

[31] X. Huang and J. Gu. A quantitative solution for constraint satisfaction. Submitted for publication. March 1991.

[32] D.S. Johnson. *Local Optimization and the Traveling Salesman Problem. In* M.S. Paterson, editor, *Lecture Notes in Computer Science, Vol. 443: Automata, Languages and Programming*, pages 446–461. Springer-Verlag, Berlin, 1990.

[33] P.C. Jackson Jr. Heuristic search algorithms for the satisfiability problem. Submitted to the third IEEE TAI Conference, Jul. 1991.

[34] S. Kirkpatrick, C.D. Gelat, and M.P. Vecchi. Optimization by simulated annealing. *Science*, 220:671–680, 1983.

[35] R.E. Korf. Depth-first iterative deepening: An optimal admissible tree search. *Artificial Intelligence*, 27:97–109, 1985.

[36] R.E. Korf. A weak method for learning. *Artificial Intelligence*, 26:35–77, 1985.

[37] R.E. Korf. Planning as search: A quantitative approach. *Artificial Intelligence*, 27:97–109, 1987.

[38] R.E. Korf. *Search: A Survey of Recent Results. In* H.E. Shrobe, editor, *Exploring Artificial Intelligence*, chapter 6. Morgan Kaufmann Publishers, Inc., San Mateo, 1988.

[39] V. Kumar. Algorithms for constraint satisfaction problems: A survey. Technical Report TR-91-28, Dept. of Computer Science, Univ. of Minnesota, 1991.

[40] S. Lin. Computer solutions of the traveling salesman problem. *Bell Sys. Tech. Journal*, 44(10):2245–2269, Dec. 1965.

[41] A. K. Mackworth. Consistency in networks of relations. *Artificial Intelligence*, 8:99–119, 1977.

[42] C.R. McLean and C.R. Dyer. An analog relaxation processor. In *Proceedings of the 5th International Conference on Pattern Recognition*, pages 58–60, 1980.

[43] S. Minton, M.D. Johnston, A.B. Philips, and P. Laird. Solving large-scale constraint satisfaction and scheduling problems using a heuristic repair method. In *Proceedings of AAAI90*, pages 17–24, Aug. 1990.

[44] J. Von Neuman and O. Morgensterm. *Theory of Games and Economic Behavior.* Princeton University Press, Princeton, 1944.

[45] N.J. Nilsson. *Principles of Artificial Intelligence.* Tioga Publishing Company, Palo Alto, California, 1980.

[46] C.H. Papadimitriou and K. Steiglitz. On the complexity of local search for the traveling salesman problem. *SIAM J. on Computing*, 6(1):76–83, 1977.

[47] C.H. Papadimitriou and K. Steiglitz. *Combinatorial Optimization.* Prentice-Hall, Englewood Cliffs, NJ, 1982.

[48] J. Pearl. *Heuristics.* Addison-Wesley, Reading, 1984.

[49] I. Pohl. *Bi-directional Search. In* B. Meltzer and D. Michie, editors, *Machine Intelligence*, pages 127–140. Elsevier, New York, 1971.

[50] G. Polya. *How to Solve It.* Princeton University Press, Princeton, 1945.

[51] P. W. Purdom. Search rearrangement backtracking and polynomial average time. *Artificial Intelligence*, 21:117–133, 1983.

[52] P. W. Purdom and C. A. Brown. An analysis of backtracking with search rearrangement. *SIAM J. Comput.*, 12(4):717–733, Nov. 1983.

[53] A. Rosenfeld, R. A. Hummel, and S. W. Zucker. Scene labeling by relaxation operations. *IEEE Trans. on Systems, Man, and Cybernetics*, SMC-6(6):420–433, June 1976.

[54] Y.G. Saab and V. B. Rao. Combinatorial optimization by stochastic evolution. *IEEE Transactions on CAD*, CAD-10(4):525–535, Apr. 1991.

[55] E.D. Sarcerdoti. Planning in a hierarchy of abstraction spaces. *Artificial Intelligence*, 5:115–135, 1974.

[56] B.M. Schwartzschild. Statistical mechanics algorithm for monte carlo optimization. *Physics Today*, 35:17–19, 1982.

[57] C.E. Shannon. Programming a computer for playing chess. *Philosophical Magazine*, 41:256–275, 1950.

[58] M.J. Shensa. A computational structure for the propositional calculus. In *Proceedings of IJCAI*, pages 384–388, 1989.

[59] P. Siegel. *Representation et Utilization de la Connaissances en Calcul Propositionel.* PhD thesis, University Aix-Marseille II, 1987.

[60] D.J. Slate and L.R. Atkin. *CHESS 4.5 – the Northwestern University Chess Program. In* P.W. Frey, editor, *Chess Skill in Man and Machine.* Springer-Verlag, New York, 1977.

[61] R. Sosič and J. Gu. How to search for million queens. Technical Report UUCS-TR-88-008, Dept. of Computer Science, Univ. of Utah, Feb. 1988.

[62] R. Sosič and J. Gu. A polynomial time algorithm for the n-queens problem. *SIGART Bulletin*, 1(3):7–11, Oct. 1990, ACM Press.

[63] R. Sosič and J. Gu. Fast search algorithms for the n-queens problem. *IEEE Trans. on Systems, Man, and Cybernetics*, SMC-21(6), Nov./Dec. 1991.

[64] R. Sosič and J. Gu. 3,000,000 queens in less than one minute. *SIGART Bulletin*, 2(2):22–24, Apr. 1991, ACM Press.

[65] R. Sosič and J. Gu. Efficient local search with conflict minimization. *IEEE Trans. on Knowledge and Data Engineering*, 1992.

[66] H. S. Stone and J. M. Stone. Efficient search techniques – an empirical study of the n-queens problem. *IBM J. Res. Develop.*, 31(4):464–474, July 1987.

[67] L. G. Valiant. A theory of learnable. *Communications of the ACM*, pages 1134–1142, 1984.

[68] D. Waltz. *Generating Semantic Descriptions from Drawings with Shadows.* PhD thesis, AI Lab, MIT, 1975.

[69] P. H. Winston. *Artificial Intelligence.* Addison-Wesley, Reading, 1984.

CHAPTER 3

APPLICATION OF GENETIC ALGORITHMS TO PERMUTATION PROBLEMS

FREDERICK E. PETRY

and

BILL P. BUCKLES
Center for Intelligent and Knowledge-based Systems
Department of Computer Science
Tulane University
New Orleans, Louisiana 70118

ABSTRACT

Genetic algorithms are a relatively new paradigm for search in A.I. which are based on the principles of natural selection. They are probabilistic algorithms that are not yet well understood. There are certain kinds of search problems, called permutation problems, for which the solution is a sequence of the input symbols. The input symbols are called genes in genetic algorithms. The ordinary rules for interchanging information between organisms in the simulated population must be modified to assure that each new individual has exactly one copy of each possible gene value. It is shown here that for permutation problems, the standard approaches to intermixing genes leads to longer search chains than necessary. Using the traveling salesman problem as a test case, it is shown that the survival rate of compact schema is directly proportional to the quality of the solution after a fixed number of iterations. Yet the standard gene intermixing methods for permutation problems, called a crossover rule, separates the parents of a new organism at almost the precise point at which the survival rate of compact schema is at a minimum. A variation is proposes that takes advantage of the knowledge of survival rates on the quality of the solution.

1. Introduction

Genetic algorithms (GAs) originated from the studies of cellular automata conducted by John Holland and his colleagues at the University of Michigan. The methods were first widely distributed by means of a book by Holland.[11] Growth in interest since then has been slow but consistent, increasing markedly over the last six years. Applications include diverse areas such as job shop scheduling,[5] training neural nets,[14] and image feature extraction or recognition.[1,16]

GAs differ from traditional search techniques in several ways. First, genetic algorithms optimize the tradeoff between exploring new points and exploiting the information discovered so far. This was proved using an analogy with the k-armed bandit problem.[11] Second, GAs have the property of implicit parallelism. Implicit parallelism means that the effect of the genetic algorithm is equivalent to an extensive search of the hyperplanes of the given space, without directly testing all hyperplane values.[8] Third, genetic algorithms are randomized algorithms, in that they use operators whose results are governed by probability. The results for any given operation are based on the value of a random number. Fourth, GAs operate on several solutions simultaneously, gathering information from current search points to direct the subsequent search. Maintaining multiple solutions concurrently makes GAs less susceptible to the problems of local maxima and noise. The discussion begins with a review of GAs for which there exist good texts on the theory[7] and application.[6]

2. Background

GAs are search procedures modeled after the mechanics of natural selection. They are randomized, but not random, search algorithms. Domain knowledge is embedded in the abstract representation of a candidate solution, termed an organism. A search over the decision space is performed via an analog of natural selection rather than a simulated reasoning process. Sets of organisms are grouped together into populations. Successive populations are called generations. A generational GA creates an initial generation, G(0), and for each generation, G(t), generates a new one, G(t+1). A abstract view of a genetic algorithm is given by

```
generate initial population, G(0);
evaluate G(0);
t := 0;
repeat
        t := t + 1
        generate G(t) using G(t-1);
        evaluate G(t);
until solution is found.
```

The operation "evaluate G(t)" refers to the assignment of a figure of merit to each component (organism) of the population and is discussed in a subsequent section. A steady-state GA differs in that instead of replacing a generation in toto, single organisms are replaced as new ones are created.

2.1. Basic Definitions

An ***organism***, or chromosome, of length n consists of a vector of the form $<x_1,x_2,\ldots,x_n>$ where each x_i is an *allele*, or gene. The domain of values from which x_i is chosen is called the *alphabet* of the problem. Frequently, the alphabet used is the binary digits {0, 1}. Alleles from two organisms called *parents* are mixed via an operator called a *crossover* rule of which there are many. Simple one point crossover of two parents at a random point, j, is illustrated by

$$<x_1\ x_2 \ldots x_j\ x_{j+1}\ x_{j+2} \ldots x_n>$$
$$+$$
$$<y_1\ y_2 \ldots y_j\ y_{j+1}\ y_{j+2} \ldots y_n>$$
$$=$$
$$<x_1\ x_2 \ldots x_j\ y_{j+1}\ y_{j+2} \ldots y_n>$$

where the resultant organism is called the *offspring* and is placed in the next generation. Appendix B contains descriptions of eight common crossover rules. A *mutation* is the random change of an allele from one alphabet value to another.

A specific organism (list of alleles) can be viewed as representative of a large number of patterns. Using # as "don't care" an example pattern or *schema* over the binary alphabet is <# # 1 1 0 #>. The organisms <1 1 1 1 0 0> and <1 0 1 1 0 0> are specific instances of this schema as well as others such as <1 # # 1 0 0>. The *order* of a schema is the number of non-# symbols it contains. Its *length* is the number of positions included within the sequence from the first through last non-# position. Thus the length of <# 1 0 # 1 1> is five and its order is four.

2.2. The GA Recombination Operators

Recombination operators are based on the mechanics of genetics. By analogy, GAs may be related to controlled breeding among, say, thoroughbred horses. The objective is to combine highly fit organisms to produce a still more fit individual. Randomization must balance two competing concerns - exploration and exploitation. A solution cannot be tested unless it appears as an organism. Thus, a reasonable number of solutions must be examined. Unlimited exploration would not be an efficient search, however. The strength of highly fit organisms must be exploited and allowed to propagate in the population. Yet, giving too much precedence to such individuals results in premature termination at a local optimum.

Fig. 1 in depicts an overview of a simple generational GA. An initial population is randomly generated and successive generations are derived by applying the selection, crossover, and mutation operators to the previous generation. The crossover and mutation operators are briefly described in the preceding subsection and additional variants are in Appendix B. The selection operator chooses two members of the present generation (and in some variants of crossover, more than two) to participate in the later operations - crossover and mutation. In diagram form, Fig. 1 shows a current generation being acted upon by the three operators to produce the successive generation.

Note in the figure that there is an intervening action called fitness function evaluation that assigns to each organism a value, noted as f_i. f_i is a figure of merit that is computed using any domain knowledge that applies. In principle, this is the only point in the algorithm that domain knowledge is necessary. Organisms are chosen using the fitness value as a guide, organisms having higher fitness values being chosen more often. Selection of "parents" is randomized as well as the application of the recombination operators. Parent selection dynamics are based on an application dependent measure of an organism known as the fitness function. The greater the fitness function value for an organism, the more likely the organism will be selected for recombination. Selecting organisms based on fitness value is a major factor in their strength.

There are two popular approaches for implementing selection. The first, called roulette selection, is to assign a probability to each organism, i, computed as the proportion, $F_i = f_i/\Sigma f_j$. A parent is then randomly selected based on this probability. A second method, called deterministic sampling, assigns to each organism, i, a value

$$C_i = \mathrm{RND}(F_i \times n) + 1 \tag{1}$$

where there are n organisms in the population. (RND means round to integer.) The selection operator then assures that each organism participates as a parent exactly C_i times.

A selection strategy called fitness scaling is often used to both prevent bias when there are only a few extraordinary organisms in a generation and to bias toward the more fit organisms when the best and average fitness values are nearly equal. One method, linear scaling, determines for each generation the constants a and b and resets the fitness of organism i to

$$f'_i = a\, f_i + b \tag{2}$$

and F_i is computed with the revised fitness. The constants are chosen such that

$$f'_{avg} = a\, f_{avg} + b \tag{3}$$

where f_{avg} is the mean fitness value. An option is to let

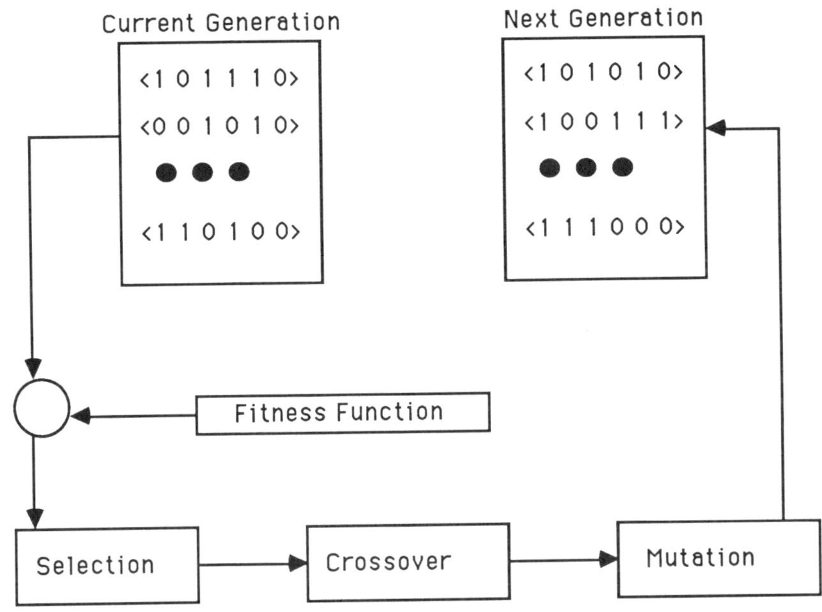

Figure 1. Components of a Generational GA

$$a = (m-1)\, f_{avg}/(f_{max}-f_{avg}) \tag{4}$$

$$b = f_{avg}\ (f_{max} - m\, f_{avg})/(f_{max}-f_{avg}) \tag{5}$$

where m is the number of offspring desired for the organism having the maximum fitness. If $f'_i < 0$ for any organism then m must be lowered.

A requirement of the above selection methods is that f_i be higher for organisms that represent better solutions. If there is an underlying objective function, OBJ, to be maximized, then that is sufficient. Assume, for the sake of illustration, that OBJ is to be minimized. First compute the OBJ_i for each organism then let $f_i = OBJ_{max} - OBJ_i$. Table 1 illustrates these fitness function concepts for an (unrealistically small) population of 5. Often the best solution from the current generation is placed unaltered into the next generation. This is known as the elitist strategy.

The mutation operator offers the opportunity for new genetic material to be introduced into a population. From the theoretical perspective, it assures that, given any population, the entire search space is connected. The new genetic material does not necessarily originate from the parents and is not introduced into the child by crossover. Rather, it occurs a small percentage of the time after crossover. The mutation operator performs, as in nature, by randomly changing alleles. For a problem over the binary alphabet, the original allele is exchanged for its complement.

Table 1. Illustration of Fitness Function Concepts

i	Organism	OBJ_i	f_i	f'_i	F_i	C_i
1	<1001110>	122	0	1.17	0.01	1
2	<0011001>	101	21	21.63	0.10	2
3	<0101100>	80	42	42.09	0.19	2
4	<1100111>	50	72	71.31	0.31	2
5	<0111011>	30	92	90.80	0.40	3

The mutation operator offers the opportunity for new genetic material to be introduced into a population. From the theoretical perspective, it assures that, given any population, the entire search space is connected. The new genetic material does not necessarily originate from the parents and is not introduced into the child by crossover. Rather, it occurs a small percentage of the time after crossover. The mutation operator performs, as in nature, by randomly changing alleles. For a problem over the binary alphabet, the original allele is exchanged for its complement.

There exist several stopping criteria for the algorithm. It may be halted when all organisms in a generation are identical, when $f_i = f_j$ for all i and j, or when $|f_i - f_j| < TOL$ for some small value TOL and all i and j. An alternative criterion is to halt after a fixed number of evaluations and take the best solution found.

2.3. The Schema Theorem

For GAs, a significant concept is that of implicit parallelism. Implicit parallelism means that search is performed over an entire hyperplane (region) of the space simultaneously via the examination of a few explicitly enumerated points. This follows from the Schema Theorem of Holland.[11] A specific organism (list of alleles) can be viewed as representative of a large number of schemata. The fundamental theorem of GAs (the schema theorem) explains that the instances of certain more fit schemata appear with exponentially greater frequency as organisms are replaced. Schemata can also be interpreted as hyperplanes in the search space.

Suppose at step i there is a population of n organisms of which m organisms are instances of schema S, i.e., $m_i(S)$. Recall with roulette wheel selection that organisms are selected for parents based on their fitness, f, where an organism, k, is selected with probability

$$f_k / \sum_{1}^{n} f_j \tag{6}$$

Then, the number of instances of schema S at the next stage is

$$m_{i+1}(S) = m_i(S) \times \frac{\overline{f(S)}}{\bar{f}} \tag{7}$$

where $\overline{f(S)}$ is the average fitness of organisms instantiating S and $\bar{f}$ is the average fitness of the entire population. This, of course, is exponential growth. After analyzing and taking into account the effects of operators such as crossover and mutation, a term α, $\alpha < 1$, is obtained leading to the modification of Eq. 7 to

$$m_{i+1} > m_i(S) \times \frac{\overline{f(S)}}{\bar{f}} \times \alpha \quad (8)$$

3. Permutation Problems

A permutation problem is one for which each allele value appears exactly once in each organism. Obviously, the binary alphabet is inadequate for representing permutation problems in an intuitive manner. Let the allele values be the letters {A, B, ... }. A sample organism of length 8 is <B C H E G A D F> . Crossover and mutation rules must preserve the permutation constraint. Appendix B contains a description of four permutation crossover rules, one of which is order crossover.

In order crossover, two random crossing sites are selected. Alleles from the first parent that fall between the two cross points are copied into the same positions of the offspring. The remaining allele order is determined by the second parent. Nonduplicative alleles are copied from the second parent to the offspring beginning at the position following the second crossing site. Both the second parent and the offspring are traversed circularly from that point. A copy of the parent's next nonduplicative allele is placed in the next available child position. An example for which the cross points are 4 and 6 is

Parent 1: <HBC | EAG | DF>

Parent 2: <ABC | DEF | GH>

Child: <CDF | EAG | HB>

Mutation by means of arbitrarily changing an allele value would not preserve the permutation constraint. The mutation rule frequently used is to interchange the values in two randomly selected positions.

The premier permutation problem is traveling salesman. The objective is to find the tour of shortest length on an undirected graph that begins at any node, visits all nodes, and returns to the starting node. That is, given n points, {A, B, . . . }, and permutations, σ_1, σ_2, . . ., $\sigma_{n!}$, the objective is to choose σ_i such that the sum of the Euclidean distances between each node and its successor is minimized. The successor of the last node in the permutation is the first one. Traveling saleman is used for the experiments described in Section 5.

The traveling salesman and other routing problems have been investigated several times using GAs.[2,4,9,17] The experiment described here is adapted from a previous publication[3] and demonstrates that performance is related to the number of short defining length schemata preserved during crossover. A short defining length schema is one for which the order is approximately equal to its length. For example, <A B # # # # # #> is short while < # # H # # # C #> is long. A specialized crossover rule, r-OPT, has been adapted from the Operations Research literature[13] by Jog, et al.[12] and is described in Appendix B. Another in the literature[10] requires a wholly different approach to the representation of a population. It is the goal of these experiments to determine the effectiveness of methods that are independent of domain knowledge.

4. Analysis of Order Crossover

Given an organism of length n, there are n^2 ways to choose a segment cut. Let the length of a cut be the number of positions within the two crossing sites. For the example of order crossover just given, the length is 3. The probability that the length, K, of a cut is 1, P[K=1], is 1/n. For any other value

$$P[K=i] = 2[n-(i-1)/n^2] \tag{9}$$

In general, the average value of K is

$$E(K) = {}^1\!/_n + \frac{2}{n^2} \sum_{i=2}^{n} i(n-(i-1))$$

$$= n + 2 - \frac{2}{n^2} \sum_{i=1}^{n} i^2$$

$$= 1 + {}^n\!/_3 + {}^1\!/_{(3n)} \tag{10}$$

A schema is of the form <A # # B C # # # # # # #>. For the traveling salesman problem, the schemata <A B # # # # # # # #>, <# # # A B # # # # #>, and <B # # # # # # # # A> are the same due to the cyclic nature of a tour. A schema for which the order, o, and the length, w, are equal is said to be compact.

A population contains many schemata. The crossover and mutation operators act in conjunction with the selection operator to put "good" schemata called building blocks together into a single organism to form a good solution. Obviously, the good schemata for a traveling salesman problem are compact. Survival of good schemata is the objective of parametrically adjusting a GA. The problem of survival is discussed elsewhere[15] and the material here is an extension of it.

If K is the length between cross points in order crossover and it is given that K > w, Oliver, et al.[15] show that the probability of survival of a schema in parent 1 is

$$\text{Prob[Survival|Parent 1]} = (K-w+1)/n \tag{11}$$

For survival of a schema in parent 2, o alleles must be present in positions corresponding to those in the schema and none of them may be within the cut of parent 1.

$$\text{Prob[Survival|Parent 2]} \cong (1-K/n)^o \tag{12}$$

The relation is approximately equal because the placement of the cut segment within the child separates the last allele taken from parent 2 from the first. The effect is negligible for large n and small w and is not taken into account in the formula. Note that for compact schemata, o and w are interchangeable in Eq. 11 and 12.

Let $S_{o,i}$ be the set of strictly compact schemata of order o in parent i within an organism. For an organism of length n, $|S_{o,i}| = n$ since the length may extend from the right end back to the left end. Combining Eq. 11 and 12, the expected value for the number of surviving schemata in an offspring is

$$M \cong n\,(1-K/n)^w + K - w + 1 \tag{13}$$

GAs are successful because they combine stability with enough perturbation to simultaneously maintain the good solutions while progressing toward better ones. Obvious hypotheses can be formulated concerning stability and perturbation and they can be expressed in terms of M. Is the best performance obtained when exploitation (i.e., stability) is given preference and the survival rate is high or when exploration is given preference and the survival rate is lower?

5. Experimental Results

Fig. 2 shows a plot of M for n=16, n=30, and n=50. In the figure, it is assumed that o=w=2. E(K) from Eq. 10 is marked for each value of n. Note that it always occurs at or near the nadir of M. A new version of order crossover was developed that allowed control of the value of E(K). That is, once one end of a segment was identified randomly, the second endpoint was chosen (also randomly) such that after many trials the average crossover segment length would be a known fixed value.

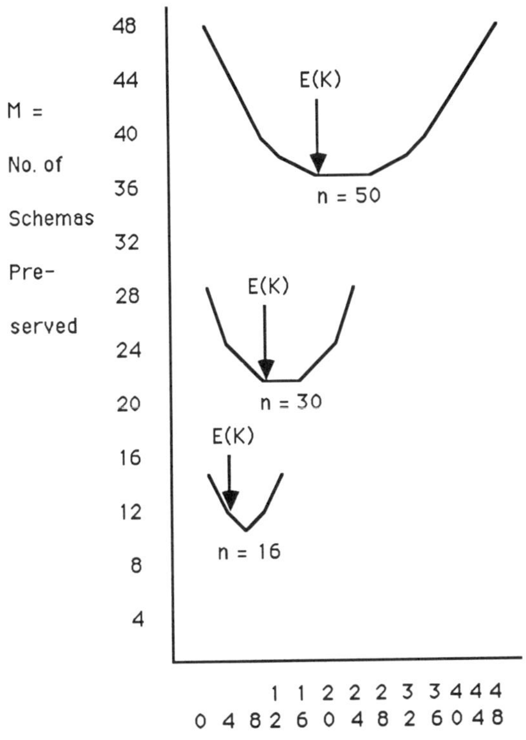

Figure 2. Plot of Average Cut Length vs. Schema Survival Rate (o=w=2)

To test each value of the controlled E(K), four tests were run, each starting with a different random number seed. Where a segment cut began near the end of an organism, it was allowed to "wrap-around." The result was taken as the average of the four runs in order to distribute the random error. The data for each problem is in Appendix A. The mutation level was fixed at 10% for all runs. Selection was implemented using the roulette wheel method. Each population was scaled. An elitist strategy was employed.

For the 16 city problem, each run consisted of 50 generations of 50 (250 evaluations). The results are shown in the plot in Fig. 3. On the graph the ordinary expected value of the length of a cut as obtained from Eq. 10 is shown via a vertical line. The average of all tests is shown by the horizontal line.

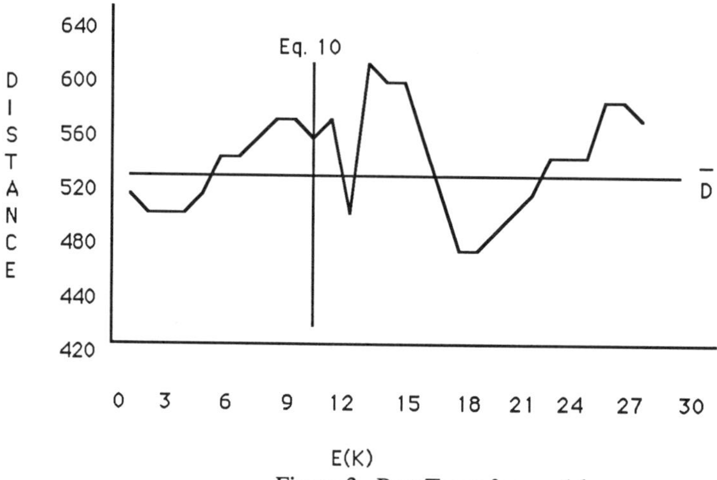

Figure 3. Best Tours for n = 16

Each run for the 30 city problem consisted of 500 generations each with a population of 100. That is, 50,000 tours were evaluated. The results are shown in Fig. 4 where each plotted point again represents the average of four independent runs.

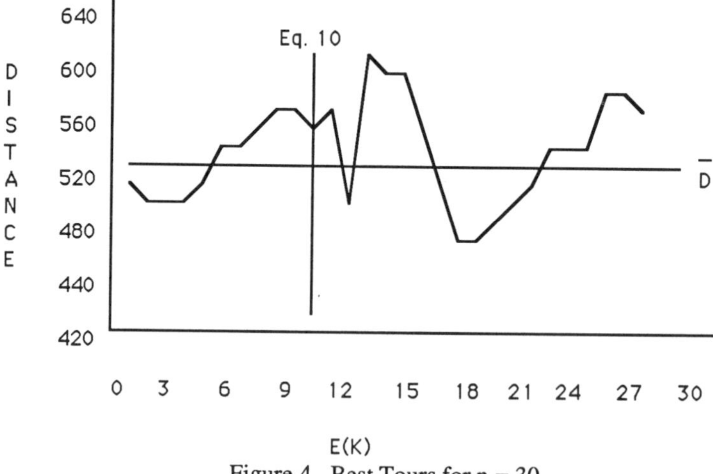

Figure 4. Best Tours for n = 30

For the 50 city problem, two independent series of tours were computed. In the first, 500 generations with populations of 100 were used (50,000 evaluations). In the second series, 1,000 generations of 100 were used (100,000 evaluations). The results are shown in Fig. 5.

Figs. 3, 4, and 5 show the result for n of 16, 30, and 50, respectively. The graphs consistently show that the performance is better for those regions in which M is high.

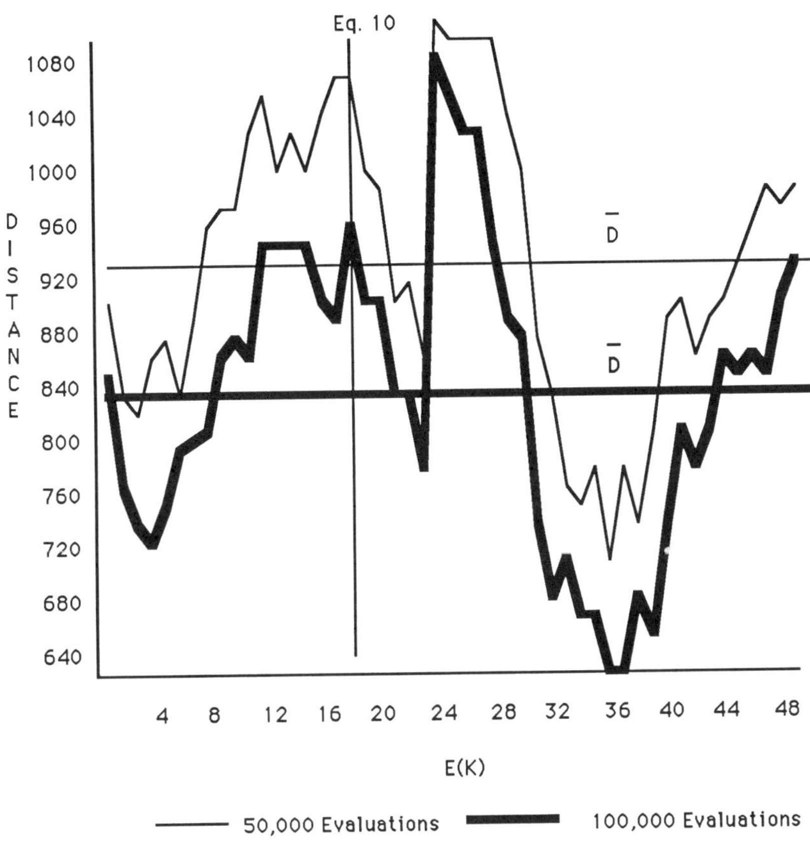

Figure 5. Best Tours for n = 50

6. Conclusions

Crossover operators specifically designed to solve the traveling salesman problem consistently achieve tours within 2-3% of the optimum with far fewer evaluations than used here.[15,17] The problem is based on compact schemata, however, and results given here show a weakness in the common permutation operators (those not based on domain knowledge). They do not maintain the correct balance between schema survival and the creation of new schema. The effect becomes more pronounced as the size of the problem grows due to a greater difference between the number of surviving schema in short or long cuts than in ones that aproximate half the organism length. It is recommended that future implementations of order crossover be modified to control the length of the average cut to be either short or long.

Our investigations did not include separation of initial search from the latter stages of optimization. It is entirely possible that mid-length cuts early, causing much perturbation, followed by controlled cuts later, emphasizing preservation, will further improve performance. This is an issue for further study.

Our less extensive testing of the PMX crossover operator showed the same trends. As noted, previous investigations[15] have indicated that for compact schemata the performance of order and PMX crossover closely approximate each other with order crossover being slightly better. An interesting future investigation would be the shortest path problem because a schema, while still compact, does not have the wrap-around characteristic.

References

1. C.A. Ankenbrandt, B. P. Buckles, and F. E. Petry, "Scene Recognition Using Genetic Algorithms With Semantic Nets," *Pattern Recognition Letters* 11 (1990) 285-293.
2. P. Baffes and L. Wang, "Mobile Transporter Path Planning," *Proc. SOAR'89* (Houston TX, 1988) 51-59.
3. B.P. Buckles, F.E. Petry, and R.L Kuester, "Schema Survival Rates and Heuristic Search in Genetic Algorithms," *Proc. Second Int. Conf. on Tools for A.I.*, (Nov. 1990, Washington, D.C.) 322-327
4. T. Cleghorn, P. Baffes, and L. Wang, "Robot Path Planning Using a Genetic Algorithm," *Proc. SOAR'88* (Houston TX, 1988) 81-87.
5. F.A. Cleveland, and S.F. Smith, "Using Genetic Algorithms to Schedule Flow Shop Releases," *Proc. Third Int. Conf. on Genetic Algorithms* (Fairfax VA, 1989) 160-169.
6. L. Davis, ed., *Handbook of Genetic Algorithms* (Van Nostrand Reinhold, New York, 1991).
7. D.E. Goldberg, *Genetic Algorithms in Search, Optimization, and Machine Learning* (Addison-Wesley, Reading MA, 1989).
8. D.E. Goldberg, "Sizing Populations for Serial and Parallel Genetic Algorithms," *Proc. Third Int. Conf. on Genetic Algorithms* (Fairfax VA, 1989) 70-79.
9. J.J. Grefenstette, R. Gopal, B. Rosmaita, and D. Van Gucht, "Genetic Algorithms for the Traveling Salesman Problem," *Proc. First Int. Conf. on Genetic Algorithms* (Boston, 1985) 160-165.
10. J.J. Grefenstette, "Incorporating Problem Specific Information in Genetic Algorithms," In *Genetic Algorithms and Simulated Annealing*, ed. L. Davis (Morgan Kaufmann, San Mateo CA, 1987) 42-60.
11. J.H. Holland, *Adaption in Natural and Artificial Systems* (University of Michigan Press, Ann Arbor MI, 1975).
12. P. Jog, J.Y. Suh, and D.V. Gucht, "The Effects of Population Size, Heuristic Crossover and Local Improvement on a Genetic Algorithm for the Traveling Salesman Problem," *Proc. Third Int. Conf. on Genetic Algorithms*, (Fairfax VA, 1989) 110-115.
13. S. Lin, and B.W. Kernighan, "An Efficient Heuristic Algorithm for the Traveling Salesman Problem," *Operations Research* 21 (1973) 498-516.
14. D.J. Montana and L. Davis, "Training Feedforward Neural Networks Using Genetic Algorithms," *Proc. Intern. Joint Conf. on Artificial Intelligence* (1989) 762-767.
15. I.M. Oliver, D.J. Smith, and J.R.C. Holland (1987), "A Study of Permutation Crossover Operators on the Traveling Saleman Problem," *Proc. Second Int. Conf. on Genetic Algorithms* (Hillsdale, NJ, 1987) 224-230.

16. W. Siedlecki, and J. Sklansky (1989) "A Note on Genetic Algorithms for Large-scale Feature Selection," *Pattern Recognition Letters* 10 (1989) 335-347.
17. D. Whitley, T. Starkweather, and D. Fuquay (1989), "Scheduling Problems and Traveling Salesman: The Genetic Edge Recombination Operator," *Proc. Third Int. Conf.on Genetic Algorithms* (Fairfax VA, 1989) 133-140.

Appendix A. Problem Data

The 16 city problem has an optimum tour of 232. The coordinates in order of the best solution are: (37,84), (41,94), (14,98), (2,99), (2,76), (25,62), (18,54), (4,50), (9,42), (13,40), (24,42), (36,38), (44,35), (54,62), (46,74).

The 30 city problem has an optimum tour of 421 according to Oliver et al.[15] The coordinates of the best solution are: (54,67), (54,62), (37,84), (41,94), (2,99), (7,64), (25,62), (22,60), (18,54), (4,50), (13,40), (18,40), (24,42), (25,38), (44,35), (41,26), (45,21), (58,35), (62,32), (82,7), (91,38), (83,46), (71,44), (64,60), (68,58), (83,69), (87,76), (74,78), (71,71), (58,69).

The 50 city problem has an optimum tour of 438. The coordinates in order of the best solution are: (41,98), (28,94), (14,98), (2,99), (4,86), (2,76), (7,64), (14,66), (25,62), (22,60), (18,54), (11,50), (4,50), (9,42), (13,40), (24,42), (25,38), (36,38), (44,35, (41,26), (45,21), (52,29), (58,35), (62,32), (70,24), (74,12), (82,7), (88,14), (92,24), (91,38, (88,44), (83,46), (71,44), (64,60), (68,58), (79,62), (83,69), (87,76), (80,80), (74,78), (71,71), (60,72, (58,69), (54,67), (54,62), (46,74), (40,76), (37,84), (40,88).

Appendix B. Crossover Rules

Crossover is the operator that is chosen more than 90% of the time during the process of creating a new generation. More than 20 versions of crossover can be identified in the literature and there are doubtless dozens more that have not been published. The crossover operators described here, except for r-OPT are the ones most frequently referenced. r-OPT is included to illustrate a crossover that uses domain knowledge.

B.1. Interleaving Crossover Using a Fixed Number of Crossover Sites

An interleaving crossover operator is one that chooses segments of alleles alternately from each parent and places them in the corresponding position in the child. Choosing a fixed number of crossover sites in advance, usually using a uniform random number generator, divides the parent organisms a priori into a fixed number of segments.

B.1.1. Simple Crossover

Simple or 1-point crossover is perhaps the most straightforward rule. A single crossover site is chosen. Alleles to the left of the site are taken in order from the first parent and alleles to the right are taken from the second parent. In the example that follows, the randomly chosen crossing site is assumed to be 5.

Parent 1: <1 1 1 1 1 | 1 1 1 1>

Parent 2: <0 0 0 0 0 | 0 0 0 0>

Child: <1 1 1 1 1 | 0 0 0 0>

B.1.2. n-Point Crossover

n-point crossover where n > 1 is a direct extension of simple crossover. n crossing sites are randomly selected which divides each parent into n+1 segments. The odd numbered segments from the first parent are placed into the corresponding segments of the offspring and likewise the even numbered segments from the second parent. Most researchers prefer an even value for n so that the first and last segments originate with the first parent. For the example that follows, n = 2.

Parent 1: <1 1 1 | 1 1 1 1 1 | 1 1>

Parent 2: <0 0 0 | 0 0 0 0 0 | 0 0>

Child: <1 1 1 | 0 0 0 0 0 | 1 1>

B.2. Interleaving Using a Random Number of Crossing Sites

In simple and n-point crossover, the parents are divided into segments a priori. An alternative is to choose randomly the parent from which the next allele is chosen. There are two crossover rules in general use that do just that. The effect is that the number of crossing sites is not chosen in advance.

B.2.1. Uniform Crossover

In uniform crossover, n uniformly distributed random numbers are chosen where n is the length of the organism and each random number is in the interval [0,1]. If the i-th random number is less than or equal to 0.5 then the next allele is chosen from the first parent. Otherwise it is chosen from the second. In the example that follows, the vector of uniformly distributed random numbers is assumed to be <0.21, 0.49, 0.76, 0.04, 0.88, 0.36, 0.17, 0.39, 0.61>. The problem alphabet is assumed to be {A B C}.

Parent 1: <B A C B A A C B C>

Parent 2: <C B A A B B A C B>

Child: <B A A B B A C B B>

B.2.2. Shuffle Crossover

A similar effect to uniform crossover can be achieved by first shuffling the alleles in the both parents using the same permuting sequence then apply an interleaving crossover rule. The offspring is unshuffled by the inverse of the original permuting sequence. While similar in effect to uniform crossover, shuffle crossover does not exhibit equivalent neighborhood and positional biases. In the example that follows, the problem alphabet is assumed to be {A B C} and the simple crossover rule is used after shuffling.

Parent 1: <B A C B A A C B C>

Parent 2: <C B A A B B A C B>

Shuffle both parents by the permutation <7 4 9 3 1 5 2 8 6> and let the randomly chosen crossing site be 3.

Parent 1: <C B C | C B A A B A>

Parent 2: <A A B | A C B B C B>

The child in shuffled form is

Child: <C B C | A C B B C B>

which, after unshuffling becomes

Child: <C B A | B B B C C C>

B.3. Permutation Crossover Rules

Permutation crossover rules are those that operate under the conditions that each organism must be a permutation of the problem alphabet. Such rules are useful if the underlying problem is task scheduling or route planning. In the examples that follow, the problem alphabet is assumed to be {A, B, C, D, E, F, G, H}.

B.3.1. Order Crossover

In order crossover, two random crossing sites are selected. Alleles from the first parent that fall between the two crossing sites are copied into the same positions of the offspring. The remaining allele order is determined by the second parent. Nonduplicative alleles are copied from the second parent to the offspring beginning at the position following the second crossing site. Both the second parent and the offspring are traversed circularly from that point. A copy of the parent's next nonduplicative allele is placed in the next available child position. An example for which the random crossing sites are 4 and 6 follows.

Parent 1: <HBC | EAG | DF>

Parent 2: <ABC | DEF | GH>

Child: <CDF | EAG | HB>

B.3.2. PMX Crossover

Initially, PMX (partially matched) crossover proceeds just as order crossover. Alleles from the first parent that fall between two randomly selected crossing sites are copied into the same positions of the offspring. The remaining allele positions are determined by the second parent during a two step process. First, alleles in the second parent not within the crossing sites are copied to the corresponding positions within the offspring. Next, each allele of the second parent within the crossing sites is placed in the offspring at the position occupied in the second parent by the allele from the first parent that displaced it. In the example below, A, H, and G displace in the offspring D, E, and F, respectively. D goes to position 1 which is the position with respect to the second parent that the displacing allele, A, occupies. E and F are placed in the positions occupied by H and G, respectively.

Parent 1: <FBC | AHG| DE>

Parent 2: <ABC | DEF | GH>

Child: <DBC | AHG| FE>

B.3.3. Cycle Crossover

Cycle crossover does not use crossing sites. A cycle is defined in a manner similar to an algebraic permutation group. To illustrate using the example below, compare the strings of parent 1 with parent 2. F displaces A, A displaces D, D displaces G, and G displaces F. This is a cycle - FADG. These alleles assume the same position in the offspring as in parent 1. Find now the first unselected allele in parent 2, i.e., C. C in parent 2 displaces B in parent 1 and B displaces C. This is a second cycle - BC. The positions of B and C in the offspring are determined by the second parent. Switching back to parent 1, there is one more cycle - HE. The positions of H and E in the offspring are the same as parent 1.

Parent 1: <F B C A H G D E>

Parent 2: <A C B D E F G H>

Child: <F C B A H G D E>

B.3.4. r-OPT Crossover

Crossover rules can be specifically designed to utilize domain knowledge. r-OPT is designed to incorporate distance information in the traveling salesman problem. Each offspring is generated from $r > 1$ parents with r-OPT crossover. The first allele is chosen arbitrarily, say from the first position of the first parent. For each subsequent allele there are, in general, r choices. For each parent, locate the allele most recently placed in the offspring. Next, find the first following allele, searching circularly, that is not already in the offspring. Consult a distance table to determine which of the chosen alleles has is the closest to the allele most recently placed in the offspring and place it in the offspring. The example that follows is of 2-OPT using the distances in Table B.1.

Parent 1: <A C G F B D E>

Parent 2: <G E F D C B A>

Child: <A C B G F D E>

Table B.1. Distances Between Points

	A	B	C	D	E	F	G
A	-	38	12	80	42	20	14
B	38	-	51	32	83	68	10
C	12	51	-	22	91	73	59
D	80	32	22	-	15	29	60
E	42	83	91	15	-	44	75
F	20	68	73	29	44	-	34
G	14	10	59	60	75	34	-

SECTION 3

LEARNING

CHAPTER 4

A LOGICAL BASIS FOR LEARNING

Emmanuel KOUNALIS

Laboratoire d'Informatique de Rouen
Université de Rouen
B.P. 118 - Place Emile Blondel
76134 Mont-Saint-Aignant
FRANCE

Michael RUSINOWITCH

Centre de Recherche en Informatique de Nancy
Université de Nancy
Campus scientifique - BP. 239
54506 Vandoeuvre-les-Nancy.
FRANCE

ABSTRACT

A central process in many kind of learning is the process of *generalization* or *concept learning* from a set of training instances (a set of examples and counterexamples) in presence of some Background Knowledge. Given a set of examples and counterexamples of a concept, the learner induces a general concept that describes all of the positive example and none of the counterexamples, and is consistent with the Background Knowledge .

We present here a logical framework to induce concept descriptions from a given set of examples and counterexamples in presence of Background Knowledge described by a set of Horn clauses. In particular we give:

1) a definition of what it means "learnable concept from examples and counterexamples in presence of Background Knowledge", and

2) a method to induce general concept descriptions from concept examples and counterexamples in Horn theories.

This work generalizes, unifies, and provides a logical framework of previous studies on the concept learning from examples paradigm.

Nous ne pouvons nous élever que par *induction* mathématique qui seule peut nous **apprendre queique chose de nouveau**. Sans l'aide de cette induction differente à certains égards de l'induction physique, mais féconde comme elle, la construction serait impuissante à créer la science.

POINCARE: Nature du raisonnement mathématique.

1. INTRODUCTION

1.1. The Problem of Concept Learning

The problem of *learning* is central to Artificial Intelligence because intelligent behavior implies an ability to adapt to new situations. Our current robots need to acquire automatic learning capacities if they are to operate in a world where changes may occur. "The ability of people to make accurate generalizations from few scattered facts or to discover patterns in seemingly chaotic collections of observations is a fascinating research topic of long-standing interest", Michalski (1983), (1984 and 1986). This ability is achieved by a process called inductive learning i.e. inductive inference from facts provided by a teacher or the environment. In this context, the most frequently studied type of learning is ***concept learning from examples*** or ***generalization*** , whose task is to induce general descriptions of concepts from specific instances of these concepts. Since a long time inductive learning has been a research topic of Artificial Intelligence (see surveys in Michalski (1984 and1986). Commercial products of AI induction research are starting to see use in industry [Michie (1985)].

A formal model for concept learning or generalization has been proposed by Plotkin (1970) and (1971). Huet (1976) and (1980) studied the algebraic properties in the case of the infinitary Herbrand universe. The key result in this theory is that, for any set of terms, there exists a unique (up to variable renaming) term that represents their most specific generalization. For instance, the most specific generalization of P(a,b) and P(b,a) is P(x,y), where a, b are constants, P is a predicate symbol and x, y are variables . Further, such generalizations may be "too" general and therefore counterexamples are required to restrict them. For instance, a better generalization of the above example would be P(x,y) / P(z,z) where this generalisation represents the ground instances (i.e., terms without variables) of P(x,y) such that x is different to y. The use of counterexamples for restricting generalizations is proposed by Vere (1980) and Mitchell (1978). Although they use counterexamples in very different ways, both consider them as a specialization device. Vere specializes an overgeneralized formula, and Mitchell avoids overgeneralizations by taking counterexamples into account. In Kodratoff (1983) the counterexamples are aimed at particularization, which means "pruning the generalization". However, the use of counterexamples to restrict a generalization may lead to generalizations which are not reasonable in the sense that all instances of the generalization of a set of examples are also instances of some counterexample. Therefore, unreasonable generalizations provide no concept to be learned.

Lassez and Marriot (1987) were the first to give a formal basis to the problem of determining whether a formula **G** of the form t / t_1, ..., t_n, where commas represent the union of the sets of the ground instances of the terms t_1, ..., t_n, is a generalization. In their viewpoint the formula **G** is a *generalization* if there exists a finite set of instances of t, whose ground instances are not instances ot t_1,...,t_n. Here t is viewed as an example where t_1, ..., t_n are counterexamples. Lassez and Marriott showed that the problem of checking whether a formula is a generalization, is decidable and they have given an effective algorithm to check it.

However, the above results do not apply anymore, if we assume the presence of background knowledge, that is, if we assume that the predicate and function symbols appearing in the examples and counterexamples are interpreted in some universe which is described by a Horn theory (in the sense that they satisfy additional properties expressed by a finite set H of Horn clauses). The problem is that a ground instance of an atom A (a generalization of a set of examples), which is not a ground instance of the counterexamples A_1, ..., A_n may be false in the intended model of a set of Horn clauses. For instance, if we suppose that a set of examples and counterexamples leads to the formula G := L(x,y) / L(s(0), 0), L(s(x), s(y)) , L(x,x), then G is a generalization, since, for example, every ground instance of the term L(s(s(z), 0) -the term L(s(s(z), 0) is an instance of L(x,y)- is a ground instance of none of L(s(0), 0), L(s(x), s(y)) , L(x,x) . On the other hand, if we assume that the symbols L, s, 0 which appears in the examples and counterexamples represent respectively the *less* predicate, the *successor* and *zero* functions for natural numbers and satisfy the set H = { ¬L(x,y) v L(x, s(y)), L(0,s(0)) } of Horn clauses (the Background Knowledge for natural numbers with the less predicate L), then the term L(s(s(z), 0) cannot obviously be a learnable concept. From immediate inspection it is not obvious at all to see that the formula G := L(x,y) / L(s(0), 0), L(s(x), s(y)) , L(x,x), provides the term L(0,s(y)) which represents the concept to be learned: "*zero is less than the successor of any number*". In order to define what it means for a formula to represent a "learnable concept" in presence of Background Knowledge, and provide a method to induce concepts, let us formulate a general paradigm for the process of generalization or concept learning from a set of training instances (a set examples and counterexamples) in presence of some Background Knowledge described by a Horn theory:

Given : **1)** a language **L** in which to describe concepts,

2) a set **H** of Horn clauses (over the language) describing the Background Knowledge,

3) a set **EX** of examples and a set **CE** of counterexamples of some 'target concept' (concept to be learned).

Determine: A concept description **G** within the language **L** that is consistent with the Background Knowledge **H** and the presented training instances **EX** $\cup$ **CE**

1.2. The Aims of the Present Chapter

We present here a logical framework to induce concept descriptions from a given set of examples and counterexamples in presence of Background Knowledge described by a set of Horn clauses. In particular we give:

1) a definition of what it means "concept to be learned from examples and counterexamples in presence of Background Knowledge", and

2) a method to induce general concept descriptions from concept examples and counterexamples in Horn theories.

Let us first try to give a definition of a "learnable concept" from a set of examples and counterexamples in presence of Background

Knowledge. Despite the abundancy of papers on learning, no one has yet defined rigorously what it means for a concept to be learnable in presence of Background Knowledge. However an answer exists since 1901, the year when R. POINCARE published an essay on the "Nature du raisonnement mathématique":

> Nous ne pouvons nous élever que par **induction mathématique** qui seule peut nous **apprendre quelque chose de nouveau.** Sans l'aide de cette induction differente à certains égards de l'induction physique, mais féconde comme elle, la construction serait impuissante à créer la science.

i.e. "The mathematical induction is the <u>only</u> tool that allows us to learn something new". In other words, a learnable concept is a formula whose proof requires some kind of induction. In compiling POINCARE'S assertion into a logical logical framework, we get that a formula **G** represents a learnable concept from a given set of training instances **EX** $\cup$ **CE** (examples **EX** and counterexamples**CE**) and the background knowledge **H** if and only if

a) it <u>matches</u> every example and no counterexample in the given set **EX** $\cup$ **CE**,

b) it <u>eliminates</u> some models (worlds) of **H** (i.e., it is not true in every interpretation which is a model of each of the axioms of the theory **H**),

c) It is <u>true</u> in the least Herbrand model (i.e, it is true in the intended interpretation) of **H**.

We must note here that these are exactly the kind of formulas that can be proved by mathematical induction. In general a formula valid in the Least Herbrand model (but false in some other models) of a given theory can be proved only by using inductive arguments. We think that these requirements capture the essence of incorporating a *new* fact into an existing theory (cf. Greiner and Genesereth (1983), and Moore (1980)).

Our work has its foundation in the work done by Kounalis and Rusinowitch (1988), (1990a) and applied to machine learning problems in (1990b), and (1990c). Let us mention some strongly related work: Plotkin (1970) and (1971) studies θ-subsumption as a proof theoretical mecanism for generalizations. Buntine (1988) suggests generalized θ-subsumption as a model theoretical mechanism to study generalizations with clausal logic. Lassez and Marriott (1987) and (1991), Maher (1990) give algorithms to decide whether a formula is a generalization and how to transform an implicit generalization into an equivalent explicit (disjunctive) one, provided that no relations between the function symbols which appear in the examples and counterexamples are allowed (i.e without background knowledge). Kounalis (1991) presents an algorithm for concept learning with equational background knowledge. Michalski (1988), describes a theory and methodology to learn concepts from examples and counterexamples. Vere (1980) gives an algorithm to generate nested implicit generalizations from examples and counterexamples. Mitchell (1978) uses finite sets of maximal and minimal terms to represent all possible generalizations of a set of examples and counterexamples. Kodratoff (1983) and (1988), and Kodratoff, Y. and Ganascia, J.G. (1984)

and (1986) use counterexamples in order to check the existence of a link between some variables and some operators.

1.3. Layout of the Chapter

In **Chapter 2**, we explain our approach to concept learning on two simple examples. In particular we show how to induce concepts in the Block world and in the elementary Number Theory.

In **Chapter 3**, we present the necessary background material for Horn Logic. In particular, we describe the framework in which we are interested, as well as the fundamental notions underlying terms, atoms, and the syntax and the semantics of Horn Logic.

In **Chapter 4**, we first present a formal definition of a "learnable concept" from a set of examples and counterexamples in presence of Background Knowledge. We next provide a basis for learning and finally present a set of inference rules that allow us to verify whether a concept is learnable.

2. OVERVIEW OF THE APPROACH: TWO EXAMPLES

Before discussing the technical details , let us describe our learning system on two simple examples:

2.1. Example 1: Block World

For example, consider the problem of learning a concept about the heights of arches built out of blocks. The following Horn theory H describes the background Knowledge about arches :

$$\neg \textbf{Higherthan}\ (x,\ y)\ \vee \textbf{Higherthan}\ (\textbf{plus1}(x),\ y)$$

$$\textbf{Higherthan}\ (\textbf{plus1}(B),\ B)$$

where Higherthan(x,y) means that the arch x is higher than the arch y, plus1(x) designs the arch which is obtained by pushing a block on the top of the arch x, and B is a constant symbol which designs the empty arch. Thus, $\neg$ Higherthan (x, y) v Higherthan (plus1(x), y) expresses the rule: if the arch x is higher than the arch y, then the arch which obtained by pushing a block on the top of arch x will be higher than arch y. On the other hand, the unit clause Higherthan(plus1(B), B) expresses the fact that the arch with one block on the top of the empty arch is higher than the empty arch.

Consider now the examples

Higherthan (plus1(B), B)

Higherthan (plus1(plus1(B)), B)

Higherthan (plus1(plus1(B)), plus1(B))

Higherthan (plus1(plus1(plus1(B)), B))

Higherthan (plus1(plus1(plus1(B)), plus1(plus1(B))))....

and the counterexamples:

Higherthan (B, B)

Higherthan (B, plus1(B))

Higherthan (B, plus1(plus1(B)))

Higherthan (B, plus1(plus1(plus1(B)))

Higherthan (plus1(B), plus1(plus1(B)))

Higherthan (plus1(B,) plus1(plus1(plus1(B))) ....

(°) The ***first step*** of our method consists of checking whether **H** is a satisfiable well-founded set of formulas. This means that H has a model and there is a natural well-founded order on the elements of the Herbrand Universe. Now, the size of literals provides such a well-founded order. For an overview of well-founded orders on terms see Dershowitz (1987).

(°) The ***second step*** consists of finding candidate formulas for describing the concept to be learned. The formulas we shall consider here are of the form **G** := A / A_1 , ..., A_n , where A is a generalization (anti instance) of the set of examples, and A_1, ..., A_n are atoms (generalizations) of the set of counterexamples. That is we are dealing with formulas involving vectors of atoms which are *anti-instances* of vectors of atoms describing sets of examples and counterexamples. The reason for considering such a kind of formulas is based on the well-known scenario of the learning from examples paradigm: Given a set of examples and counterexamples of a concept, the learner tries to induce a general concept description that induces all examples and none of the counterexamples. In this kind of situation, examples force generalization whereas counterexamples prevent overgeneralizations (the induced concept should never be so general to include any of counterexamples). This most typical form of learning leads us to think that the generalization process is incremental: The learner first must form its formulas using atoms from the complete *lattice* of atoms (with an added least element modulo variable renaming) which is defined using the anti-instance relation on atoms (see Plotkin (1970) and (1971)). He must then verify whether these formulas describe new facts with respect to the existing theory (which describes the background knowledge). If a formula is not new with respect to a given theory, then, in order to change it [either by forgetting something (i.e., further generalizing the examples) or by completing the description (i.e., further specializing the counter examples)] we shift to other elements of the complete lattice of atoms. We think that this process capture the essence of basic generalization constructions based on the *variable binding* mechanism (see Michalski (1983))

Thus, the examples and the counter examples can be generalized to get the formula:

G := Higherthan(x, y) / Higherthan(z, z) , Higherthan(B, plus1(z))

(°) Having listed the kind of formulas we are interested in, (i.e., the kind of formulas we want to check for concept description with respect to a Horn theory), our ***next step*** consists of verifying whether **G** provides a concept to learn. To check it we must first get rid of the instances of Higherthan(x, y) which are instances either of Higherthan(z, z) or of Higherthan(B, plus1(y)). To acheive this task we first consider the set I(A) of all instances of Higherthan(x, y) of depth not greater than D, where D =

max{depth(A_1), ..., depth(P_n)}, and with variables only at depth D. Next we eliminate the elements of I(A) which are instances of counterexamples. The atoms Higherthan(B, B), Higherthan(B, plus(y1)) are instances of Higherthan(z, z) and Higherthan(B, plus1(y)) respectively. Thus, the atoms Higherthan(B, B) and Higherthan(B, plus1(y1)) cannot be part of the concept description. Since, in our learning from examples process, we assume the existence of Background Knowledge described by a set of Horn formulas, it must be verified whether each of the remaining leaf labels are true in the least Herbrand model of H. This is achieved by computing an answer set A(R) for R, i.e., a finite set of substitutions, which, in essence, is a finite description of all ground substitutions which need to be considered for checking whether an atom is valid is the least Herbrand model. For our purposes, the set A(R) = {B, plus1(x) } is a suitable answer set for H. In general, the set of terms **A(R)** = { t | t is any term in T(F,X), t is of depth no greater than D(R) with variables only at depth D(R)} is said to be an **answer set** for a Horn theory R.

(°) Having computed an answer set A(R) for R, our **fourth** step consists of replacing terms in A(R) for the variables of Higherthan(plus1(x1),B) and Higherthan(plus1(x1), plus1(y1)) to get:

Higherthan(plus1(B),B)

Higherthan(plus1(plus1(x)),B)

Higherthan(plus1(B), plus1(B))

Higherthan(plus1(B), plus1(plus1(y1)))

Higherthan(plus1(x1), plus1(B))

Higherthan(plus1(plus1(x1), plus1(plus1(y1)))

(°) Having constructed the instances Higherthan(plus1(B), B) and Higherthan(plus1(plus1(x)), B) of Higherthan(plus1(x1), B) our **last step** consists of using the set of inference rules of section 4. Thus, Higherthan(plus1(x1), B) is valid in the least Herbrand model of **H**. On the other hand, Higherthan(plus1(x1), plus1(y1)) is not valid in the least Herbrand model of **H** since the ground instance Higherthan(plus1(B), plus1(B)) of it cannot be rewritten to T by using R.

Thus, **G:= Higherthan(plus1(x1), B)** is a generalization and the concept to be learned is the following: "*Any arch with at least one block is higher than the empty arch*".

2.2. Example 2: Elementary Number Theory

Consider now the following set of clauses, where NUMBER and EVEN are the predicate symbols, 0, double and s are the functions symbols. Let H be the following set of Horn clauses:

¬ NUMBER(x) v EVEN(double(x)),

NUMBER(O)

NUMBER(double(x)),

NUMBER(s(x)),

¬ EVEN(s(O))

Consider now the examples

EVEN(double(0)),

EVEN(double(s(0)))

and the counterexample

EVEN(s(0))

The examples and the counterexamples can be generalized by substituting variables for terms to get the sentence **G:= EVEN(x) / EVEN(s(w)).** Note that the term x is an anti-instance of the terms double(0)) and double(s(0) since they are instances of it (x belongs to the finite anti-instance set of double(0) and double(s(0))). Now, the fact EVEN(double(x)) which is an instance of EVEN(x) but not an instance of EVEN(s(w)) is true in the least Herbrand model of H. To see it, we note that EVEN(double(x)) is an instance of the positive literal of the first clause in H and that all instances of NUMBER(x) are true because of NUMBER(O), NUMBER(double(x)), NUMBER(s(x)) being positive unit literals in H. Our approach tries to capture this intuition as to why G1 is true in the least Herbrand model of H represent the learnable concept "*any number which is the double of a number is even*". Our approach tries to capture this intuition as to why **G1** is true in the minimal Herbrand model of H .

3. THE BASIC NOTIONS

We assume that the reader is familiar with the basic notions about Herbrand universe and Horn clauses. We introduce the essential terminology below and refer to Lloyd (1984) for a detailed introduction.

3.1. Terms, Atoms and Substitutions

The basic objects are *terms*: let F be a finite set of function symbols (**signature**) and X a set of variables. Let TF be the set of all **ground terms** constructed from F and let T(F, X) be the set of **terms** constructed from F and variables in X. V(t) stands for the set of all variables appearing in t.For any ground term t, V(t) is the empty set. Obviously TF (the **Herbrand universe)** is not empty only if F includes a nullary function symbol (**constant**).

The basic way to replace variable are *substitutions*: **Substitutions** η are endomorphisms of T(F, X) with a finite domain $dom(\eta) =\{ x \mid x\eta \neq x\}$. We denote by $t\eta$ the result of applying the substitution η to a term t. η, σ,.. will denote substitutions. Composition of substitution σ and η is denoted $\sigma\eta$. Given two terms t and s, we say that s is an **instance** of t iff $s = t\sigma$ and σ is a **match** from s to t. Further t is said to be a **generalization** (or **anti-**

instance) of s , written $t \geq s$. A term t is a **variable renaming** or a **variant** of s if there is a substitution σ such that $t\sigma = s$ and $s\sigma = t$. Note that $\geq$ gives a complete lattice on terms with an added least element, modulo variable renaming. *Also any term t has only a finite number of anti-instances up to variable renaming.*

3.2. Some Horn Logic

The relations between objects are expressed by *predicate symbols.* An **atom** (or a **positive literal**) is an expression of the form $P(t_1,t_2,\ldots,t_n)$, where the t_i are terms and P is a predicate symbol. The set of atoms is denoted by A(P, F, X), and the set of ground atoms (i.e. the **Herbrand base**) is denoted by A(P,F). A **literal** is an atom or the negation of an atom. **Clauses** are sets of literals representing their disjunctions. **Horn clauses** are clauses that contain at most one positive literal. A set of clauses is said to be **satisfiable** if it admits a first-order model. Otherwise it is said to be **unsatisfiable.** The entailement relation will be denoted by $|=$. Thus, $H |= A$ means that every first-order model of H is a model of A. We denote the set of Herbrand models of a set H of clauses as HM(H). We recall that if H is a set of Horn clauses, then it has a unique least Herbrand model which is the intersection of all Herbrand models of H. Finally an atom $P(t_1,t_2,\ldots,t_n)$ is true in the least Herbrand model of a set H of Horn clauses, denoted $H \;|=_{\mathbf{LHM}} P(t_1,t_2,\ldots,t_n)$, iff each of its ground instances of $P(t_1,t_2,\ldots,t_n)$ is true in all first-order models of H.

4. A LOGICAL BASIS FOR LEARNING

This section presents with a logical basis for learning. We first define what it means "learnable concept from examples and counterexamples in presence of Background Knowledge described by a set of Horn Clauses", and next propose a method to induce general concept description from concept examples and counterexamples.

4.1. Defining Learnable Concepts

Let **H** be a set of Horn clauses that expresses the information used in the background knowledge. Let **EX** be a set of concept examples and **CE** be a set of concept counterexamples. Assume that the atom A is a generalization (anti-instance) of the set **EX** and the atoms $A_1,...,A_n$ are (generalizations) the counterexamples. Our problem is to see whether the formula **G**:= $A / A_1 ,..., A_n$ induces a concept to be learned:

Definition 1 *(Learnable Concepts)*

Given a set H of Horn clauses, let **G** := $A / A_1 ,..., A_n$ be a formula obtained in the manner described above. If there exists at least a non-ground instance $A\sigma$ of A such that

1] $H \cup \neg A_1 \cup \neg A_2 \cup .... \cup \neg A_n \models_{\mathbf{LHM}} A\sigma$, and

2] $H \cup \neg A_1 \cup \neg A_2 \cup .... \cup \neg A_n \not\models A\sigma$,

then the atom $A\sigma$ represent a *learnable concept..*

In other words, a formula **G** induces a learnable concept $A\sigma$ from a given set of training instances **EX** $\cup$ **CE** and the background knowledge **H** if and only if

a) $A\sigma$ matches every example and no counterexample in the given set **EX** $\cup$ **CE**,

b) $A\sigma$ is false in some interpretation which is a model of each the axioms of the theory **H**,

c) $A\sigma$ is true in the least Herbrand model (i.e, it is true in the intended interpretation) of **H**

Let us illustrate definition 1 by a simple example:

Example 1

Let H be the following set of Horn clauses:

Nat(0)

¬Nat(x) v Nat(s(x)).

Let **A**σ be the formula **Nat(z)**. **Nat(z)** is not true in all models (e.g., **Z** or **Q**) of H but is true in the least Herbrand model of H.

4.2. Getting Learnable Concepts: two theorems

Let us now propose a method to induce general concept description from concept examples and counterexamples. Clearly the two main problems for testing whether the formula **G** provides a learnable concept are :

P1] The unbounded number of substitutions instances of A which need to be examinated for learnable concepts, and

P2] The undecidability of the entailment problem $|=_{LHM}$

The ***first step,*** for solving these problems, consists in removing problem 1: First, let us introduce the (polymorphic) *depth* function. The depth of a atom is the height of the tree representation of this atom. Let D = max{depth(A_1), ..., depth(A_n)}, and l et I(A) be the set {$A\sigma$ | $A\sigma$ is an instance of A, $A\sigma$ is an instance of none of A_1 ,..., A_n, $A\sigma$ is of depth not greater than D with variables only at depth D }. Then all canditates for learnable concepts are elements of I(A). If I(A) is an empty set, then G:= A/A_1 ,..., A_n provides no concept to be learned since every instance of A is also an instance of some A_1 ,..., A_n

Having eliminated the instances of A which are also instances of A_1 ,..., A_n our next step consists of verifying whether the elements of I(A) represent learnable concepts. When tackling requirements 1, and 2 of definition 1 one quickly faces the problem of deduction in the classe of the first-order models and the Least Herbrand model of a given set of Horn Clauses. Let us give some effective ways to handle this problems:

Consider the following set of inferences rules, where H is a given set of Horn Clauses:

simple1
$$\frac{A,\ B,\ C_1 \vee \neg C_2 \vee \ldots \vee \neg C_n \vee C}{B,\ C_1\theta,\ C_2\theta,\ \ldots,\ C_n\theta} \quad \textbf{(s1)}$$

if $A = C\theta$, for some clause $C_1 \vee \neg C_2 \vee \ldots \vee \neg C_n \vee C$ in H, $n > 0$ and some substitution θ

simple2

$$\frac{A,\ B,\ C}{TRUE\ ,\ B} \qquad \textbf{(s2)}$$

If $A = C\eta$ for some substitution η,

The corresponding inference relation is denoted by $|\text{-}_H$. Clearly, if H is a set of Horn clauses and A an atom , then $H|=A$ if $A|\text{-}_H$ TRUE.

Let us illustrate the use of the previous inference rules by a simple example:

Example 2

Let H be the following set of Horn clauses:

P(a)
¬Q(f(x)) v ¬P(x) v P(f(x))
Q(a))
¬Q(x) v ¬Q(f(x))

and let **A =** P(f(f(f(a)))). Then we have the following derivation.

P(f(f(f(a))))
-------------------------- (s1)
Q(f(f(f(a)))), P(f(f(a)))
-------------------------------------- (s1)
Q(f(f(f(a)))), Q(f(f(a))), P(f(a))
-- (s1)
Q(f(f(f(a)))), Q(f(f(a))), Q(f(a)), P(a)

-- (s2)

Q(f(f(f(a)))), Q(f(f(a))), Q(f(a)), TRUE

-- (s1)

Q(f(f(f(a)))), Q(f(f(a))), Q(a), TRUE

-- (s2)

:

:

TRUE

Therefore P(f(f(f(a)))) $\vdash_H$ TRUE.

The previous set of inferences rules shows how to solve the implication problem for the class of first-order models of a given set of Horn clauses.To solve the implication problem for the Least Herbrand Model we must supply a well-founded order to the background knowledge. This well-founded order is the basis for a purely deductive treatment of the learning problem:

Definition 2 *(Monotonic Orders)*

A transitive irreflexive relation > on the set of atoms A(F,P) is said to be *monotonic* if

1] > is <u>well-founded</u> (i.e., there is no infinite descending sequences $s_1 > s_2 > s_3 \ldots$ of elements of A(F,P), and

2] for any substitution σ, $s > t$ implies $s\sigma > t\sigma$.

This ordering is extended to clauses by comparing the multiset of their atoms with the multiset extension of > (see Manna and Dershowitz (1979)). Since there is no ambiguity, this extension will also be denoted by >. This leads us to a monotonic set of Clauses: A set of Horn clauses is said to be monotonic if $C\sigma > C_1\sigma$, $C_2\sigma$, $C_n\sigma$, for any substitution σ and any clause $\neg C_1 \vee \neg C_2 \vee \ldots \vee \neg C_n \vee C$ in H. For a survey of construction of monotonic orderings on atoms see Dershowitz (1987).

Example 3

Let H be the following set of Horn clauses:

Nat(0)

¬Nat(x) v Nat(s(x)).

H is monotonic because of the ordering: $Nat(s^i(x)) > Nat(s^j(x))$ iff $i >_{natural} j$ (where $>_{natural}$ is the ordering of natural numbers).Thus $Nat(s(x)) > Nat(x)$.

The ***next step*** in our construction consists in computing an answer set A(H) associated with a set H of Horn clauses i.e., a finite set of substitutions, which, in essence, is a finite description of all ground substitutions which need to be considered for checking whether an atom is valid in the least Herbrand model.

Definition 3 *(Answer Sets and Answer Instances)*

Given a set H of Horn clauses, the set of terms **AS(H)** = { t | t is any term in T(F,X) of depth no greater than depth(H) and with variables only at depth(H)} is said to be an **answer set** for H. Given a literal A, an **answer-instance** of A with respect to AS(H) is an instance of A which is obtained by substituting terms in AS(H) for the variables of A.

Example 4

Let H be the set {¬L(x,y) v L(s(x),s(y)) , ¬L(s(0),0) } of Horn clauses. Then the set AS(H) = {0, s(0), s(s(z)) } is an answer set for H. Now, if L(0,s(x)) is an atom, then the terms L(0,s(0)) , L(0,s(s(0))), and L(0,s(s(s(z)))) are the test-instances of L(0,s(x)) .

Since we want to perform implications in the least Herbrand model of a set H of Horn clauses, we must obtain a deeper characterization of this fact. The following theorem shows how to use **instances of an atom A to infer other instances of it as soon as the used instances are smaller than the one that is currently considered**. This kind of reasoning is **sound** by regarding A as an induction hypothesis. In addition, the following theorem provides us with a very general way to prove that an atom represents a learnable concept by taking into account the well-founded ordering on the ground atoms:

Theorem 1

Let H be a monotonic set of Horn clauses and let A be an atom such that $A |\!/\!-_H$ TRUE. If for any answer-instance $A\sigma$ of A there exists a Horn clause $\neg C_1 \vee \neg C_2 \vee \ldots \vee \neg C_n \vee C$ in H such that :

1) $A\sigma = C\eta$ for some substitution η,

2) For all $i \leq n$ $C_i\eta |\!-_{H \cup A}{}^{TRUE}$

Then A represents a learnable concept .

Proof: Let us assume that A is not a learnable concept. Then A is not true in the least Herbrand model of **H**. Consequently, there must exist a ground substitution σ' such that H $|\neq_{\mathbf{LHM}}$ $A\sigma'$. Let us suppose that this substitution is the smallest one with respect to >. By definition, there must exists an answer instance $A\sigma$ of A such that $A\sigma\theta = A\sigma'$. There is some substitution η such that $A\sigma\theta = C\eta\theta$ and for all $i \leq n$ $C_i\eta\theta |-_{H \cup A}$ TRUE. Since H is monotonic by hypothesis, the ground instances of A used in the derivation must be smaller (with respect to >) than the instances of the atom $A\sigma\theta$, and thus they are valid in the least Herbrand model of **H**. Therefore for all $i \leq n$ $C_i\eta\theta$ is valid in the least Herbrand model of **H** and the same is true for $C\eta\theta$. Hence we have a contradiction with the fact that H $|\neq_{\mathbf{LHM}}$ $A\sigma'$.

This theorem is the basis for our investigations of learnable concepts. Consider now the following situation: Let A be an atom and assume that there exists at least one answer instance $A\sigma$ which is not an instance of some positive literal of the set H of Horn clauses. Then A is not a learnable concept:

Theorem 2

Let H be a set of Horn clauses and A be an atom. If there exists an answer-instance $A\sigma$ of A such that $A\sigma \neq C\eta$ for any substitution η, and any clause $\neg C_1 \vee \neg C_2 \vee \ldots \vee \neg C_n \vee C$ then A is not a learnable concept.

Proof (Sketch): Let A be an atom et let us assume that some answer-instance $A\sigma$ of A is not an instance of any positive literal in H. We are going to show that there exists at least a ground substitution instanceof Aσ which is not an instance of any positive literal of H. Consider a ground instance Aσ' of Aσ obtained by substituing distinct ground terms for each variable in Aσ. These ground terms should differ in depth at least by |A| + |H| +1. Were Aσ' an instance of a positive literal of H in which every variable occurs exactly once, then the same literal would match Aσ', a contraduction. On the other hand side the definition of the previous ground substitution prevents positive literal of H in which every variable occurs more than once to apply to Aσ' . Therefore Aσ' is not true in the least Herbrand Model of H and thus is not a Learnable concept .

4.3. A General Procedure for Learning

Theorems 1 and 2 can be combined into a single procedure for verifying whether a given atom represents a learnable concept from a set of examples and counterexamples in the presence of background knowledge described by a set H of Horn Clauses. Our learning procedure modifies incrementally three sets of atoms:

1] P, a set of atoms to be proved for validity in the least Herbrand model of H.

2] C, a set of atoms which contains the premises of the clauses once they have been used.

3] B, a set of atoms that have been instanciated by elements of the answer set AS(H), and therefore can be used as induction hypotheses;

Let us present the inferences rules:

generate1

$$\frac{C,\ P \cup \{p\},\ B,\ H}{C,\ P \cup \{\cup_\eta p\eta\},\ B,\ H \cup \{p\}}$$

where $\{\cup_\eta p\eta\}$ are the set of test -instances of the atom p.

deduce1

$$\frac{C \cup \{c\},\quad P,\ B,\quad H}{C \cup \{\cup c_i\tau\},\ P,\ B,\ H}$$

if there exists a clause $\neg C_1 \vee \neg C_2 \vee \ldots \vee \neg C_n \vee C$ in H , a substitution τ such that $c = C\tau$. Clearly if n = 0, then $\{\cup c_i\tau\} = \emptyset$

deduce2

$$\frac{C,\ P \cup \{c\},\ B,\ H}{C \cup \{\cup c_i\tau\},\ P,\ B,\ H}$$

if there exists a clause $\neg C_1 \vee \neg C_2 \vee \ldots \vee \neg C_n \vee C$ in H , a substitution τ such that $c = C\tau$. Clearly if n = 0, then $\{\cup c_i\tau\} = \emptyset$

deduce3

$$\frac{C \cup \{c\},\ P,\ B,\ H}{C,\ P,\ B,\ H}$$

if c is an instance of an atom in B

transfer

$$\frac{C \cup \{c\},\ P,\ B,\ H}{C,\ P \cup \{c\},\ B,\ H}$$

if c is neither an instance of B nor an instance of a head of a clause in H

fail

$$\frac{C,\ P \cup \{p\eta\},\ A,\ H}{[]}$$

if $p\eta$ is not instance of a head of a clause in H.

The rule *generate* allows to replace conjectures by greater ones and thus using the initial conjectures as induction hypotheses. The rules *deduce1*, *deduce2*, and *deduce3* allow to prove conjectures either by using clauses in H or atoms in B. The rule *tranfer* allows to treat premises as conjectures. Finally the rule *fail* allows us detect false conjectures.

We shall say that a set of Horn clauses is *determinist* if there is no choice for the clause of H when applying *deduce 1* or *deduce 2* .

Note that the last inference rule *fail* allows a kind of **completeness** of our proof system: *Provided that a set H of Horn clauses is monotonic and determinist then we shall detect in a finite time any atom which is not a learnable concept.*

5. CONCLUSION

We have presented in this paper a very simple method to induce concepts from a given set of examples and counterexamples under the assumption that the knowledge background is described by a set of Horn clauses. The above theory can be easily extended to general clause calculi. However, some research is still needed in order to define a *learnable concept for a set of minimal models.*

REFERENCES

Buntine, W. (1988). "Generalized subsumption and its applications to induction and redundancy", *Artificial Intelligence* 36 pp. 149-176.

Dershowitz, N. (1987). "Termination of rewriting", *Journal of Symbolic Computation* 3 (1&2).

Dietterich, G.T and Michalski, R.S (1981). "Inductive Learning of Structural Descriptions: Evaluation Criteria and Comparative Review of Selected Methods", *Artificial Intelligence* 16 , pp. 257-294.

Greiner, R. and Genesereth, M. (1983). "What's new ? A semantic definition of novelty", Proc. *International Joint Conference on Artificial Intelligence*, pp. 450-454, Karslruhe.

Huet, G. (1976). Résolution d'équations dans des langages d'ordre 1, 2, ..., ω, Thèse d'Etat, Université de Paris 7.

Huet, G. (1980). "Confluent reductions: abstract properties and applications to term rewriting systems", *JACM* 27 (4), pp. 797-821.

Kodratoff, Y. (1983). "Generalizing and Particularizing as Techniques Learning", *Computer and Artificial Intelligence*, vol. 2 , pp. 417-441.

Kodratoff, Y. (1988). *Introduction to Machine Learning*, Pitman.

Kodratoff, Y. and Ganascia, J.G. (1984). "Careful Generalization for Concept Learning", Proc. *6th European Conference on Artificial Intelligence*, pp. 483-492.

Kodratoff, Y. and Ganascia, J.G. (1986). "Improving the generalization step in learning", In *Machine Learning: An Artificial Intelligence Approach*, vol. 2, Morgan Kaufman, pp. 215-244.

Kounalis, E. (1990a). A Calculus of Systems with Equality: Mémoire d'Habilitation à Diriger des Recherches en Informatique, Université de Nancy 1.

Kounalis, E. (1990b). "Learning from Examples and Counterexamples with Equational Background Knowledge", Proc. *2nd IEEE International Conference on Tools for Artificial Intelligence*, Herndon, VA, (USA), pp. 254-260. Full paper in IJTAI 1992, to appear.

Kounalis, E. (1990c). "Pumping lemmas for tree languages generated by rewrite systems", Proc. *15th Conference on Mathematical Foundations of Computer Science* (MFCS 90), Banska Bystrica, LNCS 452, Springer-Verlag, pp. 369-378.

Kounalis, E. and Rusinowitch, M. (1988). "On the word problem in Horn Theories", Proc. *9th CADE*, Argone (USA), LNCS 310, Springer-Verlag, pp. 347-357. Full paper in*Journal of Symbolic Computation.*, Mars 1991

Kounalis, E. and Rusinowitch, M. (1990a). "Mechanizing Inductive Reasoning", Proc. *8th National Conference on Artificial Intelligence*

(AAAI-90), Boston(USA), pp. 240-245. Also in the Bulletin of the European Association of Theoretical Computer Science (EATCS), n° 41, June 1990, pp. 216-226.

Kounalis, E. and Rusinowitch, M. (1990b). "Discovering New Facts in First-Order Knowledge-Based Theories", Proc. *4th International Symposium on Knowledge Engineering*, Barcelona, pp. 186-199.

Kounalis, E. and Rusinowitch, M. (1990c). "A Logical Basis for Learning in Robots' Worlds", Proc. *5th International Conference on Applications of Artificial Intelligence In Engineering*, Boston (USA), vol. 2, Manufacture and Planning, pp. 275-288.

Lassez, J.L. and Mariott, K. (1987). "Explicit representation of term defined by counter examples", *Journal of Automated Reasoning* 3, pp. 301-317.

Lassez, J.L., Maher, M. and Marriott, K. (1991). "Elimination of Negation in Term Algebras", Proc. *16th Conference on Mathematical Foundations of Computer Science* (MFCS 91), Poland.

Lloyd, W. (1984). *Foundations of Logic Programming*, Springer-Verlag.

Maher, M. (1988). "Complete axiomatizations of the algebras, rational and infinite trees", Proc. *3rd IEEE Symposium on Logic in Computer Science*, pp. 348-357.

Manna Z. and Dershowitz, M. (1979). "Proving termination with multiset ordering", *Communications of ACM* 22 (8), pp. 465-476.

Michalski, R.S. (1984 and 1986). *Machine Learning: An Artifici Intelligence Approach*, vol. 1 & 2, Springer-Verlag.

Michalski, R.S. (1983). "A Theory and Methodology of Inductive Learning", *Artificial Intelligence* 20 (1983) , pp. 111-161.

Michie, D. (1985). "Experts Systems Today", Invited talk at Conference on *Commercial Applications of Expert Systems*, Sydney.

Mitchell, T.M. (1978). Version Spaces: An Approach to Concept Learning, Ph.D. Thesis, STAN-CS-78-711, Stanford University.

Moore, R.C. (1980). "Reasoning about knowledge and action", Technical Report 191, SRI International.

Plotkin, G.D. (1970). "A Note on Inductive Generalization", in *Machine Intelligence* 5, pp. 153-163.

Plotkin, G.D. (1971). "A Further Note on Inductive Generalization", in *Machine Intelligence* 6, pp. 101-124.

Rusinowitch, M. (1989). *Démonstration automatique - Techniques de réécriture*, InterEditions.

Vere, S.A. (1980). "Multilevel Counterfactuals for Generalization of Relational Concepts and Productions", *Artificial Intelligence* 14, pp. 139-164.

CHAPTER 5

Using Genetic Algorithms for Supervised Concept Learning

WILLIAM M. SPEARS
Navy Center for Applied Research in AI
Naval Research Laboratory
Washington, D.C. 20375, USA

and

KENNETH A. DE JONG
Computer Science Department
George Mason University
Fairfax, VA 22030, USA

ABSTRACT

Genetic Algorithms (GAs) have traditionally been used for non-symbolic learning tasks. In this chapter we consider the application of a GA to a symbolic learning task, supervised concept learning from examples. A GA concept learner (GABL) is implemented that learns a concept from a set of positive and negative examples. GABL is run in a batch-incremental mode to facilitate comparison with an incremental concept learner, ID5R. Preliminary results support that, despite minimal system bias, GABL is an effective concept learner and is quite competitive with ID5R as the target concept increases in complexity.

1. Introduction

There is a common misconception in the machine learning community that Genetic Algorithms (GAs) are primarily useful for non-symbolic learning tasks. This perception comes from the historically heavy use of GAs for complex parameter optimization problems. In the machine learning field there are many interesting parameter tuning problems to which GAs have been and can be applied, including threshold adjustment of decision rules and weight adjustment in neural networks. However, the focus of this chapter is to illustrate that GAs are more general than this and can be effectively applied to more traditional symbolic learning tasks as well. [1]

To support this claim we have selected the well-studied task of supervised concept learning. [14,15,17,20] Although there have been a number of applications of genetic algorithms to supervised concept learning, they have largely avoided notice. One of the

[1] For an introduction to Genetic Algorithms, please see Goldberg. [9]

earlier efforts merged genetic algorithms with an existing concept learner.[19] Other efforts have concentrated on the combination of genetic algorithms and classifier systems to concept learning.[3,25] Finally, both Greene[10] and Janikow[13] have studied genetic algorithms (in isolation) as mechanisms for solving concept learning problems. In this chapter, we reemphasize this theme, showing how concept learning tasks can be represented and solved by GAs, and we provide empirical results which illustrate the performance of GAs relative to a more traditional method. Finally, we discuss the advantages and disadvantages of this approach and describe future research activities.

2. Supervised Concept Learning Problems

Supervised concept learning involves inducing concept descriptions from a set of examples of a target concept (i.e., the concept to be learned). Concepts are represented as subsets of points in an n-dimensional feature space which is defined *a priori* and for which all the legal values of the features are known.

A concept learning program is presented with both a description of the feature space and a set of correctly classified examples of the concepts, and is expected to generate a reasonably accurate description of the (unknown) concepts. Since concepts can be arbitrarily complex subsets of a feature space, an important issue is the choice of the concept description language. The language must have sufficient expressive power to describe large subsets succinctly and yet be able to capture irregularities. The two language forms generally used are decision trees[17] and rules[15].

Another important issue arises from the problem that there is a large (possibly infinite) set of concept descriptions which are consistent with any particular finite set of examples. This is generally resolved by introducing either explicitly or implicitly a bias (preference) for certain kinds of descriptions (e.g., shorter or less complex descriptions may be preferred).

Finally, there is the difficult issue of evaluating and comparing the performance of concept learning algorithms. The most widely used approach is a *batch mode* in which the set of examples is divided into a training set and a test set. The concept learner is required to produce a concept description from the training examples. The validity of the description produced is then measured by the percentage of correct classifications made by the system on the second (test) set of examples with no further learning.

The alternative evaluation approach is an *incremental mode* in which the concept learner is required to produce a concept description from the examples seen so far and to use that description to classify the next incoming example. In this mode learning never stops, and evaluation is in terms of learning curves which measure the predictive performance of the concept learner over time.

3. Genetic Algorithms and Concept Learning

In order to apply GAs to a particular problem, we need to select an internal representation of the space to be searched and define an external evaluation function which assigns utility to candidate solutions. Both components are critical to the successful application of the GAs to the problem of interest.

3.1. *Representing the Search Space*

The traditional internal representation used by GAs involves using fixed-length (generally binary) strings to represent points in the space to be searched. This representation maps well onto parameter optimization problems and there is considerable evidence (both theoretical and empirical) as to the effectiveness of using GAs to search such spaces.[6,9,11,22] However, such representations do not appear well-suited for representing the space of concept descriptions which are generally symbolic in nature, which have both syntactic and semantic constraints, and which can be of widely varying length and complexity.

There are two general approaches one might take to resolve this issue. The first involves changing the fundamental GA operators (crossover and mutation) to work effectively with complex non-string objects.[19] This must be done carefully in order to preserve the properties which make the GAs effective adaptive search procedures (see De Jong[7] for a more detailed discussion). Alternatively, one can attempt to construct a string representation which minimizes any changes to the GAs without adopting such a convoluted representation as to render the fundamental GA operators useless.

We are interested in pursuing both approaches. Our ideas on the first approach will be discussed briefly at the end of the chapter. In the following sections we will describe our results using the second approach.

3.2. *Defining Fixed-length Classifier Rules*

Our approach to choosing a representation which results in minimal changes to the standard GA operators involves carefully selecting the concept description language. A natural way to express complex concepts is as a disjunctive set of (possibly overlapping) classification rules (DNF). The left-hand side of each rule (disjunct) consists of a conjunction of one or more tests involving feature values. The right-hand side of a rule indicates the concept (classification) to be assigned to the examples which match its left-hand side. Collectively, a set of such rules can be thought of as representing the (unknown) concepts if the rules correctly classify the elements of the feature space.

If we allow arbitrarily complex terms in the conjunctive left-hand side of such rules, we will have a very powerful description language which will be difficult to represent as strings. However, by restricting the complexity of the elements of the conjunctions, we are able to use a string representation and standard GAs, with the only negative side effect that more rules may be required to express the concept. This is achieved by restricting each element of a conjunction to be a test of the form:

> return true if the value of feature i of the example
> is in the given value set, else return false.

For example, rules might take the following symbolic forms:

> if F1 = blue then it's a block

or

> if (F2 = large) and (F5 = tall or thin) then it's a widget

or

> if (F1 = red or white or blue) and (10 < F4 < 20) then it's a clown

Since the left-hand sides are conjunctive forms with internal disjunction, there is no loss of generality by requiring that there be at most one test for each feature (on the left hand side of a rule).

With these restrictions we can now construct a fixed-length internal representation for classifier rules. Each fixed-length rule will have *N* feature tests, one for each feature. Each feature test will be represented by a fixed length binary string, the length of which will depend of the type of feature (nominal, ordered, etc.).

For nominal features with *k* values we use *k* bits, 1 for each value. So, for example, if the legal values for F1 are the days of the week, then the pattern 0111110 would represent the test for F1 being a weekday.

Intervals for features taking on numeric ranges can also be encoded efficiently as fixed-length bit strings, the details of which can be seen in Booker. [2]. For simplicity, the examples used in this chapter will involve features with nominal values.

So, for example, the left-hand side of a rule for a 5 feature problem would be represented internally as:

F1	F2	F3	F4	F5
0110010	1111	01	111100	11111

Notice that a feature test involving all 1's matches any value of a feature and is equivalent to "dropping" that conjunctive term (i.e., the feature is irrelevant). So, in the above example only the values of F1, F3, and F4 are relevant. For completeness, we allow patterns of all 0's which match nothing. This means that any rule containing such a pattern will not match (cover) any points in the feature space. While rules of this form are of no use in the final concept description, they are quite useful as storage areas for GAs when evolving and testing sets of rules.

The right-hand side of a rule is simply the class (concept) to which the example belongs. This means that our "classifier system" is a "stimulus-response" system with no internal memory.

3.3. *Evolving Sets of Classifier Rules*

Since a concept description will consist of one or more classifier rules, we still need to specify how GAs will be used to evolve sets of rules. There are currently two basic strategies: the Michigan approach exemplified by Holland's classifier system, [12] and the Pittsburgh approach exemplified by Smith's LS-1 system. [21] Systems using the Michigan approach maintain a population of *individual rules* which compete with each other for space and priority in the population. In contrast, systems using the Pittsburgh approach maintain a population of *variable-length rule sets* which compete with each other with respect to performance on the domain task.

Very little is currently known concerning the relative merits of the two approaches. As discussed in a later section, one of our goals is to use the domain of concept learning as a testbed for gaining more insight into the two approaches. In this chapter we report on results obtained from using the Pittsburgh approach. That is, each individual in the population is a variable length string representing an unordered set of fixed-length rules (disjuncts). The number of rules in a particular individual is unrestricted and can range from 1 to a very large number depending on evolutionary pressures.

Our goal was to achieve a representation that required minimal changes to the fundamental genetic operators. We feel we have achieved this with our variable-length string representation involving fixed-length rules. Crossover can occur anywhere (i.e., both on rule boundaries and within rules). The only requirement is that the corresponding crossover points on the two parents "match up semantically". That is, if one parent is being cut on a rule boundary, then the other parent must be also cut on a rule boundary. Similarly, if one parent is being cut at a point 5 bits to the right of a rule boundary, then the other parent must be cut in a similar spot (i.e., 5 bits to the right of some rule boundary).

The mutation operator is unaffected and performs the usual bit-level mutations.

3.4. *Choosing a Payoff Function*

In addition to selecting a good representation, it is important to define a good payoff function which rewards the right kinds of individuals. One of the nice features of using GAs for concept learning is that the payoff function is the natural place to centralize and make explicit any biases (preferences) for certain kinds of concept descriptions. It also makes it easy to study the effects of different biases by simply making changes to the payoff function.

For the experiments reported in this chapter, we wanted to minimize any *a priori* bias we might have. So we selected a payoff function involving only classification performance (ignoring, for example, length and complexity biases). The payoff (fitness) of each individual rule set is computed by testing the rule set on the current set of examples and letting:

$$payoff\ (individual\ i) = (percent\ correct)^2 \tag{1}$$

This provides a non-linear bias toward correctly classifying all the examples while providing differential reward for imperfect rule sets.

3.5. *The GA Concept Learner*

Given the representation and payoff function described above, a standard GA can be used to evolve concept descriptions in several ways. The simplest approach involves using a batch mode in which a fixed set of examples is presented, and the GA must search the space of variable-length strings described above for a set of rules which achieves a score of 100%. We will call this approach GABL (GA Batch concept Learner).

Due to the stochastic nature of GAs, a rule set with a perfect score (i.e., 100% correct) may not always be found in a fixed amount of time. So as not to introduce a strong bias, we use the following search termination criterion. The search terminates as soon as a 100% correct rule set is found within a user-specified upper bound on the number of generations. If a correct rule set is not found within the specified bounds or if the population loses diversity (> 90% convergence), [5] the GA simply returns the *best* rule set found. This incorrect (but often quite accurate) rule set is used to predict (classify) future examples.

The simplest way to produce an incremental GA concept learner is to use GABL incrementally in the following way. The concept learner initially accepts a single example from a pool of examples. GABL is used to create a 100% correct rule set for this example. This rule set is used to predict the classification of the next example. If the prediction is incorrect, GABL is invoked to evolve a new rule set using the two examples. If the prediction is correct, the example is simply stored with the previous example and the rule set remains unchanged. As each new additional instance is accepted, a prediction is made, and the GA is rerun in batch if the prediction is incorrect. We refer to this mode of operation as batch-incremental and we refer to the GA batch-incremental concept learner as GABIL.

4. Empirical Studies

The experiments described in this section are designed to compare the predictive performance of GABIL with ID5R as a function of incremental increases in the size and complexity of the target concept.

4.1. *Evaluating Concept Learning Programs*

As suggested in the introduction, there are many ways to evaluate and compare concept learning programs: in either batch or incremental modes. We tend to favor incremental learning systems since the world in which most learning systems must perform is generally dynamic and changing. In this context we prefer the use of learning curves which measure the change in a system's performance over time in a (possibly) changing environment.

In the domain of supervised concept learning, this means that we are interested in situations in which examples are accepted one at a time. In this mode, a concept learner must use its current concept descriptions to classify the next example. The concept learner then compares its classification with the actual class of the example. Based on this comparison the concept learner may add that example to the existing set and attempt to reformulate new concept descriptions, or it may leave the current descriptions unchanged.

An incremental concept learner will make a prediction for each new instance seen. Each prediction is either correct or incorrect. We are interested in examining how an incremental system changes its predictive performance over time. Suppose each outcome (correct or incorrect) is stored. We could look at every outcome to compute performance, but this would only indicate the global performance of the learner (a typical batch mode statistic). Instead, we examine a small window of recent outcomes, counting the correct predictions within that window. Performance curves can then be generated which indicate whether a concept learner is getting any better at correctly classifying new (unseen) examples. The graphs used in the experiments in this chapter depict this by plotting at each time step (after a new example arrives) the percent correct achieved over the last 10 arrivals (recent behavior).

4.2. *Implementation Details*

All of our experiments have been performed using a C implementation of the GAs. In all cases the population size has been held fixed at 100, the variable-length 2-point crossover operator has been applied at a 60% rate, the mutation rate is 0.1%, and selection is performed via Baker's SUS algorithm. [1]

4.3. *Initial Experiments*

The experiments described in this section are designed to demonstrate the predictive performance of GABIL as a function of incremental increases in the size and complexity of the target concept. We invented a 4 feature world in which each feature has 4 possible distinct values (i.e., there are 256 instances in this world). This means that rules map into 16-bit strings and the length of individual rule sets is a multiple of 16.

In addition to studying the behavior of our GA-based concept learner (GABIL) as a function of increasing complexity, we were also interested in comparing its performance with an existing algorithm. Utgoff's ID5R, [24] which is a well-known incremental concept learning algorithm, was chosen for comparison. ID5R uses decision trees as the description language and always produces a decision tree consistent with the instances seen.

We constructed a set of 12 concept learning problems, each consisting of a single target concept of increasing complexity. We varied the complexity by increasing both the number of rules (disjuncts) and the number of relevant features per rule (conjuncts) required to correctly describe the concepts. The number of disjuncts ranged from 1 to 4, while the number of conjuncts ranged from 1 to 3. Each target concept is labelled as *n*D*m*C, where *n* is the number of disjuncts and *m* is the number of conjuncts.

Each target concept is associated with one experiment. Within an experiment the number of disjuncts and conjuncts for the target concept remains fixed. The variation in target concept occurs between experiments. For each of the concepts, a set of 256 unique, noise free examples was generated from the feature space and labeled as positive or negative examples of the target concept. For the more complex concepts, this resulted in learning primarily from negative examples.

For each concept, the 256 examples were randomly shuffled and then presented sequentially as described above. This procedure was repeated 10 times for each concept and for each learning algorithm. The performance curves presented are the average behavior exhibited over 10 runs. [2]

ID5R and GABIL use significantly different approaches to concept learning. Therefore, we expect their performance behaviors to differ. As the number of disjuncts and conjuncts increases, the target concept (viewed syntactically as a logical DNF expression) becomes more difficult. In general, a more complex target concept requires a larger decision tree (although this is not always true). ID5R relies upon Quinlan's information theoretic entropy measure to build its decision trees. This measure works well when individual features are meaningful in distinguishing an example as positive or negative. As the number of disjuncts and/or conjuncts increases, individual features become less informative, resulting in larger decision trees and poorer predictive performance. ID5R's information theoretic biases will therefore perform better on simpler target concepts.

GABIL, however, should perform uniformly well on target concepts of varying complexity. GABIL should not be affected by the number of conjuncts, since with our fixed-length rule representation, large conjunctions are no more difficult to find than

---

[2] It is not always possible for ID5R to make a prediction based on the decision tree. If it cannot use the tree to predict we let ID5R make a random prediction.

small ones. There is also no bias towards a small number of disjuncts. Given these biases (and lack of biases), then, it is natural to expect that while ID5R will outperform GABIL on the simpler concepts, there will exist a frontier at which the situation will reverse.

For the sake of brevity we present graphs of 7 of the 12 experiments. Figure 1 depicts the comparative results on target concept 2D1C. It is representative of the results on all the 1 and 2 disjunct concepts. Figures 2 - 7 present the comparative results of applying both GABIL and ID5R to the more difficult concepts (3 and 4 disjuncts). Recall that each point on a curve represents the percent correct achieved over the previous 10 instances (and averaged over 10 runs).

The graphs indicate that, on the simpler concepts, the predictive performance of ID5R improves more rapidly than that of GABIL. However, ID5R degrades in performance as the target concept becomes more complex, and GABIL starts to win on the 4 disjunct concepts. We expect this trend to continue with even larger numbers of disjuncts and conjuncts.

Although it is natural to expect that a simple target concept (from a syntactic viewpoint) would have a small decision tree representation, this is only a rough generalization. We were surprised to see ID5R suffer the most on the 4D1C target concept, since syntactically the concept is only moderately complex. The target concept is of the form:

if (F1 = 0001) or (F2 = 0001) or (F3 = 0001) or (F4 = 0001) then it's positive

This target concept is represented by ID5R as a decision tree of over 150 nodes. In fact, each negative example is represented by a unique leaf node in the decision tree. For this reason, ID5R cannot generalize over the negative examples, and has a good chance of predicting any negative example incorrectly. Furthermore, even the positive examples are not generalized well, resulting in prediction errors for positive examples. It is clear that the decision tree representation (which is also a bias) is poor for representing this

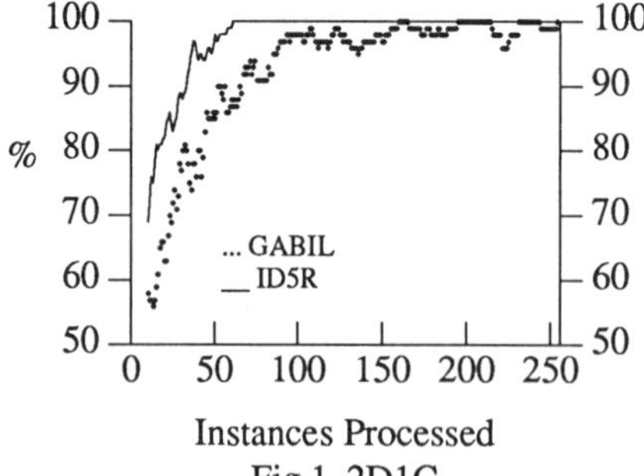

Instances Processed
Fig 1. 2D1C

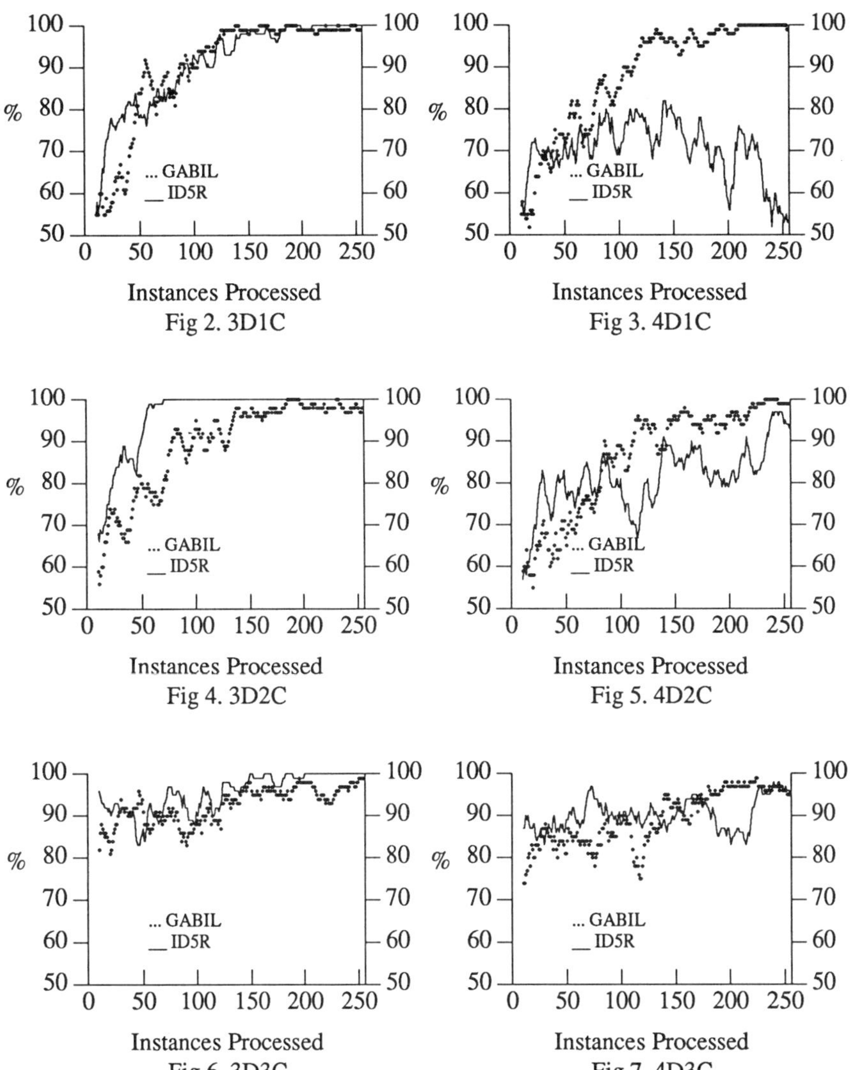

Fig 2. 3D1C

Fig 3. 4D1C

Fig 4. 3D2C

Fig 5. 4D2C

Fig 6. 3D3C

Fig 7. 4D3C

particular concept. Target concept 4D1C represents a worst case, which explains why the difference between GABIL and ID5R is greatest for this concept. A similar situation occurs for target concepts 3D1C, 4D2C, and 4D3C, although to a lesser degree.

The experiments indicate that ID5R often degrades in performance as the number of disjuncts and conjuncts increases. ID5R's biases favor concepts that can be represented with small decision trees. The information theoretic measure favors those concepts in which individual features clearly distinguish target class membership. GABIL does not have these biases, and appears to be less sensitive to increasing numbers of disjuncts and conjuncts. GABIL does not degrade significantly with increasing target concept complexity and outperforms ID5R on 4 disjunct concepts. Since the syntactic complexity of a target concept corresponds roughly with the size of its decision tree representation, we expect this trend to continue with more difficult target concepts.

5. Further Analysis and Comparisons

In other work we have compared GABIL with AQ15 [16] and Quinlan' C4.5 [18] on the *n*D*m*C target concepts and the breast cancer domain. [8,23] Most recently, GABIL has been augmented with concept learning specific operators, which are selected dynamically by the genetic algorithm while concept learning occurs. [23]. The result is a robust concept learner that is competitive with the more traditional systems.

In the future we plan to perform additional experiments involving the comparison of GABIL with other concept learning programs such as Clark's CN2, [4] Janikow's GIL, [13] and the concept learners based on neural network techniques. We also plan to implement and analyze other GA-based concept learners. The first is a variation of the current one which is truly incremental rather than batch-incremental. We feel that this change will smooth out many of the bumps in the learning curves currently due to completely reinitializing the population when an incorrect classification is made on a new example.

We are also very interested in understanding the difference between using the Pittsburgh approach and the Michigan approach in this problem domain. The current fixed-length rule representation can be used directly in Michigan-style classifier systems. We plan to implement such a system and compare the two approaches.

Finally, we noted early in the chapter that there were two basic strategies for selecting a representation for the concept description language. In this chapter we developed a representation which minimized the changes to standard GA implementations. We also plan to explore the alternative strategy of modifying the basic GA operators to deal effectively with non-string representations. In particular, we plan to use Michalski's VL1 language and compare this approach to using GAs with the current work.

6. Conclusions

This chapter presents a series of initial results regarding the use of GAs for symbolic learning tasks. In particular, a GA-based concept learner is developed and analyzed. It is interesting to note that reasonable performance is achieved with minimal bias. There is no preference for shorter rule sets, unlike most other concept learning systems. The initial results support the view that GAs can be used as an effective concept learner although they may not outperform algorithms specifically designed for concept learning when simple concepts are involved.

This chapter also sets the stage for additional comparisons between GAs and other concept learning algorithms. We feel that such comparisons are important and encourage the research community to develop additional results on these and other problems of interest.

Acknowledgements

We would like to thank Diana Gordon for her support and for many discussions on the biases in supervised concept learning systems. Diana was also instrumental in helping us design our experimental methodology. We would also like to thank John Grefenstette and Alan Schultz for many useful comments about GABIL and crossover.

References

1. J. E. Baker, Reducing Bias and Inefficiency in the Selection Algorithm, *Proceedings of the Second International Conference on Genetic Algorithms and their Applications*, (Lawrence Erlbaum, 1987), pgs. 14 - 21.
2. L. B. Booker, *Intelligent Behavior as an Adaptation to the Task Environment*, Doctoral Thesis, CCS Department, University of Michigan, (1982).
3. L. B. Booker, Triggered Rule Discovery in Classifier Systems, *Proceedings of the Third International Conference on Genetic Algorithms and their Applications*, (Morgan Kaufmann, 1989), pgs. 265 - 274.
4. P. Clark and T. Niblett, The CN2 Induction Algorithm, *Machine Learning,* **3**, 4, (1989).
5. K. A. De Jong, *An Analysis of the Behavior of a Class of Genetic Adaptive Systems,* Doctoral Thesis, Dept. Computer and Communication Sciences, University of Michigan, Ann Arbor, (1975).
6. K. A. De Jong, Genetic Algorithms: a 10 Year Perspective, *Proceedings of the First International Conference on Genetic Algorithms and their Applications*, (Lawrence Erlbaum, 1985), pgs. 169 - 177.
7. K. A. De Jong, Using Genetic Algorithms to Search Program Spaces, *Proceedings of the Second International Conference on Genetic Algorithms and their Applications*, (Lawrence Erlbaum, 1987), pgs. 210 - 216.
8. K. A. De Jong and W. M. Spears, Learning Concept Classification Rules Using Genetic Algorithms, *Proceedings of the Twelfth International Joint Conference on Artificial Intelligence*, (Morgan Kaufmann, 1991), pgs. 651 - 656.
9. D. E. Goldberg, *Genetic Algorithms in Search, Optimization & Machine Learning,* (Addison-Wesley, 1989).
10. D. Greene and S. Smith, A Genetic System for Learning Models of Consumer

Choice, *Proceedings of the Second International Conference on Genetic Algorithms*, (Lawrence Erlbaum, 1987), pgs. 217 - 223.

11. J. H. Holland, *Adaptation in Natural and Artificial Systems*, (Michigan Press, 1975).
12. J. H. Holland, Escaping Brittleness: The Possibilities of General-Purpose Learning Algorithms Applied to Parallel Rule-Based Systems. In R. Michalski, J. Carbonell, and T. Mitchell (Eds.), *Machine Learning: An Artificial Intelligence Approach*, **2**, (Morgan Kaufmann, 1986).
13. C. Janikow, *Inductive Learning of Decision Rules from Attribute-Based Examples: A Knowledge Intensive Genetic Algorithm Approach*, TR91-030, Doctoral Thesis, Department of Computer Science, University of Chapel Hill, North Carolina, (1991).
14. T. Mitchell, *Version Spaces : An Approach to Concept Learning*. Doctoral Thesis, Stanford University, Stanford, CA, (1978).
15. R. Michalski, A Theory and Methodology of Inductive Learning. In R. Michalski, J. Carbonell, and T. Mitchell (Eds.), *Machine Learning: An Artificial Intelligence Approach*, **1**, (Tioga Publishing, 1983).
16. R. Michalski, I. Mozetic, J. Hong, and N. Lavrac, The AQ15 Inductive Learning System: An Overview and Experiments. University of Illinois Report Number UIUCDCS-R-86-1260, (1986).
17. J. R. Quinlan, Induction of Decision Trees. *Machine Learning,*, **1**, 1, (1986).
18. J. R. Quinlan, Documentation and User's Guide for C4.5, (unpublished, 1989).
19. L. Rendell, Genetic Plans and the Probabilistic Learning System: Synthesis and Results. *Proceedings of the First International Conference on Genetic Algorithms and their Applications*, (Lawrence Erlbaum, 1985), pgs. 60 - 73.
20. L. Rendell, H. Cho, and R. Seshu, Improving the Design of Similarity-Based Rule-Learning Systems. *International Journal of Expert Systems*, **2**, 1, (1989).
21. S. F. Smith, Flexible Learning of Problem Solving Heuristics Through Adaptive Search, *Proceedings of the Eighth International Joint Conference on Artificial Intelligence*, (William Kaufmann, 1983), pgs. 422 - 425.
22. W. M. Spears, *Using Neural Networks and Genetic Algorithms as Heuristics for NP-Complete Problems*, Masters Thesis, CS Department, George Mason University, (1990).
23. W. M. Spears and D. F. Gordon, Adaptive Strategy Selection for Concept Learning, *Multistrategy Learning (MSL-91) Workshop*, (1991), pgs. 231 - 246.
24. P. E. Utgoff, Improved Training via Incremental Learning, *Proceedings of the Sixth International Workshop on Machine Learning*, (Morgan Kaufmann, 1989), pgs. 62 - 65.
25. S. W. Wilson, Classifier Systems and the Animat Problem, *Machine Learning*, **2**, 4, (1987).

CHAPTER 6

Extracting Procedural Knowledge from Software Systems Using Inductive Learning in the PM System

R.G. Reynolds, E.Zannoni, J.I. Maletic
Department of Computer Science
Wayne State University, Detroit, MI 48201, USA

Abstract

The issue of software reuse has been addressed by many authors in the recent years. It has been found to be a much harder task than previously thought. Some of the problems are due to the lack of emphasis placed on non-functional requirements during the software development phase, such as maintainability and understandability. Other problems arise from the difficulty of defining precise criteria for considering a software module reusable. They are usually elusive, and vary dramatically from one domain to another. This chapter presents PM, a software system the goal of which is the automation of the software reuse process. PM uses an incremental approach in performing analysis and storage of software modules, at different levels of granularity. Its fundamental characteristics are domain independence and flexibility, accomplished applying inductive learning techniques and analyzing reusable and non reusable code examples.

1: Introduction

Software reuse is predicated on the idea that problem solving knowledge encoded in the form of computer programs can be reapplied to solve related problems in the future. From this perspective, knowledge must be represented in a framework that facilitates its reuse. In terms of a software system, this corresponds to deriving a new encoding of its structure, since the source code representation does not directly support reuse. In order to achieve such a new reformulation, an understanding of the knowledge embodied in the original code is required. Here, achieving such an understanding is viewed as a knowledge acquisition task.

Biggerstaff and Richter suggest that there are four fundamental subtasks associated with the overall task of operationalizing the reuse process [1]: finding reusable components, understanding these components, modifying these components, and composing components. Each of these subproblems can be re-expressed as a knowledge acquisition problem relative to producing this new representation.

If the promise of reuse is to be fulfilled, all of these four tasks must be automated to some degree. Viewing reuse as a knowledge acquisition task facilitates its possible automation. The construction of the reuse library is one of the bottlenecks to fulfillment of this promise. Because of the continuos evolution of any software application domain, the realization of libraries supporting a flexible and correct encoding of the stored modules is not a simple goal. To incur the cost of building such a reuse library, it should be the case that its use is prolonged over time. This tends not to be the state of the art in this and many other domains. To try to address some of these problems, machine learning techniques are used to automatically acquire the knowledge needed to facilitate reuse of a software system.

The current prototype of the PM system focuses on the first two of Biggerstaff's subtasks (finding reusable components and understanding them). The current target language supported by PM is PASCAL. The process is illustrated using a software module that implements a version of Genetic Algorithms, a machine learning tool written by David Goldberg [5]. Section 2 gives an overview of the PM system as it is currently envisioned, and how each subsystem interacts and relates to reuse. Section 3 describes how the working prototype for the SRC subsystem performs assessment of the code in terms of its static structure. In section 4 the identification of reusable procedural objects or chunks based on their dynamic behavior is shown.

2: The PM System

In the current implementation of the Partial Metrics (PM) [10], the focus is on operationalizing the first two subtasks. A component diagram of the PM system is given in figure 1. The system extracts planning knowledge from a software system at three different levels of granularity: system, procedural, or code level. These three levels are represented as different passes in the figure. The goal of the first pass is to assess the reusability of the system as a whole. If a candidate is accepted for reuse at this level, it can be used as input for a second pass. In this second pass, collections of procedures can be extracted as candidates for reuse. Successful candidates can then be used as input for a third pass. In this pass, code segments can be extracted from procedural candidates.

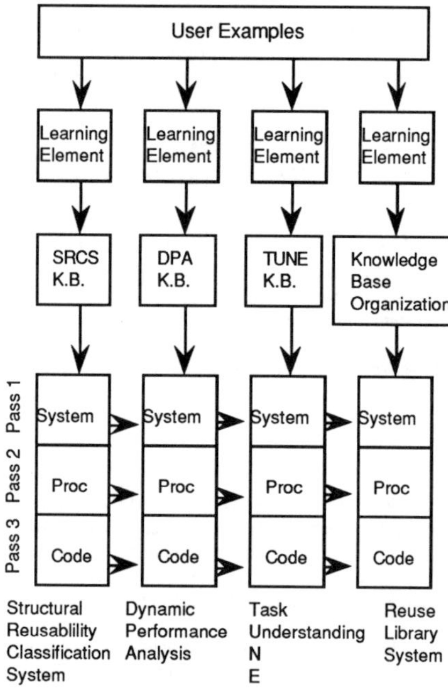

Fig.1: Component Diagram of the PM System

Each pass consists of four basic steps. New information is added at each step to a frame based description of the transaction history of the candidate. The first two steps support the isolation of reusable objects at a given level of granularity, the first phase in Biggerstaff's reuse process. First, the Structural Reusability Classification (SRC) System assesses the static structure of the candidate object, then the Dynamic Performance Analysis (DPA) System is used to isolate reusable components or chunks in the candidate system based upon their behavioral performance. The criteria used for the assessment is a function of the granularity at which the programming knowledge is extracted.

The Task Understanding (TUNE) System supports Biggerstaff's second phase of the reusability process, understanding the component to be reused. The goal here is to produce a generalized description of the context in which the candidate can be meaningfully utilized. In the current version, a faceted classification scheme is used for this purpose. The classification structure for the storage of the modules follows the approach developed by Prieto-Diaz [8].

Each of the phases described above is supported by a knowledge-base that is used to generate the reuse decisions performed in that phase. This knowledge is acquired automatically during the configuration phase of the PM system. In the configuration process, the subsystems are provided with examples of acceptable and unacceptable decisions. This approach is predicated on two basic assumptions [3].

1. It is easier to show an example of what is or is not reusable code than to precisely describe the criteria used in the judgement.

2. The criteria used to make a reuse decision in a given application are relatively straightforward but they can change dramatically from one application to another.

The reuse criteria learned for each subsystem are stored in its associated knowledge base, as shown in figure 1. That knowledge base is accessed by the corresponding subsystem during the processing of a candidate at a given level of granularity.

3: The static reusability

The assessment process performed in PM is done incrementally, with the assessment of a candidate's static structure being performed initially by the Static Reusability Classification System (SRCS). The assessment of static structure is performed prior to the behavioral assessment for two reasons. Firstly, information for the static analysis can be derived from information generated by a compiler and is less resource intensive than the behavioral analysis. Secondly, ill-structured programs that can complicate behavioral assessment at a given level of granularity are removed early on, since those programs that do not pass the first phase are withdrawn from consideration.

The criteria used to perform the static assessment process will vary with the level of granularity. At the system level the criteria will relate to the complexity of its interface to the environment. At the procedural level, the criteria relate to procedural structure and content. At the code level, the criteria relate to syntactic structures used in the implementation. In this section the current implementation of the approach used in PM to assess procedural structure will be described.

While the criteria for reuse are provided implicitly by those configuring the system in terms of positive and negative examples, the SRCS system utilizes an explicit domain model to aid in explicitly operationalizing the criteria. The domain model currently in use at the procedural level is given in Figure 2. This is an example of a software quality model, similar to those of Boehm [2], and Fenton [4]. Here, the concept of reuse is decomposed into successively more specific factors, ultimately into metrics that assess reuse in terms of a systems static structure. Details concerning the metrics used can be found in [3].

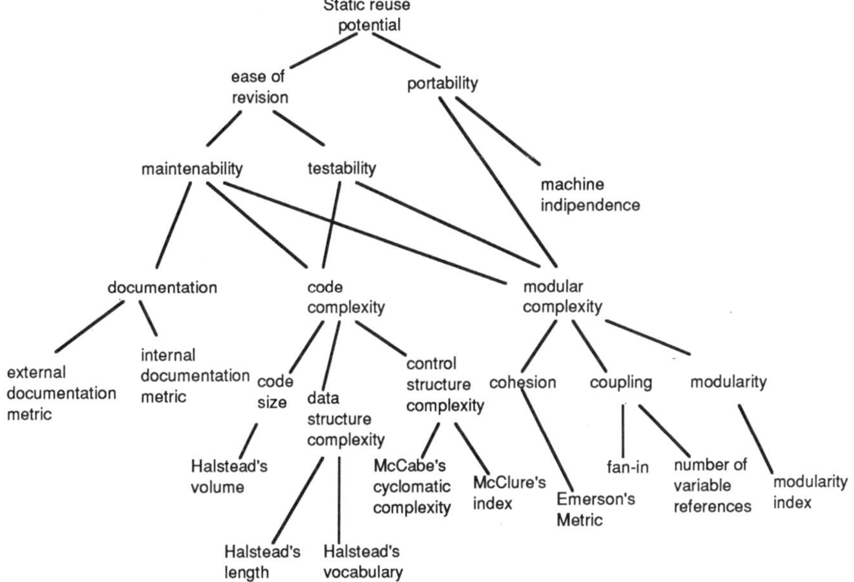

Fig. 2: Quality Model used to assess static reusability

While the model given above specifies what factors can be important in determining the reusability of software, the acceptable values of and relative importance for each will vary from one application to another. The goal of the learning element associated with the SRCS system is to acquire this information for a specific application. The source of this information is a training set of examples of reusable and not reusable code. The system attempts to generate a decision procedure, expressed in terms of values for selected metrics, that is capable of discriminating between the positive and negative examples. This is an example of an inductive concept learning problem in which the concept to be learned is static reuse.

Quinlan developed an approach to generating decision trees in a top down fashion based upon information theoretic principles [9]. The approach was implemented in a system designated as ID3. The ID3 procedure was used in SRCS in a slightly modified form as a basis for generating decision trees. One assumption made in this approach was that the attributes used in forming the decision tree be categorical in nature. Therefore, for each attribute a limited number of observational categories were established, based upon standard interpretations of these metrics taken from the software engineering literature.

The procedure utilized in the SRC system will now be described:

Let M be the set of software modules to be classified by a subtree rooted at the current node. Initially M contains modules from which the tree will be constructed.

1. If M is empty then Quit.
2. If all the modules of M are of the same class (positive examples or negative examples) or if M is empty then
   A. Designate the current node as a leafnode and label it according to the class of its objects.
   B. Quit
3. Apply an evaluation function to select an attribute A_i having possible values $A_{i1}, A_{i2}, \ldots, A_{ij}$ to partition M into j subsets. Select the attribute with the greatest discriminatory power, i.e. the degree in which an attribute partitions the objects into subsets. If no attribute is able to partition the set of objects, label it with both classes and quit.
4. Create a child node in the tree for each of the j classes.
5. For each child node recursively call this procedure

The evaluation function used to select the most appropriate attribute at each step was based on each variable's ability to sort the remaining M modules into homogeneous classes of either positive or negative examples according to their observational category for a given attribute. The extent to which an attribute was able to achieve this goal is termed its information gain. The information gain for each attribute, A_i, is calculated as: gain $(A_i)=H(p, n)-E(A_i)$.

The information gained by adding a decision node to the tree based upon attribute A_i is a function of the number of positive (p) and negative (n) examples currently associated with the parent node (H(p,n)) and the degree of homogeneity that will be expected $(E(A_i))$ within each category of A_i. H(p,n) is the entropy for the current distribution of positive and negative examples and represents the average information about the distribution received when an arbitrary example is selected. H(p,n) is calculated based upon expectation for the positive and negative examples where:

$$H(p, n) = -(\text{prob}(p) \log_2 \text{prob}(p)) - (\text{prob}(n) \log_2 \text{prob}(n))$$

Prob(p) is the probability of occurrence for positive examples while prob(n) is the probability for a negative example.

The expected information for an attribute A_i is the average of the proportion of positive and negative examples associated with each of the r categories for A_i weighted by the entropy for the distribution of positive and negative examples found in that category. Thus,

$$E(A_i) = \sum_{j=1}^{r} \frac{p_j + n_j}{p + n} H(p_j, n_j).$$

Over two hundred Pascal programs from diverse software libraries, both academic and commercial, were used to generate example decision trees. A representative decision tree produced from these examples is given in figure 3. Decision nodes that represent the partitioning based upon values for a given attribute are displayed as diamonds. Leaf nodes are represented as circles and correspond to either acceptance (+) or rejection (-) of a module as the result of following the branches dictated by the metric values for the system. Note that this decision tree requires information about each of the major subtrees in the software quality model described earlier; documentation, code complexity, and modularity. Also, based upon fan-in from the higher level concepts one would expect modularity concerns to be most important of the three, followed by code complexity issues, and then documentation. This is exactly what occurs in the example.

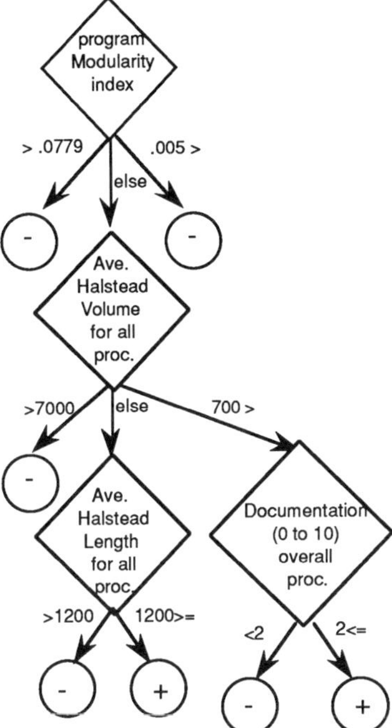

Fig. 3: An Example Decision Tree

In fact, experiments with the system have led to some general observations about the structure of the generated trees. Firstly, for any given application environment, the generated tree is relatively shallow and broad. The average number of decisions needed to classify a system is 3.1, with an average number of 7.4 internal nodes. Secondly, the decision procedure exhibited performance equal to or better than human experiments in making such discriminations, with accuracies ranging from 75% to 98% depending upon the number of training examples used. In general, a training set of 25 or more examples, evenly divided between positive and negative instances, guaranteed accuracies in excess of 90%. Thirdly, attributes associated with module complexity are most frequently found at or near the root. This reinforces the validity of the quality model used since in that model, modular structure influences three higher level factors in the underlying quality model: testability, maintainability, and portability. Lastly, although the decision trees for any given application are small, they can change dramatically in terms of the variables used from one application to the next.

Once a decision tree is configured for an application, it is stored in the knowledge base associated with the SRC system. Let us assume that the decision tree just discussed is the currently active one. Each incoming candidate system is then assessed in terms of this decision tree. In order to do this, the metric values required by the currently active decision tree are calculated. The procedural structure for an example Pascal program (Simple Genetic Algorithm) is given in figure 4. In order to simplify the diagram, procedures that are called by several others are indexed by integers in the diagram, and the names of the indexed procedures are given.

The modularity index is the first metric used to evaluate the program. This metric is the ratio of the number of procedures to the number of lines of executable code as proposed by Prieto-Diaz [8]. The value here is .07 which falls

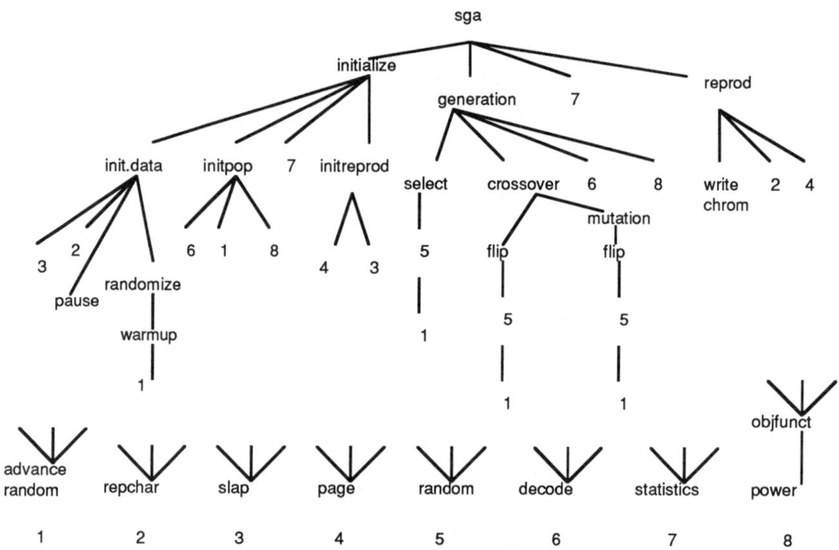

Fig. 4: Structure chart for the Simple Genetic Algorithm program

within the acceptable range. Thus, the next decision is based upon the average Halstead volume for all procedures. The value (~840) is also greater than 700 but much less than 7000. Halstead's volume is defined as

$$(\text{Length}) \log_2(\text{vocabulary}) .$$

Length is the total count of operators and operands in the procedure and vocabulary is the total number of unique operators and operands [6]. The next decision is based upon the average length, as defined above, of each procedure. The average length here is ~175 which is again within acceptable limits (1200>=). As a result, the SRC system returns the class associated with the terminal node in the path which is '+'. The program is therefore accepted at this stage and sent on to the DPA subsystem.

4: The Dynamic Performance Analysis Subsystem

The goal of this subsystem is to isolate candidate structures at a given level of granularity. The general model for this process supported here is that of chunking. Chunking involves the encoding of detailed knowledge into a more abstract form and its decoding, when necessary, to unveil the detailed information. The chunking process is motivated by the need for humans to associate specific input with more general or abstract patterns. This approach was suggested by the work of Miller [7] on the size of a human's short-term memory. His results suggested that an average person has a limit of seven plus or minus two items. This limitation can be overcome when each of the objects in short-term memory is allowed to represent an encoding of a collection of more detailed objects. For example, few people would be able to remember the string of bits 010110101100. However, if the string is linearly decomposed into three 4-bit subsequences, (0101, 1010, and 1100), then each 4-bit sequence can be encoded in its hexadecimal equivalent. The resultant set of objects, 5AC, is easy to remember. This result can then be decoded into the original, more detailed, representation if necessary.

The above example suggests that chunking consists of several distinct phases. The first phase identifies groups of domain objects sharing structural or behavioral properties, i.e. showing meaningful patterns. Each group can be viewed as an aggregate (or chunk). These aggregates should be relatively independent in order to simplify the encoding process. The decomposition of the binary sequence above can be expressed hierarchically as

```
010110101100
 /    |    \
0101 1010 1100
```

Simon observed [11] that many complex systems can be decomposed into a collection of hierarchically structured subsystems, such that the intrasystem interactions are relatively independent of intersystem ones. If there is no dependence between the inter- and intra-subsystems, then the system is said to be *completely decomposable*, as is the case for the example above. However, in term of software systems, such complete independence is rarely found because of the degree of coupling between modules (shared variables, side effects, etc.). If the independence constraint is relaxed slightly, *nearly decomposable systems* are obtained, exhibiting a few interactions, but still allowing efficient encoding to take place.

The second phase of the chunking process is encoding or abstraction. If the aggregates are independent then the encoding process is particularly straightforward since the abstraction mechanism can be applied independently to each. The presence of some interaction between components may cause the propagation of symbolic constraints produced by the chunking of one aggregate to others. In a nearly decomposable system this propagation should be relatively local in nature. The encoding of the aggregates above can be expressed as

```
0101 1010 1100
  |    |    |
  5    A    C
```

The third phase involves the storage of the chunked aggregates in a knowledge structure that enables its future use in a problem solving activity. It is assumed that the collection of chunked aggregates can be described in a hierarchical manner.

In PM, the first phase of the chunking process, the decomposition process, is supported by the DPA system. The second phase, the abstraction process, is supported by the TUNE system. The third phase, storage and retrieval, is performed by the Reuse Library System. What is actually being chunked is a function of the granularity at which the process is currently working. At the highest level of granularity the goal is to isolate independent systems. At the procedural level the goal is to identify collections of independent procedures within a larger system. At the code level the goal is to extract aggregates of code found within a procedure. The detailed procedure for extracting code aggregates has been implemented and is described in [10]. The remainder of this section will focus on how the process is currently implemented at the procedural level.

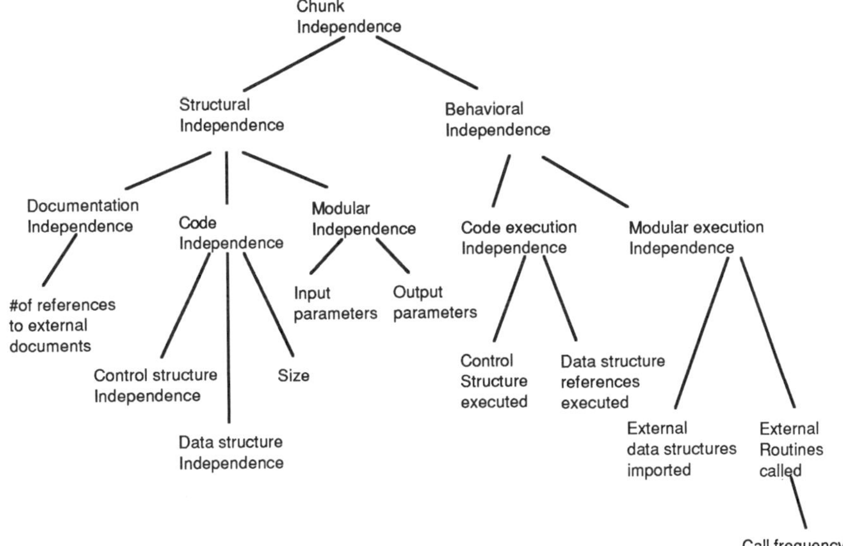

Fig. 5: Operationalizing the chunking process

The identification of chunks is also supported by a quality model. The current model is given in Figure 5. As in the SRC subsystem, the learning component will consist of building a decision tree inductively based upon assessing the structure and behavior of positive and negative examples provided by the users. This decision tree will operationalize the user's notion of independence. For our purposes let us use the simple tree given below:

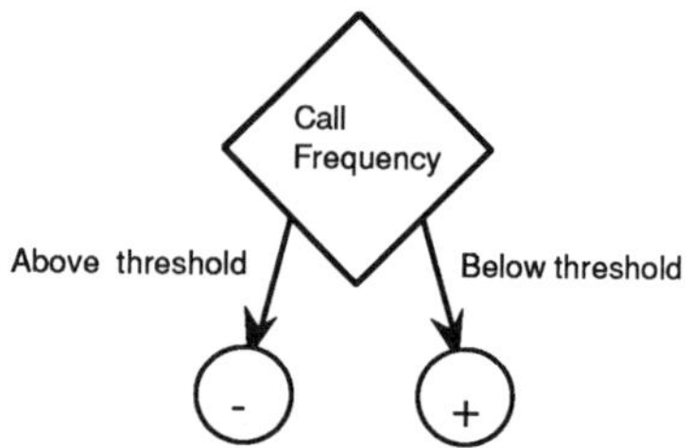

The call frequency metric for a hypothesized collection (chunk) of procedures, x, is the ratio of the total number of calls made to the procedures that are members of the hypothesized chunk, divided by the total number of calls made to x (intended as calls to the root of the subgraph corresponding to the chunk). This assesses the cohesiveness of action within the code. If no calls are made to components of a chunk (other than the root) from outside the chunk, the value for the call frequency is 1, and the collection exhibits high cohesiveness.

For a given software system, such as the SGA example here, the set of possible chunks correspond to each of the possible connected subgraphs present in the call graph. The null hypothesis here is that only the whole system itself can be chunked according to the user supplied criteria. This corresponds to chunking the whole system with the SGA main module as the root. It is considered the null hypothesis since the system had already been accepted for reuse in the previous phase. The goal here is to identify collections of component procedures that satisfy the user's criteria. In this case the criterion is that acceptable collections must exhibit a value for the call frequency metric that is below a certain threshold, in our example it is fixed to be 2.

The current version of the DPA subsystem is able to automatically generate the collection of procedures that satisfy a given constraint in the decision tree. Additional information can be in [12]. The pseudocode for the DPA main module is given below:

```
Procedure  DPA();
repeat
1.READ PASCAL SOURCE PROGRAM;
2.MODIFY SOURCE PROGRAM (INSERT "WRITE STATEMENTS") IN ORDER TO TRACE
  ROUTINE EXECUTION PATH;
3.COMPILE THE MODIFIED PROGRAM
4.EXECUTE THE MODIFIED PROGRAM (EXECUTION HISTORY IS GENERATED);
5.GENERATE A DESCRIPTION OF THE CALL GRAPH FOR THE SYSTEM. LET EACH
  PROCEDURE IN THE GRAPH REPRESENT A HYPOTHESIS THAT IT AND ALL
  PROCEDURES CALLED BY IT SHOULD FORM A CHUNK;
6.STORE EXECUTION HISTORY DATA WITH EACH HYPOTHESIZED CHUNK;
7.DERIVE APPROPRIATE STATISTICAL METRICS FOR EACH HYPOTHESIS BASED UPON
  EXECUTION HISTORY DATA;
8.PERFORM A PREORDER TRAVERSAL OF THIS TREE OF HYPOTHESES TO EXTRACT
  ACCEPTABLE CHUNKS;
9.FOR EACH SELECTED AGGREGATE, STORE APPROPRIATE INFORMATIONIN A
  FRAME.STORE THESE FRAMES AND ASSOCIATED CODE IN A FILE FOR BY THE
  TUNE SYSTEM.UNTIL (ALL SUBMITTED SYSTEMS TESTED);
end
```

In the SGA example, the system randomly generates test data for the runs. An example of such a data set is shown below:

```
SGA Parameters
Population size (popsize)          = 30
Chromosome length (lchrom)         = 30
```

```
Max # of generation (maxgen)        = 10
Crossover prob. (pcross)            = 0.6
Mutation prob. (pmutation)          = 0.03
Seed random number (0.0..1.0)       = 0.1
```

Based upon this input the system calculates the appropriate metrics required by the currently active decision tree. In this case it is just call frequency. The collected statistics averaged over all of the runs are given in Figure 6.

objects	called together	all calls	call frequency
initialize	1	21689	21689.00
initdata	1	274	274.00
randomize	1	192	192.00
warmup	1	191	191.00
initpop	1	21581	21581.00
flip	**10050**	**10541**	**1.05**
random	**10350**	**10353**	**1.0003**
objfunc	**330**	**330**	**1.00**
initreport	1	14	14.00
generation	10	31031	3103.10
select	300	10541	35.14
crossover	150	29591	197.27
mutation	9000	20591	2.29
report	10	686	68.60

Fig. 6: Selection of reusable objects for the Simple Genetic Algorithm Program

Each hypothesized chunk is labelled by its root node. The average number of calls made to the root of the chunk per run is then given followed by the total number of calls per run made to all the procedures of the chunk by any procedure of the system. The call frequency, as previously defined, is shown next. In this table the statistics for the leaf nodes are not included, since those correspond to isolate chunks of single elements. The selected hypotheses are those with a call frequency value lower than 2. The positioning of these hypothesized collections in the call graph for the SGA is given in Figure 7. Note that these aggregates are all positioned at low levels in the call graph. This is due to the particular nature of the analyzed system, since many procedures are not used in a single context, but are called from different modules. Several of the possible chunks do not present a single entry point.

Once an acceptable aggregate is identified, the system prepares a frame that describes its interfaces in term of name, type, parameter list, as well as any external data or functions that it requires. The template used to generate each frame is given in figure 8.

```
              Object : object name
   **** Object Global Variables ****
Global variable1               : Type
Global variable2               : Type
      .......................
   ******* Object Interfaces *******
Routine-Type-Qualifier: function/proc.
Routine-Name: function/procedure name
Routine-Result-Type: Type
Formal-Parameter-List:
        input variable : Type  . . .
        output variable : Type  . . .
   ******** Object Contents ********
      ............................
```

Fig. 8: The Template Description of a Candidate Code Object Produced by the DPA System

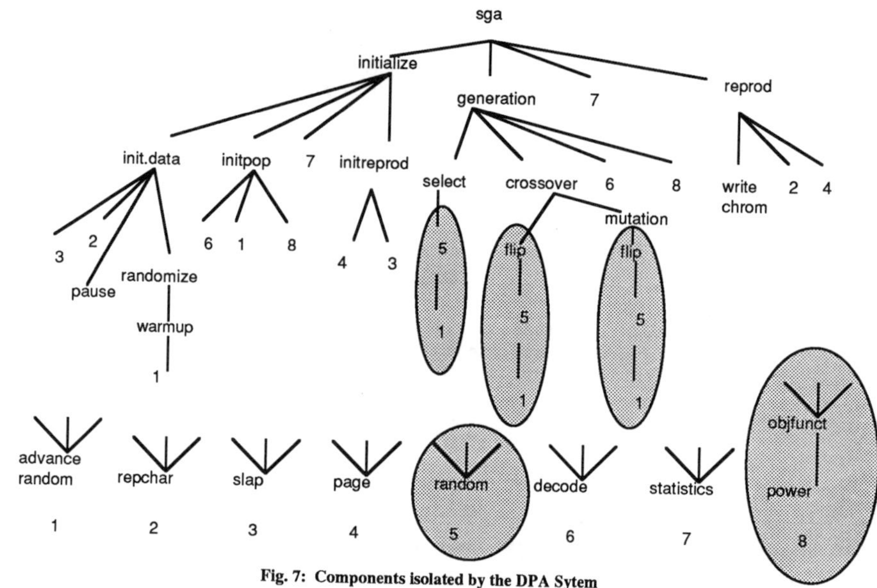

Fig. 7: Components isolated by the DPA Sytem

A description of the frame produced by the system for the FLIP module is given in figure 9. This frame is automatically placed in a file for future reference by the TUNE system.

```
****** flip ******
global  jrand          : integer
global  oldrand        :array[1..55] of real
procedure_type_qualifier     : function
procedure_name               : flip
procedure-result-type        : boolean

function flip(probability:real):boolean;
begin
  if probability = 1.0  then  flip := true
  else flip := (random <= probability);
end;
function random : real;
begin
  jrand := jrand + 1;
  if (jrand > 55) then begin
    jrand := 1;
    advance_random;
  end;
  random := oldrand[jrand];
end;
procedure  advance_random;
var     j1          : integer;
        new_random : real;
begin
  for j1 := 1 to 24 do begin
    new_random := oldrand[j1]- oldrand[j1+31];
```

```
    if (new_random <0.0) then
      new_random := new_random + 1.0;
    oldrand[j1] := new_random;
  end;
  for j1 := 25 to 25 do begin
    new_random:=oldrand[j1] - oldrand[j1-24];
    if (new_random <0.0) then
      new_random := new_random + 1.0;
    oldrand[j1] := new_random;
  end;
end;
```

Fig. 9:The description of a candidate code object produced by the DPA subsystem

5: Conclusions

In this chapter it was demonstrated how inductive learning techniques can support the acquisition of knowledge about procedural reuse, and how this knowledge can be applied to the identification of reusable procedures. In fact, it is suggested that the properties associated with reusable software components are easy to check. The problem is that the criteria can change dramatically from one application environment to another. That is why it is essential to have a system that can efficiently learn these criteria from examples provided by the user. The current PM system is able to support the learning of relevant criteria using appropriate domain knowledge as demonstrated by its processing of the SGA program.

References

[1] Biggerstaff, T., Richter, C., "Reusability Framework, Assessment, and Directions", *IEEE Software*, Vol. 4, No. 2. March 1987.

[2] Boehm, B., Brown, J., Kaspar, J., Lipow, M., "Characteristics of Software Quality", North Holland, 1978.

[3] Esteva, J.C., Reynolds, R.G., "Learning to Recognize Reusable Software by Induction", IJSEKE, Vol. 1 No.3 1991.

[4] Fenton, N. E., "Software Metrics: A Rigorous Approach", Chapman and Hall Press, London, 1991.

[5] Goldberg, D., *Genetic Algorithms in Search, Optimization and Machine Learning*, Addison-Wesley Publishing, 1989.

[6] Halstead, M.H., "Elements of Software Science", Elsevier-North Holland, New York, NY, 1977.

[7] Miller, G. , "The magical number seven, plus or minus two: Some limits on our capacity for processing information", The Psychological Review, 63(2), 1956.

[8] Prieto-Diaz, R., "A Software Classification Scheme", Ph.D. Thesis, Dept. ICS, University of California, Irvine, 1985.

[9] Quinlan, J.R., "Induction of Decision Trees", *Machine Learning*, 1: 81-106, 1986.

[10] Reynolds, R.G., Maletic, J.I., Porvin, S.,"PM: A System to Support Acquisition of Programming Knowledge", *IEEE Transactions on Knowledge Engineering and Data Engineering*, Sept. 1990.

[11] Simon, H., *The Science of the Artificial*, Cambridge, Massachusetts, M.I.T. Press, 1967.

[12] Wang, F., "Cognitive Models of Software Reuse: Extracting Procedural Knowledge in a Multiple Pass Knowledge Compiler", M.S. Thesis, Wayne State University, October 1991.

SECTION 4

PLANNING

CHAPTER 7

RESOURCE-ORIENTED PARALLEL PLANNING

SUKHAN LEE

Jet Propulsion Laboratory, California Institute of Technology, Pasadena, CA 91109 and Department of Electrical Engineering Systems, University of Southern California, Los Angeles, CA 90089-0782, USA

and

KYUSIK CHUNG

Department of Electronics Engineering, Soongsil University, Seoul, Korea

Received 25 September 1991

ABSTRACT

This paper presents a new paradigm for constructing a partially ordered plan network, referred to as "resource-oriented parallel planning (RP^2)". In resource-oriented parallel planning, goal states are grouped into a collection of goal state subsets, each of which consists of those goal states associated with a particular resource. A subplan is generated for each goal state subset by planning the flow of the corresponding resource, and thus satisfying the constraints specified by each of the goal state subsets. A complete plan is then constructed by synthesizing individual subplans based on the synchronization among subplans.

A distinctive feature of RP^2 is that each subplanner generates a conflict-free subplan by controlling the flow of a particular resource while synthesizing a complete plan in cooperation with other subplanners. This can be compared with the conventional state-oriented parallel planning, where each subplanner generates a subplan achieving a goal state while resolving conflicts among subplans in cooperation with other subplanners.

RP^2 makes use of resource reasoning in distinguishing important and unimportant resources associated with a goal. This allows each subplanner to hierarchically construct a resource-flow plan and to dynamically coordinate among subplanners in achieving a goal associated with more than one resource.

The proposed scheme not only makes it possible to generate an optimal plan in terms of the maximum parallelism or the minimum depth of a plan network, but also makes it easier to implement the concurrent generation of parallel plans in a parallel and distributed processing environment.

1. Introduction

Parallel planners or nonlinear planners such as NOAH[1], NONLIN[2], DEVISER[3], SIPE[4] and TWEAK[5] generate a partially ordered plan network achieving the given conjunctive goals. These planners are based on "state-oriented planning" in which a plan is constructed by generating a subplan for each

This paper first appeared in ***International Journal on Artificial Intelligence Tools*****, Vol. 1, No. 1 (1992).**

goal state while detecting and resolving conflicts among individual subplans in state space.

In dealing with parallel planning, the following issues should be taken into consideration: (i) the efficiency of a planning algorithm, (ii) the optimality of the resulting plan network in terms of the maximum parallelism or the minimum depth of a plan network, and (iii) the implementation of a planning algorithm in a parallel and distributed processing environment. The efficiency of parallel planning and the optimality of the resulting plan network largely depend on how conflicts among parallel actions or goals are detected and resolved. Much effort has been devoted to the development of efficient conflict detection and resolution. In particular, one method developed for efficient conflict detection and resolution is based on the domain-independent rules for resolving contradictory states, e.g. the critics with the table of multiple effects (TOME) in NOAH[1] or the improved critics based on goal structure (GOST) in NONLIN[2]. Another method is based on the domain-specific heuristics for resolving conflicting resources shared by parallel branches, e.g. the assignment of priority to the predefined resource types in SIPE[4]. However, detecting and resolving conflicts has not yet been achieved at a desired level of efficiencys[1], especially in complex system where there is a high frequency of conflicts. Furthermore, issues such as the optimality of the resulting plan network and the implementation in a parallel and distributed processing environment have not received proper attention yet.

This paper presents a new approach to parallel planning, called "resource-oriented parallel planning (RP^2)", where resources are viewed as active elements in constructing plans. In resource-oriented parallel planning, each subplanner generates a conflict-free subplan by controlling the flow of a particular resource while synthesizing a complete plan in cooperation with other subplanners. There is a duality between state-oriented parallel planning and resource-oriented parallel planning. In state-oriented planning, conflict detection and resolution is carried out after the expansion of the current plan network; whereas, in resource-oriented parallel planning, conflict-free subplans (in terms of the flow of individual resources) are constructed prior to the expansion of the current plan network (based on subplan synthesis). This makes the conflict detection and resolution simple. Furthermore, resource-oriented parallel planning makes it possible to generate an optimal plan in terms of minimum resource and makes it easier to implement the concurrent generation of parallel plans in a parallel and distributed processing environment. The latter is due to the partition of the search space into a set of resource flow subspaces.

Section 2 describes the proposed planning approach. Section 3 describes the planning procedure of RP^2. Section 4 describes resource reasoning based on which the planning procedure can improve its efficiency. Section 5 describes the details

[1]The conflict problem is handled in terms of *declobbering* in TWEAK[5]. Although it provides a theoretical principle regarding conflict detection and resolution, it does not address the implementational details for achieving efficiency in conflict detection and resolution.

of the planning procedure, particularly the construction of partial plans. Section 6 describes the issue of communication and interaction among subplanners. Section 7 compares RP^2 and the conventional approach. Section 8 describes the advantages and the disadvantages of RP^2.

2. Planning Approach

A plan P is a compound operator which transforms the initial world state W_I into the goal state W_G:

$$P : W_I \longrightarrow W_G \ . \tag{1}$$

P can be represented by a plan network or an operator network $G(P)$. $G(P)$ represents a directed graph describing a partial order of primitive operators through which (1) can be accomplished.

Our approach to parallel planning is based on the following observation: Let us denote R as the set of all the resources[2] involved in planning. R is first decomposed into a collection of disjoint resource subsets, $\{r_j, j = 1, \ldots, n | r_i \cap r_j = \emptyset \ \forall i, j \ i \neq j\}$, such that

$$R = \bigcup_{j=1}^{n} r_j \ . \tag{2}$$

Then, a plan network $G(P)$ can be decomposed into a set of partial plan networks (Resource-Flow Plan Networks) $G(p/r_j)$, $j = 1, \ldots, n$, by tracing the flow of individual r_j's in the $G(P)$ such that

$$G(P) = \bigcup_{j=1}^{n}{}^{*} \ G(p/r_j) \ , \tag{3}$$

where $\bigcup^*$ denotes the union of partial plan networks as a plan synthesis. The tracing for $G(p/r_j)$ begins with the start node and follows the edges in such a way so as to cover all the operators that change the state of r_j until it reaches the goal node, while ignoring any irrelevant operators encountered during the tracing. For instance, observe $G(P)$ in Fig. 2 where $R = \{a, b, c\}$. $G(P)$ can be decomposed into $G(p/a)$, $G(p/b)$ and $G(p/c)$, where $G(p/a) = \{$Start $\rightarrow$ unstack(c,a) $\rightarrow$ pickup(a) $\rightarrow$ stack(a,b) $\rightarrow$ Goal$\}$, $G(p/b) = \{$Start $\rightarrow$ pickup(b) $\rightarrow$ stack(b,c) $\rightarrow$ stack(a,b) $\rightarrow$ Goal$\}$, and $G(p/c) = \{$Start $\rightarrow$ unstack(c,a) $\rightarrow$ putdown(c) $\rightarrow$ stack(b,c) $\rightarrow$ Goal$\}$.

This observation leads to a new approach to parallel planning called Resource-Oriented Parallel Planning (RP^2), where P or $G(P)$ is constructed by generating and synthesizing a set of partial plans on individual resources, (p/r_j) or

[2] A resource implies a physical or logical object associated with planning, e.g. in the blocks world, blocks, robots(tools), space, time, etc. represent resources.

$G(p/r_j)_{j=1,\ldots,n}$, such that

$$P = \bigcup_{j=1}^{n}{}^{*}\, p/r_j \quad \text{or} \quad G(P) = \bigcup_{j=1}^{n}{}^{*}\, G(p/r_j)\ . \tag{4}$$

RP^2 can be compared with conventional state-oriented parallel planning[1–6] where P for conjunctive goals is constructed by generating in the backward direction and by synthesizing a set of partial plans on individual goals, $(p/g_j)_{j=1,\ldots,k}$, such that

$$P = \bigcup_{j=1}^{k}{}^{*}\, p/g_j\ , \tag{5}$$

where k denotes the total number of the conjunctive goals. Figures 1 and 2 illustrate the two planning approaches for the same blocks world problem. In Fig. 1, the planning task is decomposed in terms of resources. Then individual subplanners construct $G(p/r_j)_{r_j=a,b,c}$ to reach the flow of r_j from the initial state to the goal state while communicating with each other so as to coordinate their planning to achieve the goals, on(a,b), on(b,c), ontable(c). On the other hand, in Fig. 2 the planning task is decomposed into goal states. Then individual subplanners construct $G(p/g_j)_{g_j=\text{on}(a,b),\text{on}(b,c),\text{ontable}(c)}$[3] while communicating with each other so as to detect and resolve conflicts due to the assertion of the contradictory states of block "a", "b" or "c" among $G(p/g_j)$s (for the detailed planning procedure, see Appendix A).

There is a duality between conventional state-oriented parallel planning and RP^2. In conventional parallel planning, each subplanner generates a subplan achieving a goal state while resolving conflicts among subplans in cooperation with other subplanners. In RP^2, each subplanner generates a conflict-free, resource-flow subplan reaching the goal states while synthesizing a complete plan in cooperation with other subplanners. The tasks in either planning can be divided into two parts: one performed solely by individual subplanners (called *intra-subplanner task*) and the other performed cooperatively by a group of subplanners (called *inter-subplanner task*). In this respect, conventional parallel planning and RP^2 can be described as shown in Fig. 3, where G/goal denotes the processes to achieve a goal and C/resource denotes the process to detect and resolve conflicts associated with a resource. In conventional parallel planning, G/goal is an *intra-subplanner task* while C/resource is an *inter-subplanner task*. On the contrary, in RP^2, C/resource is an *intra-subplanner task* while G/goal is an *inter-subplanner task*. Note the duality of the two planning schemes: what *intra-subplanner tasks* achieve and what *inter-subplanner tasks* achieve in one planning scheme are reversed in the other.

[3] A phantom node [1] marked by a dotted oval in $G(p/g_j)$ indicates that the corresponding goal is achieved by linking to the start node or to an action node (marked by a box) already generated in the plan network.

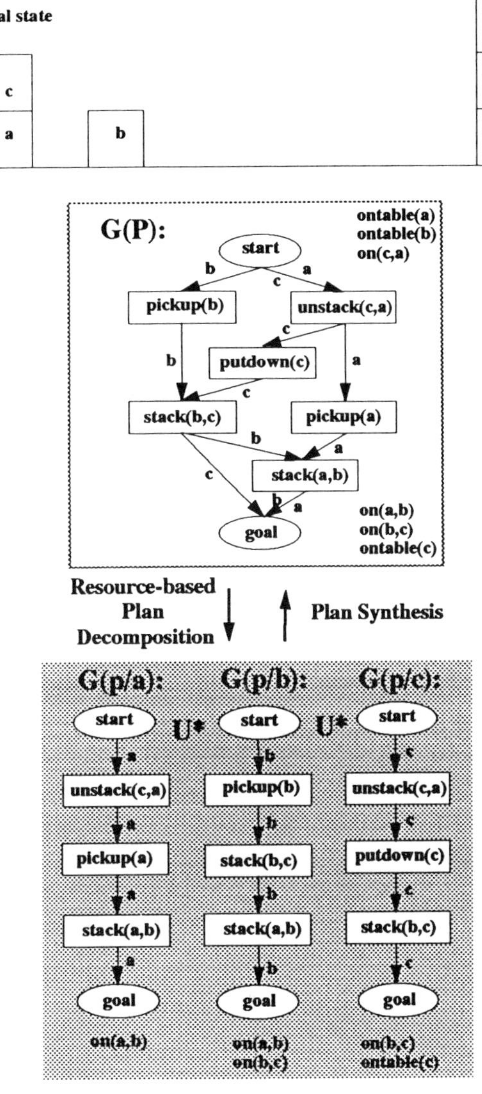

Fig. 1. Resource-oriented parallel planning.

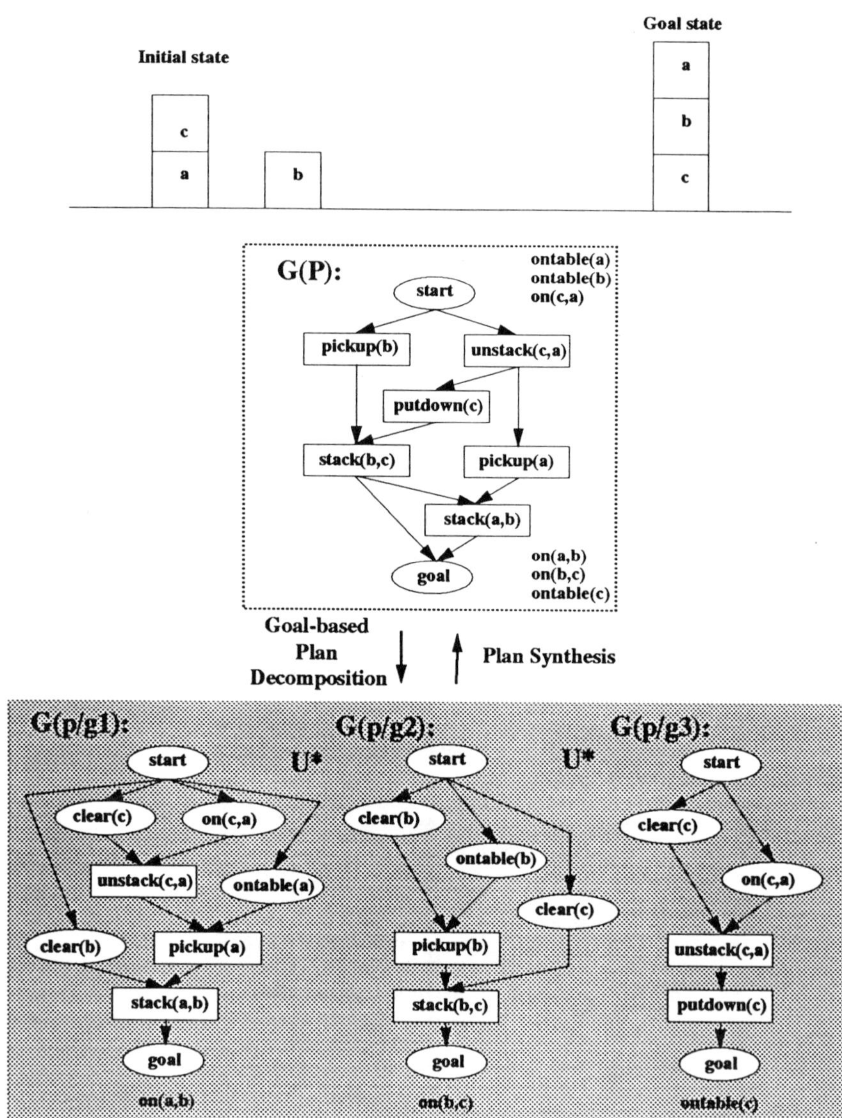

Fig. 2. Conventional parallel planning.

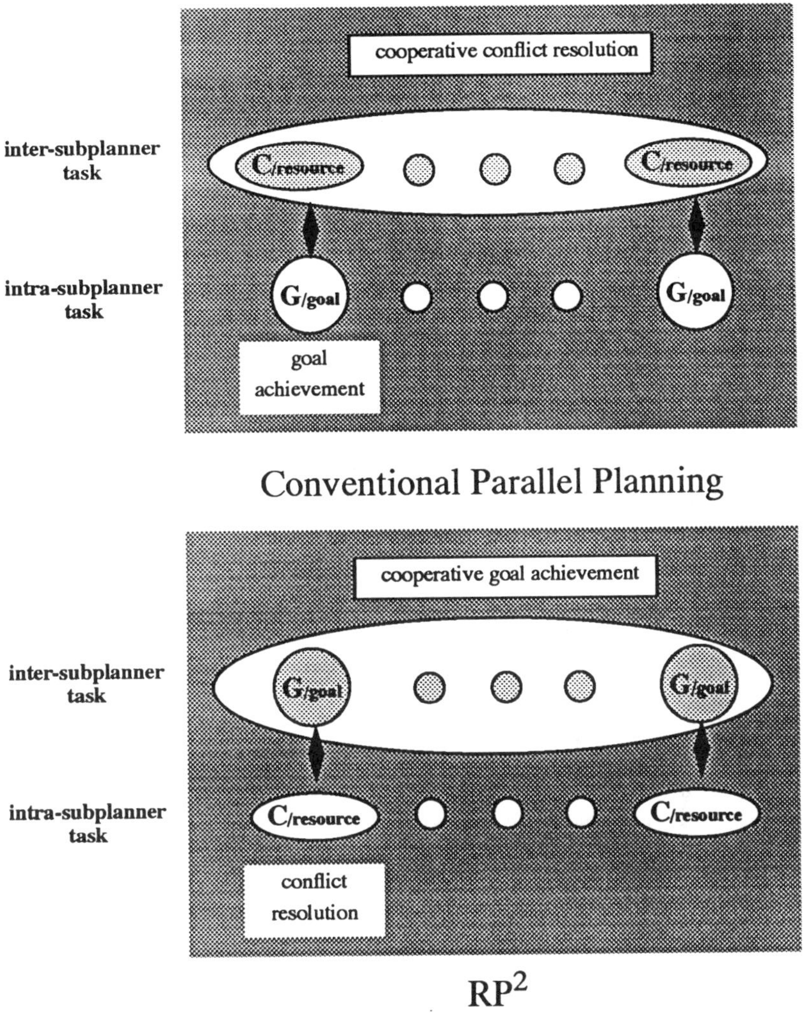

Fig. 3. Duality between conventional parallel planning and RP^2.

3. Planning Procedure

RP^2 in a parallel and distributed processing environment can be accomplished by the following procedures: (i) resource-based problem decomposition, (ii) construction of individual resource-flow plan p/r_j, based on achieving only those goals associated with r_j, (iii) communication among subplanners so as to maintain consistent and synchronized resource-flow plans, and (iv) synthesis of resource-flow plans.

During the execution of procedures (ii) and (iii), RP^2 makes use of resource reasoning in distinguishing an important resource from resources associated with a goal state. This resource distinction allows each subplanner to hierarchically construct a resource-flow plan, i.e. each subplanner can construct a skeleton plan by considering only important goals, and then refine the plan by considering the other goals. In addition, the resource distinction allows each subplanner to dynamically coordinate among subplanners in achieving a common goal, i.e. a subplanner for the important resource can form a dynamic master-slave organization, within which the associated subplanners coordinate.

The following procedure describes in detail how RP^2 can be accomplished.

The procedure of RP^2

Step 1. Decomposition of a planning task.

1. Decompose the set of all resources R into a collection of disjoint subsets of resources, $\{r_j\}_{j=1,\ldots,n}$, such that $R = \bigcup_{j=1}^{n} r_j$, where $r_i \cap r_j = \emptyset \;\; \forall i,j \;\; i \neq j$.
2. Decompose the set of goal states W_G and the set of initial states W_I into a group of goal state subsets, $\{W_G/r_j\}_{j=1,\ldots,n}$, and a group of initial state subsets, $\{W_I/r_j\}_{j=1,\ldots,n}$, respectively, such that $W_G = \bigcup_{j=1}^{n} W_G/r_j$ and $W_I = \bigcup_{j=1}^{n} W_I/r_j$. The decomposition of W_G and W_I is based on the following rule: For a goal state w_g, $w_g \in W_G$, and for an initial state w_i, $w_i \in W_I$, $w_g \in W_G/r_j$, if $w_g \sim r_j$; and $w_i \in W_I/r_j$, if $w_i \sim r_j$, where $\sim$ denotes an association relation between a state and a resource. In general, $(W_G/r_i) \cap (W_G/r_j) \neq \emptyset$ and $(W_I/r_i) \cap (W_I/r_j) \neq \emptyset$. W_G/r_j is the null set in the case where W_G is not associated with the resource r_j. The task of constructing P, $P : W_I \longrightarrow W_G$, is decomposed into a set of subtasks of constructing partial plans $(p/r_j)_{j=1,\ldots,n}$, where $\{p/r_j : W_I/r_j \longrightarrow W_G/r_j\}_{j=1,\ldots,n}$. Each subtask of constructing p/r_j is now allocated to a subplanner. Note that if W_G/r_k is the null set, then the construction of p/r_k is not required until a subgoal state associated with r_k is generated during the construction of other partial plans.

Step 2. Construction of partial plans. Each subplanner constructs a partial plan p/r_j, $p/r_j : W_I/r_j \longrightarrow W_G/r_j$, based on the following methods[4]:

1. A goal state w_g may belong to multiple goal state subsets, e.g. $w_g \in \{W_G/r_i \cap W_G/r_j \cap W_G/r_k\}$. This implies that w_g is involved in multiple subplanners, and thus there is a need to resolve which subplanner should be responsible for generating a partial plan for w_g; other subplanners involved in w_g merely combine the partial plan for w_g generated by

[4]This is one of the possible ways to construct partial plans for RP^2.

the selected subplanner with their own partial plans, which allows consistency in plan synthesis to be conserved. Note that the above process should be applied to any precondition (goal state) of operators generated during the construction of partial plans.

2. The subplanner for p/r_j will be responsible for generating a partial plan for w_g, if r_j is identified as a "primary" resource[5] associated with w_g. Those states in W_G/r_j having r_j as their primary resource are referred to as primary goals of W_G/r_j. The construction of p/r_j is then carried out hierarchically by:

   (i) the generation of an abstract plan achieving only the primary goals of W_G/r_j from the initial state, and

   (ii) the refinement[6] of the abstract plan to achieve all the non-primary goals of W_G/r_j from the initial state.

3. Any precondition of the operators generated during the construction of p/r_j, which are not associated with r_j, is regarded as true for p/r_j.

4. The subplanners communicate with each other during the construction of partial plans so as to maintain consistent and synchronized partial plans:

   (i) The subplanner for p/r_j sends its results (an operator or a set of operators) to all other subplanners for p/r_k where $r_k \sim w_g$. This is not only to share the partial results of planning but also to request the associated subplanners to achieve some preconditions of the operator(s), which are not associated with r_j or are not primary goals to the subplanner for p/r_j.

   (ii) The associated subplanners complete the requested tasks and send completion signals back to the subplanner for p/r_j. This indicates that the preconditions of the operator generated by the subplanner for p/r_j are achieved completely by all the subplanners associated with w_g.

   (iii) While completing the requested tasks, the associated subplanners may, in turn, generate subsequent new operators in order to achieve the preconditions, which may occur recursively.

Step 3. Termination. The planning procedure terminates if every subplanner completes the construction of its partial plan, $(p/r_j)_{j=1,\dots,n}$, or if any subplanner shows the nonexistence[7] of its partial plan, p/r_j. The former indicates

---

[5]See section 4 for more details.

[6]If r_j is a resource such as tool(robot) or time to be scheduled, the plan refinement means scheduling the corresponding resource.

[7]The nonexistence of any partial plan p/r_j implies the nonexistence of a plan P. This can be proved as follows: If a plan P exists, then partial plans $(p/r_j)_{j=1,\dots,n}$, exist, i.e. $\exists P \Rightarrow \{\forall j \;\; \exists p/r_j\}$. The contraposition of the fact is also true.

successful planning, where a final plan can be synthesized by combining the partial plans without repeating the common part among the plans, while the latter indicates a failure in planning.

More descriptions on resource reasoning and the construction of partial plans follow in the next two sections, with a block world example.

4. Resource Reasoning

4.1. Primary/Secondary resource

Definition. The most critical resource(s) is(are) called a *primary resource(s)* among the resources involved in achieving a goal while the others is(are) called *secondary resource(s).*

In the blocks world, the criticalities of resources can be compared by evaluating their roles in the goal state or in the actions achieving the goal, based on the following criteria[8]: (i) main/auxiliary resource, (ii) dynamic/static resource, and (iii) resource directly/indirectly manipulated by tools.

The main/auxiliary criterion can be applied by checking whether a resource is directly related to the component of a goal itself, e.g. in achieving a goal on(a,b), blocks "a" and "b" are the components of the goal. Therefore, they are called *main resources.* Conversely, robots(tools) are not directly related to the component of a goal although they are used to achieve the goal. Therefore, they are called *auxiliary resources.* A *main resource* is more critical than an *auxiliary resource* from the view of goal achievement.

The dynamic/static criterion can be applied by checking whether a resource is in motion during the execution of the actions achieving the goal, e.g. in achieving a goal on(a,b), two resources "a" and "b" are involved in operator stack(a,b) in Table 1. In this case, "a" is a moving object to be put on "b" while "b" is a supporting object. Therefore, "a" is a *dynamic resource* while "b" is a *static resource.* A *dynamic resource* is more critical than a *static resource* from the view of goal achievement.

The direct/indirect criterion can be applied by checking whether a resource is directly manipulated by a tool during the execution of the actions achieving the goal, e.g. suppose a file of blocks are moved by a robot at one time. In this case, the bottom block in the file is directly manipulated by the robot while the other blocks are not. The former is a *directly manipulated resource* while the latter is(are) an *indirectly manipulated resource(s).* A *directly manipulated resource* is more critical than an *indirectly manipulated resource* from the view of goal achievement.

In applying these criteria to evaluating the roles of resources, priority is given to the *main/auxiliary* criterion, the *dynamic/static* criterion and the *directly/indirectly*

[8]These criteria can be applied to robot assembly in the manufacturing domain. Different criteria can be used depending on the application domain.

manipulated criterion in that order[9], e.g. in a goal on(a,b), the main/auxiliary criterion is applied first. As both of them are main resources, the dynamic/static criterion is applied. "a" is a dynamic resource while "b" is a static resource. Therefore, "a" is called the *primary resource* while "b" is called the *secondary resource*[10].

In case the roles of a resource in achieving a goal differs depending on the action (operator) used, the determination of its criticality is deferred until run time. In such a case, the resource is temporarily considered to be a *secondary resource*, e.g. given a goal clear(a), it can be achieved by stack(a,?) or unstack(?,a) in Table 1, where ? denotes an uninstantiated variable. In the former, "a" is a *primary resource* while in the latter "a" is a *secondary resource*.

Table 1. Action (Operator) table.

action	*precondition*	*postcondition*
stack(x,y)	hold(x)	on(x,y)
	clear(y)	clear(x)
unstack(x,y)	on(x,y)	hold(x)
	clear(x)	clear(y)

• x or y is an object, e.g. a block or a table.

Definition. A goal state w_g is called a *primary goal (state)* to the subplanner for p/r_j if r_j is a primary resource in w_g. It is called a *secondary goal (state)* to the subplanner for p/r_k if r_k is the secondary resource in w_g.

4.2. Why is distinction needed among resources?

More than one resource can be involved in achieving a goal and a resource can be involved in achieving more that one goal. In achieving the goal or goals, the following decision-making problems occur: (i) which of the subplanners involved in achieving the goal will initiate the process to achieve the goal and take the responsibility for completely achieving the goal?, and (ii) given that more than one goal is associated with a resource, in what order will a subplanner achieve the goals? One way to handle these problem is (i) to distinguish the primary resource from the other resources associated with a goal and to select a subplanner for the primary resource[11], and (ii) to distinguish the primary goal (important goal) from goals associated with a resource and to achieve the primary goal first. The resource distinction scheme enables us to construct a partial plan in a subplanner based on a hierarchical planning scheme. This approach can improve the efficiency of the planning process by avoiding the search required for the detailed plan.

[9]The order is made based on the following reasons: (i) the decision made by the first criterion is invariant while the decisions by the other two are variant depending on the associated goal, and (ii) the second criterion evaluates the roles of resources by itself while the third criterion evaluates the roles of resources by considering their relations with a tool (an auxiliary resource).

[10]In puton(x,y) operator to achieve on(x,y), SIPE[4] classifies "x" as a resource and "y" as an argument.

[11]In case there is more than one primary resource, the subplanners associated with the primary resources need a special coordination scheme so that they can achieve the goal in a cooperative manner.

In addition, the resource distinction scheme can be applied to the cooperation among several subplanners achieving a common goal. By assigning authority to a subplanner for the primary resource, the subplanner can form and maintain a dynamic master-slave organization for the associated subplanners until the goal is completely achieved. Based on the organization, the associated subplanners can coordinate each other while achieving the goal.

5. Planning Details

Assuming that scheduling is accomplished after planning, let us focus on planning.

In the following subsections, we describe each step of parallel planning with an example of a block world in Fig. 4 (*Sussman Anomaly*), where (i) resource names are marked on the left-side of the figure, (ii) the initial and goal state are marked by oval nodes in the left and right sides, respectively, (iii) an action node is marked by a box and its number is marked on its left upperside, (iv) a precondition (postcondition) of an action is marked by an oval, (v) a thick arrow between nodes indicates a link generated by the other subplanners, and (vi) a thick-lined box indicates an action generated by the subplanner while a thin arrow indicates a link generated by the subplanner while a thin-lined box indicates an action generated by the other subplanners.

5.1. Decomposition of a planning task

First, resources are decomposed into a collection of disjoint subsets of resources, and then a planning task is decomposed accordingly. Before partitioning resources, the flow dependency among resources can be analyzed by using domain-dependent knowledge such as resource type (classification based on the functionality or similarity) or resource role (main or auxiliary). If some resources are known to be highly dependent, they are grouped into one. Otherwise, they are treated individually, e.g. auxiliary resources such as tools are grouped if they are of the same type and equal capability.

Without loss of generality, let us assume that only blocks are to be considered in planning in Fig. 4, i.e. all the other resources such as robots are available whenever required. The blocks in the example are treated individually since they are not highly dependent. As depicted in Fig. 4, W_G = {on(a,b), on(b,c), on(c,T)}[12] while W_I = {on(c,a),on(a,T),on(b,T),clear(c),clear(b)}. The task of constructing P, P: $W_I \rightarrow W_G$, is decomposed into a set of subtasks as shown in the figure:
(i) [p/r_a : { on(c,a), on(a,T) } $\rightarrow$ { on(a,b) }]
(ii) [p/r_b : { on(b,T), clear(a) } $\rightarrow$ { on(a,b), on(b,c) }]
(iii) [p/r_c : { on(c,a), clear(c) } $\rightarrow$ { on(b,c), on(c,T) }].
Each subtask is then allocated to a subplanner.

[12]This indicates block "c" is on the table T.

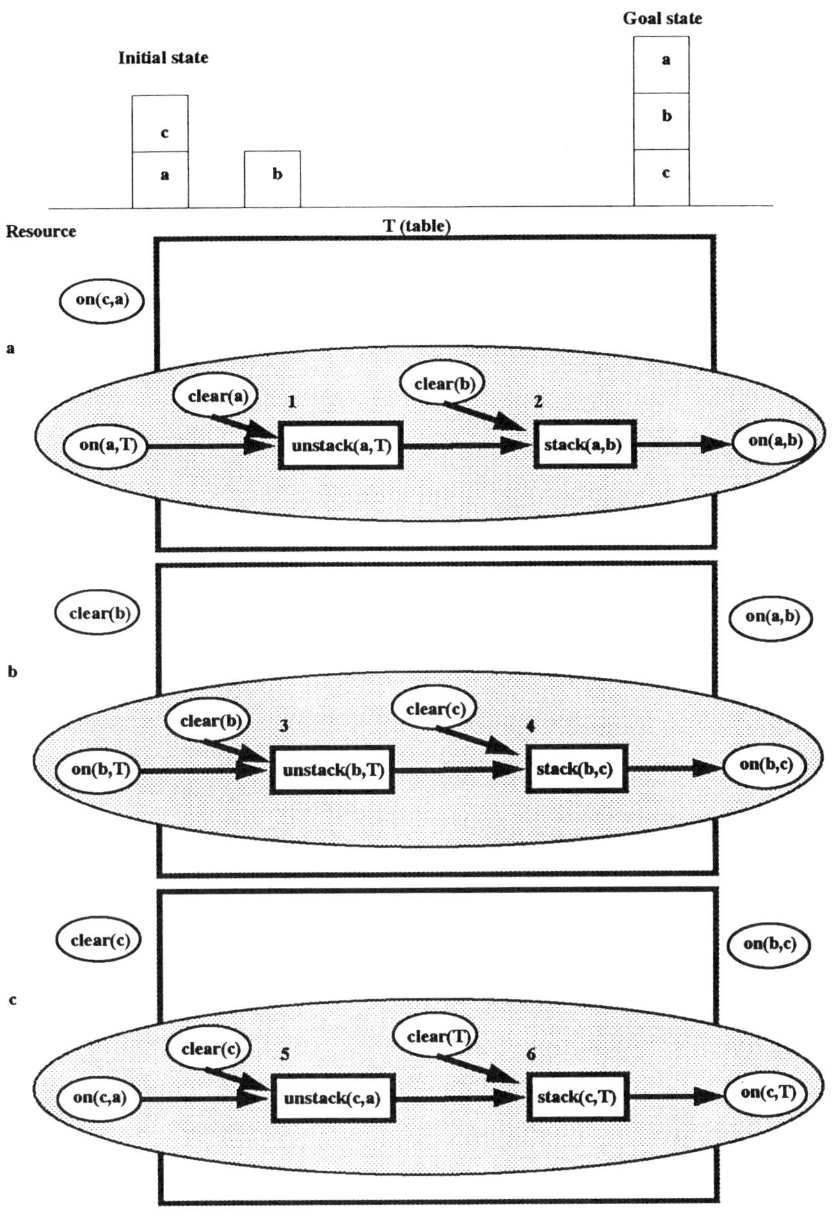

Fig. 4. Abstract plan.

5.2. Construction of partial plans

Let r_j represent a simple resource (object) on conventional parallel planning. This implies that the flow of r_j from W_I/r_j to W_G/r_j should be serial. Note that this can be exploited in constructing partial plans by keeping the intermediate p/r_j serial.

Suppose two kinds of goal sets are maintained during the planning procedure: primary goal-sets (*PGS*) consisting of primary goal states and secondary goal-sets (*SGS*) consisting of secondary goal states. The following describes the procedure for constructing a partial plan p/r_j:

Abstract planning: Distinguish primary states and non-primary states in W_G/r_j. Insert primary goal states into *PGS* and non-primary goal states into *SGS*. Generate an abstract plan to satisfy the goals in *PGS* based on backward planning, i.e. for $w_g \in PGS$, if it is satisfied by initial states, make a link between the two nodes. Otherwise, generate a new operator (action) achieving the goal and remove the goal from *PGS*. Now the preconditions of the operator become the new goals. Insert the operator's primary goals into *PGS* and the other secondary goals into *SGS*. Every time an action is generated, propagate it to the other subplanners involved in w_g. Repeat the backward planning process until all goals in *PGS* are achieved.

Plan refinement: For a goal in *SGS*, classify it into one of the following three types and achieve the goal accordingly. Repeat this procedure until all goals in *SGS* are achieved.

Type 1: r_j is associated with the goal as a secondary resource, e.g. on(r_k,r_j). In this case, wait until the subplanner for p/r_k (primary resource in the goal) achieves the goal and sends its results. On the arrival of the result, check whether it can be combined with the current p/r_j without invalidating some goal achieved earlier. If not, reject the result and request the subplanner p/r_k to reachieve the corresponding goal. Otherwise, combine the result with p/r_j and remove the goal from *SGS*. If the result includes an action, extract some of its preconditions which are associated with r_j, and then insert them into *PGS* or *SGS* accordingly.

Type 2: r_j is not associated with the goal, e.g. after stack(r_j, r_k) is generated, one of its preconditions, clear(r_k) becomes a new goals. In this case, request the associated subplanner to satisfy the goal. Actually, this has been done when the generation of the operator is propagated to the associated subplanners in abstract planning. When the result is reported from the associated subplanner, remove the goal from SGS.

Type 3: r_j is associated with the goal, however, whether r_j is a primary or secondary resource is not known prior to run-time. Check at run-time whether the goal is satisfied by the effect of its preceding step (action) in p/r_j. If so, remove the goal from *SGS*. Otherwise, determine the type of r_j considering the difference between the step (action) generating the goal and its preceding step. If r_j is a primary resource, then achieve the goal based on backward planning as in the abstract planning. Otherwise, achieve the goal by calling the procedure for Type 1.

Figure 5 illustrates how p/r_j is constructed based on the hierarchical planning. In Fig. 5a the given goals are classified as primary goals or secondary goals, and then inserted into *PGS* or *SGS*. This creates an initial plan. In Fig. 5b, the primary goal is achieved by an action (marked by a circle) and consequently, new primary goals and new secondary goals are generated. This goal achievement is repeated until all primary goals are achieved. The resulting plan is an abstract plan. The secondary goal shown in Fig. 5b can be achieved by a new action (marked by a rectangle) or the effect of the preceding step (action). Note that the new action can be internally generated or externally propagated from other subplanners. This goal achievement is repeated until all secondary goals are achieved. The resulting plan in Fig. 5c is a refined plan. Although only two preconditions are shown for an action node in Fig. 5, there can be several preconditions. In that case, planning requires several repetitions of plan refinement.

Let us see how the procedure is applied to the construction of p/r_a in Fig. 4. Given the initial and goal states associated with resource "a", the subplanner distinguishes primary goal states, on(a,b). Thus, PGS/r_a consists of a goal on on(a,b).

Abstract planning: Since on(a,b) in the goal node is not satisfied by W_I/r_a, the operator table in Table 1 is searched and stack(a,b) is selected[13]. This is denoted by node 2 in Fig. 4. In turn, stack(a,b) generates new goals, hold(a) and clear(b). hold(a) is a primary goal to the subplanner while clear(b) is a secondary goal. Therefore, hold(a) is inserted in PGS/r_a while clear(b) is inserted in SGS/r_a. Similarly, to satisfy hold(a) in node 2, unstack(a,?) is selected as denoted by node 1. This, in turn, generates new goals on(a,?) and clear(a). on(a,?) is a primary goal while clear(a) is a secondary goal. Therefore, on(a.?) is inserted in PGS/r_a and clear(a) is inserted in SGS/r_a. Because on(a,?) is satisfied by one of the initial states, on(a,T), the uninstantiated variable ? is bound to T. Thus it results in the abstract plan consisting of unstack(a,T) and stack(a,b).

When the subplanner generates actions, it also informs the associated subplanners of them. For example, after generating stack(a,b), the subplanner for p/r_a finds out that the action is associated with subplanner for p/r_b and then informs the subplanner of the action. This is not only to propagate the effect of the action in terms of r_b but also to request that the subplanner for p/r_b satisfy a precondition of the action, namely clear(b).

---

[13]If several candidate operators are available, some selection strategy is needed.

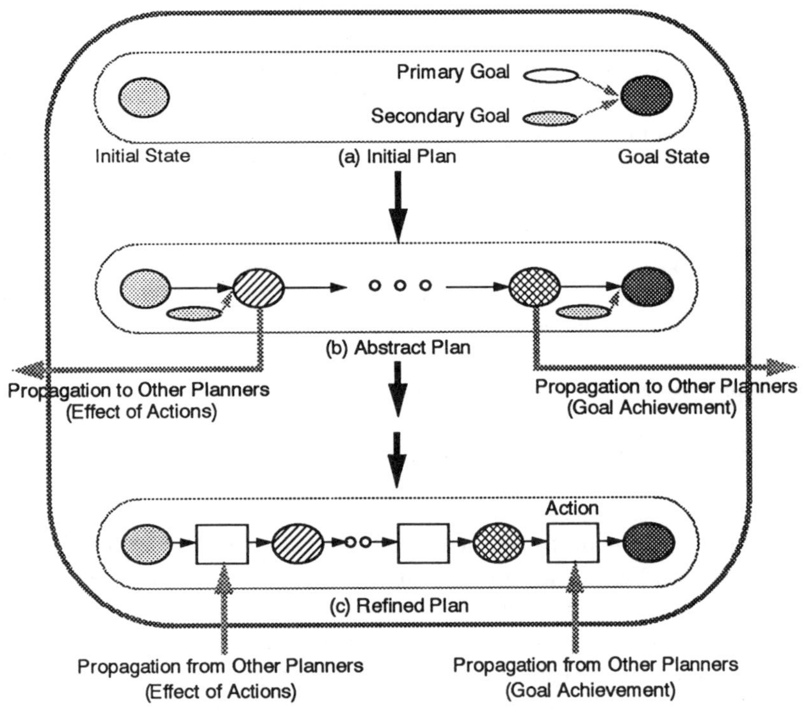

Fig. 5. Hierarchical planning in a subplanner.

Similarly each subplanner constructs its abstract plan as shown in Fig. 4. While constructing the abstract plan, each subplanner propagates its results to the associated subplanners. The snapshot when the subplanners complete the propagation is shown in Fig. 6, where the part in a shaded oval area is the abstract plan and the other part is the propagated plan. Note that each subplanner combines the propagated result with its own plan only after verifying that the propagated result does not invalidate[14] its plan.

Plan refinement: As shown in Fig. 5, SGS/r_a consists of two goals, clear(b) in node 2 and clear(a) in node 1, where clear(b) and clear(a) are classified as types 2 and 3, respectively. For clear(b) in node 2, the subplanner has requested the subplanner for p/r_b to satisfy the goal when it propagated the generation of stack(a,b) in node 2. Therefore, achieving the goal is deferred until the subplanner for p/r_b

[14]In this example, invalidation does not occur. However it can occur in the example called *creative destruction* [1], where W_I = {on(c,a),on(a,T),on(b,T),clear(b),clear(c)} and W_G = {on(c,a),on(a,b),on(b,T)}. The achievement of on(c,a) by W_I/r_c in abstract p/r_c invalidates the achievement of on(a,b) in abstract p/r_a.

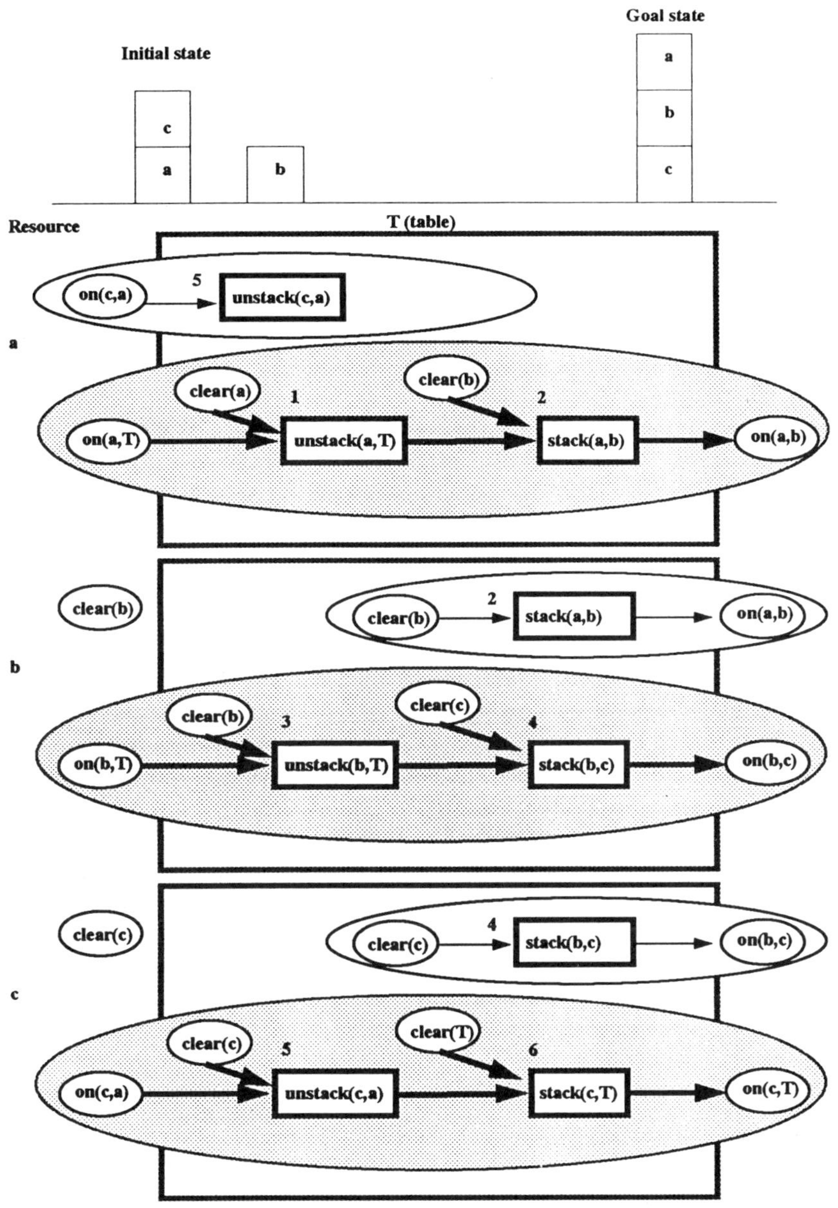

Fig. 6. After abstract plan is propagated.

sends back its result. For clear(a) in node 1, the subplanner checks whether it is satisfied by the effect of its preceding[15] step. As it is achieved by the effect of node 5, a new link is inserted between node 5 and node 1 as shown in Fig. 5.2.

Suppose node 5 is not propagated to the subplanner for p/r_a. In this case, the subplanner needs to determine the goal type of r_a. In the current p/r_a, node 1 and the initial node are two ends to be connected. The difference between the two can be extracted as on(c,a) and clear(a). Since resource "c" is a primary resource in achieving the goal, the subplanner waits for the subplanner for p/r_c to finish planning first and report the result. Suppose the subplanner for p/r_c has propagated the generation of unstack(c,a), but clear(a) is not a postcondition of the action. In this case, the subplanner for p/r_a again extracts the difference between node 5 and node 1 in terms of r_a. Then it reclassifies the type of clear(a) for node 1 and achieves the goal accordingly.

Let us see how the subplanner for p/r_b completes the plan refinement. As shown in Fig. 4, SGS/r_b consists of three goals: on(a,b) for the goal node, clear(c) for node 4, and clear(b) for node 3. Since on(a,b) is classified as type 1, the subplanner for p/r_b waits until the subplanner for p/r_a achieves the goal and sends its result. Suppose the subplanner for p/r_a has propagated the generation of stack(a,b), then node 2 is inserted in p/r_b as shown in Fig. 6. In this case, the goal of on(a,b) is achieved and the goal is removed from SGS/r_b. The precondition of the operator associated with r_b, clear(b), now becomes a goal and is inserted in SGS/r_b. For this goal, the plan refinement procedure is applied again. As it is satisfied by the effect of the preceding action (node 4), the goal is achieved so that nodes 2 and 4 are linked. If it were not satisfied by node 4, the difference between two steps (node 2 and node 4) is extracted. Then the achievement of the goal can be done by the subplanner for p/r_b or the other subplanners. For clear(c) in node 4, the subplanner for p/r_b has requested the subplanner for p/r_a to satisfy the goal during the abstract planning time. Therefore, achieving the goal is deferred until the subplanner for p/r_c sends back its results. For clear(b) in node 3, it is satisfied by the initial node and the goal is removed from SGS/r_b.

Similarly, the subplanner for p/r_c completes its plan refinement. In this procedure, clear(T) in node 6 is satisfied under the assumption that all other resources except blocks are available whenever required.

5.3. Termination

The planning procedure terminates if every subplanner constructs its partial plan $(p/r_j)_{j=1,\ldots,n}$, while completing the tasks requested from the other subplanners. A final plan can be synthesized by combining the partial plans without the repetition of the common part among the partial plans, which results from the communication while handling the dependency among the associated resources. A synthesized final plan network for the example in Fig. 4 is shown in Fig. 8.

[15]Note that intermediate plan p/r_a remains serial during planning.

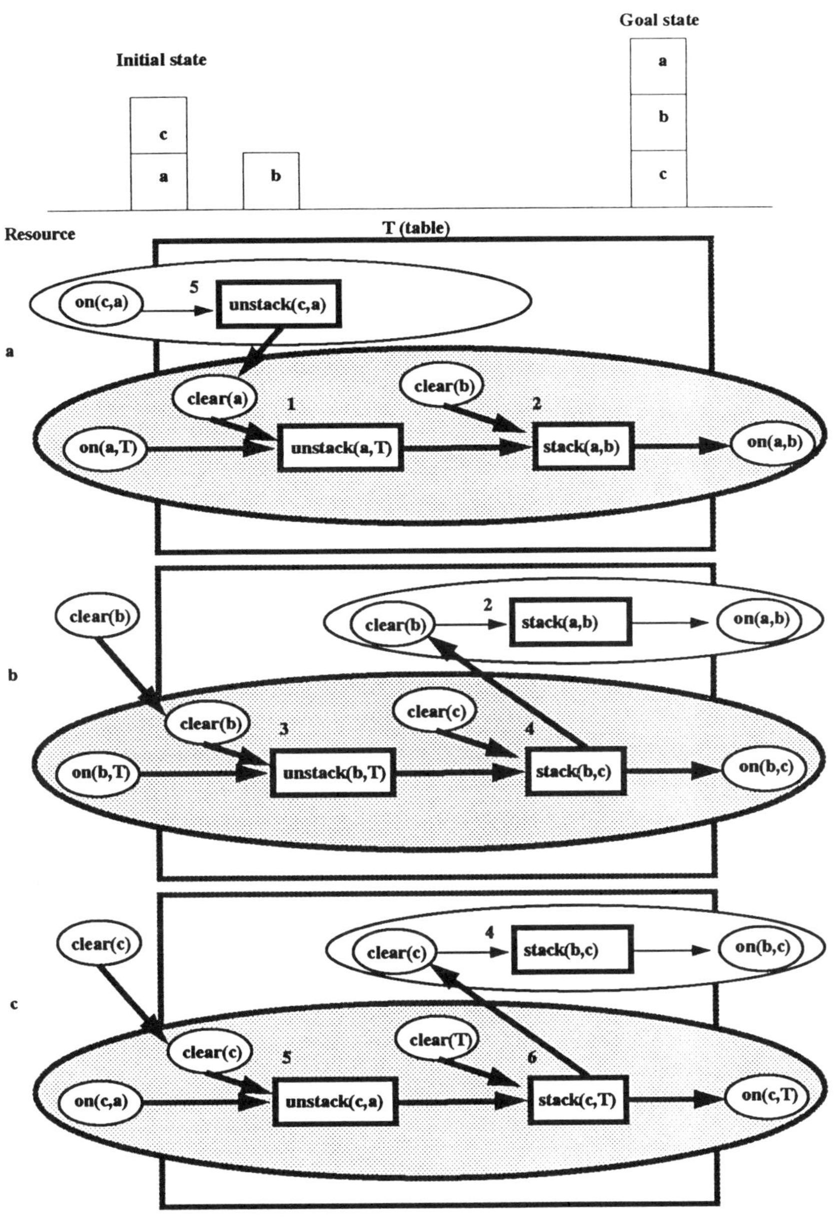

Fig. 7. Refined plan.

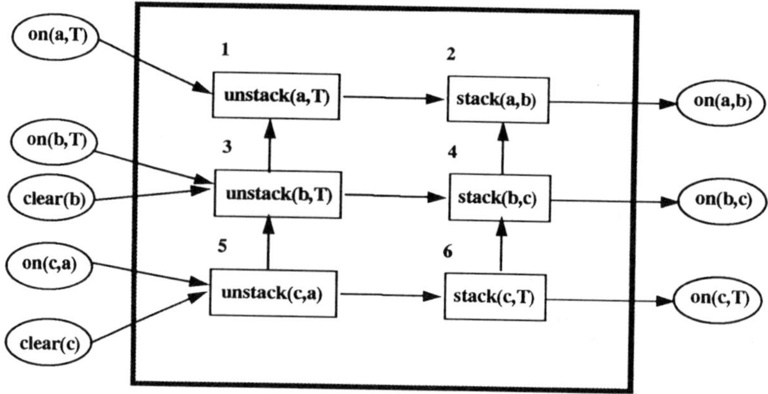

Fig. 8. Final plan.

6. Communication and Interaction

The following questions describe the degree of interaction occurring among subplanners [9]: (i) among whom the interaction takes place, (ii) when the interaction occurs, (iii) what is the content of the interaction, (iv) how the interaction is accomplished, (v) why the interaction occurs. Suppose a goal state associated with more than one resource is given in RP^2. While the goal is achieved, interaction takes place among the subplanners associated with the resources. Among the associated subplanners, the subplanner for the most critical resource initiates the process to achieve the goal. If the goal is already satisfied by the initial states, the subplanner generates a new link. Otherwise, it generates a new action (or a set of actions). Then it informs the associated subplanners of the new link or action. This initiates the interaction among the associated subplanners and the interactions will continue until the goal is completely achieved by all the associated subplanners. The content of the interaction includes the name of the goal to be achieved and information about the new link or action. This is not only to inform the effect of the action or link (result sharing) but also to request the subplanners to achieve some preconditions of the action (task assignment).

While a goal is achieved, a dynamic master-slave organization is maintained among the associated subplanners, where the subplanner for the most critical resource becomes the master and the other associated subplanners become slaves. If the master generates a link or action, it informs the salves of the generation. Also, if a slave achieves some precondition of the generated action, it is reported to the master. If all the preconditions of the generated action are achieved by the master or the slaves, it implies the complete achievement of the goal. Note that the interaction to achieve a goal is accomplished when the master receives from the associated slaves all the completion signals for the preconditions of the action.

7. Comparison with Conventional Approaches

Conventional parallel planners such as NOAH[1], NONLIN[2], DEVISER[3] and Corkill's planner[6] (a distributed NOAH) generate a partial ordered plan network, $G(P)$, based on backward planning where a cycle of linking, expansion and conflict detection/resolution is repeated until all the subgoals generated are achieved (for details, see Appendix A). While NOAH[1], NONLIN[2] and DEVISER[3] generate a nonlinear (multiagent) plan using a centralized planner, Corkill's planner generates a multiagent plan using distributed planners. As RP^2 assumes distributed planners, RP^2 can be best compared with Corkill's scheme[6]. The distinct difference between the two is in the problem decomposition. Corkill's scheme uses a goal-based decomposition approach while RP^2 adopts a resource-based decomposition approach. As a result, the decomposed tasks and the interaction among the decomposed tasks are different. In both approaches, the planning operations such as expansion, linking and conflict detection/resolution are distributed across the subplanners. Some duplicate operations are executed in the subplanners. In Corkill's scheme, each subplanner performs conflict detection and resolution in the whole set of $G(P/g_j)_{j=1,\ldots,k}$ so that conflict detection/resolution operations are duplicated. On the other hand, in RP^2, each subplanner may perform expansion operations to achieve the same goal. However, this duplication can be avoided by allowing a subplanner to perform expansion first and propagate the result to all the associated subplanners.

Both the two approaches adopt a hierarchical planning scheme; however, they apply the scheme differently: Hierarchical planning in Corkill's scheme is based on the abstraction of operators while hierarchical planning in RP^2 is based on the abstraction of preconditions (goals) in the operators. The approach in RP^2 is similar to that of ABSTRIPS[7]. However, they are different in that the criticality in RP^2 is dynamically assigned based on resource reasoning while the criticality in ABSTRIPS is assigned before planning starts.

Analytical comparison of performance

In conventional parallel planner such as NOAH or NONLIN, the total execution time of each planning operation until the completion of planning is given as follows (for details, see Appendix A):

$$T_{\text{expansion}} \approx O(N_a \times N_t)\ T_{\text{linking}} \approx O(N_a \times N_c)),\ \text{and}\ T_{\text{conflict}} \approx O((N_a)^2)\ ,$$

where N_a denotes the number of action nodes generated until the completion of planning, N_c denotes the number of cycles required for the completion of planning, i.e. the total number of goals achieved, N_t denotes the number of action (operator) types in the action table.

Let us compare the performance of RP^2 and Corkill's scheme, considering only the effects of the different problem decomposition approaches.

Let k denote the number of conjunctive goals in a planning task, n denote the number of the resource types, and α denote the average number of resources involved in an operator.

Assuming that k processors are available and each goal is assigned to a processor, let us compute the execution time of Corkill's scheme. The total number of action nodes in $G(P)$ is N_a. If we assume that the action nodes are equally distributed across $G(p/g_j)_{j=1,\dots,k}$, the average number of action nodes in $G(p/g_j)$ becomes N_a/k. While action nodes of N_a/k are generated in a subplanner, they are propagated to all the other subplanners for $G(p/g_i)_{i=1,\dots k,\text{ but } i\neq j}$. Assuming that (i) communication between a pair of subplanners takes one time unit, and (ii) it takes one time unit (by using a hashing table) to locate a node of the plan network to which the propagated result will be inserted, we can calculate communication overhead due to the propagation as follows:

$$\begin{aligned} T_{\text{Communication}} &= (N_a/k \times (k-1) \times k) \\ &= \mathrm{O}(k \times N_a)\ . \end{aligned}$$

The total execution time of each operation in a subplanner is given as follows: $T_{\text{expansion}} = \mathrm{O}(N_a/k \times N_t)$, and $T_{\text{conflict}} = O((N_a/k) \times N_a)$. As subplanners in Corkill's scheme operate in parallel while communicating with each other, the total execution time is the same as that in a subplanner, i.e. $T_{\text{Corkill}} \approx O((N_a/k) \times N_a)$.

Assuming that n processors are available and each resource is assigned to a processor, let us compute the execution time of RP^2. The total number of action nodes in $G(p/r_j)_{j=1,\dots,n}$ is $(\alpha \times N_a)$. If we assume that the nodes are equally distributed across $G(p/r_j)$s, the average number of action nodes in a $G(p/r_j)$ becomes $(\alpha \times N_a)/n$. Among the average number, (N_a/n) is the number of nodes generated by the subplanner for r_j while $((\alpha-1) \times N_a)/n$ is the number of nodes propagated to the subplanner. While action nodes of (N_a/n) are generated in a subplanner, they are propagated to its associated subplanners for $G(p/g_i)_{i=1,\dots,(\alpha-1)}$. Under the same assumption used for Corkill's scheme, communication overhead due to the propagation is as follows:

$$\begin{aligned} T_{\text{Communication}} &= (N_a/n) \times (\alpha-1) \times n \\ &= \mathrm{O}(\alpha \times N_a)\ . \end{aligned}$$

The total execution time of each operation in a subplanner is $T_{\text{expansion}} = \mathrm{O}(N_a/n \times N_t)$ and $T_{\text{conflict}} \approx \mathrm{O}(SA_{\text{avg}} \times N_g^{nz})$, where SA_{avg} and N_t^{nz}, respectively denote the average length of goal structures and the number of goals with the length of the goal structure $\neq 0$ (for details, see Appendix B). As subplanners in RP^2 operate in parallel while communicating with each other, the total execution time is the same as that in a subplanner, i.e. $T_{\mathrm{RP}^2} \approx \mathrm{O}(SA_{\text{avg}} \times N_g^{nz})$, where $SA_{\text{avg}} < N_a$ and $N_g^{nz} < \alpha \times N_c/n$. In the blocks world, $T_{\mathrm{RP}^2} \approx O(N_a)$ since $SA_{\text{avg}} \leq 1$.

The planning speed of RP^2 is $\mathrm{O}(SA_{\text{avg}} \times N_a^{nz})$ while that of Corkill's scheme is $\mathrm{O}((N_a/k) \times N_a)$. The possible speed-up in RP^2 is achieved by: (i)decomposing the planning problem in terms of resources, and (ii) constructing individual resource flow plans partly by a linear hierarchical planning algorithm (based on resource reasoning) and partly by a nonlinear planning algorithm. The linear planning algorithm is used for a subplanner to generate actions by itself, while the nonlinear planning algorithm is used to combine the partial results generated by the subplanner and propagated from the other subplanners.

Note that while constructing $G(p/r_j)$, RP^2 exploits a global constraint that the flow of r_j should be serial in the final $G(p/r_j)$. The possible drawback of RP^2 is that it is communication-boundedness, i.e. it spends as much time on communication as plan generation.

8. Conclusion

RP^2 is implemented for the blocks world domain in SUN-lisp on a sun 4/260 workstation. The software is composed of several modules: *a plan coordinator* and a set of *subplanners*. The *plan coordinator* handles the user interface, the decomposition of a planning task and the plan synthesis while the *subplanners* handle the construction of partial plans. RP^2 was tested with problems with 10 or more blocks, where communication among the modules was simulated through file I/O. The test results show that RP^2 can generate multiagent plans very efficiently in a parallel and distributed processing environment where the communication cost is not excessively high. For more details, see reference [8].

The advantages of RP^2 can be stated as follows:

- RP^2 makes use of resource reasoning in the problem decomposition, generation of partial plans, and communication among subplanners. This allows (i) parallel search among the partitioned spaces, (ii) efficient construction of partial plans, and (iii) avoidance of unnecessary communication among subplanners.
- RP^2 can generate an optimal parallel plan by minimizing the use of resources involved in each partial plan.
- The more locality that exists in the use of resources, the better the performance that can be achieved in RP^2. This is because distributed processing is possible without much communication among subplanners.

The limitations of RP^2 can be stated as follows:

- When part of the resources are heavily involved in a plan, interactions among subplanners associated with those resources will increase, thus resulting in a load balancing problem.
- When the number of resources involved in an operator are relatively large or the criticality of resources can not be compared based on resource reasoning, communication overhead among the associated subplanners will increase and create a communication bottleneck.

References

[1] E. D. Sacerdoti, *A Structure for Plans and Behavior*, American Elsevier(1977).

[2] A. Tate, *Generating Project Networks*, Proc. Int. Joint Conf. on Artificial Intelligence (1977) 888-893.

[3] S. A. Vere, *Planning in time: windows and patterns for activities and goals*, IEEE Transaction on Pattern Analysis and Machine Intell. (May 1983) 246-267.

[4] D. E. Wilkins, *Domain-independent Planning: Representation and Plan Generation*, Artificial Intell. **22** (1984) 269-301.

[5] D. Chapman, *Planning for Conjunctive Goals*, Artificial Intell. **32** (1987) 333-377.

[6] D. D. Corkill, *Hierarchical Planning in a Distributed Environment*, Proc. Int. Joint Conf. on Artificial Intelligence (1979) 168-175.

[7] E. D. Sacerdoti, *Planning in a hierarchy of abstraction space*, Artificial Intell. **5** (1974) 115-135.

[8] K. Chung, *Efficient AI nonlinear planning based on resource reasoning*, PH. D. Thesis, University of Southern California (1990).

[9] A. H. Bond and L. Gasser, *Readings in Distributed Artificial Intelligence*, Morgan Kaufmann Publishers, Inc. (1988).

Appendix A: The Time Complexity in Parallel Planning

Conventional parallel planners generate a partially ordered plan network based on backward planning where a cycle of linking, expansion and conflict detection/ resolution[16] is repeated until all the goals generated are achieved.

Procedure *Parallel Planning*

```
1.   Begin
2.     Repeat (*Backward Planning*)
3.       • Linking;
         (* If a goal (goal node) can be achieved by the effects
         of a node existing in the plan network, a link is formed
         between the two nodes unless it results in a cycle
         of nodes in the plan network *)
4.       If Linking fails then
5.         Begin
6.           • Expansion;
             (* The goal is achieved by introducing a new action
             (action node), and the preconditions of the new
             action become a new goals to be achieved *)
7.           • Conflict detection-resolution;
             (* The new action generated from expansion is
             checked against all other parallel nodes
             currently existing in the plan network
             to detect conflicts, and any detected conflicts
             are subject to immediate resolution *)
8.         End
9.       Until no more goals to be achieved
10.  End (* Parallel Planning *)
```

[16]These three operations correspond to *simple establishment, step addition*, and *declobbering*, respectively, in TWEAK[5].

The total execution time of parallel planning in a uniprocessor environment can be calculated as follows:

$$\begin{aligned} T_{PP} &= \sum_{i=1}^{N_c}\{t_{\text{expansion}(i)} + t_{\text{linking}(i)} + t_{\text{conflict}(i)}\} \\ &= T_{\text{expansion}} + T_{\text{linking}} + T_{\text{conflict}} \ , \end{aligned}$$

where N_c is the number of cycles required for the completion of planning, i.e. the total number of goals achieved.

The above equation can be further elaborated using the following assumptions:

- No backtracking occurs, i.e. the best choice is made in every decision.
- Conflicts between two actions are detected by comparing their effects.
- Any conflict between two actions in parallel branches is resolved immediately by assigning a direct precedence to the conflicting actions, i.e. by *promotion* in TWEAK[2]. This implies that all conflicts can be resolved without *white knight*[17]. Thus, the time for conflict resolution is less than the time for conflict detection.

Let N_t be the number of action types in action table, N_a be the number of action nodes generated when planning is completed, N_{pa} be the average number of preconditions in an action, and N_{sa} be the average number of postconditions in an action.

$$\begin{aligned} T_{\text{expansion}} &= \sum_{i=1}^{N_a} N_t \times (N_{sa}/2) \\ &= 1/2 \times N_a \times N_t \times N_{sa} \\ &= O(N_a \times N_t \times N_{sa}) \ , \end{aligned}$$

where i, N_t and $(N_{sa}/2)$, respectively indicate the ith expansion, the number of comparison between the current goal and the postconditions of actions required to find out all possible actions from the operator table, and the average number of condition matchings between the current goal and the postconditions of an action.

$$\begin{aligned} T_{\text{linking}} &= \sum_{j=1}^{N_c}(N_a/N_c) \times j \times (N_{sa}/2) \\ &= O(N_c \times N_a) \\ &\approx O((N_a)^2) \ , \end{aligned}$$

where j,$(N_a/N_c \times j)$, $N_{sa}/2$ respectively indicate jth cycle, the number of action nodes at cycle i assuming the number increases linearly with i, and the number

[17]Declobbering by white knight can be viewed as a reachievement of the associated goal after a backtracking. See the second to the last paragraph in p. 361 of TWEAK[5].

of comparisons between the current goal and the postconditions of action nodes to find all possible candidates in the current plan network.

$$T_{\text{conflict}} = \sum_{k=1}^{N_a} k \times \{(N_{pa} \times N_{pa}) + (N_{pa} \times N_{sa}) + (N_{sa} \times N_{pa}) + (N_{sa} \times N_{sa})$$
$$\approx O((N_a)^2) ,$$

where k, $(N_{pa} + N_{sa})^2$ respectively indicate the kth expansion, and the number of cross comparisons between pre and post conditions of the two action nodes.

Combining the above equations for $T_{\text{expansion}}, T_{\text{linking}}, T_{\text{conflict}}$, we have

$$T_{PP} \approx O((N_a)^2)$$
$$\text{for } N_{sa}, N_{pa} \leq N_t \ll N_a \approx N_c .$$

T_{PP}[18] indicates that conflict detection and resolution dominate the time complexity in parallel planning, although T_{conflict} does not include the time required to resolve complicated conflicts such as action-deadlocks. Also, note that the actual $T_{\text{expansion}}$ and T_{linking} can be less than those calculated above since exhaustive search need not be used if a good heuristic is available.

Appendix B: The Time Complexity for Conflict Detection/Resolution in RP^2

The action nodes in $G(p/r_j)$ can be divided into two groups: one group is the set of action nodes generated by the subplanner p/r_j and the other group is the action nodes generated by the other subplanners and propagated to the subplanner for p/r_j. Let us call the former the internal node group and the latter the external node group. The average number of action nodes (goals) in $G(p/r_j)$ is $\alpha \times N_a/n$ ($\alpha \times N_c/n$). Among them, N_a/n is the number of action nodes in the internal node group while $(\alpha - 1) \times (N_a/n)$ is the number of action nodes in the external node group.

In conventional parallel planning, the intermediate plan is a partially ordered network. Therefore, every time a new action node is generated, conflict detection requires the comparison of the effects or the ranges of goals (goal structure)[19] between the action and each of parallel actions in the plan network. On the contrary, in RP^2, the intermediate resource flow plan is kept linear based on a linear planning algorithm. Therefore, every time a new action node is generated or propagated, conflict detection requires the comparison of the effects between the action and some of the parallel actions in the plan network. Note that conventional parallel planning

[18] N_a in $O((N_a)^2)$ is an exponentially explosive number. The exponent of the time complexity can be reduced by using the TOME[1] table or GOST[2] table. If declobbering by white knight is included, the time complexity is $O((N_a)^3)$. Refer to the second to the last paragraph in p. 340 of TWEAK[5].

[19] The range between the node which asserts a state and the node whose goal is satisfied by the asserted state is called a goal structure[1].

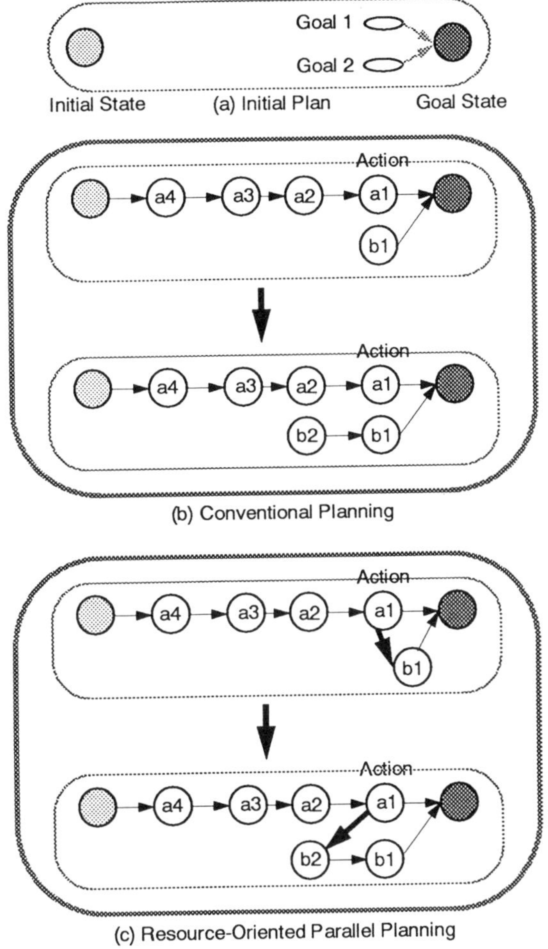

Fig. 9. Example to compare conflict detections of the two planning schemes.

requires a global comparison while RP^2 requires a local comparison, e.g. in Fig. 9a, two goals are given initially. Suppose a sequence of actions (a1, a2, a3 and a4) is generated to achieve Goal 1 while b1 is generated to achieve Goal 2. Now b2 is generated. In conventional planning (Fig. 9b), conflict detection requires comparisons between b2 and each of a1, a2, a3 and a4. In RP^2 (Fig. 9c), conflict detection requires a comparison between b2 and a1. The other comparisons are redundant since the actions of a2, a3 and a4 are not in parallel with b2 due to the inherited precedence relation between a1 and b2.

In RP^2, every time an action node (to be in the internal node group) is generated in $G(p/r_j)$ or an action node (to be in the external node group) is propagated to $G(p/r_j)$, it needs to be verified whether the action invalidates the achievement of goals achieved by any parallel actions in $G(p/r_j)$. This can be done by comparing the corresponding goal structures in a plan network. Figure 10 illustrates an example of conflict detection in RP^2. In Fig. 10b, suppose a sequence of actions (a1, a2, a3 and a4) in the internal node group is generated to achieve Goal 1 and an action b1 to achieve Goal 2 in the external node group is propagated. The ordering between Goal 1 and Goal 2 is determined initially based on resource reasoning so that there exists an ordering between a1 and b1. When an action b2 is propagated to p/r_j, it needs to compare the effects of the action and the goal achieved by a1. In Fig. 10c, suppose a sequence of actions (a1 and a2) in the internal node group is generated to achieve Goal 1 and the achievement of Goal 2 (by a state inherited from the initial state) is propagated. When an action a3 is generated, it needs to compare the effects of the action and Goal 2.

Suppose a final resource flow plan p/r_j is constructed as shown in Fig. 11a and its goal structure graph is given as in Fig. 11b. The goal structure graph illustrates that the eight goals are achieved while p/r_j is constructed. The goal structure in Fig. 11b can be divided into two types: one denoted by the solid arrow between two actions and the other denoted by the dotted arrow. The former indicates that the corresponding goal is achieved by its immediate predecessor action while the latter indicates that the corresponding goal is achieved by a state inherited from one of its predecessors (except its immediate predecessor). A dotted-line goal structure can be formed when (i) a goal is achieved by a linking operation or (ii) a goal is achieved by expansion operation, but later some parallel actions to achieve other goals are generated. For example, in Fig. 11b, suppose goals g2, g3, g5 and g7 are achieved first. Then, if g1 is achieved by an effect of action a3, the goal structure for g1 becomes a dotted-lined goal structure. In Fig. 11b, suppose g1 is achieved by action a3 first. Then the goal structure for g1 is a solid-lined goal structure. Later, if goals g2, g3 and g5 are achieved by actions a1, a2 and a3, respectively, the solid-lined goal structure for g1 is transformed into a dotted-lined goal structure. Regardless of the order in which the goal structures are formed, the number of comparisons to detect conflicts among goal structures are the same as long as the final goal structure graph is the same.

Let g_i denote a goal,

$A(g_i)$ denote the set of action nodes through which g_i can be inherited, i.e. the set of actions in parallel with the goal structure for g_i, and $SA(g_i)$ denote the size of $A(g_i)$, i.e. the number of actions in parallel with the goal structure for g_i.

For example, in Fig. 11b, $A(g1) = \{a2, a1\}$, $SA(g1) = 2$, $SA(g2) = 0$.

Let us calculate the time spent on conflict detection in the subplanner for p/r_j. Conflicts associated with g_i can be detected by checking whether g_i is violated by any node in $A(g_i)$. A goal g_i and the action nodes in $A(g_i)$ can appear in

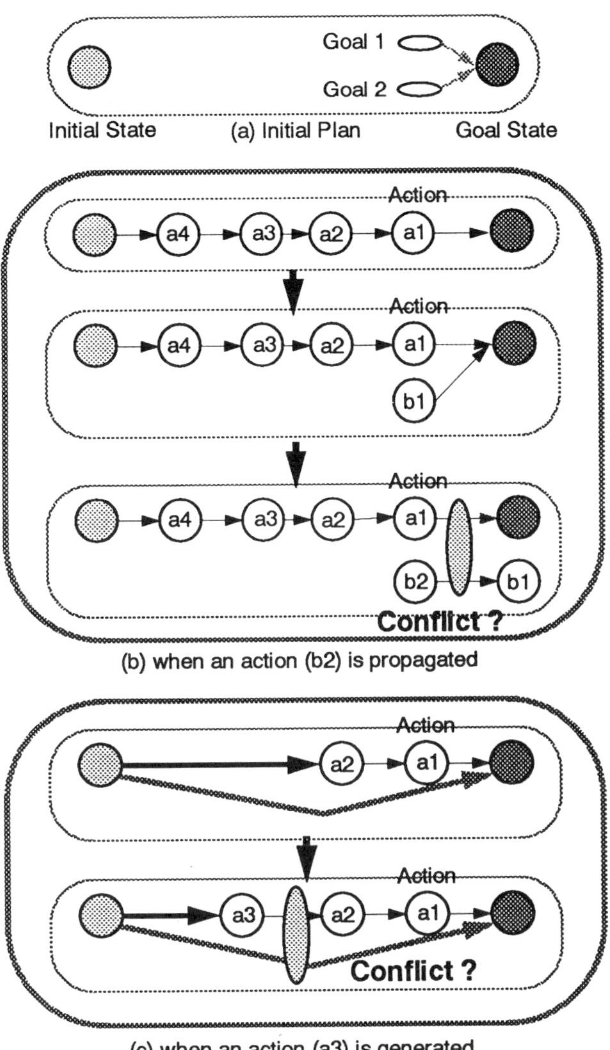

Fig. 10. Example of conflict detection in RP^2.

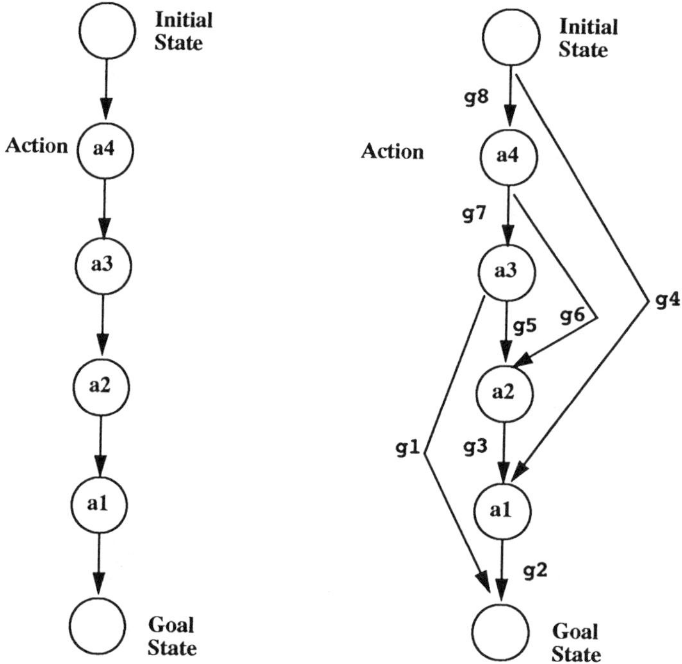

Fig. 11. A goal structure graph.

random order. Regardless of the order in which they appear, the total number of comparisons to detect the conflicts is determined by $SA(g_i)$.

The total number of comparisons for conflict detection in a subplanner for p/r_j until the completion of planning is as follows:

$$\begin{aligned} T_{\text{conflict}} &= \sum_{i=1}^{\alpha \times N_c/n} SA(g_i) \\ &= \sum_{i=1}^{N_g^{nz}} SA(g_i) + \sum_{j=1}^{N_g^{z}} SA(g_i) \\ &= \sum_{i=1}^{N_g^{nz}} SA(g_i) \end{aligned}$$

$$\approx SA_{\text{avg}} \times N_g^{nz}$$
$$< N_a \times (\alpha \times N_c/n)$$
$$(N_a \text{ is the maximum number of } SA(g_i)) ,$$

where N_g^{nz}, N_g^z and SA_{avg} respectively denote the number of goals with $SA(g_i) \neq 0$, the number of goals with $SA(g_i) = 0$, and the average length of the goal structure.

Note that SA_{avg} varies depending on the application domain and the given goal/initial states. For example, in the blocks world, $SA_{\text{avg}} \leq 1$ so that $T_{\text{conflict}} < N_c \approx N_a$. This analysis shows that RP^2 reduces the number of comparisons for conflict detection by avoiding unnecessary conflict detection.

CHAPTER 8

Path Planning for a Multi-Linked Walking Robot in a 3-D Environment

Qing Xue*, Phillip C. Y. Sheu#, and Yung-Ping Chen*

Abstract

Multi-limbed walking robots have broad potential applications in manufacturing, undersea operations, and space exploration. Although the robot path planning problem has been studied for many years, there is still no successful algorithm which can plan the path of the multi-limed walking robot by using its high maneuverability. The objective of this research is to develop a theoretical framework and practical techniques which lead to a computational efficient collision-free path planning algorithm specifically for multi-limbed walking robots.

To plan paths for multi-limbed walking robots, a shape-changeable robot model is used. In this model, the robot is represented by a set of cuboids according to its postures. A methodology which systematically represents a 3-D environment in accordance with the shape changeable robot model is also used. In path planning, the postures and motions of multi-limed walking robots are described by predicate logic. A knowledge based system is used to incorporate effectively the new robot model and workspace representation for planning collision-free paths of the multi-limed, walking robots. All efforts are designated to utilize fully the high maneuverability of the multi-limed walking robots.

1. Introduction

It is desirable to use robots to replace human beings in dangerous environment such as in nuclear reactors, under the sea, or in outer space; or to replace human beings from tedious work in manufacturing factory. The workspace in these environments is usually crowded. Therefore, a robot must demonstrate high maneuverability. Comparing to the robot with wheeled platform, a human-like multi-limbed walking robot (to make description short, we use multi-limbed robot form now on) which consists of arms and a legged mainbody is far more maneuverable. The multi-limbed robots can mimic the specific motions of human beings such as walking, crawling, or even creeping, thus avoiding collisions with obstacles in the working environment. These motions can enlarge the robot workspace, avoid degeneracy and generate large Cartesian forces. Therefore, multi-limbed robots have broad applications.

Recently, researchers have conducted many studies on multi-limbed robots [1-3]. Much attention has been focused on the kinematic [2], dynamic [3] and control aspects [1]. Robot path planning remains a fundamental problem in almost all robot applications [4]. The collision-free path planning for a robot to move from an initial position to a final position is

* with Department of Electrical Engineering, Purdue University School of Engineering and Technology at Indianapolis, Indianapolis, IN 46202

with Department of Electrical and Computer Engineering, Rutgers University, Piscataway, NJ 08855

only solved for some simple robot manipulators and mobile platforms. We have not seen any publications discussing collision-free path planning for multi- limbed robots. Here the problem of path planning for the multi- limbed robots is studied. A new robot model and corresponding workspace representation is introduced.

In the existing path planning approaches, it is always assumed that the shape of a mobile robot is fixed, so that the robot can be modeled as a circle (sphere) [5] or a polygon (polyhedron) [6,7]. If a human-like multi-limbed robot is represented by these models, the fixed volume representing the robot model would be much greater than the actual volume occupied by the robot in most cases. This will result in that a great number of feasible paths cannot be recognized in path planning. In order to solve this problem, we model the robot in such a way that the shape of the robot is changeable. In the shape-changeable robot model, the multi-limbed robot is represented by a set of cuboids with different sizes. The set of cuboids is defined according to a set of typical postures (or states) of the robot. A robot motion is defined as the motion of the cuboid, or the transition from one cuboid to another cuboid.

In order to accommodate the robot model, a corresponding workspace description need to be formalized. In the past, researchers usually avoided directly modeling the free workspace, especially in a crowded environment, because results showed that doing so would cause high computational complexity or inaccuracy for the corresponding path planning algorithm [6]. Therefore, in many path planning approaches, the configuration space (C-space) method [7] is adopted to represent the workspace. In C-space method, the robot is shrunk to a point and the obstacles are enlarged accordingly. Due to the high computational cost of transformation from world space to C-space, the C-space method works well only when the dimension of the space is small. If the C-space method is applied to the path planning of a multi-limbed robot, the dimension of the C-space will be too large and planning a path is impractical. Therefore, directly modeling the free space becomes attractive in this situation. A systematic methodology can be used to directly decompose a 3-D environment into a set of subspaces. The 3-D workspace is first projected to a set of 2-D projections according to the height of the cuboids representing the robot. The free workspace in each 2-D projection is then divided into a finite set of subspaces. Then the path planning problem is decomposed into several sub-problems where path planning in each subspace and through adjacent subspaces is studied.

A knowledge-based system approach [8,9] can be naturally adopted in the path planning. The method for planning collision-free paths in each free subspace and through the boundaries of adjacent subspaces is stored in a knowledge base. During path planning, a connection graph whose vertices are free subspaces and whose edges are robot motions will be built by using the knowledge base. Finally, a collision-free path for the robot can be searched in this connection graph.

The organization of the presentation is as follows. The model of the multi-limed walking robot will be described in Section 2. The workspace representations in accordance with the robot model is discussed in Section 3. In Section 4, the knowledge-based path planning system is described. Section 5 discusses the potential extension of this study.

2. Robot Model

In order to develop a collision-free path planning algorithm for a robot, it is essential to build a geometric model to represent the robot. Since an accurate representation of a robot requires complex mathematical expressions, some simple geometric shapes (e.g., spheres, polyhedra) are often used in the robot representations. The most common robot representation models are briefly described as follows:

1. *Sphere (Circular) Representation:* In a sphere representation, each robot is represented by the smallest sphere that circumscribes the robot. The advantage of the sphere representation is the ease of calculating the distances between two robots and between the robot and obstacles in either 2-D or 3-D Cartesian space. Therefore, the sphere model has been widely used for the representation of mobile robots [5,10].
2. *Polyhedra Representation:* A polyhedra representation of a robot can be obtained by finding the smallest polyhedron that circumscribes the robot [7,11]. This robot representation is usually more accurate than a sphere representation. However, finding the distance between two polyhedra in Cartesian space requires much more computation than the distance between two spheres.
3. *Constructive Solid Geometry (CSG) Representation:* The CSG representation describes complex solids as compositions of primitive solids [12]. These solids are organized in an ordered binary tree. When the number of primitive solids in a CSG representation is large, the CSG tree can accurately represent complex robots. Yet the CSG tree of a complex robot can be very deep, which might lead to inefficient data retrievals if there is no suitable data access support.
4. *Swept Volume Representation:* A swept volume is used to represent moving robots. A swept volume representation of a robot is a set that contains all the points in the workspace that have been swept over by the moving robot in a time interval [13]. By using the swept volume representation, the space-time problem can be reduced to a pure spatial problem. However, the accuracy of the robot representation is sacrificed severely.

From the above discussion it may be seen that among all the existing mobile robot representations, there is one similarity that the shape of the robot is assumed fixed during each motion. When a robot is equipped with legs and arms, fixed-shape robot models are always too conservative. If these models are used in collision-free path planning, many real collision-free paths would be missed. Therefore, we introduce a shape-changeable robot model to plan a collision-free path for a multi-limbed robot.

2.1. Shape-Changeable Robot Model

As discussed in last section, to model the multi-limbed robot by a fixed shape is not suitable for collision-free path planning. On the other hand, to model the robot very accurately in

Configuration space also is not suitable for collision-free path planning due to the computation burden. Therefore, some trade-off is accepted here by representing the robot by a shape-changeable model. In this model, a small set of cuboids is used to represent the robot according to its postures and motions.

2.1.1. Robot states

In the shape-changeable robot model, a set of cuboids with different sizes are used to represent a set of typical robot's postures and these typical robot's postures are defined as the states of the robot. For example, states of the robot could be stand, squat, lie etc. The reason to use a set of cuboids to represent the states of the robot in the shape-changeable robot model are as follows:

(1) since the sizes of the minimum cuboids representing the states of the robot differ drastically, the physical shape of a multi-limbed mobile robot can be described accurately,

(2) and the collision between two cuboids and between the cuboids and obstacles can easily be detected.

From a collision-free path planning perspective, only the external geometric shape of a robot needs to be considered. The structure of the robot, the relationship between the joints, etc., are regarded as internal details of the state cuboids and are not considered in the path planning process here. Since a robot with arbitrary position and orientation in the workspace can be in one of a finite number of states, the position and the orientation, P, of the robot are included as parameters of the robot state definition. For explicit representation, a state is described by predicate logic. For instance, three basic states, stand, squat and lie, can be used to describe a human-like biped walking robots, which are defined as follows:

(1) **stand**: STAND(P)=>OCCUPIED_CUBOID_SPACE(L_{st},W_{st},H_{st})$|_P$,
where L_{st}, W_{st} and H_{st} are the length, width, and height of a stand cuboid respectively and the subscript st denotes stand. The predicate OCCUPIED_CUBOID_SPACE(l,w,h)$|_P$ is true if the cuboid with length l, width w, height h, and at position and orientation P is occupied by the robot.

(2) **squat**: SQUAT(P)=>OCCUPIED_CUBOID_SPACE(L_{sq},W_{sq},H_{sq})$|_P$
where L_{sq}, W_{sq} and H_{sq} are the length, width, and height of a squat cuboid respectively and the subscript sq means squat.

(3) **lie**: LIE(P)=>OCCUPIED_CUBOID_SPACE(L_{li},W_{li},H_{li})$|_P$
where L_{li}, W_{li} and H_{li} are the length, width and height of a lie cuboid respectively and subscript li means lie.
It is assumed that $H_{st}>H_{sq}>H_{li}$.

2.1.2. The description of robot motion

Since the state of a robot is defined as a cuboid, the motion of the robot is naturally defined by a sequence of motions of a state cuboid or by transitions from one state cuboid to another state cuboid. Under this definition, each motion of the robot can be described by a rule with a precondition and a postcondition. These preconditions and postconditions are described by predicate logic. For instance, based on the three basic robot states defined earlier, some typical types of motions can be defined as (1) WALK(P_i,P_f), (2) SIDEWALK(P_i,P_f), (3) STAND_UP(P_i,P_f), (4) SQUAT_DOWN(P_i,P_f), (5) SQUAT_UP(P_i,P_f), (6) LIE_DOWN(P_i,P_f), (7) CRAWL(P_i,P_f), (8) CREEP(P_i,P_f), (9) TURN(P_i,P_f) and (10) STRIDE_ACROSS(P_i,P_f), where P_i is the initial position and orientation of the motion and P_f is the final position and orientation of the motion. For example, the motion WALK is described as follows:

Motion WALK(P_i, P_f):

Precondition: STAND(P_i) $\wedge$ EMPTY_SWEPT_VOLUME($|P_f-P_i|$,W_{st},H_{st}) $\wedge$ LESS(α,α_*^{wa})

Postcondition: STAND(P_f)

where the predicate EMPTY_SWEPT_VOLUME($|P_f-P_i|$,W_{st},H_t) is true if the swept volume caused by the stand cuboid with width W_{st} and height H_{st} moving from P_i to P_f is obstacle-free and this swept volume will be found by a path planning algorithm, the predicate LESS(x,y) is true if $x < y$, α is the slope of the floor and α_*^{wa} is the largest slope of the floor on which the robot can walk.

The advantage of the shape-changeable robot model is that it can provide a relatively accurate representation to the high maneuverable multi-limbed robot. Since cuboids with different sizes are used to represent different postures of the robot, more states can be defined for the description of the robot in different types of environments. The more robot states that are defined, the more precise description the robot will have. Consequently the path description of the robot will become more accurate. However, if the number of states is too big, the system may become too complicated to manage.

3. Workspace Model

The quality of a collision-free path planning algorithm depends on not only good representation of a robot but also the good representation of the workspace. In every particular collision-free path planning algorithm, the method to describe the workspace is related to the robot model.

3.1. Current robot workspace descriptions

The purpose of choosing a good workspace representation is to make the robot path planning computational simple and/or accurate. The commonly adopted workspace descriptions are discussed below.

1. *Configuration Space Method*: Conceptually, the configuration space method shrinks a spherically- or polyhedrally-represented robot to a point, while at the same time expanding the polyhedral obstacles in the workspace according to the shape of the robot relative

to a reference point. Once configuration space obstacles are obtained, the collision-free path of the robot can be searched in the configuration free space [7]. This approach works very well when a robot is represented by a fixed-shape object and have translational motions. When rotations of the robot are allowed during its motion, the grown obstacles have an extra dimension for each degree of rotational freedom. Therefore, the computational complexity of the path planning algorithm for rotational motions of a robot is high. Since constructing a configuration space heavily depends on the shape of the robot, it will require additional dimensions to approach the path planning problem when using a shape-changeable robot model.

2. *Critical Curve Method:* The first exact solution to the path planning problem (or the piano mover's problem) is developed in [5]. Obstacles to the robot in the workspace are represented by critical curves. Each critical curve is a curve traced by the reference point of the fixed-shape robot which is represented by a circle or a polygon while the robot moves in contact with an obstacle. Then the free space is partitioned into many regions by critical curves. A collision-free path is searched in the connectivity graph of these regions. The computational complexity of the path planning algorithm associated with this free space representation is $O(n^{2^{(d+6)}})$, where n is the number of edges of the obstacles and d is the number of degrees of freedom of the robot. For the classical piano mover's problem in three dimensions, where d = 6 corresponding to 3 translational and 3 rotational degrees of freedom, the complexity becomes $O(n^{4096})$ [6]. Besides the problem of high computational complexity, the construction of critical curves depends on the fixed shape of the robot. Therefore, the computational complexity of this method is even higher and becomes impractical when used for solving path planning problem with a shape-changeable robot model.

3. *Generalized Cones Method*: Representing the free space in a two dimensional robot workspace by a union of generalized cones is introduced in [14], where each generalized cone is represented as a node in a connectivity graph. A collision-free path is represented by the minimal set of nodes which connects the node containing the start location and the node containing the goal location. The computation time using the generalized cone free space representation is extremely short in practice. Unfortunately, this method does not work well in a very cluttered environment since it is an approximate method. Besides being decomposed to generalized cones, the free space can also be decomposed into several rectangular areas [15], or overlapped convex polygons [16].

4. *Potential Field Method*: Potential field representation of a workspace is widely adopted when the analytical calculation is used to find a collision-free path. This representation is also attractive for combining collision-free path planning with robot control [17]. In the potential field approach, the target position and orientation of a robot are modeled as the source of an attractive force, and obstacles are modeled as sources of repulsive forces. The actual motion of a robot is determined by the resultant vector, which is the sum of the forces acting on the robot. This approach provides a simple elegance for avoiding

obstacles in a local context, but it is very difficult to solve global path planning problems due to the local minima trap.

5. *Octree Method:* The octree representation of a workspace has often been adopted in the collision-free path planning when heuristic database search techniques are used [18]. An octree is a special tree data structure. Starting with a cubical region of the robot work space, the search space is recursively decomposed into eight smaller cubes. The decomposition process continues until a collision-free path is found or a desired resolution is reached. Although the octree representation makes the path search process fast, to map an object into an octree requires a large amount of computations. Moreover, an object needs to be mapped to an octree again if its geometric position is changed.

Since we modeled robots as a set of cuboids, we seek a way to construct the workspace to accommodate the robot model in order to develop a general and computational simple path planning algorithm. All existing workspace descriptions are based on a fixed-shape robot model. Using these workspace descriptions to develop a path planning algorithm for a multi-limbed robot will result in very high computational complexity. Hence, we use a new method to describe the work space based on the shape-changeable robot model.

3.2. Workspace description in shape-changeable robot model

In our approach, the robot states are represented by a set of cuboids with different sizes. It can be observed that when the cuboid robot contacts an obstacle, no matter what shape the obstacle has, the robot "feels" that the obstacle has the shape of a polyhedra column. Therefore, in this approach we assume that the obstacles in the 3-D environment are represented by polyhedral columns. Our strategy to represent the 3-D workspace is to systemically decompose it into smaller subspaces so that the path can be planned easily in each subspace. We first try to project the 3-D environment into a set of 2-D spaces based on the height of state cuboids. Subsequently, the free space of each 2-D space will be decomposed into a set of polygons. The details are discussed in the following subsections.

3.2.1. 2-D projections of 3-D workspace

The motion of a robot is defined as the motion of a state cuboid or a transition between a pair of robot state cuboids. Therefore the height of a basic motion described in Section 2.1.2 is defined as the maximum of the heights of its initial cuboid and final cuboid. Since obstacles are represented by polyhedra columns and the walking robot should always touch the ground, if we use the height H of a robot state and corresponding motion to cut the part of the polyhedra column obstacles that is higher than H, and project the remaining parts to the x-y (horizontal) plane, the collision-free paths for the robot state and corresponding motions in the 3-D environment are the same with those in this 2-D projection. Moreover, it should be noted that projections corresponding to different robot states result in different 2-D spaces. For example, if there is a small door on a wall and the height of the door is greater than the height of the state cuboid LIE(P) and corresponding motion CREEP, but less than the height of the state cuboid STAND(P) and corresponding motion WALK, the position of the door in the horizontal projection of the wall is in the free space for state LIE(P) and motion CREEP, but is not in the free space for state STAND(P) and motion WALK.

To illustrate how to find the 2-D projection for each robot state and corresponding motions, we still use the three states STAND(P), SQUAT(P) and LIE(P) defined earlier as an example. The state cuboids and corresponding motions associated with these three states have three height levels: H_{st} (associated with the state STAND(P)), H_{sq} (associated with the state SQUAT(P)), and H_{li} (associated with the state LIE(P)). Then the 3-D workspace can be horizontally projected to three 2-D spaces called lie-2D-projection, squat-2D-projection, and stand-2D-projection, respectively, based on the three height levels. The obstacles in each 2-D projection are called lie-obstacles, squat-obstacles and stand-obstacles, respectively. Besides obstacles, in some area of a 3-D workspace the robot may need extra effort to pass through. For example, if there is a ramp on the floor, the robot may creep through, but with certain difficulty. To represent these difficulties, the corresponding regions in the 2-D projection are associated with difficulty factors.

Based on the above discussion, the lie-2D-projection and the lie-obstacles can be obtained by the following procedure:

Step 1: Remove all parts of the 3-D workspace that are higher than H_{li}. Subsequently, project the remaining parts of the 3-D workspace to the x-y plane.

Step 2: Check the angle α of the floor to the x-y horizontal plane. Project the zones on the floor with $\alpha > \alpha_*^{cr}$ to the x-y plane, where α_*^{cr} is the largest angle with which the robot can possibly creep through. The projected zones correspond to the lie-obstacles.

Step 3: Project the zones on the floor with $0 < \alpha < \alpha_*^{cr}$ to the x-y plane. The projected zones correspond to regions with a creep difficulty factor D^{cr} (i.e., it represents the degree of difficulty for the robot to creep in this zone).

The squat-2D-projection can be obtained in the similar manner as the lie-2D-projection. The squat-obstacle and regions with crawl difficulty factor are specified in the squat-2D-projection. The stand-2D-projection can also be obtained in the similar manner as the lie-2D-projection. The stand-obstacle and regions with walk difficulty factor are specified in the stand-2D-projection.

However, since a robot can perform the motion STRIDE_ACROSS (which is a motion in the stand level that allows the robot to stride across an obstacle with height less than h_{sa} and width less than w_{sa}), in order to represent completely the stand-2D-projection, besides including the similar steps in the procedure described for the lie-2D-projection, one extra step is needed.

Step 4: Project the objects whose height is less than h_{sa} and whose width is less than w_{sa} in the 3-D workspace to x-y plane. The regions corresponding to the projections of these objects in the stand-2D-projection are considered as the free space but assigned to a difficulty factor D_{sa} (i.e., it represents the degree of difficulty for the robot to stride across the obstacle).

After decomposing the 3-D workspace into a set of 2-D spaces, the problem of planning a collision-free path for a robot in a 3-D environment is reduced to that of planning of collision-free paths for the robot in each 2-D projection and the motion from one 2-D projection to another 2-D projection.

3.2.2. Representation of the free space in each 2-D projection

In order to plan a collision-free path for a robot in a 2-D projection of the 3-D workspace, the 2-D projection space is further decomposed so that the free space in a 2-D projection can be represented by a set of polygons. In a 2-D projection space, a *wall* is defined to be serially connected piece-wise line segments which are the boundaries of the obstacles in the 2-D projection space. A *channel* in the 2-D projection is then defined to be the free space between two walls. The free space in a 2-D projection space may have many channels. To find all the channels in the free space, the method in [19] can be used.

After finding all the channels in the 2-D projection space, the path planning problem is broken down to plan the path for the robot through channels. When a robot is inside a channel, it can see convex corners and concave corners on the walls of the channel (see Figure 1(a)). All regions in the channel that the robot has difficulty to pass through are associated with convex corners. Therefore, based on the position of convex corners, the entire channel can be divided into a set of small convex polygons called *channel elements*. Consequently, the path planning problem is further decomposed into finding the path of the robot through each channel element and the connections of adjacent channel elements.

Suppose there is a channel between two walls W_1 and W_2; the algorithm for dividing the channel into channel elements is given as follows:

Step 1: Find all convex corners on wall W_i, where i= 1,2.

Step 2: For each convex corner v_i^m on W_i, where $m = 1,\ldots,q_i$ and q_i is the number of the convex corners on W_i, choose a point P_j^m on W_j ($j = 1,2,\ j \neq i$) so that

$$|v_i^m P_j^m| = \min\left\{|v_i^m, v_j^n|,\ |v_i^m, A_k|\right\}$$

where $|\ .\ |$ is a norm operation. v_j^n is a convex corner on W_j where $n= 1,\ldots, q_j$ and q_j is the number of the convex corners on W_j. A_k is the projection point from v_i^m to each line segment on W_j where $k = 1, \ldots, p_j$ and p_j is the number of line segment on W_j. Each $v_i^m P_j^m$ is called a barricade in the channel and the space between the two barricades inside the channel is called a channel element.

It can be shown that a barricade between two channel elements is the locally narrowest part in the channel, and two barricades do not intersect. Therefore, each channel element is a convex polygon. We can determine if the robot can pass through a channel by checking whether it can pass through these barricades in the channel.

In order to determine whether a robot can pass through a channel, the channel elements are classified based on their geometric features. Assuming that there is a channel element between two barricades and two pieces of walls s_1 and s_2 (see Figure 1(b)), according to the definition of channel elements, the line segments on s_1 and s_2 should not contain any convex vertices. Therefore, only three forms of line segments on the pieces of the walls correspond to each channel element:

(1) there are several line segments on s_1 or s_2 which form several concave corners,

(2) s_1 or s_2 only consists of one line segment, and

(3) there is no line segment on the s_1 or s_2, i.e., two barricades have a common end.

Based on the combination of these three forms, eight basic patterns of the channel elements can be obtained in (see Figure 2(a)). Since a barricade is a connection of a pair of channel elements, there are at most 64 possible adjacency patterns between two adjacent channel elements. For instance, the connection of channel elements in pattern 1 and 4 forms an adjacency pattern. The barricade between patterns 1 and 4 is denoted barricade 1-4 (see Figure 2(b)).

4. Knowledge-based system approach

Based on the shape-changeable robot model and the channel description of the workspace, the path planning problem can be decomposed into a set of small problems. Each small problem is to determine whether the robot can pass through a barricade in a 2-D projection, or whether the robot can be transferred from one 2-D projection to another 2-D projection. Since channel elements and barricades have relatively simple geometric shape, we can find a set of if-then rules and procedures to solve each small problem. However, since the geometric features of each channel element and barricade are different, the rules and procedures for them are unique and ad hoc. Therefore there is a large amount of knowledge which related to path planning in the barricades and channel elements. To manage this large amount of knowledge and to infer the final solution from it, the knowledge-based system is naturally adopted. Input for the knowledge-based path planning system includes the geometric information of the work space, the specification of a multi-limbed robot, and the initial and final positions of the robot. The output of the system is a collision-free path. Since there is a finite number of barricade patterns, it is possible to complete the knowledge-based system for finite defined robot states and motions and thus find a converged path for the robot.

The knowledge-based system contains four major components: a global database, an interpreter, a knowledge base, and a controller (see Figure 3). The global database contains all the geometric information of the workspace and the robot. The interpreter translates the geometric information of the workspace to the channel elements based on labeling algorithm [20] and algorithms given in Section 3.2.2. The knowledge base contains all knowledge about how the robot passes each barricade and how the robot will be transferred from one 2-D projection to another 2-D projection. The controller uses the geometric information about the channel elements and the barricades obtained from the interpreter to match suitable rules in the knowledge base. If a collision-free motion between two channel elements is generated by the rules and procedures in the knowledge base, this collision-free motion will be recorded in a connection graph. In the connection graph, a vertex is a channel element and an edge is a collision-free motion of the robot. To construct the knowledge-based, path planning system, two key problems remain: how to build a knowledge-base and how to generate a connection graph. These problems are discussed in the following subsections.

4.1. The connection graph

As mentioned above, the interpreter translates the geometric data of the workspace to channel elements and the relationship between channel elements. The knowledge base determines which barricades the robot can pass. This information must be memorized so that a collision-free path can be found. A connection graph is used for this purpose here. The connection graph consists of several connection subgraphs, each of which is associated with a 2-D projection of the 3-D workspace. A vertex of the connection subgraph is a channel element in the associated 2-D projection space. An edge exists between two adjacent vertices in the connection subgraph if there is a collision-free motion of the robot between the vertices in a 2-D projection. An edge exists between two adjacent vertices in different subgraphs if there is a collision-free motion changing the robot from one state to another. For example, if a robot can pass a barricade between a pair of channel elements in the stand-2D-projection by walking, then the edge exists between these two corresponding vertices and can be labeled as motion WALK. Similarly, when motion SQUAT_DOWN is collision-free, an edge is defined which connects one vertex in the stand connection subgraph and one vertex in the squat connection subgraph. The edge associated with each motion can be assigned with a unique motion difficulty factor. Once a connection graph is generated, a collision-free path for the shape-changeable robot can be searched within it.

4.2. Building the path planning knowledge base

To generate the connection graph, we need to know (1) how the robot, modeled as cuboids with different sizes, can pass through each barricade in each 2-D projection of the 3-D workspace, and (2) how the robot can be transferred from one 2-D projection to another 2-D projection of the robot's workspace. Since passing through different patterns of barricades may involve different procedures and rules, the patterns of the barricades must be studied individually. The knowledge about how to pass each pattern of barricades is stored in the knowledge-base.

The procedure for determining the rules to generate motions between two adjacent channel elements in the same 2-D projection is based on the geometric information of these two channel elements. The rules for passing barricade 1-4 are discussed as an example. The geometric futures of barricade 1-4 are that (1) both walls of the channel element in pattern 1 consist of only one line segment and (2) one wall of the element in pattern 4 is a line segment and the other wall consists of several line segments that form a set of concave corners (see Figure 4). For convenience, in Figure 4, we denote the angles of the concave corners as θ_j, where j = 1,...,h and h is the number of the concave corners on a wall of the channel element in pattern 4. The line segment on the other wall of the channel element in pattern 4 is denoted as l_1. The wall of the channel element in pattern 1 connected to l_1 is denoted as l_2. Barricades which are on the boundary of the channel element in pattern 1 are denoted as B_1 and B_2. B_2 is assumed to be the barricade between the channel element in pattern 1 and the channel element in pattern 4. The other barricade of the channel element in pattern 4 is denoted as B_3. In order to plan the path for a robot which is projected to a 2-D plane as a rectangle to pass through the barricade, the critical configuration approach in [21] may be used. In [21], path planning for a rectangle to passes a corner formed by two lanes (which are not necessarily parallel, see Figure 5) is discussed. The results show that if the value of the robot's width, the sizes of the lanes, and the angle of the corner (θ) are given, in order to pass through the corner, the robot can only have a length less than the maximum allowable length a^*. The analytic solution to calculate a^* is provided in [21]. If the length of the given robot is less than a^*, two procedures, PROCEDURE I for the angle of the corner θ within [0°, 90°] and PROCEDURE II for the angle of the corner θ within [90°, 180°], are given [21] for planning the path of the robot through the corner.

In order to plan the path for the robot to pass barricade 1-4, the upper limit a_j^* of the robot's length for each corner θ_i must be calculated. If one of a_j^* is less than the length of the robot, then the robot cannot pass this barricade. If all of a_j^*'s are larger than the length of the robot, PROCEDURE I and PROCEDURE II are modified based on interaction between the adjacent corners. Modified PROCEDURE I and PROCEDURE II can be used to plan a path for the robot. Based on this discussion, the path planning rules for barricade 1-4 are given as follows (Here it is assumed that both channel elements can contain the robot. If one of channel elements cannot contain the robot, more adjacent channel elements need to be considered and more rules are needed):

RULE 1:

IF this is barricade 1-4,
and the line segments l_1 and l_2 are aligned,
and the line segment B_1, B_2 and B_3 are longer than the width of the robot,

THEN the robot can pass through the barricade by aligning its centerline in parallel with line segments l_1 and l_2.

RULE 2:

IF this is barricade 1-4,
and the line segment l_1 and l_2 are aligned,

and one of the line segment B_1, B_2 and B_3 is shorter than the width of the robot,

THEN there is no collision-free path for the robot to pass through barricade 1-4.

RULE 3:

IF this is barricade 1-4,
and one of the upper limit of the length of the robot, a_j^*, for a corner in the barricade is less than the length of the robot,

THEN there is no collision-free path for the robot to pass through the barricade.

RULE 4:

IF this is barricade 1-4,
and all the upper limits of the length of the robot a_j^* for the corners in the barricade are larger than the length of the robot,

THEN the collision-free path can be generated by modified PROCEDURE I for $\theta_i \in [0^o, 90^o]$ and modified PROCEDURE II for $\theta_i \in [90^o, 180^o]$.

The generation of rules for motion between channel elements which are not in the same 2-D projection is also based on the geometric information of two corresponding channel elements. In particular, it is based on the geometric shape and the size of the overlapped area of these two channel elements, the size of the robot and the swept volume of the robot motion. In order to complete the knowledge base, the channel elements and barricades must be studied individually. After all the rules are found for the knowledge base, this knowledge-based system can be used to construct the connection graph. Finally, a collision-free path for the robot in the entire free space can be searched in the connection graph.

5. Discussion

In previous sections, we have discussed the knowledge-based path planning system. It is shown that the shape-changeable robot model can easily be used in the knowledge-based, path planning system. This work can be extended to the following directions:

(1) Improve the shape-changeable robot model: It is desirable to formulate theoretically a relationship between the number of states defined and the accuracy achieved in the shape-changeable model. To reduce the complexity of the knowledge-based system, a method is needed to generate the minimum set of robot states for a given workspace and the robot task.

(2) Improve the workspace description: For a more complicated environment, e.g., a stairway, the method for the decomposition of the 3-D workspace cannot be effectively used and thus the method of work space modelling should be modified. One possible solution to this problem is to allow the projection of the 3-D workspace to planes other than ground.

(3) Expand the knowledge base for trajectory planning: Trajectory planning for a robot involves planning a path of the robot and planning the timing for robot position along the path. Here the knowledge-based system is used for planning the collision-free path only. The internal characteristics of the robot, such as kinematics and dynamics, are not considered. In fact, the joint force calculations, which involve robot kinematics and dynamics, can be considered as rules and can be incorporated into the knowledge-based system for trajectory planning. Research in this direction may effectively give a new approach to trajectory planning.

(4) On-line planning and learning: The aforementioned path planning method decomposes a complicated problem into a set of simple problems. Channel element and barricade generation are based on the known environment information. In fact, channel elements and barricades can be obtained by sensory feedback, and the 2-D projections and the connection graph can be constructed gradually during robot motion. This is actually a learning process for the robot [22].

6. Conclusion

Robot path planning is a fundamental problem in robotics research. Although this problem has been studied for many years, there is still no successful algorithm for robot path planning with many degrees of freedom, such as with a multi-limbed working robot. This research provided a fundamental framework for new robot modelling, and workspace description. Specifically, the shape-changeable robot model provides a new approach to utilize the maneuverability of the multi-limbed robot in the path planning process. The knowledge-based, path planning system is an open-ended system. New planning knowledge can be gradually added to the system without affecting the old knowledge. The robot model and workspace description can also be modified without affecting the overall structure of the system. It is believed that human beings and living creatures learn path planning using this method.

References

[1]. C. A. Klein and S. Kittivacharapong, "Optimal Force Distribution for the Legs of a Walking Machine with Friction Cone Constraints," *IEEE Trans. Robotics and Automation*, Vol 6, pp 73 - 85, Feb. 1990.

[2]. S. Y. Aleshinsky and V. M. Zatsiorsky, "Human Locomotion in Space Analyzed Biomechanically Through a Multi-Link Chain Model," *J. Biomechanics* Vol. 11. pp 101-108, 1978.

[3]. R. L. Huston and C. E. Passerello, "ON the Dynamics of a Human Body Model," *J. Biomechanics*, Vol. 4, pp 369 - 378, 1971.

[4]. J.T. Schwartz and C. K. Yap, "Advances in Robotics," *Lawrence Erlbaum Associates*, Hillsdale, New Jersey, 1987.

[5]. J. T. Schwartz and M. Sharir, " On the Piano Movers' Problem: III. Coordinating the Motion of Several Independent Bodies: The Special Case of Circular Bodies Moving Amidst Polygonal Barriers," *The International Journal of Robotics Research,* Vol.2, No.3, pp 46-75, Fall 1983.

[6]. J. T. Schwartz and M. Sharir, "On the Piano Movers' Problem: I. The Special Case of a Rigid Polygonal Body Moving Amidst Polygonal Barriers," *Commun. Pure Appl. Math.*, Vol.36, pp 345-398, 1983.

[7]. T. Lozano-Perez, "Spatial Planning: A Configuration Space Approach," *IEEE Trans on Computer, Vol C-32, No. Feb 1983.*

[8]. N. G. Bourbakis, "A Heuristic, Real-Time Path Planning for Collision-Free Navigation in a Dynamic Multiple Robots Unknown Environment," *Proc. International Conference on Tools for Artificial Intelligence*, Virginia, Oct. 1989.

[9]. C. L. Dym, "Issues in the Design and Implementation of Expert System," *AI EDAM*, Vol. 1, NO. 1, pp 37 - 46, 1987.

[10]. C. K. Yap, "Coordinated the Motion of Several Discs," *Technical Report No.105*, New York University Computer Science Department, Courant Institute of Mathematical Science, 1984.

[11]. L. Gouzenes, "Strategies for Solving Collision-free Trajectories Problems for Mobile and Manipulator Robots," *The International Journal of Robotics Research*, Vol 3, No. 4, pp 51 - 65, 1984.

[12]. A. A. G. Requicha, "Representations for Rigid Solid: Theory, Methods, and Systems," *J. ACM Computer Survey* Vol, 12, No. 4, pp 437 - 463, December 1980.

[13]. P. Tournassoud, "A Strategy for Obstacle Avoidance and its Application to Multi-robot Systems," *Proc. IEEE International Conference on Robotics and Automation*, pp 1124 - 1229, San Francisco, CA, 1986.

[14]. R. A. Brooks, "Solving the Find-Path Problem by Good Representation of Free Space," *IEEE Transactions on System, Man, and Cybernetics*, SMC-13, 190 - 197, March/April

1983.

[15]. J. S. Singh and M. D. Wagh, "Robot Path Planning Using Intersecting Convex Shapes: Analysis and Simulation," *IEEE J. Robotics and Automation*, Vol. RA-3, No. 2, pp. 101-108, Apr, 1987.

[16]. R. Chatila, "Path Planning and Environmental Learning in a Mobile Robot System," *Proc. European Conf. on Artificial Intelligence*, Orsay, France, 1982.

[17]. Y. K. Hwang and N. Ahuja, "Path Planning Using a Potential Field Representation," *Proc. of IEEE Int. Conf. on Robotics and Automation,* pp 648-649, April 1988.

[18]. B. Faverjon, "Obstacle Avoidance Using an Octree in the Configuration Space of a Manipulator," *IEEE International Conference on Robotics*, pp 504 - 512, 1984.

[19]. S. H. Suh and K. G. Shin, "A Variational Dynamic Programming Approach to Robot-Path Planning With a Distance-Safety Criterion," *IEEE Journal of Robotics and Automation*, Vol. 4, No. 3. June 1988.

[20]. E. Rich, "Artificial Intelligence," *McGraw-Hill Book Company*, 1983.

[21]. C. T. Lee, "Critical Configuration Path Planning and Knowledge- Based Task Planning for Robot Systems," Ph. D. Thesis, Purdue University, May 1990.

[22]. B. J. Oommen, S. S. Iyengar, S. V. N. Rao, and R. L. Kashyap, "Robot Navigation in Unknown Terrains Using Learned Visibility Graph. Part I: The Disjoint Convex Obstacle Case," *Proc. National Conference on Artificial Intelligence*, Philadelphia, 1986.

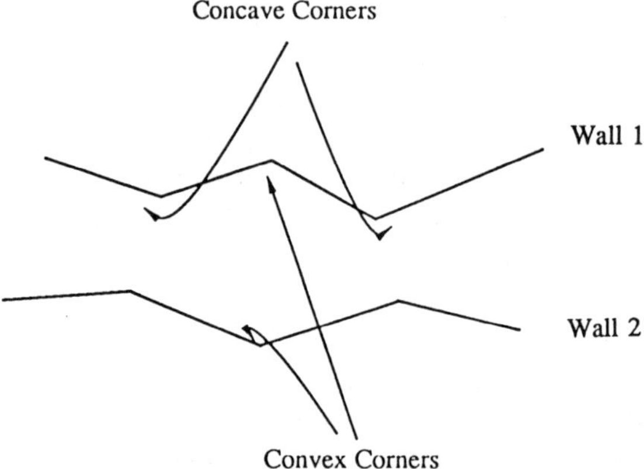

Figure 1(a): A channel with convex corners and concave corners.

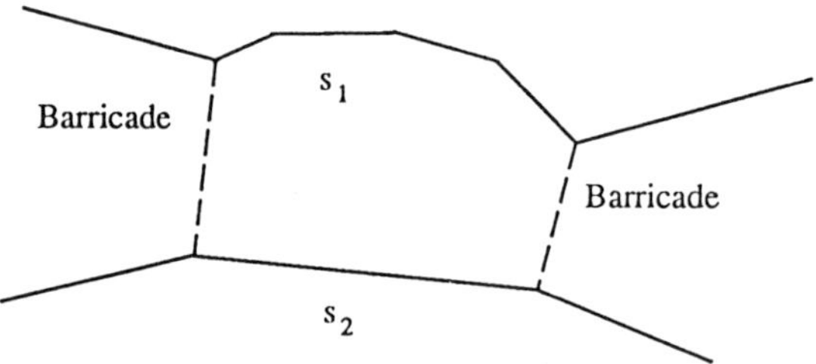

Figure 1(b): a channel element constructed by two barricades and two pieces of walls, s_1 and s_2.

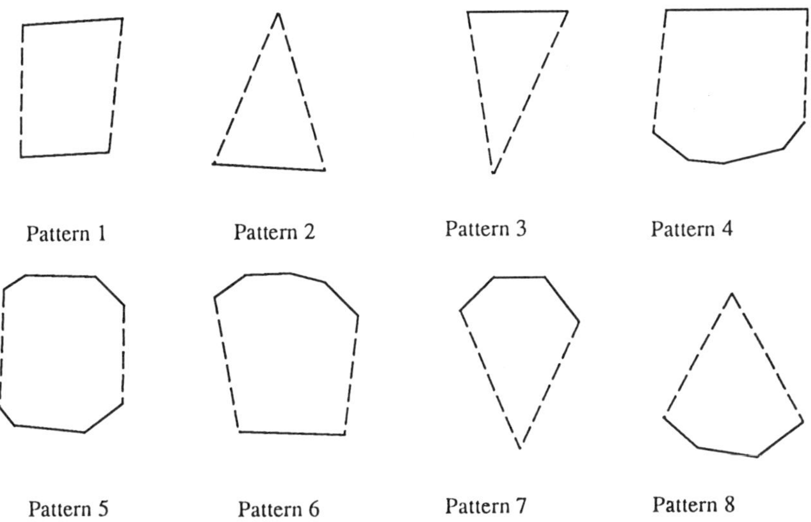

Figure 2(a): Eight patterns of channel elements.

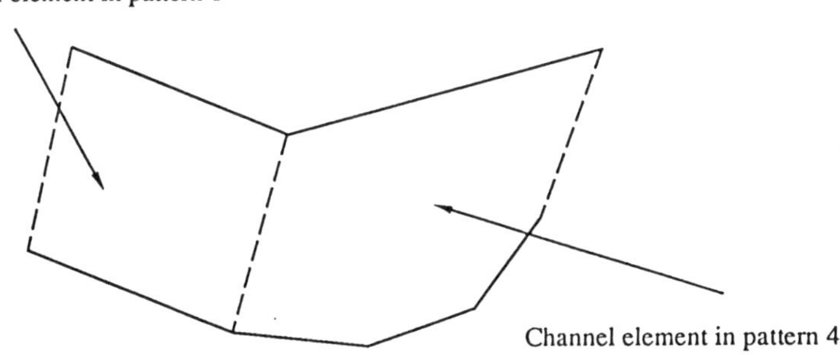

Figure 2(b): Barricad 1-4 formed by a channel element in pattern 1 and a channel element in pattern 4.

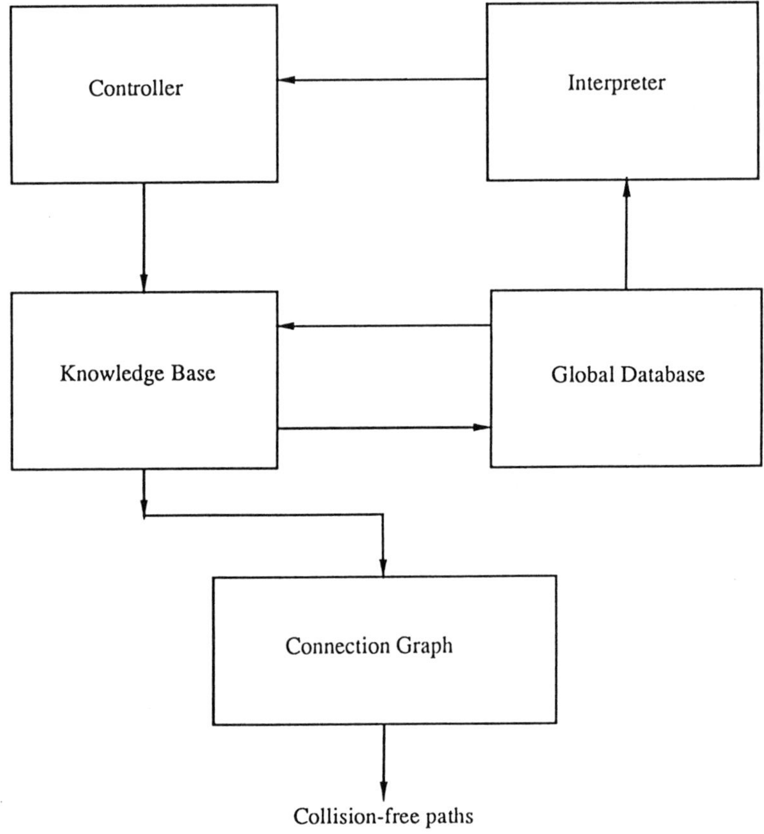

Figure 3: The structure of the knowledge-based path planning system.

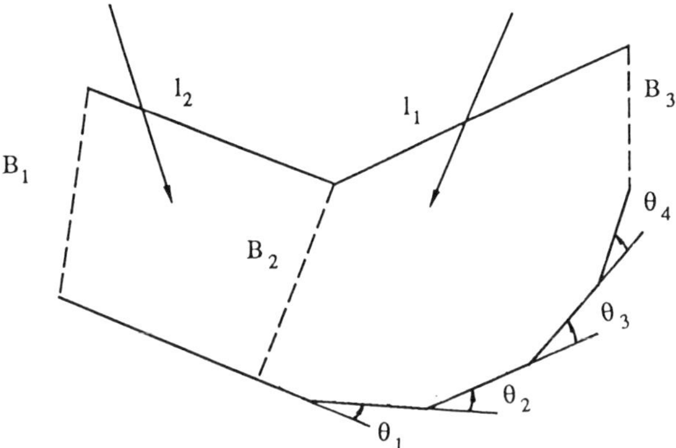

Figure 4: The barricade in pattern 1-4 with labeled notations.

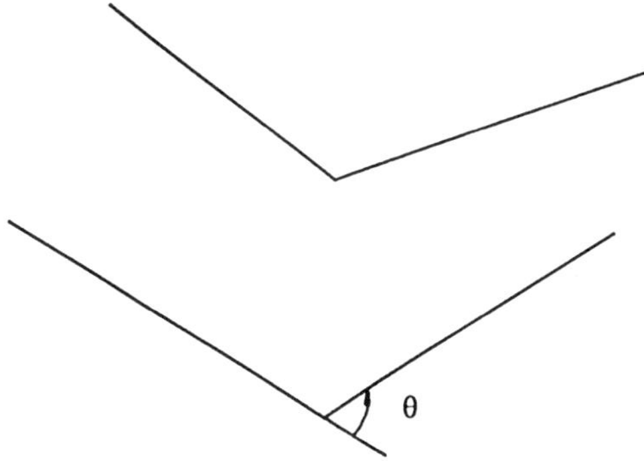

Figure 5: A corner used in [21] which formed by two lanes.

SECTION 5

AI LANGUAGES

CHAPTER 9

ADVANCED PARSING TECHNOLOGY FOR KNOWLEDGE-BASED SHELLS

JAMES R. KIPPS
Department of Information and Computer Science
The University of California, Irvine
Irvine, CA 92717, USA

ABSTRACT

With the exception of "natural language" front-ends, formal syntax and parsing techniques are aspects of knowledge-based shells that receive little attention. Although they are rarely even acknowledged as issues in shell development, syntax and parsing play a significant role in determining how a shell is used and regarded by programmers. The syntax of a knowledge-based shell formally defines the textual format for knowledge expression. The quality of a syntax is characterized by its expressiveness, clarity, and readability. The parsing technology available to the shell developer is a limiting factor in achieving a sophisticated and high-quality syntax. Commonly available parser generators, based on restrictive SLR, LR(1), and LL(1) technologies, severly inhibit "human friendly" syntaxes; few of these are even available for LISP-based systems. In this chapter, I present a parser generator for advanced applications, such as developing a knowledge-based shell, and describe the parsing technology on which it is based.

1. Introduction

1.1. Syntax and Knowledge-Based Shells

Commercial vendors of knowledge-based shells typically package their wares as programming environments for building expert systems. At the heart of each such environment is a knowledge-based programming language (KBPL). As with conventional programming languages, KBPLs have a syntax and semantics. The semantics of a KBPL defines how knowledge is represented and interpreted, as well as how the interpretation of knowledge is controlled. The syntax of a KBPL defines how knowledge is expressed. The quality of a syntax can be measured in terms of the the ease with which ideas can be conceptualized and written and by the clarity with they can later be read and understood. Although the semantics of knowledge representation and interpretation have been explored extensively in both the academic and commercial communities, formal syntaxes and parsing technologies for knowledge expression have received little attention.[a]

One factor that contributes to this seeming lack of interest in syntactic issues is that many vendors believe they can shield their customers from the underlying KBPL with intelligent graphical interfaces, thus making the quality of their KBPL's syntax a nonissue. Of course, there is always a certain subset of end-users who disagree with or feel limited by a vendor's view of "intelligent" and who wish to bypass the interface completely. In addition, the syntax is still an issue for the vendor's support personnel, who often have to deal directly with the KBPL.

A more significant factor, however, is the difficulty of implementing parsers for "human-friendly" syntaxes. For C-based shells, the ready availability of LR(1) and LL(1) parser generators has actually made this situation worse by forcing language designers to adapt to their limitations. For LISP-based shells, where existing parser generators are *not* so readily available, KBPLs often adopt a LISP-like syntax and rely on the LISP reader for parsing. The troubling aspect of this is that parsing technologies are available that can be used to develop a new generation of parser generators for KBPLs and other advanced languages. LR(1) and LL(1) parsing technologies are over two decades old. New parsing technologies have been developed since that can be used to generate practical parsers for KBPLs with sophisticated syntaxes. An example of one such technology is Tomita's algorithm[1] for general LR (GLR) parsing, which is defined as a variation on standard LR techniques. The RAND Advanced Compiler Kit (RACK)[2] is a new parser generator for GLR applications and is based on Tomita's algorithm.

1.2. Beyond LR(k)

AI research necessarily spawns the development of advanced programming languages and systems as vehicles for experimentation and demonstration of concepts. LISP[3], PROLOG[4], and OPS5[5] are three lasting examples, but there are many others, including GPS[6], PLANNER[7], KRL[8], EMYCIN[9], and ROSIE[10]. The KBPLs of most commercial knowledge-based shells have their roots in one or more such languages. All of these languages have a syntax and a parser subsystem for translating input programs into an interpretable representation.

The construction of parsers for syntaxes of even limited sophistication is a non-trivial task without a parser generator. As depicted in Fig. 1, a parser generator is a system that outputs a parser program. The parser translates source input, written in some target language, into a usable form. The input to the parser generator is a file of grammar rules describing the syntax of the target language. Generation is depicted with solid arrows, and data flow through the parser program is depicted

[a]This excludes work on "natural language" front-ends and menu-driven parsing.

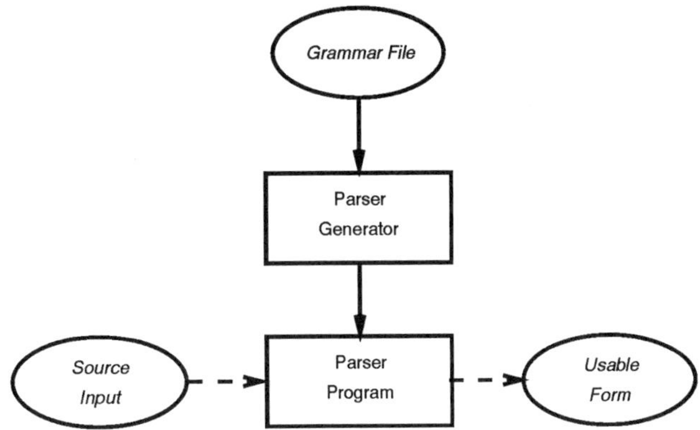

Fig. 1. Generic parser generator.

with dashed arrows. YACC[11] is an example of a commonly used parser generator for languages developed under UNIX.[b]

Because KBPLs are intended for encoding of expert knowledge, language developers should strive for higher-levels of sophistication than are found in conventional programming languages. Unfortunately, commonly available parser generators, such as YACC, are limited to LR(k) and LL(k) grammars (typically for $k \leq 1$), which severely restrict the level of sophistication of a language. (An LR(k) grammar describes a language whose sentences can be recognized in a single backup-free pass if at most k tokens of look-ahead are available.) While LR(1) grammars can cover most conventional programming languages, there are many interesting languages for which no LR(k) grammar exists, for any k. The example that initiated much of this work is ROSIE, an English-like language for building expert systems.

Samples of rules written using ROSIE's syntax are shown in Fig. 2. Propositions and actions have the syntax of English sentences and imperative clauses. Data elements can be referenced with noun phrases and anaphoras. Verb and noun phrases can be modified by prepositional phrases, and noun phrases can further be modified by relative clauses. In addition, programming blocks are delimited by punctuation marks (i.e., commas, semicolons, and periods) rather than begin-end statements or curly braces. On the whole, this gives ROSIE a highly readable yet highly ambiguous English-like syntax, requiring a parser with arbitrary look-ahead and parse-time disambiguation.

During the development of ROSIE, we experimented with several parsing techniques. The first was based on a multi-track algorithm[12]. Another used an unpublished technique developed by Ross Quinlan. Later, these approaches were discarded in favor of a new technique[13] that eventually evolved into the RACK parser generator[14].

[b]UNIX is a trademark of Bell Laboratories.

```
If any red battalion does advance toward any strategic
        objective that is undefended,
    move a blue battalion to that objective and
    report 'that battalion was directed to that objective'.

For each blue battalion (BBTL) in Sector #15,
    advise BBTL to 'move to Red River Crossing' and
    assert BBTL was given a new directive.
```

Fig. 2. Sample ROSIE rules.

1.3. RACK: The RAND Advanced Compiler Kit

RACK is a "next generation" parser generator for use in building advanced programming languages, such as KBPLs. RACK provides a general tool for specifying the grammatical structure of source programs, as well as code to be invoked when particular structures are recognized. RACK turns the specification into a parser program that handles the input process. **RACK parsers are unique in their ability to recognize non-LR(k) languages**. Using RACK, language designers can focus on "human factors" in crafting their syntaxes without otherwise being restricted by the parsing technology.

RACK generates practical parsers. RACK parsers are based on Tomita's algorithm for fast general context-free parsing. The execution speed and memory requirements of RACK parsers compare favorably with parsers generated by YACC. On LR(1) languages, the performance is identical. On non-LR(k) languages or when $k > 1$ (languages for which YACC cannot generate a parser) RACK parsers have near-YACC performance on input segments that require no look-ahead. When look-ahead is required, performance is impacted by a small factor.

1.4. Summary

In the remainder of this chapter, I present the RACK parser generator and describe the parsing technology on which it is based. First, I review conventional parsing concepts, define terminology, and outline standard LR parsing and its limitations. Second, I discuss GLR parsing, informally define Tomita's algorithm, and clarify concepts in Tomita's algorith with a annotated example. Third, I present RACK and its significant features. Finally, I show an empirical analysis comparing RACK parsers to parsers generated by YACC.

2. Background

2.1. Practical Parsing

Throughout this chapter I assume familiarity on the part of the reader with concepts from compiler construction and formal language theory. Nonetheless, a review of these concepts is helpful to understanding the explanation of the Tomita's algorithm that appears in Section 3.

Parsing techniques have been actively studied since the early days of computer science. Context-free grammars (CFGs)[15,16] have been used extensively for describing the syntax of programming and natural languages, and numerous algorithms have been developed to recognize sentences in languages so described. Some of these algorithms are general, e.g., Earley's algorithm[17] and the Cocke-Younger-Kasami algorithm[18], in the sense that they are applicable to all or most CFGs; others, such as the LL, operator precedence, predictive, and LR parsing algorithms,[19] are more restricted and are applicable to only a small subclass of CFGs, including the grammars of most conventional programming languages. These latter algorithms are more efficient than the former because they take advantage of inherent features in the class of grammars they recognize; parsers based upon these algorithms are often referred to as practical parsers.

Most practical parsers analyze the syntax of their input in a single, deterministic pass, without need of backup. Each input token is examined only once, and, at the time it is examined, there is sufficient information available to make all necessary parsing decisions. In his famous paper, Knuth[20] established a family of CFGs known as LR(k) grammars and provided an effective test to determine, for a given positive integer k, whether a grammar belonged to the LR(k) class. The connection to practical parsers mentioned above is that an LR(k) grammar describes a language, all of whose sentences can be parsed in a single backup-free parse, if at most k symbols of look-ahead are available.

2.2. Terminology

A *language* is a set of strings over a finite set of symbols called called *terminals* (or *tokens*); tokens appear in lowercase, e.g., a, b, c. A *context-free grammar* is used as a formal device for specifying which strings are in a language; hereafter, grammar is used to mean context-free grammar. Besides tokens, a grammar uses another set of symbols called *nonterminals*; nonterminals appear in uppercase, e.g., A, B, C. Tokens designate the lexical categories of the language, i.e., the elementary interpretation of input character strings, such as identifiers, numbers, and operators. Nonterminal symbols designate the syntactic categories of the language, i.e., the interpretation of token sequences, such as expressions, statements, and subroutines. Together the tokens and nonterminal symbols of a language make up its *vocabulary*; individual vocabulary symbols appear as uppercase letters in italics, e.g., A, B, C, while strings of zero or more vocabulary symbols appear as Greek letters, e.g., α, β, γ. The empty string is ϵ.

A grammar consists of a finite set of rewrite rules or *productions* of the form

$$\mathtt{A} \rightarrow \alpha$$

where the A component is called the *left-hand side* of the production, and the α component is called its *right-hand side.* The nonterminal that stands for "sentence" is called the *root* (R) of the grammar. Productions with the same nonterminal on their left-hand side are called *alternatives* of that nonterminal. For example,

$$\begin{aligned} \mathtt{A} &\rightarrow \alpha \\ \mathtt{A} &\rightarrow \beta \\ \mathtt{A} &\rightarrow \gamma \end{aligned}$$

are alternatives of A. Productions of the form

$$\mathtt{A} \rightarrow \epsilon$$

are called *null productions.*

The rest of the definitions are given with respect to a particular grammar G, called the *source grammar.* We write

$$\alpha \Rightarrow \beta$$

if $\exists \gamma, \delta, \eta, \mathtt{A}$ such that $\alpha = \gamma \mathtt{A} \delta$ and $\beta = \gamma \eta \delta$ and $\mathtt{A} \rightarrow \eta$ is a production. We write

$$\alpha \stackrel{*}{\Rightarrow} \beta$$

(α *derives* β) if $\exists \alpha_0, \alpha_1, \cdots, \alpha_m$ $(m \geq 0)$ such that

$$\alpha = \alpha_0 \Rightarrow \alpha_1 \Rightarrow \cdots \Rightarrow \alpha_m = \beta.$$

The sequence $\alpha_0, \cdots, \alpha_m$ is called a derivation (of β from α).

A *sentential form* is a string α such that the root $R \stackrel{*}{\Rightarrow} \alpha$. A *sentence* is a sentential form consisting entirely of terminal symbols. The *language defined by a grammar, L(G),* is the set of G's sentences. Any sentential form may be represented in at least one way as a *derivation tree,* reflecting the steps made in deriving it (though not the order of the steps). The *degree of ambiguity* of a sentence is the number of its distinct derivation trees. A sentence is *unambiguous* if it has degree 1 of ambiguity. A grammar is *unambiguous* if each of its sentences is unambiguous.

A *recognizer* is an algorithm that takes as its input a string and either *accepts* or *rejects* it, depending on whether the string is a sentence of the language defined by the source grammar. A *parser* is a recognizer that outputs the set of all legal derivation trees of a string upon acceptance.

2.3. Review of LR Parsing

In this section, I review concepts in standard LR parsing, the exact definition and operation of which can be found in Aho and Ullman[19], by presenting a generic LR

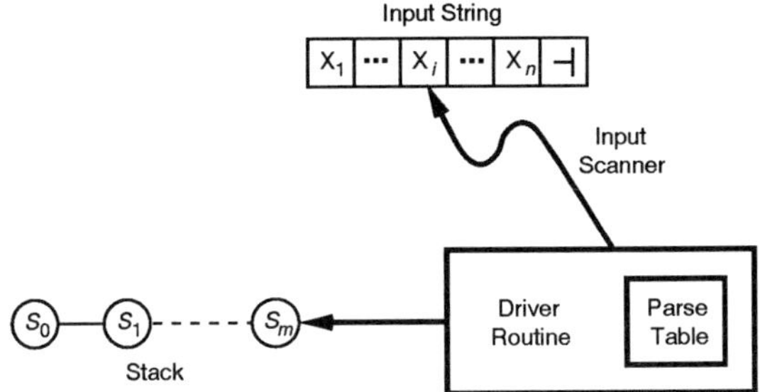

Fig. 3. Generic architecture of an LR parser.

parser as a recognizer. LR parsers derive their name from the fact that they scan their input from *L*eft-to-right and construct a *R*ightmost derivation tree in reverse. For all but trivial examples, LR parsers are too complex to implement by hand. However, their implementation is straightforward to automate, giving rise to a class of software tools called LR parser generators. Such tools take a context-free grammar as input and output an LR parser for the language described.

LR parsers can be thought of as consisting of two parts: a driver routine and a parse table. Typically, the parser produced by an LR parser generator will always contain the same driver routine; only the parse table changes. In this way, LR parser generators are actually parse table generators.

Figure 3 depicts a generic LR parser. It has a input string, a stack, and a parse table. The input string $x_1 \cdots x_n$ is scanned from left-to-right, one token at a time. Each stack element records a symbol s, called a *parse state* (or *state*).[c] The mth element, labeled s_m, is at the top-of-stack and is referred to as the state of the parser.

The parse table consists of two parts, an action table and a goto table, which are implemented as look-up functions, ACTION and GOTO. The action table maps states and tokens to parser actions. ACTION(s,x) takes a state s and input token x and returns one of four parser actions:

1. Shift to state s'.
2. Reduce using production p.
3. Accept.
4. Error.

The goto table maps states and nonterminal symbols to states. GOTO(s,D) takes a state s and nonterminal symbol D and returns a state s', which corresponds to the action 'shift to state s'.'

Each move of the driver routine is determined by consulting the action table entry for s_m (the state on the top of the stack) and x_i (the input token being scanned). The moves resulting from the four parser actions listed above cause the driver to behave

[c]Stack elements can also record other useful information, such as the sequences of the derivations made in reaching a state.

as described below.

1. If ACTION(s_m,x_i) = 'shift to state s',' the driver executes a shift move by creating a new top-of-stack element for state s'. Afterwards, the input scanner is advanced to x_{i+1}, making it the new current input token.
2. If ACTION(s_m,x_i) = 'reduce using production p,' the process executes a reduce move. A reduce move corresponds to the recognition of a rightmost derivation of production p. Production p has the form

$$D_p \rightarrow C_{p1} \cdots C_{p\bar{p}}$$

where $\bar{p}$ is the length of its right-hand side. The top $\bar{p}$ stack elements, $s_{m-(\bar{p}-1)} \cdots s_m$, correspond to the vocabulary symbols $C_{p1} \cdots C_{p\bar{p}}$. The driver routines executes a reduce action by removing these $\bar{p}$ elements from the stack, which makes $s_{m-\bar{p}}$ the new top-of-stack. Having recognized the nonterminal D_p, the driver then executes a shift action to the state s' (where GOTO($s_{m-\bar{p}}$,D_p) = s') by creating a new top-of-stack element for s'. The input scanner is *not* advanced, and the current input token is unchanged.
3. If ACTION(s_m,x_i) = 'accept,' the driver halts and returns success.
4. If ACTION(s_m,x_i) = 'error,' the driver calls an error handler, e.g., to display a message indicating where the error was detected in the input string.

The driver routine first initializes the stack with a stack element for the start state of the parse table, designated as state 0, and then sets the input scanner to the first token, x_1, of the input string. Finally, the driver repeatedly executes the moves determined by the action table entry for its state and the current input token until the input string is accepted or rejected.

As an example, consider the simple English-like grammar shown in Fig. 4. The nonterminals `S`, `NP`, `VP`, and `PP` correspond to the syntactic classes: sentence, noun phrase, verb phrase, and prepositional phrase; the tokens `det`, `noun`, `verb`, and `prep` correspond to the lexical classes: determiner, noun, verb, and preposition. Each sentence in this language contains a noun phrase, followed by a verb phrase, followed by an arbitrary number of prepositional phrases.

The parse table for the example grammar is shown in Fig. 5. In building the parser table the grammar is augmented by a 0th production

$$D_0 \rightarrow \mathtt{S}\dashv$$

where nonterminal `S` is the root of the grammar; the symbol '⊣' is a special terminal that denotes end-of-sentence and appears only as the last symbol of an input string. Entries in the action table have the meaning:

sh$s$ – shift to state s.
re$p$ – reduce using production p.
acc – accept.
blank – error.

Entries s in the goto table have the meaning: 'shift to state s.'

(1) S → NP VP
(2) S → S PP
(3) NP → noun
(4) NP → det noun
(5) PP → prep NP
(6) VP → verb NP

Fig. 4. Example LR grammar.

State	Action Table					Goto Table			
	det	noun	verb	prep	⊣	NP	PP	VP	S
0	sh3	sh5				8			1
1				sh2	acc		7		
2	sh3	sh5				6			
3		sh4							
4			re4	re4	re4				
5			re3	re3	re3				
6				re5	re5				
7				re2	re2				
8			sh9					11	
9	sh3	sh5				10			
10				re6	re6				
11				re1	re1				

Fig. 5. LR parse table.

Figure 6 traces the nine moves made by the driver when parsing the input

`I saw the man`

Assume that `I` and `man` are instances of the token `noun`, `saw` of the token `verb`, and `the` of the token `det`. The $n + 1$st input token '⊣' denotes end-of-sentence.

The stack column shows the contents of the stack (as ordered states) at the beginning of each move; top-of-stack is the rightmost state. Under the input column, a dot '∘' prefixes the input token being scanned. When a segment of the input has been recognized in a derivation of some nonterminal (i.e., after a reduce move), it is replaced by that nonterminal. The action column shows the action table entry for each move; for reduce moves, the subsequent goto table entry is also shown.

In move 1, the parser is in state 0 scanning the first input symbol `I(noun)`. ACTION(0,`noun`) = sh5, so the driver executes a shift move, making state 5 the current state; the input scanner is advanced to `saw`. In move 2, the driver is in state 5 scanning `saw(verb)`. ACTION(5,`verb`) = re3, so the driver executes a reduce move. Because the length of the right-hand side of production 3 (`NP` → `noun`) is equal to one, one element (for state 5) is removed from the stack. This makes state 0 the current state. The driver then consults the goto table entry for state 0 and `NP`. GOTO(0,`NP`) = 8, so the driver executes a shift move to state 8. In move 3, the current state is state 8 and `I` has been replaced by `NP`, but the input scanner is still at `saw`. Moves 3 through 9 are determined in a manner similar to moves 1 and 2.

2.4. Limitations of Standard LR Parsing

Standard LR parsing only recognizes a restricted set of context-free grammars. The general restriction is that the grammars must be unambiguous with k symbol look-ahead. Since context-free languages are inherently ambiguous[21], there will always be a set languages for which no LR(k) grammar exists for any k, some of which will nonetheless be interesting and desirable.

To illustrate this limitation, consider the two productions shown in Fig. 7 defining an *if-then-else* statement. The first production will be called the *simple-if* rule and

	Stack	Input	Action	
1.	0	∘I saw the man ⊣	sh5	
2.	0 5	NP ∘saw the man ⊣	re3	GOTO(0,NP) = 8
3.	0 8	NP ∘saw the man ⊣	sh9	
4.	0 8 9	NP saw ∘the man ⊣	sh3	
5.	0 8 9 3	NP saw the ∘man ⊣	sh4	
6.	0 8 9 3 4	NP saw the man ∘⊣	re4	GOTO(9,NP) = 10
7.	0 8 9 10	NP saw NP ∘⊣	re6	GOTO(8,VP) = 11
8.	0 8 11	NP VP ∘⊣	re1	GOTO(0,S) = 1
9.	0 1	S ∘⊣	acc	

Fig. 6. Moves of an LR parser.

(1) STMT → if COND STMT

(2) STMT → if COND STMT else STMT

Fig. 7. Two ambiguous productions: (1) *simple-if*, and (2) *if-else*.

the second the *if-else* rule. Any CFG containing these rules will be ambiguous, since the input segment

if *cond* if *cond stmt* else *stmt*

can have two derivations. The first

if *cond* { if *cond stmt* } else *stmt*

has the *else* part attached to the outermost *if* statement; the second

if *cond* { if *cond stmt* else *stmt* }

has it attached to the innermost *if*.

The ambiguity created by these productions will be detected by an LR parser generator as *shift/reduce* and *reduce/reduce* conflicts. A conflict arises when an entry in the action table can contain two or more alternative parser actions. In this case, there will be two conflicting parser actions for all action table entries under the token `else`: One is a reduce action, which leads to the first derivation; the other is a shift action, which leads to the second derivation. Some parser generators will call an error on encountering a conflict. Others, such as YACC, can be forced by declaration to select one action or the other, which I refer to as *compile-time* disambiguation.

Most modern programming languages are defined such that the second derivation is the correct one. That is, each *else* part is attached to the innermost un-*else*'d *if* statement. By telling YACC to prefer the shift action on encountering an `else` token, it is possible for YACC to generate a parser that recognizes a language so defined. The reason that most language designers prefer this definition is because it makes their languages LR(1). Languages that adopt the alternative definition, i.e., in which the rightmost *else* part is attached to the leftmost un-*else*'d *if* statement, are non-LR(k) and cannot be recognized with a standard LR parser.

To understand why the alternative definition is non-LR(k), consider the input segment

if *cond* if *cond stmt* ∘else *stmt*

where the driver is scanning the token `else`, as indicated by the dot. The driver can immediately reduce by the *simple-if* rule, getting

if *cond simple-if* ∘else *stmt*.

After scanning past the last *stmt*, the driver can then reduce by the *if-else* rule. This set of actions leads to the first derivation, which is correct for this input.

Now, consider the input segment

if *cond* **if** *cond stmt* ○**else** *stmt* **else** *stmt*.

The same set of actions would lead to

if-else ○**else** *stmt*

which is incorrect. In this instance, the driver should have shifted past the first **else** token to the second **else** and then reduced using the *if-else* rule, giving

if *cond if-else* ○**else** *stmt*

which will lead to a correct derivation. Thus, the alternative language is non-LR(k) because the driver cannot correctly decide to shift or reduce on the first **else** token without scan past some arbitrary number of symbols in *stmt* to the next **else** token.

As another example of a non-LR(k) language, suppose we wished to enhance our English-like language to allow noun phrases to consist of an arbitrary number of prepositional phrases. We can do this by adding the production

NP → NP PP

to the grammar in Fig. 4. This simple change makes the grammar non-LR(k). What this means to our example is that the action table will contain two double-action entries, denoting the two uses of a prepositional phrase. Since the driver is a deterministic process with only a single stack, it can follow one of these actions but not both. To follow both, the drive must become nondeterministic, using some form of search to parse the input. Capturing this nondeterminism is the essence of Tomita's algorithm and general LR parsing.

3. General LR Parsing

3.1. Unbounded Look-Ahead

The primary constraint imposed by the restricted context-free parsing algorithms used in practical parsers involves the amount of look-ahead they allow in order to resolve ambiguities. A language is ambiguous if more than one derivation tree exists for any sentence in the language. If *disambiguation rules* exist for selecting the "right" derivation, then the ambiguity is *resolvable*. Resolvable ambiguity is an important aspect of a language. The grammar of a language gives it syntactic structure. Ambiguity relaxes the rigidity of this structure and promotes brevity expression.

Examples of resolvable ambiguities found in conventional programming languages include arithmetic expressions and if-then-else statements; examples found in natural language include the attachment of prepositions and relative clauses. An ambiguous language trades syntactic precision for conciseness, informality, and readability. However, when its ambiguities are resolvable, then the language regains its precision, at least at a mechanical level. When the disambiguation rules agree with the intuitive expectations of users, then precision is also regained at the human level. Although some practical parsers, such as those produced by YACC, permit a small degree of ambiguity in the languages they recognize, there are still languages such as ROSIE, which have reasonable and understandable disambiguation rules but which cannot be recognized by these parsers.

Highly ambiguous languages, such as ROSIE, require the power of a general context-free parser. This power comes in the form of *unbounded* look-ahead. The general context-free parsing algorithms, such as Earley's algorithm[17] and the Cocke-Younger-Kasami algorithm[18], typically pursue all derivations of an ambiguous sentence. Once found, *parse-time* disambiguation can decide which was the correct derivation and discard the others. For an LR parser, this would be equivalent to being able to look ahead an arbitrary number of tokens before making any parsing decision. Unfortunately, most of the general algorithms do not make practical parsers.

The general context-free parsing algorithms are necessarily less efficient than the restrictive algorithms because they must simulate a multiple-path, nondeterministic pass over the input tokens. While many of the general algorithms can be shown to theoretically run as efficiently as the restricted algorithms on a large subclass of CFGs, the actual run-time performance parsers based on these algorithms is too slow to considered them practical.

In 1985, Tomita[1] introduced a general context-free parsing algorithm defined as a variation on standard LR parsing, i.e., a table-driven, bottom-up parsing algorithm. The benefit of this approach is that it eliminates the need to expand alternatives of a nonterminal at parse time (i.e., what Earley calls the *predictor* operation). For Earley's algorithm, the predictor operation is one of two $O(n^2)$ components. While eliminating this operation does not change the upper-time bound of $O(n^3)$, it does make the difference with regard to implementing a practical parser.

Although Tomita's algorithm belongs to the same complexity class as Earley's and other general algorithms[22], in realistic applications it is unlikely to ever realize worse than $n \log n$ time. This is because the sentences of "useful" languages are normally intended to be human readable as well as machine readable. This places a natural limit on the complexity of the input a parser might expect to receive. Because Tomita's algorithm takes advantage of parse tables similar to those found in practical parsers, implementations of this algorithm have the potential for run-time performance that is comparable to the restricted algorithms, while retaining the power to recognize a far wider range of languages.

3.2. Tomita's Algorithm

The following is an informal description of Tomita's algorithm as a recognizer. Tomita views his algorithm as a variation on standard LR parsing. The algorithm takes a shift-reduce approach, using an extended LR parse table to guide its actions. The change the algorithm makes to the parse table is to allow it to contain multiple

(1) S → NP VP
(2) S → S PP
(3) NP → noun
(4) NP → det noun
(5) NP → NP PP
(6) PP → prep NP
(7) VP → verb NP

Fig. 8. Example non-LR(k) grammar.

State	Action Table					Goto Table			
	det	noun	verb	prep	⊣	NP	PP	VP	S
0	sh5	sh7				9			1
1				sh2	acc		8		
2	sh5	sh7				3			
3			re6	re6,sh2	re6		4		
4			re5	re5	re5				
5		sh6							
6			re4	re4	re4				
7			re3	re3	re3				
8				re2	re2				
9			sh10	sh2			4	12	
10	sh5	sh7				11			
11				re7,sh2	re7		4		
12				re1	re1				

Fig. 9. LR parse table with multiple-action entries.

actions per entry, i.e., at most one shift or accept action and any number of reduce actions. Thus, the parse table can no longer be used for fully-deterministic parsing; some search may have to be done. The algorithm simulates a nondeterministic parse with pseudo-parallelism. It scans an input string $x_1 \cdots x_n$ from left to right, following all paths in a breath-first manner and merging like subpaths when possible to avoid redundant computations.

An example non-LR(k) grammar is shown in Fig. 8. This is a variation of the grammar seen earlier in Fig. 4. Again, the nonterminals S, NP, VP, and PP define the syntactic classes: sentence, noun phrase, verb phrase, and prepositional phrase; and the preterminals det, noun, verb, and prep define the lexical classes: determiner, noun, verb, and preposition.

The parse table for this grammar is shown in Fig. 9. It is constructed in a manner similar to the parse table seen earlier in Fig. 5, with the exception that shift/reduce and reduce/reduce conflicts appear as multiple-action entries; parser actions have the same meaning. The parse table in Fig. 9 has two multiple-action entries in states 3 and 11 under the column labeled prep.

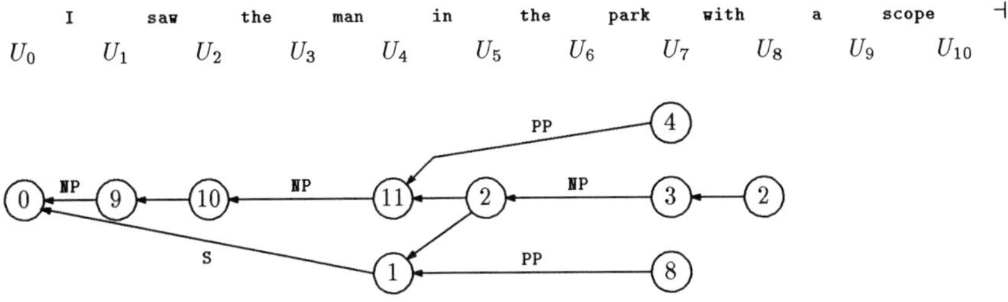

Fig. 10. Example graph-structured stack.

Tomita's algorithm operates by maintaining a number of parsing *processes* in parallel. Each process has a stack, scans the input string from left-to-right, and, thus, behaves basically the same as the driver routine of a standard LR parser. Each stack element is labeled with a parse state and points to its parent, i.e., the previous element on a process's stack. We call the top-of-stack the current state of a process.

Each process does not actually maintain its own separate stack. Rather, these "multiple" stacks are represented using a single directed acyclic (but reentrant) graph called a *graph-structured stack*, an example of which is shown in Fig. 10. Each stack element corresponds to a vertex of the graph. (In Fig. 10, circles represent the vertices of the graph, where each circle is labeled with a parse state s.) Each leaf of the graph acts as a distinct top-of-stack to a process. (There are three processes depicted in Fig. 10: one in state 4, one in state 2, and one in state 8.) The root of the graph acts as a common bottom-of-stack. The edge between a vertex and its parent is directed toward the parent. (As a convenience to the reader, edges in Fig. 10 are labeled when they denote the recognition of a nonterminal.) Because of the reentrant nature of the graph (as explained below), a vertex may have more than one parent. (In Fig. 10, the vertex under U_5 has two parent vertices.)

The leaves of the graph grow in stages. Each stage U_i corresponds to the symbol x_i from the input string. After x_i is scanned, the leaves in stage U_i are in a one-to-one correspondence with the algorithm's *active* processes. Each active process references a distinct leaf of the graph and treats that leaf as its current state. On scanning x_{i+1}, an active process can (1) add an additional leaf to U_i or (2) add a leaf to U_{i+1}. Only processes that have added leaves to U_{i+1} will be active when x_{i+2} is scanned. (In Fig. 10, x_i = `with`; two leaves have been added to U_i and one to U_{i+1}.)

In general, a process behaves in the following manner. On x_i, each active process (corresponding to the leaves in U_{i-1}) executes the entries in the action table for x_i given its current state. When a process encounters multiple actions, it *splits* into several processes (one for each action), each sharing a common top-of-stack and each executing a distinct action. When a process encounters an error entry, the process is discarded (i.e., its top-of-stack vertex sprouts no leaves into U_i by way of that process). All processes are synchronized, scanning the same symbol at the same time. After a process shifts on x_i into U_i, it waits until there are no other processes that can act on x_i before scanning x_{i+1}.

The Shift Action. A process (with top-of-stack vertex v) shifts on x_i from its current state s to some successor state s' by

1. creating a new leaf v' in U_i labeled s';
2. placing an edge from v' to its top-of-stack v (directed towards v);
3. making v' its new top-of-stack vertex (in this way changing its current state).

Any successive process shifting to the same state s' in U_i is *merged* with the existing process to form a single process whose top-of-stack vertex has multiple parents, i.e., by placing an additional edge from the top-of-stack vertex of the existing process in U_i to the top-of-stack vertex of the shifting process. The merge is done because, individually, these processes would behave in exactly the same manner until a reduce action removed the vertices labeled s' from their stacks. Thus, merging avoids redundant computation. Merging also ensures that each leaf in any U_i will be labeled with a distinct parse state, which puts a finite upper-bound on the possible number of active processes. This limits the size of the graph-structured stack and eliminates the possibility of exponential explosion in the number of active parsing processes.

The Reduce Action. A process executes a reduce action on a production p by following the chain of parent links down from its top-of-stack vertex v to the ancestor vertex from which the process began scanning for p, essentially "popping" intervening vertices off its stack. Since merging means a vertex can have multiple parents, the reduce operation can lead back to multiple ancestors. When this happens, the process is again split into separate processes (one for each ancestor). The ancestors will correspond to the set of vertices at a distance $\bar{p}$ from v, where $\bar{p}$ equals the number of symbols in the right-hand side of production p. Once reduced to an ancestor, a process shifts to the state s' indicated in the goto table for D_p (the nonterminal on the left-hand side of production p) given the ancestor's state. A process shifts on a nonterminal much as it does a terminal, with the exception that the new leaf is added to U_{i-1} rather than U_i. (A process can only enter U_i by shifting on x_i.)

The algorithm begins with a single initial process whose top-of-stack vertex is the root of the graph-structured stack. It then follows the general procedure outlined above for each symbol in the input string, continuing until there are either no leaves added to U_i (i.e., no more active processes), which denotes *rejection*, or a process executes the accept action on scanning the $n+1$st input symbol '$\dashv$,' which denotes *acceptance*. (Figure 10 shows an instance of a graph-structured stack in which three vertices were added to U_7 as a result of reduce actions while scanning `with`; a vertex was added to U_8 as a result of a shift action on `with` in state 3.)

3.3. Annotated Example

To further illustrate the mechanics of Tomita's algorithm as a recognizer, consider the following example, which uses the grammar in Fig. 8 and parse table in Fig. 9 to analyze the sentence

`I saw the man in the park with a scope ⊣`

Assume `I`, `man`, `park`, and `scope` are instances of the token `noun`, `saw` is an instance of `verb`, `in` and `with` are instance of `prep`, and `a` and `the` are instances of `det`.

The diagrams that follow trace the growth of the graph-structured stack from U_0 through U_{10}. Each circle is a vertex of the graph labeled by a parse state. The line segments connecting vertices are edges created by shift actions (i.e., from the state of the left vertex, on the grammar symbol labeling the segment, and into the state of the right vertex). Backward arrows indicate a reduce action back to the vertex at the head of the arrow, where each arrow is labeled p_i, indicating that an instance of the ith production was recognized. After reducing back to the earlier vertex, a shift is done on nonterminal D_i (the left-hand side of the ith production).

Initially, there is a single active process, denoted by a single vertex in U_0 labeled 0. The only action from state 0 on `I` is `sh7`, so [1] the process creates a new vertex labeled 7 in U_1. The only action in state 7 on `saw` is `re3`, so the process reduces back one vertex (the length of production 3) as indicated by the backward arrow. From state 0 [2], the process shifts to state 9 on `NP`, state 10 on `saw`, state 5 on `the`, and state 6 on `man`. From state 6, it reduces back two vertices using production 4.

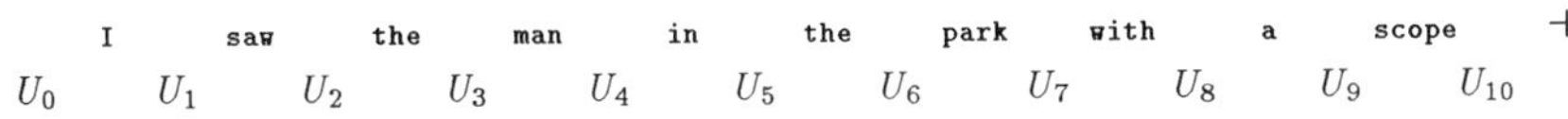

1. Scanning x_2 = `saw(verb)`

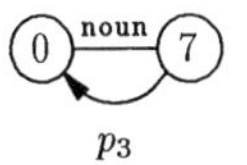

2. Scanning x_5 = `in(prep)`

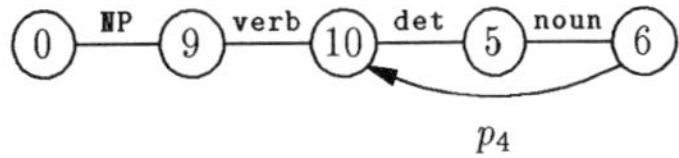

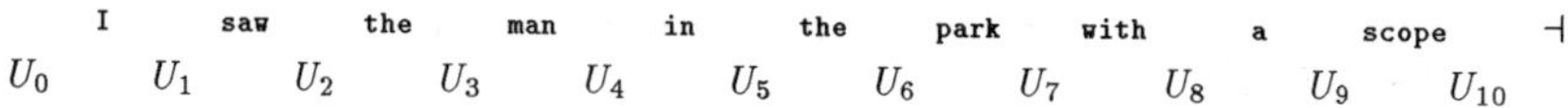

3. Scanning x_6 = `the(det)`

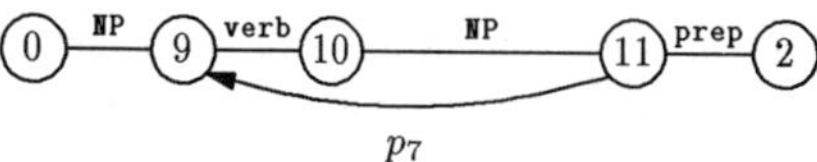

4. Scanning x_6 = `the(det)`

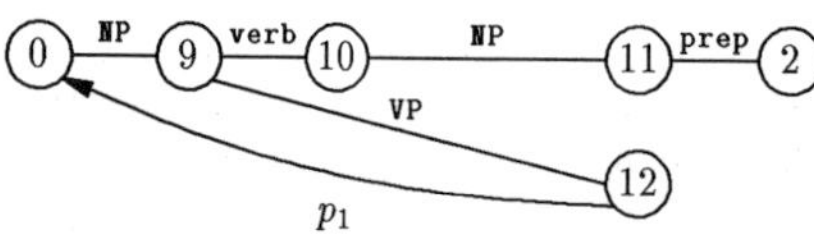

5. Scanning x_8 = `with(prep)`

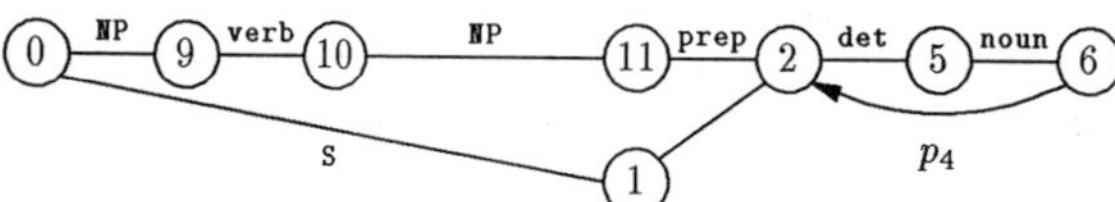

6. Scanning x_8 = `with(prep)`

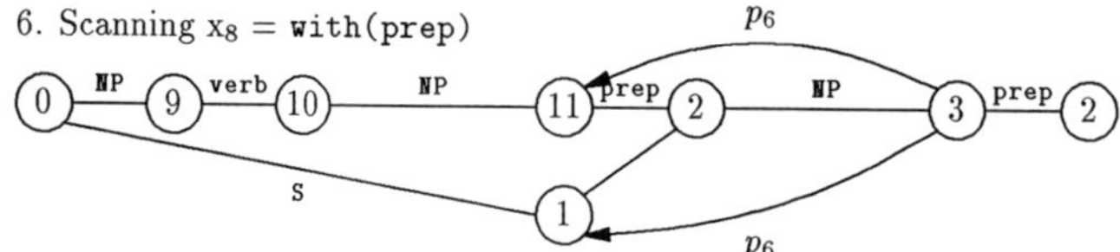

From state 10 [3], the process shifts to state 11 on `NP`, where it finds two actions on `in`, `sh2` and `re7`. The process splits in two. In [4], one process follows the shift action, while the second follows the reduce action. In [5], the second process has shifted on `in`, entering the same state as the first and merging with it into a single process again. This merged process shifts first on `the` and then `park` to state 6, where it reduces on `with` using production 4. In [6], the process encounters another two-action state. It splits in two: one process follows the shift action; the other follows the reduce action. As the latter process goes back past the earlier merged vertex, it splits once more.

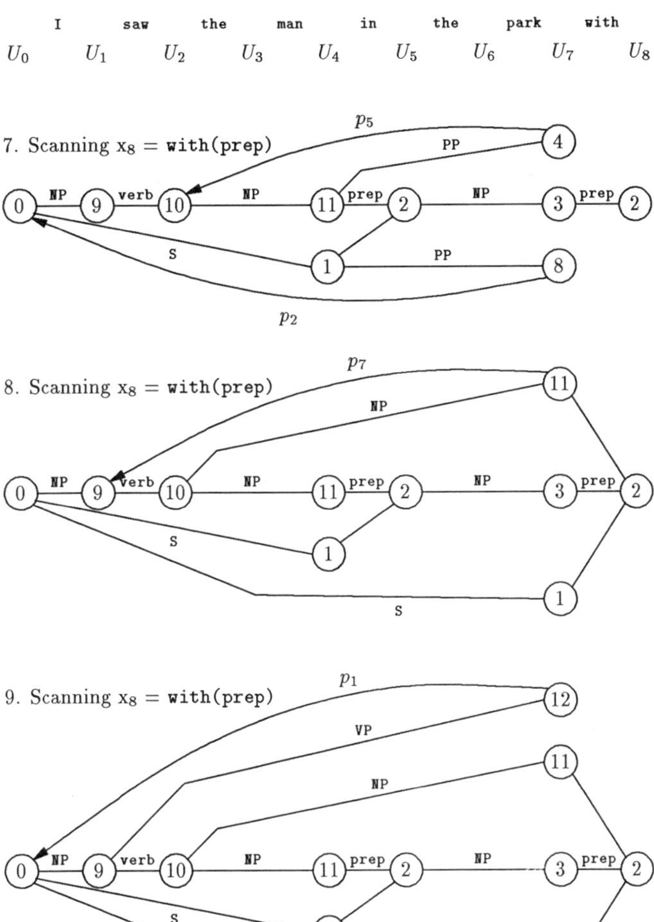

In [7], these processes reduce again. Finally in [8], they shift on `with` to merge with the process that originally followed the shift action earlier in [4]. Note that the process in state 11 also has reduce action on `with`. It splits and reduces twice: first (in [8]) using production 7 and then (in [9]) using production 1.

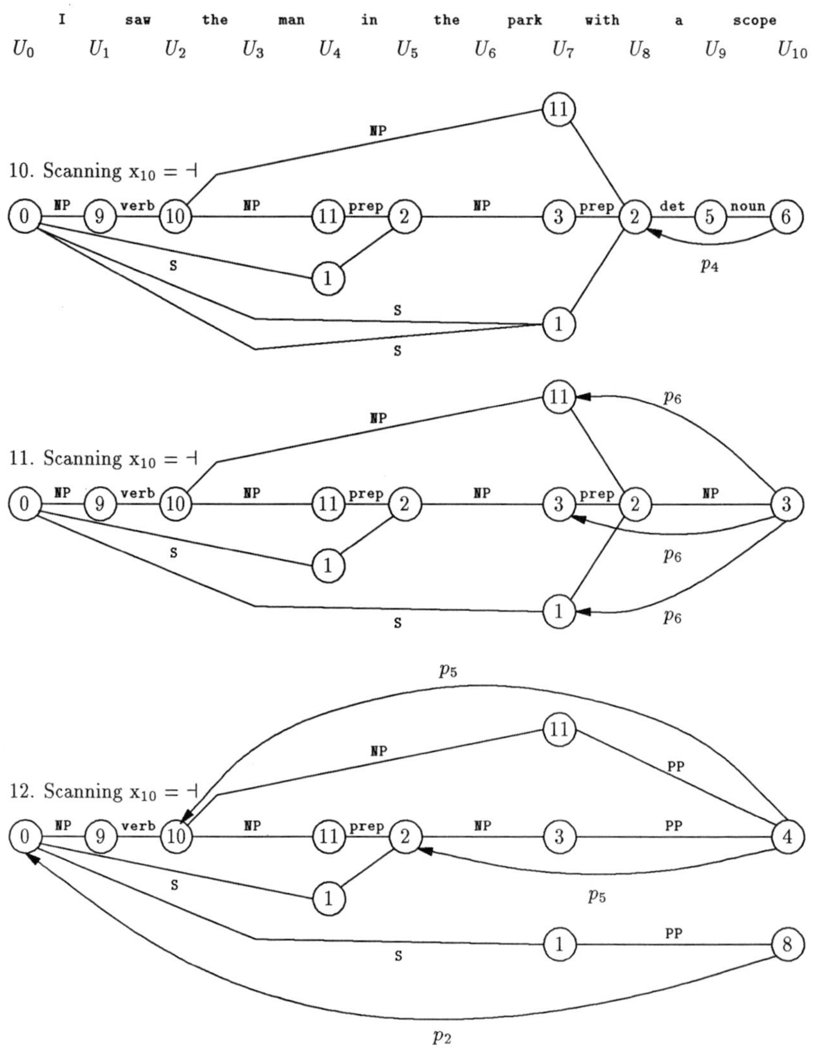

Eventually in [10], this process shifts to state 1 on S. Because another process has already made the same shift, the recognizer detects an ambiguity and discards the second process. Meanwhile, the three processes that merged on `with` at state 2, shift on `the` and `scope` to state 6, and reduce on '⊣' using production 4. In [11], the merged processes reduce back past the merging vertex, where they split back into three separate processes, two of which re-merge on PP in [12].

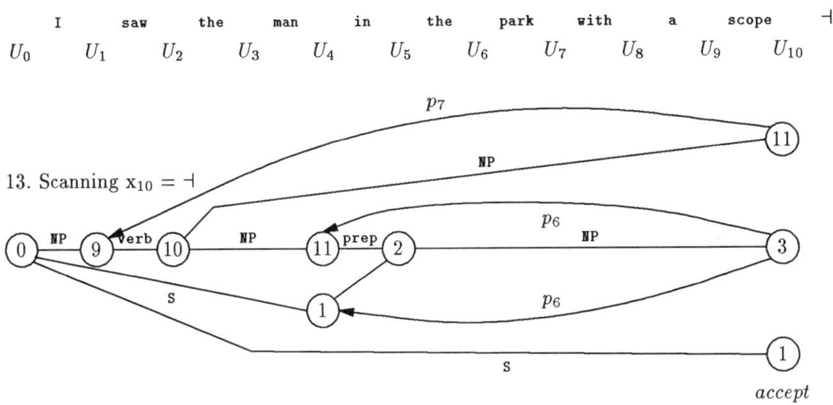

Finally in [13], one of the processes reaches a state with an accept action on '⊣'. The sentence is recognized as belonging to the language.

3.4. Computation Complexity and Practical Performance

A formal analysis of Tomita's algorithm[22] shows that has a worst-case time complexity of $O(n^{\bar{p}+1})$, where n is the length of the input string and $\bar{p}$ is the length of the longest production in the grammar. Thus, Tomita's algorithm has a time complexity of $O(n^3)$ for CFGs with productions of length no greater than two, such as grammars in Chomsky normal form[23]. This same analysis also shows a modification to Tomita's algorithm that has a worst-case complexity of $O(n^3)$ for all CFGs.

On the pragmatic side, CFGs that induce such worst-case behavior are rare. An example of one worst-case grammar is shown in Fig. 11. When parsing a string of x's, this grammar causes Tomita's algorithm to exhibit $O(n^5)$ behavior. It is highly unlikely that the productions and sentences required to induce worst-case behavior will ever occur in realistic applications. In addition, the same analysis cited above shows that there are two subclasses of CFGs, *unambiguous grammars* and *bounded-state grammars*, that Tomita's algorithm can recognize in $O(n^2)$ and $O(n)$ time, respectively. These two subclasses subsume all LR(k) grammars and many non-LR(k) grammars. Assuming that realistic grammars and sentences will combine aspects of both unambiguous and bounded state grammars, Tomita's algorithm should have an average time complexity of $O(n^2) \cup O(n)$ in most cases.

(1) S → S S S S
(2) S → S x
(3) S → x

Fig. 11. Example worst-case CFG.

4. RACK: The RAND Advanced Compiler Kit

4.1. Overview

The RAND Advanced Compiler Kit (RACK) generates parsers that are based on Tomita's algorithm for GLR parsing. RACK also generates scanner programs for transforming input characters into tokens. RACK provides a general tool for describing the input of source programs. The RACK user specifies a grammar that defines the lexical and syntactic structure of the input as well as code to be invoked when particular structures are recognized. RACK turns the specification into a parser and scanner program that handles the input process.

RACK is written to be fully upward compatible with YACC. Programmers familiar with YACC should have no difficulty learning to use the additional features available in RACK. These features include arbitrary look-ahead and parse-time disambiguation, multiple start symbols, a lexical scanner generator, and an interpreter for interactive debugging and grammar development. RACK is implemented in portable C. RACK parsers can be generated as either C or LISP programs.

4.2. Operations

The input to RACK is a grammar file. Its output is a parser program file and a scanner program file. The user specifies the *implementation* language in which the parser and scanner are to be encoded. Presently, RACK supports three implementation languages: C, Common Lisp, and Standard Lisp. The relationship of RACK to the parser and scanner are depicted in Fig. 12. Generation is depicted with solid arrows, and data flow through the parser and scanner is depicted with dashed arrows.

The grammar file contains the *grammar symbols*, *lexical rules*, and *grammar rules* that describe the language to be recognized. This is called the *target* language. The lexical rules are used to generate the scanner program, while the grammar rules are used to generate the parser program.

The parser and scanner are intended to operate as a front-end to a user program, e.g., the compiler or interpreter of a KBPL, a database manager, or even another parser generator. The user program invokes the parser with the function `yyparse()` when it needs to translate textual input into a representation that it can easily access and use. The parser repeatedly requests tokens from the scanner, which it invokes with the function `yylex()`, until it has either recognized a sentence in the target language or recognized an error condition. The scanner reads characters from an input device and returns a token whose character pattern matches the longest sequences of input characters.

The grammar file also contains declarations that configure certain aspects of the parser and scanner, rule actions that are applied upon recognizing instances of lexical rules or grammar rules, and auxiliary subroutines that support code generation operations and interface the parser to the user program. The rule actions and auxiliary subroutines must be coded in the implementation language.

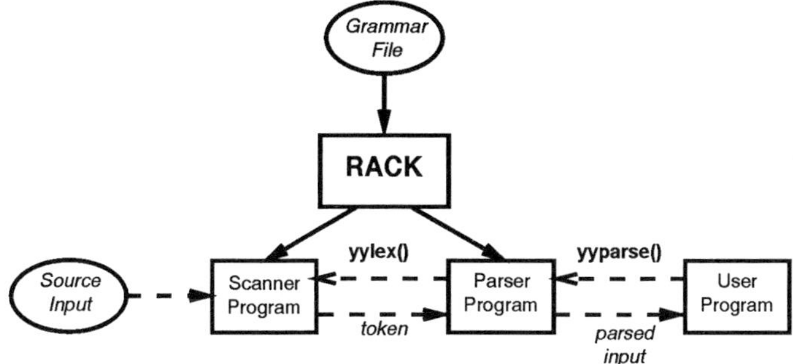

Fig. 12. Relation of RACK to parser and scanner.

Depending on the input grammar, RACK parsers can take one of two forms. If the grammar is LR(1), then the parser generated by RACK will be similar to the parser YACC would generate. This means there is no penalty for using RACK on existing YACC grammars. On non-LR(k) grammars or when $k > 1$ (grammars for which YACC cannot generate a parser), RACK generates a GLR parser. A GLR parser has two modes of operation: *deterministic* and *nondeterministic*. In its deterministic mode, the parser behaves like a standard LR parser, although with more overhead than a YACC parser. When the parser encounters a multiple-action entry in the parse table, it enters the nondeterministic mode. In this mode, the parser follows all possible derivations of the input tokens in parallel, keeping track of the parallel parsing processes with Tomita's algorithm. Eventually the parser scans past the ambiguous input segment, at which point it will switch back to the more efficient deterministic mode.

4.3. Resolving Ambiguities

The significance of having a tool such as RACK is that it eliminates the primary constraint imposed by existing parser generators on the expressiveness and readability of a language. This constraint involves whether ambiguities are allowed in the language and the time at which ambiguities must be resolved.

An LR parser generator detects ambiguities as shift/reduce and reduce/reduce conflicts. Conflicts can be resolved in three ways:

1. Rewriting the grammar.
2. Compile-time disambiguation.
3. Parse-time disambiguation.

All three options require careful consideration of the language being described, as well as some thought toward the behavior of the resulting parser. While rewriting the grammar works in many cases, it can result in complicated grammars and slow parsers. Also, because context-free languages are inherently ambiguous[21], there are some conflicts that can never be resolved in this manner.

When the correct choice of action can be determined at compile time (i.e., when compiling the grammar into a parser program), then the second option is always recommended. Compile-time disambiguation leads to smaller, faster parsers. Conflicts resulting from arithmetic expressions and if-then-else statements are typically resolved at compile time. Sometimes, as with the non-LR(k) language described in Section 2.4, there is insufficient information at compile time to make the correct choice. Parse-time disambiguation lets the parser follow each action until it has seen sufficient tokens to make the correct choice.

YACC supports compile-time disambiguation only, while most other parser generators report conflicts as errors. RACK supports both compile-time and parse-time disambiguation. Its compile-time disambiguation strategy is modeled after that used in YACC. Its parse-time disambiguation strategy is to compare alternative derivation trees and select the tree using the highest priority grammar rule at the highest level. A better strategy, which may be added in the future, would allow parse-time disambiguation based on the value of semantic attributes attached to grammar rules and lexical elements. This strategy would increase the power of RACK parsers to the level of ATN parsers.

4.4. Other Significant Features

Besides its look-ahead and parse-time disambiguation capabilities, RACK supports four significant features that distinguish it from other parser generators and make it more appropriate for KBPLs and other advanced applications. These include: multiple start symbols, a scanner generator, an interface to both C and LISP, and an interactive grammar interpreter.

Multiple Start Symbols

Multiple start symbols provide a way of having a single parser that recognizes more than one top-level syntactic construct. A start symbol of a grammar is a distinguished nonterminal that represents the concept of a sentence. The purpose of having a parser is to recognize sentences and to take some action, such as code generation, upon recognition. Historically, only one nonterminal can be a start symbol of a grammar. Sometimes, however, it is convenient to have multiple start symbols.

For example, consider building an interpreter for some ALGOL-like programming language. The start symbol for this language would be something like `prog`, for program; assume that a program consists of subroutines, a subroutine consists of statements, and statements of expressions. We will need a parser for loading programs into the interpreter, but it would also be convenient to allow the user to input statements and expressions from the keyboard. Rather than having three separate parsers, i.e., one for recognizing programs, another for statements, and a third for expressions, all of which share much of the same syntax, multiple start symbols allow the same parser to be used for recognizing all three.

```
%token NOUN DET VERB PREP
%lex
%input %nocase
%internal %nocase
%%
NOUN : I | MAN | PARK | SCOPE
DET : A | THE
PREP : IN | WITH
VERB : SAW
%%
s :  s pp | np vp
np :  NOUN | DET NOUN | np pp
pp :  PREP np
vp :  VERB np
```

(a) RACK/ISG grammar.

```
W  [ \t]
%%
{W}*[iI]             { return(NOUN); }
{W}*[mM][aA][nN] { return(NOUN); }
{W}*[pP][aA][rR][kK]
                     { return(NOUN); }
{W}*[sS][cC][oO][pP][eE]
                     { return(NOUN); }
{W}*[aA]             { return(DET); }
{W}*[tT][hH][eE] { return(DET); }
{W}*[iI][nN]         { return(PREP); }
{W}*[wW][iI][tT][hH]
                     { return(PREP); }
{W}*[sS][aA][wW] { return(VERB); }
```

(b) LEX grammar.

Fig. 13. Comparison of lexical grammars.

Multiple start symbols are implemented in RACK parsers by creating separate start and accept states for each start symbol. Where the start symbols share syntax, they also share states in the parse table. Multiple start symbols add little to the size of parse tables and do nothing to hinder execution time of the parser. This feature is unique to RACK.

The Scanner Generator

Like YACC, RACK parsers rely on a lexical analyzer (or scanner) function, called `yylex()`, for scanning input tokens. Unlike YACC, RACK supports an integrated scanner generator (ISG); YACC users must rely on LEX[24] (a commonly-used scanner generator for UNIX applications), or they must code their scanner by hand. The design of ISG is oriented towards a tight integration with RACK; LEX is designed for general-purpose regular expression matching and is only loosely integrated to YACC.

Figure 13 compares the input specifications for ISG and LEX. A full RACK/ISG grammar for the tokens and sentences of the simple English-like language seen earlier is shown in Fig. 13(a); an equivalent LEX grammar (for the tokens only) is shown in Fig. 13(b). The declaration section of the RACK/ISG grammar specifies that input tokens can appear in mixed case. In ISG scanners, tokens are separated by an arbitrary number of whitespaces by default.

The scanner generator supported by RACK has several advantages over LEX. First, ISG is simpler to use. A lexical grammar for input tokens is specified with rules that are similar to those used in specifying the syntactic grammar, and rule actions that simply return the token type are supplied automatically. Treatment of case dependencies can also be specified by declaration. Second, ISG scanners are smaller and faster than LEX grammars; ISG optimizes standard lexical operations. Third, ISG interfaces to C, Common Lisp, and Standard Lisp; LEX only interfaces to C.

Interfacing C and LISP

RACK allows users to declare whether the scanner and parser are to be implemented in C, Common Lisp, or Standard Lisp. The code generation portion of the parser is performed by actions attached to grammar rules; actions must be coded in the implementation language of the parser.

When parsing a sentence, rule actions are executed as soon as possible. For LR(1) grammars or in deterministic mode, rule actions are executed after each reduce action; in nondeterministic mode, rule actions are executed after disambiguation according to a postorder traversal of the selected derivation tree. RACK supports a mechanism (i.e., the dollar-sign variables of YACC) for accessing and passing values during code generation. As shown in Section 4.5, grammars for LISP-coded parsers can take advantage of the backquote macro during code generation.

The Grammar Interpreter

Grammars can be developed and debugged using the grammar interpreter option. With this option, RACK generates an interactive parser that allows a user to step through the execution of the parser and examine its actions. Among other features, the grammar interpreter lets users inspect the state of the parse, examine derivations made, and unwind to an earlier point in the parsing process and resume. The interpreter also lets users add and delete grammar rules and symbols dynamically, thus supporting iterative grammar development.

4.5. Example: RACK Grammar

To further illustrate some of the features discussed above, consider the example RACK grammar file shown in Fig. 14. This grammar file defines a simplistic English-like language, called SCOPE. By convention, tokens appear in uppercase, e.g., `NOUN`, `VERB`, and `PREP`, and nonterminals appear in lowercase, e.g., `s`, `np`, and `vp`. The implementation language for SCOPE is Common Lisp.

The grammar file starts with four parser declarations. The first two declarations tell RACK not to resolve shift/reduce or reduce/reduce conflicts at compile time, except for those involving nonterminal `s`. The third declaration identifies the tokens of SCOPE. One-character tokens, such as `';'`, do not need to be declared. The fourth declaration specifies the start symbols. SCOPE has two start symbols: `s_seq`, which is used to recognize a sequence of sentences `s` separated by semicolons, and `np_seq`, which is used to recognize a sequence of noun phrases `np`.

```
%resolve %none
%except s
%token NOUN, VERB, DET, PREP, AND
%start s_seq, np_seq

%lex
%rename yygetlex
{
(defun yylex()
  (let ((n (yygetlex)))
    (setf yylval (coerce yytext 'string))
    n))
}
%input %nocase
%input %nocase
%output %upcase
%eos '\n'

%%

NOUN : I | MAN | PARK | SCOPE
DET : A | THE
PREP : IN | WITH
VERB : SAW
AND : AND
';' : ';' .* '\n'

%%

s_seq : s { (format t "~A~%" $1) }
      | s { (format t "~A~%" $1) } ';' s_seq
      | error ';' { (format t "~%?") } s_seq;

np_seq : np { (format t "~A~%" $1) }
       | np { (format t "~A~%" $1) } ';' np_seq
       | error ';' { (format t "~%?") } np_seq;

s : s AND s    { `(<and> ,$1 ,$3) }
  | s pp       { `(<s>   ,$1 ,$2) }
  | np vp      { `(<s>   ,$1 ,$2) };

np : DET NOUN { `(<np>  ,$1 ,$2) }
   | NOUN     { `(<np>  ,$1) }
   | np pp    { `(<np>  ,$1 ,$2) };

vp : VERB np  { `(<vp>  ,$1 ,$2) };

pp : PREP np  { `(<pp>  ,$1 ,$2) };
```

Fig. 14. Example RACK grammar file: SCOPE.

The declaration `%lex` introduces the scanner declarations. The parser expects to receive tokens from a scanner function called `yylex`, where tokens are represented by integer codes. Other values can also be associated with tokens by assigning those values to the variable `yylval`. The first declaration tells RACK to rename the scanner function to `yygetlex`. Following this is a code segment defining `yylex` in terms of `yygetlex`. After recognizing a token, the scanner function assigns a list of the token characters to the variable `yytext`. Here, `yylex` is defined to assign these characters as a string to `yylval` before returning the code `n` of the recognized token; these strings are used later in grammar rule actions.

The three declarations following this specify how the scanner is to handle alphabet characters: the first declares that there are no case changes for input characters; the second declares that alphabet characters in the right-hand side of lexical rules are case independent; the third declares that input characters are to be output in uppercase. The final scanner declaration, `%eos '\n'` designates newline to be the end-of-sentence character.

The first set of double precent signs (`%%`) separates the scanner declarations from the lexical rules. Each lexical rule associates a character pattern, which appears to the right of the colon, with a token, which appears to the colon's left. For instance, the rule

```
NOUN : I | MAN | PARK | SCOPE
```

associates the disjunctive character pattern `I | MAN | PARK | SCOPE` with the token `NOUN`. Each time the parser request a token via `yylex`, the scanner function *recognizes* the character pattern that matches the longest sequence of input characters and returns the integer code of the token associated with that pattern; the input characters matched by the pattern are removed from the input stream. If no pattern matches and the first input character is a whitespace, it is discarded and the scanner function tries again; in this way, whitespace characters act as separators. If the first input character is not whitespace, then it is treated as a one-character token and its the character code is returned.

The first five lexical rules have the same general form and behavior, their patterns match sequences of alphabet characters. The sixth rule

```
';' : ';' .* \n
```

is somewhat different. Its pattern matches a semicolon, followed by zero or more characters, followed by a newline character. When this pattern is recognized, the scanner function returns the integer code for the one-character token `';'`, which is its character code. This rule is used to discard newline characters that would otherwise be recognized as the end-of-sentence character.

The second set of double percent signs separates the lexical rules from the grammar rules. Each grammar rule associates a sequences of tokens, nonterminals, and actions, which appear to the right of the colon, with the nonterminal defined by the rule, which appears to the colon's left. Alternatives of a nonterminal can be spliced into a single rule when separated by bars (|).

Grammar rule actions are delimited by curly braces and must be written in the implementation language. Within an action, expressions of the form $\$i$ are variables that refer to the value associated with the i element on the right-hand side of the rule. For instance, in the rule

```
pp :   PREP np   '(<pp> ,$1 ,$2) ;
```

the variable `$1` refers to the value associated with the token `PREP` and `$2` refers to the value associated with the nonterminal `np`. If an action terminates the right-hand side of a rule, its value will be associated with the nonterminal on the left-hand side of the rule. In this way, data structures can be created and passed between grammar rules. Rule actions are executed as soon as unambiguously possible.

The grammar file for SCOPE specifies six grammar rules; the first four have three alternatives each. The first rule defines the nonterminal `s_seq` as consisting of one or more instances of nonterminal `s` separated by semicolons. The rule actions in the first two alternatives of this rule output the value associated the leading `s` as soon as it is recognized. The third alternative is for error handling. If a syntax error is detected during the recognition of `s`, the parser looks for such a rule as a means for graceful recovery. In this case, the rule action indicates that the user should re-type the input. The second grammar rule is similar to the first. The last four grammar rules define the syntactic structure of conjunctive sentences (`s`), noun phrases (`np`), verb phrases (`vp`), and prepositional phrases (`pp`). When any of these rules are recognized, their actions create a list structure representing the syntactic construct recognized.

Given the grammar file seen in Fig. 14, RACK generates a scanner file, called `yylex.lsp`, and parser file, called `yytab.lsp`. When these files are loaded into Common Lisp, the parser can be invoked with the function call

```
(yyparse yy_s_seq)
```

which recognizes instances of the first start symbol, or it can be invoked with the function call

```
(yyparse yy_np_seq)
```

which recognizes instances of the second start symbol. A sample run is shown below.

```
> (yyparse yy_s_seq)
i saw a man in the park with a scope;
(<S> (<S> (<S> (<NP> I) (<VP> SAW (<NP> A MAN)))
          (<PP> IN (<NP> THE PARK)))
     (<PP> WITH (<NP> A SCOPE)))
i saw a man in the park and the man in the park saw the scope in the park
(<AND> (<S> (<S> (<NP> I) (<VP> SAW (<NP> A MAN)))
            (<PP> IN (<NP> THE PARK)))
       (<S> (<S> (<NP> (<NP> THE MAN) (<PP> IN (<NP> THE PARK)))
                 (<VP> SAW (<NP> THE SCOPE)))
            (<PP> IN (<NP> THE PARK))))
```

As specified by the grammar file in Fig. 14, SCOPE allows prepositional phrases to be attached to both sentences and noun phrases, which means that input sentences such as

`i saw a man in the park`

has more than one derivation. Using parse-time disambiguation, SCOPE is defined so as to attach prepositional phrases to noun phrases only if they cannot be attached to a sentence. This definition is designated in the grammar by the order of alternatives for nonterminals `s` and `np`.

RACK orders productions as it reads them from the grammar file. Productions appearing first have a higher precedence than those appearing later. When the parser derives one or more derivations for the same nonterminal from the same input segment, it selects the derivation whose most recently recognized production has the highest precedence. When more than one such derivation exists, it continues making a left-to-right, top-down comparison until only one derivation remains.

By ordering the alternatives of `s` so that '`s pp`' appears before '`vp np`,' we tell RACK to prefer long sentences over short sentences. Likewise, by making '`np pp`' the last alternative of `np`, we tell RACK to prefer short noun phrases over long noun phrases. In this way, a parser for the SCOPE language will only attach a prepositional phrase to a noun phrase when it cannot be attached to a sentence.

4.6. Empirical Analysis: RACK versus YACC

Empirical results that compare the performance of RACK parsers to parsers generated by YACC are reported in Tables 1 and 2. Values shown correspond to primitive operations executed, including shift, reduce, and stack for YACC parsers, and shift, reduce, stack, disambiguate, and other overhead operations for RACK parsers. In each test, the size of the executable was under 32K for YACC parsers and under 41K for RACK parsers. These tests were run on a Sun 3/60 using C-coded parsers. The benchmark grammar, shown in Fig. 15, is a slight variation on SCOPE.

Table 1 measures the effect on a RACK parser as it switches between its deterministic and nondeterministic modes, increasing sentence size and increasing the number of ambiguous sentence segments. The input segment d is unambiguous, while the input segment n is ambiguous with two derivations. Thus, the first set of sentences has 2^n derivations (for $n \in \{10, 20, 30\}$), the second set has 4^n derivations, and the third has 8^n derivations.

The YACC parser was generated using compile-time disambiguation, while the RACK_n parser was generated using compile-time disambiguation on sentence sequences, only. The RACK_d parser was generated with full compile-time disambiguation; it is presented to compare RACK's GLR parser when running in deterministic mode only to a YACC parser. As indicated by Table 1, the steps required to parse sentences increase linearly for both the YACC and RACK_d parsers, where the RACK_d parser has a greater level of overhead. The RACK_n parser, because it enters the non-

```
%resolve %none
%except s
%token NOUN DET VERB PREP
%lex
%%
NOUN : I | MAN | PARK | SCOPE
DET : A | THE
PREP : IN | WITH
VERB : SAW
%%
s : s pp | np vp | s s
np : NOUN | DET NOUN | np pp
pp : PREP np
vp : VERB np
```

Fig. 15. Benchmark grammar.

d = `i was a man`
n = `i was a man with a scope`

sentences	**YACC**	**RACK$_d$**	**ratio**	**RACK$_n$**	**ratio**
$\{ddn\}^{10}$	725	831	1.2	1335	1.8
$\{ddn\}^{20}$	1445	1661	1.2	2970	2.1
$\{ddn\}^{30}$	2165	2491	1.2	4905	2.3
$\{dnn\}^{10}$	845	971	1.2	1910	2.3
$\{dnn\}^{20}$	1685	1941	1.2	4420	2.6
$\{dnn\}^{30}$	2525	2911	1.2	7530	3.0
$\{nnn\}^{10}$	965	1111	1.2	2475	2.6
$\{nnn\}^{20}$	1925	2221	1.2	5850	3.0
$\{nnn\}^{30}$	2885	3331	1.2	10125	3.5

Table 1. Degrees of ambiguity: 2^n, 4^n, and 8^n.

deterministic mode, naturally has worse performance. However, the performance ratio of the RACK$_n$ parser to the YACC parser, which appears as the last column of Table 1, shows that the cost of parsing ambiguous input is a low factor that increases slowly with the degree of ambiguity.

By adding a second prepositional phrase to the ambiguous input segment n, its degree of ambiguity is increased to five; the degree of ambiguity in the input sentences increases proportionally. Table 2 measures the effect of this increase on performance. As indicated, even after significantly increasing the degree of ambiguity, the performance ratio between RACK and YACC still increases by only a small factor.

The empirical results shown above are intended to measure the performance cost of GLR parsing using RACK. That is, the cost of using sophisticated non-LR(k) grammars over the restricted grammars that can be supported by existing parser generators. In evaluating these results, it is important to keep in mind that most

d = `i was a man`

n = `i was a man in the park with a scope`

sentences	YACC	RACK	ratio
$\{ddn\}^{10}$	845	2005	2.4
$\{ddn\}^{20}$	1685	4310	2.6
$\{ddn\}^{30}$	2525	6915	2.8
$\{dnn\}^{10}$	1085	3250	3.0
$\{dnn\}^{20}$	2165	7100	3.3
$\{dnn\}^{30}$	3245	11550	3.6
$\{nnn\}^{10}$	1325	4485	3.4
$\{nnn\}^{20}$	2645	9870	3.7
$\{nnn\}^{30}$	3965	16155	4.1

Table 2. Degrees of ambiguity: 5^n, 25^n, and 125^n.

of the time spent in translation is in code generation and optimization, not parsing. Real time is not shown because the numbers did not have sufficient precision to be meaningful; for all test shown here, the YACC parsers always ran in under two seconds, and the RACK parsers in under six seconds. The results of these tests support the assertion that RACK generates practical parsers for non-LR(k) languages.

5. Conclusion

In this chapter, I presented the RACK software system as a parser generator for advanced languages, such as the KBPLs of knowledge-based shells. I reviewed standard parsing technologies and described the new technology on which RACK parsers are based. Finally, I demonstrated an application of RACK to a simple English-like grammar and showed empirical results comparing the run-time performance of RACK parsers to parsers generated by YACC.

RACK has been fully implemented in approximately 20,000 lines of C code and is documented with a comprehensive reference manual. Currently, RACK is being applied to the development of DTAS[25], an application-specific language for VLSI design. DTAS uses a concise and expressive syntax for describing the functional decomposition of digital logic circuits; its grammar consists of more than 475 rules and a half-dozen alternative start symbols. RACK is also being applied to a natural-language application in the User-Assisted Translation of Operational Plans (UATOP) project[26].

While no plans have been made to extend the capabilities of RACK as described here, there are several directions that future work could take. RACK could be extended to recognize attribute grammars; this capability would support semantic disambiguation and improve type checking, error detection, and code generation tasks. RACK could be extended to allow dynamic grammar manipulations; this capability would support powerful, LISP-like macro facilities. RACK could also be extended to provide improved error-handling and recovery mechanisms and to interface other languages.

Since the mid-1960s, the syntactic aspects of programming languages have drawn little interest as a topic of research. This apathy is unfortunate, because it has resulted in language features that come at the expense of clear syntax: human factors are frequently disregarded in favor of "computer factors." The ready availability of LR(1) and LL(1) parser generators has actually made this situation worse by forcing language designers to adapt to their limitations. It is my hope that the availability of such tools as RACK may spark new interest in exploring the power of syntax for improving the expressiveness, readability, and general utility of computer languages developed in the coming years.

Acknowledgements

The RACK parser generator was developed by the author while a member of the research staff of the Information Sciences Department at The RAND Corporation. Elements of this work originated with the ROSIE project, which was supported by the Defense Advanced Research Projects Agency under contract number MDA-903-85-C-0030. Development of the RACK parser generator was funded entirely as RAND-Sponsored Research. The author is indebted to Louis Miller, Iris Kameny, Jed Marti, Ed Hall, Jon Hertzog, and others at RAND for their efforts in securing this support.

References

1. M. Tomita, *An Efficient Context-Free Parsing Algorithm for Natural Languages and Its Applications.* PhD thesis, Computer Science Department, Carnegie Mellon University, Pittsburg, PA, (1985).
2. J. R. Kipps, "The RAND Compiler Kit (RACK): Reference Manual and Users Guide," RAND Note N-3100-RC, The RAND Corporation, (1991).
3. J. McCarthy, "Recursive Functions of Symbolic Expressions and Their Computation by Machine," *Communications of the ACM*, **7**, (1960), pp. 184–195.
4. D. H. D. Warren and L. M. Pereira, "PROLOG–The Language and Its Implementation Compared to LISP," *Proceedings of the Symposium on Artificial Intelligence and Programming Languages*, (1977).
5. C. L. Forgy, "The OPS5 User's Manual," TR CMU-CS-81-135, Computer Science Department, Carnegie Mellon University, Pittsburg, PA, (1981).
6. G. W. Ernst and A. Newell, *GPS: A Case Study in Generality and Problem Solving*, (Academic Press. New York, NY, 1969).

7. C. Hewitt, "PLANNER: A Language for Proving Theorems in Robots," *Proceedings of the Second IJCAI*, (1971).
8. D. G. Bobrow and T. Winograd, "An Overview of KRL: A Knowledge Representation Language," *Cognitive Science*, **1(1)**, (1977).
9. W. van Melle, E. H. Shortliffe, and B. G. Buchanan, "EMYCIN: A Domain-Independent System that Aids in Constructing Knowledge-Based Consultation Programs," *Machine Intelligence: Infotech State of the Art*, **9(3)**, (1981).
10. J. R. Kipps, B. Florman, and H. A. Sowizral, "The New ROSIE Reference Manual and User's Guide," RAND Report R-3448-DARPA/RC, The RAND Corporation, (1987).
11. S. C. Johnson, "YACC–Yet Another Compiler Compiler," CSTR 32, Bell Laboratories, Murray Hill, NJ, (1975).
12. E. T. Irons, "Syntax Graphs and Fast Context-Free Parsing," Research Report 71-1, Department of Computer Science, Yale University, New Haven, CT, (1971).
13. J. R. Kipps, "A Table-Driven Approach to Fast Context-Free Parsing," RAND Note N-2841-DARPA, The RAND Corporation, (1988).
14. J. R. Kipps, "RACK: A Parser Generator for AI Languages," *Proceedings of IEEE International Conference on Tools for AI*, (1990), pp. 430–435.
15. N. Chomsky, "Three Models for the Description of Language," *IRE Transactions on Information Theory*, **2(3)**, (1956), pp. 113–124.
16. J. W. Backus, "The Syntax and Semantics of the Proposed International Algebraic Language of the Zurich ACM-GAMM Conference," *Proceedings of the International Conference on Information Processing*, (1959), pp. 125–132.
17. J. Earley, *An Efficient Context-Free Parsing Algorithm*. PhD thesis, Computer Science Department, Carnegie Mellon University, Pittsburg, PA, (1968).
18. D. H. Younger, "Recognition and Parsing of Context-Free Languages in Time n^3," *Information and Control*, **10(2)**, (1967), pp. 189–208.
19. A. V. Aho and J. D. Ullman, *The Theory of Parsing, Translation and Compiling*, (Prentice-Hall, Inc. Englewood Cliffs, NJ, 1972).
20. D. E. Knuth, "On the Translation of Languages from Left to Right," *Information and Control*, **8**, (1965), pp. 607–639.
21. S. Ginsburg and J. S. Ullian, "Preservation of Unambiguity and Inherent Ambiguity in Context-Free Languages," *Journal of the ACM*, **13(3)**, (1966), pp. 364–368.
22. J. R. Kipps, "Analysis of Tomita's Algorithm for General Context-Free Parsing," *Proceedings International Workshop on Parsing Technologies*, (Pittsburg, PA), (1989), pp. 193–202.
23. N. Chomsky, "On Certain Formal Properties of Grammars," *Information and Control*, **2(2)**, (1959), pp. 137–167.

24. M. E. Lesk, "LEX–A Lexical Analyzer Generator," CSTR 39, Bell Laboratories, Murray Hill, NJ, (1975).
25. J. R. Kipps and D. D. Gajski, "Automating Technology Adaptation in Design Synthesis," *Applications of Learning and Planning Methods*, ed. N. G. Bourbakis, (World Scientific Publishing Company, Singapore, 1991).
26. J. R. Kipps and J. Marti, "Extracting Data from Operation Orders," RAND Note N-3300-A, The RAND Corporation, (1991).

CHAPTER 10

OBJECT-ORIENTED NATURAL LANGUAGE PROCESSING SYSTEMS

MAMDOUH H. IBRAHIM
Artificial Intelligence Services, Electronic Data Systems Corporation
Troy, MI, 48007, USA

Abstract

In this article, the potential of using object-oriented programming (OOP) in developing natural language processing (NLP) systems is illustrated through discussion of TARO, an interactive object-oriented tool for building natural language processing systems. TARO is implemented in KSL, an object-oriented language developed at Electronic Data Systems (EDS), to build natural language interfaces for databases and expert systems. TARO takes advantage of the inheritance and polymorphism of OOP to provide an NLP environment in which testing and refinement of complex components can be achieved without major program modifications. By utilizing the encapsulation feature of OOP, TARO provides the opportunity to integrate semantic and syntactic analysis at the same time, rather than in separate stages. This integration dramatically reduces the number of syntactic interpretations that must be considered during a parse operation. Future work in using the object-oriented paradigm to represent discourse interpretations are being investigated.

1. Introduction

Natural language processing was and still is one of the most serious challenges for many researchers in the AI field. The success achieved in automating dictionary look-up and language translation in the fifties, though limited, provided a false hope that natural languages can be easily processed with the available linguistic theories and computer technology.

To address these problems, the field of computational linguistics emerged as a separate field for linguists and computer scientists to focus on the goal of building computer systems that deal with natural languages. Frequently, advances in software engineering and in linguistic models that take advantages of the state-of-the-art in computer hardware have contributed to advances in natural language processing.

For example, early progress in the development of systems for syntactic parsing and analysis was made using conventional computer languages and environments. However, developments in semantic analysis and discourse interpretations were severely limited until the power of symbolic computing (Lisp) and interactive environments were recognized and exploited. The introduction of frame-based languages made it possible to explore implementations based on frames and scripts, while the wide-spread use of Prolog for logic programming opened the door for development of knowledge representation schemes that were difficult to implement before.

Object-oriented programming has only recently gained recognition as a powerful paradigm for organizing and incrementally modeling complex problems. Coupled with workstation technology and interactive programming environments, the paradigm provides an opportunity for developing better integrated and hopefully more powerful natural language processing systems.

Natural language processing encompass many aspects, all of which are very challenging. Text analysis and understanding, natural language interfaces, and machine translation enjoy much of the attention of researchers and industry developers. However, other disciplins are not far behind. Current research activities tackle the more difficult problems of speech recognition and generation, automatic text generation, and representation of world knowledge and common sense for use by natural language systems. In this article we will focus mainly on text analysis, where we will illustrate how the concepts of the object-oriented paradigm can enhance and facilitate building natural language processing systems.

Ideally, any natural language processing system that deals with textual material should include three basic linguistic components: (i) morphological analysis and dictionary operations, (ii) syntactic analysis, and (iii) semantic interpretation. The interaction between these components can vary from one system to another based on the linguistic model used and the particular implementation of the system. For the most part, the concrete research results and the commercially developed systems address the first two components: morphological analysis and dictionary operations and syntactic analysis. Although much effort went into the third component, semantic interpretation, implemented systems still lack the power to process general natural languages on the same level as human do.

From software engineering point of view, advances in knowledge representration schemes contributed to the development of knoweldge structures for representing linguistic concepts and their relationships. These proved to be valuable for semantic interpretation. The best known of these representations schemes are predicate logic, semanitc-nets, frames and script systems.

Furthermore, several programming environments were developed to facilitate the implementation of complex natural language systems. For example, Prolog with its pattern matching and deductive capablities provided a new environment for developing more sophisticated systems. More recently, object-oriented programming has emerged as a powerful paradigm for organizing and developing complex systems.

The rest of this chapter is divided into three sections. Section 2 describes the three linguistic components: morphological analysis and dictionary operations, syntactic analysis, and semantic interpretation. Section 3 presents a brief discussion of semantic nets, frames and scripts, and logic and object-oriented programming concepts as they may apply to natural language processing. Section 4 presents an overview of TARO, the class hierarchy definition of its components, the process for building a parser incrementally and its operations, and a brief discussion of how semantic analysis can be integrated. Finally, potential extensions and future work are presented in section 5.

2. Linguistic Components

The process of analyzing natural language texts could be divided into three basic linguistic components: the morphological analysis and dictionary operations, syntactic analysis, and semantic interpretation. The first of these deals with breaking down the textual material into its elementary components—sentences and words—and the look-up of these words in a a particular lexicon specific to the language analyzed. The second component establishes the syntactic form represented by the words. This process takes into consideration the order of the words, their syntactic forms and the syntactic rules of the language. The semantic interpretation components is responsible of transforming the syntactic constructs generated by the syntactic analysis component to a formal framework representing text meaning.

In addition to the above three components, discourse constraints and interpretation has been established as an important component of any complete natural language processing system that attempts to understand utterance in context. However, discussion of discourse and nonlinguistic factors that need to be considered for language processing will not be discussed here. For the interested reader, selected papers in this area can be found in Readings in Natural Language Processing[1].The rest of this section addresses the three basic linguistic components.

2.1. Morphological Analysis and Dictionary Operations

The first step of any natural language processing system is to recognize and identify the words, the smallest conceptual elements of the text to be analyzed. Once the words are identified, they should be decomposed into word stems and affixes. The decomposition process is analogous to "tokenization" in compiling source code, although much more complex. This decomposition leads to substantial reduction in the space required for dictionaries; only word stems and their possible affixes can be stored in the dictionary rather than storing all words of the language

For example, the word "boys" can be decomposed to "boy" and the suffix "s" indicating plural number, "finished" can be decomposed to "finish" plus the suffix "ed" indicating past tense, and "playing" can be decomposed to "play" and the suffix "ing" indicating present continuous tense. However, the word "king" cannot be decomposed into "k" and "ing", thus the morphological rules must handle such exceptions with care.

Also, spelling rules must be used in some cases to reconstruct the stems produced by standard suffix-removal rules. For example, "leaving" should produce "leave" as a stem rather than "leav", and "canning" should produce "can" rather than "cann". For further reading on algorithms for stem reconstruction see Lovins' paper[2].

Selected lexicons or dictionarys, appropriate for the text under analysis, are then consulted to look-up lexical information about the word. Recently, electronic versions of major dictionaries, such as the New Oxford English Dictionary and Longman's Dictionary of Contemporary English[3,4], became available. These dictionaries contain information about word spelling, pronunciation, lexical categories and syntactic feature, word defintions, and word synonyms among other information.

Simple text analysis methods are primarily based on syntactic information, including lexical word categories (noun, verb, adjective, etc.) and syntactic feature information (e.g., gender, number, tense, etc.) which must be part of the dictionary. Other sophisticated systems require semantic information that must also be attached to the dictionary entries. Thus many text processing systems develop their own lexicon and populate it with the necessary information required by the system.

Some text processing systems provide the user with the capability of updating the dictionary; thus allowing the dictionary to be tailored to the type of text being analyzed. This allows lists of not found words in the text to be generated automatically. These lists include misspelled words and words that are not in the dictionary. The user is then asked to either correct the misspelled words or update the dictionary to include the not found words.

2.2. *Syntactic Analysis*

Syntax deals with the structural properties of texts. Syntactic analysis determines the details of sentence structure and characterizes the structural relations between its components. The process by which this analysis is performed is called parsing, and the component responsible of performing parsing in a language processing system is called the parser.

The parser task is to determine if the sentence conforms to a grammar (set of rules) that describe the language and, if so, it produces a structure that reflects the productions that were applied to generate it. A grammar is called Context-free if the rules apply regardless of the context. Otherwise, it is called context sensetive grammar.

A large body of work on context-free parsing has been developed for the purpose of construction of compilers for computer languages[5] and an efficient algorithm for parsing general context-free languages[6] is described in the literature.

Generally, context-free grammar for phrase structures cannot account for many linguistic facts. Refinement to include some feature agreement, such as subject-verb agreement in number, can be implemented by adding rules specifying the singular and plural forms. Because of its simplicity and for the purpose of this article, we will use context-free grammar to illustrate some of the parsing principals in the following discussion.

Using a grammar that describes the structures of strings in a language, the parser assigns a structure, called a parse tree, to each grammatical sentence. For example, given the grammar shown in Figure 1, the sentence "The children play a game" can be parsed to produce the parse tree shown in Figure 2.

```
1) S      -->   NP    VP
2) NP     -->   Det   N
3) VP     -->   V     NP
4) Det    -->   "the" | "a"
5) N      -->   "children" | "game"
6) V      -->   "play"
```

Figure 1. A simple grammar for subset of the English language.

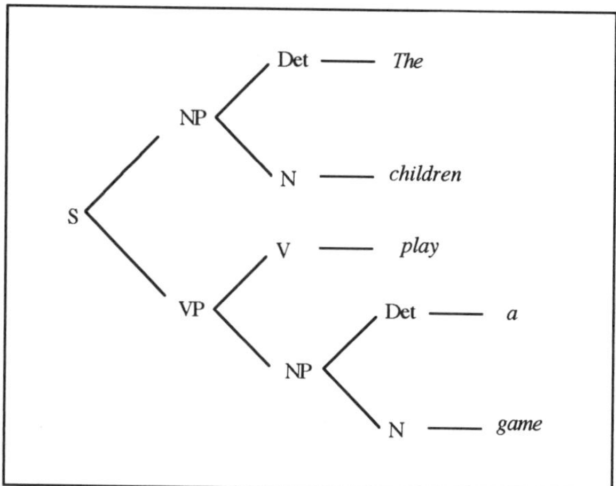

Figure 2. A parse tree for a sentence.

It is important to notice that for a given language there may exist many grammars. Though these grammar describe the same language, they may produce different parse trees for the same sentence, or they may vary in their parsing efficiency. Thus writing or selecting a grammar that is appropriate for the purpose of a particular language processing system is very important for the success of that system. However, grammar writing is outside the scope of this chapter and will not be discussed further.

For parsing a sentence using a grammar There are two main parsing strategies available in principle for parsing a sentence using a grammar:top down and bottom up. The top-down strategy is a hypothesis driven approach in which parsing begins with the start symbol (S in the grammar of the above example) applying the grammar rules in a forward direction until the terminal symbols correspond to the words of the sentence being parsed.On the other hand, the bottom-up strategy is a data driven approach in which individual text words are initially considered, and attempts are made to group them into successively larger components by applying the rules of the grammar backward and until a single parse tree has been produced.

The same structures generated as output of a parsing process can be found by both top-down and bottom-up parsing, but the difference is in the amount of work to be done. For example, a strictly top-down, left-to-right parsing strategy is inefficient when the parser encounters actual sentence words that do not satisfy the decomposition of the initial hypothesis selected during the forward applications of the grammar rules. At this point the anlaysis is abandoned and the parser starts all over by selecting another intial set of hypotheses.

For example, the correct parse tree for the two sentences:

"Have the students take the exam today!" and
"Have the students taken the exam today?"

can be determined only after encountring the form of the verb "take"[7] (assuming the parser looks at the words one at a time from left to right). In the first sentence "Have" is the main verb of an imperative sentence, while it is an auxiliary verb of the interrogative second sentence. The inefficiency of this approach is due to the fact that one alternative is selected to begin with, then if it proves to be the wrong choice after the rest of the sentence is encountered, backtracting is performed to consider new interpretations. Backtracking can be avoided by using look-ahead features that anticipate the sentence structure to the right of the current analysis point. However, this complicates the system.

On the other hand, the bottom-up approach may also be inefficeint when parsing certain sentences. This is because strict bottom-up parsing will not allow the use of previously confirmed information in simplifying the rest of the analysis steps. For example, when using a bottom-up parser to analyze the sentence: "He can cause trouble" the parser will not be able to determine that the word "can" cannot be a noun, while this alternative could be ruled out if the parser is allowed to use information obtained by confirming that the previous word "He" is a pronoun that can not be followed by a noun.

To avoid the problems encountered when applying one approach by itself, sometimes they are combined into one method called bottom-up parsing with top-down filtering. In this method, parsing proceds bottom-up with guidance from tables precomputed for a particular grammar to eliminate constituents that will never be combined into higher-level structures in the grammar.

One of the best-known parsing mechanism is the Augmented Transition Network (ATN)[8]. In this parser, the grammar is represented by a network of nodes representing states, and branches specifying transitions between states. The branches are labeled with names for word classes like noun, verb, adjective, etc. The class of labels that can be attached to the branches of the network can be augmented to specify any combination of the following: specific words, recursive calls to subordinate ATNs, test operations on both the current input and on already identified constituents, and procedures that build structures contributing to the final parse tree.Figure 3 illustrates an ATN network for a subset of the English language grammar.

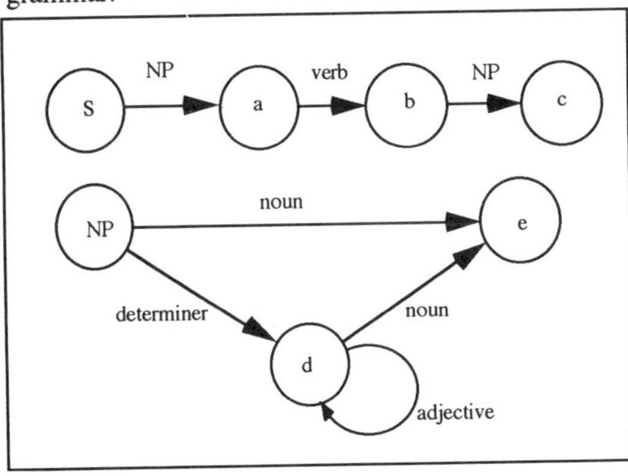

Figure 3. An example of an ATN network.

In the this example, tests on the labels are assumed to be always true. However, ATN allows tests, possibly semantic, to be specified on the labels. For example, when the first NP is encountered its number is stored in a special register. Then the branch labeled "verb" could have an additional test that checks the number of the particular verb found is equal to the value stored in the register. Other semantic tests can also be performed this way.

Active chart parser[9] is another efficient parser that takes the idea of a well formed substring table (chart), which is a passive lattice consisting of one edge per constituent (either initial or discovered), and makes it active by using edges to record partial or incomplete hypothesized constituents as well. The chart can be visualized as a network of vertices representing points in the sentence linked by edges representing constituents. Initially, the chart has only the edges representing the words of the sentence and their lexical categories. As constituents are found by the parser, they are added to the chart. The parser uses the chart by entering a new constituent whenever a rule succeeds and looking in it for constituents whenever there is a nonterminal at the beginning of the remainder. The parser can use an edge found in the chart starting at the current point, and advances to the end of that edge without reparsing the constituent represented by that edge.

In active chart parser, in addition to keeping a list of all complete edges that represent constituents found, another list of active edges are also maintaned that represent points along the way in looking for constituents to be complete. Each active edge will have a remainder that indicates what still need to be found. The parser stops when a constituent is found that contains all the words of the sentence. Active chart parsers reduce work duplication (constituents are computed only once) and make it possible to design flexible strategies for deciding the order in which to try the rules. For a servey of syntactic analysis techniques see Winograd[10] volume on syntax.

2.3 Semantic Interpretation

Semantics refer to the study of meaning in language. Semantic interpretation is the process of mapping natural languages, or their syntactic analyses, onto some representation of their meaning. Semantic interpretation is very important component in any language processing system since syntactic analysis alone cannot resolve natural language ambiguities using purely structural rules.

There are several ways to produce semantic interpretation of a sentence. The following paragraphs discuss briefly representatives of semantic interpretation techniques such as semantic grammars, case grammars, and conceptual dependency.

Semantic grammars.

Semantic grammars are specialized context-free grammars that are capable of analyzing only certain type of texts. These grammars use deeper and more detailed knowkedge that cover only a narrow subject domain. Most systems built using this approach intended for analyzing queries to retrieve information from specialized databases.

The best known example of this semantic grammar is the LADDER system[11] which provides a natural language interface to a distributed database dealing with ships and their attributes. A sample of this grammar is illustrated in Figure 4.

S	-->	*what is the* ATTRIBUTE *of* SHIP
ATTRIBUTE	-->	*speed* | *length* | *beam* | *class*
SHIP	-->	*the* SHIP-NAME | *ships of class* CLASS-NAME
SHIP-NAME	-->	*kennedy* | *enterprise*
CLASS-NAME	-->	*kitty hawk* | *lafayette*

Figure 4. A sample semantic grammar.

In this example, concepts such as length or class are unambiguous since the context in which this grammar operates deals with ships. So when the query "what is the length of the kennedy" is encountered, it is interpreted according to this grammar to be the length of the ship kennedy not the person named kennedy.

Although this type of grammar is very successful in resolving ambiguity in narrow domain when dealing with small number of rules, it is unmanageable when the number of rules grows large. The grammar also can not be used in dealing with other subject matter than what it was build for. Nevertheless, semantic grammars are suitable for producing restricted natural language interfaces quickly, but they will never produce a general solution for natural language understanding.

Case Grammars.

Case grammars[12,13] are another approach to combining syntactic analysis and semantic interpretation. Generally, case grammars operate with relatively shallow knowledge that cover a wide area.

In such grammar, constructs are characterized by lexical heads. For example, nouns function as heads for noun phrases, and verbs as heads for sentences. Each head class is associated with certain roles (cases). Examples of such roles are AGENT (initiator of an event), OBJECT or PATIENT (entity that is acted upon), INSTRUMENT (cause of the event or object used), etc.

Parsing using case grammar is expectation driven. It works by comparing the expectations embodied in case frames attached to head classes with the case identifiers attached to the words of the sentence. This requires entries in the lexicon to identify case frames for the head classes and case identifiers for other significant words. Once the verb of the sentence (the head class) is encountered, the parser, attempts to fill in the slots of its case frame using the appropriate elements of the sentence that have case identifiers matching the case specifications.

AGENT	who does the breaking
OBJECT	that is being broken
LOCATIVE	place of the event
INSTRUMENT	used for breaking
TIME	time of the breaking event

Figure 5. Simplified case frame for the verb "BREAK".

For example, if the verb "BREAK" is associated in the lexicon with the case frame shown in Figure 5, then the sentence "Bill broke the window with a hammar" can be semantically interpreted as shown in Figure 6.

```
(broke (AGENT Bill)
       (OBJECT window)
       (INSTRUMENT hammar)
```

Figure 6. Semantic interpretation of a sentence.

Notice that parsing using case grammars depends heavily on the correctness of the lexical entries associated with each verb in the lexicon.

Case grammars are successful in resolving most of the syntactic ambiguities. This is because the case identifiers of the words are matched to the slots of the corresponding case frame of the verb, and they will be guaranteed to fill in the slots that match the intended meaning of the words. However, case grammars cannot analyze semantically ambiguous sentences that can only be resolved by contextual information or special knowledge of discourse.

ATNs provide a suitable structure for parsers using case grammars. For example, Simmons[14] describes a system that uses ATN parser to translate English sentences into a semantic net representing the case structures of the sentences. Case grammar can also be embeded within other overall formalisms. For example, it served as the basis for a major transformational analysis of English, the UCLA Grammar[15].

Conceptual Dependency.

Conceptual dependency (CD) is a full meaning representation formalism developed by Roger Schank[16]. It differs from the previous two approaches to semantic interpretation in that it de-emphasizes the role of syntax and concentrates on constructing the meaning structures.

Parsing using conceptual dependency bears a strong resemblace to parsing using case grammar, both are driven by expectations that are set up by the main verb of the sentence. However, the roles of CD are filled by conceptual entities (acts and objects) rather than syntactic constituents (NPs and clauses). CD goes beyond case frames, by defining a system of primitives and rules to manipulate them that capture the meaning of the sentence, rather than having a case frame for every verb.

The theory behind CD assumes that all verbs (actions) can be reduced in meaning to combinations of a small group of primitive ACTS. Each ACT has a fixed number of arguments associated with it, e.g., actor, recipient, object, etc. For example, the sentence "John gave Mary a book" would have the representation*:

---

*A graphical representation for CD were introduced by Schank[16], but will not be discussed here.

(ATRANS)

ACTOR:	John
DONER:	John
RECIPIENT:	Mary
OBJECT:	book

In this representation, the meaning of the verb "gave" is represented by the ATRANS primitive ACT, which indicates Abstract TRANSfer (of possession) of an object. Other verbs, such as "take", are also represented by ATRANS, but have their slots filled differently. A typical set of primitive actions were given by Schank[17] is as follows:

ATRANS	Transfer of an abstract relationship (e.g., give)
PTRANS	Transfer of physical location of an object (e.g., go)
PROPEL	Application of physical force to an object (e.g., push)
MOVE	Movement of a body part by its owner (e.g., kick)
GRASP	Grasping of an object by an actor (e.g., throw)
INGEST	Ingesting an object by an animal (e.g., eat)
EXPEL	Expulsion of an object from the body of an animal (e.g., cry)
MTRANS	Transfer of mental information (e.g., tell)
MBUILD	Building new information out of old (e.g., decide)
SPEAK	Producing of sounds (e.g., say)
ATTEND	Focusing of a sense organ toward a stimulus (e.g., listen)

Some of the CD roles are filled with an act instead of an object. For example, a key is not allowed to fill the INSTRUMENT role of an action. Instead, other action (such as turning the key) in which the key is a central participant may be used to fill the INSTRUMENT role. Examples of these roles that can be filled by conceptualizations (i.e., other acts) are CAUSE, REASON, etc.

An important component in any parser using CD is the verb-ACT dictionary which contains entry for each environment in which a verb can appear. For example, the verb-ACT dictionary may have three entries associated with the verb "want".These entries correspond to the different usage of the verb "want": stative (want something to happen), transitive (want an object), or intransitive (want a person).

To map a sentence into its CD, first the main verb and noun of the sentence are identified through a syntactic parser. Next, the appropriate entry from the verb-ACT dictionary is selected. The rest of the sentence is then analyzed to find components that fit into the empty slots of the verb structure selected from the dictionary.

A series of parsers were built based on CD. MARGIE[16] was the first in this series. It handled very simple sentences. MARGIE was followed later by SAM and PAM[17] that use CD in higher knowledge representations called scripts and plan-based schemes.

CD demonstrated the advantages of using primitive-based, semantic representations in dealing with natural language systems. However, it requires a vast amount of semantic information in order to be able to produce a complete and correct semantic interpretations within any given context.

3. Representational and Computational Issues

The previous section addressed linguistic knowledge and models that must be considered when deeling with natural language processing. To construct computational systems that can process natural languages, we must consider not only linguistic issues, but also computational models that allow knowledge representation and data structuring.

The AI literature is full of research directed toward knowledge representation. In this section, we discuss some of these knowledge representation schemes that have been used for natural language processing. Also, we discuss programming paradigms that provide, in addition to knowledge representation, software engineering advances that facilitate building natural language processing systems. In the remainder of this section we focus first on two representation schemes, semantic nets and frames and scripts. Next, we present logic programming emphasizing its contribution to natural language processing. Finally, we introduce the concepts of the object-oriented paradigm as the latest advance in programming techniques that can benefit language processing systems.

3.1. Semantic Networks

As is the case with any representation, semantic nets, first developed by Quillian[18] and Raphael[19], provide a way to denote objects and describe the relations among them. For illustrative purposes, objects of semantic nets are denoted by labeled circles (called nodes) and the relations are denoted by labeled archs between the nodes (called links).

The difference between any node-link network and semantic nets is that in the later, labels represent meaningful information. For example, Figure 7 illustrates a semantic net that describes an object, my-desk, and its associated relations.

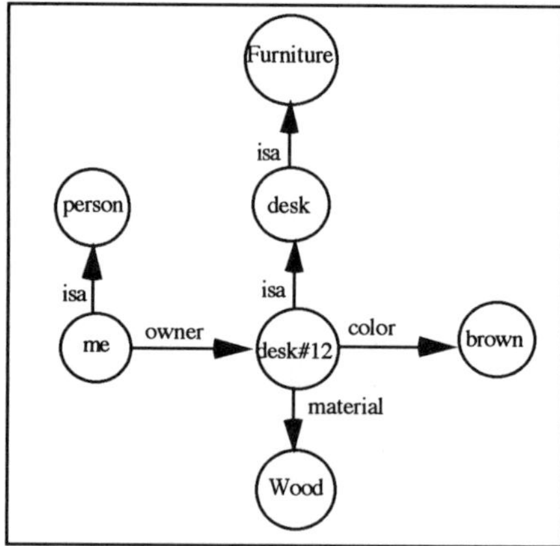

Figure 7. An example of a semantic net.

Semantic nets provide a convinient structure for representing information in such a way that allows later reasoning with the knowledge. For instance, in the previous example it is easy to find answer to questions such as who owns desk#12? and what color is desk#12? and so on.

Because of their expressive power, semantic nets were used to represent the contents of natural language sentences through describing the aspects of particular events. For example, using case grammar, the sentence "Bill gave Mary a book" can be represented by the semantic net illustrated by Figure 8.

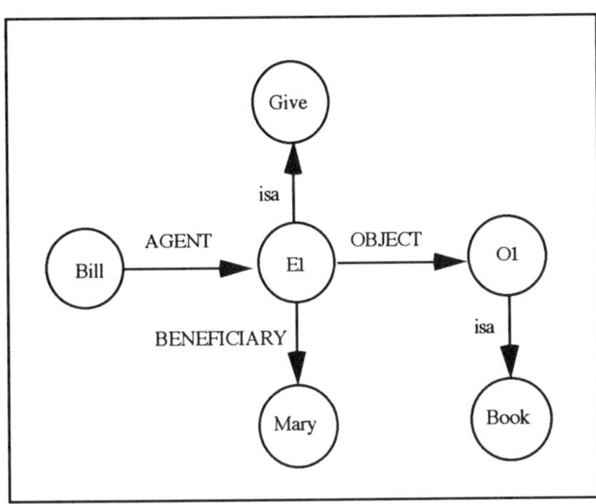

Figure 8. A semantic net representation of a sentence.

Note in the above example, E1 and O1 are specific instances of the concepts Give and Book, respectively. Links associated with specific instances describe properties of that instance, while links associated with concepts describe general properties that apply to the majority of the instances of that concept.

Several natural language systems used semantic nets for semantic interpretation. One reason is that semantic nets lend themselves to a natural implementation of ATNs. SHRDLU[20] is an example of a natural language system that utilizes semantic nets for its knowledge representation. SHRDLU is an integrated program that deals with a specific domain, the blocks world. SHRDLU represents physical objects and allows the user to use natural language to ask questions about the state of the world and what is possible within this world. The system is made up of three major components, a syntactic parser based on ATN, a semantic processor to interpret word meanings, and a logical deductive segment that finds answers to user questions.

Another example of a system using semantic net is descibed by Simmons[14] which uses an ATN paeser to translate English sentences into a semantic net representing the case structures of the sentences. The semantic nets can then be used to answer questions about the sentences.

Semantic nets are a powerful tool for knowledge representation. However, one of thier major limitations is the difficulty of manipulating large, complex network structure. One approach to overcome this difficulty is to partition the network into groups of related nodes and their links[21]. By collapsing these groups, each to be represented by one node, the network is simplified, and reasoning can shift to the lower level when detail information is required.

Semantic nets have been used for other purposes such as learning[22], but discussion of these other uses is beyond the scope of this article.

3.2. Frames and Scripts

The notion of frames extends the concept of partitioning semantic nets. We can think of a frame as a collection of semantic net nodes and slots that together describe an object, act, or event. Frames, first introduced by Minsky[23] are conceptual objects that are used as an organizational mechanism for grouping pieces of knowledge into logically consistent blocks.

A frame consists of a collection of slots that describe the object represented by the frame. In turn, the slots point to other frames describing other objects. Conditions, default values, and procedural information are all valid fillers for the slots of frames. The flexibility in using different types of slot fillers makes the frame representation a very powrful tool for representing knowledge. For example, default values supply typical information in the absence of specfic values. Procedural attachement can be invoked when slot values change or to indicate how to compute slot values when required. An example of a typical frame to represent a Date object is illustrated in Figure 9. In this example the slots of the frame are the YEAR, which carry 1989 as default, the MONTH, and the DAY. When a particular Date frame is instantiated, the default value of the YEAR is automatically used from the Date frame. Other slot values must be filled individually to complete the frame.

YEAR: 1989
MONTH:
DAY:

Figure 9. A Date frame.

Frame languages like KRL[24] and KL-ONE[25] were developed to manipulate frames and to implement operations such as frame matching. These languages provide frame hierarchies that allow inheritance of properties from higher level frames, and type checking of values that can fill a slot to enforce certain constraints.

Several systems were built that take advantage of frame representation. The first, GUS[26], was an experimental, extended natural language interaction system. Gus played the role of travel agent with a user planning a simple trip in California. Initial database for GUS was extracted from the Official Airline Guide and the data were stored in a suitable frame format. Although GUS operated in a limited domain and was considered an experimental system, it proved that frame representaition schemes are an impovement over those using semantic nets.

By restricting the use of frame-like structure, Schank and his students introduced the notion of script[17] as a sequence of stereotyped sequence of events that can help explain understanding stories. Like frames, scripts consist of slots that contain associated information. However, slots of a script have special roles. For example, the slot Entry Conditions describes the conditions that must be satisfied before processing the script, the slot Roles represents the people who are involved in the events described by the script, and the slot Scenes describes actual sequence of events that constitute the script with the events represented in CD formalism. Other slots describe the objects involved in the events described by the script and the results that will occur after the events of the script occur. Figure 10 illustrates simplified version of the restaurant script (taken from Schank[17]).

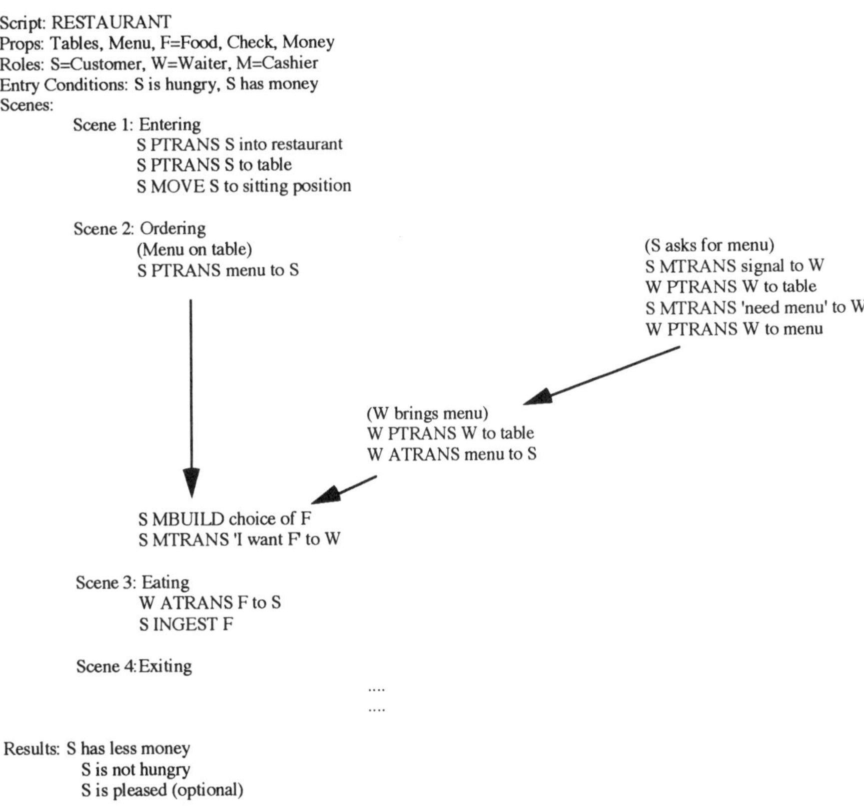

Figure 10. Illustration of a simplified Restaurant Script.

Note that the slot contain script variables like F, for food, S, for customer, etc. will need to be bound during the process of understanding a story.

The first step in a process that use scripts is to identify and activate the appropriate script. The first few sentences play an important role in selecting and confirming the choice of the relevant scripts. Next, sentences are matched with the script elements, binding script variables along the way.

Several systems were build by Schank and his students based on CD and scripts. SAM[27] is a system that could read newspaper stories on certain topics and produces instantiated script structures representing the contents of the story. SAM consists of three modules: ELI, an English language parser which maps the sentences into CD representation; PP-Memory, which identifies the individuals refered to in the text; and the Script Applier, which decides and instantiates the appropriate scripts at any point in the process. PAM[28] is another such high level representation system that understands stories in terms of plan-based schemes.

Scripts are useful in answering questions about events that were not explicitly observed. Also, scripts provide a coherent interpretation from a collection of observations. However, with all the potential that scripts offered, implemented systems that use scripts were all limited. Their success is primarily due to the narrow domains for which they were build. Further research is still needed to support the range of functionality that is characteristic of human language understanding.

3.3. Logic Programming

Since much of language analysis is based on representing facts and reasoning about them, predicate logic immediately seems appealing as a semantic representation. This is because predicate logic is supposed to be able to represent the logical form of any sentence, which will lend themselves to being used in reasoning.

With predicate calculus very well studied in the literature, many researchers used it to represent natural language statements. Predicate calculus language consists of a set of constant terms; a set of variables; a set of predicates each taking a specified number of arguments; the connectives IF, AND, OR, and NOT; and the quantifiers EXISTS and FORALL. The terms of the language can be constants, variables or functions applied to the correct number of terms. Finally, the formulas of the language are:

i) A predicate applied to the correct number of terms;
ii) If p and q are formulas then (if p q), (and p q), (or p q), and (not p).
iii) If x is a variable, and p is a formula, then (exists (x) p), and (forall (x) p).

In predicate calculus, initial facts are called axioms. To deduce new facts from the axioms, predicate calculus has rules of inference. Examples of these rules are the modus ponens (given (if p q) and p then deduce q) and the universal instantiation (if something is true of everything, then it is true for any particular thing). Using these rules and the established axioms, new axioms are deduced and the process continues until deducing the fact one wanted. For example, if we have the following:

```
(1)   (instant tweety canary)          !tweety is a canary
(2)   (forall x (if                    !all canaries are yellow
              (instant x canary)
              (color x yellow)))
```

Then we can deduce from (2) using the universal instantiation

```
(3)   (if (instant tweety canary)
              (color tweety yellow))
```

Then using the modus ponens on (3) along with (1) we deduce that

```
(4)   (color tweety yellow)
```

Complementing predicate calculus with resolution procedures and unification algorithms and backtracking opened the door for developing powerful languages for logic programming. The dialect that is most successful is Prolog[29]. Prolog programs consist of set of relations among objects. Each relation is composed of a set of clauses. Usually the relations will contain variables, and part of the proof process involves finding the appropriate binding for these variables that make the relation true. Prolog interpreter uses backtracking to find variable bindings.

The development of Prolog has raised hope in using logic programming for natural language processing. Many parsers were developed in Prolog to take advantage of programming with logic. For a comprehensive discussion of the use of Prolog to represent grammars see the article by Pereira and Warren[30].

Unfortunately, predicate logic, in general, and Prolog, in particular, cannot represent all kind of knowledge. For example, relative information, uncertainty, inference of facts from the absence of others, and beliefs are difficult to represent with predicate logic. A variety of techniques for handling these problems were developed, including: nonmonotonic reasoning, probabilistic reasoning, fuzzy logic, and the concept of belief spaces. However, because the scope of these topics is beyond that of this article, they will not be discussed here.

3.4. The Object-Oriented Paradigm

Object-oriented programming has recently gained the acceptance of the computer science community as the best paradigm for organizing and dealing with very complex systems. The paradigm compliment the concept of frames with notions such as abstraction, encapsulation, and inheritance to create objects that communicate through sending and receiving messages.

Object-oriented programs represents elements of a problem domain as objects. An object incorporates both data and functional characteristics. All operations are performed by sending messages to objects to invoke behaviors. Objects that represent entities of a problem typically incorporate other objects as components. Encapsulation refers to the separation of the implementation of a component from its usage so that local changes can be explored without having widespread impact. Polymorphism is the property that allows the interchange of objects that observe the same external protocol. It enables sending the same messages to objects of different classes. For example, in a natural language processing system (as we will see in the description of TARO next section), a dictionary can be represented as an object containing words; a word is an object containing other objects that define the part of speech, gender, etc. Access to a dictionary, and thus the words in the dictionary, is accomplished through sending messages to the dictionary. The dictionary can be replaced by another, differently structured dictionary, without adverse impact as long as the new dictionary complies with the same message protocol.

For the purpose of this article, we will introduce KSL[31], a reflective object-oriented programming language developed by the Research and Development group of Electronic Data Systems (EDS), and is implemented in a workstation-based interactive programming environment (EDS/OWL[32]). KSL provides class-based inheritance, where objects are described by classes. An object is an instance of the class that describes it. A new class can be created by specialization of an existing class. The new class will inherit all of the behaviors of the existing class. Additional behaviors can be defined and inherited behaviors can be redefined as required on the new class. Note that in KSL, object data are stored in slots and the object functional characteristics are called methods. Both slots and methods are referred to more generally as object behaviors.

In KSL, everything is an object, including classes, behaviors, and program instructions; thus KSL can operate on itself, which makes it reflective. This quality enables classes, behaviors, and instructions to be created and modified programmatically. It also enables objects to be both components of the problem model and active elements in the program execution process, thus allowing dynamic modification of a program.

The reflective capability of KSL—the ability of the language to operate on itself—makes it particularly suitable for the problems presented by NLP. KSL is used to develop a Text Analysis and Representation with Objects (TARO) system discussed in the next section.

4. Building Object-Oriented NLP Systems

This section describes TARO a tool for building natural language processing systems which is implemented in KSL. TARO takes advantage of the inheritance and polymorphism of OOP to provide an NLP environment in which testing and refinement of complex components can be achieved without major program modifications. Much of the extensibility of TARO is a result of the reflectivity of KSL, which allows grammar rules and classes of lexical constituents to be defined and tested interactively. TARO provides the opportunity to perform semantic and syntactic processing at the same time, rather than in separate stages, by utilizing the encapsulation feature of OOP. This integration dramatically reduces the number of syntactic interpretations that must be considered during a parse operation. These are very important features when building and testing a natural language system.

4.1. Introduction to TARO

TARO operates on a set of context free grammar rules, a set of associated semantic rules, a lexicon, an input mechanism for the sentences to be processed, and a working memory that contains the structures generated during the parsing process. The major components of TARO are depicted in the class hierarchy in Figure 11.

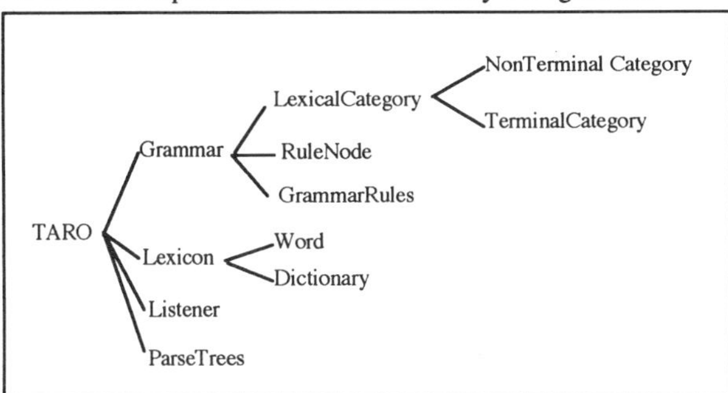

Figure 11. TARO object class hierarchy.

A grammar in TARO is represented by an instance of the GrammarRules class. Each grammar rule is represented by a RuleNode object. The NonTerminalCategory and the TerminalCategory subclasses describe the lexical objects on which the grammar rules operate. Behaviors defined on these classes provide information specifying the lexical type and the word positions in a sentence for each lexical object. Further specializations of these classes provide a lexical object representation for the grammar symbols.

A Listener in TARO is the recipient of the sentence to be processed. Specialization of the Listener class allows capturing and forming sentences from different types of input, e.g., speech input or input from a text database. The Parse behavior defined on this class can be specialized to allow the use of different parsing strategies. The built-in parser of TARO uses a technique similar to the active chart parser discussed by Winograd[10] and the parsing algorithm presented by Tomita[33]. It retains all of the generated partial and complete lexical structures, does not use backtracking, and does not duplicate construction of the same syntactic constituents. Unlike the active chart, the built-in parser uses a bottom-up parsing strategy in order to avoid problems caused by left-recursive rules. For a particular parse operation, a Listener must be associated with a dictionary and a grammar. Specialization of Dictionary and GrammarRules can be developed to allow parsing in different domains.

Working memory for TARO is represented by a ParseTrees object; it becomes the parser output. Attributes are added to the ParseTrees class during the process of building the grammar to reflect the addition of new terminal and non-terminal lexical categories--a process that is supported by the reflectivity of KSL. The objects representing the lexical constituents in working memory provide an object representation for the lexical structures of the parsed sentence. In addition to the syntactic information, these objects incorporate semantic behaviors—both data and functions—which are used during the parse.

Working memory can be accessed to obtain the lexical objects that represent a full sentence or any partial constituent. The parser output can be displayed in a network form using the graphical facilities provided by the interactive environment of EDS/OWL.

To illustrate we use an example context free grammar, given by Winograd[10] and shown in Figure 12, to parse the sentence "the rabbit with a saw nibbled on an orange".

S	-->	NP VP
NP	-->	Determiner NP2
NP	-->	NP2
NP2	-->	Noun
NP2	-->	Adjective NP2
NP2	-->	NP2 PP
PP	-->	Preposition NP
VP	-->	Verb
VP	-->	Verb NP
VP	-->	Verb PP

Figure 12. Example context free grammar.

The display of the S (sentence) lexical objects generated after parsing the example is shown in Figure 13. All the lexical objects are prefixed and suffixed by the beginning and ending word numbers of their constituents. Details of elements that appear in the structures toward the top of the display are not repeated unless an expanded view is requested.

4.2. Incremental Grammar Building

Incremental definition of the parser components is an important feature of TARO because it contributes to the rapid prototyping and extensibility. The following paragraphs focus on the process of building a grammar for the standard parser.

When grammar symbols are introduced to TARO, classes are created to represent the general behaviors of the corresponding lexical types. For example, Noun, Verb, etc., become subclasses of TerminalCategory, and S, NP, VP, etc., become subclasses of NonTerminalCategory as shown in Figure 14. Also, the ParseTrees class is modified to add a slot that corresponds to each added symbol, thus associating the grammar symbols with working memory.

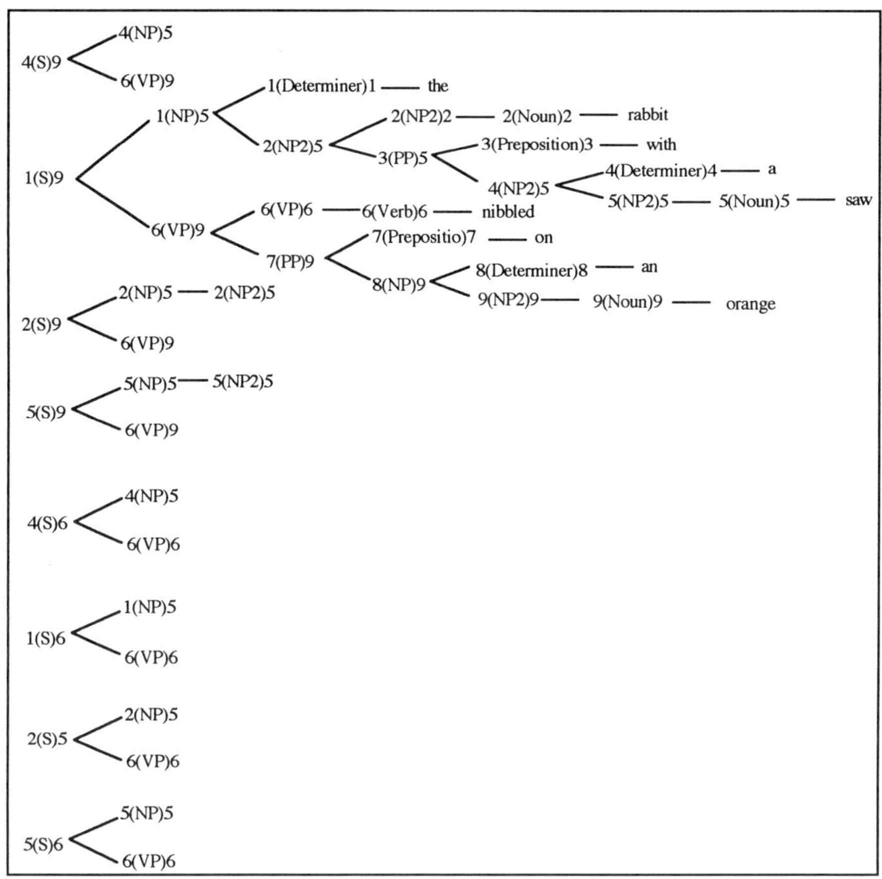

Figure 13. The S contents display.

Grammar rules are represented by instances of the *RuleNode* class, which defines the mechanism of the matching process. Lexical objects, created by the rules, are described by further specialization of the *NonTerminalCategory* subclasses. These specialized classes are defined incrementally as the rules are specified. For each rule, the class representing the lexical category of its left hand side is specialized to create a subclass that represents the lexical objects created by this rule. For example, in Figure 14 the *NP_1* and *NP_2* classes are created when the first and second NP rules of the example grammar are added. Note that both NP_1 and NP_2 are of the NP lexical category type but represent two different

NP grammar rules. Semantic behaviors for a particular grammar rule can then be defined on the associated class.

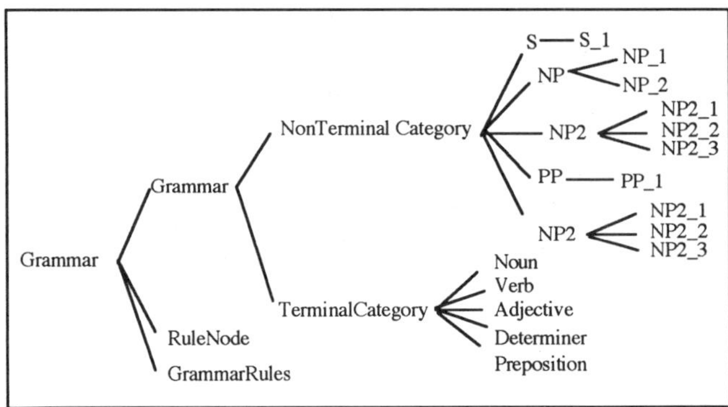

Figure 14. The class hierarchy for the example grammar.

A grammar browser, shown in Figure 15, displays a graphical representation of the grammar. This browser is used to inspect and manipulate the grammar rules interactively and to gain access to the behaviors defined on the lexical category classes.

To improve the efficiency of the matching process, the grammar rules are partitioned according to the lexical category of the last symbol in their right hand side. Rules ending with the same symbol are incorporated into a *PossibleRules* behavior defined on the class representing the lexical category of that symbol. For example, the *PossibleRules* behavior of the *Noun* class contains pointers to all rules ending with a Noun, only the NP2_1 rule in this grammar. Similarly, the *PossibleRules* behavior of the *NP2* class points only at the RuleNodes representing NP_1, NP_2, and NP2_2 because they end with NP2.

4.3 Syntactic Representation with Objects

The parsing of a sentence is initiated by sending a Parse message to a *Listener* object. In the standard parser, words of the input sentence are processed from left to right and the corresponding *Word* objects are retrieved from the *Dictionary*. Each *Word* object is used to instantiate a corresponding terminal lexical object which is then inserted in the corresponding slot in working memory. For example, when the word "saw" is encountered, two terminal lexical objects of the *Noun* and *Verb* classes are instantiated and inserted in the Noun and Verb slots of the *ParseTrees* object.

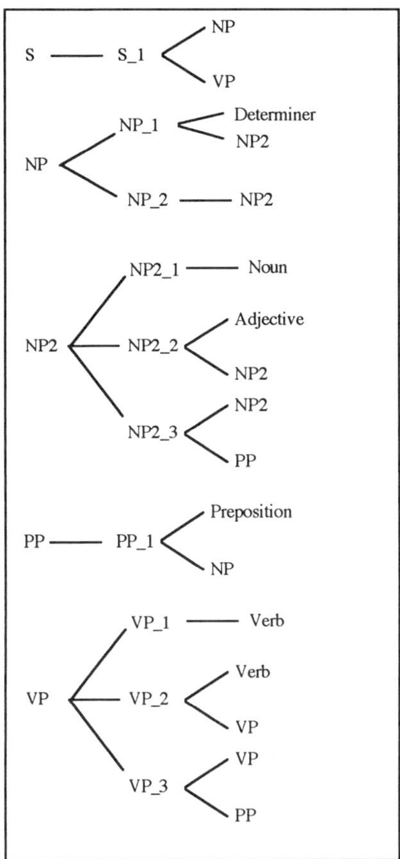

Figure 15. The Grammar Browser.

The addition of a new lexical object to working memory triggers the matching process for the grammar rules that end with the type of the added object. These rules are referenced by the *PossibleRules* behavior of the lexical object class. The process of matching a rule involves a search for constituents that match the right hand side of the rule. Matched rules are fired creating new lexical objects which are added to working memory. The matching process is repeated for each added object until no new rules are triggered. The parser then continues with the next word from the input sentence.

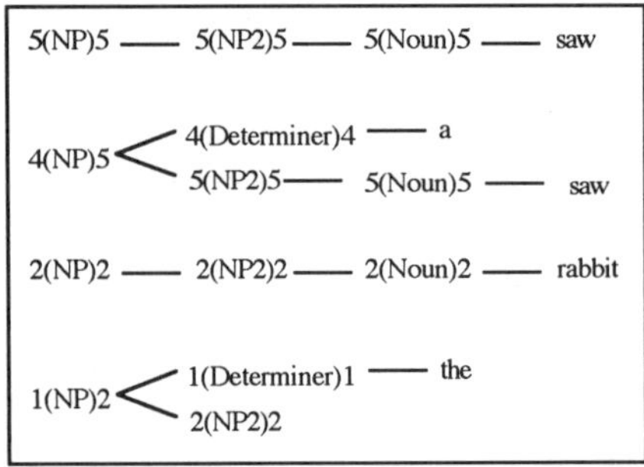

Figure 16. Partial display of the NP constituents.

As shown in Figure 16, if the 2(Noun)2 object representing the word "rabbit" is encountered while parsing the example sentence, then only the NP2_1 rule is triggered as referenced by the *PossibleRules* behavior of the *Noun* class. The rule is matched and fired adding a 2(NP2)2 object to working memory. This addition triggers the NP_1, NP_2, and NP2_2 rules referenced by the *PossibleRules* behavior of the *NP2* class. Both NP_1 and NP_2 match and are fired creating 1(NP)2 and 2(NP)2, respectively. However, NP2_2 is not matched because no preceding Adjective constituent exists at this time in working memory. Similarly, the PP_1 rule triggered by the addition of 1(NP)2 and 2(NP)2 fails causing the parser to proceed with the next word from the sentence.

Note that a word sequence constraint eliminates the matching of constituents that are not in sequential order. For example, when the 5(NP2)5 is encountered, it will be combined only with 4(Determiner)4, representing the word "a", to create 4(NP)5 and not with the 1(Determiner)1 which represents the word "the". In addition, the lexical constituents matching the right hand side of a rule must satisfy associated semantic constraint behaviors before the rule is fired.

4.4. Semantic Integration

The object representation of TARO permits the integration of semantic analysis in several components. First, the semantics of each word can be attached as attributes of the word object in the Dictionary and can be used to determine the role of the word in a certain context. Second, since the lexical categories created by each grammar rule are represented as objects of different classes, semantic analysis associated with a particular rule can be added as behaviors on the corresponding class. The inheritance feature of OOP allows sharing the semantic behavior definitions. For example, the semantic behaviors that are common to all noun phrases are defined on the NP class and are inherited by all of its subclasses. On the other hand, semantic behaviors defined for a particular NP rule can be defined as specialized behaviors on the class created for that rule.

In the standard TARO parser, the ability to integrate semantic analysis with syntactic analysis has been implemented for simple agreement features such as Number, Gender, Person, and Case as behaviors on the words of the dictionary. Agreement checks and propagation are implemented as behaviors on the lexical category classes. The agreement check behaviors are invoked when a grammar rule is lexically matched. If the semantic behaviors of the matched constituents satisfy the agreement check behaviors, then the rule is fired. Otherwise the rule is rejected reducing the number of possible syntactic interpretations that could be generated. The propagate agreement behaviors are invoked as a result of firing a rule. These behaviors propagate the appropriate semantic information to the added lexical objects.

Role behaviors incorporate additional semantics. They specify the roles which the constituents of a rule play within a sentence. The definition of these behaviors parallels the definition of the lexical class hierarchy. For example, when the S_1 rule is fired, the NP constituent is assigned the Subject role and the VP constituent is assigned the Verb role in the parsed sentence.

Currently, we are in the process of using TARO to build a grammar checker for English text by adding an expert system component to examine the partial constituents generated during the parser operation. This component will use heuristic rules to determine the validity of a sentence structure and suggest corrections if necessary.

Morphological behaviors will be considered for the Dictionary class to utilize the roots of words, reducing the number of dictionary entries. The dictionary words can also contain behaviors that use morphological analysis to help determine the proper lexical category of a word. Idioms can be represented as specializations of the Word class and can then be treated as a terminal lexical category.

5. Conclusions and Future Work

In this article we presented TARO, a tool for building, testing, and extending natural language systems. TARO provides a foundation for the integration of syntactic and semantic processing that will continue to be modular and extensible as its capabilities are expanded. This potential, is largely the result of the use of object-oriented programming.

Encapsulation and polymorphism allow new lexical categories to be added, while developing a natural language system, without changes to the rest of the system. In addition, these two object-oriented features allow TARO to modify or replace NLP components with new ones that incorporate different functionality with minimum impact on the other components of the system. The inheritance feature, which provides reusability of code and propagation of changes, assists in defining the scope of the application of semantic agreement rules.

The reflectivity of KSL allows dynamic extension and refinement of the grammar and the dictionary components. It also allows, through specialized behavior types, the integration of procedural, rule-based, and logic programming. These capabilities of TARO enable linguists to easily add, modify, and test varieties of grammars and parsing techniques, and at the same time try different semantic approaches while prototyping NLP systems.

Future work will introduce additional semantic analysis at the word level. Rieger[34] and Small[35] reported on a word expert approach for parsing. This approach fits naturally into TARO. The representation of words as objects allows the definition of expert behavior on each word to determine its contextual meaning and role. Another direction will focus on implementing a technique similar to the lexical functional grammar discussed by Winograd[8] which will incorporate additional semantic representation into the parsing process.

6. Acknowledgement

The Author would like to acknowledge the contribution of Fred Cummins, Bill Bejcek, and Scott Woyak in the development of KSL and EDS/OWL.

7. References

1. B. J. Grosz, K. S. Jones and B. L. Webber, *Readings in Natural Language Processing*, (Morgan Kaufmann, Los Altos, California, 1986).
2. J. B. Lovins, "Development of a Stemming Algorithm,"*Mechanical Translation and Computational Linguistics*, 11:1-22, (March and June 1968), pp. 11-31.
3. H. Kucera, "Uses of on-line Lexicons," *Information in Data, First Conference of the University of Waterloo Center for the New Oxford English Dictionary,* (Waterloo, Canada, November 1985), pp. 11-24.
4. H. Alshawi, B. Boguraev and T. Briscoe, "Towards a Dictionary Support Environmnet for Real Time Parsing," *Proceedings of the Second Conference of the European Chapter of the ACL,* (Geneva, Switzerland, March 1985), pp. 27-29.
5. A. V. Aho and J. D. Ullman, *The Theory of Parsing, Translation and Compiling, Vol. I: Parsing*, (Prentice-Hall, Englewood Cliffs, N.J., 1972).
6. S. L. Graham, M. A. Harrison and W. L. Ruzzo, "An Improved Context-Free Recognizer," *ACM Transactions on Programming Languages and Systems*, **2:3** (July 1980), pp. 415-462,.
7. M. P. Marcus, *A Theory of Syntactic Recognition for Natural Language*, (MIT Press, Cambridge, MA, 1980).
8. W. A. Woods, "Transition Network Grammmars for Natural Language Analysis," *Communications of the ACM* **13** (1970), pp. 591-606.
9. M. Kay, "Algorithm Schemata and Data Structures in Syntactic Processing," *in Proceedings of the Symposium on Text Processing*, (Nobel Academy, 1980).
10. T. Winograd, *Language as a Cognitive Process: Syntax*, (Addison-Wesley, Reading, Mass., 1983).
11. G. G. Hendrix, E.D. Sacerdoti, D. Sagalowicz, and J. Slocum, "Developing a Natural Language Interface to Complex Data," *ACM Transactions on Database Systems* **3:2**, (June 1978), pp. 105-147.
12. C. Fillmore, "The Case for Case," in *Universals in Linguistic Theory*, eds. E. Bach and R. T. Harms, (Holt, New York, 1968).
13. B. Bruce, "Case Systems for Natural Language," *Artificial Intelligence* **6**, (1975).
14. R. F. Simmons, "Semantic Networks: Their Computation and Use for Understanding English Sentences," in *Computer Models of Thought and Language*, eds. R. C. Schank and K. M. Colby, (Freeman, San Francisco, 1973).
15. R. P. Stockwell, P. Schachter, and B. H. Partee, *The Major Syntactic Structures of English,* (New York: Holt, Rinehart and Winston, 1973).

16. R. C. Schank, *Conceptual Information processing*, (North Holland, Amsterdam, 1975).
17. R. C. Schank and R. P. Abelson, *Scripts, Plans, Goals, and Understanding*, (Erlbaum, Hillsdale, N.J., 1977).
18. R. Quillian, "Semantic Memory," in *Semantic Information Processing*, ed. M. Minsky, (MIT Press, Cambridge, Mass., 1968).
19. B. Raphael, "A Computer Program for Semantic Information Retrieval,"in *Semantic Information Processing*, ed. M. Minsky, (MIT Press, Cambridge, Mass., 1968).
20. T. Winograd, *Understanding Natural Languages*, (Academic Press, New York, 1972).
21. G. G. Hendrix, "Encoding Knowledge in Partitioned Networks," in *Associative Networks*, ed. N. V. Findler, (Academic Press, New York, 1979).
22. P. H. Winston, *Artificial Intelligence*, (Addison Wesely, Reading, Mass., 1977).
23. M. Minsky, "A Frame for representing Knowledge," in *The psychology of Computer Vision*, ed. P. Winston, (McGraw-Hill, New York, 1975).
24. D. G. Bobrow, and T. Winograd, "An Overview of KRL: A Knowledge Representation Language," *Cognitive Science* **1:1**, (1977).
25. R. Brachman and J. Schmoltz, "An Overview of the KL-ONE Knowledge Representation System," *Cognitive Science* **9**, (1985), pp. 171-216.
26. D. G. Bobrow, R. M. Kaplan, M. Kay, D. A. Norman, H. Thompson, and T. Winograd, "GUS, a Frame-driven Dialog System," *Artificial Intelligence* **8:2**, (1977), pp. 155-173.
27. R. Cullingford, "SAM," in *Inside Computer Understanding*, eds. R. C. Schank and C. K. Riesbeck, (Erlbaum, Hillsdale, N.J., 1981).
28. R. Wilensky, *Planning and Understanding: A computational Approach to Human Reasoning*, (Addison-Wesely, Reading, MA, 1983).
29. D. H. D. Warren, and L. M. Pereira, "Prolog-The Language and Its Implementation Compared to Lisp," in *Proc. Symposium on Artificial Intelligence and Programming Languages. SIGPLAN Notices* **12:8** and *SIGART Newsletter* **64**, (1977).
30. F. C. N. Pereira, and D. H. D. Warren, "Definite Clause Grammars for Language Analysis-A Survey of the Formalism and a Comparison with Augmented Transition Networks," *Artificial Intelligence* **13:3**, (May 1980), pp. 231-278.
31. M. H. Ibrahim, and F. A. Cummins, "KSL: A Reflective Object-Oriented Programming Language," *Proceedings of the International Conference on Computer Languages*, (Miami, FL, 1988), pp. 186-193.
32. F. A. Cummins, W. E. Bejcek, M. H. Ibrahim, D. J. O'Leary, and S. W. Woyak, "OWL 3.0 Reference Manual," *Internal Technical Report # AAI-87007*, (EDS Research and Development, Troy, MI, August, 1987).
33. M. Tomita, "An Efficient Cintext-ree Parsing Algorithm for Natural Languages," *Proceedings of the Nith International Joint Conference on Artificial Intelligence*, (1985), pp. 756-763.
34. C. Rieger S. and Small, "Word Expert Parsing," Proceedings of the Sixth International Joint Conference on Artificial Intelligence, (1979), pp. 723-728.
35. S. Small, "Viewing Word Expert Parsing as Linguistic Theory," Proceedings of the Seventh International Joint Conference On Artificial Intelligence, (1981), pp. 70-76.

CHAPTER 11

Spoken Language Translation*

Hiroaki Kitano
Center for Machine Translation
Carnegie Mellon University
Pittsburgh, PA 15213 U.S.A.

Abstract

Real-time translation of spoken language has been one of the ultimate goals of the natural language, artificial intelligence, speech recognition, and machine translation research. Recent advancement of the related research fields come to the point that we can build experimental small-scale prototype system which translate spoken utterace in one langauge into another language and produce audio output. This chapter discusses technical issues of spoken language translation and describes one of the first experimental system developed so far. Also, we will describe the most up-to-date natural language processing technologies using massively parallel machines.

1. Introduction

Development of a speech-to-speech translation system or *interpreting telephony* is one of the ultimate goals of research in natural language, speech recognition, and artificial intelligence. The task of speech-to-speech translation ultimately requires recognition and understanding of speaker-independent, large-vocabulary, continuous speech in the context of mixed-initiative dialogues. It also needs to accurately translate and produce appropriately articulated audio output in real-time (figure 1).

Accomplishment of the task requires the collective effort of various researchers. Speech recognition modules need to exhibit highly accurate and real-time performance under a speaker-independent, continuous speech, large vocabulary condition. A machine translation module consists of parsing and generation, and must be capable of interpreting very elliptical (where some words are not said) and ill-formed sentences which may appear in real

*This work is, in part, supported by the National Science foundation under grant MIP-900111 and by the Pittsburgh Supercomputer Center under grant IRI-910002P.

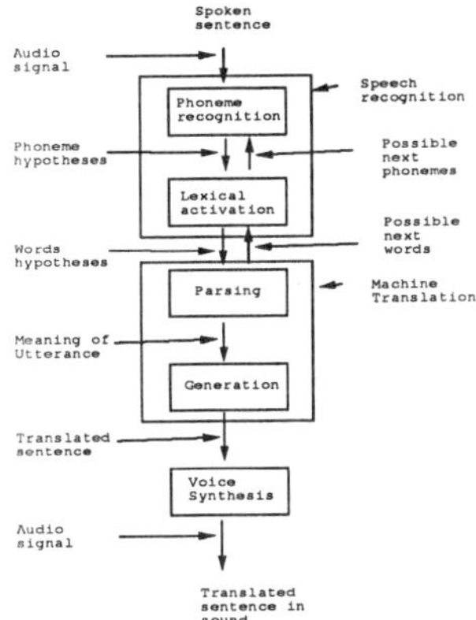

Figure 1: Process flow of Speech-to-speech translation

spoken dialogues. In addition, an interface between the parser and the speech recognition module must be well designed so that necessary information is passed to the parser, and an appropriate feedback is given from the parser to the speech recognition module in order to to improve recognition accuracy. In figure 1, we assumed that an interface is made at both phoneme hypothesis and word hypothesis levels, so that prediction made by the parser can be immediately fed back to the phoneme recognition device. No speech recognition module is capable of recognizing input speech with perfect accuracy, thus it sometimes provides a false word sequence as its first choice. However, it is often the case that a correct word is in the second or third best hypothesis. Thus, phoneme and word hypotheses given to the parser consist of several competitive phoneme or word hypotheses each of which are assigned the probability of being correct. With this mechanism, the accuracy of recognition can be improved because it filters out false first choices of the speech recognition module and selects grammatically and semantically plausible second or third best hypotheses. To implement this mechanism, the parser needs to handle multiple hypotheses in a parallel rather than a single word sequence as seen in text input machine translation systems. For a translation scheme, we use interlingua, i.e. language independent representation of meaning of the sentence, so that translation into multiple languages can be done efficiently. A generation module needs to be designed so that appropriate spoken sentences can be generated with correct articulation control. In addition to these functional challenges, it should be noted that the real-time response is the major requirement of the system, because speech-to-speech dialog translation systems would be used for real-time transactions, imposing a far more severe performance challenge than for text-based machine translation systems.

Furthermore, since the comprehensive system must handle two-way conversations, the system should have bi-directional translation capability with an ability to understand interaction at the discourse knowledge level, predict possible next utterance, understand what particular pronouns refer to, and to provide high-level constraints for the generation of contextually appropriate sentences involving various context-dependent phenomena. To attain

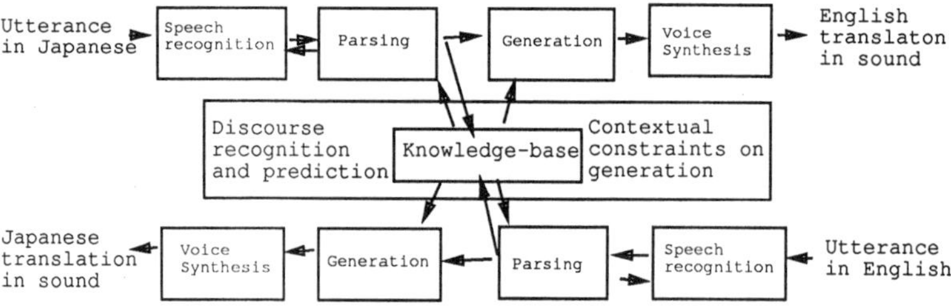

Figure 2: Overall process flow of Speech-to-speech dialog translation system

these features, the overall picture of the system should look like figure 2. The knowledge-base in figure 2 is used for keeping track of discourse and world knowledge established during the conversation, and is continuously up-dated during processing. It is now clear that development of a speech-to-speech translation system requires a new set of technologies: it is not just an assembly of existing speech recognition, machine translation, and voice synthesis systems.

Although it is evident that the development of such a system is not a trivial task and completion is not in our sight, recent advancement in related areas, especially in speech recognition and natural language processing, made it possible for us to build a prototype of a speech-to-speech translation system. So far, three experimental systems have been developed: ΦDmDialog which we will describe in this dissertation, SpeechTrans [Tomabechi et. al., 1989], another experimental system developed at the Center for Machine Translation based on the phoneme-based generalized LR parser [Saito and Tomita, 1988], and SL-Trans [Ogura et. al., 1989] [Morimoto et. al., 1990] by ATR Interpreting Telephony Research Laboratories.

ΦDmDialog is an experimental speech-to-speech dialog translation system developed at the Center for Machine Translation at Carnegie Mellon University. This is one of the first experimental speech-to-speech translation systems currently up and running. The system employs a parallel marker-passing algorithm as the basic architecture of a model. Speech processing, natural language, and discourse processing are integrated to improve the speech recognition rate by providing top-down predictions on possible next inputs. A parallel incremental generation scheme is employed, and a generation process and the parsing process run almost concurrently. Thus, a part of the utterance may be generated while parsing is in progress. Unlike most machine translation systems, where parsing and generation operate by different principles, our system adopts common computation principles in both parsing and generation, and thus allows integration of these processes. The system has been publicly demonstrated since March 1989.

The SpeechTrans [Tomabechi et. al., 1989] prototype uses a generalized LR parser extended to phoneme processing [Saito and Tomita, 1988]. Like ΦDmDialog, it assumes noisy phoneme input. Since noisy phonemes contain errors in their phoneme sequences, SpeechTrans uses a confusion matrix to create possibly correct phoneme-sequence hypotheses. It further employs a semantic-oriented grammar with a notation similar to that of Lexical Functional Grammar. The results of parsing are represented in an interlingua, a language-independent representation of meaning, and then sent to the generation module. SPEECHTRANS translates Japanese utterances into English. The system operates in a doctor-patient domain and handles such utterances as *Atamaga itai* ("I have a headache.")

SL-TRANS ([Morimoto et. al., 1990] and [Ogura et. al., 1989]) is a prototype system for interpreting telephony at ATR Interpreting Telephony Laboratories in Japan. SL-TRANS employs HMM-LR parsing in which a hidden Markov model phoneme verifier provides probability measures to a predictive LR parser [Kita et. al., 1989]. The LR parser provides top-down constraints on phoneme recognition since the parser has an intra-clause grammar (a Bunsetsu grammar). However, unlike ΦDMDIALOG and SPEECHTRANS, the LR parser does not perform semantic analysis. It is used only to provide word sequence hypotheses to a unification-based parser pipelined to the LR parser. The parser is based on a chart parser and employs a head-driven phrase structure grammar. By separating the parser for speech processing and semantic analysis, SL-TRANS allows use of a fully linguistic formalism in a straightforward manner; but this is at the cost of being redundant with two independent parsing processes. Currently, SL-TRANS translates spoken Japanese into English and operates in the ATR's conference registration domain.

2. ΦDMDIALOG: An Experimental Speech-to-Speech Translation System

The ΦDMDIALOG system is an experimental speech-to-speech dialogue translation system with following technical features:

Almost concurrent parsing and generation: Unlike traditional methods of machine translation in which a generation process is invoked after parsing is completed, our model concurrently executes the generation process during parsing [?]. Both the parsing and generation processes employ parallel incremental algorithms. This enables our model to generate a part of the input utterance during the parsing of the rest of the utterance.

Dynamic participation of discourse and world knowledge: The model attains highly interactive processing of knowledge from the morphophonetics level to the discourse level by distributively representing that knowledge in a memory network on which actual computations are performed. Discourse plan hierarchies for each participant of the dialog provide the ability to handle complex mixed-initiative dialog, and enable our system to perform discourse processing which are essential for simultaneous interpretation.

The cost-based ambiguity resolution scheme: We adopted the cost-based scheme [Kitano et. al., 1989a] to attain a highly interactive and uniform mechanism of ambiguity resolution. In this scheme, the least-cost hypothesis is selected from among other hypotheses. The idea behind this scheme is to consider parsing and generation as processes of a dynamic system which converge into a global minima through a path with the least cost. The scheme is consistent with several psycholinguistic studies[Crain and Steedman, 1985] [Ford, Bresnan and Kaplan, 1981] [Prather and Swinney, 1988].

Integration of Case-Based and Constraint-Based Processing: Case-based and constraint-based processing are integrated using feature aggregation and constraint satisfaction methods. The integration of case-based and constraint-based processing provides specificity of prediction and productive syntactic and discourse processing.

Massively parallel model: The model is built on a hybrid parallel paradigm [Kitano, 1989c] which is a parallel processing scheme which integrates a marker-passing algorithm and a connectionist network in a consistent manner. The marker-passing section of our model captures the flow of information during processing, and the connectionist network acts as a discriminator which selects one hypothesis out of multiple hypotheses. The marker-passing division of the model borrowed some ideas from the direct memory access (DMA) paradigm[Riesbeck and Martin, 1985] in the initial stage of our research; however, significant theoretical modification has been made, thus, these two models should be regarded as different models. The choice of the massively parallel computation scheme was one of the crucial factors in implementing our model.

Among these features, particularly important is the notion of memory-based (or case-based) approach to natural language processing. Memory-based natural language processing is an idea of viewing natural language processing as a memory activity. For example, parsing is considered as a memory-search process which identifies similar cases in the past from the memory, and to provide interpretation based on the identified case. It can be considered as an application of Memory-Based Reasoning (MBR) [Stanfill and Waltz, 1988] and Case-Based Reasoning (CBR) [Riesbeck and Schank, 1989] to natural language processing[1].

The ΦDmDialog system described in this chapter has been implemented in on an IBM RT-PC workstation and HP-9000 workstation using CommonLisp and MultiLisp run on Mach OS. Speech input and voice synthesis are done by connected hardware systems such as Matsushita Institute's Japanese speech recognition device [Morii et. al., 1985] and DECTalk. Concept hierarchy of the memory network is based on [Tsujii, 1985], with domain-specific and other general knowledge added. Parallelism is simulated on these serial machines. Implementations on actual parallel machines are described in later chapters.

The performance of the ΦDmDialog system is proven to be excellent when implemented on massively parallel machines. The model has been implemented on the IXM2 associative memory processor and the Semantic Network Array Processor (SNAP). In both cases, the parsing or translation process completes at the order of a few milliseconds. The CM-2 version is currently being implemented, and expected to attain similar performance. The performance on the IXM2 and SNAP are clearly one of the best performances ever accomplished.

---

[1]For arguments concerning superiority of the memory-based approach over the traditional approach, see [Nagao, 1984], [Riesbeck and Martin, 1985], and [Sumita et. al., 1990].

2.1. An Overview of the Model

This section describes the basic organization and the algorithm of the model. The ΦDmDialog system is composed of a memory network which represents various levels of knowledge involved in the speech-to-speech processing task, and markers which carry information in the memory network. Also, a connectionist network with a localist implementation performs spreading activation for sub-symbolic processing with complements symbolic processing by the marker-passing. Although the connectionist network has been experimentally incorporated in the system, this dissertation focus on processing by the marker-passing scheme.

2.1.1. Memory Network

The memory network incorporates knowledge from morphophonetics to plan hierarchies for each participant of a dialog. This knowledge includes both abstract knowledge and specific cases of utterances and discourses. Knowledge on specific cases is important since we assume that a considerable portion of human language comprehension and production is strongly case-based. Each node is a *type* and represents either a concept (Concept Class node; CC) or a sequence of concepts (Concept Sequence Class node; CSC). Strictly speaking, both CCs and CSCs are a *collection* or *family* since they are, most of time, sets of classes. CCs represent such knowledge as phonemes (i.e. /k/ /a/), concepts (i.e. *Conference, *Event, *Mtrans-Action), and plans (i.e. *Declare-Want-Attend). When a strict linear-order constraint is imposed, CSCs represent sequences of concepts and their relations such as phoneme sequences (i.e. /k a i g i/), concept sequences[2] (i.e. `<*Conference *Goal-Role *Attend *Want>`) or plan sequences (i.e. `<*Declare-Want-Attend *Listen-Instruction>`)[3] of two participants of the dialog[4]. They are summarized in 1. Each type of node creates instances during parsing which are called concept instances (CI) and concept sequence instances (CSI), respectively. CIs correspond to 'discourse entities' as described in [Webber, 1983]. Nodes are connected through several types of links. A guided marker-passing scheme is employed for inference in the memory network.

Lexical Entry In our model, lexical items are represented by Concept Sequence Class nodes applied to the lexical level which we call *lexical nodes*. Each lexical node has knowledge of how each word should be pronounced in the form of a phoneme sequence. For example,

---

[2]Concept sequences are the representations of the integrated syntax/semantics level of knowledge in our model. These sequences can be used to represent abstract knowledge or specific cases. We assume use of phrasal lexicons [Becker, 1975] [Hovy, 1988] as generic patterns that are induced from a large sample of utterance cases and map between specific surface representations and semantics.

[3]This should not be confused with 'discourse segments' [Grosz and Sidner, 1990]. In our model, information represented in discourse segments is distributively incorporated in the memory network.

[4]Use of plan hierarchies of each speaker as discourse knowledge is another unique feature of our model. Most other studies of dialog have been dedicated to one-speaker initiative domains[Cohen and Fertig, 1986][Litman and Allen, 1987].

	Phonology	Syntax/Semantics	Discourse
CSC	Phoneme Sequence	Concept Sequence	Discourse Plan Sequence
CSI	——	Instance of Concept Sequence	Instance of Discourse Plan Sequence
CC	Phoneme	Concept	Discourse Plan
CI	——	Instance of Concept	Instance of Discourse Plan

Table 1: Types of Nodes in the Memory Network

```
(defLEX '(kaigi
   (is-a (conference))
   (language (japanese))
   (surface (kaigi))
   (gen-phon (ka i gi))
   (sequence (k a i * i))))
```

```
(defLEX '(conference
   (is-a (conference))
   (language (english))
   (surface (conference))
   (gen-phon (conference))
   (sequence (K AA N F R AX N S))))
```

Figure 3: Lexical Nodes for 'Kaigi' and 'Conference'

definitions for a lexical node for a Japanese word 'Kaigi' (conference) and an English word 'Conference' are shown in figure 3.

This represents 'kaigi' as a Japanese lexical representation of a concept 'conference', its surface representation used for written text processing is 'kaigi', a symbol sequence used for generation process is 'ka i gi', and a recognition phoneme sequence is 'k a i * i'[5]. By the same token, a lexical node for 'conference' has an expected phoneme sequence 'K AA N F R AX N S' and other information similar to the case of the Japanese lexical node shown in the figure. Each word has its own lexical node containing such information, and these definitions are compiled into the memory network.

Ontological Hierarchy Class/subclass relation is represented in the memory network in form of the ontological hierarchy. Each CC represents specific concept and they are connected through IS-A links. The highest (the most general) concept is **entity* which

[5]'*' represents nasal phoneme.

```
(<NP> <==> (<NP> <PostP>)
 (((x0 head) == x1)
  ((x0 case) == (x2 case)))
```

Figure 4: Grammar using LFG-like notation

```
(<attend-action> <== (<attend> <event>)
    ((x0 = x1)
     ((x0 ACTION) = (x1 root))
     ((x0 OBJECT) = x2)))
```

Figure 5: Grammar using Semantic-oriented notation

entail all possible concepts in the network. Subclasses are linked under the **entity* node, and each subclass node has their own subclasses. As a basis of the ontological hierarchy, we use the hierarchy developed for the MU project [Tsujii, 1985], and domain specific knowledge and other knowledge necessary for processing in the system has been added.

Grammar Rules Grammar rules can be written using notations similar to Lexical-Functional Grammar (figure 4) or using more semantic-oriented encoding (figure 5). Also, mixing levels of abstraction in a grammar rule is permitted in our model (figure 6). Although the use of such a semantic-oriented grammatical encoding method may be linguistically controversial (it would provides less linguistic generalization than other formalisms such as Lexical Functional Grammar or Head-driven Phrase Structure Grammar), this is one of the best way to write grammar for speech input parsing due to its perplexity reduction effects. Perplexity is a measure of the complexity of the task similar to an average branching factor; a small perplexity measure means a task is rather simple. Generally, smaller perplexity improves accuracy and response speed of the speech recognition module. We extend the idea of the semantic-oriented grammar to allow direct encoding of a surface string sequence into a *specific case* of utterances. Use of specific cases with stochastic measurement has a significant contribution in perplexity reduction while strong constraints at the syntactic/semantic level can directly influence the speech processing level.

```
(<i-want-attend-event> <== (I want to *circumstance)
   (((x0 ACTOR) = x1)
     ((x0 ACTION) = x2)
     ((x0 OBJECT) = x4)))

(<*circumstance> <== (register for the *event)
   (((x0 ACTOR) == (x0 ACTOR))
    ((x0 ACTION) == x1)
    ((x0 OBJECT) == x4)))
```

Figure 6: Grammar using mixture of surface string and generalized case

2.1.2. Markers

Markers are entities which carries information, and pass through the memory network in order to make inference and predictions. Our model uses five types of markers:

- Activation Markers (A-Markers), which show activation of nodes.
- Prediction Markers (P-Markers), which are passed along the conceptual and phonemic sequences to make predictions about nodes to be activated next.
- Contextual Markers (C-Markers), which are placed on nodes with contextual preferences.
- Generation Markers (G-Markers), each of which contain a surface string and an instance which represents the surface string.
- Verbalization Markers (V-Markers), which anticipate and keep track of verbalization of surface strings.

These markers are summarized in table 2. A-Markers carry information on a concept instance node, probability/cost measure, linguistic and semantic features, etc. P-Markers contain constraint equations, feature structures, and a probability measure of the hypothesis. Figure 7 shows an example of information carried by an A-Marker and a P-Marker.

G-Markers are created at the lexical level and each contains a surface string, linguistic and semantic features, a cost measure, and concept instance nodes. G-Markers are passed up through the memory network. At a certain point of processing, surface strings of G-Markers are concatenated following the order of concept sequence class nodes, and a final string of the utterance is created. When incremental sentence production is performed, V-Markers record part of the sentence which is already verbalized and anticipate the next possible verbalization strings. Figure 8 shows an example of a G-Marker and a V-Marker.

```
(A-MARKER0236
 (Probability: 0.14)
 (CI: Conference045)
 (Concept: Conference)
 (Feature: nil)
 (Type: Event)
)


(P-MARKER0196
 (Probability: 0.50)
 (Constraints: ((x0 = x2)
((x0 subj) = x1))
 (Feature: nil)
)
```

Figure 7: Example of an A-Marker and a P-Marker

Marker	Passing Direction	Information
A-Markers	IS-A	Instance, features, cost
P-Markers	The next element on CSCs	Constraints, cost, instances
G-Markers	IS-A	Instance, feature, cost, lexical realization
V-Markers	The next element on CSCs	Constraints, cost, instances, verbalized words
C-Markers	Contextual links	Activation level

Table 2: Markers in the Model

The basic concept introduced in our model, which is substantially different from other marker-passing models, is a use of a probabilistic and structured parallel marker-passing. Each marker carries a probability measure that weights how likely the hypothesis (represented in the marker) is true. It also contains symbolic data such as linguistic feature, a pointer to a discourse entity, and constraints. Inclusion of rich information in markers dramatically increased the capability of the marker-passing scheme, compared with traditional marker-passing which merely carried bit-vectors or an identifier of an activation source. Propagation of a probability measure enables stochastic analysis (which is essential in processing speech inputs) and propagation of syntactic and semantic features and discourse entities enables sound linguistic analysis.

Our model uses five types of markers. These markers are (1) Activation Markers (A-Markers), which show activation of nodes, (2) Prediction Markers (P-Markers), which are passed along the conceptual and phonemic sequences to make predictions about nodes to be activated next, (3) Contextual Markers (C-Markers), which are placed on nodes with

```
(G-MARKER0886
 (Probability: 0.67)
 (CI: John021)
 (Concept: Male-Person)
 (Feature: ((Gendar: Male)
    (Number 3sg)))
 (Type: Object)
)
```

```
(V-MARKER0180
 (Probability: 0.50)
 (Constraints: ((x0 actor) = x1)
((x0 object) = x3)
 (x0 = x5))
 (Feature: ((Actor (CI: John021)
   (Gendar: Male)
   (Number 3sg))))
 (Surface String: "Jon ha")
)
```

Figure 8: Example of a G-Marker and a V-Marker

contextual preferences, (4) Generation Markers (G-Markers), which each contain a surface string and an instance which the surface string represents and (5) Verbalization Markers (V-Markers), which anticipate and keep track of the verbalization of surface strings. Information on which instances caused activations, linguistic and semantic features, and probabilistic measures are carried by A-Markers. The binding list of instances and their roles, probability measures, and constraints are held in P-Markers. G-Markers are created at the lexical level and passed up through the memory network. At a certain point of processing, surface strings of G-Markers are concatenated following the order of a CSC and a final string of the utterance is created. When incremental sentence production is performed, V-Markers record part of sentences which are already verbalized and anticipate next possible verbalization strings.

2.1.3. Baseline Parsing Algorithm

The basic cycle of our model is:

Activation: Nodes are activated either by external inputs or as a result of accepting a CSC. A new A-Marker (for parsing) and a G-Marker (for generation) are created containing

$$\overset{P}{<e_0}\, e_1\, e_2\, e_3 \cdots e_n > \Rightarrow < e_0\, \overset{P}{e_1}\, e_2\, e_3 \cdots e_n >$$

A (a) Simple Prediction

$$< \overset{P}{e_0}\, \overset{P}{e_1}\, e_2\, e_3 \cdots e_n > \Rightarrow < e_0\, e_1\, \overset{P}{e_2}\, \overset{P}{e_3} \cdots e_n >$$

A (b) Dual Prediction

Figure 9: Movement of P-Markers

relevant information.

Marker Passing: Markers are passed up through IS-A links. Features are aggregated through this process.

Collision: When an A-Marker or a G-Marker activate a node with a P-Marker or a V-Marker, a collision takes place. Information stored in the A-Marker or G-Marker is combined with that of the P-Marker or G-Marker. Recalculation of costs, probability measures, and constraint satisfaction are conducted at this stage.

Prediction or Acceptance of CSC: After the collision, the P-Marker or V-Marker is moved to the next element of the CSC and makes a prediction as to what may be activated next. In the event that the P-Marker or V-Marker is at the last element of the CSC, the CSC is accepted, and a new A-Marker or G-Marker is created which contains information stored in the P-Marker or G-Marker. This creation of a new marker is the activation stage of the next cycle.

Movement of P-Markers is important in understanding parsing in our model. The movement of G-Markers for generation will be described in a later section. The movements of P-Markers on a CSC are illustrated in figure 9. In (a), a P-Marker (initially located on e_0) is hit by an A-Marker and moved to the next element. In (b), two P-Markers are used and moved to e_2 and e_3. In dual prediction, two P-Markers are placed on elements of the CSC (on e_0 and e_1). This dual prediction is used for phonological processing.

Figure 10 shows movement of a P-Marker on the layers of CSCs. When the P-Marker at the last element of the CSC gets an A-Marker, the CSC is accepted and an A-Marker is passed up to the element in the higher layer CSC. Then, a P-Marker on the element of the CSC collides with an A-Marker, and the P-Marker is moved to the next element. At this time, a P-Marker which contains information relevant to the lower CSC is passed down and placed on the first element of the lower CSC. This is a process of accepting one CSC and predicting the possible next word and syntactic structure.

We will further illustrate this basic parsing algorithm using a simple memory network, as in Figure 11. Part (a) of the figure shows an initial prediction stage. P-markers are placed on `*person` in a CSC at the syntax/semantics level. Also, the other P-marker is placed on the first element of CSCs at the phonological level. In In part (b) of Figure 11, a word, `john`, is activated as a result of speech recognition, and an A-marker is passed up through IS-A link.

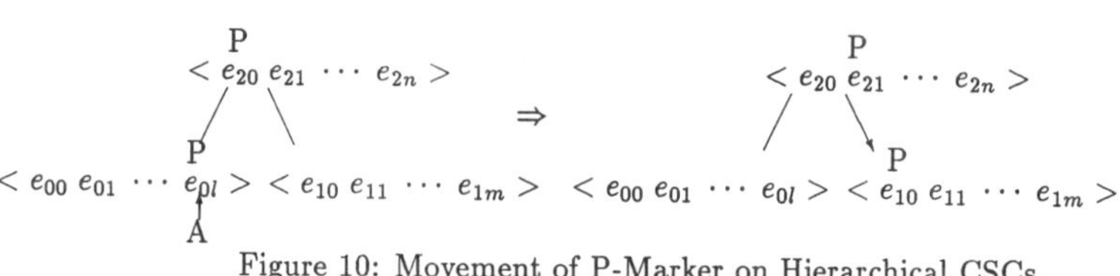

Figure 10: Movement of P-Marker on Hierarchical CSCs

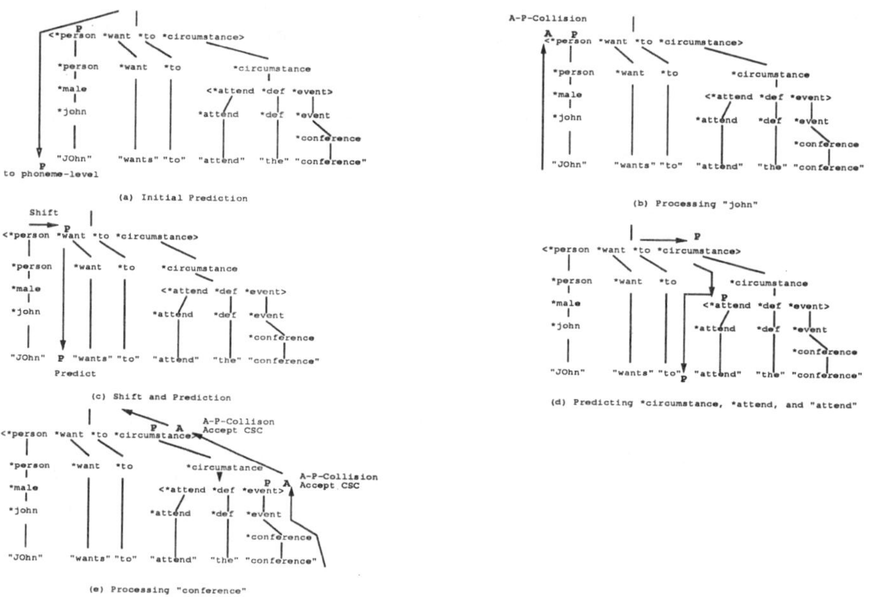

Figure 11: A simple parsing example.

It reaches to *person in the CSC, which has the P-marker. An A-P-collision takes place and features in the A-marker are incorporated into the P-marker following the constraint equation specified in the CSC. Next, the P-marker shift takes place; this may be seen in part (c) of the figure. Now the P-Marker is placed on *want. Also, the prediction is made that the possible next word is wants. Part (d) shows a movement of P-markers after recognizing to. In (e), the last word of the sentence, conference, comes in and causes an A-P-collision at *event. Since this is the last element of the CSC <*attend *def *event>, the CSC is accepted and a new A-marker is created. The newly created A-marker contains information on build up by a local parse with this CSC. Then, the A-marker is propagated upward, and it causes another A-P-collision at *circumstance. Again, because *circumstance is the last element of the CSC <*person *want *to *circumstance>, the CSC is accepted, and interpretation of the sentence is stored in a newly created A-marker. The A-marker further propagates upward to perform discourse-level processing.

2.2. Speech Input Processing

The integration of speech recognition and natural language processing is one of the most important topics in spoken language processing. The benefit of integrating speech recognition and natural language processing is that it improves the recognition rate of the speech inputs in two ways. First, the integration provides more appropriate assignment of *a priori probability* to each hypothesis so that several highly ambiguous hypotheses can be differentiated from expectations, and the correct one may be selected. Second, it imposes more constraints to reduce search space. Given the same computational power, reduction of search space results in improvement of the recognition rate. Thus, the quality of the *language model* is an important factor. Since our goal is to create accurate translation from speech input, a sophisticated parsing and discourse understanding scheme is necessary.

In our system, we assume that an acoustic processing device provides a symbol sequence for a given speech input. In this paper, we assume that a phoneme-level sequence is provided to the system[6]. The phoneme sequence given from the phoneme recognition device contains substitution, insertion and deletion of phonemes, as compared to a correct transcription which contains only expected phonemes. We call such a phoneme sequence a *noisy phoneme sequence*. The task of phonological-level processing is to activate a hypothesis as to the correct phoneme sequence from this noisy phoneme sequence. Inevitably, multiple hypotheses can be generated due to the stochastic nature of phoneme recognition errors. Thus, we want each hypothesis to be assigned a measure of its being correct. In the stochastic models of speech recognition, the probability of each hypothesis is determined by $P(y|h) \times P(h)$. $P(y|h)$ is the probability of a series of input sequences being observed when a hypothesis h is articulated. $P(h)$ is an a priori probability of the hypothesis derived from the language

[6]We use Matsushita Institute's Japanese speech recognition system[Morii et. al., 1985] for current implementation. However, this does not mean that our framework is incapable of attaining phoneme recognition. In fact, an introduction of probabilistic time-synchronous marker-passing would add a speech processing capability comparable to the Hidden Markov Model. Alternatively, neural network-based phoneme recognition such as TDNN [Waibel et. al., 1989] is highly conformal to our framework.

kaigi ni sanka shitai nodesu	*youshi ha arimasuka*	*oname wo onegai shimasu*
DAI*I*IPAUTAQPAINO*EKU	BJOHIRAARI*ATAWA	O*A*AEJOORE*EISI*AS@
BAII*IPAA=KAS@PAINODUSU	JOSJUWAARINAOQZAA	WO*A*AEJOORE*EEHJANA
BAII*I*IPAU=KAIQPAI*O*ESU	IOUSIWAARIMAUQKA	WONA*AEJOBO*E*EIHJAH@
KAIIMIPAA=KAS@PEEI*ODESU	JOOSIHAKARI*AUQKA	O*A*AEJO*O*E*EEISINAKU
KAI*I*IPAA=ZAS@PAIWO*USJU	IOOSJUWAWARI*AACA	O*A*AEJOO*E*EEIHJAZU

Figure 12: Examples of Noisy Phoneme Sequences

model. Apparently, when phonological-level processing is the same, the system with a sophisticated language model attains a higher recognition rate, because a priori probability differentiates among hypotheses of high acoustic similarity which would otherwise lead to confusion. At the same time, we want to eliminate less-plausible hypotheses as early as possible so that the search space is kept within a certain size. We use syntactic/semantic and discourse knowledge to impose constraints which reduce search space, in addition to probability-based pruning within the phonological level. A priori probability will be given by a P-Marker passed down from the higher-level processing.

This section describes phonological-level activities. We assume a noisy phoneme sequence, as shown in figure 12, to be the input of the phonological-level processing. In order to capture the stochastic nature of speech inputs, we adopt a probabilistic model similar to that used in other speech recognition research. First, we describe a simple model using a static probability matrix. In this model, probability is context-independent. Then, we extend the model to capture context-dependent probability. In subsequent sections, we describe the language model of our system, and how predictions are provided to the speech processing level to attain integrated processing.

2.2.1. The Organization of Phonological Processing

The algorithm described as a baseline algorithm is deployed on phonetic-level knowledge. In the memory network there are CSCs representing the phoneme sequence for each lexical entry. The dual prediction method is used in order to handle deletion of a phoneme. Probability measures involved are: a priori probability given by the language model, a confusion probability given by a confusion matrix, and a transition probability given by a transition matrix.

A priori probability is derived from the language model and is a measure of which phoneme sequence is likely to be recognized. A method of deriving a priori probability is described in the section on syntax/semantic parsing, discourse processing, and prediction.

A confusion matrix defines the output probability of a phoneme when an input symbol is given. Given an input sign i_i, the confusion matrix a_{ij} determines the probability that the sign i_i will be recognized as a phoneme p_j. It is a measure of the distance between symbols and phonemes as well as a measure of the cost of hypotheses that interpret the symbol i_i as the phoneme p_j. In the context-dependent model, the confusion matrix will defined as a_{ijk} which gives a probability of a symbol i_i to be interpreted as a phoneme p_j at a transition t_k. We call such matrix a *dynamic confusion matrix*.

A transition matrix defines the transition probability which is a probability of a symbol i_{i+1} to follow a symbol i_i. For an input sequence $i_0\ i_1\ \cdots\ i_n$, the a priori probability of the transition between i_0 and i_1 is given by b_{i_0,i_1}. Since we have a finite set of input symbols, each transition can be indexed as t_k. The transition probability and the confusion probability are intended to capture the context-dependency of phoneme substitutions – a phenomena whereby a certain phoneme can be actually articulated as other phonemes in certain environments.

2.2.2. The Context-Independent Model

First, we will explain our algorithm using a simple model whose confusion matrix is context-independent. Later, we will describe the context-dependent model which uses a dynamic confusion matrix. Initially, P-Markers contain a priori probability (π_l) given by the language model. In ΦDMDIALOG, the language model reflects full natural language knowledge from syntax/semantics to discourse. The P-Markers are placed on each first and second element of CSCs representing expected phoneme sequences. For an input symbol i_i, A-Markers are passed up to all phoneme nodes that have a probability(b_{ij}) greater than the threshold (Th). When a P-Marker, which is at the i-th element, and an A-Marker collide, the P-Marker is moved to the i+1-th and i+2-th elements of the sequence (this is a dual prediction). When the next input symbol i_{i+1} generates an A-Marker that hits the P-Marker on the i+1-th element, the P-Marker is again moved using the dual prediction method. The probability density measure computed on the P-Marker is as follows:

$$ppm(i) = ppm(i-1) \times t_{s_{i-2},s_{i-1}} \times c_{p_{i-2},s_{i-2}} \quad (1)$$

$$ppm(1) = ppm(0) \times t_{onset,i_0} \quad (2)$$

$$ppm(0) = \pi_l \quad (3)$$

Here $ppm(i)$ is a probability measure of a P-Marker at the i-th element of the concept sequence class node, which is a probability of the input sequence being recognized as a phoneme sequence traced by the P-Marker. And t_{onset,i_0} is a transition probability from the onset to the first phoneme, i.e. probability of the phoneme to be given as a first phoneme of inputs.

In figure 13, an input sequence is $i_0\ i_1\ \cdots\ i_n$. p_{ij} in the diagram denotes a phoneme P_j at the i-th element of the CSC. p_{ij} is a state rather than an actual phoneme, and P_j in the CSC refers to the actual phoneme. P-Markers at p_{00}, p_{01}, p_{02}, and P-Markers on the 0-th element of the CSCs referring to P_0, P_1, and P_2, respectively, are hit by A Markers. Eventually, P-Markers are moved to the next elements of CSCs. For instance, p_{00} will move to $p_{10}, p_{11}, p_{20}, p_{21}$ depending on which CSC the P-Marker is placed on. Probabilities are computed with each movement. A P-Marker at p_{11} has the probability π_0. When

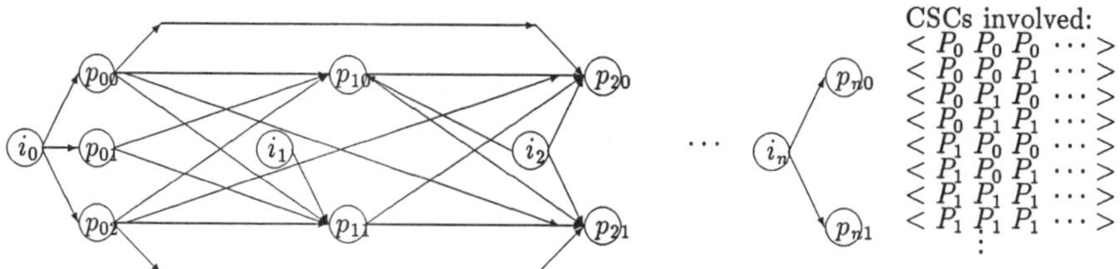

Figure 13: Phoneme-level State Transition

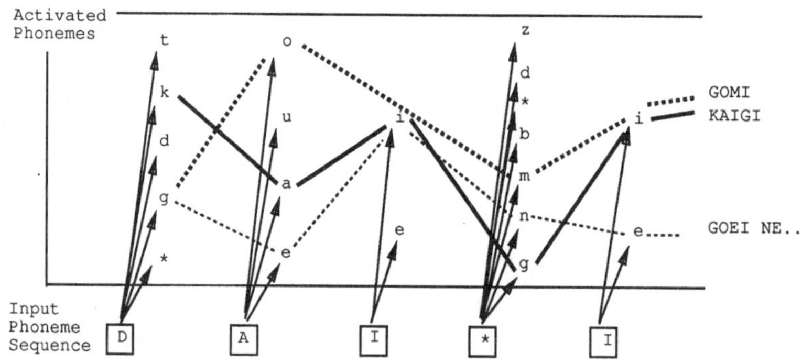

Figure 14: Phoneme Processing

the P-Marker receives an A-Marker from i_1, the probability is re-computed and it will be $\pi_0 \times b_{i_0,p_{00}} \times a_{p_{i_0},p_{i_1}}$. Transitions such as $p_{00} \rightarrow p_{21}$ and $p_{00} \rightarrow p_{20}$ insert an extra phoneme which does not exist in the input sequence. Probability for such transitions is computed in such a way as: $\pi_0 \times b_{i_0,p_{00}} \times a_{i_0,\phi} \times b_{i_2,p_{20}} \times a_{\phi,i_2}$. A P-Marker at p_{10} does not get an A-Marker from i_1 due to the threshold. In such cases, a probability measure of the P-Marker is re-computed as $\pi_0 \times b_{i_0,p_{00}} \times a_{i_0,noise}$. This represents a decrease of probability due to an extra input symbol.

P-Markers at the last element (p_n) and one before the last (p_{n-1}) are involved in the word boundary problem. When a P-Marker at p_n is hit by an A-Marker, the phoneme sequence is accepted and an A-Marker which contains the probability and the phoneme sequence is passed up to the syntactic/semantic-level of the network. Then, the next possible words are predicted using syntactic/semantic knowledge, and P-Markers are placed on the first and the second element of the phoneme sequence of the predicted words. When a P-Marker at p_{n-1} is hit by an A-Marker, the P-Marker is moved to p_n and, independently, the phoneme sequence is accepted, due to the dual prediction, and the first and the second elements of the predicted phoneme sequences get P-Markers.

Figure 14 shows a simplified view of this process. We suppose an input phoneme sequence to be 'DAI*I...'. Each input phoneme activates phoneme hypotheses based on a confusion matrix. For example, an input phoneme 'D' activates phoneme hypotheses 't', 'k', 'd', 'g', and '*' with corresponding probability measures. For the sake of simplicity, the transition probability is not drawn in this figure. A path shown by a thick solid line shows a lexical hypothesis for KAIGI (conference), a thick dashed line shows GOMI (garbage), and a thin dashed line shows GOEI NE.. (guard and a part of a following word). In activating lexical hypothesis GOMI, the third input phoneme 'I' is considered to be a noise, and, thus, a path ignores either 'i' or 'e' activated by 'I'. On the other hand, a path for GOEI has a transition that adds a phoneme which does not appear in the input phoneme sequence; a phoneme 'o' is inserted while transiting from 'g' to 'e'.

2.2.3. The Context-Dependent Model

The context-dependent model can be implemented by using the dynamic confusion matrix. The algorithm described above can be applied with some modifications. First, A-Markers are passed up to phonemes whose maximum output probability is above the threshold. Second, output probability used for probability calculation is defined by the dynamic confusion matrix. The probability measure is computed by:

$$ppm(i) \;=\; ppm(i-1) \times a_{i_{i-2},i_{i-1}} \times b_{p_{i-2},i_{i-2},k} \tag{4}$$

where k denotes a transition from i_{i-2} to i_{i-1}. It is interesting that our context-dependent model is quite similar to the *Hidden Markov Model (HMM)* when the transition of the state of P-Markers are synchronously determined by, for example, certain time intervals. We can implement a forward-passing algorithm and the Viterbi algorithm [Viterbi, 1967] using our model. This implies that when we decide to employ the HMM as our speech recognition model, instead of a current speech input device, it can be implemented within the framework of our model.

2.3. Syntactic/Semantic Parsing

Unlike most other language models employed in speech recognition research, our language model is a complete implementation of a natural language parsing system. Thus, complete semantic interpretations, constraint checks, ambiguity resolution and discourse interpretations are performed. The process of prediction is a part of parsing in our model, thereby attaining an integrated architecture of speech input parsing. In syntactic/semantic processing, the central focus is on how to build the informational content of the utterance and how to reflect syntactic/semantic constraints at phonological-level activities. Throughout the syntactic/semantic-level and the discourse-level, we use a method to fuse constraint-based and case-based approaches. In our model, the difference between a constraint-based process and a case-based process is the level of abstraction; the case-based process is specific and the constraint-based process is more abstract. The constraint-based approach is represented by various unification-based grammar formalisms [Pollard and Sag, 1987] [Kaplan and Bresnan, 1982]. We employ a mixed approach which uses syntactic and semantic constraints at three levels of abstraction; specific cases, generalized cases, and syntactic rules[7]. In our model, propagation of features and unification are conducted as *feature aggregation* by A-Markers and *constraint satisfaction* is performed by operations involving P-Markers. The case-based approach is a basic feature of our model. Specific cases of utterances are indexed in the memory network and reactivated when similar utterances are given to the system. One of the motivations for case-based parsing is that it encompasses *phrasal lexicons* [Becker, 1975][8]. The scheme described in this section is applied to discourse-level processing and attains an integration of the syntactic/semantic-level and the discourse-level.

2.3.1. Feature Aggregation

Feature aggregation is an operation which combines features in the process of passing up A-Markers so that minimal features are carried up. Due to the hierarchical organization of the memory network, features which need to be carried by A-Markers are different depending upon which level of abstraction is used for parsing. When knowledge of cases is used for parsing, features are not necessary because this knowledge is already indexed to specific discourse entities. Features need to be carried when more abstract knowledge is used for parsing. For example, the parsing of a sentence *She runs* can be handled at different levels of abstraction using the same mechanism. The word *she* refers to a certain discourse entity so that very specific case-based parsing can directly access a memory which recalls previous memory in the network. Since previous cases are indexed into specific discourse entities, the activation can directly identify which memory to recall. When this word *she* is processed in a more abstract level such as PERSON, we need to check features such as number and gender. Thus, these features need to be contained in the A-Marker. Further abstraction requires more features to be contained in the A-Marker. Therefore, the case-based process and the constraint-based process are treated in one mechanism. Aggregation is a cheap operation since it simply adds new features to existing features in the A-Marker. Given the fact that unification is a computationally expensive operation, aggregation is an efficient mechanism for propagating features because it ensures only minimal features are aggregated when features are unified.

Feature aggregation is applied in order to interface with different levels of knowledge. At the phonological level, only a probability measure and a phoneme sequence are involved. Thus, when an A-Marker hits a CC node representing a certain concept, i.e. *female-person-3sg* for *she*, the A-Marker does not contain any linguistically significant information. However, when the A-Marker is passed up to more abstract CC nodes, i.e. *person*, linguistically significant features are contained in the A-Marker and unnecessary information is discarded. When a sentence is analyzed at the syntactic/semantic-level, propositional content is established and is passed up to the discourse-level by an A-Marker, and some linguistic information

[7]In fact, we are now developing a cross-compiler that compiles grammar rules written in LFG for the universal parser [Tomita and Carbonell, 1987] into our network. Designing of a cross-compiler from HPSG to our network is also underway.

[8]Discussions on benefits of phrasal lexicons for parsing and generation are found in [Riesbeck and Martin, 1985] [Hovy, 1988].

which is necessary only within the syntactic/semantic-level is discarded.

2.3.2. Constraint Satisfaction

Constraint is a central notion in modern syntax theories. Each CSC has *constraint equations* which define the constraints imposed for that CSC depending upon their level of abstraction. CSCs representing specific cases do not have constraint equations since they are already instantiated and the CSCs are indexed in the memory network. The more abstract the knowledge is the more it contains constraint equations. Feature structures and constraint equations interact at two stages. At the prediction stage, if a P-Marker placed on the first element of the CSC already contains a feature structure that is non-nil, the feature structure determines, according to the constraint equations, possible feature structures of A-Markers that subsequent elements of the CSC can accept. At an A-P-Collision stage, a feature structure in the A-Marker is tested to see if it can meet what is anticipated. If the feature structure passes this test, information in the A-Marker and the P-Marker are combined and more precise predictions are made as to what can be acceptable in the subsequent element. For *She runs*, we assume a constraint equation *(Agent num = Action num)* associated with a CSC representing a generalized case which has, for example, `<*Agent *Action>` for a concept sequence. When a P-Marker initially has a feature structure that is nil, no expectation is made. In this example, at an A-P-Collision, an A-Marker has a feature structure containing *(num = 3s)* constraints for the possible verb form which can follow, because the feature in the A-Marker is assigned in the constraint equation so that *(Agent num 3s)* requires *(Action num 3s)*. This guarantees that only the verb form *runs* can be legitimate[9]. When predicting what comes as an *Action, P-Markers can be passed down via IS-A links and only lexical entries that meet a constraint *(Action num 3s)* can be predicted. When we need to relax grammatical constraints, P-Markers can be placed on every verb form, but are assigned higher a priori probabilities for those which meet the constraint. A unification operation can be used to conduct operations described in this section. As a result of parsing at the syntactic/semantic-level, the propositional content of the utterance is established. Since our model is a memory-based parsing model, the memory network is modified to reflect what is understood as a result of previous parsing.

2.4. Discourse Processing

2.4.1. Plan-Based Dialogue Understanding

We use hierarchical plan sequences, represented by CSCs, to understand dialogues and to predict possible next utterances. Plan hierarchies are organized for each participant of the dialog in order to capture complex dialog which often takes place in a mixed-initiative dialog. This is one of the major differences of our model from other discourse models.

[9]When we use abstract notation such as NP or VP, the same mechanism applies and captures linguistic phenomena.

Each element of the plan sequence represents a domain-specific instance of a plan or an utterance type [Litman and Allen, 1987]. Major differences which distinguish our model from simple scripts or MOPs [Schank, 1982] as used in past memory-based models are: (1) our plan sequences can be dynamically created from more productive knowledge on dialog and domain as well as previously acquired case knowledge, whereas scripts and MOPs are simple predefined sequential memory structures, and (2) a plan sequence has an internal constraint structure which enables constraints to be imposed to ensure coherence of the discourse processing. These features attain hierarchical organization of discourse knowledge and productivity of knowledge depending upon the level of abstraction. Abstract plan sequences are similar to plan schemata described in [Litman and Allen, 1987] in that they represent generic constraints and relationships between an utterance and a domain plan. They are parameterized and domain-independent knowledge of discourse plans. When an element of the plan sequence of this abstraction is activated, the rest of the elements of the plan sequence have constraints imposed, derived from the information given to the activated elements. This ensures coherence of the discourse. On the other hand, specific plan sequences representing the discourse cases are already indexed in the memory as a result of instantiating abstract knowledge based on past cases of discourse and, therefore, they contain domain-specific knowledge. When such a plan sequence is activated, it simply predicts the next plan elements because these specific plan sequences are regarded as records of past cases, and, thus, most constraints are already imposed and the sequence is indexed according to the specific constraints.

2.4.2. Script-based Discourse Understanding

In addition to plan-based discourse understanding, the model entails a script-based discourse understanding which is an extended version of a script or memory organization packet-(MOP) based story understanding [Schank, 1982]. In this approach, a sequence of utterances is represented as CSC at a discourse level tangential to the plan-based model; here, however, each utterance is also linked to nodes representing speech acts and domain plans. This part of the model accounts for canned conversations in which speakers do not really re-compute the planning behind the utterance.

Aspects which distinguish our model from simple scripts or MOPs as used in past models are (i) utterance sequences can be dynamically created from more productive knowledge on dialogue and domain as well as previously acquired case knowledge, whereas scripts and MOPs are simple predefined sequential memory structures; and (ii) an utterance has an internal constraint structure which enables constraints to be imposed to ensure discourse processing coherence. Again, the level of abstraction may vary in each CSC representing a discourse script. Some CSCs may involve elements linked to specific instances of utterance, or others may use elements linked to abstract nodes representing utterance types.

2.5. Prediction from the Language Model

Predictions are provided in a top-down manner. When A-Markers are passed up, a probability measure for each hypothesis is carried up. At each collision between an A-Marker and a P-Marker, a prediction is associated, and P-Markers are passed down. During this process, a probability measure should follow $P_0 = \sum_i P_i$ in branching and merging. A parameter for each branch needs to be learned through exposure to a large corpus of utterances of an applied domain. Case-based parsing provides the most specific prediction and gives high a priori probability. Prediction by more abstract knowledge provides less specific predictions and gives weaker a priori probability compared to predictions by more specific cases. Introduction of cases for prediction has proven to be useful since it reduces perplexity to 2.44 where the perplexity measure by using a bi-gram grammar was 3.60. Some probabilities are assigned for words which are not predicted from a case-based process, but are predicted from a unification-based process, so that even utterances which have been unexpected by the case-based process can be handled. With a certain threshold value, we obtained an experimental result which shows that the top-down prediction effectively reduced perplexity. With a small test set which has a perplexity of word choice of 247.0 with no constraints, the perplexity was reduced to 19.7 with syntactic and semantic constraints, and further reduced to 2.4 with discourse-level constraints. However, the effect of perplexity reduction by adding the discourse-level knowledge would be less effective when we apply our method in a large mixed-initiative dialog domain. This problem will be discussed in section 14. The perplexity can be controlled by the threshold value. Introduction of a threshold relaxation method would take advantage of the probabilistic approach to prediction. A high threshold is assumed at the beginning of a search to narrow down a search space; if no solution is found the threshold is lowered and the search space is widened to find a solution. This idea is similar to layering prediction [Young et. al., 1989] and probabilistic marker speed control [Wu, 1989].

2.6. Cost-based Ambiguity Resolution

A cost-based scheme of ambiguity resolution[Kitano et. al., 1989a] has been adopted in ΦDmDialog. In the cost-based theory, the hypothesis with the least cost will be selected. The cost-based theory rests on the idea that, in dynamic systems, the state of the system converges into the most stable point (the global minima) through the path with the least workload. We believe such a law of physics is applicable at the abstract level since cognitive processes are manifestations of a dynamic system which consists of large numbers of neurons, the brain. In addition, several psycholinguistic studies [Crain and Steedman, 1985] [Ford, Bresnan and Kaplan, 1981] [Prather and Swinney, 1988] were taken into account in deriving the cost-based theory. The cost-based disambiguation scheme applies to both the parsing and the generation process. In a speech input natural language system, ambiguities caused by noisy speech inputs are added along with lexical and structural ambiguities. The cost-based approach enables us to handle these different levels of ambiguity in a uniform manner. This has not been attained in the past models of ambiguity resolution. In the parsing process, costs are added when: (1) substitution, deletion and insertion of phonemes are performed to activate certain lexical items from noisy speech inputs (this part is handled using probabilistic measures as described earlier), (2) new CIs are created, (3) CCs without contextual priming are used for further processing, and (4) the memory network is modified to satisfy constraints. Costs are subtracted when: (1) prediction has been made from discourse knowledge, and (2) CCs with contextual priming have been used.

$$\begin{aligned} CSC_i &= \sum_j CC_{ij} + \sum_k constraints_k + bias_i && (5)\\ CC_j &= LEX_j + instantiateCI - priming_j && (6)\\ LEX_l &= -C\log P && (7)\end{aligned}$$

whereas $CC_{ij}, constraints_k, bias_i$ denote a cost of the j-th element of CSC_i, a cost of assuming the k-th constraints, and the lexical preference of CSC_i. $LEX_j, instantiateCI, priming_j$ denote a cost of the lexical node LEX_j, a cost of creating new CIs by referential failure, and contextual priming, respectively. P denotes the probability measure of phonological level activities, and is converted into cost using $-C\log P$ where C is a constant.

2.6.1. Initial Conditions

Our model parses utterances under a given context. Thus, the cost assigned to a certain hypothesis is not always the same. It is dependent on the context, the initial conditions according to which the utterance is given to the system. The discourse context which is the initial condition of the system is determined based on the previous course of discourse. Major factors are the state of the memory network modified as a result of processing previous utterances, contextual priming, and predictions from discourse plans. The memory network is modified based on the knowledge conveyed by the series of utterances in the discourse as described briefly in the previous section. Contextual priming is imposed either by using C-Marker passing or by the connectionist network. The mechanism of assigning preference is based on top-down prediction using discourse knowledge. Such predictions are reflected as an a priori probability at the speech processing level.

2.6.2. Phonological Processing

The phonological level has been handled with a probability measure. When a probability is introduced, the process which requires more workload is less likely to be chosen. Thus, qualitatively, higher probability means less cost and lower probability means higher cost. Probability/cost conversion equations are[10]:

$$\begin{aligned} P &= e^{\frac{-cost}{C}} && (8)\\ cost &= -C\log P && (9)\end{aligned}$$

[10]The equations are based on the Maxwell-Boltzmann distribution $P = e^{\frac{-\epsilon_n}{kT}}$.

A version of our implementation uses a cost-based scheme because the use of probability requires multiplication, whereas the use of cost requires only addition which is computationally less expensive than multiplication. It is also a straightforward implementation of our model which perceives parsing as a physical process (an energy dispersion process). For such cases, we introduce an *accumulated acoustic cost (AAC)* as a measure of cost which is computed by:

$$aac(i) \quad = \quad aac(i-1) + cc_{i_{i-1},p_{i-1}} + tc_{i_{i-2},i_{i-1}} - pe \tag{10}$$

where $aac(i), cc_{i_{i-1},p_{i-1}}, tc_{i_{i-2},i_{i-1}}$, and pe are an AAC measure of the P-Marker at the i-th element, confusion cost between i_{i-1} and p_{i-1}, transition cost between i_{i-2} and i_{i-1}, and phonetic energy, respectively. Phonetic energy reflects an influx of energy from an external acoustic energy source.

2.6.3. Reference to the Discourse Entity

When a lexical node activates any CC node, a CI node under the CC node is searched for. This activity models reference to an already established discourse entity [Webber, 1983] in the hearer's mind. If such a CI node exists, the reference succeeds and this parse will be attached with no cost. However, if no such instance is found, reference failure results. If this happens, an instantiation activity is performed creating a new instance with certain costs. As a result, a parse using a newly created instance node will be attached with some cost.

2.6.4. Contextual Priming

Either a C-Marker-based method or a connectionist network method is used for contextual priming. In the C-Marker-based scheme [Tomabechi, 1987], some CC nodes designated as Contextual Root Nodes have a list of contextually relevant nodes. C-Markers are sent to these nodes as soon as a Contextual Root Node is activated. Thus each sentence, phrase or word might influence the interpretation of succeeding sentences, phrase or words. When a node with a C-Marker is activated by receiving an A-Marker, the activation will be propagated with no cost. Thus, a parse using such nodes would have no cost. However, when a node without a C-Marker is activated, a small cost is attached to the interpretation using that node. However, the problem of this C-Marker-based scheme is that it cannot capture the dynamic nature of contextual priming — phenomena such as backward priming and a winner-take-all process cannot be simulated. The connectionist network is adopted with some computational costs in order to overcome these problems. When a connectionist network is fully deployed, every node in the network is connected with weighted links. A competitive excitation and inhibition process is performed to select one hypothesis[Waltz and Pollack, 1985]. Although both A-Markers and G-Markers carry cost information, their actual value changes over time according to the change in the activation level of the lexical and conceptual nodes.

2.6.5. Constraints

Constraints are attached to each CSC. These constraints play important roles during disambiguation. Constraints define relations between instances when sentences or sentence fragments are accepted. When a constraint is satisfied, the parse is regarded as plausible. On the other hand, the parse is less plausible when the constraint is unsatisfied. Whereas traditional parsers simply reject a parse which does not satisfy a given constraint, links between nodes are built or removed, forcing them to satisfy constraints. A parse with such forced constraints will record an increased cost and will be less preferred than parses without attached costs.

2.7. Interlingua with Multiple Levels of Abstraction

ΦDmDialog is an interlingua system in which meaning representations are assumed to be language independent. However, unlike other machine translation systems which employ a single level of abstraction in parsing and generation, ΦDmDialog uses multiple levels of abstraction. For instance, the KBMT-89 system [Nirenberg et. al., 1989a] uses Lexical Functional Grammar (LFG) as a basis for parsing and generation, but it does not use any phrasal lexicons or semantic-grammars along with with the LFG rules. On the contrary in ΦDmDialog, *specific case*, *generalized case* and *unification grammar* co-exist. This is illustrated in Figure 2.7. There, line (α) represents the process of translating a specific case, i.e. a representation of a particular source language sentence. The level of abstraction increases as we move up to line (β), which traces translation of what we call "generalized cases" or conceptual representations (given as `<*person *want *to *circum>`). At the most abstract level, (γ), we rely on a unification-based grammar. Translation occurs at the lowest — the least abstract — possible level. At all levels, however, CCs which are linked to CSCs represent language-independent concepts. Each CSC, at any level of abstraction, is associated with constraint equations which create meaning representations. When a CSC is a specific case (level α), its meaning representation is directly associated.

Advantages of using multiple levels of abstraction are as follows. The approach:

1. Improves performance by performing translations whenever possible at a level closer to the surface; there is no need for expensive unification or constraint-based processes.

2. Ensures scalability since new sentence structures can be handled simply by adding CSCs.

3. Attains high performance with massively parallel machines because, in most cases, translation can be done by finding specific or generalized cases during parsing and by invoking corresponding cases in the target language. This essentially converts time-complexity into space-complexity, which is not a problem with massively parallel machines.

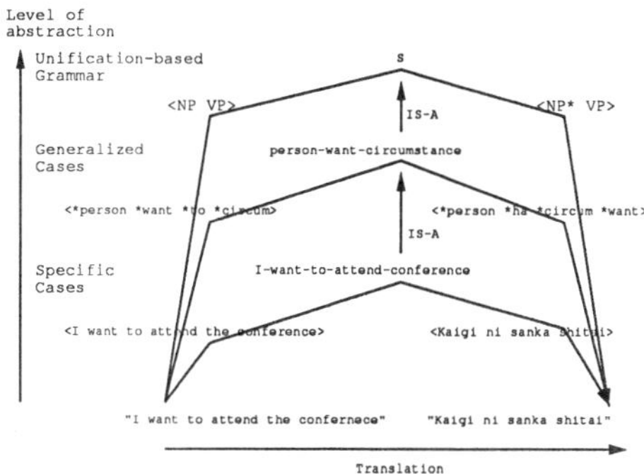

Figure 15: Translation paths at different levels of abstraction

Knowledge at different levels of abstraction can be integrated by the *feature aggregation* scheme described in Section 5. With feature aggregation, parsing and generation are attempted with the most specific cases, which involve no or only a small amount of feature unification (or constraint satisfaction). If a specific case is not found, the A-marker propagates upward and searches for more abstract cases or those which involve more expensive constraint satisfaction processes. When none of the cases is applicable for the input, the unification- or constraint-based process is invoked; this is stored at the highest level of abstraction in the memory network. The levels of abstraction are by no means discrete. Levels between, say, specific case and generalized case are permissible. In such cases, a CSC may represent a sequence such as `<I want to attend *EVENT>`, which is a mixture of a specific case and a generalized case. CSCs representing specific cases are mostly used for "canned expressions" and CSCs at more abstract levels cover a wider range of expressions. It is also possible to use specific cases for analysis and general cases for generation, and vice versa, if necessary. Since the system translates at the most specific level of abstraction, computational costs are automatically kept to a minimum.

2.8. Generation

The generation algorithm of ΦDMDIALOG can be characterized by its highly integrated processing and its capability of simultaneous interpretation. The generation algorithm employs a parallel incremental model which is coupled with the parsing process in order to perform simultaneous interpretation. In addition, the case-based process and the constraint-based process are integrated in order to generate the most specific expressions using past cases and their generalization, while maintaining syntactic coverage of the generator.

2.8.1. A Basic Generation Algorithm

Generally, natural language generation involves several stages: content delineation, text structuring, lexical selection, syntactic selection, coreference treatment, constituent ordering, and realization. In our model, the content is determined at the parsing stage, and most other processes are unified into one stage, because, in our model, lexicon, phrase, syntactic fragment, and sentence are treated in the same mechanism. There is no need to subdivide the generation process into text structuring, lexical selection and syntactic selection. The common thrust in our model is the hypothesis activation-selection cycle in which multiple hypotheses are activated and where one of them is finally selected. This cycle is adopted throughout parsing and generation. Lexical and syntactic hypotheses are activated at the same time and one hypothesis among them is selected to form a final output string. Thus, the translation process of our model can be viewed in the following processes:

Concept Activation: A part of the parsing process. Individual concepts represented by CCs are activated as a result of parsing speech inputs. A-Markers are created and passed up by activating the concept.

Lexical and Phrasal Hypotheses Activation: Hypotheses for lexicons and phrases which represent the activated concept are searched for, and G-Markers are created and passed up as a result of this process. Usually, multiple candidates are activated at one time.

Propositional Content Activation: A part of the parsing process, by which propositional content of the utterance is determined.

Syntactic and Lexical Selection: Selection of one hypothesis from multiple candidates of lexicons or phrases. First, the syntactic and semantic constraints are checked to ensure the correctness of the hypotheses, and the last selection is made using cost/activation-based selection.

Realization: The surface string (which can be either a sequence of words or a sequence of phonological signs) is formed from the selected hypothesis and sent to the speech synthesis device.

The movement of V-Markers is important in understanding our algorithm. First, a V-Marker is located on the first element of the CSC. When a G-Marker hits the element with the V-Marker, the V-Marker is moved to the next element of the CSC (Figure 16a). In the case where the G-Marker hits an element without a V-Marker, the G-Marker is stored in the element. When another G-Marker hits the element with a V-Marker, the V-Marker is moved to the next element. Since the next element already has a G-Marker, the V-Marker is further moved to the subsequent element of the CSC (Figure 16b). In figure 16c, $\bar{e_1}$ is a *closed class lexical item*[11]. When a G-Marker hits the first element, a V-Marker on the first element is moved to the third element by passing through the second element which

[11]Closed class lexical items refer to function words such as *in, at, of, to* in English and *ga, ha, wo* in Japanese.

(a)
$$\overset{V}{<}\ \underset{G\uparrow}{e_0}\ e_1\ e_2 \cdots e_n > \Rightarrow <\ \overset{V}{e_0\ e_1}\ e_2 \cdots e_n >$$

(b)
$$\overset{V}{<}\ e_0\ \underset{G\uparrow}{e_1}\ e_2 \cdots e_n > \Rightarrow <\ \underset{G\uparrow}{e_0}\ \overset{V}{\underset{\uparrow G}{e_1}}\ e_2 \cdots e_n > \Rightarrow <\ e_0\ e_1\ \overset{V}{e_2} \cdots e_n >$$

(c)
$$\overset{V}{<}\ \underset{G\uparrow}{e_0}\ \bar{e}_1\ e_2 \cdots e_n > \Rightarrow <\ e_0\ \overset{V}{\bar{e}_1}\ e_2 \cdots e_n >$$

Figure 16: Movement of V-Marker in the CSC

$$\overset{V}{<\ a_{20}\ a_{21} \cdots a_{2n} >} \qquad \Rightarrow \qquad \overset{V}{<\ a_{20}\ a_{21} \cdots a_{2n} >}$$
$$<\ a_{00}\ a_{01} \cdots \overset{V}{\underset{G}{a_{0l}}} >\ <\ a_{10}\ a_{11} \cdots a_{1m} > \quad <\ a_{00}\ a_{01} \cdots a_{0l} >\ \overset{V}{<}\ a_{10}\ a_{11} \cdots a_{1m} >$$

Figure 17: Movement of V-Marker in the Hierarchy of CSCs

is a closed class item. In this case, the element for the closed class item need not have a G-Marker. The lexical realization for the element is retrieved when the V-Marker passes through the element.

There are cases in which an element of the CSC is linked to other CSCs as seen in figure 17. In such instances, when the last element with a V-Marker gets a G-Marker, that CSC is accepted and a G-Marker that contains relevant information is passed up through an IS-A link. Then an element of the higher layer CSC gets the G-Marker and a V-Marker is moved to the next element. Since the element is linked to the other CSCs, constraints recorded on the V-Marker are passed down to lower CSCs. This movement of the V-Marker allows our algorithm to generate complex sentences.

Let us illustrate the generation process using the simple example shown in Figure 18. In keeping with earlier examples, the input sentence is *John wants to attend the conference.*

First, part (a) of the figure shows the concept activation stage: `john` is activated and an A-marker is created. The A-marker propagates and activates a CC node, `*john`. This is a part of parsing process.

Part (b) is a lexical hypothesis activation stage: a G-marker is created at the lexical node under the CC `*john`. The G-marker contains surface realization of the concept `*john` which is `jon`, along with other linguistic information. Then, the A-marker and the G-marker propagate upward. The A-marker traverses toward CSCs representing English syntax, and the G-marker traverses towards the CSC representing Japanese syntax. On the CSC `<*person` *ha ...>, a V-marker is already placed on the first element of the CSC. The G-marker and the V-marker collide at *person.

Next, part (c) of Figure 18 shows the V-marker shift. Since the element *ha is a closed-class item, it retrieves the lexical realization of *ha which is 'ha', and the V-Marker is moved to *event. At this point, the V-marker contains the surface string 'Jon ha' along with other syntax and semantic information. This is a partial realization of the surface string.

Part (d) shows the processing of *want* and *attend*. This is the concept activation stage and the lexical hypothesis activation stage. Due to the difference in word order in English and Japanese, the V-marker is not placed on *want and *attend in the CSC for Japanese. G-markers propagated from *shitai* ("want") and *sanka* ("attend") simply stay at each element of the CSC until the V-marker arrives.

The processing of *kaigi* triggered by input word *conference* is shown in part (e). A G-marker and a V-marker collide at *event, and the V-marker is moved to *ni. Since *ni is a closed-class item, its surface realization is appended to the V-marker and the V-marker further moves to *attend. Now, *attend already has a G-marker, and so a G-V-collision takes place there and the V-marker moves to *want. Again, *want already has a G-marker and a G-V-collision occurs. Since *want is the last element of the CSC, the V-marker contains the surface realization created by this local generation process: 'Jon ha kaigi ni sanka shitai'. This is the realization stage. Although the possible translation is created, it does not mean that this is the translation of the input sentence because the whole process is based on lexical-level translation, and no result of analysis from the parsing stage is involved. At this stage, it is generally the case that multiple generation hypotheses are activated.

When parsing of the sentence, as a whole or as a local phrase, is complete, its interlingua representation is constructed. It should be noted that for each CSC, there is a CC node which represents its concept (see Figure 19). As a result of parsing (whether of a complete sentence or of a local phrase), certain CC nodes will be activated and one will be selected as a CC representing the meaning of the sentence (or a phrase). This is the propositional content activation stage. Then, the target language CSC under the CC will be selected as a translation of the input sentence. This is the syntactic and lexical selection stage. This time, a constraint check is performed to ensure the legitimacy of the sentence to be generated. When there are more than one CSCs active under the CC, the one with lowest cost in the G-marker is selected.

2.8.2. Hypotheses Activation

When a concept is recognized by the parsing process, hypotheses for translation will be activated. The concept can be an individual concept, a phrase or a sentence. In our model, they are all represented as CC nodes, and each instance of the concept is represented as a CI node. The basic process is that for each of the activated CC, LEX nodes[12] in the target language will be activated. There are several cases:

[12]LEX nodes are a kind of CSC. They represents lexical entry and phonological realization of the word.

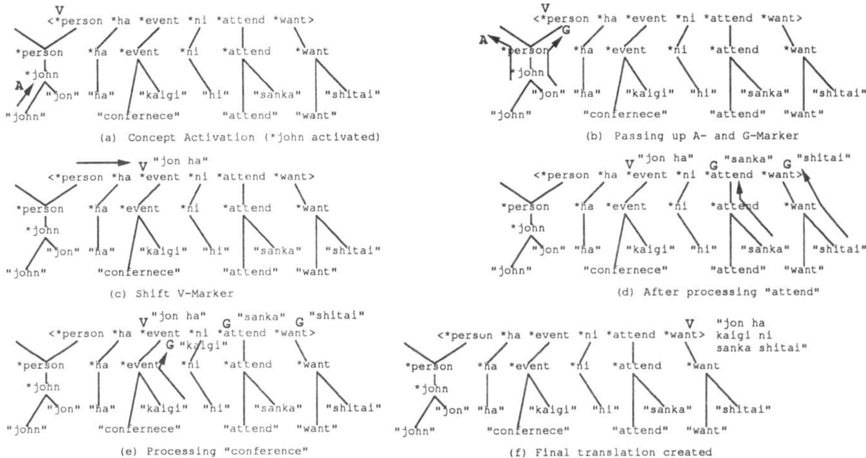

Figure 18: A simple example of the generation process.

Word-to-Word: This is a case when a word in the source language can be translated into a word in the target language. In figure 19a, the word LEX_{SL} activates CC_1. $LEX1_{TL}$ is activated as a hypothesis of translation for LEX_{SL} interpreted as CC_1. A G-Marker is created at LEX_{TL} containing a surface realization, cost, features, and an instance which the $LEX1_{TL}$ represents (CI). The G-Marker is passed up through an IS-A link. When a CC_1 does not have $LEX1_{TL}$, CC_2 is activated and $LEX2_{TL}$ will be activated. Thus, the most specific word in the target language will be activated as a hypothesis.

Word-to-Phrase: When a CC can be represented by a phrase or sentence, a CSC node is activated and a G-Marker which contains that phrase or sentence will be created. In figure 19b, LEX_{SL} activates CC_1 which has $CSC1_{TL}$. In this case, $CSC1_{TL}$ will be activated as a hypothesis to translate LEX_{SL} interpreted as CC_1.

Phrase-to-Word: There are cases where a phrasal or sentence expression can be expressed in one word in the target language. In figure 19c, CSC_{SL} activates CC_1 which can be expressed in one word using $LEX1_{TL}$. $LEX1_{TL}$ will be activated as a hypothesis for translating CSC_{SL}.

Phrase-to-Phrase: In cases where the expression in both languages corresponds at the phrase-level, the phrase-to-phrase translation mechanism is adopted. In figure 19d, CSC_{SL} will be translated using $CSC1_{TL}$ via CC_1. Such cases are often found in greetings or canned phrases.

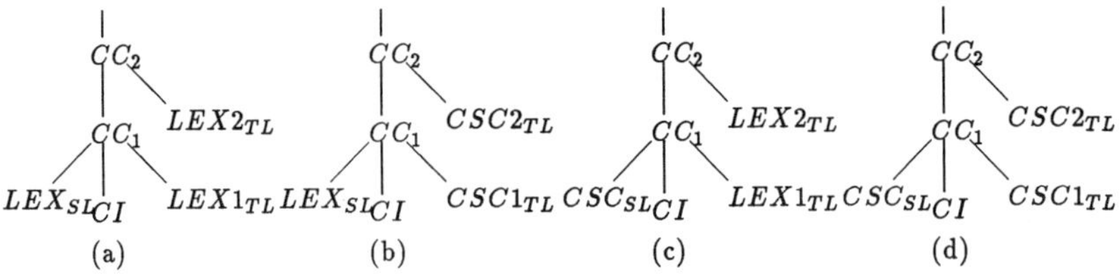

CC_2 $LEX2_{TL}$ CC_1 LEX_{SL} CI $LEX1_{TL}$
(a)

CC_2 $CSC2_{TL}$ CC_1 LEX_{SL} CI $CSC1_{TL}$
(b)

CC_2 $LEX2_{TL}$ CC_1 CSC_{SL} CI $LEX1_{TL}$
(c)

CC_2 $CSC2_{TL}$ CC_1 CSC_{SL} CI $CSC1_{TL}$
(d)

Figure 19: Activation of Syntactic and Lexical Hypotheses

2.8.3. Syntactic and Lexical Selection

Syntactic and lexical selections are conducted involving three processes: feature aggregation, constraint satisfaction, and competitive activation. Feature aggregation and constraint satisfaction correspond to a symbolic approach to syntactic and lexical selection which guarantees grammaticality and local semantic accuracy of the generated sentences, and the competitive activation process is added in order to select the best decision among multiple candidates. Features are carried up by G-Markers using feature aggregation. At each CSC, constraint satisfaction is performed in order to ensure the grammaticality of each hypothesis. Hypotheses which do not meet grammatical constraints are eliminated at this stage. Grammatical constraints are imposed using constraint equations, an example of which is *(agent num) = (action num)* which requires number agreement. Among hypotheses which are grammatically sound, one hypothesis is selected using the cost-based scheme; i.e. the hypothesis with the least cost will be selected. Priming of each hypothesis can be done by C-Marker passing or by the connectionist network. There are cases in which hypotheses from case-based and constraint-based process are both activated. In such cases, the system prefers the hypothesis from the case-based process, unless ungrammaticality is observed.

2.9. Simultaneous Interpretation: Generation while Parsing is in Progress

Development of a model of simultaneous interpretation is a major goal of the project which makes our project unique among other researches in this field. We have investigated actual recordings of simultaneous interpretation sessions and simulated telephone conversation experiments, and made several hypotheses as to how such activities are performed, as a basis for designing the ΦDmDialog system.

The process of simultaneous interpretation is a knowledge-intensive and a highly interactive process requiring the dynamic participation of various knowledge sources. Simultaneity of interpretation emerges from the fact that interpreters actually start translation even before the whole sentence is spoken by the speaker. We hypothesize that such activity is made possible because simultaneous interpreters process parsing and generation almost concurrently, and their knowledge, especially discourse and world knowledge, enables appropriate prediction and selection of hypotheses as to the meanings of utterances.

From the practical aspect, the simultaneous interpretation capability is essential for real-

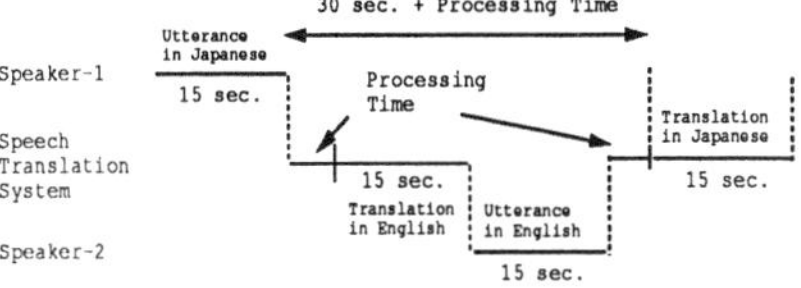

(a) Transaction with Conventional Sequential System

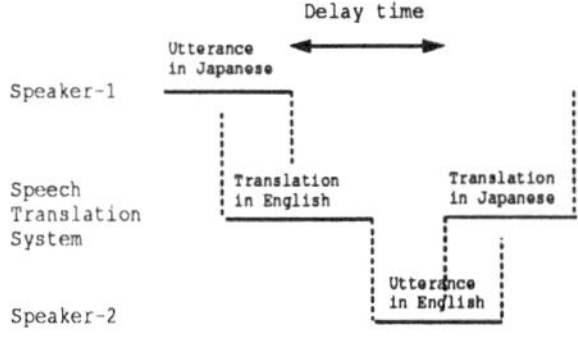

(b) Transaction with Simultaneous Interpretation System

Figure 20: Transaction with Conventional and Simultaneous Interpretation Architecture

time deployment of the system. In real dialogs, the length of each utterance can be considerably long. Utterances of sentences where each took 10-15 seconds are frequently observed. This imposes critical problems in deploying sequential parse-and-generation type architectures. Supposing that one utterance is 15 seconds in length, the hearer would need to wait more than 15 seconds to start hearing the translation of her/his dialog partner's utterance. Then, assuming that she/he responds with an utterance of 15 seconds in length, the first speaker would have to wait at least 30 seconds to start hearing her/his dialog partner's response. We believe that unless speech-to-speech translation systems overcome this problem, practical deployments are hopeless.

The approach we would take is to simulate actual simultaneous interpreters at work. From the analysis of actual simultaneous interpretation sessions, we know that:

- Translation began even in the middle of the input sentence.
- The interpreter uses a phrasal lexicon of canned expressions.
- Translation generally starts after a phrase is spoken.
- Long sentences are translated into multiple sentences. This is typically observed in Japanese-to-English translation.
- The interpreter is making strong guesses as to what will be said.

We can therefore derive several requirements that the generator of a simultaneous interpretation system must satisfy:

- The system must have incremental parsing capability.
- The system must be able produce sentences incrementally.
- The system must have opportunistic sentence planning capability to avoid syntactic dead-ends.
- The system must be able to divide one sentence into multiple sentences.
- The system must be able to predict what may be said.

The basis for simultaneous interpretation capability is the use of a parallel incremental model of parsing and generation, which has been described in previous sections, so that these can run almost concurrently with certain interactions. Of course, formulation of each part of the sentence takes place after it is processed and its meaning is determined. However, it is concurrent in the sense that the generation process does not wait until the entire parse is completed, so the translated utterance is generated incrementally[13]. Lexical selection and partial production of utterances are conducted while parsing is in progress. Thus, in some inputs, a part of the utterance can be generated before parsing of the entire sentence is completed. We do this by verbalizing a surface string or phonological realization of the instance whose role is determined, i.e. not ambiguous, and delay verbalization of ambiguous instances until they are disambiguated. The part of the sentence which is verbalized is recorded in a V-Marker and the V-Marker is moved to the next possible verbalization element. This avoids redundant verbalization. Only the element with a V-Marker can be verbalized in order to ensure the consistency of the produced sentence.

3. Massively Parallel Implementation

This section describes massively parallel implementation of the ΦDmDialog model. Currently, we have two implementation of the model: one system on the semantic network array processor SNAP, and the other system on the IXM2 assocviative memory processor. While there are obvious architectural constraints in each hardware, some modifications has been made to implement the original model on these machines. In either implementations, however, we have attained milliseconds order performance in parsing and translation.

3.1. Implementation on Semantic Network Array Processor

A version of the ΦDmDialog has been implemented on the Semantic Network Array Processor (SNAP). The goal of our work is to develop a scalable and high-performance natural language processing system which utilizes the high degree of parallelism provided by the

[13]Unlike an incremental generation by IPG[Kempen and Hoekamp, 1987], which assigns procedures to each syntactic category, our algorithm uses markers to carry information. Also, concepts to be expressed are incrementally determined as parsing progresses.

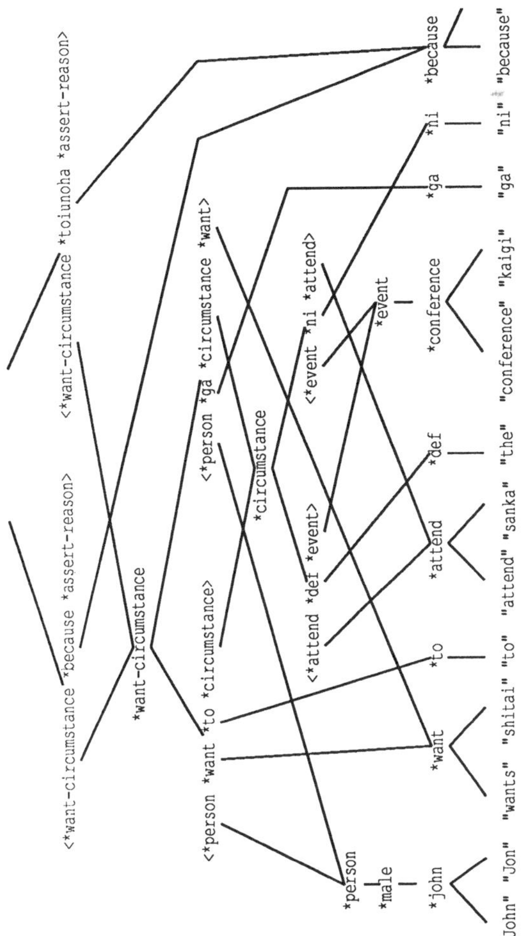

Figure 21: A part of the memory network

Input utterance	Translation
John	
wants	jon ga (John role-agent)
to	
attend	
the	
conference	
because	kaigi ni sanka shitai (want to attend the conference)
he	
is	toiunoha (because)
interested	kare ga (he role-agent)
in	
interpreting telephony	tuuyaku denwa ni kyoumi ga arukara desu (interested in interpreting telephony)

Table 3: Simultaneous interpretation in ΦDmDialog

SNAP machine. In order to accomplish the high-performance natural language processing, we have designed a highly parallel machine called Semantic Network Array Processor (SNAP) [Moldovan et. al., 1990] [Lee and Moldovan, 1990], and implemented an experimental machine translation system called DmSNAP using a parallel marker-passing scheme. DmSNAP is a SNAP implementation of the ΦDmDialog speech-to-speech dialogue translation system [Kitano, 1991a], but with some modifications to meet hardware constraints. Despite its high performance, our system carries out sound syntactic and semantic analysis including lexical ambiguity, structural ambiguity, pronoun reference, control, unbounded dependency, and others.

In the next section, we describe briefly the SNAP architecture, then, describe design philosophy behind the DmSNAP followed by descriptions on implementation and linguistic processing. Finally, performance are presented.

3.1.1. SNAP Architecture

The Semantic Network Array Processor (SNAP) is a highly parallel array processor fully optimized for semantic network processing with marker-passing mechanism. In order to facilitate efficient propagation of markers and to ease development of applications, a set of marker propagation instructions has been microcoded. SNAP supports propagation of markers containing (1) bit-vectors, (2) address, and (3) numeric value. By limiting content of markers, significant reduction in cost and resource has been attained without undermining performance requirements for knowledge processing. Several AI applications such as natural language processing system, classification system [Kim and Moldovan, 1990], and rule-based system has been developed on SNAP.

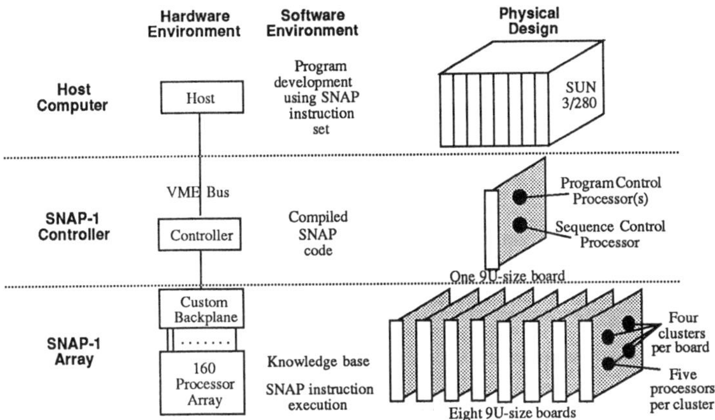

Figure 22: SNAP Architecture

The Architecture SNAP consists of a processor array and an array controller (figure 22). The processor array has processing cells which contain the nodes and links of a semantic network. The SNAP array consists of 160 processing elements each of which consists of TMS320C30 DSP chip, local SRAM, etc. Each processing elements stores 1024 nodes which act as virtual processors. They are interconnected via a modified hypercube network. The SNAP controller interfaces the SNAP array with a SUN 3/280 host and broadcasts instructions to control the operation of the array. The instructions for the array are distributed through a global bus by the controller. Propagation of markers and the execution of other instructions can be processed simultaneously.

Instruction Sets A set of 30 high-level instructions specific to semantic network processing are implemented directly in hardware. These include associative search, marker setting and propagation, logical/arithmetic operations involving markers, create and delete nodes and relations, and collect a list of nodes with a certain marker set. Currently, the instruction set can be called from C language so that users can develop applications with an extended version of C language. From the programming level, SNAP provides data-parallel programming environment similar to C* of the Connection Machine [Thinking Machine Corporation, 1989], but specialized for semantic network processing with marker passing.

Propagation Rules Several marker propagation rules are provided to govern the movement of markers. Marker propagation rules enables us to implement guided, or constraint, marker passing as well as unguided marker passing. This is done by specifying type of links that markers can propagate. All markers in DmSNAP are guided markers, thus they are controlled by propagation rules. The following are some of the propagation rules of SNAP:

- *Seq(r1,r2)* : The *Seq* (sequence) propagation rule allows the marker to propagate through *r1* once then to *r2*.
- *Spread(r1,r2)* : The *Spread* propagation rule allows the marker to travel through a chain of *r1* links and then *r2* links.
- *Comb(r1,r2)* : The *Comb* (combine) propagation rule allows the marker to propagate to all *r1* and *r2* links without limitation.

3.1.2. DmSNAP

DmSNAP is a SNAP implementation of the ΦDmDialog speech-to-speech dialogue translation system. Naturally, it inherits basic ideas and mechanisms of the ΦDmDialog system such as memory-based approach to natural language processing and parallel marker-passing. Syntactic constraint network is introduced in DmSNAP whereas ΦDmDialog has been assuming unification operation to handle linguistic processing.

Parallel Marker-Passing One other feature inherited from the ΦDmDialog is use of parallel marker-passing. In DmSNAP, however, a different approach has been taken with regard to the content of markers propagate through the network. Since ΦDmDialog has been designed and implemented on idealized simulation of massively parallel machines, markers carry feature structure (or graph) along with other information such as probabilistic measures, and unification or a similar heavy symbolic operations has been assumed at each processor element (PE). In the DmSNAP, content of the marker is restricted to (1) bit markers, (2) address markers, and (3) values [14]. Propagation of feature structures and heavy symbolic operations at each PE, as seen in the original version of the ΦDmDialog, are not practical assumptions to make, at least, on current massively parallel machines due to processor power, memory capacity on each PE, and the communication bottleneck. Propagation of feature structures would impose serious hardware design problems since size of the message is unbounded (*unbounded message passing*). Also, PEs capable of performing unification would be large in physical size which causes assembly problems when thousands of processors are to be assembled into one machine. Even with machines which overcome these problems, applications with a restricted message passing model would run much faster than applications with an unbounded message passing model. Thus, in DmSNAP, information propagated is restricted to bit markers, address markers, and values. These are readily supported by SNAP from hardware level.

Syntactic Constraint Network Syntactic constraint network (SCN) is a new feature which has not been used in the previous works in memory-based NLP. SCN is used to

[14] We call a type of marker-passing which propagates feature structures (or graphs) an *Unbounded Message Passing*. A type of marker-passing which passes fix-length packets as seem in DmSNAP is a *Finite Message Passing*. This classification is derived from [Blelloch, 1986]. With the classification in [Blelloch, 1986], our model is close to the Activity Flow Network.

handle syntactic phenomena without undermining benefits of memory-based approach. Although, unification has been the central operation in the recent syntactic theories such as LFG [Kaplan and Bresnan, 1982] and HPSG [Pollard and Sag, 1987], we prefer SCN over unification-based approach because unification is computationally expensive and it is not suitable for massively parallel implementation. Although there is a report on an unification algorithm on massively parallel machines [Kitano, 1991b], still it is computationally expensive, and takes up major part of computing time even on SNAP. In addition, there is a report that unification is not necessary the correct mechanism of enforcing agreement [Ingria, 1990]. Also, the classification-based approach [Kasper, 1989], which pre-compiles a hierarchy of feature structures in the form of a semantic network, can carry out similar task with less computational cost [Kim and Moldovan, 1990]. Finally, current unification hard-rejects failure which is not desirable from our point. We want the system to be robust enough that while recognizing minor syntactic violation, it keep processing to get meaning of the sentence.

In the syntactic constraint network model, all syntactic constraints are represented in the finite-state network consists of (1) nodes representing specific syntactic constraints (such as 3SGPRES), (2) nodes representing grammatical functions (such as SUBJ, OBJ, and OBJ2 for functional controller), and (3) syntactic constraint links which control state-transitions and the passing of information among them. Although, unification has been used to (1) enforce formal agreement, (2) percolate features, and (3) building up feature structure, we argue that these functions are attained by independent mechanism in our model. Formal agreement is enforced by activation and inhibition of nodes through active syntactic constraints. Percolation of feature is attained by passing of address through memory and syntactic constraint networks. It should be noted that not all features now being carried by unification grammar need to be carried around in order to make an interpretation of sentences. Our model only propagates necessary information to relevant nodes. Finally, instead of building up features, we distributively represent meaning of the sentence. When parsing is complete, we have a set of new nodes where each represents an instance of concept and links defines relation among them.

3.1.3. Linguistic Processing in DMSNAP

We will explain how DMSNAP carries out linguistic analysis using two sets of examples:

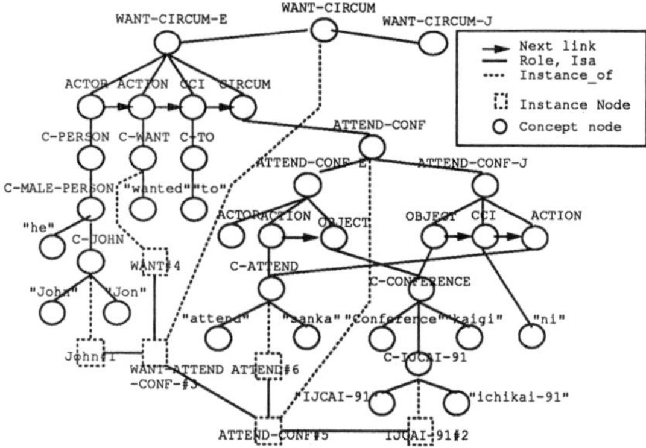

Figure 23: Part of Memory Network

	Example I
s1	John wanted to attend IJCAI-91.
s2	He is at the conference.
s3	He said that the quality of the paper is superb.

	Example II
s4	Dan planned to develop a parallel processing computer.
s5	Eric built a SNAP simulator.
s6	Juntae found bugs in the simulator.
s7	Dan tried to persuade Eric to help Juntae modify the simulator.
s8	Juntae solved a problem with the simulator.
s9	It was the bug that Juntae mentioned.

The examples contain various linguistic phenomena such as: lexical ambiguity, structural ambiguity, referencing (pronoun reference, definite noun reference, etc), control, and unbounded dependencies. It should be noted that each example consists of a set of sentences (not a single sentence isolated from the context) in order to demonstrate contextual processing capability of the DMSNAP.

These sentences in examples are not all the sentences which DMSNAP can handle. Currently, DMSNAP handles substantial portion of the ATR conference registration domain (vocabulary 450 words, 329 sentences) and sentences from other corpora.

Basic Parsing and Generation - Translation The essence of DMSNAP parsing and generation algorithm is described using sentence `s1`. A part of memory network involved in this explanation is shown in figure 23. `C-` denotes concepts; and "..." denotes surface string in the lexical node. Notice that only a part of the memory network is shown and no part of the syntactic constraint network is shown here. Also, the following explanation does not describe activity of the syntactic constraint network part. This will be described in a relevant part later.

Initially, the first CSE in every CSC on the memory network gets a P-MARKER. This P-MARKER is passed down ISA links. The CCs receiving a P-MARKER are C-PERSON and C-ATTEND. Also the closed class lexical items (CCI) in the target language propagate G-MARKER upward ISA links.

Upon processing the first word 'John' in the sentence s1, C-JOHN is activated so that C-JOHN gets an A-MARKER and a CI JOHN#1 is created under C-JOHN. At this point, the corresponding Japanese lexical item is searched for, and JON is found. A G-MARKER is created on JON. The A-MARKER and G-MARKER propagate up through ISA links (activating C-MALE-PERSON and C-PERSON in sequence) and, then, ROLE links. When an A-MARKER collides with a P-MARKER at a CSE, the associated case role is bound with the source of the A-MARKER and the prediction is updated by passing P-MARKER to the next CSE. This P-MARKER is passed down ISA links. In this memory network, the ACTOR roles of concept sequences WANT-CIRCUM-E is bound to JOHN#1 pointed by the A-MARKER. This is made possible in the SNAP architecture which allows markers to carry address as well as bit-vectors and values, where many other marker-passing machines such as NETL [Fahlman, 1979] and IXM2 [Higuchi et. al., 1991] only allow bit-vectors to be passed around. Also, G-MARKERs are placed on the ACTOR role CSE of WANT-CIRCUM-J. The G-MARKER points to the Japanese lexical item jon.

After processing 'wanted' and 'to', a P-MARKER is passed to CIRCUM and, then, to ATTEND-CONF. At this point, a source language (English) expression for the concept ATTEND-CONF is searched for and ATTEND-CONF-E is found. The first CSE of ATTEND-CONF-E gets a P-MARKER. After processing 'attend' and 'IJCAI-91', ATTEND-CONF-E becomes fully recognized[15] so that a CSI having CIs is created under ATTEND-CONF-E. Then the associated concept ATTEND-CONF is activated. An A-MARKER is passed up from ATTEND-CONF to the last element of the CSR WANT-CIRCUM-E. As the result, the CSR WANT-CIRCUM-E and its CC WANT-CIRCUM are activated in sequence. Therefore the parsing result is represented by the activated CC WANT-CIRCUM and the associated CSI. Also, upon processing 'IJCAI-91', the concept C-CONFERENCE is activated and then C-MARKERs are passed to nodes connected to C-CONFERENCE by CONTEXT links. This is an operation for contextual priming.

When the parsing is done, a V-MARKER is passed to the target language (Japanese) expression WANT-CIRCUM-J from WANT-CIRCUM, and, then, to the first CSE of WANT-CIRCUM-J. Since the first CSE has a G-MARKER pointing to JON, jon becomes the first word in the translated Japanese sentence and then the V-MARKER is passed to the next CSE. This operation is repeated for all CSEs in the CSC. Finally, the Japanese sentence t1 is constructed for the English sentence s1.

With this algorithm, the first set of sentences (s1, s2 and s3) is translated into Japanese:

[15] *fully recognized* means that the CSC can be *reduced*, in the shift-reduce parser's expression.

t1 Jon ha ichikai-91 ni sanka shitakatta.
t2 Kare ha kaigi ni iru.
t3 Kare ha ronbun no shitsu ga subarashii to itta.

Anaphora Anaphoric reference is resolved by searching for discourse entity as represented by CIs under a specific type of concept node. Sentence s2 contains anaphora problems due to 'He' and 'the conference'. When processing 'He', DMSNAP searches for any CIs under the concept C-MALE-PERSON and its subclass concepts such as C-JOHN. In the current discourse, JOHN#1 is found under C-JOHN. JOHN#1 and IJCAI-91#2 are created when the s1 is parsed. An A-MARKER pointing to JOHN#1 propagates up through ISA links. Likewise, IJCAI-91#2 is found for C-CONFERENCE. In this sentence, there is only one discourse entity (CI in our model) as a candidate for each anaphoric reference, thus a simple instance search over the typed hierarchy network suffices. However, when there are multiple candidates, we use the centering theory by introducing forward-looking center (*Cf*), backward-looking center (*Cb*), etc [Brennan et. al., 1986]. Also, incorporating the notion of the *focus* is straightforward [Sidner, 1979].

Lexical Ambiguity DMSNAP is capable of resolving this lexical ambiguity through use of *contextual priming* using the contextual marker (C-Marker) [Tomabechi, 1987] and the cost-based disambiguation [Kitano et. al., 1989a]. Sentence s3 contains a word sense ambiguity in the interpretation of the word 'paper' as either a technical document or a sheet of paper. Upon reading 'paper', C-THESIS and C-PAPER are activated. At this time, C-THESIS has a C-MARKER. The C-MARKER comes from activation of C-IJCAI-91 and C-CONFERENCE, in previous sentences, which has contextual links connecting concepts relevant to academic conference such as C-THESIS. The meaning hypothesis containing C-THESIS costs less than the one with C-PAPER so that it is selected as the best hypothesis.

Control Control is handled using the syntactic constraint network. Sentence s7 is an example of sentence involving *functional control* [Bresnan, 1982]. In s7, both *subject control* and *object control* exist – the subject of 'persuade' should be the subject of 'tried' (*subject control*), and the subject of 'help' should be the object of 'persuade' (*object control*). In this case, CSCs for *infinitival complement* has CSE without NEXT link. Such an CSE represents *missing subject.* There are SUBJ, OBJ, and OBJ2 nodes (these are *functional controller*) in the syntactic constraints network each of which store pointer to the CI node for possible controllee. Syntactic constraint links from each lexical items of the verb determine which functional controller is active. Activated functional controller propagate a pointer to the CI node to unbound subject nodes of CSCs for infinitival complements. Basically, one set of nodes for functional controller handles deeply nested cases due to *functional locality.*

Take an example from s7, when processing 'Dan', a pointer to an instance of 'Dan' which is C-DAN#1 is passed to SUBJ node of functional controller. Then, when processing 'tried', a SC-Marker propagates from the lexical node of 'tried' to SUBJ through SC-link, and the SUBJ node is being activated. Then, the pointer to C-DAN#1 in the SUBJ node propagate to SUBJ role node (or ACTOR node) of the CSC for infinitival complement. After processing 'to', the CSC for infinitival complement is predicted. Temporal bindings take place in each predicted CSC. When processing 'persuade', however, OBJ gets activated since 'persuade' enforces *object control*, not *subject control*. Thus, after 'Eric' is processed, a pointer to an instance of 'Eric' propagate in to the already active OBJ node, and then propagate to SUBJ role node (or ACTOR role node) of each CSC for infinitival complement. This way, DMSNAP performs *control*.

Structural Ambiguity Structural ambiguity is resolved by the cost-based ambiguity resolution method [Kitano et. al., 1989a]. The cost-based ambiguity resolution takes into account various psycholinguistic studies such as [Crain and Steedman, 1985] and [Ford, Bresnan and Kaplan, 1981]. Sentence s8 contains a structural ambiguity in the PP-attachment. It can be interpreted either:

$[_S$ *juntae* $[_{VP}$ *solved* $[_{NP}$ *the problem* $]$ $[_{PP}$ *with* $[_{NP}$ *the simulator* $]]]$, or

$[_S$ *juntae* $[_{VP}$ *solved* $[_{NP}$ *the problem* $[_{PP}$ *with* $[_{NP}$ *the simulator* $]]]]]$.

In this case, two hypotheses are activated at the end of the parse. Then, DMSNAP computes the cost of each hypothesis. Factors involved are contextual priming, lexical preference, existence of discourse entity, and consistency with world knowledge. In this example, the consistency with the world knowledge plays central role. The world knowledge is a set of knowledge of common sense and knowledge obtained from understanding previous sentences. To resolve ambiguity in this example, the DMSNAP checks if there is a problem in the simulator. Constraint checks are performed by bit-marker propagation through CONSTRAINT links and EQROLE links. Since there is a CI which packages instances of ERROR and SNAP-SIMULATOR then the constraint is satisfied and the second interpretation incurs no cost from constrain check. However, there is no CI which packages instances of JUNTAE and SNAP-SIMULATOR. Therefore the first interpretation incurs a cost of constraint violation (15 in our current implementation). Thus DMSNAP is able to interpret the structural ambiguity in favor of the second interpretation.

Unbounded Dependency There are two ways to handle sentences with unbounded dependency. The first approach is straightforward memory-based approach which simply store a set of CSCs involves unbounded dependency. A large set of CSCs would have to be prepared for this, but its simplicity minimized computational requirements. Alternatively, we can employ somewhat linguistic treatment of this phenomena within our framework. The syntactic constraint network has a node representing TOPIC and FOCUS which usually bound to the displaced phrase. An address of CI for the displaced phrase (such as 'the bug' in the example s9) is propagated to the TOPIC or FOCUS nodes in the syntactic constraint network. Further propagation of the address of the CI is controlled by activation of nodes along the syntactic constraint network. The network virtually encodes a finite-state transition equivalent to {COMP—XCOMP}*GF-COMP [Kaplan and Zaenen, 1989] where GF-COMP denotes grammatical functions other than COMP. The address of the CI bound to TOPIC or FOCUS can propagate through the path based on the activation patterns of the syntactic constraint network, and the activation patterns are essentially controlled by markers flow from the memory network. When the CSC is accepted and there is a case-role

Sentence	Length (words)	Number of machine cycle	Time at 10 MHz (msec)
s2: He is at ...	4	6500	0.65
s3: He said that ...	10	15000	1.50
s5: Eric build ...	5	5500	0.55
s6: Juntae found ...	6	10500	1.05
s8: Juntae solved ...	7	16500	1.65

Table 4: Execution times for DmSNAP

not bound to any CI (OBJECT in the example), the CSE for the case-role bound with the CI propagated from the syntactic constraint network.

3.1.4. Performance

DMSNAP complete parsing in the order of milliseconds. While actual SNAP hardware is now being assembled and to be fully operational by May 1991, this section provides performance estimation with precise simulation of the SNAP machine. Simulations of the DMSNAP algorithm have been performed on a SUN 3/280 using the SNAP simulator which has been developed at USC [Lin and Moldovan, 1990]. The simulator is implemented in both SUN Common LISP and C, and simulates the SNAP machine at the processor level. The LISP version of the simulators also provides information about the number of SNAP clock cycles required to perform the simulation.

There are two versions of DMSNAP, one written in LISP and one in C. The high-level languages only take care of the process flow control, and the actual processing is done with SNAP instructions. The performance data summarized in Table 2 was obtained with the first version of DMSNAP written in LISP. Furthermore, with a clock speed of 10 MHz, these execution times are in the order of 1 millisecond. These and other simulation results verify the operation of the algorithm and indicate that typical runtime is on the order of milliseconds per sentence.

3.2. Implementation on IXM2 Associative Memory Processor

ASTRAL is the IXM2 implementation of the ΦDMDIALOG model. Two implementations will be described: a parser with a flat syntactic patterns, and a parser with a hierarchical memory network. The first implementation took an extreme view that all possible syntactic structure is pre-expanded in a flat memory structure. This is the most memory intensive version of the model. The latter model is moderate strategy to use some abstraction in encoding a memory network which is closer to the ΦDMDIALOG. Experimental results were impressive. Syntactic recognition complete at the order of a few milliseconds. Scaling

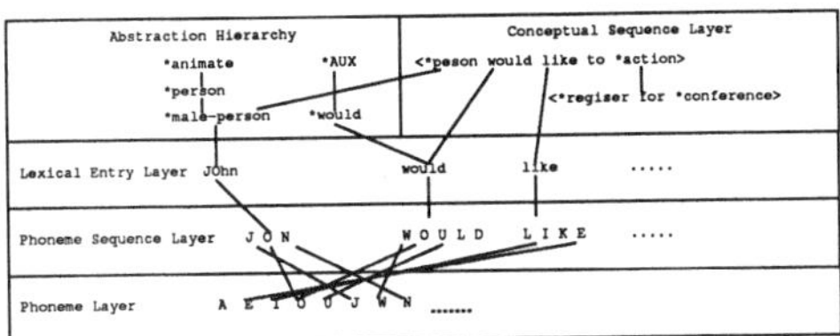

Figure 24: Overall Architecture of the Parsing Part

property seems to be desirable since only a linear degradation is observed with the scaling up of the memory-base.

3.2.1. The Massively Parallel Associative Processor IXM2

IXM2 is a massively parallel associative processor designed and developed by one of the authors at the Electrotechnical Laboratory [Higuchi et. al., 1991]. it is dedicated to semantic network processing using marker-passing.

IXM2 consists of 64 processors, called *associative processors*, which operate with associative memory each of which has a memory capacity of 256K words by 40 bits. Each associative processor is connected to other associative processors through network processors.

An associative processor consists of an IMS T800 transputer, 8 associative memory chips, RAM, link adapters, and associated logic. When operated at 20 MHz clock, T800 attains 10 MIPS [Inmos, 1987]. Each associative memory chip is a 20 Kbit CAM (512 words × 40 bits) manufactured by NTT [Ogura et. al., 1989]. The IXM2 has 64 such processors, thus attaining 256K parallelism which is far larger than 64K parallel of the Connection Machine [Hillis, 1985]. This high level of parallelism allows us to implement practical memory-based systems.

Network processors are used to handle communication between associative processors. There is one top-level network processor which deals with communication among the lower-level network processors, and 8 lower-level network processors each of which is connected to 8 associative processors. Unlike most other massively parallel architectures which use N-cube connections or cross-bar connections, IXM2 employs a full connection so that communication between any two processors can be attained by going through only 2 network processors. This full connection architecture ensures high communication bandwidth and expandability which are critical factors in implementing real-time applications. Each interconnection attains high speed serial links (20 Mbits/sec) which enable the maximum transfer rate per link at the speed of 2.4 Mbytes/sec.

3.2.2. ASTRAL

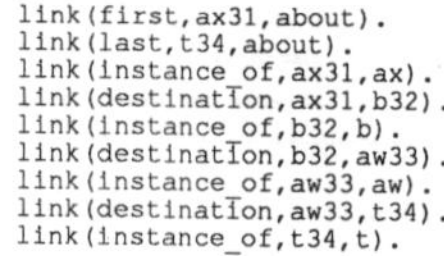

```
link(first,ax31,about).
link(last,t34,about).
link(instance_of,ax31,ax).
link(destination,ax31,b32).
link(instance_of,b32,b).
link(destination,b32,aw33).
link(instance_of,aw33,aw).
link(destination,aw33,t34).
link(instance_of,t34,t).
```

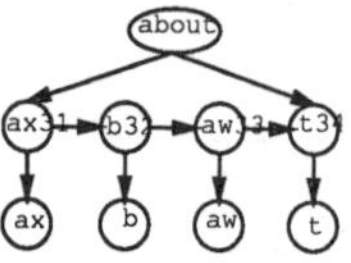

Figure 25: Network for 'about' and its phoneme sequence

ASTRAL[16] is an implementation of the memory-based translation on IXM2. The overall architecture is shown in figure 24. The memory consists of four layers: a phoneme sequence layer, a lexical entry layer, abstraction hierarchy, and a concept sequence layer.

Phoneme Layer: Phonemes are represented as nodes in the network, and they are connected to each instance of phoneme in the phoneme sequence layer. Weights are associated to links which represent the likelihood of acoustic confusion between phonemes.

Phoneme Sequence Layer: The phoneme sequence of each word is represented in the form of a network. This part is shown in figure 25.

Lexical Entry Layer: The lexical entry layer is a set of nodes each of which represents a specific lexical entry.

Abstraction Hierarchy: The class/subclass relation is represented using IS-A links. The highest (the most general) concept is **all* which entails all the possible concepts in the network. Subclasses are linked under the **all* node, and each subclass node has its own subclasses. As a basis of the ontological hierarchy, we use the hierarchy developed for the MU project [Tsujii, 1985], and domain specific knowledge has been added.

Concept Sequence: Concept sequences which represent patterns of input sentences are represented in the form of a network. Concept sequences capture linguistic knowledge (syntax) with selectional restrictions.

Figure 25 shows a part of the network. The figure shows a node for the word 'about', and how the phoneme sequence is represented. The left side of the figure is a set of IXM instructions to encode the network in the right side on the IXM2 processor. Refer [Higuchi et. al., 1991] for details of the mapping of semantic networks to IXM2. We have encoded a network including phonemes, phoneme sequences, lexical entries, abstraction hierarchies, concept sequences which cover the entire task of the ATR's conference registration domain. The vocabulary size is 405 words in one language, and at least over 300 sentences in the corpus have been covered. The average fanout of the network is 40.6. The weight value has not been set in this experiment in order to compare the performance with other parsers which do not handle stochastic inputs. In the real operation, however, a fully tuned weight

[16]ASTRAL is an acronym for the *<u>As</u>sociative model of <u>Tra</u>nslation of <u>L</u>anguage.*

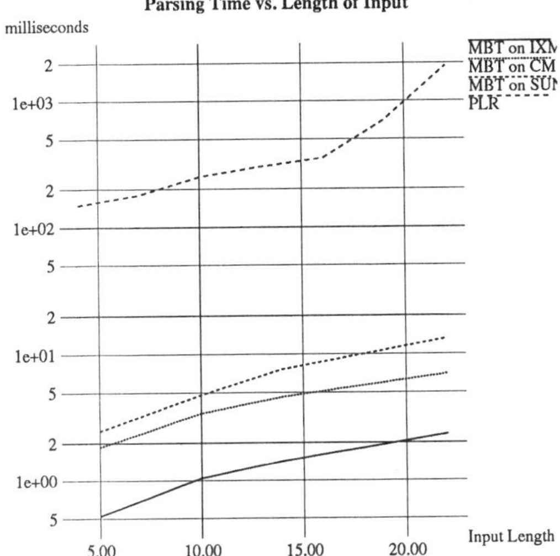

Figure 26: Parsing Time vs. Length of Input

is used. The implementation in this version uses a hierarchical memory networks thereby attaining a wider coverage with smaller memory requirements[17].

The table for templates of the target language is stored in the host computer (SUN-3/250). The binding-table of each concept and concept sequence, and specific substrings are also created. When the parsing is complete, the generation process is invoked on the host. It is also possible to compute distributively on 64 T800 transputers. The generation process is computationally cheap since it only retrieves and concatenates substrings (which is a lexical realization in the target language) bound to conceptual nodes following the patterns of the concept sequence in the target language.

3.2.3. Performance

We carried out several experiments to measure the system's performance. Figure 26 shows the parsing time against sentences of various lengths. Parsing at milliseconds order is attained. PLR is a parallel version of Tomita's LR parser. The performance for PLR was shown only to provide a general idea of the speed of the traditional parsing models. Since machines and grammars are different from PLR and our experiments, we can not make a direct comparison. However, its order of time required, and exponentially increasing parsing time clearly demonstrate the problems inherent in the traditional approach. The memory-

[17]An alternative method of covering wider inputs is to use similarity-based matching as seen in [Sumita et. al., 1990]. Combining such an approach with our model is feasible.

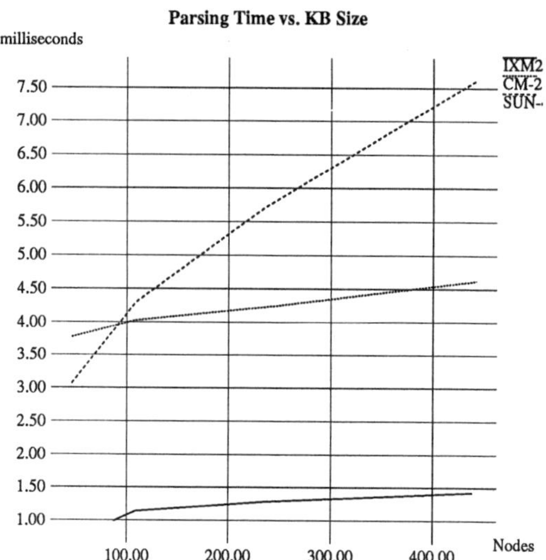

Figure 27: Parsing Time vs. KB Size

based approach on IXM2 (MBT on IXM2) shows a magnitude faster parsing performance. Also, its parsing time increases almost linearly to the length of the input sentences, as opposed to the exponential increase seen in the PLR. Notice that this graph is drawn in log scale for the Y-axis. CM-2 is slow in speed, but exhibits similar characteristics with IXM2. The speed is due to PE's capabilities and machine architecture, and the fact that CM-2 shows a similar curvature indicates the benefits of the MBT. The SUN-4 shows a similar curve, too. However, because the SUN-4 is a serial machine, its performance degrades drastically as the size of the KB grows, as discussed below.

Scalability is demonstrated in figure 27. The parsing time of a sentence with 14 input symbols is shown for various sizes of KBs. The size of the KB is measured by the number of nodes in the network. The performance degradation is less than linear due to the local activation of the algorithm. This trend is the opposite of the traditional parser in which the parsing time grows beyond linear to the size of the grammar KB (which generally grows square to the size of grammar rules, $o(G^2)$) due to a combinatorial explosion of the serial rule applications. CM-2 shows a similar curve with IXM2, but is much slower due to the slow processing capability of 1-bit PEs. The SUN-4 has a disadvantage in a scaled up KB due to its serial architecture. Particularly, the MBT algorithm involves an extensive set operations to find nodes with the A-P-Collision, which is suitable for SIMD machines. Serial machines need to search the entire KB which lead to the undesirable performance as shown in the figures in this section.

4. Discussions

4.1. Integration of Speech and Natural Language Processing

Although top-down prediction from the language model is known to improve speech recognition accuracy, the appropriate method of providing prediction is still an open question. In our system, we introduced (1) utterance cases and (2) discourse knowledge as sources of predictions.

Use of cases reduces perplexity because predictions from cases are more specific than predictions from linguistic knowledge, and more constrained than a bi-gram grammar. In an experimental grammar which has a test set perplexity of 3.66 with a bi-gram grammar, the perplexity for the same test set was reduced to 2.44 by using cases of utterances. Probabilities carried by markers from each level of processing are merged when they meet at certain nodes as predicted, and decide a final a priori probability distribution. Although this method successfully reduces the perplexity measure in the test set used in the experiment, there is some question as to its effectiveness when it applied to larger domains.

While there are considerable doubts regarding the effectiveness of using syntactic and semantic levels of knowledge alone for prediction, use of pragmatic and discourse knowledge, such as discourse plans [Litman and Allen, 1987] and discourse structure [Grosz and Sidner, 1990], gain attention with the hope that introduction of these higher levels of constraints may help by further reducing perplexity, and thus attain higher recognition rates. As a matter of fact, [Young et. al., 1989] reports that perplexity was reduced dramatically by introducing discourse knowledge using a layering prediction method, and that the semantic accuracy of the recognition result was 100%. The introduction of discourse knowledge would be useful for highly goal-oriented and relatively limited domains such as the DARPA resource management domain. We have investigated the effectiveness of using predictions from the discourse level in the ATR conference registration domain, because the ATR domain is a mixed-initiative and less goal-oriented domain.

We have carried out an experiment using a small corpus of 3 dialogs consisting of 92 utterances. For the test set of perplexity of 19.7 using syntax and semantic constraints, the addition of discourse knowledge reduced the measure to 2.4. This result alone is a significant success, and seems to confirm the effectiveness of using discourse knowledge. However, effectiveness of predictions from discourse knowledge largely depends upon the task domain and the coverage of the corpus compared to dialogs in real deployment. There are three basic problems:

First, although use of discourse knowledge generally helps in reducing perplexity, this assumes that patterns of dialogs, i.e. transition patterns among subdomains, are relatively limited so that discourse level knowledge can further constrain possible next word choice. We have investigated patterns of subdomain transitions in the ATR corpus in order to examine how this assumption holds in our domain. We took 30 dialogs from the ATR corpus to measure perplexity of subdomain transitions. The total number of utterances in 30 dialogs was 1325. 31 subdomains and 177 transitions were identified. For each subdomain, there were several subdomains within them, but we did not count these details. We simply counted major transitions between relatively abstract subdomains. Each subdomain consisted of utterances ranging from 2 utterances to over 50 utterances. Perplexity of the test set without constraint was 4.95 (note that this is not a word choice perplexity). A test set perplexity of subdomain choices was reduced to 3.44 by using a bi-gram grammar at the subdomain transition level. Yet, on average, the system has to select a domain from 11 hypotheses in order for a new subdomain to transit. Moreover, none of the dialog transitions were equal to any other dialog transitions, which implies that perplexity of the task with a larger corpus of data would be significantly larger than that which we encountered in our experiment. It should be noted that a considerable portion of syntactic structures and vocabulary are shared among subdomains, so that even if the possible next subdomain is reduced to 1/3 of all subdomains, this does not mean possible next words can be reduced to 1/3. Therefore, unfortunately, we must conclude that the use of discourse knowledge which captures transition patterns among subdialog domains, i.e. statistical transition models, bi-grams at the discourse level, and goal calculations, would have only a limited impact in reducing perplexity in mixed-initiative domains with larger topic space.

Second, the nature of mixed-initiative dialog makes accurate prediction even more difficult. Unlike the DARPA resource management domain, the ATR domain is a mixed-initiative dialog where the two participants in the dialog have their own intentions and goals. This is one of the inherent characteristics of the task which speech-to-speech translation system is expected to process. Here is an example taken from the ATR corpus:

Secretary: Please give me your card name and number.

Questioner: It's American Express, the number is 123-45678-90123. Would the proceedings be published?

Secretary: Yes, it will be published in July. Can I charge a registration fee to your AMEX account?

Questioner: Yes, and send me a registration form please.

Secretary: OK. I need your name and phone number, too.

A domain of this subdialog seems to be a credit card charge, but it has subdialogs of asking if the proceedings will be published and asking for a registration form to be sent out. Although predictions of speech acts may be attainable since more than 80% of the interaction is based on the Request-Inform discourse plan, predictions on which subdomain the dialog may switch into and when it may happen are hopelessly difficult. In the above dialog, how can we predict that the questioner may ask if the proceedings will be published in the middle of a dialog on a credit card? This means that although stronger preferences can be placed on some of the subdomains, the system must be able to expand its search space to nearly the entire domain so that sudden switching of subdomains in such complicated dialog structures can be handled. When this happens, the perplexity measure would drastically increase. In the case of our experimental set it should fall somewhere in the middle between 2.4 and 19.7.

However, obviously, expanding search space to entire domains significantly undermines the recognition rate. We still do not have an answer to this problem.

Third, prediction failures run the risk of undermining recognition rates by pruning out a correct hypothesis in favor of incorrect but predicted hypotheses. Chances of making wrong predictions depend upon the coverage of the corpus collected from real dialogs. If the corpus covers a sufficient portion of possible dialog transitions, the chances of making wrong predictions would be much lower. In the ATR's conference registration domain which involves various topics such as sightseeing, dinner, and hotel reservations, covering all possible subdomains and transitions is nearly impossible. Actually, one dialog of the corpus involves how to spend time with geishya girls at Kyoto! While covering all possible transitions is not feasible, the problem remains of how to avoid selecting wrong but predicted hypotheses when an unexpected utterance is made. We believe that higher level knowledge can help only a little with this problem, and that it can even be harmful in some cases. The only solution we suggest is to improve speech recognition at lower levels.

In summary, the language model cannot be 100% correct in providing a priori probability to the speech processing level. Use of discourse knowledge is effective only with a task of a relatively limited domain, and it would be less effective in mixed-initiative and wide domains with which we intend to deal. Given the fact that a highly accurate prediction of what may be told next is not feasible, we still need to improve the speech recognition system's accuracy without depending on higher levels of knowledge sources such as discourse knowledge.

4.2. Design of Massively Parallel Systems

There are some design issues important to massively parallel AI applications. Some of the issues affect design decisions of the overall design ideas and some issues affects choice of the hardware.

1. Gaining massive parallelism
2. Deciding where to gain parallelism
3. Mapping from logical world to physical world
4. Avoiding PE overload
5. Minimizing Communication

First, a high level of parallelism needs to be attained in order to take advantage of the massively parallel machines. However, if we simply map current AI systems which extensively rely on piecewise rule applications, the level of parallelism attained can only be medium at best. The memory-based approach fits perfectly with massively parallel machines because matching of an input against all cases will be considered in parallel by SIMD operation. For example, the traditional view of natural language processing has been relying upon grammar rules to analyze sentences. However, in reality, natural language is a bulk collection of exceptions, and many serious NLP systems have a large set of rules which cope with each exceptions. Memory-based parsing and memory-based translation theory is a superior and practical model for building practical NLP systems to be delivered to the real-world.

Second, the designer should notice that not all processes can be parallelized. The processes which can be parallelized differ from one architecture to another. For example, the array processor architecture (such as CM-2 and SNAP) can parallelize activation of more than one nodes, but thise architecture does not send markers in parallel – each marker will be send out sequentially from one node. The associative processor (such as IXM2) can send markers in parallel, but activation of nodes will be in serial in each driving PE, thus parallelism will be only 64 for this operation. In some cases, creating/deletion of nodes and links requires controller interrupts which makes this part of process serial. Designers should be well aware of the characteristics of each architecture and should avoid turning a massively parallel machine into a serial machine.

Third, logical structure of the semantic networks is not necessary mapped directly on physical allocation. Suppose we have a node with 10 fanout. All 10 neighbour nodes are within one hop on the logical map. However, if the PE has only 4 physically connected neighbour PEs, at least 6 of the logical neighbours will be allocated on PEs which are more than one hop.

Fourth, there are hardware constraints. For example, if marker-passing algorithm requires propagation of addresses or other information, each node needs to have memory to store the information, or the information will be simply lost. Physical constraints on the memory capacity limits numbers of markers which can be legally acceptable to each node. In addition, fine-grained massively parallel machines do not have powerful PEs assigned to each node, so that heavy operations such as unification would kill entire performance of the system.

Fifth, minimization of communication is critical in designing high performance massively parallel AI systems. Although the massively parallel machine circumvented a Von-Neumann bottleneck, it encounters a communication bottleneck. In some case, over 95% of entire computing time was consumed in communication of data between processors. Physically, a communication between processor is an expensive operation.

These are some of the design issues for massively parallel AI applications. This list may give the impression that designing a massively parallel AI system is a hard task, but it is not true. It simply requires a paradigm change of the view toward intelligent processes. We had been relying on somewhat rule-based and serial thinking, which may be due to hardware constraints of the serial machines we have so far. The alternative view which is more oriented toward memory-based and parallel thinking, enables us to build more practical AI applications, and once one get used to massively parallel thinking, and it would be a viable alternative to many of the current AI approaches.

5. Conclusion

Translation of the spoken utterances is a challanging and significant research goal. It requires extensive in-depth research as well as concentration of wide range of technologies from computer architecture to linguistics. We have finally come to the point where we can start building experimental systems which actually perform spoken language translation. Of course, the systems are still primitive and far from practical use. However, development of prototype systems has substantial research significancance at this moment.

First, it is significant because it clearly illustrate limitations of the current technologies and present a set of new problems which need to be solved. Our recent finding, in this regard, is that robustness in parsing is farmore important issue than we have anticipated. Of course, we knew that robust parsing is essential, but the robustness required in the real world use would involve treatment of false start, phrase insertions, discourse markers, etc. These issue has not been the research target in the robust parser research. This is just one example. Through the development and the evaluation of the ΦDmDialog system, we have found a set of new and challanging research tasks which would keep us busy for years to come.

Second, the system building is essential in accumlating and gathering knowledge in various fields. We need speech processing, natural language processing, hardware architecture, and other field in order to build a system which works. This would inevitably require communication and collaboration of researchers in different field. Joint projects of this sort would foster cross-fertilization of futher research in each domain as well as interdeciplinary domains.

The ΦDmDialog project was one of such examples. The ΦDmDialog system is one of the first speech-to-speech translation systems, and the first to demonstrate a possibility of simultaneous interpretation.

The model has several significant features. First, it is based on a massively parallel computational model which provides considerably higher performance using parallel computers. Second, it integrates the parsing and generation processes, which enables it to translate input utterances even before the whole sentence is spoken to the system. The generation process is lexically guided and uses both surface and semantic information carried by G-Markers and A-Markers. Predictions and tracking of verbalization are made by V-Markers. Third, discourse knowledge has been fully incorporated in the model. This allows effective simultaneous translation and prediction of next possible utterances. Fourth, a cost-based disambiguation scheme and a connectionist network have been useful faculties in dynamically selecting one hypothesis among multiple hypotheses.

Several experiments has been conducted by using the ATR corpus of telephone dialogs. We confirmed that the use of utterance cases and discourse knowledge contributes towards reducing perplexity. However, at the same time, we found that the effect of perplexity reduction by discourse knowledge in a larger domain is severely restricted due to the inherent unpredictability of subdomain transitions in mixed-initiative dialogs. In order for our model to generate translated sentences simultaneously, resolution of ambiguity at the earliest possible moment is desirable. Extra ambiguities caused by the addition of speech processing pose serious problems which need to be resolved. Since limitations of the usefulness of discourse knowledge in reducing perplexity have been found in mixed-initiative domains, we need to conduct research on a better speech processing module and methods of reducing search space without heavily depending upon discourse knowledge.

Of course, our model is, by no means, complete and we have a long list of future research issues. However, we believe that the importance of developing an actual prototype is in the fact that we have actually faced these problems and identified what need to be done next.

On the serial machine, one of the most significant problem was its performance. On serial machines, such as IBM RT-PC, it took 3 to 20 seconds to translate from speech-to-speech even when the vocabulary is less than 100. With the vocabulary of 450 words, it took over a minutes. The solution to this is to use actual massively parallel machines.

The massively parallel memory-based translation attains real-time translation when implemented on a massively parallel machine. Our experiments using the SNAP and the IXM2 show that parsing is completed on the order of a few milliseconds, whereas the traditional parsers requires a few seconds to even a few minutes. The main reason for this performance is the data-parallel nature of the memory-based translation paradigm where a parallel search is carried out for all sentence patterns (represented as conceptual sequences). The system not only attains milli-second order parsing performance, but also exhibits a desirable scaling property. The parsing time required grows only sublinearly to the size of the knowledge-base loaded. This scaling property is the real benefit of using a massively parallel machine. Also, we can state that the memory-based approach is promising for large-scale domains.

References

[Becker, 1975] Becker, J. D., *The Phrasal Lexicon,* Bolt, Beranek and Newman Technical Report 3081, 1975.

[Bisiani et. al., 1989] Bisiani, R., Anantharaman, T., and Butcher, L., *BEAM: An Accelerator for Speech Recognition,* CMU-CS-89-102, 1989.

[Blelloch, 1986] Blelloch, G. E., "CIS: A Massively Parallel Concurrent Rule-Based System," *Proceeding of AAAI-86,* 1986.

[Brennan et. al., 1986] S. Brennan, M. Friedman, and C. Pollard, "A Centering Approach to Pronouns," *Proceedings of the ACL-86*, 1986.

[Bresnan, 1982] Bresnan, J., "Control and Complementation," *The Mental Representation of Grammatical Relations,* The MIT Press, 1982.

[Carberry, 1985] Carberry, M., *Pragmatic Modeling in Information System Interfaces,* Ph. D. Thesis, Department of Computer and Information Science, University of Delaware, Newark, DE., 1985.

[Charniak, 1983] Charniak, E., "Passing Markers: A theory of contextual influence in language comprehension," *Cognitive Science,* 7 (3), 171-190, 1975.

[Charniak, 1988] Charniak, E., "A Neat Theory of Marker-Passing," *Proceedings of AAAI-88,* 1988.

[Cohen and Fertig, 1986] Cohen, P. and Fertig, S., 'Discourse Structure and the Modality of Communication,' In *International Symposium on Prospects and Problems of Interpreting Telephony*, 1986.

[Cottrell, 1988] Cottrell, G., "A Model of Lexical Access of Ambiguous Words," In Small, S. et. al. (Eds.) *Lexical Ambiguity Resolution,* Morgan Kaufmann Publishers, 1988.

[Crain and Steedman, 1985] Crain, S. and Steedman, M., "On Not Being Led Up The Garden Path: The Use of Context by the Physhological Syntax Processor," In *Natural Language Parsing,* 1985.

[DeMara and Moldovan, 1990] R. Demara and D. Moldovan, "The SNAP-1 Parallel AI Prototype", Technical Report PKPL 90-15, University of Southern California, Department of EE-Systems, 1990.

[De Smedt, 1989] De Smedt, K., "Distributed Unification in Parallel Incremental Syntactic Tree Formation," In *Proceedings of the Second European Workshop on Natural Langauge Generation,* 1989.

[Fahlman, 1979] S. Fahlman, *NETL: A System for Representing and Using Real-World Knowledge,* The MIT Press, 1979.

[Fikes and Nilsson, 1971] Fikes, R., and Nilsson, N., "STRIPS: A new apporach to the application of theorem proving to problem solving," *Artificial Intelligence,* 2, 189-208, 1971.

[Ford, Bresnan and Kaplan, 1981] Ford, M., Bresnan, J. and Kaplan, R., "A Competence-Based Theory of Syntactic Closure," In Bresnan, J. (Ed.), *The Mental Representation of Grammatical Relations,* MIT Press, 1981.

[Furuse et. al., 1990] Furuse, O., Sumita, E., Iida, H., "A method for realizing Transfer-Driven Machine Translation," *Workshop on Natural Language Processing,* IPSJ, 1990 (in Japanese).

[Grosz and Sidner, 1985] Grosz, B. and Sidner, C., "The Structure of Discourse Structure," *CSLI Report No. CSLI-85-39*, 1985.

[Grosz and Sidner, 1990] Grosz, B. and Sidner, C., "Plans for Discourse," In Cohen, Morgan and Pollack, eds. *Intentions in Communication,* MIT Press, Cambridge, MA., 1990.

[Higuchi et. al., 1991] Higuchi, T., Kitano, H., Handa., K., Furuya, T., Takahashi, H., and Kokubu, A., "IXM2: A Parallel Associative Processor for Knowledge Processing," *Proceedings of AAAI-91,* 1991.

[Hillis, 1985] Hillis, D. W., *The Connection Machine,* The MIT Press, Cambridge, MA, 1985.

[Hovy, 1988] Hovy, E. H., *Generating Natural Language Under Pragmatic Constraints,* Lawrence Erlbaum Associates, 1988.

[Ingria, 1990] Ingria, R., "The Limit of Unification," *Proceedings of ACL-90,* 1990.

[Inmos, 1987] Inmos, *IMS T800 Transputer,* 1987.

[Kaplan and Bresnan, 1982] Kaplan, R. and Bresnan, J., "Lexical-Functional Grammar: A Formal System for Grammatical Representation," In Bresnan, J. (Ed.), *The Mental Representation of Grammatical Relations,* MIT Press, 1982.

[Kaplan and Zaenen, 1989] Kaplan, R. and Zaenen, A., "Long-distance Dependencies, Constituent Structure, and Functional Uncertainty," 1989.

[Kasper, 1989] R. Kasper, "Unification and Classification: An Experiment in Information-Based Parsing," *Proceedings of the International Workshop on Parsing Technologies,* Pittsburgh, 1989.

[Kempen and Hoekamp, 1987] Kempen, G. and Hoenkamp, E., "An Incremental Procedural Grammar for Sentence Formulation," *Cognitive Science*, 11, 201-258, 1987.

[Kita et. al., 1989] Kita, K., Kwabata, T. and Saito, H., "HMM Continuous Speech Recognition using Predictive LR Parsing," In *Proc. of ICASSP - IEEE International Conference on Acoustic, Speech, and Signal Processing,* 1989.

[Kitano, 1991a] Kitano, H., "ΦDMDIALOG: An Experimental Speech-to-Speech Dialogue Translation System," *IEEE Computer,* June, 1991.

[Kitano, 1991b] H. Kitano, "Unification Algorithm for Massively Parallel Computers," *Proceedings of the International Workshop on Parsing Technologies*, Cancun, 1991

[Kitano, 1989c] Kitano, H., "Hybrid Parallelism: A Case of Speech-to-Speech Dialog Translation," In *Proceedings of IJCAI-89 Workshop on Parallel Algorithms for Machine Intelligence,* 1989.

[Kitano et. al., 1989a] Kitano, H., Tomabechi, H. and Levin, L., "Ambiguity Resolution in DMTRANS PLUS," In *Proceedings of the Fourth Conference of the European Chapter of the Association for Computational Linguistics,* 1989.

[Kim and Moldovan, 1990] J. Kim and D. Moldovan, "Parallel Classification for Knowledge Representation on SNAP" *Proceedings of the 1990 International Conference on Parallel Processing*, 1990.

[Lee, 1988] Lee, K.F., *Large-Vocabulary Speaker-Independent Continuous Speech Recognition: The SPHINX System*, Ph.D. Thesis, Carnegie Mellon University, 1988.

[Lee and Moldovan, 1990] W. Lee and D. Moldovan, "The Design of a Marker Passing Architecture for Knowledge Processing", *Proceedings of AAAI-90*, 1990.

[Lin and Moldovan, 1990] C. Lin and D. Moldovan, "SNAP: Simulator Results", Technical Report PKPL 90-5, University of Southern California, Department of EE-Systems, 1990.

[Litman and Allen, 1987] Litman, D. and Allen, J., "A Plan Recognition Model for Subdialogues in Conversation," *Cognitive Science 11* (1987), 163-200.

[Moldovan et. al., 1990] Moldovan, D., Lee, W., and Lin, C., *SNAP: A Marker-Passing Architecture for Knowledge Processing,* Technical Report PKPL 90-1, Department of Electrical Engineering Systems, University of Southern California, 1990.

[Morii et. al., 1985] Morii, S., Niyada, K., Fujii, S. and Hoshimi, M., "Large Vocabulary Speaker-Independent Japanese Speech Recognition System," In *Proceedings of ICSSP - IEEE International Conference on Acoustics, Speech, and Signal Processing,* 1985.

[Morimoto et. al., 1990] Morimoto, T., Iida, H., Kurematsu, A., Shikano, K., and Aizawa, T., "Spoken Language Translation: Toward Realizing an Automatic Telephone Interpretation System," *Proceedings of InfoJapan-90,* Tokyo, 1990.

[Nagao, 1989] Nagao, M., *Machine Translation: How Far Can It Go?,* Oxford, 1989.

[Nagao, 1984] Nagao, M., "A Framework of a Mechanical Translation between Japanese and English by Analogy Principle," *Artificial and Human Intelligence,* Elithorn, A. and Banerji, R. (Eds.), Elsevier Science Publishers, B.V. 1984.

[Nirenberg et. al., 1989a] Nirenberg, S. (Ed.), *Knowledge-Based Machine Translation,* Center for Machine Translation Project Report, Carnegie Mellon University, 1989.

[Ogura et. al., 1989] Ogura, K., Sakano, T., Hosaka, J., and Morimoto, T., *Spoken Language Japanese-English Translation Experimental System (SL-TRANS),* TR-I-0102, ATR Interpreting Telephony Research Laboratories, 1989.

[Ogura et. al., 1989] Ogura, T., Yamada, J., Yamada, S. and Tanno, M., "A 20-K bit Associative Memory LSI for Artificial Intelligence Machines," *IEEE Journal of Solid-State Circuits,* Vol. 24, No. 4, 1989.

[Pollard and Sag, 1987] Pollard, C. and Sag, I., *Information-Based Syntax and Semantics,* Volume 1, CSLI Lecture Notes, 13, 1987.

[Prather and Swinney, 1988] Prather, P. and Swinney, D., "Lexical Processing and Ambiguity Resolution: An Autonomous Processing in an Interactive Box," In *Lexical Ambiguity Resolution,* Small, S. et. al.(Eds.), Morgan Kaufmann Publishers, 1988.

[Quillian, 1968] M. R. Quillian, "Semantic Memory," *Semantic Information Processing,* M. Minsky(Ed.), 216-270, The MIT press, Cambridge, MA, 1968.

[Riesbeck and Martin, 1985] Riesbeck, C. and Martin, C., "Direct Memory Access Parsing," *Yale University Report 354,* 1985.

[Riesbeck and Martin, 1986] Riesbeck, C. and Martin, C., "Direct Memory Access Parsing," *Experience, Memory, and Reasoning,* Lawrence Erlbaum Associates, 1986.

[Riesbeck and Schank, 1989] Riesbeck, C. and Schank, R., *Inside Case-Based Reasoning,* Lawrence Erlbaum Associates, 1989.

[Saito and Tomita, 1988] Saito, H. and Tomita, M., "Parsing Noisy Sentences," In *Proceedings of COLING-88,* 1988.

[Sato and Nagao, 1990] Sato, S. and Nagao, M., "Toward Memory-based Translation," *Proceedings of COLING-90,* 1990.

[Schank, 1982] Schank, R., *Dynamic Memory: A Theory of Learning in Computer and People,* Cambridge University Press, 1982.

[Sidner, 1979] C. Sidner, *Towards a Computational Theory of Definite Anaphora Comprehension in English Discourse,* Ph. D. Thesis, Artificial Intelligence LAb., M.I.T., 1979.

[Small et. al., 1988] Small, S., et. al. (Eds.) *Lexical Ambiguity Resolution,* Morgan Kaufmann Publishers, Inc., CA, 1988.

[Stanfill and Waltz, 1988] Stanfill, C. and Waltz, D., "The Memory-Based Reasoning Paradigm," *Proceedings of the Case-Based Reasoning Workshop,* DARPA, 1988.

[Stanfill and Waltz, 1986] Stanfill, C. and Waltz, D., "Toward Memory-Based Reasoning," *Communications of the ACM,* 1986.

[Stanfill, 1988] Stanfill, C., "Memory-Based Reasoning Reasoning Applied to English Pronunciation," *Proceedings of the AAAI-88,* 1988.

[Sumita et. al., 1990] Sumita, E., Iida, H., and Kohyama, H., "Example-Based Approach in Machine Translation," *Proceedings of InfoJapan-90,* 1990.

[Tanaka and Numazaki, 1989] Tanaka, H. and Numazaki, H., "Parallel Generalized LR Parsing based on Logic Programming," *Proceedings of the First International Workshop on Parsing Technologies,* Pittsburgh, 1989.

[Thinking Machine Corporation, 1989] Thinking Machine Corporation, *Model CM-2 Technical Summary,* Technical Report TR89-1, 1989.

[Tomabechi, 1987] Tomabechi, H., "Direct Memory Access Translation," In *Proceedings of the International Joint Conference on Artificial Intelligence (IJCAI-87)*, 1987.

[Tomabechi et. al., 1989] Tomabechi, H., Saito, H. and Tomita, M., "SpeechTrans : An Experimental Real-Time Speech-to-Speech Translation," In *Proceedings of the 1989 Spring Symposium of the American Association for Artificial Intelligence,* 1989.

[Tomita, 1986] Tomita, M., *Efficient Parsing for Natural Language,* Kluwer Academic Publishers, 1986.

[Tomita and Carbonell, 1987] Tomita, M. and Carbonell, J. G., "The Universal Parser Architecture for Knowledge-Based Machine Translation," In *Proceedings of the International Joint Conference on Artificial Intelligence (IJCAI-87)*, 1987.

[Tsujii, 1985] Tsujii, J., "The Roles of Dictionaries in Machine Translation," *Jouhou-syori* (Information Processing), Information Processing Society of Japan, Vol. 26, No. 10, 1985. (In Japanese)

[Viterbi, 1967] Viterbi, A.J., "Error Bounds for Convolutional Codes and an Asymptotically Optimum Decoding Algorithm," In *IEEE Transactions on Information Theory,* IT-13(2): 260-269, April, 1967.

[Waibel et. al., 1989] Waibel, A., Hanazawa, T., Hinton, G., Shikano, K. and Lang, K., "Phoneme Recognition Using Time-Delay Neural Networks," IEEE, *Transactions on Acoustics, Speech and Signal Processing,* March, 1989.

[Waltz, 1987] Waltz, D., "Application of the Connection Machine," *Computer,* Jan., 1987.

[Waltz, 1990] Waltz, D., "Massively Parallel AI," *Proceedings of AAAI-90,* 1990.

[Waltz and Pollack, 1985] Waltz, D. L. and Pollack, J. B., "Massively Parallel Parsing: A Strongly Interactive Model of Natural Language Interpretation," *Cognitive Science,* 9(1): 51-74, 1985.

[Webber, 1983] Webber, B., "So What Can We Talk About Now?" In Brady, M. and Berwick, R. (Eds.), *Computational Models of Discourse*, The MIT Press, 1983.

[Wu, 1989] Wu, D., "A Probabilistic Approach to Marker Propagation," In *Proceedings of the International Joint Conference on Artificial Intelligence (IJCAI-89),* 1989.

[Young et. al., 1989] Young, S., Ward, W. and Hauptmann, A., "Layering Predictions: Flexible Use of Dialog Expectation in Speech Recognition," In *Proceedings of the International Joint Conference on Artificial Intelligence (IJCAI-89),* 1989.

CHAPTER 12

ARTIFICIAL INTELLIGENCE LANGUAGES AND PROGRAM EXECUTION EFFICIENCY

by

Samuel O. Aletan and Susan N. Twohig
Louisiana Tech University
College of Engineering
Department of Computer Science
Ruston, LA 71272
soa@engr.latech.edu

ABSTRACT

This chapter is concerned with the roles that languages, architectures, and algorithms play in the execution efficiency of artificial intelligence (AI) related problems. The examples used in this chapter are based on one observation of the execution efficiency of programs written in ADA, C, FORTRAN, PASCAL, and PL/1 to solve the 8 queens and traveling salesman problems. C is the only language that is available on all the machines used; therefore, greater emphasis was placed on C. Three algorithms which determine the optimal solution to the traveling salesman problem are examined. The first two, an iterative algorithm and a recursive algorithm, must compare all paths to find the shortest path. The third algorithm, a branch and bound algorithm, does not have to examine all paths, and is, therefore, feasible for larger data sets. We also examined two algorithms which produce near optimal solutions. These algorithms are not new, but they shed some light on the importance of algorithms in the efficiency of programs executed on conventional machines. The programs written based on these algorithms were run on several machines that included both complex instruction set computers (CISCs) and reduced instruction set computers (RISCs). Execution times were compared, and the assembly code generated by some of the machines were examined. Based on the execution times, we found that some of the factors that can be used to evaluate conventional machines in executing programs written in high level languages (HLLs) are of little use in evaluating the efficiency of conventional machines in executing AI-related problems. Although languages, system software, and architectures do influence the execution efficiency of programs, the role of programmer's experience and algorithms seem to have the most influence. Faster computers and improved system software must be complemented with better algorithms and strategies in order to solve, or at the very least slow down, the combinatorial explosion that makes solutions to some AI problems unsolvable in linear time.

1. INTRODUCTION

The basic procedure programmers follow when solving problems on computers involve the following steps [Aletan, 1988]:

- State the problem to be solved.
- Select or develop algorithms to solve the stated problem.
- Code the algorithms in a language of choice or assigned language.
- Translate the program (compile/interpret).
- Execute the translated code and debug the program if need be.
- Obtain the final/correct or acceptable solution.

These steps can be viewed as the transformational/executional process.

In order to carry out this procedure, some resources are required. These resources include:

- Programmer(s) to develop or select the algorithms, code them, execute, and debug the program.
- Architecture (computer) that will execute the program. Architecture has many components that include:
    1. Compiler/interpreter for translating the source code to an object code.
    2. Operating system for managing the computer's resources and coordinating the computer's activities.
    3. Virtual machine and hardware for representing and eventually executing the code.

Programmers have a great deal of control over some of the steps involved in the problem solving procedure. Programmers have influence on languages and algorithms selection, and coding. On the other hand, the compile/interpret and execute portion of the procedure are in the architecture domain. The architecture has more influence on how well these steps are carried out. Both the programmers and architecture have influence on how well errors are detected and corrected. Languages, compiler/interpreter, operating system, algorithms, and architecture are all interrelated in this process, and their efficiency will determine the overall efficiency of the whole procedure. As one proceeds from problem definition to execution, it becomes increasingly difficult to improve efficiency. The selection of poor algorithms or adoption of poor strategies cannot be completely compensated for with compilation and execution efficiency.

In this chapter, we discuss the interrelationships between these tools —architecture, algorithms, and languages — in solving AI related problems. The 8 queens and traveling salesman problems will be used as examples to illustrate the influence of languages, architectures, algorithms, and programmers experience on programs' execution efficiencies. The two problems are not meant to represent the entire AI problems but they are used for discussion of the dependency of the various resources involved in solving AI problems.

The 8 queens and traveling salesman problems are widely used as examples in many AI books. These two problems, and others such as Monkey and Bananas, Tower of Hanoi, Missionaries and Cannibals, Chess, and Cryptarithmetic can be considered classics because they are commonly used to illustrate the process involved in solving AI problems [Rich, 1983; Nilson, 1980]. These problems can be viewed as a core that can be used to develop approaches to solving AI problems. The 8 queens problem falls in the category of AI problems that are recoverable, i.e., a path that leads to a dead end without a solution could be reversed by backtracking and choosing another path without going back to the beginning stage. It is possible, in many cases, to generate a sequence of steps that when taken can lead to a solution. There is a definite outcome, solution, for the 8 queens problem.

The traveling salesman problem differs from the 8 queens. For problems such as the traveling salesman, planning can only generate a sequence of steps that has a good probability of resulting in a desired solution except if we are willing to do an exhaustive search. This can be very expensive because, the traveling salesman problem is a classical NP-complete problem that has many characteristics that are similar to many real world problems [Naps and Singh, 1986]. "No NP-Complete problem can be solved by any known polynomial algorithm, an algorithm requiring a number of steps that grows as a polynomial in the size of input" [Papadimitriou and Steiglitz, 1982]. All NP-complete problems suffer from combinatorial explosion. That is, as the number of instances increases, the time to solve the problem increases exponentially. Exponential time algorithms "include certain non-polynomial time complexity functions, like $n^{\log n}$, which are not normally regarded as exponential functions" [Garey and Johnson, 1979].

1.1. Languages and Architectures

Information Processing Language (IPL) was the first language explicitly designed for coding algorithms developed to solve non-numeric problems. The design of LISP was influenced by IPL, FORTRAN, and ALGOL. LISP and PROLOG are currently the most widely used AI languages. There are many other AI languages, such as Smalltalk and OPS, that are not as widely used as LISP and PROLOG. AI is a broad discipline and there is not a single language that can meet all of AI's requirements. An AI language must have three capabilities — action, description, and reasoning. Usually, languages that have one of these capabilities would more than likely lack the other two. For example, PROLOG is basically a declarative language that is suitable for storing knowledge. On the other hand, PROLOG is weak in action and description. Languages of many paradigms — imperative, functional, object-oriented, and logic — are used to write AI programs.

There are currently two microprocessor architecture design philosophies: CISC and RISC. CISC is a conventional technique of supporting software by implementing critical functions in hardware and complex instructions that are similar to high level statements in programming languages. RISC on the other hand is based on the philosophy of supporting software with primitive instructions most of which can execute in one clock cycle, and implement functions in hardware only if it doesn't negatively impact the execution time of the basic primitive instructions. Most architectures are moving towards the middle of these two design philosophies but each of the philosophies is currently used to design architectures. For example, the Intel 80486 and Motorola MC68040 based systems can be classified as CISC systems even though the design philosophy incorporates some RISC ideas. Also, the IBM RS/6000 and SPARCstation systems are RISC-based systems. Some of the features of the IBM RS/6000 are similar to features that are available on CISC architectures.

AI products are becoming application-driven rather than technology driven. Integration of AI and conventional software is becoming a determining factor in choosing a language for a given AI project. Most AI software are being deplored on conventional (general purpose machines based on CISC or RISC architectures) rather than specialized machines. Conventional machines such as SUN, DEC, and HP workstations and PCs are readily available to researchers and users of AI products compared to specialized machines such as LMI, TI Explorer and Symbolics [Pleszkun and Thashutaveetil, 1987]. This approach is becoming the norm as AI-technology is spreading beyond the high-tech companies to smaller companies such as the ones in the banking and insurance industries. Some of these companies do not have LISP or PROLOG experts and they will do the best they can with conventional languages such as C and PASCAL or Shells. The major difficulty with using conventional languages in AI programming is the languages' lack of the logic or symbolic facilities that make AI languages such as LISP or PROLOG a little more efficient or easier to use at the development stage.

Most AI programming starts off as an exploratory process. LISP is dynamically typed and ideally suited for incremental program development. This makes LISP a language of choice for fast prototyping of software systems. A great deal of investment has been put into the development of tools to make it easy to build, test, and modify prototypes on a timely basis. The AI process is different from the conventional process given earlier — define problem, develop algorithm, code algorithm, compile or interpret, execute, and debug. The AI process requires an inductive instead of a deductive procedure. Exploratory programming involves problem specification, coding of prototypes, exploration, and freezing and optimization of the prototype [Kreutzer and McKenzie, 1991]. Prototypes may be turned into working application programs or in a few instances, thrown away once a full understanding of what they were designed for have been attained.

The characteristics of programs written for AI are quite different from those of programs written to solve scientific or business problems (conventional software). These differences are the main reasons why LISP and other AI languages, including PROLOG, are quite different from procedural languages. The attributes of generic AI system include generality, addivity, explanation facility, and flexibility [Schutzer, 1987]. The differences between conventional and AI software are summarized in Table 1. AI software tries to simulate how humans reason and solve problems. But many things that people do are too vague to transform to computational data, and humans use what is generally referred to as "common sense" which is sometimes difficult to explain. Many of the things humans do are not simply accessible to awareness.

Experts use inexact reasoning due to the facts that more exact techniques are not known, or because exact techniques are not applicable to problem being solved. It is possible that enough data can not be obtained. AI must be able to deal with imprecise knowledge. It is also possible that the data to be processed are so large that it becomes practically impossible for computers to process them within the time constraints allowed for the problem. This constraints could be due to the sequential nature of the data. The primitive structures of the data could also be a problem because they lack real "reasoning" of how the data will be used or interpreted. AI may accept a satisfactory answer where conventional programming requires an optimal solution.

Table 1: Differences Between Conventional and AI Programming.

Attribute	Conventional Programming	AI Programming
Knowledge	Precise	Imprecise
Solutions Sought	Optimal	Satisfactory
Definition of Solution Steps/Technique	Exact/Algorithmic	Inexact/Heuristic Search
Control/Data	Mixed	Separated
Processing	Numeric	Symbolic and Concepts
Viewpoint	Quantitative	Plausible and Logical Reasoning
Changes	Rare	Frequent

Conventional programming requires a step by step of how to solve a problem. They are predictive, procedural, and algorithmic in nature. Programmers must predict with certainty all possible situations that their program will encounter; any deviation from the way data is processed must be inserted by a programmer at a very precise point in his/her program. Many of the problems that fall in the purview of AI are ill-defined and cannot be specified algorithmically. Heuristic search is sometimes utilized with strategies to limit the amount of computational efforts required to find a solution. Conventional programming does not require its data to be separated from its control mechanisms. AI programming separates data from control mechanisms. The way in which knowledge is stored is a major difference between conventional and AI approaches. In AI, the factual data must be stored with their "meaning" or relationships between various objects [Bernold and Albers, 1985]. AI programming is more concerned with symbolic and concepts processing rather than number processing that are more common for conventional systems.

Conventional systems tend to solve problems that are difficult or time consuming for humans. Although AI systems could be designed to solve problems that are time consuming for humans or repetitive enough to be error prone due to fatigue that humans may suffer, many of AI efforts are directed towards performing tasks that are easy for humans to carry out. Some of these tasks are navigating through a cluttered environment, driving a vehicle, understanding spoken instructions, recognizing forces and scenery, learning a job by watching and trying it out, utilizing "common sense" to resolve conflicts, and many others. These type of problems are very tasking for computers. On one hand humans carry out these functions easily without a great deal of thought. On the other hand, the processes in carrying out these functions are not well understood. Many real-world concepts involve indefinite number of components and they may also involve unbounded number of steps.

2. EXECUTING AI-RELATED PROBLEMS

There are three basic choices for programmers who are to solve AI related problems:

- Code the problems in LISP or in any other widely used AI HLLs and execute the programs on a LISP machine (AI machine such as Symbolic 3600) or execute the programs on architectures designed to efficiently support the language used.
- Code the problems in LISP or any of the other widely used AI HLLs and execute the programs on conventional (general purpose) machines.

- Code the problems in some other HLLs and execute the programs on general purpose machines.

The ideal solution will be to use the best available high level language (HLL) for each project or problem and execute the programs on machines that best support the structures and attributes of that HLL. In most instances, the ideal solution will not be possible because of practical reasons such as cost. The fact that LISP is the language of choice for most AI experts who are conversant in LISP indicates that the availability of LISP machines will be ideal or very close to it. But LISP machines are scarce because their costs are higher than those of general purpose machines, and they cannot efficiently support programs written in imperative languages like C, ADA, FORTRAN, PASCAL, etc.

The second choice is a more prevalent practice among AI experts because of costs, i.e., code problems in one of the widely used AI languages such as LISP or PROLOG and execute the programs on general-purpose machines. LISP is a natural language for a great number of operations that are performed in AI-related tasks. One of the well documented research effort on the performance of LISP was conducted by Richard Gabriel [Gabriel, 1986]. In addition to this research, many researchers had observed that programs written in LISP perform poorly on conventional machines [Anderson et al., 1987]. LISP does not run efficiently on conventional machines because of the semantic gap between list-manipulating languages like LISP, poor compilers, and lack of hardware support for memory management. Even though new LISP compilers are more efficient than their predecessors, observations still show that general purpose machines are less efficient, compared to LISP machines, in executing programs written in LISP.

On AI machines, such as Symbolics 3600, the execution of LISP primitives are supported directly in hardware [Moon, 1987]. The power of AI machines are not only from this direct hardware support of the execution of LISP primitives but also from their development (knowledge engineering), text editing, program libraries, memory management, interactive programming, and graphics. Systems such as the FAIM-1 symbolic multiprocessing system was to significantly improve the performance of AI systems over conventional systems such as the VAX 11/780 by one hundred or more times [Anderson et al., 1987]. The major drawbacks for AI machines continue to be high cost and poor performance in executing programs that are written in conventional languages. The major drawback of conventional machines in executing programs written in LISP is slower execution speed. This is partly because of the uniqueness of LISP compared to most other HLLs [Layer and Richardson, 1991].

Some of the attributes of LISP that distinguish it from conventional HLLs such as C, COBOL, FORTRAN, PASCAL, and PL/I are:

- There is a heavy reliance on the use of recursion as control structure. LISP is unparalleled in its ability for expressing recursive algorithms which manipulate dynamic data structures.
- Numbers and characters manipulations are supported but most algorithms are geared towards list processing. This characteristics is more of a consequence of the application area, AI, for which LISP was designed.
- Linked lists and property lists are the basic data structures supported. Other data structures such as arrays are supported but linked lists and property lists are the major data structures.
- There is support for a wide variety of primitives for the creation, destruction and modification of linked lists and property lists.
- Programs can be created dynamically, and descriptor processing can be done at execution time.
- The basic unit from which programs are formed are expressions which are composed of functional calls. On the other hand, programs are formed by expressions which are used to form statements in programs written with procedural languages.
- Function parameters are transmitted either by value (more prevalent) or by name, depending on the classification of the function.
- Referencing of nonlocal elements is primarily based on the most recent association rule.

The uniqueness of LISP is the motivation for the design of LISP machines in order to efficiently support programs written in LISP. But unfortunately, only a few installations can afford to buy and maintain LISP machines.

The third choice, code the problems in one of the imperative languages and execute them on general-purpose machines, is probably the most common practice of the three choices. More people are conversant in one or more imperative HLLs than in LISP and other widely used AI languages. The issue of compatibility is always a concern, and an installation may choose an imperative language because most of their other software is written in imperative languages. In addition, the AI and other system software (including the software that will be developed for the fifth generation computers, FGCs) will be integrated with conventional software (software written in imperative languages). In other words, AI and conventional software will coexist on computers and they must be supported efficiently. Faster execution speed is crucial to some AI systems which may require parallel architecture, and the efficiency of each processing unit is essential to the efficiency of a parallel processing machine. It is not good enough to cover up the inefficiency of a uniprocessing system by adopting a multiprocessing system.

3. ARCHITECTURES AND LANGUAGES USED

The computers used for the observations reported in this paper were an IBM 4341 mainframe, an IBM RT/PC, a Zenith 80386, a MicroVax II, and a Sun 3/60 Workstation. These systems are briefly discussed below:

1. The 4341 has 16 32-bit general purpose registers, 24-bit addressing, and 16 megabytes of real memory as well as 16 kilobytes of cache. The instruction set consists of 182 instructions, and cycle times range form 115 to 230 nanoseconds. The 4341 (mainframe) runs under VM/SP operating system (O/S) release 5 with compilers for most of the widely used HLLs such as FORTRAN, PASCAL, and PL/I.
2. The IBM RT/PC is based on the IBM 32-bit microprocessor RISC architecture. Most RISC instructions require only one or at most two cycles. The RT/PC has 16 32-bit general purpose registers and four megabytes of fast memory. Our system runs under the advanced interactive executive (AIX) O/S version 2.1 with compilers for C and FORTRAN. The RT/PC is the only RISC system of all the machines listed here. It has 118 instructions, a floating point co-processor, a floating point accelerator, and a memory management processor. Some of the features of the RT/PC disqualifies RT as a "true" RISC machine; its more of hybrid machine.
3. The Sun 3/60 Workstation has a 68020 processor with 32-bit addressing, 32-bit data busses, and 16 32-bit general purpose registers. It has four megabytes of memory with eight megabytes available on the server. There are 105 basic instructions and 18 different addressing modes.
4. The Zenith 80386 has a 16 megahertz processor with one megabyte of memory and 16 32-bit general purpose registers, 16 and 32-bit addressing are available, and the 80386 has 157 instructions with a clock cycle of 62.5

nanoseconds. The MicroVax II implements a 32–bit architecture with 32–bit bus structures. It features a single-chip 78032 microprocessor, one megabyte of memory, 16 32–bit general purpose registers, and an instruction set of 304 instructions. The MicroVAX II used runs under micro-VMS O/S 4.4 with compilers for C, PL/I, and LISP.

The languages in which the algorithms were implemented were PL/I, C, PASCAL, Ada, and FORTRAN. PL/I is run on the MicroVax II, optimized and un-optimized, and on the 4341. The RT, the 80386, the MicroVax II, and the Sun are used to run C, and all but the 80386 run optimized and un-optimized. PASCAL is run on the 80386 and the 4341. Ada is run on the Sun, optimized and un-optimized, and on the 80386. FORTRAN is run on the RT, optimized and un-optimized, and on the 4341.

4. 8 QUEENS PROBLEM

The 8 queens problem involves the placing of eight queens on a standard chessboard in such a way that no queen can capture any of the other queens; the first queen position will be given. In other words, there can be only one queen in any row, column, or diagonal. See Figure 1. This type of problem falls into the class of problems that are known as combinatorial and scheduling problems. A great number of scheduling problems are thought to be intractable. A good knowledge of the problem domain is crucial to efficient solutions to these types of problems.

4.1. Languages and Programmers

The 8 queens problem was assigned to some students and the result from four of the students are shown in Table 2. The four students were: Douglas Schales, George Tahtouh, Chien-Lih Lin, and Shyan Chen [Aletan, 1988]. The students were told to use any language they want. The choice of languages varied — C, LISP, PL/I, FORTRAN, and PASCAL. The programs are listed in Table 2 using each language's first or the first two letters and the programmers last name's first letter, and a number to indicate the number of programs written in a particular language as listed in the table. Douglas Schales wrote the C (C-S1), PL/I (PL-S1), and PASCAL (PA-S1) programs. George Tahtough wrote two FORTRAN (FO-T1 and FO-T2), three PL/I (PL-T2, PL-T3, and PL-T4), and a LISP (LI-T1) programs. Chien-Lih Lin wrote two PASCAL (PA-L2 and PA-L3), and a LISP (LI-L2) programs. Shyan Chen wrote a LISP (LI-C3) program.

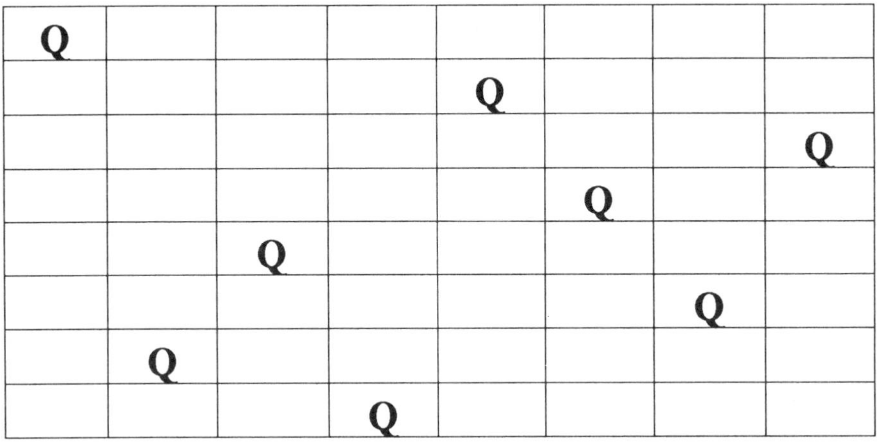

Q							
				Q			
							Q
					Q		
		Q					
						Q	
	Q						
			Q				

Figure 1: One Solution For The 8 Queens Problem

Table 2: Execution Times for the 8 Queens Problem

Programs	IBM 4341		MicroVAX II		IBM RT		Algorithms
	Noopt	Opt	Noopt	Opt	Noopt	Opt	
C-S1	n/a	00.29	00.50	00.47	00.37	00.32	Recursive
FO-T1	00.19	00.11	00.27	00.25	00.30	00.17	Iterative
FO-T2	58.97	27.13	61.75	51.45	35.88	22.98	Iterative
PL-S1	00.58	00.53	00.61	00.52	n/a	n/a	Recursive
PL-T2	46.22	43.26	108.47	57.17	n/a	n/a	Recursive
PL-T3	32.20	27.13	94.52	48.44	n/a	n/a	Iterative
PL-T4	00.48	00.47	00.53	00.40	n/a	n/a	Recursive
PA-S1	00.36	00.21	00.71	00.66	n/a	n/a	Recursive
PA-L2	00.11	00.10	00.22	00.20	n/a	n/a	Recursive
PA-L3	00.08	00.07	00.22	00.16	n/a	n/a	Iterative
LI-T1	120.00	n/a	03.44	03.47	n/a	n/a	Recursive
LI-L2	n/a	n/a	01.76	01.71	n/a	n/a	Recursive
LI-C3	n/a	n/a	01.22	01.19	n/a	n/a	Recursive

4.2. Results

The IBM RT/PC execution times were very competitive with that of the IBM 4341 mainframe. A complete comparison can not be made between the two machines because our RT/PC does not have most of the compilers that are available on 4341. Programs FO-T1, FO-T2, PL-T2, and PL-T4 were written by the same programmer but FO-T1 and PL-T4 ran faster than FO-T2 and PL-T2 respectively. After the programmers turned in their initial results, all the results were put together and they were shown to the programmers. One of the programmers, the author of FO-T2 and PL-T2, was not pleased with his execution time. He rewrote the two programs essentially with the same algorithm but a better strategy. His knowledge of the problem domain had increased compared to when the problem was originally assigned. In FO-T2 and PL-T2, the entire board (sixty-four positions), see Figure 1, was searched before a queen was placed. The author avoided exhaustive search in FO-T1 and PL-T4 to improve execution speed. The major difference between PA-L2 and PA-L3 was that PA-L2 used recursion to backtrack while PA-L3 used a stack (functions were used to simulate PUSH and POP) to do backtracking iteratively.

Interpreted LISP performed very poorly as compared to compiled LISP. LISP execution times compared very poorly to other HLLs; the only exceptions are FO-T2, PL-T2 and PL-T3 whose poor performances were algorithm/strategies related. These three programs (FO-T2, PL-T2, and PL-T3) performed poorly across all machines both with iterative and recursive algorithms. Both FORTRAN and PASCAL performed very well. One of the shortcomings of FORTRAN is the lack of support for recursion. Some problems that are easily solvable with recursive algorithms cannot be coded in FORTRAN because of this deficiency.

The influence of system software (compilers in this case) were very obvious with FO-T2 on the IBM machines. This effect was also present with PL-T2 and PL-T3 on the MicroVAX II machine. The optimized code for these programs executed at almost one-half the execution time of their non-optimized code. But it is worth noting that the optimized code for FO-T2 and PL-T2 still ran slower than the non-optimized code of their counterpart, FO-T1 and PL-T4. The non-optimized code for FO-T1 on the slowest machine of the three machines tested, MicroVAX II, ran faster than the optimized code for FO-T2. The importance of judicious choice of algorithms, data structures, and implementation strategies cannot be overstated. Although LISP is the most popular AI language, an alternative language may be called for if execution efficiency is crucial for an AI software and the software is to run on conventional machines. The more the programmers' familiarity with the problem to be solved, the better the chance for developing an efficient solution to a problem. It is also necessary for the programmers to have some knowledge about the capabilities (strength and weaknesses) of the machine(s) on which their software will run.

5. TRAVELING SALESMAN PROBLEM

The traveling salesman problem involves a salesman who is assigned a number of cities to visit. Beginning from his home city, he must visit each city exactly once, and then return to his home city, minimizing the total distance. The length of time to solve this problem becomes exponential as the number of cities increases, because for each number of cities, the number of tours to compare is (n-1)!. Currently, there is no algorithm available which can solve this problem in less than exponential time. Three algorithms for solving the traveling salesman were coded and their execution efficiency on five architectures were observed. One of the algorithms is iterative, another one is recursive and the other one is a branch and bound algorithm. The branch and bound was implemented with both a tree data structure and array structure.

5.1. Algorithms and Languages

The first optimal algorithm examined used an iterative method to generate the permutations of the first n - 1 integers [Goodman and Hedetniemi, 1977]. The second algorithm used a recursive subroutine to create tours by extending a partial tour which originally contains only the starting city [Tremblay and Sorenson, 1984]. Both the iterative and recursive algorithms must compare all tours to determine the optimal tour. The third algorithm which finds an optimal solution, the branch and bound algorithm, does not have to examine each tour, and is, therefore, feasible to use for larger data sets. The specific algorithm used is attributed to Little, Murty, Sweeny, and Karel (the flowchart is shown in Figure 2) [Goodman and Hedetniemi, 1977]. The algorithm was implemented using a tree data structure and, also, using an array to simulate a tree. While this algorithm is better than the previous two, it is still exponential and is very data-dependent.

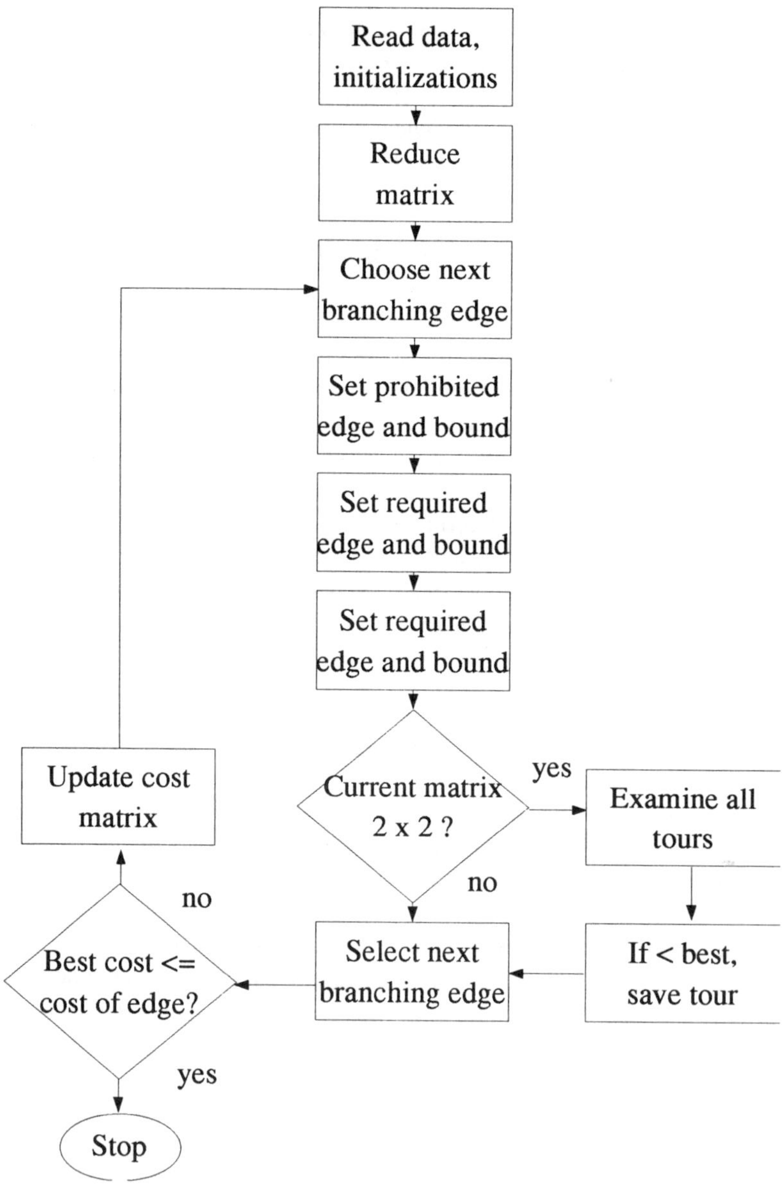

Figure 2: Flowchart of the Branch and Bound Algorithm

As all algorithms, even the branch and bound, eventually become exponential, algorithms have been developed which do not obtain the optimal tour but do obtain a good tour. One of the simplest of these algorithms is a greedy algorithm which builds a tour by always adding to the tour the next city with the lowest cost which has not yet been visited [Goodman and Hedetniemi, 1977]. A greedy tour can be improved with a procedure called 2–opting, which examines each set of four cities and, if possible, rearranges to improve the tour [Aho et al., 1983]. Greedy algorithms can be solved in polynomial time but do not guarantee an optimal solution.

5.2. Results

Most of our evaluations in this paper were devoted to the performance of the five architectures, listed above, in executing the various algorithms coded in several high level languages. Some of the architectures were not able to handle twelve or more cities in reasonable time. Some systems simply ran out of storage.

5.3. Optimal Algorithms

Tables 3–7 show the execution times in seconds for the three optimal algorithms. Recursion and tree data structures are not available in FORTRAN. Table 3 shows that PL/I ran slower on the MicroVax II than it did on the 4341 (especially for ten or more cities), resulting in the worst times for all algorithms. The only exception is the twenty cities with the branch and bound implemented with a tree data structure. The tree version of the branch and bound algorithm ran slower than the array version on both machines. The recursive routine ran faster than the iterative routine on the 4341 and slower on the MicroVax II.

Table 3: Execution Times for Traveling-Salesman Programs Written in PL/I

MicroVax Unoptimized						
# of Cities	5	8	10	12	15	20
Iterative	0.68	2.58	160.35			
Recursive	0.68	2.77	211.18			
BandB(array)	0.68	1.66	2.81	3.05	7.73	150.73
BandB(tree)	0.68	1.71	2.97	3.51	7.99	173.57

MicroVax Optimized						
# of Cities	5	8	10	12	15	20
Iterative	0.60	2.54	150.39			
Recursive	0.62	2.91	203.18			
BandB(array)	0.60	1.57	2.23	3.01	5.90	137.34
BandB(tree)	0.68	1.41	2.52	3.57	6.89	159.51

4341						
# of Cities	5	8	10	12	15	20
Iterative	0.30	2.42	184.66			
Recursive	0.30	2.91	143.32			
BandB(array)	0.33	1.57	1.26	1.80	5.49	125.46
BandB(tree)	0.33	1.41	1.37	1.90	5.99	174.49

Table 4 shows that for smaller cases, the RT and the Sun were able to run C fastest. For larger cases, the RT executes fastest. Optimization cut execution time about half on the RT and the MicroVax II. The 80386 and the MicroVax II performed about the same on smaller cases, with the 80386 becoming faster as the number of cities increased. The tree version of the branch and bound algorithm ran faster than the array version only on smaller data sets. The array version ran faster as the number of cities increased. The recursive routine usually ran slower than the iterative routine, except on the 80386.

Table 4: Execution Times for Traveling-Salesman Programs Written in C

RT Unoptimized						
# of Cities	5	8	10	12	15	20
Iterative	0.12	0.59	46.26			
Recursive	0.10	0.79	64.12			
BandB(array)	0.09	0.40	0.53	0.83	2.85	66.85
BandB(tree)	0.06	0.54	0.76	1.03	3.35	109..84
RT Optimized						
# of Cities	5	8	10	12	15	20
Iterative	0.10	0.41	31.05			
Recursive	0.08	0.62	43.79			
BandB(array)	0.07	0.26	0.29	0.38	1.20	25.72
BandB(tree)	0.06	0.27	0.36	0.40	1.39	50.32
80386						
	5	8	10	12	15	20
Iterative	0.30	0.99	56.65			
Recursive	0.99	1.54	35.87			
BandB(array)	1.21	1.37	1.32	1.81	2.85	37.68
BandB(tree)	0.99	1.31	1.54	1.65	2.80	55.47
MicroVax Unoptimized						
# of Cities	5	8	10	12	15	20
Iterative	0.33	1.32	82.41			
Recursive	0.32	1.67	105.02			
BandB(array)	0.33	0.86	1.11	1.52	4.33	100.32
BandB(tree)	0.36	0.96	1.19	1.58	4.70	130.62
MicroVax Optimized						
# of Cities	5	8	10	12	15	20
Iterative	0.30	0.99	56.66			
Recursive	0.32	1.37	80.52			
BandB(array)	0.31	0.66	0.81	1.03	2.65	57.10
BandB(tree)	0.32	0.75	0.88	1.10	2.93	83.35
Sun Unoptimized						
# of Cities	5	8	10	12	15	20
Iterative	0.08	0.50	38.00			
Recursive	0.07	0.50	43.70			
BandB(array)	0.06	0.39	0.30	0.50	1.50	36.20
BandB(tree)	0.06	0.49	0.40	0.50	1.90	59.10
80386						
# of Cities	5	8	10	12	15	20
Iterative	0.08	0.40	35.80			
Recursive	0.06	0.50	39.70			
BandB(array)	0.06	0.25	0.30	0.50	1.40	35.50
BandB(tree)	0.05	0.26	0.40	0.60	1.70	56.80

The PASCAL implementations executed smaller data sets fastest on the 4341 and larger data sets fastest on the 80386. The 4341 ran the recursive routine faster than the iterative routine on all data sets, while the 80386 ran it faster only on small data sets. The array version of the branch and bound algorithm always executed faster than the tree versions on the 4341 and faster for larger data sets on the 80386.

Table 5: Execution Times for Traveling-Salesman Programs Written in PASCAL

4341						
# of Cities	5	8	10	12	15	20
Iterative	0.04	1.14	95.76			
Recursive	0.04	0.92	69.30			
BandB(array)	0.06	0.45	0.67	1.02	3.36	75.74
BandB(tree)	0.08	0.53	0.85	2.78	4.57	83.89

80386						
# of Cities	5	8	10	12	15	20
Iterative	0.66	1.65	34.92			
Recursive	0.66	1.54	47.31			
BandB(array)	1.05	1.12	1.31	1.49	2.86	36.25
BandB(tree)	0.83	1.08	1.32	1.54	2.80	61.85

Table 6 shows that ADA on the SUN ran faster than ADA on the 80386. This was expected because the ADA compiler on the SUN was developed many years after the JANUS ADA for the 80386-based systems was released. The tree version of the branch and bound algorithm executed faster than the iterative routine on the SUN and slower on the 80386 for ten cities. The tree version of the branch and bound algorithm executed faster than the array version for smaller data sets and slower for larger data sets on both machines.

The SUN was able to run optimized C faster than the RT on the recursive routine and on the other algorithms using smaller data sets. C ran faster than Ada on the SUN. The recursive routine ran faster than the iterative routine when coded in Ada and slower when coded in C. The array version to the branch and bound algorithm executed faster than the tree version in both languages. Optimization on the SUN did not decrease execution time as much as it did on the RT.

Table 6: Execution Times for Traveling-Salesman Programs Written in ADA

Sun Unoptimized						
	5	8	10	12	15	20
Iterative	0.09	0.80	71.30			
Recursive	0.08	0.80	61.80			
BandB(array)	0.08	0.30	0.40	0.60	2.30	55.30
BandB(tree)	0.07	0.30	0.50	0.70	2.40	71.70

Sun Optimized						
	5	8	10	12	15	20
Iterative	0.09	0.80	71.00			
Recursive	0.08	0.80	61.50			
BandB(array)	0.07	0.30	0.40	0.60	2.20	55.20
BandB(tree)	0.06	0.30	0.50	0.70	2.40	71.30

80386						
	5	8	10	12	15	20
Iterative	1.54	4.42	160.10			
Recursive	1.32	4.45	171.95			
BandB(array)	1.65	2.36	2.69	4.34	8.13	61.68
BandB(tree)	1.53	2.53	2.86	4.45	9.01	211.79

Table 7 shows that FORTRAN on the RT ran faster than FORTRAN on the 4341 in most cases, and the difference became more pronounced as the number of cities increased. Optimization slightly improved execution times on the RT. On the RT, the iterative algorithm usually ran faster in C while the branch and bound algorithm usually ran faster in FORTRAN. The RT usually showed the best execution times of all machines, and either C or FORTRAN perform well.

Table 7: Execution Times for Traveling-Salesman Programs Written in FORTRAN

RT Unoptimized						
	5	8	10	12	15	20
Iterative	0.09	0.80	71.30			
BandB(array)	0.08	0.30	0.40	0.60	2.30	55.30

RT Optimized						
	5	8	10	12	15	20
Iterative	0.09	0.80	71.00			
BandB(array)	0.07	0.30	0.40	0.60	2.20	55.20

4341						
	5	8	10	12	15	20
Iterative	1.54	4.42	160.10			
BandB(array)	1.65	2.36	2.69	4.34	8.13	61.68

The 4341 ran PASCAL faster than FORTRAN and PL/I. PL/I ran the slowest of all languages. The FORTRAN version of the branch and bound algorithm using an array ran fastest. The 4341 was able to run faster using recursion, and the array version of the branch and bound ran faster than the tree version. The 4341 ran slower overall than the SUN and the RT.

The 80386 ran C fastest and ADA slowest. The PASCAL implementation of the branch and bound algorithm using an array ran faster than the C or ADA implementations. The recursive routine usually executed slower than the iterative routine, and the array version of the branch and bound usually executed faster than the tree version in all languages.

The MicroVax II ran the slowest of all machines, and C, in all cases observed, ran faster than PL/I. The recursive routine executed slower than the iterative routine, and the array version of the branch and bound algorithm executed faster than the tree version. Optimization significantly improved execution times in both languages, but all times were much greater than times for the other machines.

These results show that the RT, 80386, and SUN performed well in solving the traveling salesman problem. C performed well on all the machines. It seems C would outperform FORTRAN with larger data set. But, the lack of support for coding recursive algorithms is a drawback for FORTRAN because some AI-related problems require recursion for their solutions. Optimization greatly influences execution time on the RT. The SUN also performs well when running C. Of all the algorithms which find the optimal solution, the branch and bound algorithm implemented with an array is the best choice. This algorithm is only feasible, however, for cases up to 24-city data set, and is very data-dependent. The only machine that was able to run a 24-city data set was the RT, with the FORTRAN implementation of the branch and bound algorithm using an array requiring 104.30 seconds. The other machines either ran out of space or time. The recursive and iterative algorithms are only feasible for cases up to ten, regardless of the data, and the iterative routine seems to be the better choice. The FORTRAN version of the iterative algorithm using a 12-city data set took almost 2 hours of execution time on the RT. This exponential growth of times is one reason why the greedy algorithms were developed.

5.4. Greedy Algorithms

If an optimal tour is not necessary, the greedy algorithms are very efficient. They provide good tours in much less time. Table 8 and Table 9 show execution times in seconds for the greedy algorithms using a 24-city data set. Table 10 shows the improvement between algorithms for all the data sets.

Table 8: Execution Times of Greedy Algorithm for Data Set of 24

	4341	80386	RT	MicroVax	Sun
PASCAL	0.10	1.15			
Unoptimized FORTRAN	0.10		0.15		
Optimized FORTRAN			0.13		
Unoptimized C		1.54	0.11	0.68	0.10
Optimized C			0.10	0.68	0.10
Unoptimized PL/I	0.40			1.74	
Optimized PL/I				1.67	
Unoptimized ADA		2.14			0.10
Optimized ADA					0.10

Table 9: Execution Times of 2-opting Algorithm for Data Set of 24

	4341	80386	RT	MicroVax	Sun
Pascal	0.10	1.15			
Unoptimized FORTRAN	0.10		0.20		
Optimized FORTRAN			0.15		
Unoptimized C		1.56	0.17	0.68	0.10
Optimized C			0.15	0.68	0.10
Unoptimized PL/I	0.40			1.84	
Optimized PL/I				1.71	
Unoptimized Ada		2.15			0.10
Optimized Ada					0.10

The Greedy algorithms execute in polynomial time, and, even though they can not guarantee the optimal solution, they do find a good solution. In some cases, the greedy algorithm even found the optimal solution. 2-opting does not improve cost much, but does not significantly increase execution time. The Sun consistently worked best on these algorithms using C or ADA. FORTRAN on the RT and PASCAL on the 4341 also performed well.

Table 10: Improvement in Cost

Number of Cities	Optimal	Greedy	2-opting
5	7750	7750	7750
8	2370	2565	2505
10	640	755	755
12	5241	6274	5958
15	5584	6482	6427
20	6786	8774	8613
24	7685	9835	9556

6. INSTRUCTION ANALYSIS

M. J. Flynn has described measures for an "ideal" high-level language architecture. According to Flynn, all instructions can be classified as M-type which move data around in storage, P-type which perform sequencing and comparisons, or F-type which perform functions such as arithmetic and logical operations. Using these types, Flynn has determined three ratios: an M-ratio, the ratio of M-type instructions to F-type; a P-ratio, the ratio of P-type instructions to F-type; and a NF-ratio (nonfunctional ratio), the ratio of the sum of M- and P-type instructions to F-type. All ratios for an "ideal" machine would be zero, as M- and P-type instructions are considered "overhead" [Flynn, 1978]. For comparison, assembly codes for the branch and bound algorithm using an array were obtained. Table 11 shows the Flynn ratios for each machine.

Table 11: Flynn Ratios

		M-ratio	P-ratio	NF-ratio
RT Unoptimized				
	FORTRAN	1.5766	0.4792	2.0558
	C	1.2449	0.2797	1.5247
RT Optimized				
	FORTRAN	2.0763	0.5485	2.6248
	C	1.6781	0.4002	2.0783
MicroVax Unoptimized				
	PL/I	0.2514	0.8464	1.0978
	C	1.0513	1.3761	2.4274
MicroVax Optimized				
	PL/I	0.3338	1.1531	1.4869
	C	1.2270	1.6378	2.8649
Sun Unoptimized				
	Ada	2.5103	1.9845	4.4948
	C	1.3253	0.5301	1.8554
Sun Optimized				
	Ada	2.5668	1.7914	4.3583
	C	1.3976	0.5233	1.9209
80386				
	Pascal	2.5741	1.1389	3.7130
	Ada	3.1048	1.2157	4.3205
	C	1.7601	0.6217	2.3816
4341				
	Pascal	2.8327	2.3236	5.1564
	FORTRAN	3.2787	0.9191	4.1978
	PL/I	0.9920	0.3972	1.3892

The lowest Flynn ratios resulted from PL/I code on the MicroVax II. The MicroVax II uses fewer data movement instructions than the other machines and is able to perform multiple operations, such as array referencing, in one instruction. Optimization increases the Flynn ratios because more operations are moved to registers for speed, but these operations are still considered memory movement. The best ratios came from PL/I, while the worst came from PASCAL and ADA. The worst ratios came from PASCAL on the 4341. The RISC architecture would be expected to suffer the most because of its requirements to adopt a load/store strategy. This disadvantage is offset by the fact that variables that are placed in registers are referenced several times before they are stored back in to the memory.

Flynn's analysis may not be a good measure for this type of problem, however, because more data movement and comparison operations are required than arithmetic and logical operations. An analysis of the branch and bound algorithm showed that most of the execution time is spent in the segment of the algorithm which chooses a next branching edge (See Table 12). Table 13 shows the number and types of instructions needed for each machine and each language for this segment.

Table 12: Edge Choosing Segment of Branch and Bound Algorithm in C

```
min = -1
 for(i=2,i<=level;++i)
      {for(j=2;j<=level;++j)
              {if(work[i][j]==0)
                    {d=max;
                     for(k=2;k<=level;++k) if (k!=i&&work[i][k]<d) d
                     dd = d;
                     d  = max;
                     for(k=2;k<=level;++k) if (k!=i&&work[k][j]<d) d
                     dd = dd + d;
                     if (dd>min)
                          {min = dd;
                           row = i;
                           col = j;}}}}
```

Table 13: Instructions Required By RT

FORTRAN Unoptimized		FORTRAN Optimized		C Unoptimized		C Optimized	
l	60	l	44	l	116	l	63
st	22	st	23	sli	25	st	31
cas	21	sli	14	cas	23	sli	20
sli	20	c	13	st	18	lr	17
a	15	cas	11	a	15	clrcb	13
c	13	lr	10	c	13	c	13
ai	5	a	9	clrcb	8	a	12
ble	5	ai	5	ble	5	cas	11
lis	4	ble	5	lis	4	lis	5
bgt	4	ais	4	bgt	4	ble	5
ais	4	bgt	4	ais	4	bgt	4
beq	2	lis	4	beq	2	ais	4
bge	2	beq	2	bge	2	beq	2
lr	2	bge	2	cal	1	bge	2
ci	1	ci	1	ci	1	cal	1
cal	1	cal	1	bne	1	ci	1
bne	1	bne	1			bne	1
TOTALS	182		153		242		205

Table 14: Instructions Required By 80386

C		Pascal		Ada	
MOV	52	MOV	67	MOV	106
CMP	10	CMP	14	ADD	21
JMP	7	JMP	9	JMP	20
ADD	6	ADD	6	CMP	18
MUL	5	SHL	5	JNE	10
SHL	5	MUL	5	CALL	9
INC	4	JZ	5	PUSH	9
JZ	3	INC	4	POP	9
JLE	3	JLE	3	XCHG	8
JGE	2	JG	2	DEC	6
JG	2	JGE	2	MUL	5
		JNZ	2	INC	4
		XOR	1	JLE	4
				JL	2
				AND	2
				JE	1
				INTO	1
				JG	1
TOTALS	99		125		236

Table 15: Instructions Required By SUN Workstation

C Unoptimized		C Optimized		ADA Unoptimized		ADA Optimized	
movl	43	movl	43	movea.l	51	move.l	45
addl	16	addl	16	move.l	44	movea.l	41
asll	10	asll	10	trapv	21	trapv	19
cmpl	9	cmpl	9	cmp.l	13	cmp.l	13
lea	5	moveq	5	cmpi.l	10	cmpi.l	10
jgt	4	jle	5	trapgt.	10	trapgt.	10
addql	4	lea	5	adda.l	10	adda.l	10
jra	4	jra	4	beq.b	6	beq.b	6
jge	2	addql	4	muls.l	5	muls.l	5
jeq	2	jeq	2	lea.l	5	lea.l	5
tstl	1	jge	2	asl.l	5	asl.l	5
jne	1	jne	1	bgt.w	4	bgt.w	4
jle	1	tstl	1	addq.l	4	addq.l	4
				bra.w	4	bra.w	4
				moveq.l	4	moveq.l	4
				neg.b	4	neg.b	4
				sne.b	2	sne.b	2
				slt.b	2	slt.b	2
				move.b	2	move.b	2
				and.b	2	and.b	2
				tst.b	2	tst.b	2
				add.l	1	add.l	1
				tst.l	1	tst.l	1
				bne.w	1	bne.w	1
				ble.b	1	ble.b	1
				clr.l	1	clr.l	1
				ble.b	1	ble.b	1
TOTALS	102		107		214		205

Table 16: Instructions Required By MicroVax II

C Unoptimized		C Optimized		PL/I Unoptimized		PL/I Optimized	
movl	14	movl	16	cmpp4	30	cmpp4	30
cmpl	9	cmpl	9	brw	17	brw	17
addl3	6	bleq	4	movp	16	movp	16
mull3	5	mull3	3	ashp	15	ashp	13
bleq	3	addl3	3	blss	12	blss	12
brw	3	aobleq	3	cvtpl	10	clrl	7
beql	3	brw	3	mull2	10	cvtlp	7
bgtr	2	bgtr	2	cvtwl	8	bgeq	6
bgeq	2	beql	2	cvtlp	8	mull2	6
aobleq	2	mnegl	1	clrb	6	bleq	5
acbl	2	tstl	1	incb	6	addp6	5
tstl	1	addl2	1	bgeq	6	cvtpl	5
		acbl	1	addp6	5	brb	4
		bneq	1	bleq	5	bgtr	4
		bgeq	1	addl2	5	addl2	3
				bgtr	4	beql	3
				brb	4		
				bbc	3		
				beql	2		
				mcomb	2		
				blcb3	2		
				subp6	1		
				bneq	1		
				bbs	1		
TOTALS	52		50		179		143

Table 17: Instructions Required By 4341

	FORTRAN		PASCAL		PL/I	
	L	67	L	21	MVC	11
	ST	32	ST	20	ZAP	10
	C	14	CH	11	CVB	9
	SR	12	A	9	CP	7
	A	10	C	9	MH	7
	BCR	7	LR	8	AR	7
	LA	6	BAL	7	LR	5
	BALR	6	BNL	6	ST	5
	BC	6	MH	4	LA	4
	BXLE	6	AH	4	STE	3
	SLL	5	B	4	XI	3
	M	5	LA	4	BH	2
	LR	5	SLA	3	AP	2
			BL	3	BNH	2
			AR	3	MVI	2
			MVC	3	LE	2
			BE	2	SE	2
			LH	1	BNE	1
			LTR	1	LH	1
			BNE	1	CVD	1
			SR	1	BE	1
			BL	1	BNL	1
			BNH	1	OI	1
					L	1
					BALR	1
TOTALS		81		127		91

The preceding tables show that most of the machines use more load, store, and move instructions. The exception is the MicroVax II, and, therefore, it has the best Flynn ratios. The MicroVax II using C generates the fewest instructions of all the machines. PL/I on the MicroVax II uses almost three times as many instructions, and this is reflected in execution times.

The FORTRAN code from the RT uses less instructions than the C code, and, again, this is reflected in execution times. Even though the RT needs many instructions, most of these instructions execute in one cycle. There are 205 instructions generated by the C optimizing compiler on the RT and only 50 instructions by the C optimizing compiler on the MicroVAX. The FORTRAN optimizing compiler on the RT generated 153 instructions and the FORTRAN compiler on the 4341 generated only 81 instructions. The ability of RISC architectures to execute instructions in few cycles contributed to the RT's execution improvements over the CISC architectures such as the MicroVax II.

The SUN, the 80386 and the 4341 all need many load, store, and move instructions to perform the segment of code shown in Table 12, and, since instructions on these machines require multiple cycles, all of the machines, in most of the cases observed, ran slower than the RT. The implementation which generated the fewest instructions on all three machines also executed fastest. This shows that algorithms have a great impact on performance. The machines that generated the fewest number of instructions do not always have the best execution times.

The 8 queens and traveling salesman problems are typically considered to be artificial intelligence type problems. These problems require much more memory as well as efficient memory management, but do not require many arithmetic operations. RISC systems with efficient load/store architecture seems appropriate for this type of application in terms of execution speed. But RISC architectures are not known for their efficient use of memory. Some artificial intelligence problems require large amount of storage; in these instances, CISC architectures could be favored. Flynn's ratios, however, are not as representative for artificial intelligence-related problems as they would be for a numerical type problems. More indepth research is needed to find out the appropriateness of CISC and RISC architectures in executing artificial intelligent problems.

7. CONCLUSION

The characteristics of programs written for AI are different from that of conventional software which are dominated by scientific and business programs. Execution efficiency of AI software is not only dependent on architectural attributes but also on programmer's experience, and careful selection of algorithms. The 8 queens problem and many other AI related problems are known as combinatorial problems. But the 8 queens problem can always be solved with exhaustive search. The traveling salesman problem and other NP-complete problems must be approached through architectural innovations and algorithm improvements and developments. There are fairly good algorithms such as the branch and bound algorithm, which can significantly delay the combinatorial explosion. The results documented in this paper show that RISC architectures, such as the IBM RT, could be a good choice to run this type of problem if execution speed is a concern. But, if memory usage is of primary concern, then the CISC architectures should be considered. Our observation showed that Flynn's ratios which may be reasonable as a measure of architectures effectiveness in other application areas, such as scientific applications, are of little use when executing AI-related problems. We intend to extend our efforts to include PROLOG, larger AI-related problems, and more RISC architectures such as the SPARCstations 1 and 2, and HP 720 workstations. We can not reach a definite conclusion due to the number and small size of the problems that we have analyzed but we can state the following preliminary conclusions:

1. LISP is not as efficient as procedural languages on conventional machines. But LISP is an excellent language for exploratory programming and most AI programming starts off as an exploratory process.
2. C seems to be a viable language for coding AI-related problem. Optimization by the compilers can greatly improve execution times
3. ADA seems to have a potential for coding AI-related problems but better compilers are needed
4. FORTRAN has a decisive disadvantage because it lacks support for coding recursive algorithms
5. PL/I seems to be a poor language for coding AI-related problems when we are concerned about execution speed
6. RISC architectures seem to have advantages for fast execution and better optimization for C and FORTRAN code. Optimizing compiler is part of the

RISC design strategies and the pay off is obvious in our observations. A major disadvantage with RISC architectures is storage consumption; RISC architectures, in general, consumes more storage (generate more instructions) than CISC architectures for most problems.

7. Programmer's familiarity with the problem to be solved is important for developing an efficient solution to a problem.
8. Careful selection of algorithms, data structures, and implementation strategies are crucial to execution efficiency.

BIBLIOGRAPHY

[1] Aho, Alfred V., et al. (1983). Data Structures and Algorithms. Addison-Wesley: Reading.

[2] Aletan, Samuel (1988). "The Influence of Algorithms and Languages VS Programmers Experience on Programs Execution Efficiency," Modelling and Simulation Conference. May 5–6, pp. 1131–1135.

[3] Anderson, Judy M., et al. (1987). "The Architecture of FAIM-1,"IEEE Computer. Volume 20, Number 1, January, pp. 55–65.

[4] Bernold, Thomas and Gunter Albers, editors. (1985). Artificial Intelligence: Towards Practical Application. Elsevier Science Publishers: B. V. (North-Holland), GDI.

[5] Flynn, M. J. (1978). "A Canonic Interpretive Program Form For Measuring 'Ideal' HLL Architectures," Computer Architecture News. Volume 6, Number 8, April.

[6] Gabriel, Richard P. (1986). Performance and Evaluation of LISP Systems. Second Edition, The MIT Press: Cambridge, Massachusetts.

[7] Garey, Michael R. and David S. Johnson. (1979). Computers and Intractability A Guide to the Theory of NP-Completeness. W.H. Freeman and Company: San Francisco.

[8] Goodman, S. E. and S. T. Hedetniemi. (1977). Introduction to the Design and Analysis of Algorithms. McGraw-Hill Book Company: New York.

[9] Kreutzer, Wolfgang and McKenzie Bruce. (1991). Programming for Artificial Intelligence - Methods, Tools, and Applications. Addison-Wesley Publishing Company: New York.

[10] Layer, K. D. and C. Richardson. (1991). "LISP Systems in the 1990's," Communications of the ACM. September, pp. 48–57.

[11] Moon, David A. (1987) "Symbolics Architecture," IEEE Computer. Volume 20, Number 1, January, pp. 43–52.

[12] Naps, Thomas L. and Bhagat Singh. (1986). Introduction to Data Structures with PASCAL. West Publishing Company: St. Paul.

[13] Nilson, N. J. (1980). Principles of Artificial Intelligence. Tioga Publishing Company: Palo Alto, CA.

[14] Papadimitriou, Christos H. and Kenneth Steiglitz. (1982). Combinatorial Optimization: Algorithms and Complexity. Prentice-Hall, Inc.: Englewood Cliffs.

[15] Pleskun, Andrew R. and Mathew J. Thashuthaveetil. (1987). "The Architecture of LISP Machines," IEEE Computer. Volume 20, Number 3, March, pp. 35–44.

[16] Rich, Elaine. (1983). Artificial Intelligence. McGraw-Hill Book Company: New York.

[17] Schutzer, D. (1987). Artificial Intelligence An Applications-Oriented Approach. Van Nostrand Reihold Company Inc., New York.

[18] Tremblay, Jean-Paul and Paul G. Sorenson. (1984). An Introduction to Data Structures with Applications. McGraw-Hill Book Company: New York.

SECTION 6

AI ARCHITECTURES

CHAPTER 13

THE ANALYSIS AND SYNTHESIS OF INTELLIGENT SYSTEMS

WILLIAM ARDEN
TELOS Corporation
55 North Gilbert Street
Shrewsbury, New Jersey 07702

ABSTRACT

A generalized cognitive system is defined mathematically, which is then isomorphically translated into a corresponding Petri Net Structure. The Petri Net Representation is then examined for a variety of binary compositions with other such Petri Net Representations. The closure properties of these compositions are then discussed. Following, is an examination of the structural properties of the machine represented cognitive systems. These methods are reflected upon and proposed as the means of analyzing and synthesizing cognitive systems in machine implementable form. Implementation considerations and interpretation are also given for these Cognitive Machine Nets as they are termed.

ACKNOWLEDGMENT

I wish to thank Telos Corporation for its support in the production of this document.

SECTION 1 - INTRODUCTION

1.1 PROLOGUE

This paper proposes a means of synthesizing and analyzing computational machines based upon cognitive systems. However, before we proceed to the formal development of this means with its resulting benefits, let us quickly review some of the work in the field. This should suggest the rationale behind the approach of this paper.

Constructing human brainlike machines has been of interest for some time. The emergence of the notion of building machine models based upon biological nerve cells and their interconnection was given by the seminal work of Warren McCulloch and Walter Pitts, in their 1943 paper "A Logical Calculus of the Ideas Immanent in Nervous Activity" [48]. Again in 1947, they published a second work entitled "How We Know Universals" [49]. This work explored network architectures that could recognize various patterns. These papers combined greatly motivated the beginnings of the cybernetics era.

Later in the 1950's, serial computers were becoming available and learning was being demonstrated on them to some extent. Arthur Samuel gave credence to learning automata with his computer programs for playing checkers [63].

Then in 1962, Frank Rosenblatt defined the perceptron which is perhaps the earliest connectionist model of learning automata [59]. Perceptrons demonstrated methods of parallel computation and programmed learning, but were inadequate in representing knowledge. Fortunately, following Rosenblatt's work and primarily in the 1970's, many powerful ideas were introduced in a new, discipline termed knowledge engineering (Post Facto). These included semantic networks, frames, relational data bases, logical production systems and expert systems [52].

Meanwhile, cognitive science was converging in interest. Learning was being formulated under the discipline of mathematical psychology, [59]. Finally, James L. McClelland, David Rumelhart and the PDP Research Group published their two-volume text "Parallel Distributed Processing, Explorations in the Microstructure of Cognition" [47]. This two-volume set represented the comprehensive compilation of neural network (which, as we have shown, dates back to the 1943 McCulloch and Pitts paper) research under the discipline of cognitive science.

However, most of the work described in the PDP series presented single and uniform learning rules. Marvin Minsky the Donner Professor of Science at MIT has stated "No single method or learning trick will make a machine be versatile enough. Instead, a very smart machine must be built more like a corporation or community. It will need an intricate network of interlocking checks and balances, in which every part is supervised by other systems, each of which must learn when and how to use the resources available" [51]. Minsky has termed such a machine to be a "Society of Mind" and has published a recent book by that title. Minsky, who has founded MIT's Artificial Intelligence laboratory, General Turtle Inc., LOGo Computer Systems Inc. and Thinking Machines Corp., further states that while many new neural net and cognitive models are being suggested that include notably Boltzmann Machines, there is at present little in the way of means to analyze their respective properties [52].

This paper proposes a means of synthesizing and analyzing a general class of cognitive models. It does so through the powerful methods of Petri Net modeling which, while presently sophisticated, have yet to be employed to their potential in such applications [57]. Other methods which offer promise in this area include the usage of topological graphs with attributes [72].

1.2 BACKGROUND

We will first consider a generalized cognitive system, as depicted in Figure 1. As can be seen, the cognitive system described is essentially composed of knowledge representations called knowledge atoms and feature representations. We will denote the knowledge atoms as α_j for each, and the features as R_i for each. Now, as observed in the figure, there is something called a Distal Environment.

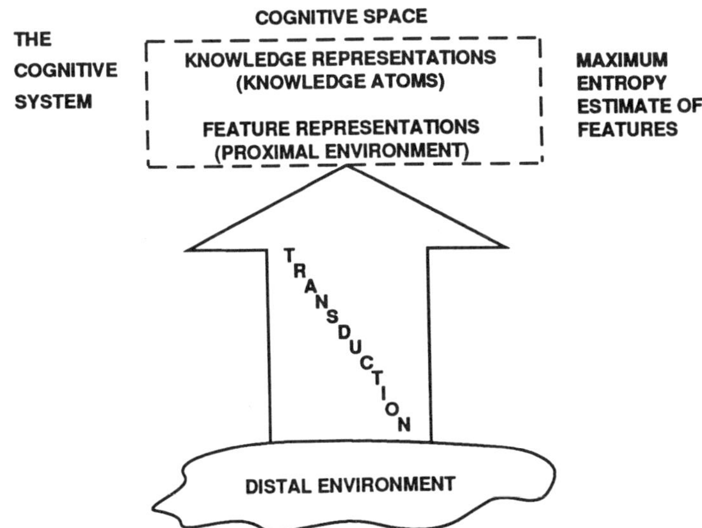

Figure 1. Overview of Cognitive System Within its Environment

This is the "world" or environment apart and outside the cognitive system. In the case of animals, this would be termed their habitat, environment or ecosystem. We note in the figure a process called transduction. This is the process of taking environmental stimuli or emanations and transducing or converting it into a form that is representable by our features representations. For example, consider the microphone. It performs transductions by transducing acoustic signal into electrical signals that are readable by an electrical system.

Returning to the cognitive system, we will state its task as basically to formulate a magnitude estimation of a stimulus cluster [70] or equivalently some good estimate of its distal environment. It does this by learning. Each of the features are stimulated or not stimulated ($R_i \in \{1, 0\}$, respectively) with a certain probability distribution called P. This is known as the proximal environment. Learning occurs by weighting certain knowledge atoms with a weighting factor λ. Basically, each time a knowledge atom is activated (the knowledge atoms are either activated or not activated) a memory trace or update to λ is made. This is done by a Completion Function. At a given state, the completion function C will take those R_i (features) stimulated and those a_i[1] (knowledge atom activations present) and update (stimulate) other R_i's, thereby recognizing patterns. These newly recognized patterns, in turn, activate other knowledge atoms that again update the weighting factor λ. What has not been mentioned is that the knowledge atoms are connected with the features by a set of connections $K_{\alpha i j}$ from an α_i to an R_j (see Figure 2). These connections go as stimulating, absent, or inhibiting denoted as $K_{\alpha i j} \in \{1, 0 -1\}$, respectively. Given these connections K_α to knowledge atoms, we conduct our completions such that the probability of Shannon missing information is maximized. The Shannon missing information is defined as entropy as defined in statistical physics. Hence, we say that we conduct completions such that the maximum entropy estimate (denoted π) is updated such that it is further maximized. This process ensures us that maximal missing information in the Shannon sense or, equivalently, maximal homogeneity is enforced. This allows the cognitive system to suppose the maximal randomness of the environment and not impose its own order or inhomogeneities.

---

[1] Both knowledge atoms and features may be activated. A knowledge atom activation is properly denoted $a_j = 1$ where $a_j \in \{0, 1]$. Similarly a feature activation is denoted $R_i = 1$ where $R_i \in \{0, 1\}$.

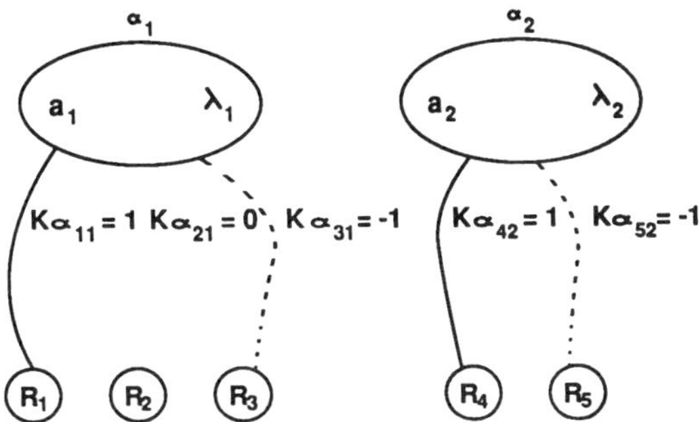

Figure 2. A Graph of a Simplified Cognitive System

We have now discussed the entire cognitive system by its basis $(R_i, a_j, \alpha_j, K_{\alpha ij}, \lambda_{\alpha j}, P, \pi, C)$. We also formulate this same cognitive system as the quintuple (R, P, O, π, C), where the O is taken as a collection of basic observable events or observables. These observable events are in fact observable to the cognitive system given appropriate knowledge atoms α_j and connections $K_{\alpha ij}$. Hence, we take O as:

$$O = \{\alpha_j, K_{\alpha ij}\}. \tag{1-1}$$

The maximum entropy estimate π is taken as:

$$\pi = \{\lambda_\alpha \mid \text{maximum entropy estimates are further maximized with updates}\} \tag{1-2}$$

or

$$\pi = \{\lambda_\alpha \mid \lambda_\alpha \to \pi\} \tag{1-3}$$

Therefore, π is specified by the λ_α such that the λ_α's approach π. The only other item not directly shown in our basis for the cognitive system is the knowledge atom activations: a_j. These will be given by the completion function C, which we will define as:

$$C: R \times A \to R \times A \text{ such that } \pi \text{ is maximized}$$

$$\text{where } A = \{a_j\} \tag{1-4}$$

C is therefore

$$C = \langle \{R_i, a_j\}, \{R_k, a_l\} \rangle \mid \pi \to \max \pi \tag{1-5}$$

or is, in fact, ordered tuples of activated and deactivated features and knowledge atoms. Here, with each new feature update, many previously deactivated features will be activated by the cognitive system; hence, recognition will occur.

Now, we have briefly discussed our generalized cognitive system, which is distilled from various works in connectionism [47], [56], [45], [35], [24]. We cite that the primary flaw of connectionism is that it does not currently allow for incorporating many specialized cognitive systems into what Minsky has termed a "society of mind." Further, as Minsky has pointed out, these connectionist models of cognitive systems are so far largely unanalyzable [52]. What we propose to do is to take this generalized cognitive system and model it with a Petri Net Representation (PNR). This will allow us to aggregate or compose the PNR-modeled cognitive systems via Petri Net forms of composition. Further, it will allow us to analyze these PNR modeled cognitive systems via Petri Net Analysis techniques. We have kept the cognitive system completely general so that different completion functions or learning algorithms may be introduced to specialize these cognitive systems. These specialized cognitive systems may, therefore, be aggregated into a "Society of Mind."

We intend to be mathematically formal in this treatment and so, instead of assuming a PNR for the cognitive system, we will first algebraically categorize the cognitive system math model and perform an appropriate isomorphic generation of the PNR. This will guarantee that the PNR is essentially equivalent algebraically and, therefore, a good representation of the cognitive system. Further, the methods of isomorphic generation of PNR's based upon cognitive system math models will allow for similar treatments of cognitive systems not in the class of our generalized cognitive model.

To begin with cognitive systems in our class of generalized cognitive systems, we will only need one form of algebraically associative binary composition that we will call aggregation, denoted @ (see paragraph 2.2). Aggregation will, in general, be the means of connecting different cognitive systems. Recall that for most number systems we typically have +, −, x, ÷. Recall, also, that a number system such as the integers has an identity unit denoted 1 which is 0 for addition as:

$$a + 0 = a \tag{1-6}$$

and 1 for multiplication as:

$$a \times 1 = a \tag{1-7}$$

We will similary define an identity unit for our cognitive system so that:

$$C_s \;@\; 1 = C_s \tag{1-8}$$

where C_s is the cognitive system. We will call this self generation because the resulting C_s from the C_s aggregated with 1 is identical.

Now we have a set C_s, and an associative composition (we impose that it be associative) called aggregation and an identity unit 1. We, in fact, have discovered the algebraic structure and class of the cognitive system. It is a Monoid. A Monoid is, in fact, simply a set together with an associative binary composition and an identity unit. Monoids are, in fact, very primitive algebraically. Most algebraic structures encountered are Groups, Rings, or Fields. However, Monoids are very important to automata theory. In this regard, we can formalize our cognitive system as an automata and, therefore, is capable of automation aggregation or growth by fixed rules.

Since we can mathematically formalize our cognitive system with aggregation and self-generation as a Monoid, the isomorphic generation of a PNR will be straightforward. Isomorphism for Monoids involves a one-to-one onto mapping (called bijection) where the mapping η obeys the following rules of homomorphism:

$$\eta(x@y) = \eta(x)@\eta(y) \qquad (1\text{-}9)$$

and

$$\eta(1) = 1 \qquad (1\text{-}10)$$

What this means is that for each item of the cognitive system we must have a corresponding item in our PNR (and only corresponding items) such that aggregation and self-generation is the same for cognitive systems and PNR's of those cognitive systems. We will merely require that aggregation be the same for both PNR's and cognitive systems by imposing this as a requirement upon aggregation. We do this also for our identity unit 1 by stipulating that self generation be an exact copy for both PNR's and cognitive systems.

Considering this, we will examine roughly how we will find Petri Net items in correspondence with the cognitive system. Let us return to our feature representations the R_i. We will include also for these R_i's endogeneous features which must be activated by knowledge atoms, and exogenous features which must be activated by transduction. We state this as:

$$R = \{R_{en}, R_{ex}\} = \{R_i\} \qquad (1\text{-}11)$$

where we will only concern ourselves now with the R_i, which may be either endogenous or exogenous. We see that these features may be represented by Petri Net places. Their activation or deactivation may be given by placing (creating) or removing (destroying) a token on them. We will let this be a red token.

As for knowledge atoms, we see that they too may be places. How do we distinguish, then, between features and knowledge atoms? Let us place a permanently residing blue token on a place for the knowledge atom. Further, allow this blue token to be weighted by the corresponding weighting factor λ. The blue token then distinguishes between features and knowledge atoms, while at the same time allows the knowledge atoms to have memory trace by weighting this blue token.

Now, we will consider the connections between knowledge atoms and features. We recall that these are either stimulating, absent, or inhibiting. Here, we must use Petri Net input arcs, transitions and output arcs for stimulating connections, a null connection denoted λ_c and also absent for an absent connection and a Petri Net inhibitor input arc, transition and output for an inhibiting connection. All this is shown by Figure 3. In observing Figure 3, we see that red tokens are also used on knowledge atoms. These are for the activation or deactivation of the knowledge atom activations. Thus, the red tokens are 2-state markings serving the same purpose on both knowledge atoms and features.

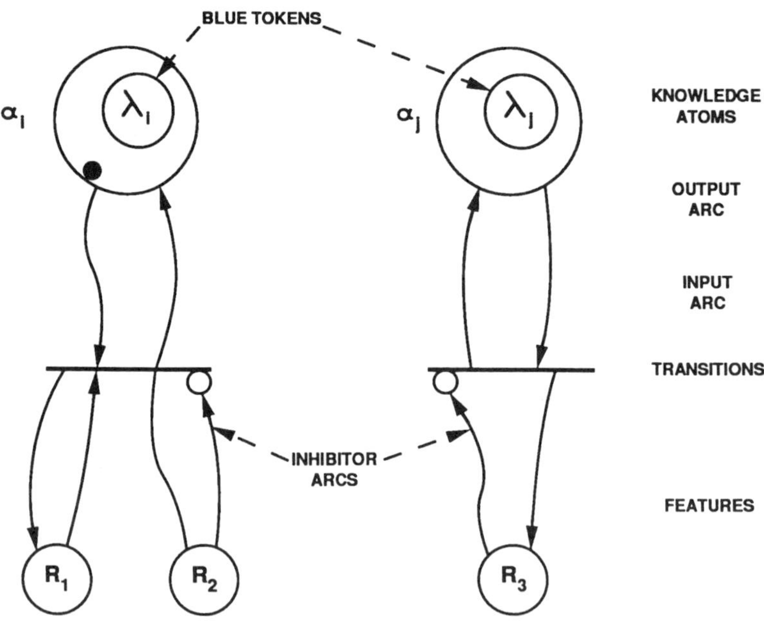

Figure 3. A Simple Cognitive Machine Net

All that remains is to find a correspondence for P, π, and C in the PNR. We do this by using an identity map. The identity map simply gives P, π, and C the same meaning in the PNR, but under its new interpretation. The new interpretation is that red tokens will appear in features by transduction with probability P and that the PNR will have a firing rule which creates or destroys red tokens by the completion function C maximizing π. We note that, since red tokens appear with probability P in features, this firing rule is stochastic.

This is the essential background to what is to follow. In the next section, we will do formal definitions and a mathematically formal isomorphic generation.

Following this we will talk about the Petri Net Language of our PNR cognitive systems (we will call Cognitive Machine Nets or CMN's). Here, we create an alphabet of transitions which have fired. The language is merely a set of strings over this alphabet. We further require that for our CMN's a decision is chosen (appropriate transitions are fired). This basically gives us a L-Type Petri Net Language. Standard Petri Net Analysis is also provided for the CMN's. In general, the Petri Net treatment is very conventional.

The formal treatment is to follow. Since this treatment is very abstract, an example of a CMN is given in paragraph 2.5.

SECTION 2 - ISOMORPHIC GENERATION

To begin, we do not start with a math model of a cognitive system and a math model of a PNR and prove their isomorphism. Rather, we begin by specifying a basis for the Cognitive Math Model and defining its Monoid such that a bijective (a 1 to 1 onto mapping) generation is performed such that the homomorphic rule:

$$\eta(1) = 1 \text{ and} \tag{2-1}$$

$$\eta(x@y) = \eta(x)@\eta(y) \text{ is obeyed;} \tag{2-2}$$

where 1 is the unit (as the number 1 for a group over the reals with binary composition of multiplication and similarly as the number 0 for the group over the reals with the binary composition of addition).

This then is isomorphic generation in that the resulting space is isomorphic as the obvious consequence of its isomorphic (bijective and homomorphic) generation.

The primary rationale for this approach is that should other cognitive systems come into question that are not in the class of our generalized cognitive model, then the methods of this paper would still apply. (This is addressed in the Section 6.)

2.1 DEFINITION AND BASIS OF A COGNITIVE SYSTEM

Given a Cognitive System as the quintuple (R, P, O, π, C) [47] where:

R is a set of feature representations defined as:

$$R = R_{ex} \times R_{en} \tag{2-3}$$

R_{ex} being the collection of exogenous features and R_{en} the collection of endogenous features, wherein we will specify as follows:

$$R = \{R_i\} = \{R_{ex}, R_{en}\} \tag{2-4}$$

P is to be taken as a probability distribution on the R_i and is known as the proximal environment.

O is a collection of basic observable events we will specify by the knowledge vector $K_{\alpha j}$ with the knowledge atom α_j, or

$$O = \{\alpha_j, K_{\alpha ij}\} \tag{2-5}$$

π is a maximum entropy estimate to be specified by λ_α as

$$\pi = \{\lambda_\alpha \mid \lambda_\alpha \to \pi\} \tag{2-6}$$

C is a completion function specified by:

$$C: \; R \times A \rightarrow R \times A$$

where A is the collection of knowledge atom activations $\{a_j\}$, and R is a collection of feature representations $\{R_i\}$ such that π is maximized.

Given this definition of a Cognitive System, we observe that a basis for the Cognitive System is:

$$(R_i, a_j, \alpha_j, K_{\alpha ij}, \lambda_{\alpha j}, P, \pi, C)$$

which will serve as suitable for the generation of an isomorphic extended Petri Net representation.

2.2 THE MONOID OF A COGNITIVE SYSTEM

We will define an associative binary composition which we will term as aggregation:

@ such that for

$$B_1 = (R_1, P_1, O_1, \pi_1, C_1) \tag{2-7}$$
$$B_2 = (R_2, P_2, O_2, \pi_2, C_2) \tag{2-8}$$
$$\text{and} \quad B_3 = (R_3, P_3, O_3, \pi_3, C_3) \tag{2-9}$$

we will have

$$(B_1 \,@\, B_2) \,@\, B_3 = B_1 \,@\, (B_2 \,@\, B_3) = B = \{R, P, O, \pi, C\} \tag{2-10}$$

where:

$$R = \{R_1, R_2, R_3\} \tag{2-11}$$
$$P = \{P_1, P_2, P_3\} \tag{2-12}$$
$$O = \{O_1, O_2, O_3\} \tag{2-13}$$
$$C = \{C_1, C_2, C_3\} \tag{2-14}$$
$$\pi = \{\pi_1, \pi_2, \pi_3\} \tag{2-15}$$

Further, we will define an identity unit 1 which will perform an operation termed self-generation as:

$$C_{s1}@1 = C_s, \; C_{s2}@1 = C_{s2}, \text{ etc.} \tag{2-16}$$

The Cognitive System together with operations of aggregation and self-generation define the Monoid M_B as the triple:

$$M_B = \{B_1, @, 1\} \tag{2-17}$$

where:

$$B = \{R, P, O, \pi, C\} \text{ is the cognitive system.} \tag{2-18}$$

We will term the Monoid M_B the cognitive space of B.

2.3 GENERATION OF A PETRI NET REPRESENTATION

Here we use the basis of the cognitive system defined in paragraph 2.2 to generate the Petri Net[1] Representation (PNR) by a bijective rule η and later impose that the homomorphic rules

$$(B_1 , B_2) = \eta(B_1)\eta(B_2) \qquad (2\text{-}19)$$

$$\text{and} \quad \eta(1) = 1 \text{ are obeyed.} \qquad (2\text{-}20)$$

Accordingly, the PNR will be isomorphic to the cognitive space and it too will be a Monoid. The bijective rule will apply as follows:

For each R_i, create a unique place (p_i) without a token and call this a feature.

For each α_j, create a unique place (p_j) with a permanently residing blue token and call this a knowledge atom.

Connections $K_{\alpha i j}$ and their respective Petri Net elements are shown in Figure 4. This is formally stated below:
For $K_{\alpha i j} \varepsilon \{1, 0, -1\}$ map as follows:

$$K_{\alpha i j} = 1 \rightarrow I(t_n) = \{p_i , p_j\}, t_n , O(t_n) = \{p_i , p_j\} \qquad (2\text{-}20a)$$

as a connection and here interpret $K_{\alpha i j} = 0$ as the absence of a connection to knowledge atom so that this map is trivially $\{0\} \rightarrow$ an existent absence connection which will be shown as a deleted connection (denoted: λ_c). Let $K_{\alpha i j} = -1 \rightarrow I^-(t_m) = \{p_i , p_j\}, t_m , O(t_m) = \{p_i , p_j\}$ as an anti-connection where $I^-(t)$ is an inhibitor arc and where each triple $I(t)$, t, $O(t)$ or $I^-(t)$, t, $O(t)$ is unique for each α and call these triples interconnects. We will observe here that the bijections of $K_{\alpha i j} = \{1, 0, -1\}$ are with connections, absent connections, and anticonnections, respectively.

---

[1]A Petri Net is a quadruple: {P, T, I , O} where P is a set of places, T is a set of transitions, and I may be taken as a set of Input arcs (from places to transitions) and O is a set of output arcs (from transitions to places). Petri Nets typically have firing rules and these have markings μ of tokens. Sometimes the tokens are weighted (to have numerical value). Extended Petri Nets have included colored tokens and inhibitor arcs (inverting the input or output values). The Petri Net we generate will be an extended Petri Net using colored tokens and inhibitor arcs in addition to the Standard Petri Net quadruple: {P, T, I, O} with marking μ, weighting W and firing rule.

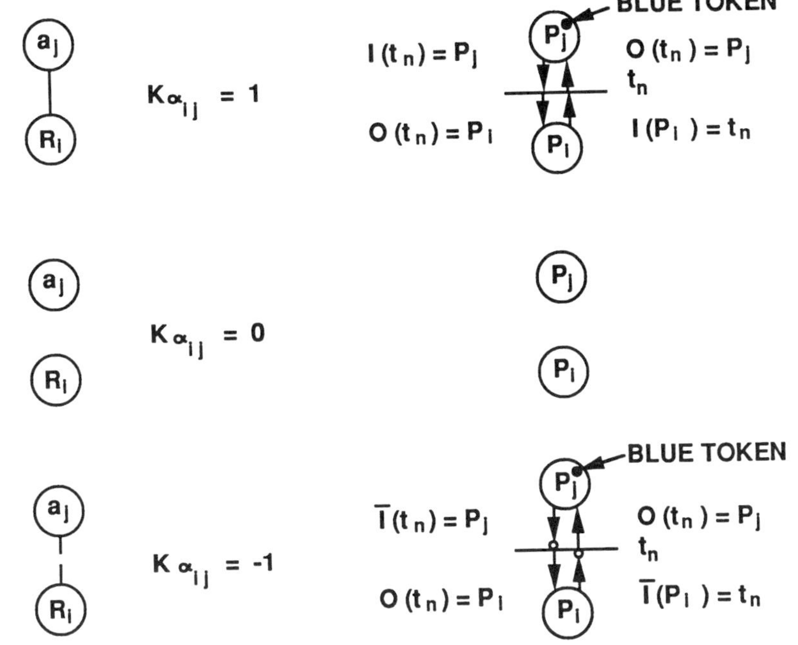

Figure 4. Cognitive System Connections and their Isomorphic (Equivalent) Petri Net Elements. P_i and P_j are Places while t_m and t_n are Transitions. The $I(t_n)$ are Input Arcs, $\overline{I}\ (t_n)$ Input Inhibitor Arcs, and $O(t_n)$ Output Arcs.

Given knowledge atom activations $a_{\alpha j}$ we will do as follows:

For $a_{\alpha j} = 1$ place a red token on the corresponding α_j place, (2-21)

and for $a_{\alpha j} = 0$ do not place this token there. (2-22)

For each $\lambda_{\alpha j}$ weight the corresponding α_j blue token with the $\lambda_{\alpha j}$ value by an identity map.

The probability distribution P will govern feature activations as follows:

For P, use the same rule to place or not place tokens on a given feature, i.e.:

P: $R_i = 1$, create a token (2-23)
P: $R_i = o$, destroy a token if present, and do not place a token there. (2-24)

As a result, the distribution P will be identical in both the cognitive space and the PNR.

For π as specified by the $\lambda_{\alpha j}$'s , let it too be identical in the PNR by an identity map.

For C specified by C: $R \times A \rightarrow R \times A$ such that π is maximized, use the map $C \rightarrow C'$ such that C' maximizes $\pi' \varepsilon B$ by the same C (call it C') under the new interpretation of R and A. Hence C is mapped to C' by an identity map and C' is equivalent to C under its interpretation in the PNR. This is the formal way of saying that C' of the PNR is identical to C of the cognitive system.

As a result,

$$C_n = \{\{I, T, O\}, \{\lambda_c\}, \{I^-, T, O\}\} \quad (2\text{-}25)$$

is the set of connections where λ_c is a null connection. Further, P_α is the set of places with permanent blue tokens (knowledge atoms) with weighting W and marking μ of red tokens.
Also P_f is the set of places without blue tokens (features) with marking μ of red tokens. We now have the quintuple:

$$E = \{C_n , P_\alpha , P_f , \mu, W\} \quad (2\text{-}26)$$

This quintuple E is the result of our isomorphic mapping into Petri Net Elements. We will usually state E as:

$$E = \{C_n , P, \mu, W\} \quad (2\text{-}27)$$

where $P = \{P_\alpha , P_f\}$ and $P_\alpha = \{P, \mu_B\}$

$$\mu_B \equiv \text{a permanent blue token marking on each place.} \quad (2\text{-}28)$$

Further, let

$$\eta(B_1) = E_1 \quad (2\text{-}29)$$

$$\eta(B_2) = E_2 \quad (2\text{-}30)$$

and for

$$B = \{B_1 \ @ \ B_2\} \quad (2\text{-}31)$$

$$\eta(B) = \eta(B_1) \ @ \ \eta(B_2) = E_1 \ @ \ E_2 = E \text{ and } \eta(1) = 1 \quad (2\text{-}32)$$

Here we are imposing that aggregation be the same for cognitive systems as it is for the PNR of the cognitive system. We are also imposing this same requirement upon self-generation.

Thus, the triple {E, @, 1} is a Monoid that we will call the Machine Space which is isomorphic to the Monoid that we call the cognitive space. Hence, the Machine Space and Cognitive Space are equivalent as under isomorphisms, as a consequence of its isomorphic generation which was simply a bijective generation (for each object of the cognitive system, a corresponding Petri Net object was created) with homomorphism imposed (that aggregation and self-generation be the same for both PNR of cognitive systems and the cognitive systems themselves).

2.4 INTERPRETATION

We have arrived at the quintuple:

$$E = \{C_n, P_\alpha, P_f, \mu, W\} \tag{2-33}$$

as the result of our isomorphic generation.

Essentially, we now have a set of connections C_n between knowledge atoms P_α (blue token marked places) and features P_f (places without blue tokens). These knowledge atoms are updated according to stochastic firing rules governed by π and C and specified by the weighting W on the blue tokens and the creation or destruction of red token specified by μ. This is depicted in Figure 3. We observe that, in general, tokens are not moved as in their deterministic Petri Net "cousins." Rather, they are created or destroyed. This is a consequence of the stochastic firing rule preserved under isomorphic generation.

The PNR of our generalized cognitive system as depicted in Figure 3 strongly suggests the following neurological interpretation [35], [22]:

a. Inputs to transitions as axons
b. Outputs of transitions as dendrites
c. Places as neurons (The dichotomy of blue token marked places and non-blue token marked places as that of efferent and afferent neurons, respectively)
d. Transitions as synapses.

We will notice that in Figure 3, all links from transitions are bidirectional. This is a consequence of our isomorphism. However, we may allow for uni-directional links. To motivate the allowance of uni-directionality, we cite the instance of such by axons and dendrites. As a result, we will consider a class of PNR of cognitive systems termed Cognitive Machine Nets (CMN's) which may allow for uni-directionality of link. Meanwhile, in examining the properties of cognitive systems on a whole, we may easily preserve a consistent isomorphism with CMN's that have bidirectional links. Should a generalized cognitive system be proposed with uni-directional links, the isomorphically generated CMN need only preserve the sense (input or output) of the uni-directional link.

2.5 AN EXAMPLE

In this paragraph, we will give an example of a simple cognitive system represented in Petri Net form as a CMN. This cognitive system is represented as a CMN in Figure 5.

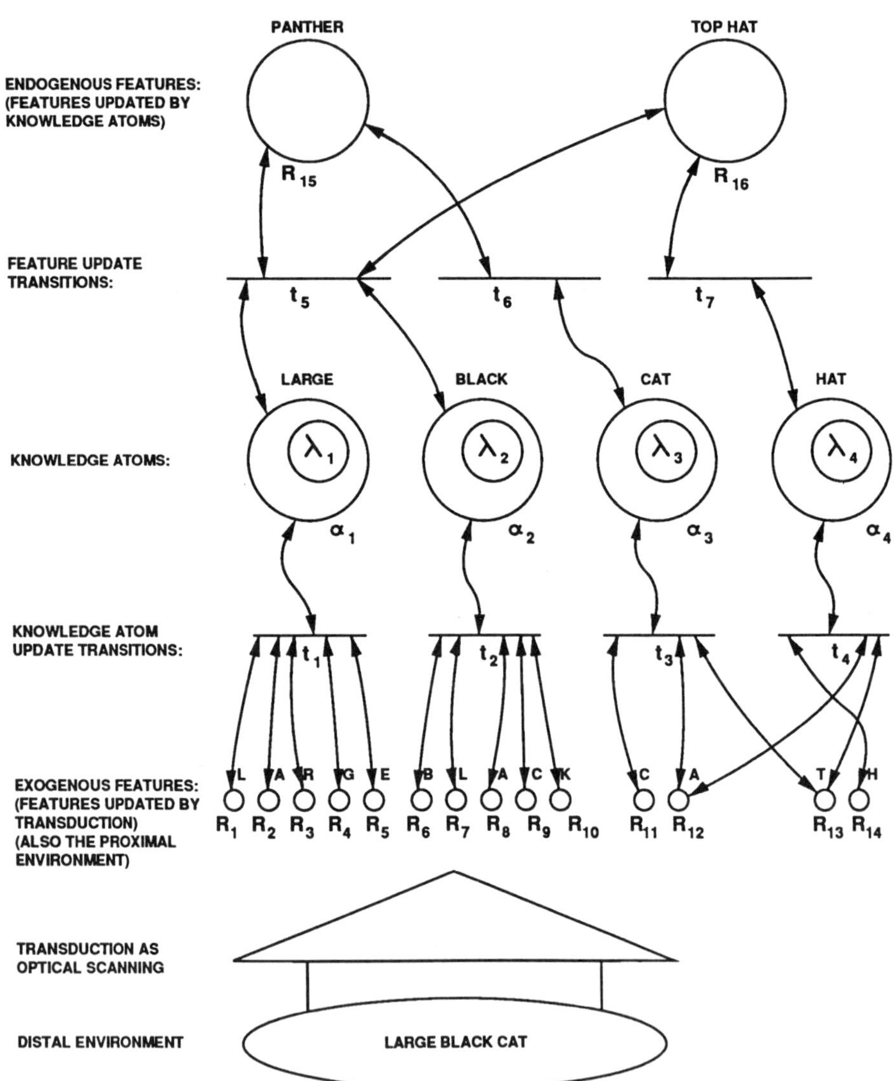

Figure 5. An Example Harmonium Machine

We will discuss it first as a cognitive system or C_s. Given our definition of a C_s as the quintuple: $(R, P, \tilde{O}, \pi, C)$, we see from the figure that:

$$R \equiv \{R_{ex}; R_{en}\} = \{R_1, R_2 \ldots R_{14}; R_{15}, R_{16}\} = \{R_i\} = \{R_1, R_2, \ldots R_{16}\} \tag{2-34}$$

$P \equiv$ the Proximal environment is the probability distribution of the activation of $R_1 \ldots R_{14}$ by the optical scanner (2-35)

$O \equiv$ the set of observables is here {large, black, cat, hat} given by connections K_α and knowledge atoms α (2-36)

Before we go on and show π and C, we will first mention that choices of π and C will specify types of cognitive systems and vice versa. Here, we will choose a harmonium machine described in the PDP series Volume 1 [47].

For the harmonium machine, we have C such that:

$$\text{probability } (a_i = 1) = \frac{1}{1 + e^{-I/T}} \tag{2-37}$$

and

$$\text{probability } (R_i = 1) = \frac{1}{1 + e^{-J/T}} \tag{2-38}$$

where $a_i = 1$ is a knowledge atom activation and $R_i = 1$ is a feature activation and T is a parameter called the Computational Temperature usually set at T = 1 and lowered to force decisions.

Also here:

$$I_\alpha = \Sigma\, W_{i\alpha}\, r_i - \lambda_\alpha \tag{2-39}$$

and

$$J_i = 2 \cdot \Sigma\, W_{i\alpha}\, a_\alpha \tag{2-40}$$

and

$$W_{i\alpha} = (K_\alpha)_i \frac{\lambda_\alpha}{|K_{\alpha i}|}$$

where K is a proportionality constant to be chosen as $1>K>1-2/[\max_\alpha |K_\alpha|$ (2-41)

Here the subscript α denotes a particular knowledge atom and R_i a particular feature.

This C is chosen because it maximizes π for harmonium machines. π for harmonium machines is

$$e^{H(r,\ a)}$$

where H is the harmony between features updates and knowledge atom activations. We will merely state H(r, a) as:

$$H(r,\ a) = \Sigma_\alpha\ K_\alpha\ \lambda_\alpha\ h(r,\ K_\alpha) \tag{2-42}$$

and

$$h(r,\ K_\alpha) = \frac{r \cdot K_\alpha}{|K_\alpha|} - K \tag{2-43}$$

where K is the constant seen before: $1>K>1-2/[\max_\alpha |K_\alpha|]$.

We will not go into the details of this formulation as it diverts us from the intentions of our example. The interested reader should see the chapter on Harmony Theory in the PDP series [47]. Let us simply state that the completion function given will serve to maximize π.

We have now specified the C_s = {R, P, O, π, C}. Let us return to the figure and see how it behaves as a CMN. Firstly, red tokens will appear with probability P on our places $R_1 \ldots R_{14}$ with each pass of the optical scanner. These are the feature activations. Our transitions $t_1 \ldots t_4$ will fire according to the completion function for knowledge atom updates. Similarly, transitions $t_5 \ldots t_7$ will fire according to the completion function for feature updates. For several passes of the optical scanner the blue tokens of the knowledge atoms will begin to weight by λ. In fact, this CMN can be trained by weighting λ_3 to recognize the cursive word cat. This CMN will then correctly decide Panther instead of Top Hat and overall recognition will have been performed.

What we notice from this example is that the PNR readily models the C_s. Beyond this, the C_s in PNR form is now capable of undergoing the powerful techniques of Petri Net Synthesis and Analysis which are to follow.

SECTION 3 - SYNTHESIS

3.1 PRELIMINARY REMARKS

The operations of aggregation will be defined via the technique of Petri Net Languages. The power of this technique lies in its ability to specify and automatically synthesize Petri Nets. Path expressions have already been developed for the automatic generation of Petri Nets [44]. Further investigation may result in methods of generating cognitive systems based on path expressions derived from tomographic brain trace imaging techniques. Such a cognitive system may provide valuable insights to Brain Science [23], [24].

Further, the analysis of path expressions and Petri Net Languages has been shown to demonstrate system-specific properties [60] and the usage of Language-preserving transformations could facilitate the optimization of such systems while preserving their functionality [18], [57]. However, the primary motivation for the definition of the operations of aggregation via Petri Net Languages is that the alphabet of transitions is key to specifying those operations.

3.2 THE L-TYPE PETRI LANGUAGE OF THE COGNITIVE MACHINE NET

Recall that we defined a Petri Net Representation (PNR) as:

$$E = \{C_n, P, \mu, W\} \qquad (3\text{-}1)$$

We will refer to E as the Cognitive Machine Net (CMN).

Now given E, we then need an initial state we will call μ_1: an alphabet Σ, a labeling function σ such that σ: $T \rightarrow \Sigma$, and a final state which we will denote as μ_f. This then will comprise the Petri Language of our CMN. We will consider μ_1 to be the first red token introduced to the CMN. We will force the singularity of the token by generating (and destroying) tokens in time along a real numbered axis (we will call this <u>dense time</u>); therefore, the probability of a token being created or destroyed at the same time is zero, and so μ_1 is unique. We will consider σ to be any labeling such that:

$$T \rightarrow \{\lambda, T_0, T_1, T_2, \ldots T_n\}, \text{ where } \lambda \text{ is a null label.}$$

We will then require that $\mu_f \in F$ where F is a finite set of final markings (see Note 1), where each marking is unique from another. Further, this defines what is known as an L-type Petri Net Language.

NOTE 1: This is akin to the requirement that for a cognitive system based upon statistical physics that a sufficient lowering of the computation temperature will force a decision [4], [43], [53], [54], and [56].

Now, with regard to the labeling function σ, we have three types of labeling: free, Non-λ, and λ transitions. Under free labeling, each transition is distinctly labeled; under Non-λ, not every transition need be distinctly labeled; and for λ-transitions there is a null labeling $\sigma(t_j) = \lambda$ where λ is deleted from all sentences in the language. These three labelings define, respectively, the classes L^f (L-type free), L (L-type Non-λ), and L^λ (L-type λ transitions).

Each of the three languages are constructed by the set of strings formed by concatenations of the alphabet and each has a particular usage. L^f describes the functionality of the overall system; L could be used to describe completions of features (distinctively labeling knowledge atom to feature transitions while arbitrarily labeling feature to knowledge atom transitions). This could also be done similarly for knowledge atom upates (the converse). Both labelings would preserve the completion process. Meanwhile, L could be used by labeling with λ-transitions to separate the language into a knowledge atom updater or a feature completer.

3.3 AGGREGATING COGNITIVE MACHINE NETS

We will use the results derived from the Petri Net Language of the cognitive machine net. Since our machine net is an Extended PNR with a stochastic firing rule (given by a completion function), the compositions and operations to be shown will differ somewhat from those of the standard Petri Net form. The compositions to be shown are all binary and are to be considered as special cases of aggregation as described earlier. The binary compositions will be as follows:

a. Concatenation:
This will be combination sequentially as:

$$L_1 L_2 = \{x_1 x_2 \mid x_1 \in L_1, x_2 \in L_2\} \qquad (3\text{-}2)$$

where L_1 & L_2 are both L-type Petri Net Languages and x_1 & x_2 are strings.

b. General Union:

$$L_1 \text{ OR } L_2 = \{x \mid x \in \{x_1, x_2\}^*\} \qquad (3\text{-}3)$$

where $x_1 \in L_1$, $x_2 \in L_2$ and $\{x_1, x_2\}^*$ is the set of all strings composed of x_1 and x_2.

NOTE 2: This is the only composition not in the literature. It is necessitated by the stochastic nature of the machine nets.

c. Restricted Union:

$$L_1 \text{ XOR } L_2 = \{x \mid x \in L_1 \text{ XOR } x \in L_2\} \qquad (3\text{-}4)$$

d. Concurrency:

$$L_1 || L_2 = \{x_1 || x_2 \mid x_1 \in L_1, x_2 \in L_2\} \qquad (3\text{-}5)$$

An example is

$$\text{for } L_1 = \{ab\}, L_2 = \{c\} \qquad (3\text{-}6)$$
$$L_1 || L_2 = \{abc, acb, cab\} \qquad (3\text{-}7)$$

e. Intersection:

$$L_1 \cap L_2 = \{x \mid x \in L_1 \text{ and } x \in L_2\} \qquad (3\text{-}8)$$

This equation will apply to lockstep identical execution modes, which will only apply to a machine net operating with a self-generated counterpart. Certain properties of intersection are discussed in the section on its closure properties.

These five compositions will serve as the basis for aggregating machine nets. Naturally, they will apply for repeated composition.

A special merit of this approach to specifying the binary compositions (via a language specification) is that the class of L-type Petri Net languages is rich and powerful and, therefore, our machine nets which are cognitive (isomorphically) may be composed with other L-type language Petri Nets [34]. For example, the composition of concatenation of a target recognizer neural net with a Kalman filter would serve to recognize such objects as Soviet ICBM's in boost phase while providing the earliest intercept points.

3.4 OPERATIONS UPON COGNITIVE MACHINE NETS

The operations of reversal, complement, and substitution are well known in the Petri Net literature. These operations are of a special significance for CMN's. We will discuss each individually.

a. Substitution. In general, there are three candidates for substitution, i.e., knowledge atoms (places with blue tokens), features (places without blue tokens), and transitions. The requirements we will place upon substitution will apply to many-to-1 mappings (for example, a subnet substituted for a feature) and 1-to-many mappings (for example, a transition substituted for a subnet). They are as follows:

(1) Finiteness: That the cardinality of all places and transitions to be substituted for be finite.

(2) Non-Vacuity of Language: Each subnet to be substituted must contain at least a single transition.

(3) Homomorphism: All subnets for substitution must obey the homomorphic rule that

$$\eta(a@b) = \eta(a)@\eta(b) \text{ and} \tag{3-9}$$

$$\text{trivially } \eta(1) = 1^1 \tag{3-10}$$

which we call self-generation, where η is the substitution rule and a and b are both subnets and ab their specific aggregation (one of the types already discussed).

(4) Interconnect: All remote nodes must consist of the Petri element replaced, i.e., place or transition.

It is through the operation of substitution that the notion of cognitive schema naturally arises. Figure 6 depicts this. It will be through schema substitution that hierarchies of cognition will be attained.

b. Reversal. Reversal in the Petri Net Sense is simply the operation of reversing the strings of transitions. While this operation is simple in nature, it is of importance in that reversal simulates back-propagation, where strings are generated as a means of simulating the environment (by completing features). This is used in many learning algorithms. We consider reversal in both the Petri Net sense and Stochastic sense (see closure properties of Reversal).

c. Complement. To begin, we take the alphabet Σ and the set of all strings over the alphabet Σ* and let L be the language defined on the Cognitive Machine Net. Then:

$$L^- = \Sigma^* - L \tag{3-11}$$

is the set of all strings in Σ* which are not in L. L^- is, therefore, the complement of L.

Complement may be used to examine those strings of transitions which do not fire by taking L to be the set of strings of transitions which do fire. This will give insight into what might be termed "neurologically impaired" pathways in brain models as well as probalistically (o<p<<1) non-reachable sets for the CMN's and, therefore, model correctness.

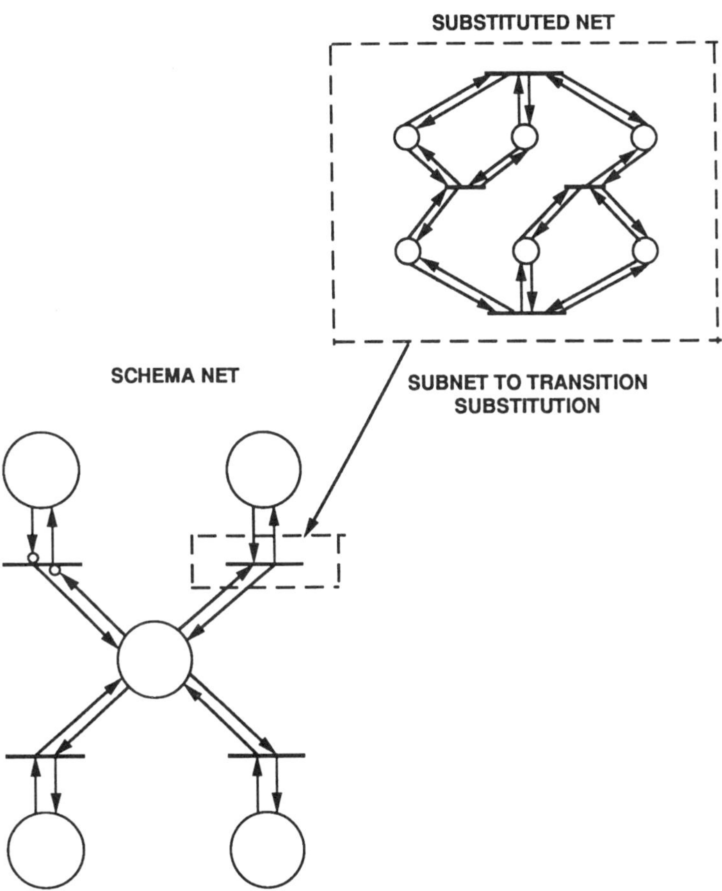

Figure 6. Schema Substitution

SECTION 4 - ANALYSIS

One of the shortcomings of the various neural net systems has been the lack of analytical means to evaluate their performance [51], [52]. However, due to our formulation of Cognitive Systems as Petri Net Representations (PNR's) the general arsenal of Petri Net Analysis applies. We will discuss the analysis of our CMN's by their Closure Properties, Structural Properties, and Sizing and Timing. Some of the Petri Net Analysis is somewhat unconventional in that our PNR's are extended Petri Nets with stochastic firing rules.

4.1 CLOSURE PROPERTIES

Closure properties will be discussed for the five forms of aggregation and three forms of operation given under synthesis. In general, all proofs will be by construction. Closure will be discussed only for aggregation and operation upon CMN's. Certainly aggregation and operation with non-CMN's is of interest and should provide useful; but is, at the same time, out of the scope of this text since many possibilities would have to be addressed for even a fair assessment.

Since our formulations of aggregation and operation were via language characteristics, so will our discussion of their closure properties be conducted.

4.1.1 Aggregation

The following subparagraphs discuss the closure properties for the five forms of aggregation:

a. Concatenation

Given $L_1 L_2 = \{x_1 x_2 \mid x_1 \in L_1, x_2 \in L_2\}$ (4-1)

We will show $L_1 L_2$ is a Petri Net Language or equivalently that for $L = L_1 L_2$ there exists:
(1) An initial state μ_i
(2) A labeling function $\sigma: T \rightarrow \Sigma$
(3) A final state μ_f.

We shall stipulate here that feature tokens be introduced in time as formulated by the real numbers (recall that we call this dense time). We recall that the probability of any two tokens being introduced at exactly the same time is, therefore, zero. Let the first token introduced be μ_i and construct γ_2 (the second CMN) so that γ_1 (the first CMN) can introduce a token to it. There will finally result in a $\mu_f \in F$ of γ_2 the set of final markings. Additionally, let σ_1 of L_1 and σ_2 of L_2 be preserved. The $L_1 L_2$ is itself a Petri Net Language L.

b. General Union

Here we have:

$$L_1 \text{ or } L_2 = \{x \mid X \in \{x_1, x_2\}^*\} \quad (4\text{-}2)$$

where $x_1 \in L_1$ and $x_2 \in L_2$
Let the first red token be introduced in dense time in either CMN's γ_1 or γ_2. Construct γ such that γ_1 or γ_2 may cross generate or destroy tokens. I(t), $I^-(t)$ or O(t) will be defined for $p \in P_1 \in \gamma_1$ and $t \in T_2 \in \gamma_2$ and for $p \in P_2 \in \gamma_2$ and $t \in T_1 \in \gamma_1$. Then, $\mu'_f \in F' = F_1 \cup F_2$ is the final marking and $\sigma = \sigma_1 \cup \sigma_2$ is the labeling function.
L_1 or L_2 is, therefore, a Petri Net Language L and so there is closure.

c. Restricted Union

Given:

$$L_1 \text{ XOR } L_2 = \{X \mid x \in L_1 \text{ XOR } x \in L_2\} \quad (4\text{-}3)$$

We will define μ_i as under general union and preserve σ as

$$\sigma' = \sigma_1(t_i) \text{ for } t_i \in T \in \gamma_2 \quad (4\text{-}4)$$
$$\text{and } \sigma' = \sigma_2(t_j) \text{ for } t_j \in T \in \gamma_2 \quad (4\text{-}5)$$

Let $F' = F_1 \cup F_2$ and $\mu_f \in F'$. Then L_1 XOR L_2 is a Petri Net Language L and so is closed under restricted union.

d. Concurrency

Here we have:

$$L_1 || L_2 = \{x_1 || x_2 \mid x_1 \in L_1, x_2 \in L_2\} \quad (4\text{-}6)$$

For concurrent operation, we will invoke our notion of dense time such that μ_i is the first red token to appear in either CMN γ_1 of L_1 or CMN γ_2 of L_2. The new labeling function σ' will preserve σ_1 and σ_2 as before. However, in order to allow for true concurrency, we will let $\mu_f' = \langle \mu_{f1}, \mu_{f2} \rangle \in \langle F_1, F_2 \rangle$, where $\langle a,b \rangle$ denotes ordered tuples of a and b. This will allow for completion of the concurrent process so that μ_f' is indeed the final marking. $L_1 || L_2$ is then a Petri Net Language L closed under concurrency.

e. Intersection

For intersection we have:

$$L = L_1 \cap L_2 = \{x \mid x \varepsilon L_1 \text{ and } x \varepsilon L_2\} \qquad (4\text{-}7)$$

We will recall that for CMN's γ_1 and γ_2, intersection applies to γ_1 and γ_2 as $\gamma_1 1 = \gamma_2$, or equivalently where γ_2 is the self-generated image of γ_1. This implies both identical proximal environments (identical probability distributions of the feature space updated by environmental transduction). However, this does not imply that initial tokens μ_i need appear identically in time or by feature.

We will call this difference for self-generated CMN's perspectivity. Perspectivity alone should be an important aspect in such areas as dual-focal image recognition.

Now returning to μ_i, we have explained that it exists and is unique. μ_f is similarly existent and unique as the final marking by letting it be the first marking εF_1, the set of finals markings.

Moreover, $\sigma_1 = \sigma_2$ and $L = L_1 \cap L_2$ is closed and, therefore, L is a Petri Net Language. We should, however, note that since a language L is a set of strings over an alphabet and that $L = L_1 \cap L_2$ where the strings represent actual transitions fired must be a proper subset of the set:

$$L^* = \{T_1{}^*, T_2{}^* \mid T_1 \varepsilon L_1 \text{ and } T_2 \varepsilon L_2\} \qquad (4\text{-}8)$$

and more so in general $x_1 \neq x_2$ where $x_1 \varepsilon x_1{}^*$ the set of strings over T_1 and $x_2 \varepsilon x_2{}^*$ similarly. These differences between identical self-generated CMN's are, importantly, due to perspectivity.

4.1.2 Operation

The following subparagraphs discuss the closure properties for the three forms of operation:

a. Substitution. We will recall that for CMN's we stipulated that substitution obey rules of:

(1) Finiteness
(2) Non-Vacuity of Language
(3) Homomorphism
(4) Interconnect.

Let μ_i be the first token created regardless of whether or not it is placed upon the substituted subnet or hierarchical parent. Similarly, let μ_f, the final token, be the first token to be created in a decision class F or, equivalently, $\mu_f \varepsilon F$ where μ_f is generated. All that remains is to define σ' of the parent CMN with substituted child CMN having σ_p and σ_c, respectively. We simply state σ' as:

$$\sigma' = \{\sigma_p : T_p \rightarrow \Sigma_p \text{ given } T_p \text{ of the parent}\} \\ \{\sigma_c^P : T_c^P \rightarrow \Sigma_c^P \text{ given } T_c^P \text{ of the child}\}. \quad (4\text{-}9)$$

CMN's are, therefore, closed under substitution. We should keep in mind that rules 1, 2, and 3 provide us this closure. Rule 1 is necessary for $\mu_f \varepsilon F$ to be reached, while rule 2 disallows a "nulling" of a parent net that might consist of a resultant net without transitions. Homomorphism preserves aggregation, while interconnectedness makes the operation possible.

b. Reversal. With reversal in the Petri Net Sense we show closure trivially by letting $\mu_i = \mu_f$, $\mu_f = \mu_i$ and $\sigma = \sigma'$. However, we should mention that for a more general notion of reversal in the sense of back propagation we let μ_i be the first knowledge atom to generate a red token and μ_f be in F the set of decision features to be completed. Meanwhile, $\sigma = \sigma'$. We call this reversal in the stochastic sense. Reversal is obviously closed in both regards.

c. Complement. We will only comment here that "Closure under complement for the L-type Petri Net Languages is an open problem" [57], and that Crespi-Reghizzi and Mandrioli [19] have shown there exist Petri Net Languages not closed under complement.

4.2 STRUCTURAL PROPERTIES

While the closure properties ensure the means of synthesizing CMN's, the structural properties allow for the testability of such CMN's. The structural properties we will discuss are:

a. Boundedness
b. Conservation
c. Liveness
d. Reachability
e. Coverability
f. Complexity
g. Decidability.

Since the CMN is a stochastic automata, these properties must be interpreted in a stochastic sense as probabilities going to zero (not true), or P → 1 (true) and P → .5 (maximal missing information or maximal ignorance) and so on. In certain cases, we may even have P = 0 or P = 1 (determinism) with respect to such things as the existence of blue tokens. The informed reader may point to the Theory of Chaos and remind us that a deterministic finite automata such as a conventional computer is capable of generating purely random numbers in the math sense (by their distribution). This is clearly beyond the scope of this paper and, therefore, we shall only regard these properties and our CMN's for that matter as stochastic.

Each of the seven properties will be defined in the succeeding subparagraphs and since they will vary by maximum likelihood estimates (π's), completion functions (c's), and architectures of CMN's, the author will only attempt brief remarks upon their nature with regard to CMN's.

Before we begin, we will define a concept fundamental to many of the properties under investigation. This concept is called the Reachability set: R(E), where E is our PNR:

$$E = \{C_n, P, \mu, W\} \tag{4-20}$$

We define R(E) as follows:

R(E) is the smallest set of marking such that:

1. $\mu \in R(C_n, P, \mu)$
   and
2. if $\mu' \in R(C_n, P, \mu)$ and $\mu'' = \delta(\mu', t_j)$ for some $t_j \in T$ then $\mu'' \in R(C, \mu)$

where $\delta(\mu', t_j)$ is the next state function which we define as the μ'' creation or that the probability of t_j firing with marking μ' is strictly greater than zero.

Therefore, the Reachability set in our case is that set of markings whose conditional probabilities are all greater than zero.

4.2.1 **Boundedness**

First, we begin with a definition of K-safeness:

A place $p_i \in P$ of E with initial marking μ_i, is K-safe if for all $\mu \in R(C_n, P, \mu)$, $\mu(p_i) \leq K$. Further, a place is bounded if it is K-safe and if all places are bounded, then the PNR E is itself bounded. We should note that all our feature places are necessarily 1-safe, which is termed simply, safe. However, our blue tokens may be incrementally weighted in dense time and are, therefore, neither necessarily safe, K-safe nor bounded; however, most cognitive scientists do agree that knowledge atom weighting should be bounded [35], [47]. Boundedness will probably be important to CMN's with realistic weighting coefficients.

4.2.2 Conservation

A PNR E will be strictly conservative if for all $\mu' \in R(E)$

$$\sum_{\text{for } p_i \in P} \mu' \cdot (p_i) = \sum_{\text{for } p_i \in P} \mu \cdot (p_i) \qquad (4\text{-}11)$$

This will never occur for CMN's because our tokens are either created or destroyed and not moved. Therefore, all CMN's have the property of being not strictly conservative. However, consider the following:

A PNR E is <u>conservative with respect to a weighting vector</u>,

$W = (W_1, W_2 \ldots W_n)$ where n = the number of blue tokens and $W_i \geq 0$ if for all $\mu' \in R(C_n, P, U)$ then:

$$\sum_{\substack{i \text{ for } p_i \\ \text{with blue} \\ \text{token}}} W_i \cdot \mu'(p_i) = \sum_{\substack{i \text{ for } p_i \\ \text{with blue} \\ \text{token}}} W_i \cdot \mu(p_i) \qquad (4\text{-}12)$$

This, of course, depends on the weighting scheme which is at the CMN designer's discretion.

4.2.3 Liveness

A transition is said to be <u>live</u> in a marking μ if it is potentially fireable or, equivalently, its probability of firing is greater than zero, given marking μ. If a transition is not live, then it is dead. We should expect that CMN's with dead transitions do not have either appropriate knowledge atoms or features for the stimulus transduction present.

We also introduce here the notions of levels of liveness and let them be normalized for CMN's as:

$$10 \cdot (\text{Probability of Firing})$$

so that values range from 0 to 10, or from dead to absolutely live. Levels of liveness should reflect appropriateness of CMN models [13].

4.2.4 Reachability

Given a PNR E with marking μ and a successive marking μ', then μ' is <u>reachable</u> if $\mu' \in R(E)$.

Those markings which are not reachable should reflect the correctness of the CMN as representative of the environment. Then again, the CMN designer may want to place restraints upon certain blue token markings for the purpose of discernment.

4.2.5 Coverability

A PNR E is said to be coverable if for marking μ' and successive marking $\mu'' \in R(E)$ that for a given μ then $\mu'' \geq \mu'$.

In general, if inhibitor arcs, as well as regular arcs, were used in an appropriate fashion together with the proper weighting function, CMN's could be constructed to be coverable. Coverability may be used as a criteria for monotonically increasing learning.

4.2.6 Complexity

Complexity in the Petri Net Literature refers to the time or space complexities for algorithms that solve the problems of the first five structural properties. This complexity is certainly of interest. However, for our CMN's, other forms of complexity will likely be of interest including the cardinality of P, T, I, O, the range and domain of W, the upper limit of W, etc. For example, the overall complexity of the human brain is oftentimes alluded to by the size estimate of its composition requiring about 10 billion neurons.

4.2.7 Decidability

Because we can formulate decision classes for final markings, all CMN's are capable of selecting a decision or solution. This was inherent in our discussion of their closure properties. This is of special significance in that a solution can always be proposed by CMN's, although it may not be the correct one! The solvability or, equivalently, the strict decidability of the problem will then reside on the confirmation of the proposed solution [20]. In certain problems such as the next undiscovered prime number, the confirmation should be polynomial in time with parallel processing.

In this respect, certain NP complete problems should be solvable in polynomial time using CMN's with deterministic counterparts for confirmation. A methodology for this will likely oftentimes be by assuming alternative hypothesis and recognizing counterexamples.

4.3 SIZING AND TIMING

A convenient method of sizing will be the assignment of unitary sizes to Knowledge Atom Places (KAP's) and to Feature Assigned Places (FAP's). Simple summation over KAP's and FAP's will be one size estimate.

Another, which should be of interest, is interconnect size which may be formulated as the cardinality of $\{I, O, I^{-}\}$. Similarly, the cardinality of T will reflect sizing of something analogous to synapses.

Timing is readily determined by its correspondence with the real numbers for token generation and destruction. As is evident, our CMN's are readily timed and sized [27].

SECTION 5 – IMPLEMENTATION CONSIDERATIONS

This chapter will explore some of the possible and alternative means of implementing our CMN's. We will approach this from the broad perspectives of software and hardware implementations.

CMN's may be implemented for a single processor system. No doubt, modern tasking languages for time slice techniques which support complexity management are best for this endeavor. The Ada language with its tasking-rendezvous and procedural capability would be a recommended language for CMN simulation. Nevertheless, as the number of places in the feature space linearly increases, the number of interconnects would tend to increase exponentially. This would result eventually in severe limitations on the size of the feature space.

On the other hand, a platform of a multiprocessor or multicomputer architecture might be used with an available language (Alsys, United Kingdom, is developing Ada for a transputer-based multicomputer) [9]. This would then extend the available feature space. However, this approach would still be limiting in that ordinary fetch-execute cycling would have to be performed over relatively large numerical routines in order to generate the stochastic signals. Still, this platform would offer a basically ideal test bed for varying CMN's.

Now, in considering the hardware implementations of CMN's we generally expect the following properties:

a. Greater throughput
b. Feature space limitations primary dependent upon cost
c. Completions (c) and maximum likelihood estimates (π) fixed
d. Interconnects primarily fixed.

Yet, the increased throughput may serve as the driving factor towards a totally hardware implementation. Silicon would offer good packing densities, and thin film programmable synapses have reached densities of 10^9 synapses per square cm [69]. Gallium Arsenide would deliver microwave operating frequencies, although it would have lesser packing density.

Meanwhile, optical technology (along with its concurrent 10^{15} cycles/sec bandwith) progressively moves into the forefront as the best candidate implementation technology for Neural Nets or in our case CMN models. One such optical neural computer [70] has demonstrated enormous potential for interconnects primarily due to lights non-interfering coherence properties. R. C. Johnson, a neural net researcher, reports that "Last week O-E/LASE '88 conference here saw the marriage of optical computing and neural nets" [37].

On the other hand, a collection of devices is emerging which have characteristics of CMN elements. These include the following:

a. Neural chips comprising a crossbar switch with programmable resistive interconnections [38]
b. Programmable Synaptic Arrays [69]
c. Gated Dipole Flip Flops [39]
d. Sigmoid Function Differential Amplifiers [39].

Most of these devices are only of moderate to low complexity and warrant much more of a network architect than a device physicist.

We will conclude this section by making a few very general observations about our CMN's. Firstly, red tokens are strictly two-state devices and, therefore, suggest implementation in binary digital flip-flops, whether clocked or not. Secondly, blue tokens represent n-ary discrete or n-ary digital devices which suggest counters whether fixed or floating point. Therefore, all tokens would most likely best be implemented into digital hardware.

Interconnects would, in general, be conductive pathways and even free space propagation for the optical case. The introduction of tokens in dense time will probably require collision detection/resolution schemes.

Now, consider the transition or synapse. This has non-linear and oftentimes sigmoidal characteristics and is stochastic. A device which should hold promise for such an element should be a non-linear analog quantum device. Its quantum behavior should reflect that of the stochastic process to be modeled. In this regard, the device physicist may be called upon along with the network architect. For the time being, however, a non-linear sample and hold amplifier should suffice.

Also, worthy of mention is that high resistivities (@ 1 MΩ) have shown good fault tolerance [69] for neural chips.

SECTION 6 - CONCLUDING REMARKS

The methods of analyzing and synthesizing machine representation of cognitive systems have been discussed based on the generalized model. Nevertheless, the methods presented in this paper would still apply for cognitive systems outside our model so long as the cognitive system under question could be formalized as a mathematical model.

Naturally, in creating a "Society of Mind" in the Minsky sense, we would seek many forms of cognitive models, some for control, as well as for learning in general. Nevertheless, we must remind ourselves that our basis cognitive model may be individuated for a variety of π's and C's (maximum likelihood estimates and completion functions or learning algorithms, respectively). In this regard, it may best serve us to concentrate on the multifarious cognitive models possible from the generalized cognitive system.

SECTION 7 - BIBLIOGRAPHY

[1] D. Adams, "A Model for Parallel Computations," Parallel Processor Systems, Technologies and Applications, New York: Spartan Books, pp. 311-334, (1970).

[2] T. Agerwala, "Some Applications of Petri Nets," Proceedings of the 1978 National Electronics Conference, **Vol. 23**, pp. 149-154, Oct. 1978.

[3] T. Agerwala, and M. Flynn, "Comments on Capabilities, Limitations and 'Correctness' of Petri Nets," Proceedings of the First Annual Symposium on Computer Architecture, New York: ACM, pp. 81-86, (1973).

[4] J. A. Anderson, "Cognitive and Psychological Computation with Neural Models," IEEE Trans. Syst. Man, Cybern., **Vol. SMC-13**, pp. 799-815, Sept. 1983.

[5] T. Araki, and T. Kasami, "Some Decision Problems Related to the Reachability Problem for Petri Nets," Theoretical Computer Science, **Vol. 3**, No. 1, pp. 85-104, Oct. 1976.

[6] H. Aso and M. Kimura, "Absolute Expediency of Learning Automata," Inform. Sci., **Vol. 17**, No. 2, pp. 91-112, (1979).

[7] P. Azema, R. Valette, and M. Diaz, "Petri Nets as a Common Tool for Design Verification and Hardware Simulation," Proceedings 13th Design Automation Conference, New York: IEEE, pp. 109-116, June 1976.

[8] H. Baker, Jr., "Petri Nets and Languages," Computation Structures Group Memo 68, Project MAC, Massachusetts Institute of Technology, Cambridge, Massachusetts, 6 pages, May 1972.

[9] J. Barnes, Conversations with in Arlington VA, March 1988.

[10] P. Bernstein, and D. Tsichritzis, "Models for Description of Computer Systems," Proceedings of the Eighth Annual Princeton Conference on Information Sciences and Systems, Princeton University, Princeton, New Jersey, pp. 340-343, March 1974.

[11] G. Berthelot, "Checking Liveness of Petri-Nets," Parallel Computers - Parallel Mathematics, Amsterdam: North- Holland, pp. 217-220, March 1977.

[12] G. Berthelot, and G. Roucairol, "Reduction of Petri Nets," Proceedings of the Fifth Symposium on Mathematical Foundation of Computer Science, Lecture Notes in Computer Science, **Vol. 45**, Berlin: Springer-Verlag, pp. 202-209, Sept. 1976.

[13] E. Best, "On the Liveness Problem of Petri Net Theory," ASM/6, Computing Laboratory, University of Newcastle upon Tyne, Newcastle upon Tyne, England, June 1976.

[14] E. Best, "Path Programs," Lecture Notes in Computer Science, Berlin: Springer- Verlag, (1980).

[15] T. Bredt, "Analysis of Parallel Systems," Technical Report 7, Digital Systems Laboratory, Stanford University, Stanford, California, 59 pages, August 1970; also IEEE Transactions on Computers, **Vol. C-20**, No. 11, pp. 1403-1407, Nov. 1971.

[16] W. Brinsfield, and R. Miller, "On the Composition of Parallel Program Schemata," Conference Record 1971 12th Annual Symposium on Switching and Automata Theory, New York: IEEE, pp. 20-23, Oct. 1971.

[17] F. Commoner, A. Holt, S. Even, and A. Pnueli, "Marked Directed Graphs," Journal of Computer and System Sciences, **Vol. 5**, No. 5, pp. 511-523, Oct. 1971.

[18] L. Cox, Jr., "Predicting Concurrent Computer System Performance Using Petri Net Models," Proceedings of the 1978 ACM National Conference, New York: ACM, pp. 901-913, Dec. 1978.

[19] S. Crespi-Reghizzi and D. Mandrioli, "Petri Nets and Szilard Languages," Information and Control, **Vol. 33**, No. 2, pp. 177-192, Feb. 1977.

[20] M. Davis, "Computability and Unsolvability", New York: McGraw-Hill, 210 pages, (1958).

[21] G. Fahlman and G. Hinton, "Connectionist Architectures for Artificial Intelligence," p. 100, Jan. 1987.

[22] J. L. Feldman and J. D. Cowman, "Large-scale Activity of Neural Nets II: A Model for the Brainstem Respiratory Oscillator," Biol. Cybern., **Vol. 17**, pp. 39-51, 1975.

[23] K. Fukushima, S. Miyake and T. Ito, "Neurocognitron: A Neural Network Model for a Mechanism of Visual Pattern Recognition," IEEE Trans. Syst., Man, Cybern., **Vol. AMC-13**, pp. 826-834, Sept. 1983.

[24] K. Fukushima, "A Model of Associative Memory in the Brain," Kybernetik, **Vol. 12**, pp. 58-63, (1973).

[25] H. Genrich, and K. Lautenbach, "Facts in Place/Transition- Nets," Proceedings of the Seventh Symposium on Mathematical Foundations of Computer Science 1978, Lecture Notes in Computer Science, **Vol. 64**, Berlin: Springer-Verlag, pp. 213-231, Sept. 1978.

[26] H. Genrich and E. Stankiewicz-Wiechno, "A Dictionary of Some Basic Notions of Net Theory," Lecture Notes in Computer Science, Berlin: Springer-Verlag, (1980).

[27] S. Ghosh, "Some Comments on Timed Petri Nets," AFCET Journees sur les Reseaux de Petri (AFCET Workshop on Petri Nets), Paris, France, pp. 213-226, March 1977.

[28] K. Gostelow, "Computation Modules and Petri Nets," Proceedings of the Third IEEE-ACM Milwaukee Symposium on Automatic Computation and Control, New York: IEEE, pp. 345-353, April 1975.

[29] S. Grossberg, "Neural Network Research: From a Personal Perspective," Electronic Engineering Times, pp. A12-A40, March 7, 1988.

[30] S. Hampson and D. Kibler, "A Boolean Complete Neural Model of Adaptive Behavior," Biol. Cybernetics., **Vol. 49**, pp. 9-19, (1983).

[31] J. Haugeland, "Mind Design," MIT Press, (1987).

[32] R. Hect-Nielson, "Neurocomputing: Picking the Human Brain," IEEE Spectrum, pp. 36-41, March 1988.

[33] D. Hillis, "The Connection Machine," Scientific American, pp. 108-115, June 1987.

[34] J. Hopcroft, and J. Ullman, Formal Languages and Their Relation to Automata, Reading, Massachusetts: Addison- Wesley, 242 pages, (1969).

[35] J. J. Hopfield, "Collective Processing and Neural States," Modeling and Analysis in Biomedicine. Singapore: World Scientific, (1984).

[36] M. Jantzen, "On the Hierarchy of Petri Net Languages," R.A.I.R.O. Theoretical Informatics, **Vol. 13**, No. 1, pp. 19-30, (1979).

[37] R. C. Johnson, "Optics and Neural Nets: Marriage of Convenience," Electronic Engineering Times, pp. 41, Jan. 18, 1988.

[38] R. C. Johnson, "Lockhead Targets Neural Nets," Electronic Engineering Times, pp. 51, Dec. 14, 1987.

[39] R. C. Johnson, "Gated Dipoles may be Flip-Flop of Nervous System," pp. 49-50, Nov. 16, 1987.

[40] R. Karp, and R. Miller, "Parallel Program Schemata," RC-2053, IBM T. J. Watson Research Center, Yorktown Heights, New York, 54 pages, April 1968; also, Journal of Computer and System Science, **Vol. 3**, No. 4, pp. 167-195, May 1969; preliminary draft, IEEE Conference Record of the 1967 Eighth Annual Symposium on Switching and Automata Theory, New York: IEEE, pp. 55-61, Oct. 1967.

[41] R. Keller, "Generalized Petri Nets as Models for System Verification," Technical Report 202, Department of Electrical Engineering, Princeton University, Princeton, New Jersey, 50 pages, August 1975.

[42] V. Kotov, "An Algebra for Parallelism Based on Petri Nets," Proceedings of the Seventh Symposium on Mathematical Foundations of Computer Science 1978, Lecture Notes in Computer Science, **Vol. 64**, Berlin: Springer-Verlag, pages 39-55, Sept. 1978.

[43] S. Lakshmivarahan, "Learning Algorithms Theory and Applications". New York: Springer-Verlag, (1981).

[44] P. Laur and R. Campbell, "A Description of Path Expressions by Petri Nets," Technical Report 64, Computing Laboratory, University of Newcastle upon Tyne, England, May 1974.

[45] D. S. Levine, "Neural Population Modeling and Psychology: A Review," Math. Biosci., **Vol. 66**, pp. 1-86, (1983).

[46] W. A. Little and G. L. Shaw, "Analytic Study of the Memory Storage Capacity of a Neural Network," Math. Biosci., **Vol. 39**, pp. 281-290, (1978).

[47] J. McClelland, D. Rumelhart and the PDP Research Group, "Parallel Distributed Processing, Explorations in the Microstructure of Cognition," **Vol. 1**, **Vol. 2**, MIT Press, (1986).

[48] W. McCulloch and W. Pitts, "A Logical Calculus of the Ideas Immanent in Nervous Activity," Bulletin of Mathematical Biophysics, **Vol. 5**, pp. 115-137, (1943).

[49] W. McCulloch and W. Pitts, "How We Know Universals," Bulletin of Mathematical Biophysics, **Vol. 9**, pp. 127-147.

[50] R. Miller, "A Comparison of Some Theoretical Models of Parallel Computation," Report RC-4230, IBM T. J. Watson Research Center, Yorktown Heights, New York; also, IEEE Transactions on Computers, **Vol. C-22**, No. 8, pp. 710-717, August 1973.

[51] M. Minsky, "Artificial Intelligence," Electronic Engineering Times Anniversary Issue, pp. A65-A69, Nov. 1987.

[52] M. Minsky, S. Papert, "Perceptron, Expanded Edition," MIT Press, (1988).

[53] B. J. Oommen, "Ergodic Learning Automata Capable of Incorporating A Priori Information," IEEE Transactions on Systems, Man and Cybernetics, **Vol. SMC-17**, No. 4, July/August.

[54] M. Oonuki, "Firing Probability of Neural Networks: First- Order Differential Equation," J. Theor. Biol., **Vol. 58**, pp. 59-81, (1976).

[55] P. Peretto, "Collective Properties of Neural Networks, a Statistical Physics Approach," Biol. Cybern., **Vol. 50**, pp. 51-62, (1984).

[56] P. Peretto and J. J. Niez, "Stochastic Dynamics of Neural Networks," IEEE Transactions on Systems, Man and Cybernetics, **Vol. SMC-16**, No. 1, Jan/Feb. 1986.

[57] J. Peterson, "Petri Net Theory and the Modeling of Systems," Prentice Hall, (1981).

[58] C. Petri, "General Net Theory," Proceedings of the Joint IBM/University of Newcastle upon Tyne Seminar on Computing System Design, Computing Laboratory, University of Newcastle upon Tyne, Newcastle upon Tyne, England, pp. 131-169, Sept. 1976.

[59] Z. Pylyshyn, "Computation and Cognition," MIT Press, (1986).

[60] W. Riddle, "The Equivalence of Petri Nets and Message Transmission Models," SRM/97, Computing Laboratory, University of Newcastle upon Tyne, England, August 1974.

[61] F. Rosenblatt, "Principles of Neurodynamics," Spartan Books, New York, (1962).

[62] A. Salomaa, "Formal Languages", New York: Academic Press, 322 pages, (1973).

[63] A. Samuel, "Some Studies in Machine Learning Using the Game of Checkers," IBM Journal of Research and Development, **Vol. 3**, No. 3, pp. 210-223, (1959).

[64] J. Sifakis, "Homomorphisms of Petri Nets: Application to the Realization of Fault-Tolerant Systems," Technical Report 90, Institute of Applied Mathematics and Computer Science, Grenoble, France, Nov. 1977.

[65] D. Tank and J. Hopfield, "Collective Computation in Neuronlike Circuits," Scientific American, pp. 104-114, Dec. 1987.

[66] G. Toulousi, "Neural Networks," Nature 327:662, June 25, 1987.

[67] Y. Z. Tsypkin and A. S. Poznyak, "Finite Learning Automata," Eng. Cybern., **Vol. 10**, pp. 478-490, (1972).

[68] J. Von Neumann, Collected Works, Vol. 5, p. 304, Pergamon, New York, (1963).

[69] ___________, "Programmable Synaptic Arrays for Electronic Neural Network," NASA Tech Briefs, Jan. 1988.

[70] ____________, "Stimulus Context and Absolute Magnitude Estimation: A Study of Individual Differences," Perception and Psychophysics, **Vol. 50**, No. 1, July 1991

[71] ____________, ____________, Scientific American 256: 88-95, Mr "87.

[72] N.G. Bourbakis, ARTEMIS - An Automated Software Environment for Analysis, Design and Simulation of Computing Systems, International Journal on SEKE, 1992 (to be forthcoming)

CHAPTER 14

Artificial Intelligence Languages and Architectures: Past, Present, and Future

by

Samuel O. Aletan

Department of Computer Science

College of Engineering

Louisiana Tech University

Ruston, LA

1. INTRODUCTION

Artificial Intelligence (AI) is the study of what intelligence is and the process of creating computing systems that are more useful and smart. AI is an interdisciplinary field which includes psychology, philosophy, linguistics, electrical engineering, and computing science. These disciplines and branches of AI are shown in Figure 1. Other engineering disciplines are also actively involved in some of the branches of AI. For example, mechanical engineering plays an important role in the design of robots. AI researchers in psychology, philosophy, and linguistics are collectively referred to as information processing psychologists or cognitive scientists [37]. The cognitive scientists are interested in understanding what intelligence is, how it is acquired and used. Their central activity involves the modeling of human information processing. The computing science, electrical engineering, and other related engineering fields are more interested in building computing systems that perform at high levels of behavior — building machines that are more useful and smart. Their central activity involves efforts to make computing systems behave intelligently. In AI, it is not enough to prove theorems formally; it is also necessary to design, implement, and convert the theorems into a functioning system.

The theories offered by the cognitive scientists are numerous but they are still inconsistent and incomplete. The lack of concrete theories as to how the human mind works has been a stumbling block in the efforts to transform the available theories into a computational database. To further complicate things, some of the problems that fall within the purview of AI do not have precise algorithms to solve them. Therefore, the solutions to some AI problems are inexact, and cannot be expressed precisely as can most problems in scientific and engineering fields. In addition, most of the computations required to solve some AI problems are non-numeric in nature. Some of these problems are also complex and ambiguous. Some AI branches, such as vision, do require some numeric computation; therefore, a dedicated AI system cannot totally discount numeric computations.

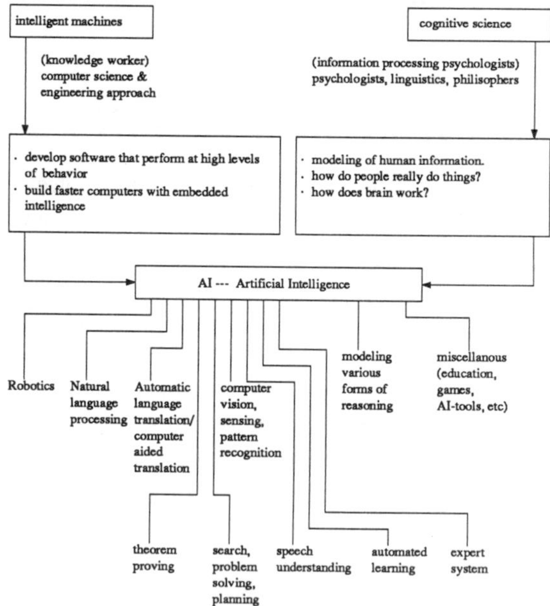

Figure 1 AI disciplines and subfields

1.1. Branches of AI

AI is an interdisciplinary field and the most notable branches are listed in Table 1. The theories for some of these branches of AI such as speech understanding, reasoning, learning, and vision have proven to be very difficult to formulate and transform into computational database. AI researchers have not enjoyed overwhelming success in these areas of AI. AI researchers have achieved more success in the branches of AI such as theorem proving, search, problem solving, and planning. The most success has been achieved, to date, in expert systems (ES). The branches of AI are interdependent on each other. For example, advances in reasoning, learning, speech understanding, and natural language processing will have a great impact in expert systems, and designing of intelligent and more flexible robots. These branches (reasoning, learning, speech understanding, natural language processing, knowledge acquisition, and vision) poses the most difficulties for computers. The influences of each of the branches and disciplines

Table 1 Major Branches of AI

Automated Learning
Speech Understanding
Natural language processing
Automatic language translatin, and computer-aided translation
Computer vision, sensing, and pattern recognition
Knowledge representation
Robotics
Theorem proving
Automated Programming
Search, problem solving, and planning
Expert system
Miscellaneous (AI approaches to education, game playing, etc.)

of AI shown in Figure 1 will become more explicit in the evaluation of languages and architectures that are required in the pursuit of the goal of AI — to build machines with embedded intelligence.

The branches of AI shown in Figure 1 are inconclusive; the areas of research associated with AI are dynamic. For instance, early research in robotics was not AI-based, but was instead involved in solving lower level manipulator control problems [6]. It is also possible that in the future, some branches of AI, such as expert systems, may be considered as conventional software rather than AI. Research activities in areas such as vision, and efforts to build intelligent and robust robots, have moved robotics into the realm of AI. Other areas that are closely associated with AI include adaptive systems, database systems, image processing, graphics, and pattern recognition. In the future, some of these may become a part of AI research. AI will continue to be a dynamic multidisciplinary field as it has been since the earlier efforts by Charles Babbage, John von Neumann, Claude Shannon, and Alan Turing. Modern AI research started in the mid to late 1950's by a few group of researchers including Newell, Simon, Misky, Shaw, and McCarthy. Since the earlier work by these and other researchers, AI has gone through many phases of developments. The first organized study of AI was in 1956 at Dartmouth.

1.2. The phases of AI development

The history of AI was divided into a variety of phases starting from 1842 to the present. These phases are [8] :

- 1842–1960 — Prehistory period with activities involving work done by Charles Babbage and Alan Turing.
- 1958–1965 — Dawn age, with activities that included development of a program for solving geometric analogy problems and another program for doing symbolic integration.
- 1963–1970 — Dark age, with very little activity due by-and-large to over expectation.
- 1968–1975 — Renaissance age with the development of expert systems such as MYCIN.
- 1973–1980 — Partnerships age with the realization that researchers in other field such as linguistics and psychology were needed as partners in efforts to meet AI goal.
- 1978–Present — Entrepreneur and commercialization age with several AI products being marketed.

A broader categorization of modern AI development phases was given in [31]. These development phases are shown in Figure 2.

Exploration phase — This phase involved the development of working models that were used to validate new concepts put forward by AI theorists in relation to computational intelligence. this phase included the dawn, dark, and renaissance age as stated earlier.

Prototype phase — This phase involved the development and use of LISP machines as more complex problems were attempted. LISP machines were computers designed as language directed computers for executing programs written in LISP. Several important initiatives commenced during this phase; these initiatives included the fifth generation computer project (FGCP) launched in Japan, the strategic computing initiative, and a standard LISP definition by a U.S. government sponsored committee. This phase corresponds to the partnership age as stated earlier.

Commercialization phase — This phase involves the marketing of AI products, continuing work on the development of FGCP. There is a realizations that AI software must be integrated with conventional software. Other activities in this phase includes efforts to improve user interfaces, integration with databases, training, more concerns for system performance and cost, and software maintenance. Most of these activities were not as important in the two earlier phases of AI development as they are currently. The commercialization/industrialization of AI should be considered a major step forward in the application of computers.

Figure 2 Development Phases of AI

Both AI software and hardware have been advanced. These advances are influencing research efforts in areas such as parallel processing, supercomputing, networking, and distributed processing. There are four major disciplines that must continue to improve in order to make progress towards the design of computers with some level of intelligence. These disciplines are [35] :

1. Several branches of AI, including vision, speech recognition, and human oriented input-output in natural language.
2. New innovations in computer architecture and enhancement of current architectural techniques.
3. Software engineering with development of new languages, enhancement of current languages, and design of operating systems that will have facilities to support execution of programs on parallel architectures. Also, there must be efficient means for acquiring, storing and accessing knowledge.
4. Very large scale integration (VLSI) with adoption of faster devices such as Gallium Arsenide and Josephson Junctions for the implementation of architecture designs.

The rest of this chapter is devoted to topics in software engineering and computer architecture. The development of AI languages will be briefly discussed. This will be followed by a brief discussion of some of the current AI computers, and analysis of the execution efficiency of three AI-related problems coded in conventional languages and executed on conventional architectures. The last two sections of this chapter are devoted to the discussion of some LISP-based architectures, and the future trends in AI languages and architectures.

2. MAJOR AI TOOLS: LANGUAGES and ARCHITECTURES

Two of the major tools utilized in building and executing AI programs are programming languages and architectures. The effort to build tools for developing and executing programs started very early in AI's development. LISP and modern research in AI can be considered siblings because they were introduced at about the same place and time. LISP was designed to code AI-related problems. The development of PROLOG was also affected by the needs of AI. In its basic form, PROLOG was designed with theorem proving as its foundation. Prolog in its purest form is really an expression of the first-order predicated calculus. This is the basis on which programs are written; as sets of axioms and statements of the result to be proven as true or false [8]. The development of AI languages such as LISP and PROLOG and the earlier research into AI, affected the need to develop special architectures to support the development and execution of programs written to solve AI-related problems. The earlier research established some basic needs necessary to support AI. One of these basic needs was met by the design of LISP machines. The establishment of these tools — LISP and PROLOG, and LISP machines — has not eliminated the active roles of conventional languages and architectures in AI research. Conventional languages and architectures remain strong participants in the efforts to build intelligent machines and make AI components as part of an overall computing system.

2.1. AI Languages

There is nothing in a HLL that says that a particular HLL is an AI language. But suitability of a language for a particular task, programmer's experience with a language, software development and maintenance cost, concern for efficiency, and the band wagon effect will play a role in the popularity of a languge. Industry and government backing are also major influencies in the poularity of a language .

LISP

LISP is currently the most established high level language (HLL) for writing AI programs [27]. LISP assumed its current position as a language of choice for AI researchers with little or no competition from other languages. This was attributed to the limited number of AI researchers (less than 50) that were involved in AI research during the early years of AI development [27]. After the initial introduction of LISP around 1958, LISP quickly began to mutate. Several versions of LISP were developed including Bolt and Beranek & Newman LISP (BBN LISP), InterLISP-D from Xerox, MACLISP, FRANZLISP, and many others. Currently, Common LISP is the standard adopted for LISP. LISP, in its purest form, can be considered a functional programming language. But over the years LISP has been extended and refined to suit the needs of AI programming [24]. Current LISP is more of a procedural language, but unlike conventional procedural languages such as FORTRAN, and Ada, LISP is functional. LISP can be classified as a procedural-functional language. The syntax and semantics of LISP are formed from the mathematical theory of recursive functions. LISP is characterized by some unique attributes that include:

- Lists and property lists are the fundamental data structures in LISP.
- LISP was designed for symbolic processing rather than numbers and characters.

- Programs can be treated and executed dynamically. In other words, LISP supports runtime creation, redefinition, and compilation of new procedures.
- LISP employs run time type checking; it supports dynamic variable typing.
- The basic unit from which programs are formed are expressions composed of functional calls.
- The functional nature of LISP encourages the use of many small functions. Programs written in LISP are organized as a collection of functions that call each other.
- Programs written in LISP usually have a lot of searching and pointer dereferencing operations.
- Recursive use of conditional expressions as a sufficient tool for building computable functions.
- LISP structures can store objects of any type; this makes the storage reusable.
- The use of garbage collection mechanism to handle the dynamic storage requirements of programs written in LISP.

LISP is currently the second oldest HLL in widespread use; Fortran is the oldest HLL still in widespread use. The operational features considered to be unmatched by other HLL, and the time-sharing program set up by the National Science Foundation and Stanford where the main program was written in InterLisp, were two of the reasons why LISP has gained widespread use. LISP is seen as a convenient vehicle for higher level systems for symbolic and AI computations. Four reasons were given for this [26]:

- LISP's runtime system that gives access to the features of the host computer and its operating system. LISP has been called the assembly language of AI [9].
- The internal list structure of LISP is a good target for compiling from yet higher level languages.
- LISP's compatibility with computers that produce binary or assembly level program.
- The availability of LISP's interpreter as a command language for driving other programs.

One of the major contributions of LISP was seen as the concept of interpreting a program as it was read or typed [33]. The availability of an interpreter and the lack of any form of declaration makes it very natural to use LISP in a time sharing environment. Although the first interactive LISP was on a PDP–1 in 1963, the most important implementations were those on PDP–6 and PDP–10. The influence of LISP on the structures of these machines was evident with the half word instructions and stack instructions that were implemented. Researches were later able to use the Decsystem-20 family. The researchers at M.I.T. contributed to the popularity of these machines in AI laboratories [26]. In the early years of AI, many programs were implemented in LISP, with each implementation taking advantage of the built-in facilities for manipulating symbolic data structures. In the later years when higher-level formalisms such as production systems, logic theorem provers, and rule-based expert systems were developed, LISP became the principal implementation HLL [24]. Most of the software on some LISP machines was written in LISP. For example, the MIT LISP machine used LISP to code its debugger, compiler, graphics support, EMACs-like editor, etc. [13]. Many modern environments for expert systems are implemented in LISP. Some pioneering expert systems were also written in LISP; these include MYCIN, and DENDRAL [27]. The popularity of LISP within the AI community in the U.S. was not seriously challenged until another AI language, PROLOG, that was developed in Europe (France) in 1971 made its way to the U.S. in the early 1980.

PROLOG

PROLOG was not made available to the public for many years after its initial design but it has also become a favored AI tool. In its purest form, PROLOG is basically an expression of the first-order predicate calculus in terms of which programs are written. Programs written in PROLOG are not to be executed statement-by-statement but they are rather set of known facts and relationships about the problem(s) being solved. Programs can be viewed as declarative assertions about a problem domain. It is not always required to see the solution to a problem as a step-by-step sequence of statements; this is one of the distinction between PROLOG and procedural languages such as COBOL and C. Programming in PROLOG requires the programmer to specify known facts about the problem(s) and relationships, and then ask questions about the problem(s) and relationships. Because of these features and the fact that PROLOG is based on first-order predicate calculus, PROLOG is probably the best known logic programming language.

The popularity of PROLOG can be credited to two major activities:

- The development of a robust interpreter for PROLOG produced by the department of AI of the University of Edinburgh. The interpreter was built on the DEC-System 10 and could operate in both interpretive and compiled modes [24].
- The adoption of PROLOG by the Japanese as the basis for their FGCP.

There are several other important activities that are fueling the growing popularity of PROLOG and one of these is the availability of PROLOG on PCs. When Borland International's Turbo PROLOG was released around 1986, as many as 100,000 copies were sold within a year [27]. The availability of PROLOG on PCs positions PROLOG as a viable language for writing commercial AI products. PROLOG has been used in many applications including relational databases, theorem proving, site planning, high-level specification languages, biochemical analysis, natural language understanding, expert systems, automatic code generation, and program verification. Some of the expert systems that were written in PROLOG are MI, Mecho, ORBI, and Chat System. The ease of integrating various components of expert systems, compactness of expression with efficient implementation, and the dual semantics made available in PROLOG are three of the advantages for using it in coding expert systems [11]. Currently, LISP is still ahead of PROLOG among AI audience in the U.S. But in Europe, PROLOG enjoys better success. Some governments, such as Hungary, encourage the use of PROLOG. Britain and Japan were at one time or another investigating the possibilities of using PROLOG in production planning, industrial process control, and strategy control for flexible automation systems [11]. PROLOG may be used in applications other than AI even though PROLOG is a more specialized language than LISP.

Other HLLs

LISP and PROLOG are not the only HLL used to code AI algorithms. Other HLL languages such as Smalltalk and OPS have been used. Conventional HLLs ranging from BASIC to ADA have also been used. While conventional HLLs are procedural in nature, languages such as Smalltalk, Flavors, OPS, Loops, and Common Object use object-oriented paradigms. In contrast to LISP and PROLOG, which have their origins in abstract mathematics, object-oriented languages have their origins in software engineering and simulation. The first object-oriented language, Smalltalk, was developed by Alan Kay and his colleagues at Xerox Palo

Alto Research Center in the early 1970's [24]. Object-oriented programming is expected to play the same role that structured programming played in the 70's. In programs written in Smalltalk everything is represented as an object, an active computational structure of arbitrary complexity. Smalltalk supports inheritance of class properties and message passing mechanism. For instance, the number 6 is a member of the class integers and therefore inherits integer operation such as *, –, +, and so on. Smalltalk supports the development of modular code and uses strong typing to both data elements and code for their manipulation. Object-oriented languages support information hiding, operator overloading, on-line documentation, and embedded language.

Ideas from object-oriented programming have been used in other languages such as SIMULA and ADA. ADA, a procedural language, supports features such as information hiding and operator overloading. Object-oriented methodology is becoming a major player in AI programming arena especially in development of hybrid AI environments. KEE, ART, and NEXPERT are hybrid object-oriented / rule-based knowledge engineering languages. The expert system XCON, developed in 1980 by DEC and Carnegie Mellon University (CMU), was written in OPS5. OPS5 is a production system modeling language developed at CMU. There are other AI languages that are not widely used; these include IPL, PLANNER, CONNIVER, SAIL, and FUZZY. Most of these are specialized languages for a particular branch or related area of AI.

Many AI problems have been solved with programs written in BASIC, FORTRAN, and even COBOL and many other conventional (imperative) HLLs. The major problem with these conventional languages is that they do not know how to handle uncertainty and do not have all the logic or symbolic facilities that make LISP or PROLOG more efficient at the program development level. Some of these languages do not even have facilities to support recursion. But more people know or are exposed to more conventional HLLs than to LISP, PROLOG or Smalltalk. Also, programs written in conventional HLLs are more efficient on conventional architectures. A good programmer can work around inefficiencies or lack of a facility in a language. But programmers' options are limited if efficiency is hardware related, such as lack of good support for garbage collection which is common on most conventional architectures when executing programs written in LISP.

One of the first expert system shells written, Expert-Ease, was written in

FORTRAN; IMPACT, another expert system, was written in COBOL; and an internal expert system for teaching music developed by IBM was written in PASCAL [27]. Programmers experience with a language, architecture, and problem domain can overcome most of the drawbacks of conventional languages [1]. The major problem is that most AI problems are often ill-defined and require a great deal of time during the development phase. The most appropriate language for a particular task will depend on the task to be performed, programmers' experience, and architecture(s) available for executing the task. Languages play a greater role at the development level, and architectures and system software play a decisive role at the execution level.

2.2. Development of AI Computers

There are two basic choices for researchers or programmers who are to write AI programs without any AI machine (LISP machine) :

1. Code programs in LISP and execute them on non-AI (conventional) machines which are usually less efficient in executing programs written in LISP.
2. Code programs in some other conventional, usually imperative / procedural, HLL and execute them on non-AI machine. Execution of programs may be more efficient because non-AI machines (conventional, which are usually general purpose, machines) are more sympathetic (better matched) to the structures of procedural HLLs.

The first choice can be extended to all the non-procedural / non-imperative HLLs which usually receive little or no attention when conventional architectures are designed. Conventional architecture designs generally pay more attention to the needs of the more widely used imperative HLLs. The ideal solution would be to use the best available HLLs for the given project and execute the programs on machines that best support the structures and attributes of the programs written in these HLLs. But in most instances, an ideal solution is very rare. The first choice, of the two listed, is the most common, because LISP and other AI languages are used more by AI researchers, just like COBOL and FORTRAN are used more in solving business and scientific problems respectively. But if efficiency is of utmost importance, then the second choice becomes a viable alternative. The widespread availability of general purpose (conventional) machines and the fact that more people are familiar with procedural HLLs, than any AI language, are compelling reasons for opting for the second choice. But this choice must be made with consideration of the fact that a great deal of AI research is, at the beginning, exploratory and this type of work can benefit from a language that can be used interactively. Secondly, most procedural HLLs lack the types of structures and attributes that are required to "easily" build AI programs.

Early LISP Implementations

After LISP was developed in the late 1950's, LISP was first available only on expensive mainframe time sharing systems for many years. But as stated earlier, the first interactive LISP on the PDP-1 computer was introduced in 1963, and the most important implementations of LISP, were those on the PDP-6, DEC system-10 and 20. LISP influenced the architecture of these systems because the half word instructions and the stack instructions of these machines were developed with the efficient support of LISP in mind. These were the machines of choice for AI research in the early years of AI development. Another one of the earliest implementation of LISP was on the IBM 704. It was this implementation from which the LISP functions CAR (contents of the address part of the operand) and CDR (content of the decrement part of the operand) were coined. The IBM 704 LISP, which was introduced in 1960/1961, was extended to the IBM 7090 and later to the IBM 360 and 370 [26]. All of these conventional computers were not very efficient in executing programs written in LISP. Conventional machines are designed to have efficient arithmetic data path, whereas programs written in LISP depend more on symbolic rather than numeric operations.

3. CONVENTIONAL ARCHITECTURES VS CONVENTIONAL HLLs AND LISP

Three small AI-related problems were evaluated with the objective to: Code programs in both LISP and conventional HLLs and run them on conventional computers in efforts to see how conventional HLLs perform against LISP. As we have stated earlier, for many years the DEC system 10/20 series were the main stay systems for AI researchers. But the lack of speed and adequate address space (18–bit address space) were two of the major problems faced by the DEC systems. But with advances in software (especially compiler design), VLSI technology, and tools to support LISP environment, there are improvements on todays systems.

But current architectures are still designed, by and large, based on the criteria to support procedural HLLs. Any type of support for LISP is usually through software with very little hardware support.

3.1. Problems Solved

The three problems that we evaluated were: 8–queens, Knights tour, and traveling salesman (TS). Although these problems did not result in large programs, they did give us some preliminary results as to the efficiency of conventional architectures in executing AI-related problems coded in procedural HLLs and LISP. A conclusive result can only be reached with larger problems because storage usage and management are important issues in the evaluation of architectures support in the execution of AI programs. A brief description of the three problems are:

Knight's Tour

The objective of the Knight's Tour problem is to start at an initial square on an 8X8 board, and move, using the moves of a Knight in chess, to the squares on the board visiting all the squares once. A round trip solution imposes the restriction that the final resting position must be one legal Knight move from the initial position.

8–Queens

The objective of the 8–queens problem is to start at an initial square on an 8X8 chessboard and place a queen. Then place other queens on the chessboard in such a way that no queen can capture any others. A solution to this problem imposes the restriction that the chessboard cannot have more that one queen on any given row, column, and diagonal.

Traveling Salesman

The objective of the TS problem may be stated like this- given a road map of several cities, begin from a starting city and find the optimum route such that each city will be visited. The solution to this problem imposes the restriction that each city must be visited only once except the starting city because the journey must terminate at the starting city.

3.2. HLLs

The HLLs used to code the three problems are Ada, C, FORTRAN, LISP, Pascal, and PL/I. Five of these HLLs are procedural languages and they are expected to have better performance on conventional (general-purpose) architectures. LISP is a non-procedural language as stated earlier.

Systems Utilized

In all the observations we made, four machines were involved. The machines used in the first observation are:

1. IBM 4341 (mainframe) running under VM/SP operating system (O/S) release 5 with compilers for most of the widely used HLLs such as FORTRAN, Pascal, and PL/I.
2. Digital Equipment MicroVAX II running under micro-VMS O/S 4.4 with compilers for C, PL/I, and LISP.
3. Zenith PC with 80286 microprocessor running under the MS DOS. There are compilers for most of the widely used HLLs on PCs, this includes FORTRAN, Pascal, and C.
4. IBM RT/PC running under the advanced interactive executive (AIX) O/S version 2.1. Our system has compilers for C and FORTRAN.

In the first observation, our emphasis was on the influence of programmers and architectures on program execution efficiency. A full detail of our observation is given in [1]. The four machines observed are complex instruction set computers (CISCs) except the IBM RT/PC. The IBM RT has 118 instructions, a floating point co-processor, a floating point accelerator, and a memory management processor. The RT is referred to as a reduced instruction set computer (RISC) even though some of its features are also common on CISCs.

The 8–queens problem was the problem analyzed in the first observation. The 8–queens problem may be classified as one of the problems known as combinational and scheduling problems. Some scheduling problems are thought to be intractable. The key to an efficient solution of these types of problems is a good knowledge of the problem domain, a judicious selection of algorithms, and sound logic to implement the algorithms. Most of the activities involved in the selection of algorithms and strategies, and the actual coding of the algorithms are, to some extent, within programmers control. These activities are within the purview of what we called "programmers domain". The rest of the activities involved in solving a problem — compilation/interpretation, execution, and debugging are within what we called "architecture domain". Programmers have more influence on efficiency with activities within the programmers domain; architectures and systems software have more influence on efficiency than programers within the architecture domain [1].

Table 2 Processing times (seconds) [Optimized-Opt, Non optimized-Noopt]

	IBM 4341		MicroVAX II		IBM RT		PC
	Noopt	Opt	Noopt	Opt	Noopt	Opt	
CC-S1R	N/A	00.29	00.50	00.47	00.37	00.32	03.18
PA-S2R	00.36	00.21	00.71	00.66	N/A	N/A	01.75
PL-S3R	00.58	00.53	00.61	00.52	N/A	N/A	N/A
FO-T1N	00.19	00.11	00.27	00.25	00.30	00.17	03.37
FO-T2N	58.97	27.13	61.75	51.45	35.88	22.98	981.62
LI-T3R	120(interpreted)		03.44	03.47	N/A	N/A	08.52
PL-T4R	46.22	43.26	108.47	57.17	N/A	N/A	N/A
PL-T5N	32.20	27.13	94.52	48.44	N/A	N/A	N/A
PL-T6R	00.48	00.47	00.53	00.40	N/A	N/A	N/A
LI-L1R	N/A	N/A	01.76	01.71	N/A	N/A	05.82
PA-L2R	00.11	00.10	00.22	00.20	N/A	N/A	N/A
PA-L3N	00.08	00.07	00.22	00.16	N/A	N/A	N/A
LI-C1R	N/A	N/A	01.22	01.19	N/A	N/A	03.30
AD-K1R	N/A	N/A	N/A	N/A	N/A	N/A	03.02

The Programmers/HLLs/Programs

Five programmers were told to write the 8–queens program and use any language of their choice that any of the four machines we have at our disposal support. One of the programmers was asked to run one of his programs, which he wrote in C, on all the four machines. C was the only HLL that we have compilers for on each of our four machines. There were fourteen programs written by the five programmers (Douglas Schales, George Tahtouh, Chien-Lih Lin, Martin Kanski, and Shyan Chen).

The names given to the programs listed in Table 2 were derived as:

- First two letters of the language the given program was written, e.g., CC for C, and PA for Pascal.
- The next letter in the name represents the first letter of the last name of the author of the program.
- The first digit in the name represents the number given to the programs written by each author, starting from 1, 2, 3, and so on.
- The last letter in the program's name represents the type of algorithm that a program adopted, R for recursive algorithm and N for nonrecursive algorithm.

For example, PL-T4R means this program was written in PL/I, the author was Tahtouh, it's the fourth program written by this author, and the program implemented a recursive algorithm.

Compiler Optimization

The compile and link times were included in the earlier report [1]. Compiler optimization had the most obvious impact with programs that were implemented with non-recursive algorithms especially the programs written in FORTRAN (FO-T2N on the IBM 4341), and PL/I on the MicroVAX II. But it is also obvious from this observation that compiler optimization cannot compensate for a poor choice of algorithm and implementation strategies. For example, the processing times of FO-T1N and PL-T6R, and FO-T2N and PL-T4R are evidence of this fact. FO-T1N and PL-T6R are improved versions of FO-T2N and PL-T4R. The basic algorithms, recursive for PL-T4R and nonrecursive for FO-T2N, remain unchanged but their logic and implementation strategies were altered for FO-T1N and PL-T6R. In FO-T2N and PL-T4R, the entire board (sixty-four positions) was searched before a queen was placed. But after the programmer responsible for these two programs was informed of the poor performance of his programs compared to that of other programmers, he made some changes and created FO-T1N and PL-T6R. The programmer had gained better understanding of the problem to be solved, and how to best solve the problem when he created FO-T1N and PL-T6R as compared to when FO-T2N and PL-T4R were written. The unoptimized code for FO-T1N was better than the optimized version of FO-T2N. Optimization is very important but judicious selection of algorithms and implementation strategies are even more important.

Compiled LISP programs (MicroVAX II) are faster than interpreted LISP (IBM 4341 and PC). This is not unexpected; interpreters are more useful during program development and compilers will be more efficent for production runs. The unoptimized codes for LI-L1R and LI-C1R have better execution times than the optimized and unoptimized versions of LI-T3R. The programmer's understanding of a problem contributed to the selection of better implementation strategies for LI-L1R and LI-C1R. From the data in Table 2, it seems that some architectures support some HLLs better than others. For example, the optimized code of the programs written in FORTRAN on the IBM 4341, and the programs written in PL/I on the MicroVAX showed dramatic improvements.

Architectures

Our second observation was based on our interest to find out how a particular architecture supports several HLLs. the MicroVAX II was our target architecture. We were able to use five HLLs — Ada, C, LISP, Pascal, and PL/I. We were also interested in PROLOG but we do not have a PROLOG compiler for our MicroVAX II systems. The instruction set of the MicroVAX II is a subset of the instruction set of the VAX architecture. The MicroVAX is a CISC system. It supports about three hundred instructions. It has ten addressing modes, and sixteen 32–bit general purpose registers [10]. There are several processor and input/output registers. There is support for many data types including: Character string, Floating point, Packed decimal, Integer, Numeric string, Queue, and variable length bit field.

Execution Times

In addition to the 8–queens problem, the Knight and TS Problems were added. The execution times for these problems are shown in Table 3. The times for the Knight Tour and TS are for one execution. Times for the 8–Queens are for 1000 executions, except for LISP, which is for 20 executions. LISP had the worst execution times for the three problems. The execution time for twenty executions was over three minutes; the highest execution time of over six minutes recorded for Pascal was for one thousand executions. The second highest execution time for the TS problem was less than six minutes and the highest execution time was almost three days (2 days and 19 hours) recorded for the TS problem written in LISP. It is important that the match between problems, algorithms, and architectures be evaluated so that the proper language(s) and architectures be assigned to the problems to be solved. The poor performance of LISP cannot be attributed only to language/architecture relationships but also to the LISP environment on the architecture, MicroVAX II in this case. The major problem seems to be the lack of efficient garbage collection on the MicroVAX II. The system spent more time salvaging storage than in executing code for the problem being solved. It is of utmost importance that memory management operations for LISP environment be efficient.

Table 3 Execution Times on MicroVax II

Language	*Queens*	*Knights*	*Salesman*
Ada	04:44.86	00:01.58	02:05.43
C	02:43.38	00:01.06	05:19.40
LISP	03:41.73	00:13.95	67 hours
Pascal	06:55.96	00:01.84	02:25.72
PL/I	03:27.58	00:02.35	01:20.79

Instructions Generated by HLLs Compilers

The types of the instructions generated for the three problems are shown in Tables 4, and 5. Some instructions types have been combined to reduce the listings for each Table. For example, ADD(L2, L3, W2, W3), and ACBW were listed separately in [2] but they have been combined in Tables IV, and V. In the Tables, KN, TS, and 8–Q are used for Knight, travelling salesman, and 8–queens problems, respectively. The variations in types of instructions generated by each HLL's compiler are noticeable between different HLLs and problems. The LISP compiler generated the least amount of unique instructions. But the LISP compiler also generated the most amount of instructions. Among the procedural HLLs, the Ada Compiler generated more instructions in each of the three problems. The C compiler generated the least amount of instructions in each of the three problems. The types of instructions generated by the Ada and C compilers are very similar.

Table 4 Instruction usage by Ada, C, and LISP compilers

	ADA			C			LISP		
Instructions	KT	TS	8-Q	KT	TS	8-Q	KT	TS	8-Q
ADD(L2,L3,W2,W3)	17	14	3	9	8	3	7	8	9
AOBLEQ				4	1	1			
ASHL	5			7					
BRANCHES	70	60	19	17	16	9	33	19	19
CALLS	15	8	2	10	11	2			
CLR(B,W,L,Q)	29	17	10	12	12	5	11	9	12
CMP(W,L)	28	38	11	12	11	5			
INC(B,W,L)	21	12	6	3	8	2			
JMP/JSP	/8	/17	/6	/1	/1	/1	/119	44/83	10/43
MNEGL							16		
MOVA/MOV(B,W,L)	21/56	12/45	1/13	8/10	11/11	1/5	16/282	29/266	9/201
MOVC3/MOVZ(BL,BW)	7/	5/3							
MULL(2,3)	4	7			7				
PUSH(AB,AL,L)	23	18	2	20	20	1			
RET	4	3	2	3	2	2			
SUB(L2,L3,W3)	4	12	2	2	2	4	1		2
TST(L,W)	16	6	3	5	5	4	28	11	9

The most prominent instructions among these HLLs and problems are (based on the instructions generated by each compiler): BRANCH, MOVE/PUSH, CALL/JUMP TO SUBROUTINE, and COMPARE. Four instructions —BRANCH, JUMP, JUMP TO SUBROUTINE, and MOVE — accounted for ever 90% of the instructions generated by the LISP's compiler. The PL/I's compiler generated the following instructions almost exclusively: ADD COMPARE and BRANCH WORD, CONVERT WORD TO LONG WORD, MOVE ZERO TO LONG WORD, CALL WITH STACK, and CALL WITH GENERAL ARGUMENT LIST. Also, the Pascal's Compiler was the only compiler that made use of the INDEX, NOP(no operation), and MOVE COMPLEMENTED LONGWORD instructions.

Table 5 Instruction usage by Pascal and PL/I

	PASCAL			PL/I		
Instructions	KT	TS	8-Q	KT	TS	8-Q
ADD(L2,L3,W2,W3)/ACBW	7/1	8/	2/	10/5	13/3	3/3
AOBLEQ	3		3			
BRANCHES	19	26	11	31	18	11
CALLG/CALLS	/19	1/8	/2	8/2	4/2	/2
CLR(B,W,L,Q)	9	5		19	15	5
CVTW(L)/CMP(L,W)	/8	/16		13/11	17/9	9/5
INC(B,L)/INDEX	1/11	1/10	2/6	1/		2/
JMP/JSB				9/17	3/10	1/1
MOVA(B,W,L)/MOV(B,W,L)	3/36	13/27	6/9	36/63	18/32	1/9
MCOML		16				
MOVC3/MOVZ(BW,BL,WL)		8/3		/8	4/8	
MULL(2,3)/NOP	/12	4/7	/9	8/	8/	
PERROR/PTRAP		1/3				
PUSH(AB,AL,L)	41	16	2	8	6	2
RET	1	1	1	3	3	1
SUB(L2,L3,W3)	2	3	3	7	4	3
TST(L,W)	3	1	3	3	1	4

Preliminary Observations

The most obvious observation was the lack of efficient support for LISP on conventional architectures. For example, garbage collection operation was time consuming on the MicroVAX II. Garbage collection is very important for LISP environment and the problem will even be greater for more complex problems. Other major observations are:

- We can use any HLL to code AI problems. The strength of LISP is not only in the data structures; LISP is a valuable tool during the development phase of software because it can be interpreted and used interactively.
- The instructions that are generated varied between HLPLs; this supports the idea of HLL directed architectures such as the LISP machines.

- Most of the instructions generated by each of the compilers are simple instructions. The use of RISC systems may be a viable choice.
- The selection of HLLs to code AI algorithms is important but efficiency is more dependent on programmers experience about the problem to be solved, the architecture to be used, and the ability to select algorithms and implementation strategies that will yield the best performance. In other words, efficiency is more dependent on the activities that are performed within the programmer's domain.
- Compiler optimizations can contribute to execution and storage usage efficiency but compiler optimizations cannot compensate for lack of efficient algorithms and implementation strategies.

4. AI INFLUENCE ON HARDWARE

The advances in technology, successes from the exploratory phase of AI, and the realization of lack of adequate support for LISP on conventional machines were the major factors that led to the design of LISP machines. LISP machines are designed to efficiently support the creating, executing, and debugging of programs written in LISP. The lack of adequate support of LISP on conventional machines was a consequence of the semantic gap between LISP structures and conventional hardware. Any closing of this semantic gap was expected to improve computational efficiency. One of the objectives for the design of LISP machines was to reduce the semantic gap between the structures of hardware and LISP. In the earlier stage of AI evolution, execution speed was not a major concern; rather, the concern was finding out what was theoretically and practically realizable. There was also emphasis on how quickly prototype solutions could be developed. But as AI researchers tackle more complex problems and AI products are been commercialized, there is a need for faster computers with large memory space. New architectures were and are being designed and proposed in order to meet these needs.

4.1. LISP Machines

The major objective of the designers of the LISP machines was to design hardware and software that will efficiently support the developement, execution, and debugging of both system and application software written in LISP. LISP machine designs started at MIT's AI laboratory in 1974 with the design of CONS. This was followed by the design of CADR in 1978. The machine was a single user computer implemented with a specialized processor. Some of the key primitives of LISP were implemented directly in hardware or firmware. The major design objective of the machine were :

1. improved performance
2. reduced cost, and
3. better microprogram debugging.

The MIT machines eventually led to the development and design of other LISP machines. The MIT LISP machine was licensed to LISP Machines Inc., (LMI) and Symbolics [17].

One of the pioneers in the design of LISP machines is Xerox. The work of Xerox researchers has had influence on the commercialization of LISP machines. The earlier design efforts at Xerox PARC inspired other designers of LISP machines; Xerox earlier designs included the DORADO and DOLPHIN. The first Commercial LISP machine was probably the Xerox 1100 series introduced in 1981. Other earlier LISP machines included the Symbolics 3600, LAMBDA (both introduced in 1983); and in 1984 Tektronix 4400 series, and Texas Instruments (TI) explorer were introduced. Some research-based designs are SPUR, and Smalltalk on RISC (SOAR). These machines/processors addressed the performance and memory limitations of early LISP implementations on conventional architectures such as DEC system-10 and DEC system-20 families of time-shared machines. The LISP machines attempt to close the semantic gap between LISP and conventional architectures. Several issues guided the design of these LISP machines and some design issues are unique to some of the LISP machines. LISP machines must address the following issues [28]:

1. heap maintenance
2. environment maintenance
3. efficient list representation
4. fast function calls

These issues were addressed with various implementation strategies; these strategies include:

1. Implementation of instruction sets that are geared to frequent LISP operations.
2. Tagged architecture and pointer encoding.

3. Some form of hardware support for memory management (garbage collection).
4. Some form of function-to-function calling protocol allowing dynamic redefinitions.

A brief description of the features of some of these LISP machines/processors is given below.

Symbolics 3600

The first Symbolics LISP machine, LM-2, was introduced in 1981; the LM-2 was a commercial version of the MIT LISP machine [25]. The Symbolics 3600, introduced in 1983, was a successor to the LM-2 and it was two to eight times as powerful as the LM-2. The Symbolics 3600 has a stack based tagged architecture, and some LISP functions such as MEMBER and CAR are directly implemented in hardware or firmware. The Symbolics 3600 provides hardware support for about thirty-four data types including integers, symbols, list calls, complex numbers, arrays, floating point, and rational numbers. The Symbolics 3600 direct support for LISP can be summarized into six specific areas [30]:

1. Hardware and firmware support for data types as stated earlier.
2. Hardware support for garbage collection; each memory page has an associated page-tag that indicates if that page contains pointers to memory areas of interest to the garbage collector [28].
3. Hardware implemented generic operations (tagged architecture).
4. LISP primitives implemented directly in hardware or firmware as stated earlier.
5. Stack with virtual buffer capability; there are function return instructions that allow the return of multiple values.
6. Demand-paged multi-level virtual memory 28 bit addressing with a 36–bit pointer stored into a 36–bit word, eight extra bits are used for distinguishing data types and also for memory management activities.

The Symbolics 3600 had more functions implemented in hardware than LM-2.

4.2. RISC Architectures

Most of the LISP machines are based on CISC architectures. But there have been few processors designed to support AI languages, mostly LISP and in at least one case Smalltalk, that are based of RISC architectures. Three of these processors are SOAR, SPUR, and MIPS-X. A brief description of SOAR follows.

SOAR This processor was also designed at Berkeley. The objective of the designer was to come up with an architecture that can execute programs written in Smalltalk better than current VLSI microcomputers [36]. SOAR was defined as a stack-based virtual machine with register windows to support function calls. Each window has eight registers for local variables; on the other hand, each window for RISC II has twelve registers for local variables. Statistical data showed that Smalltalk uses fewer local variables than C. Operations that generally slow down the execution of programs written in Smalltalk were identified and supported. These operations include: type checking, object oriented storage management, and procedure calls. SOAR does not support byte-addressing like RISC I. There are separate instructions for extracting or inserting bytes from words. Each SOAR instruction is 32 bits long and most instructions, with the exception of load, return, and store operations, require only one cycle. The purpose of tags in SOAR is to improve performance; this is in contrast with traditional objectives which are to catch errors and support implementation of generic instructions. Each SOAR instruction has a bit that either enables or disables tag checking. Untagged instruction will allow programs written in imperative languages such as C and Pascal to run on SOAR. SOAR is claimed to be the first architecture with tagged and untagged versions of its instructions[36].

4.3. Parallel/Multiprocessor Architectures

Most of the LISP directed architectures are based on uniprocessing with control flow mechanism. But more and more multiprocessing systems are being introduced. The MIPS-X was designed for general purpose multiprocessing in a shared memory environment. Designs have shown that six to eight processors may share the same memory without noticeable performance degradation because of bus contention [18]. The SPUR was also designed for parallel processing.

SPUR This Processor was developed at Berkeley as a project to extend the philosophy of RISCs I and II (RISCs I and II were the first two processors designed at Berkeley to demonstrate the viability of RISC design principles). SPUR was designed to support LISP while RISCs I and II were designed based on statistical data collected on programs written in C and Pascal. The major difference between RISC II and SPUR lies with SPUR's implementation of more functions in hardware. These functions included hardware tags (register is 40 bit wide, 32 bit for data and 8 bit for tag), support for conditional branches beyond RISC II provisions, parallel type checking on CAR and CDR operations, run-time checking for integer arithmetic and garbage collection. Register windows, 138 registers with 32 registers per window similar to those implemented in RISCs I and II, were implemented so that the overhead associated with register save and restore during function calls and returns could be minimized. SPUR implemented more complex operations in hardware than most RISC architectures. This increase in hardware support was the consequence of the design objective to support LISP. SPUR has three custom CMOS chips: the cache controller, CPU, and floating-point processor [20].

MIPS-X This processor was designed at Stanford University. It was a successor to an earlier design, MIPS (Multiprocessor without Interlocking Pipeline Stages). It has RISC features such as simple instruction set with single-cycle execution for each instruction, and Load and Store architecture (only load and store operations can access the memory, all other operations are performed in registers). But it has only 32–general purpose registers (no overlap windows like the SPUR). There is also a small, 512 word, on-chip instruction cache. There is only one addressing mode (base plus displacement). MIPS-X uses software for tag checking [32].

For a small number of processors, the processing rates of multiprocessors are scalable on the number of active processors per system. Processors such as SPUR and MIPS-X, that were designed with multiprocessing as part of their architecture design criteria, have advantages over general purpose microprocessors such as the MC68030 and Intel 86386 when they are used to build multiprocessing systems. One of the advantages is ease of interface between processors. Technological advancement made it possible to have more transistors on the SPUR as compared to RISC II. The additional transistors were used for an on-chip instructions cache, tagging for LISP data, and a low-overhead interface to a floating-point coprocessor [20]. There will be more discussion on other types of architectures that have been proposed or designed to support AI in the next section.

The development of LISP machines was supplemented with the development of tools for the rapid and incremental development of AI software. LISP, by nature, is an interactive language but compiled code can be executed faster, in most cases, than interpreted code. The availability of LISP machines must be supported with the appropriate tools that will allow for the improved progam organization, editing, and debugging than on conventional systems. But the execution speed of AI programs has also improved on conventional, by and large, due to the advances in AI tools. There are better compilers for LISP today than in the 1970s and early 1980s. The improvement of execution speed on conventional systems has been countered with the need to solve more complex problems. LISP, in particular, requires a different programming environment than conventional languages. For the LISP environment, interactive tools are very important to programmers exploring the structure of programs with which they are not familiar and for maintaining large software. We will have more to say in the next section concerning the differences between conventional and AI software.

5. FUTURE TRENDS IN AI LANGUAGES AND ARCHITECTURES

One viable way to attempt to forecast the future languages and architectures is to look at current languages, architectures, and AI demands as we currently know them. Most of the resources required by AI researchers are due to researchers' efforts to solve more complex problems, and integrate different AI branches into functioning systems. There is also the need to integrate AI software with conventional software, and to continue research in design of architectures that will result in improved cost/performance ratio of AI computing systems. The ultimate goal is to build intelligent systems.

5.1. Selecting HLLs

LISP is the oldest AI language and the most popular within the AI community in the U.S., but PROLOG is also growing in popularity. In addition to LISP and PROLOG, there are many other languages that have been used for one reason or the other in one or more projects of importance. As we have stated earlier, future systems will consist of both conventional and AI software. There are many reasons why a particular language is selected for a given project and some of these reasons are:

1. Ease of use.
2. Availability of experts for the particular language.
3. Concern for the development and maintenance cost of programs.

4. Compatibility with other software.
5. Popularity of a language.
6. Execution efficiency.

These are just a few of the reasons why a language may be favored over other languages. The importance of each criteria will vary from project to project. For example, in some cases, cost could be the major criteria used to select a language.

Uniqueness of AI Software

There are four basic categories of HLLs — imperative, production, declarative, and object-oriented. Conventional languages such as Ada, Pascal, FORTRAN, COBOL, BASIC, and so on, are generally referred to as imperative languages. Languages such as LISP and PROLOG are referred to as declarative languages. These two languages can further be classified as functional (LISP) and logic (PROLOG) languages. The advantages of imperative languages include the facts that more people are familiar with one or more of these HLLs, and programs written in one of these HLLs can usually run efficiently on conventional architectures. The basic differences between conventional software (usually written in imperative HLLs) and AI software (usually written in declarative, production, or object-oriented HLLs) are listed in Table 6 [17].

AI problem solving is usually guided by empirical rules — trial and error, and rules of thumb — which are called heuristics [17]. Domain knowledge is used extensively in AI programs and the controls that guide searches are usually separated from its domain knowledge. AI languages attempt to stay away or minimize any form of side effects. This is unlike conventional programs that can cause ripple effects when changes are made in one part of a program. In conventional programs, domain knowledge and control mechanism are intermixed. A detailed, precise and absolute, step by step algorithm is required in solving a problem to be coded in one of the imperative HLLs. Recursive algorithms are commonly used in AI programs; on the other hand, iterative and loop constructs are more common in conventional programs.

Table 6 Major Differences between AI and Conventional Software

AI	Conventional
Control structure usually separate from domain knowledge	Information and control are usually integrated
Mostly symbolic processing	Mostly numeric processing
Heuristic search (solutions are not implicit, deal with ill-defined knowledge structures)	Algorithmic (solution steps are explicit, predict with certainty all possible situations)
Satisfactory answers are usually acceptable	Best possible solution is usually sought
Some incorrect answers are tolerated	Precise answeres are required
Programs are frequently modified; they must be easy to modify, update, and enlarge	Programs are difficult to modify; so, they are not frequently modified
Recursive routines are commonly used	Nonrecursive routines are more common ; some HLLs do not support recursion

AI programs deal with concepts, sentences, and words; results are often not guaranteed to be correct, but results that are not totally correct are acceptable just as in human problem solving environments [17]. AI programs are sometimes written for problems that are complex, uncertain, and ambiguous, and for which there is no well defined solution. Most of the programs written for AI are almost always of an experimental and evolutionary in nature. Development time and cost of AI programs are expected to be higher than that of conventional programs. Tools and environments for developing, executing, and debugging AI programs require a special purpose support in contrast to conventional programs which can be developed, executed, and debugged on general purpose systems.

Declarative HLLs

Most conventional (imperative) languages lack the essentials to be effective as AI language because they were not designed with AI needs as their principal concern. AI languages are designed specifically for symbol processing and the initial designs of some of these languages have poor support for arithmetic, interative, and array processing. The declarative, production , and object-oriented languages were designed with needs of a branch or multiple branches of AI in mind. In some instances, new ideas in AI can result in the design and introduction of a new language that can be used to code algorithms in a natural manner. LISP and PROLOG are the major languages that represent functional and logic programming paradigms, respectively. The terms functional-, applicative-, dataflow-, and reduction languages are used interchangeably. Declarative languages are expected to alleviate the software crisis, and make programming and program understanding much easier [7]. For instance, functional programming is expected to relieve today's twin crisis of AI-oriented computing:

1. the need to reduce the cost of software, and
2. the need to find computer designs that make much better use of the opportunities provided by VLSI and parallelism.

Declarative languages give programmers the capability to define a problem's solution without been entangled with the detailed instructions of how the solution is to be formulated. Programs written in declarative languages can be shorter, more concise, more powerful, and understandable compared to programs written in imperative languages [31].

Object-Oriented and Production System HLLs

One of the major reasons for the introduction of object-oriented programming was to simplify AI programming. Smalltalk is an example of object-oriented language. Programs are represented as objects and messages. Smalltalk introduces the notion of data abstraction and inheritance. Smalltalk allows objects to perform their own computations and send messages to each other [15]. Smalltalk provides a complete programming tool kit and programs can be developed interactively. Smalltalk is often used for rapid prototyping, expert systems, and many other AI applications [15]. OPS — Official Production System — was developed at CMU in the mid 1970's. OPS was developed as an outgrowth of research done in psychology for understanding human memory and cognition. The OPS model offers an important link between strong and weak heuristics methods for problem solving; production systems provide the means to encode human expertise in the form of rules and designing pattern-driven search algorithm [24]. Many versions of OPSS (a version of OPS) are implemented in LISP and they are usually implemented as an interactive, general programming environment [15]. OPS has been used effectively in writing expert systems and many other AI applications. For example, XCON an expert system developed by Digital is written in OPSS. OPS is a viable language for any type of rule-based application.

5.2. Future AI HLLs

In brief, trends in HLL designs can by classified into one of three groups [33]:

1. Move to succinctness by having more powerful operators. APL is a prime example in this class of languages.
2. Move to generalized structures by having everything for everybody. These are HLLs that can be classified as general purpose languages such as PL/I, and Ada. These languages are, normally, designed by committees.
3. Move to specialization by having only the attributes that a language need to efficiently support the coding of programs in a given application domain. PROLOG is an example in this class of languages. Future AI languages will take this route.

The future AI environments will have multiple HLLs from all current programming paradigms — imperative, functional, logic, production system, and object-oriented. AI language must provide three capabilities: action, description, and reasoning. There is no language that is strong in all three areas. For instance, PROLOG is a reasoning-oriented language but it is not strong in description and action. LISP, on the other hand, has some features of conventional languages. New languages have been developed to combine the strengths of LISP and PROLOG. LOGLISP and QUTE are two of these languages [37]. There are also versions of PROLOG (PARLOG, and Concurrent PROLOG), and LISP (Concurrent LISP) developed in order to allow for natural parallel programming.

AI programs are usually large and complex, and they are exploratory by nature. Five of the attributes that AI languages must process are: support for symbolic processing, flexibility of control, tools to support exploratory programming, late binding and constraint propagation, and a well-defined semantics [24]. The language must also support modularity, be extensible, use high-level constructs, support prototyping, program must be readable, and provision for interpreted and compiled modes. There's no language that meet all these requirements, but current AI languages (logic, functional, object-oriented, and system production) meet more of these requirements than imperative languages. But imperative languages will be used in most of the software that will be available in the near future. Some of the reasons for this are:

1. Automatic conversion of programs from one language to another will be available, e.g., C to LISP, Fortran to ADA, etc. [12].
2. A large audience is using imperative languages while many AI languages such as Q3, PLANNER, MICROPLANNER, CONNIVER, KRL, NETL, SIAL, POP-2, and FUZZY are not widely used or available beyond AI researchers community.
3. There are facilities to include or call functions written in one programming paradigm from a different programming paradigm. Programs written in C can be called from programs written in LISP.
4. Conventional and AI software will be integrated, and for a given installation, the AI software may be a small portion of the entire software system.

We think LISP and PROLOG will remain the work horse of AI programming. In our environment, where there are no AI architectures, conventional languages may be used to write AI-related problems. Languages developed for AI will be more of a specialized languages rather than a general purpose language. The future of AI software will be very dependent on the availability of sophisticated compilers and interpreters for AI languages, operating system with facilities for supporting parallel processing, development of techniques to obtain, code and access knowledge, and better software engineering methodology for developing and maintaining large and complex software. We must develop tools that will give programmers and users the appearance that they are working with a knowledgeable assistant. Tools are the key to the future of AI software.

5.3. Trends in AI Hardware

The usual trend in computing is for advances in technology to be used to design new and more powerful computers, and then for software to find means to make the best use of the resources that are available on the new computers. The introduction of LISP machines was a dramatic change from the conventional trend; architectures were specifically designed to support a language, LISP in this case. As AI products move out of the laboratory into the commercial world, and as AI researchers get closer to realizing the goal of building an intelligent system, it is obvious that conventional architectures will not be adequate to handle and execute the enormous amount of information that must be processed. All AI software will not require faster speed and larger memory, but some AI programs are complex and most of these complex problems require faster speed and larger memory. We have to move from uniprocessor and sequential architectures to multiprocessors and parallel architectures. LISP machines are simply a stepping stone. Future architectures will have to be homogenous systems with capabilities for distributed processing.

The computational needs of many branches of AI such as vision, pattern recognition, speech understanding, and machine learning are great. Some AI problems are NP-complete. The computational consumption for these problems grow exponentially with problem size. A prime example of a problem with NP-complete characteristics is the TS problem discussed earlier. Solutions to this type of problems will result in combinatorial explosion (amount of time needed to solve a problem will grow exponentially with data size). This combinatorial explosion is obvious by looking at Figure 3 [2]. The execution times for five, six, seven, eight, nine, ten, and eleven cities for the TS problem are 0.27, 0.35, 0.62, 1.88, 8.59, 45.13, and 320.47 seconds respectively. AI researchers are putting their efforts into finding solutions that will delay the explosion (have the time-versus-problem-size curve grow linearly for a longer period of time). The goal is to delay, as long as possible, the combinatorial explosion.

Massively Parallel Architectures

There are several proposals, some of which have actually been designed and are functioning, for massively parallel architectures. Most conventional architectures use a single instruction single data (SISD) computational model. This model is inadequate for many reasons; two of these reasons are:

1. The physical speed limit of electronic devices is dictated by the basic limit set by the laws of physics. Signal propagation in a machine can approach 2/3 the speed of light. Different technologies may be used to get this limit but that is about all we can do right now.
2. The structural limitations caused by the current design technique of separating memory from the CPU and the sequential control unit. This problem becomes more pronounced as memories and problem sizes increase.

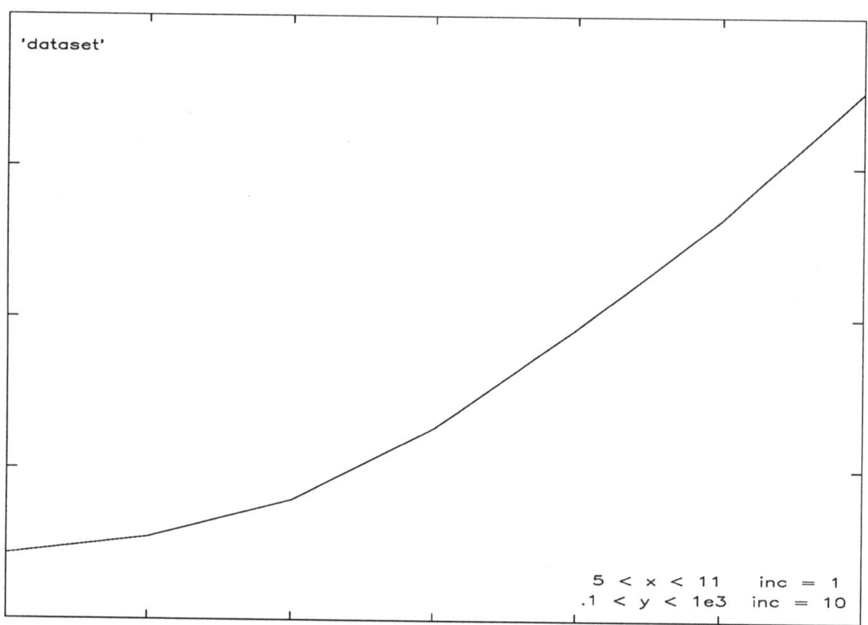

Figure 3 Logarithmic graph demonstrating exponential growth in execution time for TS Problem

In order to improve execution speed, a single instruction multiple data (SIMD) model is used. The ILLIAC IV, IBM GF11, CRAY series, and CDC Cyber 205 are prime examples. To further improve execution speed and to introduce "true" parallelism, multiple instruction multiple data (MIMD) computational model is used. The MIMD can further be classified as a model with a private memory (each processing element, PE, having their own memory; this is also referred to as loosely coupled processors) or a model with a shared memory (all PEs access the same memory, also referred to as tightly coupled processors). The model with a private memory is also referred to as message passing model. There is also a control mechanism that is distinguishable in addition to data mechanism. The four control mechanisms are control driven (von Neumann architectures), pattern-driven, demand-driven, and data-driven (dataflow architectures). These control mechanisms are listed in order of less explicit control. The data and control mechanisms and some of the languages available in some of the models are listed in Table 7 [3].

	Data Mechanisms and some Languages	
Control	**Shared Memory**	**Distributed Memory**
Control driven	[von Neumann machines] FORTRAN, COBOL, Ada, APL, PL/I, Pascal, C, Modula, Concurrent Pascal, Multilisp	[Communicating Process] CSP, Ada, Occam
Pattern driven	[logic] PROLOG	[actors] Actors
Demand driven	[graph reduction]	[string reduction] FP(functional programming), SASL, LISP
Data driven	[dataflow I-structure]	[dataflow tokens] VAL, ID, SISAL, LAU, LUCID, VALID

Table 7 Computational Models

Concurent Pascal and Multilisp are Pascal and Lisp versions with parallel constructs. Occam was the language on which Transputer, a CMOS processor designed for implementing multiprocessing systems, design was based. Most of the languages listed under von Neumann are widely used; on the other hand the other languages, especially those listed under demand-driven and data-driven are not. The driving force behind these alternatives to control driven architectures and imperative languages is the need to extract parallelism both in hardware and software. AI is probably receiving the most intense attention in terms of architectural designs. One of the reasons for this attention is the belief that AI represents the cornerstone of the next (fifth) generation computers. The fifth generation computers (FGC) is exemplified by the FGCP in Japan. The goals of FGCP include:

1. Develop a new generation of computers based on logic that are thousands or millions of times faster than conventional computers in doing symbolic processing.
2. Implement basic mechanisms for retrieving and managing a knowledge base in hardware and software.
3. Accept inputs and produce outputs in the form of pictures, diagrams, speech, and conventional means (better person-machine interface).
4. Automatic internal indexing, reasoning, and learning.
5. Develop supporting environments to alleviate the "software crisis" and enhance programmers productivity.

The FGCP is based on logic and Prolog is the language of choice. But there are other researchers who believe that the FGCP should be based on an evolutionary approach rather than revolutionary approach. These researchers believe that control driven, with which we have had more experience, can be built to meet our needs by finding solutions to the problems that plague current control driven architectures.

There must be technological advancements in four major areas- AI, software engineering, VLSI, and architectures- in order to realize the goals of the FGCs. There must be progress in several areas of AI including vision/image processing, language processing/speech recognition, machine learning, knowledge-based expert systems, and knowledge acquisition, representation, and accessing. Several architectures have been designed or proposed to meet the needs of these diverse but related branches of AI. The basic approaches that are followed in designing AI architectures are shown in Figure 4 [4, 22].

LANGUAGE-/SOFTWARE-BASED ARCHITECTURES

- List-Processing (LISP)-based Architectures
(SPUR, Symbolic 3600 Series, LMI Lambda, Xerox 1100 Series, TI Explorer...)
- Prolog-based Architectures
(PIM [FGCP], PIE, PLM (Aquarius),...)
- Functional Programming-based Architectures
(Rediflow, ALICE, C-LISP Machine, FFP...)

KNOWLEDGE-BASED ARCHITECTURES

- Semantic-Network-based Architectures
(NETL, Connection Machine, Thistel,...)
- Rule-based Architectures
(DADO, PSM, NON-VON,...)
- Object-based Architectures
SOAR, iAPX432, Dragon, FAIM-1...)
- Nerual-network-based Architectures
(Boltzmann, Neural circuits,...)

INTELLIGENT-INTERFACE-BASED ARCHITECTURES

- Speech-Recongnition-based Architectures
(Harpy, HEARSAY, NEC DP-100,...)
- Pattern-Recognition/Image-Recognition-based Architectures
(PIPE, PUMPS, ZMOB, Tospics,...)
- Computer-Vision-based Architectures
(WARP, HERMES, TALOS, Butterfly, VICOM-VME,...)

Figure 4 Design Approaches to AI Computer Architectures

Language-/Software-based Architectures

Most of our earlier discussions of LISP machines fall into the category of list-processing (LISP) architectures. The architectures listed under Prolog-based architectures are not as mature as those for LISP machines. The selection of

PROLOG for the FGCP will improve and increase the activities on PROLOG-based architectures. The Aquarius architecture was conceived as a project to determine how a large improvement in performance can be achieved in a system dedicated to solve some difficult problems. These problems consist of both numerical intensive calculations and substantial symbolic manipulations; both problems will have an algorithm that requires computing over a search space [9]. Aquarius is a heterogeneous MIMD machine with each PE tailored to the requirements of the intended applications. Initially, each PE will be a floating point processor, parallel PROLOG processor, or an I/O processor. The system uses a restricted dataflow control mechanism. The first experimental processor of this project was the programmed logic machine (PLM). PLM was attached to the NCR/32 processor which acted as the host. The design of PLM was based on PROLOG and it had a tagged architecture. The designers of Aquarius adopted a unique design by having a three tier system:

1. The programming logic level of control at the top.
2. Control driven architecture in the middle.
3. Fine granularity dataflow at the bottom.

Functional Programming-based Architectures Rediflow is an hybrid architecture that combines control driven, dataflow, and data driven mechanisms. The designers felt that in a given problem, there could be a large portion that is sequential in nature and the control driven mechanism will be more appropriate for that segment of the program. The Rediflow was to be an interconnected set of private memory processors. A global address was provided to support the pointer mechanism used by the graph reduction model. The design is similar to the transputer's arrangements (they called it Xputer — a processor, a memory, and a moderately intelligent switch that ties together with its four neighbors in a rectangular mesh) [3]. The system uses message passing to communicate with processors in other nodes. Rediflow has a feature that enables it to perform dynamic load balancing. The system was to have medium-grain parallelism and could have between 100 and 10,000 processors.

ALICE (Applicative Language Idealized Computing Engine) is a general purpose multi-processor parallel production system based on an extended graph reduction model. ALICE was designed to provide direct support for expression substitution model of computation that are used in declarative languages. ALICE can also support imperative languages even though HOPE was the language that influenced the design of ALICE the most. The prototype of ALICE was a desktop that could run about 100 times faster than conventional machine with comparable complexity (assuming that the problems being solved have high degree of parallelism). ALICE was to be based on the Transputer using 112 Transputer chips [31].

Semantic-based Architectures

The connection machine was designed to manipulate knowledge stored in semantic networks in parallel. Although the prototype, CM-1, was designed for the stated purposes, the designer, Thinking Machines Corporation, realized that the machine could be used as a general purpose computer. The prototype had 65,536 1–bit processors and another system was to have 100,000 processors. Connection machine can be viewed as a design that tries to correct the bottleneck problem (one big processor and one big memory) by having a large number of small processors distributed throughout the memory. Other views see connection machines as a system that pushes parallelism to its limit and as a model of the brain with a highly parallel collection of slow processes. C, LISP, and FORTRAN are available for the CM-1. These languages have been extended to allow parallelism. A floating-point processor has been added to every two node points on the CM-2 which is a successor to the CM-1. This addition of floating-point processors seems to be a realization that AI architectures must provide for floating-point operations even though most AI operations require symbolic processing. The floating-point processors were expected to be able to have a peak of 2.5GFLOPs; actual experiments have shown only 1GFLOPs [3]. NETL was an earlier system designed to perform operations similar to the ones that CM-1 was designed. NETL uses marker passing (1–bit markers) but the Connection Machine uses true message passing. The processors in the Connection Machine are more powerful than those in NETL.

Rule-based Architectures

DADO is a fine-grain, parallel, tree-structured MIMD parallel processor designed to efficiently support the execution of expert system, as well as multiple and independent systems. Tree interconnection schemes offer simplicity and are well suited to the layout of VLSI chips [3]. Its major disadvantage is the possibility of traffic jams at the root if there is a great deal of communication among PEs located at the tree's leaves. DADO2 has 1023 PEs based on the Intel 8751, a 1–chip 8–bit microcomputer. A commercial version of this can have between 3 and 8191 PEs; each PE is a 32–bit Motorola 68020 [3]. Each PE can operate in one of two modes, SIMD or MIMD, at any given instance under software control. Some of the languages that are available on DADO are OPS5, and parallel versions of C, FORTRAN, and LISP. The NON-VON is also a massively parallel tree-structured architecture with capabilities to efficiently support relational database operations. NON-VON uses small PEs similar to those used for the CM-1 Connection machines. The PEs are custom-designed, each VLSI chip can hold between 8 and 16 of the small PEs. This system can operate as SIMD, multiple SIMD or MIMD.

Object-based Architectures

We have discussed SOAR (Smalltalk on a RISC) which is a uniprocessor for Smalltalk. iAPX 432 was designed by Intel to support object-oriented languages; the design of iAPX 432 was specifically based on Ada. iAPX 432 is a CISC processor with stack and three address instruction. The design can support multiprocessor configurations. The FAIM-1 is a multiprocessing system designed to significantly improve the performance of AI systems. The goal of the designers was to have a system that is about 100 times faster than conventional machines such as VAX 11/780. The design of FAIM-1 was driven both by AI needs and desire to have an affordable system that is cost-effective. The design includes a language (OIL), programming environment, an architecture, and a resource allocation strategy. FAIM-1's objective was to take advantage of parallelism at all levels. OIL can be looked upon as the machine language for FAIM-1 and also as a concurrent high-level symbolic processing language. Programs written in OIL are a collection of objects that communicate through messages with the level of parallelism specified in the message. OIL has attributes that are available in several languages such as LISP and PROLOG. The computational model on which OIL was based was directly supported in hardware. The system has a stack-based tagged architecture. FAIM-1 supports memory management with hardware to relieve the system's software of this time consuming and frequently performed task.

Neural-Network-based Architectures

Most of the massively parallel architectures available today are digital multiprocessor (symbolic) systems. The other type of architectures, those that qualify to be categorized under the Neural-network-based architectures, are analog neural network systems (non-symbolic) [16]. One of the problems that continues to plague symbolic-based (digital) computers used for solving AI problems is the combinatorial explosion. The current supercomputers cannot, in a timely fashion, solve large NP-complete problems. It is expected that solutions to some intractable AI problems, which are presently not solvable on conventional systems, may be solved with the successes of neural networks research. The Boltzmann architecture was designed to support efficient searches for combinations of hypotheses that maximally satisfy some input data and some stored constraints [14]. The architecture uses value-passing capability and probabilistic PEs.

Speech-Recognition-based Architectures

In the early 1970's, the Defense Advanced Research Project Agency (DARPA) initiated several projects to develop speech-understanding systems [34]. The goals of the project include: design systems that would be able to accept continuous speech from several speakers, systems should require minimum training by each speaker, and system should be able to operate on 100–word vocabulary with less than 10–percent semantic error rate. The computing system to support this project must be able to perform 100 million instructions per second. Harpy and Hearsay-II were two of the systems that met the goals set for the project. It is anticipated that in the future, processor that can process a billion instructions per second would be available; this would enhance the chance of having "true" continuous speech recognition systems.

Pattern-Recognition/Image-processing-based Architectures

The Pipelined Image-Processing Engine (PIPE) is a multistage pipelined image-processing system for research in vision [23]. The input to this system can come from many sources such as analog or digital television cameras. Sequences of images can be processed in real time and output can be sent to devices such as monitors, robot vision systems, and image-processing machines. The system is designed with two pipelines to perform local neighborhood operations on iconic images. The first pipeline is that of images that proceed from PE to PE, and the other pipeline is for the neighborhoods within each PE. PIPE is a SIMD but can also act in a limited way as MIMD. PUMP is another system, a multiuser system in which many task-processing units are allocated from a pool. Each PE is tailored to a specific task, and images are processed by passing them through a series of various PEs. PIPE, on the other hand, is made up of series of identical stages that can perform many different operations on images. Cytocomputer is a system that has many things in common with PIPE. It performs neighborhood and table look-up operations, but does not have many of the other features that PIPE has. It cannot process more than one image in an operation. The system has proved to be very useful for low-level image processing [23].

The Pyramid is a SIMD made up of a pyramidal array of PEs that are attached to a general-purpose computer. Each PE is connected to 13 other elements, comprising of four children at a level below, its parent at the level above, and the remaining eight are the neighbors at the same pyramid level. The direct link to the four children is an advantage for Pyramid over PIPE in terms of faster communications for the Pyramid. Another system, ZMOB, is a more general parallel processor. It has 256 processors connected by a ring-shaped high-speed communications system. The communications link combine both cross-bar and broadcast media. The speed of the communications link make each processor seem to be connected to each other. ZMOB is an MIMD with private memory. Each PE is a Z-80 processor, each of which has 62K RAM of memory, 2K EPROM, hardware multiply, floating point processor, and serial and parallel communication ports [38]. Due to the small amount of memory available to each processor and for the lack of shared memory the host computer must play an important role to compensate for this. ZMOB allows different computations to be performed at the same time, on the same or on different data. For image processing, images are usually broken up into parts and distributed to different PEs. ZMOB is more powerful than PIPE, but PIPE is more suited (specialized) to its task of processing low-level images.

Computer-Vision-based Architectures

The design of architectures for vision is very important to the future success of AI research and applications. The goal of AI researchers, to build an intelligent machine, cannot be achieved without a vision system. The architectures for vision systems must provide large amount of storage, and faster execution speed than current general purpose computers. The required speed can be provided by specialized parallel architectures. Current vision processing units can be classified as bit-serial processors or multibit-multiprocessors. The bit-serial systems, such as WARP, are SIMD machines. They require a powerful host to do miscellaneous tasks including input-output operations [4]. The Warp is a one-dimensional systolic array with a 32–bit processor for each cell. Each Warp can have ten or more identical cells. Each cell is implemented as a programmable horizontal microengine with its own sequencer and a control store of 8K instructions [3]. Two floating point processors (Weitek 32–bit PE) were used. Each cell can transfer as much as 80MBytes in a second to and from its immediate neighbors. A ten-cell Warp was reported to have processed 1024–point complex Fast Fourier Transforms (FFT) at a rate of one FFT every 600 microseconds [3]. The multibit—multiprocessor systems are MIMD machines. Some of these systems, such as FLIP and PIPE, also rely on host computers or coprocessors to perform various miscellaneous tasks, others such as DIAS and HERMES do not have a host computer[4]. HERMES has a RISC-based bit-sliced systolic array architecture with three structural levels of processors: low-level with 8–bit processors, mid-level with 16–bit processors, and high—level with 32–bit processors. One of the uniqune attribute of HERMES is the feature that allows image data to be read in parallel. An elaborate discussion of HERMES and references to some vision systems such as PICAP, GOP, TALOS, HOMOGENEOUS, etc are given in [4, 19, 5]. Future vision systems must definitely address the problems associated with 3–D configurations. Parallel systems utilizing the speed advantage of RISC processors, like the HERMES, will play an important role in future vision systems.

5.4. Future Computing Needs

There is agreement among scientists that future computing needs will require parallel architectures. The development of future computing needs will be influenced by advances in microelectronics, exploiting these advances in microelectronics to design parallel architectures, and building software that provide parallelisms and significant intelligence.

Architectures

Most of today's computers are based on uniprocess or designed for sequential and deterministic numerical computations. Next generation computers, which will have AI as their foundation, will require parallel and distributed processing with decentralized control. The future architectures will be homogeneous computers with various control mechanisms. Some part of the future computing architectures are represented by the FGCP and other similar projects in Europe (European Strategic Program for Research in Information Technologies, ESPRIT); the British project on software engineering, intelligent knowledge based systems, VLSI circuitry, and man-machine interfaces; U.S. (Microelectronics and Computer Technology Corporation, and DARPA Strategic Computing and Survivability). Each of these projects have their own national flavors and there is no agreement as to the strategy to follow. The only common ground is that architectures will support parallelism; MIMD will be supported in contrast to the SIMD architectures that are common on most of the current supercomputers. The architectures will also support symbolic processing because processors must deal with operations involving sentences, speech, images, graphics, and so on. For instance, the FGCP will consist of many integrated systems including the following [37]:

1. Input — user language that include speech, natural language, picture graph, etc.
2. Software system — Intelligent Programming System and knowledge-based programming system that will utilize logic programming language and knowledge representation language.
3. Architecture — problem solving inference machine and knowledge-based machine. These two machines will be represented by symbol manipulation machine, numerical computation machine, and database machine.

Two approaches that have been advocated for the design of future architectures are [34]:

1. Design a general purpose parallel architecture and figure out how to match different algorithms to the machine's structures. This is similar to the approach taken in designing most conventional architectures.
2. First design parallel algorithms and then design the architectures to execute these algorithms efficiently.

Either of these approaches can also be adapted with a revolutionary or evolutionary strategy. The revolutionary strategy is based on the assumptions that [35] :

1. Knowledge-base expert system will be an important application area in the 1990's and beyond.
2. The most effective machine language for expert system is logic programming.

3. Knowledge processing requires parallel processing for high-performance.
4. Fifth generation computing will be completely different from conventional computing (sequential, and centralized controlled computing).

This strategy is supported by AI and academic computing communities and this is the strategy choosing for the FGCP. The second strategy is based on evolutionary approach that will build on and enhance current architectures. This strategy is based on the assumption that [34]:

1. Communication and cooperation of heterogenous processors and processes will be the important concern in the 1990's.
2. The most primitive, general, and most understood general form of computation is the control flow mechanism.
3. Decentralized processing will require recursive structuring of computer systems.
4. Fifth generation computing will be an extension of current systems with efforts to correct current known problems.

This strategy is supported by the data communications and microelectronics industries. The major concern is how to connect heterogenous PEs in a decentralized system.

It seems logical that the evolutionary strategy, a decentralized heterogenous PEs connected to work in parallel, will have the earliest success in achieving the goals of the next generation computing. The main advantage of this is the experience that has been accumulated over the years. The various forms of control mechanisms in addition to control flow — reduction or demand-driven, and dataflow — will also be part of the fifth generation computing. The groups working on the FGCP are investigating all three control mechanisms. Both CISC and RISC architectures will play a role in the future systems. The granularity chosen for an architecture will play a role in using CISC or RISC principles to design the PEs. The choice of implementation technology and granularity will influence the PEs structure, function, speed, cost, and reliability. RISC will take advantage of technologies such as Josephson Junctions and Gallium Arsenide. MOS VLSI will dominate the earlier years of FGCs.

It may be possible to place several PEs on a single die, like the NON-VON, if fine grain is chosen and each PE could be based on RISC. Having several PEs on the same chip will be beneficial for PEs that need to communicate frequently with each other. Large-grain systems would probably have only one or two PEs on each die. Any advancement in semiconductor technologies could be used to provide more memory and registers for each PEs rather than squeezing more PEs on the same chip. The PEs could be based on CISC ; each PE would have more computational power to handle complex computations with little or no communication overhead. Communication is a major issue in parallel architectures because the gains expected from concurrency could be wiped out by long delays in communication. There are various communication topologies that are currently being used or investigated including tree, rings, boolean n-cubes, and circuit-switching, such as Omega networks or banyan networks.

The level of concurrency is another issue of importance in parallel architecture. How many PEs are optimum? We may be able to solve most of our problems on conventional architectures with few PEs, but some problems will require concurrency that can only be provided by systems with thousands of PEs. Both too little and too much parallelism are costly. In expert systems, for instance, only a few problems require that more than a few branches of reasoning be pursued concurrently. But in some instances, many thousands or even millions of PEs may be needed to perform an exhaustive search [34].

In our view, future architectures, at least in the U.S., will make use of decentralized control systems based on parallel and distributed processing. Both symbolic and numeric computations will be required. There will be some architectures based on data driven and demand driven control mechanisms but this decade (1990s) will be dominated by control driven architectures. It is possible that both data driven and demand driven architectures will be replaced with hybrid architectures that will combine the advantages of both mechanisms. An example of this approach is the Rediflow architecture discussed earlier. Most architectures will be specialized because of the diversity of the various AI branches and other conventional application disciplines.

Algorithms

The easiest task in the design of the fifth generation computers could be the hardware design, especially if the decentralized control driven mechanism is adopted. One of the reasons for this is the fact that architects have accumulated a great deal of experience with control driven architectures. On the other hand, algorithms and software that will make the optimum use of the hardware resources will pose a lot of challenges. The advantage that we can expect from concurrency is limited especially for very complex and NP-complete problems. Some problems will require a broad knowledge ; there must be some control structures (algorithms, heuristics, and strategies for applying the heuristics) to limit the search space. In many real world problems, there are simply too many branches of possible paths to an eventual solution or solutions to keep the search from combinatorial explosion. Concurrency can help improve computational efficiency but it cannot help extend the solvable problem size. We need better algorithms, heuristics, models, and implementation strategies to eliminate, limit, or delay the effect of combinatorial explosion. In addition to NP-complete problems, there are several AI branches such as vision, pattern recognition, speech understanding, and machine learning, which require a great amount of computational resources.

The development of better algorithms or improvement of current algorithms is necessary in order to make the best use of hardware resources and to make the resource requirements of programs manageable. The algorithms that are selected must be matched with the underlying architectures on which the algorithms will be executed. The ideal goal is to attain a speedup that is proportional to the number of PEs in each architecture. This goal faces challenges that require compromises between speed, storage, and communication needs. We can expect the best contribution in situations where the problems being solved have solutions that require polynomial time on sequential computers. Problems that are intractable with combinatorial explosion cannot currently be solved in polynomial time unless we have exponential number of PEs which is currently impractical. The success of FGCs is very dependent on our ability to develop better algorithms, heuristics, and control strategies to deal with a few of the real-world problems that qualify as "intractable". We must match algorithms with architecture structures because what is best on one particular architecture may not necessarily be the best on another one.

Software

The largest challenge of fifth generation computing will be the intelligent software required to utilize the parallel and massively parallel architectures that will be built. Some of the problems we must resolve are: languages, tools, productivity, and integration of AI and conventional software. LISP and PROLOG are the languages of choice in the AI community, but in commercialization of AI products, users who may not be comfortable with either of these languages may want to extend their systems. We think the four programming paradigms discussed earlier — imperative, functional (also referred as dataflow, applicative, or reduction languages), logic, and object-oriented programming — will coexist in the fifth generation computing environment.

Most of the software will be written in imperative languages because there is a large software base that already exist. One of the advantages of declarative languages (functional and logic) is the potential to take advantage of parallelism that an architecture may offer. Variations of some imperative languages have been developed to give programmers the opportunity to specify operations that should or could be performed concurrently. Two of these languages are Parallel Pascal and Parallel FORTRAN. There is a version of C, C++, that was designed to be used as object-oriented language. The fact that more people use imperative languages and they are reasonably efficient on conventional machines make us to conclude that imperative languages will be here for years to come. Some companies are even re-writing some of their AI products, which might have been written in LISP, in imperative languages such as C. Similar to the idea discussed earlier about hybrid architecture, there are also hybrid languages that combine the features of PROLOG and LISP. The goal is to have languages that can provide most of the three capabilities required of AI languages — reasoning, description, and action. LogLisp and QUTE are two languages that combine the features of PROLOG and LISP. There are currently other AI languages that are not widely used because they are special purpose languages or they are designed for a specific machine. Some of the languages that will fit this characterization are OIL (designed for FAIM), Occam (designed for Transputer), and KRL and KL-ONE (for knowledge representation). The strength of special purpose languages is that they provide a higher level of abstraction and in so doing, make it easier to write and understand programs.

The availability of the proper tools that can be shared on different machines is very essential to the success of future generation computing. Tools such as O/S, compilers, debuggers, shells, editors, and many other utility programs are important to the success of future computing. The next generation computers will require distributed O/S's that can coordinate many PEs without becoming a bottleneck. Each node may have its own O/S, but they must all be coordinated with the O/S of other nodes or computers so that they can share computational resources. Some problems are nondeterministic; distributing and balancing these problems on parallel systems will be a challenge for an O/S. Parallel architectures will require efficient task allocation techniques. Static allocation has less overhead during execution time while dynamic allocation seems natural but has more overhead because of the need to dynamically assign tasks to PEs and perform dynamic load-balancing. We must balance the overhead caused by load-balancing with the expected improvement that load-balancing will yield. A strategy that combines static and dynamic load-balancing may be a viable alternative. Efficient garbage collection is a must for any machine that executes AI software. Hardware support for memory management is essential.

Compilers/interpreters will take on added responsibilities; for one thing, future software will be larger and more complex. The compilers may be responsible for task allocation in addition to code generation and optimization. Debuggers and editors are essential; they must appear as intelligent tools to help programmers create, modify, correct, and maintain programs. Debugging parallel code is a very difficult task. It is a real challenge to develop debuggers which will probably call for multiple windows to be displayed at once in order to observe the status of several PEs simultaneously. Debugging could indirectly influence the number of PEs that an architecture will support. The importance on debuggers and editors can not be overstated especially for AI software that is exploratory in nature. Rapid prototyping will be a key component in the development of future software.

The maintenance of software will even be more important. On one hand, we will have longer and more complex software programs to deal with; on the other hand, these software will be integrated together with many of them written in diverse languages. It has been observed that some organizations spent as much as 70% of their time on correcting errors in, and making changes to their existing programs [34]. The current software engineering tools are seldom used in software industry. In some cases, management lacks software background and therefore, they are less accommodating in the purchase and use of these tools. Secondly, most of the tools are designed for programs written in structured languages and a large protion of current software are written in unstructured languages including assembly languages. These current tools must be modified and new ones developed to accommodate programs written in declarative and object-oriented programming languages. If current tools are fully utilitized it could contribute enormously to software productivity. Some of the techniques for improving productivity are [34]: tools for tracing, debugging and verifying programs; libraries that will permit many applications to be constructed basically from well-tested building blocks, automatic code generators, or very high-level languages that can translate specifications into machine executable code; and structured programming methodologies. Most of these techniques are well known but they must be changed to suite parallel processing environments.

The building of reuseable and shareable tools is of utmost importance to the success of the next generation computing environment. How to make these PEs communicate efficiently, share loads equitably with no idle PE when possible, coordinate and synchronize the activities of the PEs, design and maintain large complex software, and increase productivity and reliability are challenges that the software engineers must address. We can learn a lesson from the improvements that are present in today's conventional machines in executing programs written in LISP. The improvement is not only due to the increase in computer speed compared to what we had on the PDP-6 for instance, but also to the advances and knowledge gained about the computation principles and mechanisms as it relates to languages. This knowledge gained has effected improvement in LISP itself, and in the design of interpreters and compilers for LISP. We have also developed the understanding that AI programs are usually large, complex, nondeterministic, use recursive algorithms more often, and sometimes require a great deal of computational resources. The first few years after the introduction of the FGCs, we must put forth efforts to study the relationships between software (languages, applications and system programs), algorithms, and hardware architectures. This will enable us to provide better tools in the form of hardware and software for the future computational needs.

6. CONCLUSION

The development of AI products is moving from the AI laboratories to the commercial world where more challenges must be met. There are also research efforts to design the FGCs with AI as its cornerstone. The objectives of the FGCs include the building of knowledge based systems. It is a fact that AI research can and has been performed on conventional architectures using conventional languages to code programs, but AI requires special architectures and languages. The hardware must consist of parallel PEs that can cooperate in executing a given task or tasks. Some of the challenges in designing parallel architectures are deciding on number of PEs to have in a system, the granularity to adopt, synchronization and coordination of PEs, communications between PEs, and the computational model to use. The development of parallel architectures is of less concern compared to the software concerns. Having parallel architectures are not to be taken as panacea for knowledge-based systems. We do not have experience on how to write programs that can utilize one thousand or more PEs simultaneously. We do not have experience either on how to predict, in an inexpensive fashion, as to the problems that can best be implemented on a given architecture. We must match algorithms with architectures, and must make sure the control techniques of the programming model also matches the control technique implemented on the underlying machine. The future computing environment will consist of several heterogeneous parallel and surprisingly sequential computers with distributed processing capabilities. There will not be one language but rather several languages and the challenge will be how to integrate programs together to function as a unit. Emphasis should be placed on parallel programming, development of tools to help improve productivity and reliablity of software, and development of parallel algorithms including heuristics and control strategy. The early success, at least in the U.S., will come from control driven parallel architectures.

Bibliography

[1] Aletan, S. The Influence of Algorithms and Languages VS Programmers Experience on Programs Execution Efficiency. *Modelling and Simulation Conference* (May 5-6 1988), 1131–1135.

[2] Aletan, S. Current and Future Trends in Artificial Intelligence Architectures and Programming Languages. In *Tools for Artificial Intelligence* (October 23-25 1989), pp. 215–221.

[3] Almasi, G. S., and Goltlieb, A. *Highly Parallel Computing*. The Benjamin/Cummings Publishing Company, 1989.

[4] Bourbakis, N. G., and et al. A RISC-bit-sliced design of the HERMES multilevel vision system. *Journal of Microcomputer Applications 11* (1988), 155–167.

[5] Bourbakis, N. G., and et al. Multiprocessors and Microprocessor Vision System. *International Journal of Microprocessor and Microsystems 11* (1990), 155–167.

[6] Cercone, N., and McCalla, G. AI: Underlying Assumptions and Basic Objectives. In *Computers for Artificial Intelligence Applications* (1986), IEEE Computer Society Press, pp. 12–22.

[7] Darlington, J., and Reeve, M. *ALICE and the Parallel Evaluation of Logic Programs*. IEEE Computer Society Press, 1985.

[8] Delahaye, J. P. *Formal Methods in Artificial Intelligence*. John Wiley & Sons, 1987.

[9] Despain, A. M., and Patt, Y. N. *Aquarius – A High Performance Computing System for Symbolic/Numeric Applications*. IEEE Computer Society Press, 1986.

[10] Digital Equipment Corporation. *VAX Architecture Handbook*.

[11] Eisenstadt, T. O. . M. *Artificial Intelligence: Tools, Techniques, and Applications*. Harper & Row Publishers, 1984.

[12] Elliot, L. B., and Holliday, F. L. Automating Conversion : FORTRAN to Ada via Ada. *Computer Language 4* (1987), 63–70.

[13] Fahlman, S. Computing Facilities for AI: A Survey of Present and Near-Future Options. *AI Magazine* (1980-1981), 16–23.

[14] Fahlman, S. E., and et al. Massively Parallel Architectures for AI : NETL, THISTLE, and BOLTZMANN Machines. In *The Proceedings of the Annual National Conference on Artificial Intelligence* (August 1983), pp. 109–113.

[15] Fields, S. Surveying AI Languages. *PC AI 1* (1987), 28–35.

[16] Firebaugh, M. W. *Artificial Intelligence, A Knowledge-Based Approach.* Boyd & Fraser Publishing Company, 1988.

[17] Gevarter, W. B. *Intelligent Machines An Introductory Perspective of Artificial Intelligence and Robotics.* Prentice Hall, 1985.

[18] Gimarc, C. E., and Milutinovic, V. M. A Survey of RISC Processors and Computers of the Mid-1980s. *IEEE Computer 20* (September 1987), 59–69.

[19] Gowrishankar, T. R., and et al. Specification for the Development of a Knowledge-based Image-interpretation System. *Engineering Application of AI 3* (1990), 79–90.

[20] Hill, M., and et al. Design Decisions in SPUR. *IEEE Computer 19* (1986), 8–22.

[21] Hillis, D. W. The Connection Machine : A Computer Architecture Based on Cellular Automata. In *Tutorial : Computer for Artificial Intelligence Applications* (1985), IEEE Computer Society Press, pp. 491–506.

[22] Hwang, K., and et al. Computer Architectures for Artificial Intelligence Processing. *IEEE Computer 20* (January 1987), 19–27.

[23] Kent, E. W., Shneier, M. O., and Lumia, R. PIPE (Pipelined Image-Processing Engine). *Journal of Parallel and Distributed Computing* (1985).

[24] Luger, G. F. *Artificial Intelligence and the Design of Expert Systems.* The Benjamin/Cummings Publishing Company, 1989.

[25] Manuel, T. LISP and Prolog Machines are Proliferating. *Electronics* (November 3 1983), 266–271.

[26] McCarthy, J. History of LISP. *SIGPLAN Notices 13* (August 1987), 217–222.

[27] Newquist III, H. Will the Real AI Language Please Stand Up. *Computer Language 4* (July 1987), 58–59.

[28] Pleszkun, A. R., and Thazuthaveetil, M. J. The Architecture of LISP Machines. *IEEE Computer* (March 1987), 35–44.

[29] Sacerdot, E. D. The Copernican View of Artificial Intelligence. *Sun Technology 2* (1989), 46–52.

[30] Schwartz, D. C. The LISP Machine Architecture. In *GDI Technology Assessment and Management Artificial Intelligences Towards Practical Applications*, T. Bernold and A. Gunter, Eds. Elsevier Science Publisher, 1985.

[31] Smith, K. New computer breed uses transputers for parallel processing. *Electronics* (February 24 1983).

[32] Steenkiste, P., and Hennessy, J. Lisp on a reduced-instruction-set processor : Characterization and optimization. *IEEE Computer 21* (1988), 34–45.

[33] Taylor, D. Languages Past, Present & Future. *Computer Language 4*, 12 (December 1987), 57–62.

[34] Torrero, E. *Next Generation Computers*. IEEE Press, 1985, pp. 94–99.

[35] Treleaven, P. C. The New Generation of Computer Architecture. In *Proceedings of the 10th Annual International Symposium on Computer Architecture* (June 1983), pp. 402–409.

[36] Ungar, D., and et al. Architecture of SOAR : Smalltalk on a RISC. In *The 11th Annual International Symposium on Computer Architecture, Conference Proceedings (IEEE & ACM)* (June 5-7 1984), pp. 188–197.

[37] Wah, B., and Li, G.-J., Eds. *Artificial Intelligence Languages and Programming*. IEEE Computer Society Press, 1985, pp. 57–61.

[38] Weiser, M., and et al. Status and performance of the zmob parallel processing system. In *Tutorial : Computers for Artificial Intelligence Applications* (1985), IEEE Computer Society Press, pp. 423–426.

CHAPTER 15

Performance Analysis of an Asynchronous Dataflow Computing Machine for Parallel Machine Learning

John Carter, Susantha Herath*, Jayantha Herath
Electrical and Computer Engineering Department
Drexel University, Philadelphia, PA 19104

*Computer Science Department
Southwest Texas State University, San Marcos, TX 78666.

Abstract - This paper proposes dataflow algorithmic transformations and dataflow architectures for implementing parallel machine learning computations with applications in robotics. Learning plays an essential role in the process of building intelligent machines. To give a broad overview of machine learning, the basic methods of learning are described. It is desirable to find a machine architecture which is more suited to parallel machine learning than traditional sequential or parallel processors. An asynchronous, fine-grained, and highly parallel architecture is proposed as the architectural basis for autonomous learning systems. The machine's behavior is measured by simulating two competing robots in a dynamic environment where one of the robots is able to perform a weak form of learning. A transformation is made from the robot domain to a game playing domain so that the goals of the computer program simulation are easily seen. Dataflow algorithmic transformations are used to exploit the parallelism and map the learning algorithm to the dataflow architecture. The machine's performance is measured, the results are evaluated, and the conclusion is made that dataflow algorithmic transformations and dataflow architectures are well-suited to parallel learning in an asynchronous and dynamic environment.

Key Words - Dataflow Architectures, Dataflow Algorithmic Transformations, Machine Learning Computations, Robotics, Game Playing, Multiprocessor performance

1. INTRODUCTION

The ability to perform well at learning is an integral part of intelligent behavior. Therefore, machine learning is important in the design of intelligent systems. Such systems must operate successfully in unstructured and structured surroundings and respond to unanticipated situations with the ability to imitate the components of human intelligence. They must make decisions with incomplete or uncertain information and be loaded with competing constraints to solve the problems and reach the correct conclusions. These systems are finding increasing use in controlling unmanned systems. The ability to sense-process-act is an integral part of intelligence. Autonomous vehicles or robots are a combination of sensing, processing and decision-making algorithms. These systems integrate planning, real-time control, vision, and actions. Once human intelligence is well enough understood to be reduced to algorithmic form, it can be realized on digital computers. Tasks such as the development of new classification methods, classifying noisy data sets and new examples, comparing the learning approaches by measuring the rate of learning and implementing a wide variety of learning algorithmic applications and intelligent subsystems require extensive computer processing of data.

There are three major requirements to develop practical learning autonomous systems. The first is a powerful, yet flexible or scalable parallel architecture. Secondly, there needs to be a programming environment which can make use of the large amount of symbolic machine learning algorithms available and be able to run them on various parallel machines without making source code modifications. Finally, there needs to be more research into the applicability and performance of machine learning algorithms on parallel machines. The use of parallel machines for machine learning holds promise, but current parallel processors have difficulties such as the managing shared memory resources and the costly time needed to synchronize the processing elements. This limits the number of useful processors in this type of machine to a small number. Additionally, most of the programming environments available for the parallel processor are machine architecture specific. This limits the usefulness of the applied algorithms. The programming environment for parallel processing must free the programmer from being responsible for exploiting the parallelism of the program. It should also free the programmer from handling processor synchronization and memory-sharing, as well.

Dataflow algorithmic transformations and dataflow architectures are proposed for implementing parallel machine learning with the application of learning robotics. The following sections describe its implementation. Section 2 of this paper outlines several techniques used by machine learning systems. Section 3 describes the learning robot problem and the robot/game playing domain transformation which illustrates characteristics inherent in many practical machine learning computations. Section 4 proposes the dataflow algorithmic transformations and asynchronous dataflow architectures for parallel machine learning computations and describes the ID world program development environment for simulation. Section 5 provides the performance measurements of dataflow computing for learning robotics. Section 6 presents the conclusions.

2. MACHINE LEARNING TECHNIQUES

There are many techniques used in the field of machine learning [7]. It is difficult to strictly classify these techniques because most involve some portion of the other techniques. However, it is beneficial to group these techniques into some general classes which reflect the main method of learning used.

2.1. Rote Learning

The simplest form of learning is rote learning, in which solutions to particular problems are stored for future use. Examples include most scientific programs and databases. In scientific programs, computers learn how to solve a problem by the explicit algorithms given by the programmer. In the same way, databases learn facts by explicit instruction. Note that in this method, all learning is completed before any tasks are started.

2.2. Learning by Induction

Induction is used when learning is accomplished by drawing conclusions based on a set of facts. Induction also involves modifying a conclusion to include a set of facts. Although without background knowledge a problem cannot be solved, inductive learning uses experience more than background knowledge in its solution to the problem [6].

2.3. Learning through Examples - Symbolic

Symbolic methods are characterized by the use of symbols. These symbols can be of any form, but typically for a computer they are made up of characters. Symbolism is what is used to describe the tasks which are executed by a computer program. The developers of symbolic learning systems generally use computer languages which simplify the use of symbols. These languages include Lisp and Prolog. Storage methods for this knowledge include the use of decision trees. Expert systems use decision trees in classifying the symbolic knowledge.

2.4. Learning through Examples - Neural Networks

Neural networks consist of a large array of processing elements which can be grouped into input, output, and hidden layers. All of the nodes are part of the learning process, where the outputs of the system are based on the connections of the nodes to each other and the weights assigned to each of these connections. The weights of the connections are determined by applying training examples to the input elements and adjusting the weights of the connections so that the outputs correspond to the desired outputs. There are two general forms of neural network models: 1) Each processing element learns one (and only one) concept apiece and 2) A group of processors learn the concepts.

2.5. Comparison of Neural and Symbolic Learning Algorithms

Although they represent very different techniques in the solution of machine learning problems, neural architectures and symbolic learning systems are frequently applied to similar learning problems (learning by example). Two learning approaches are compared by measuring the rate of learning and the success of classifying new examples [4]. ID3 (symbolic) and perceptron (neural) run significantly faster than back-propagation (neural) in both learning and classifying performance. The accuracy in the classification process was about the same for all three methods, with back-propagation noted as being slightly better in classifying noisy data sets.

2.6. Learning by Observation and Discovery

Learning by observation and discovery involves having the machine observe the environment and record facts pertaining to it. Unlike learning by advice, the machine knows very little about what information is important. Additionally, the goal of what is to be learned is not necessarily explicit. However, there is not enough time and memory space to get meaningful results from a general observation technique in a large domain space; in fact, this technique is not very practical in a very limited domain. The primary motivation behind the use of this technique is to illustrate a method of learning which some believe that humans use. As research has shown, a large amount of knowledge is needed in order to be able to learn efficiently. Additionally, even a very large amount of information is useless with weak methods of organization, to say nothing of prioritizing, combining, etc.!

2.7. Learning by Deduction

When conclusions are drawn about a certain class by observing only a few members of the class, this is learning by induction. In contrast, deductive learning takes the knowledge about a class and applies this to a specific member of the class. This method preserves truth more than inductive learning. Two examples of this form of learning are taking advice and explanation-based learning.

One attempt to have computers to learn in the same way as humans is to develop the ability to learn by advice. Humans get advice from watching others and by reading books. Notice that unlike learning by experimentation, learning by advice requires a separate source (or expert) for the data (or advice).

Explanation-based learning (or analytic learning) systems use background knowledge and a domain description language to describe the examples presented to it. This is a form of deductive learning because all of the learning is drawn from known truths (no learning can take place if the examples can not be described). The advantage of explanation-based learning is that only one negative example in the use of a heuristic is necessary to correct the heuristic and an explanation is generated at the same time.

2.8. Learning by Analogy

Humans have the ability to relate past experiences to the present circumstances even when they are not directly related. For instance, a person had a past experience at a high school baseball game when the team was tired and run down and consequently played a game with a lot of errors. When the same person feels tired before speaking engagement, he may see the need to get rest so as to avoid a poor performance. Creating a new concept based on the similarities and differences between the current problem and the old concept is learning by analogy. The same technique can be applied to symbolic learning methods as well.

3. PARALLEL MACHINE LEARNING IN ROBOTIC PROCESSING

This study concentrates on the suitability of the dataflow architecture for use in a learning robotics environment. Two robots, X and Y, are envisioned as competing in a dynamic environment. Successful behavior represents intelligence. The robots have very little background knowledge about their surroundings or their goals. The robots only know that they have to make some sort of movements in acheiving the goal. Additionally, they are only told what the basic types of movements are. When one robot makes it to the goal or if both robots play to a draw, the competition is completed and the supervisor (or teacher) tells the robots which one won, or in the case of a draw, that there was a tie.

Robot X has the capability to perform some weak form of learning. The method used is observation and discovery with reinforcement from a teacher. The learning is accomplished by instructing Robot X that if it won or tied in the competition, then to assume that whatever it did during the course of the competition was the correct move to make. Note that there are no relative values assigned to each of the moves -- they all have equal weight. Also, there is no concept of winning by a lot or a little.

It is important to consider that the robots are in a dynamic situation: each robot acts independantly. This means that the movements of each robot affect the possible movements of the other robots. One way to visualize this is to imagine that each robot, in the course of attempting to reach their goal, puts stumbling blocks in the path of the other robot.

Observation and discovery is a very weak and inefficient method in learning. What makes it useful for this simulation are three things: 1) The learning is reinforced by a teacher (but very weakly - only enough to specify whether the goal was reached, 2) It has a very limited domain (there are not a lot of "distractions" in the observation and discovery process), and 3) If successful learning can be accomplished under these conditions, it will give greater flexibility for possible future modifications to the architecture and the algorithms.

3.1. The Domain Transformation from Robots to Game Playing

Although the basic ideas of the robot competition are easy to visualize, how to implement these concepts in a computer program is not as easy to visualize. For this purpose, a domain transformation to a simple game of Tic-Tac-Toe is proposed. This game fulfills the assumptions made about the robot competition in an earlier section. Each robot takes the respective positions of X and O. The competition area is reduced to a Tic-Tac-Toe grid. Since X and O move independently of each other (and can block the other's movements by their own), this effectively simulates a dynamic competition field. The problem will now be viewed as a Tic-Tac-Toe game and used to generate the desired performance results.

3.2. The Tic-Tac-Toe Implementation

The algorithm, taking the position of X, learns how to play a better game of tic-tac-toe. In the learning portion of the algorithm, X and O take turns picking open positions and moving there. After each move, the playing board is checked for a win or a tie. A win occurs when one player has three of its marks in a row. A tie occurs when there are no open positions and no winner. When the outcome of the game is decided, X attempts to learn how to win by assigning a value to the board positions it held in the game. If X wins or ties, it increases the value of all X positions; if it loses, it decreases the value. Notice that this is a very weak form of learning, in that order of the moves is not considered, among many other things. This demonstrates the loose learning capability of learning by observation and discovery. This algorithm is an example of reinforced learning, but since the decisions made by X (the learner) are reinforced based solely on the outcome (not the individual moves, etc.), the reinforcement is considered weak reinforcement.

A Sample game is shown below with x making the first move and also winning the game:

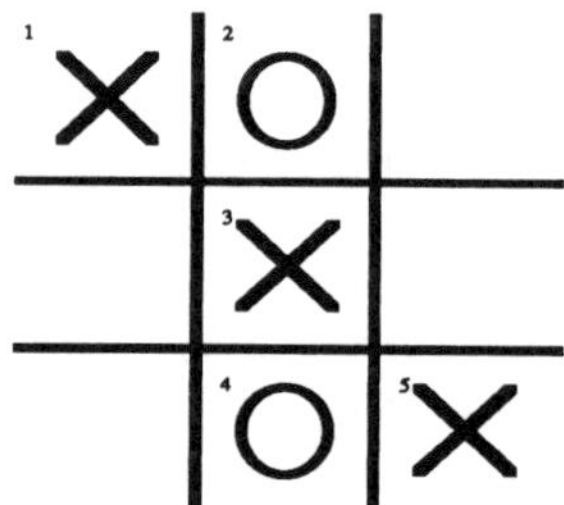

Figure 1. - A Sample Tic-Tac-Toe Game.

The Tic-tac-toe program is composed of six functions. In order to better understand the algorithm, an overview of the functions is given below:

random - given an initial seed, compute a random integer value from 0 to 8, returning a new seed and the integer values.

Calls: none
Called by: learn, realgame, main

findrandomopenpos - given a seed and an array containing the game grid, find a random open position for either an X or O move.

Calls: random
Called by: learn, realgame

winortie - given an array containing the game grid, compute whether an x win, a tie, or an o win has occurred.

Calls: none
Called by: learn, realgame

learn - given a number of learning passes and a seed value, compute and return a value array which holds the relative values for each board position.

Calls: random, findrandomopenpos, winortie
Called by: main

realgame - given a value array and a seed value, play a game using the learned value array in making moves for x (not o), returning the array with the final board positions and the outcome.

Calls: random, findrandomopenpos, winortie
Called by: main

main - given a seed value, the number of learning passes and the number of games to play, return the the value array learned and the outcome of the games played (the number of wins by x, by o, and the number of ties.

Calls: random, learn, realgame
Called by: none

After a number of games for learning, the algorithm plays some games using the values learned by X and then records the number of X wins, ties and O wins. X picks a random open position of the highest value in choosing its moves. For the data presented in this article, the algorithm, in ten learning iterations, ascribed a value for the positions such that the corners and the center position were worth more (this is the desired result!). The outcome after playing ten games was X: 8 wins, Ties: 0, and O: 2 wins. Clearly this is not an incredible result because X, with the first move each game, has a decided advantage playing only by chance, but as discussed earlier, the technique of observation and discovery is only marginally useful in most domains. However, the usefulness of the algorithm is that it demonstrates the performance of a learning technique on a highly-parallel asynchronous machine.

An example run of the algorithm had the following initial call:

Main, with parameters: seed = 65332
n_learn = 10
n_games = 10

which returned the following values:

value = (2 1 5
3 5 3 - (The Tic-Tac-Toe value grid.)
6 4 6)
xwins = 8
ties = 0
owins = 2

The average of a group of 10 runs (each with different seeds) yielded:

value = (3 1 5
2 5 2
4 4 2)

As can be seen, the algorithm is beginning to learn that the center and corner positions are more valuable. Of course, this weak form of learning is not able to infer the importance of having three in a row as a key element to winning.

4. DATAFLOW COMPUTING FOR PARALLEL LEARNING SYSTEMS

4.1. Dataflow Algorithmic Transformations

Task partitioning of an algorithm that leads to better processor utilization is a major challenge in programming parallel and distributed systems. Applications involve iterative computations to improve the quality of the decisions or recursive computations adopted at different levels of resolution. It is interesting to unravel the computation cycles and evaluate their performance of the implementations. Dataflow algorithm transformation techniques such as unfolding and look-ahead will form the basis of unraveling the cycles and increasing the level of concurrency in special-purpose processors and vector and multi-processor implementations. Unfolding exploits the inter-iteration concurrency and precedence constraints. Lookahead transformations recast the recursive computations and create additional concurrency in the algorithms. The combination of program unfolding with look-ahead converts the algorithms into forms which possess greater concurrency.

Machine learning computations have considerable potential for parallel execution. The effective exploitation of parallelism can be performed using dataflow transformation techniques. Therefore, methods to transform machine learning computations to corresponding dataflow graphs is required such that the operations can be executed on a dataflow-based machine. These transformations are procedures which disintegrate complicated computations into several simpler computations that are executable on the dataflow machine. Several static and dynamic dataflow computing models [3] have been proposed for implementing the dataflow computing concept in practical machines. These models support the building of highly parallel and asynchronous computing machines, but differ in their approach as to how the computing should proceed. The tagged token dynamic computing model, more efficient in exploiting parallelism to a large degree, is used in this simulation study. In this model, a tag assigned to each token distinguishes its identity and allows multiple re-entrancy. Identically tagged tokens enable the execution of an operation. Each node can be created at run time and several instances of a node can be fired at a time. Recursion and iteration are represented directly. Successive cycles of an iteration are allowed to overlap by unfolding loops. Functional languages can be used to represent the high level data dependancy of the learning computations. These functional descriptions are transformed to machine-executable low-level dataflow graphs. These languages do not reflect von Neumann properties or the machine structure and can be used effectively to represent learning computations and evaluate them in neural-dataflow computing machines.

4.2. Functions of the General Dataflow Processing Unit

General asynchronous dataflow machines consist of a large number of dataflow processing units (PUs). Figure 2 illustrates the functional block diagram of a dataflow processing unit. The PU consists of multiple pipeline preprocessing units for slow knowledgeable deliberative computations and fast reactive computations, an excution unit and a distribution unit. The

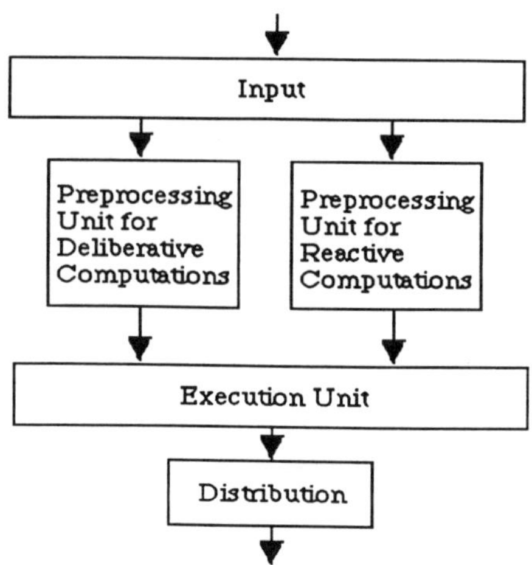

Fig. 2. Functional block diagram of a dataflow processing unit.

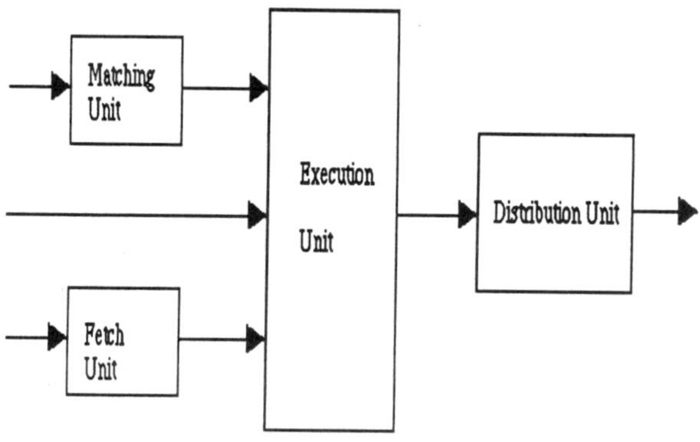

Fig. 3. The preprocessing unit for reactive computations.

execution unit performs the execution and structure handling. Figure 3 shows the preprocessing unit for fast reactive computations. The dataflow processing unit must consist of mechanisms to recognize the data tokens to an operation, fetch operations, execute operations, and distribute resulting data tokens. To satisfy these requirements, a dataflow processing unit basically consists of a matching unit, an instructions fetch unit, an execution unit and a distribution unit. The matching unit sequentially matches and synchronizes the operands for execution. The basic computing cycle of double operand operations consists of matching operands, fetching instructions, executing instructions, and dispatching results to destinations. Single operand operations can be executed directly in the execution unit. Matching a large number of operations narrows the pipeline between the matching unit and the execution unit. One advantage of this parallel architecture over other architectures is that it handles the processor synchronization problem by being data-driven. This data-driven characteristic makes the machine asynchronous in execution and suitable for algorithms without a consistent level of parallelism.

4.3. The MIT Tagged-Token Dataflow Architecture

In order to assess the performance of a machine learning algorithm on a parallel machine, an algorithm which uses the technique of observation and discovery to learn how to win the game of tic-tac-toe was used. This algorithm was run on a parallel machine simulator and the performance results were evaluated. The test bed is based on the Id functional language and the MIT tagged-token dataflow architecture (TTDA) [1]. The Id language is used to represent the high level concepts of the learning algorithm. Id world [6] was used as the parallel machine simulator. It emulates the architecture of the TTDA (see Fig. 4). Dataflow machines are data-driven and asynchronous, which makes them suitable for algorithms which do not have a consistent level of parallelism. Dataflow machines do not have shared storage mechanisms. This protects against side effects and allows independent computations to be done in parallel. Id, a high-level functional language, is designed to support parallel machines, but does so implicitly; the programmer does not need to manage the parallel resources. In addition, it is deterministic.

The original MIT dataflow machine consisted of 32 networked Texas Instruments LISP Explorer machines. The next development of the TTDA-based machine is the Monsoon machine [3], designed to show the practical scalability and programmability of a TTDA. The Monsoon was built in cooperation with Motorola and consists of a network of processors. The follow-on to the Monsoon machine is a 1-1000 processor machine where each processor will consist of an 88110 RISC processor with added synchronization circuitry.

The simulator used for this research is based on a theoretical TTDA. The top level structure of this machine is shown in Fig. 4. The packet network shown here can consist of as few as one processing element and one I-structure memory. This memory is a memory module which includes a memory controller and unique method of addressing. An I-structure is passed by reference, as a token, when traveling through the machine. Each location in the I-structure element

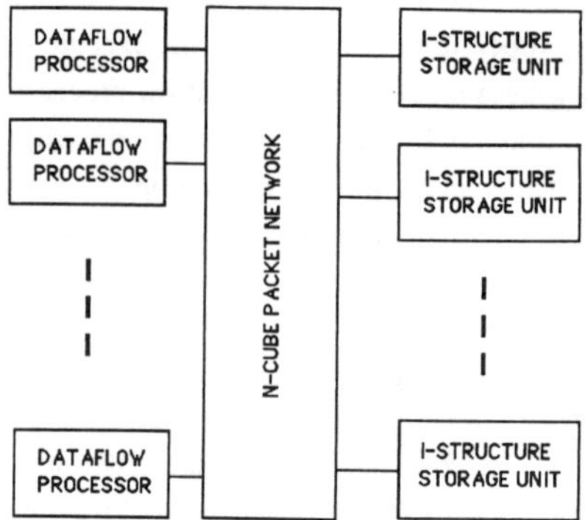

Fig. 4. The tagged token dataflow architecture.

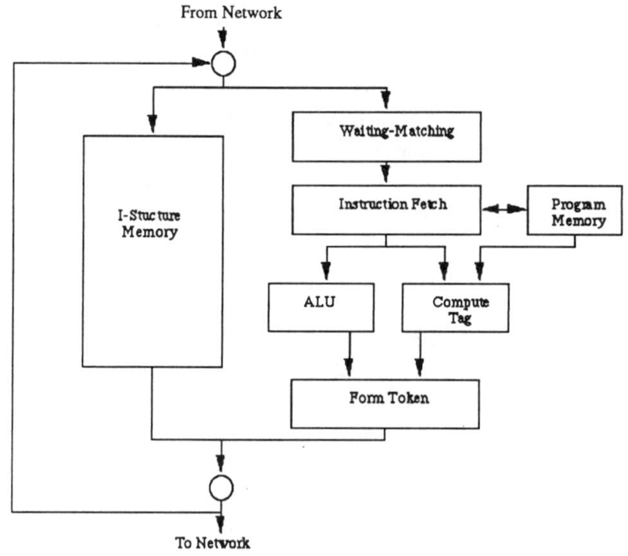

Fig. 5. The MIT TTDA processing element.

is write-once, read-many.

Each processing element (PE) in the TTDA is connected to the other PEs and the I-structure units by means of an n-cube packet network. Figure 5 shows the basic structure of a processing element in the TTDA. There are four basic units in the pipeline for each processor: 1) Waiting-Matching, 2) Instruction Fetch, 3) ALU/Compute Tag, and 4) Form Token. The functions of these units are similar to the explanation given in section 4.2.

The waiting-matching unit collects tokens in preparation for execution. For monadic operators, no waiting or matching is needed: the token is immediately passed down the pipe. For dyadic operations, when a token enters the waiting-matching unit the pool of waiting tokens is checked to see if there is a match. If there is, both tokens are passed down the pipe; if not, the waiting token is assigned to the waiting token pool. The pool can be managed by either associative memories or a heap structure.

The instruction fetch unit acts on the tag associated with the tokens just passed from the waiting-matching unit by fetching the instruction the tags indicate from the program memory. The instruction fetch unit passes on the instruction opcode, the operands and the destination for the result to the ALU/Compute Tag unit.

The third unit in the pipe consists of two processors: a conventional ALU and a tag-computing ALU. The first ALU performs the arithmetic or logic operation specified by the opcode upon the operand(s). The second ALU computes a new tag for the result of the first ALU based on its context and destination.

The Form Tokens unit combines the result and new tag into a new token. The new token is sent to either the top of the pipeline or out onto the network to either an I-structure unit or another PE.

4.4. The ID World Program Development and Simulation Environment

ID World provides a programmer with a high-level language which is suitable for programming a parallel machine and also provides a simulator for the TTDA. The program development environment consists of ID (the programming language) and the simulator for the TTDA machine. The simulator not only runs the ID code, but allows the operator to vary the simulated machine's characteristics. These characteristics include: 1) The number of processors, 2) The communication latencies, and 3) The degree of loop unfolding.

ID has many features which make it ideal for programming machine learning algorithms on a parallel machine. ID is: 1) General Purpose, 2) Functional, 3) Deterministic, 4) Recursive, 5) Capable of being run on different parallel machines without source code modifications, and 6) Able to extract available parallelism in the source code without help from the programmer.

5. PERFORMANCE OF DATAFLOW COMPUTING FOR LEARNING ROBOTICS

System modeling, performance evaluation and prediction are complex tasks in dataflow architectures. This is due to their unconventional properties such as instruction-level synchronization and context switching, split-phase memory transactions, deep pipelines and specific instruction sets. A very limited amount of experimental results is available for these machines - even for those dataflow prototypes that have actually been constructed. An experimental approach was chosen to investigate the performance of dataflow computing for numerically intensive parallel machine learning algorithms. The benchmark application is described in section 3. Appendix A shows the Id code and Appendix B for the pseudocode. The functional descriptions of the high level data dependancy of the machine learning algorithms are transformed into a machine-executable low-level dataflow graphs. However, the granularity of the high-level language programming blocks are not explicitly optimized to balance computation and communication - a natural and logical fine-grained decomposition of the problem is used instead. Finally, the performance is evaluated and the limitations of fine-grained general-purpose dataflow computing are identified.

5.1. Analysis of the Inherent Advantage for X Having the First Move

Because X always makes the first move, it always has an inherent advantage. This is because half the time, X has one more mark on the game board than does O. In order to determine what this advantage is, a run of 100 games was initiated, where X had performed no learning ("RealGameTest"). The result was: Xwins: 59, Ties: 12, and Owins: 29. The conclusion is that X enjoys a 2-to-1 advantage over O without any learning.

From this simulation run the parallelism profile, the critical path length of the algorithm, and the waiting tokens profile were collected. Figure 5 (The parallelism profile for RealGameTest) shows the number of operations happening at a given unit of time. The total area under the curve, then, is the total number of instructions executed. As the graph shows, the greatest number of operations at any time during the execution of the program is 650. The conclusion is that to execute this algorithm efficiently on a parallel machine, more than 650 processors are not needed or wanted. The graph also shows the critical path length of the algorithm (approximately 3900 instructions). The critical path length is the longest sequential sequence of instructions in the parallel execution of the algorithm. This number determines the shortest possible execution time of the algorithm. The other important information that the graph gives is the shape of the curve. In the ideal case, the parallelism profile will look like a rectangle. Note that this same curve would not be ideal when the upper limit on the curve is caused by the unavailability of more processing elements. Since in the real world, algorithms are not capable of executing exactly the same number of instructions at every point in the algorithm, a "real-world ideal" parallelism profile would be a thick bell curve. Our graph for this example (Fig. 6), closely resembles this.

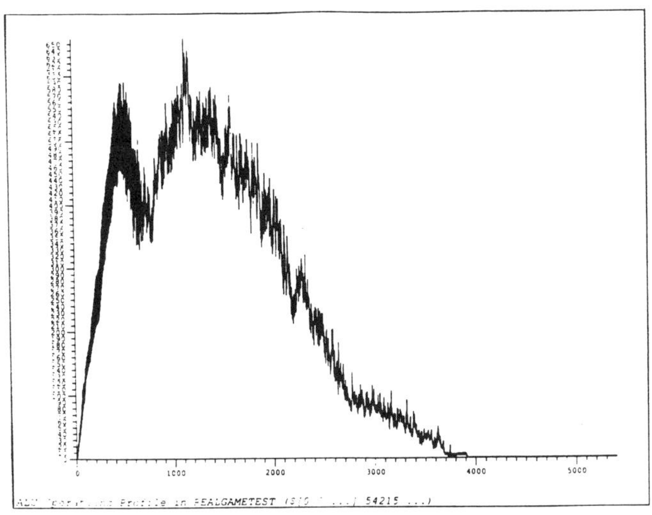

Fig. 6. The parallelism profile for RealGameTest.

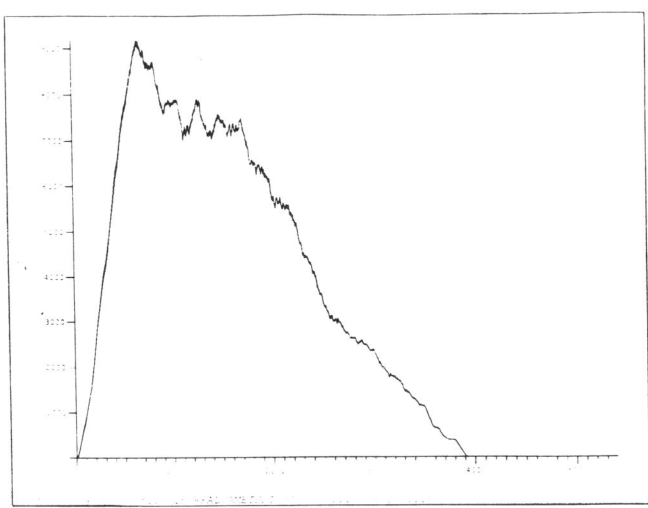

Fig. 7. The waiting tokens profile for RealGameTest.

The Waiting-Tokens profile for RealGameTest is shown in Fig. 7. This graph shows the number of tokens waiting to be processed at each given time unit of the execution of the program. In the ideal case, there would be no tokens waiting to be processed.

In any case, the RealGameTest graph shows us a number of things. First, the parallel machine must have enough storage to store the largest number of tokens which are waiting at any time. For this algorithm, that would be approximately 9000 tokens. The peaks in the graph also show the bottlenecks in the processing. This is particularly true when the number of waiting tokens are high relative to the number of operations being executed. One example of this in the RealGameTest execution is between unit times 500 and 1000.

5.2. A Sample Run of Ten Learning Iterations and Ten Game Iterations

Using an Iterative Algorithm.

In this section, a basic example is provided, using an iterative solution to the 3x3 Tic-Tac-Toe problem. In this example X learns for 10 iterations and then plays 10 games with O. The basic idea of how X learns is described next. X has a "value" grid, which contains a value for each position on the Tic-Tac-Toe board. Before any learning is accomplished, these values are all 0. During the course of learning it is expected that the X value grid will reflect the fact that the center and corner positions are, in general, more valuable.

In our simulation run of ten learning iterations, X ascribed a value for the positions such that the corners and the center position were worth more (this is the desired result!). The outcome after playing ten games was Xwins: 8, Ties: 0, and Owins: 2. X gained on its inherent advantage (2-to-1) over O by beating it 4-to-1.

This example run of the algorithm called Main with the following parameters: seed = 65332, n_learn = 10, and n_games = 10. This returned the following values: Xwins = 8, Ties=0, Owins=2, and value = (2 1 5 3 5 3 6 4 6) (Value is a linear array which represents the two dimensional Tic-Tac-Toe grid values for the desireability of a position). As can be seen, the algorithm is beginning to learn that the center and corner positions are more valuable. Of course, this weak form of learning is not able to infer the importance of having three in a row as a key element to winning.

In Fig. 8, the critical path length is shown for the tic-tac-toe algorithm with different latencies and number of processors. The term latency encompasses many areas of communication. The graph shows that for the uniprocessor case the critical path length is very high. As the number of processors increases, the critical path length decreases (until no more parallelism can be extracted). Increased latency decreases the amount of possible parallelism because without the necessary data (slowed by some communication latency), there reaches a point where additional processors are of no additional benefit because no data are ready for calculations. For this algorithm in the zero latency case, processors over 16 in number would generally not be useful.

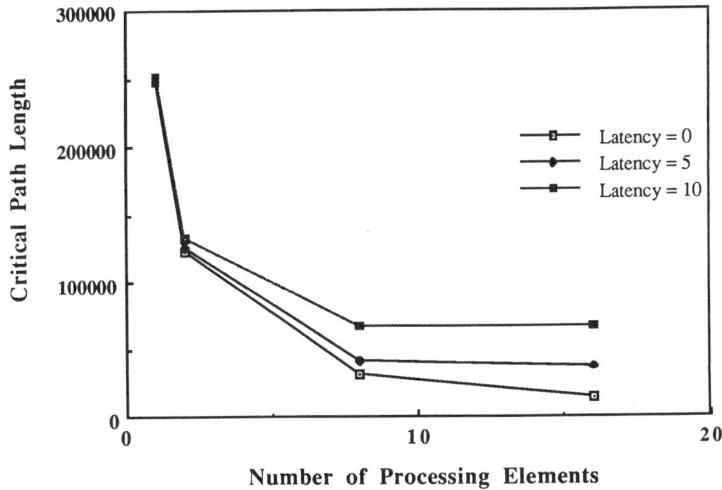

Fig. 8. Critical path length

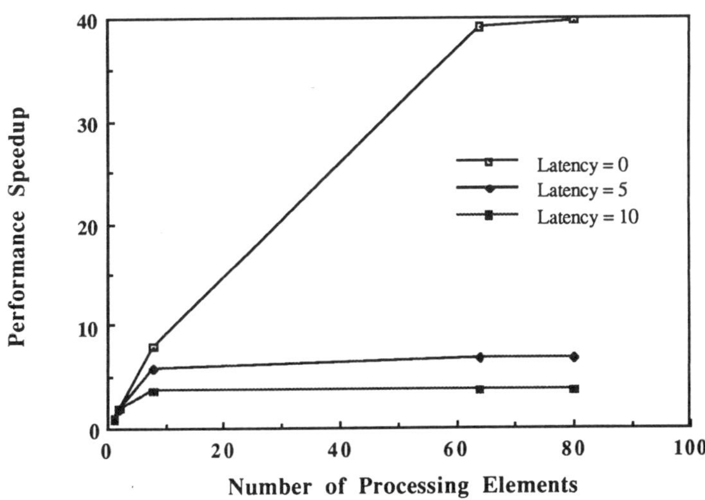

Fig. 9. Performance speedup.

Figure 9 illustrates the speedup to the execution based on the number of processors and the latency in the system. The speedup is defined as the total instruction count (the same as the number of instructions executed by a uniprocessor machine) divided by the critical path length of the parallel machine. Obviously the speedup can never be greater than the number of processors in the parallel machine. As this graph illustrates, very high latencies make this algorithm not very well suited for parallel machines. But in the case of low latencies, the use of up to 64 processors would be very beneficial in decreasing the total execution time of the algorithm.

Figure 10 shows the utilization of the processors. Utilization is defined as the speedup times 100% divided by the number of processors. This graph is useful in planning the number of processors which would be the most cost-effective in the building of a dedicated machine for this algorithm.

The parallelism profile is illustrated in Fig. 11. The graph illustrates how the parallelism in this algorithm is not very regular, suggesting that the use of an asynchronous machine (such as was used in this simulation) is the preferred choice.

5.3. Learning Ability

In this section the learning curve for this algorithm is determined (and thereby justifying the amount of learning iterations previously used). It should be noted that the rate of learning will depend on the initial seed value.

To acquire the learning curve (Fig. 12), a group of 11 runs of the iterative solution to the Tic-Tac-Toe problem was run. Each run used the same seed (2143) and ran the same number of games (10), but for each run the number of learning iterations was increased by 1 (i.e. 0-10 learning iterations).

The graph shows that for this learning cycle, the concept was learned by the sixth learning iteration. If further learning iterations were executed, it could be that the concept could weaken. But this will be temporary in nature.

6. CONCLUSION

Machine learning uses many of the same techniques that humans use to learn. Unfortunately, there has been an inability to develop learning systems which can combine all these techniques to an advantage. Except for very limited domains, machine learning performance comes no where near the performance of human learning. Despite these realizations, many interesting and useful systems have been developed.

Parallel machine learning can be very useful to all levels of intelligence processing systems. For real-time processing performance, the learning robotic processing requires massive parallel processing. To fully exploit the VLSI strength, dataflow algorithmic transformations and architectures are proposed in this paper. Most parallel machine learning computations for robotic

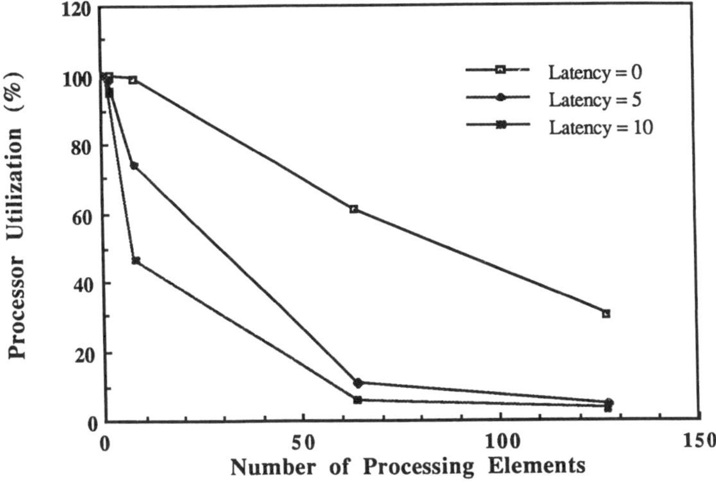

Fig. 10. Processor utilization.

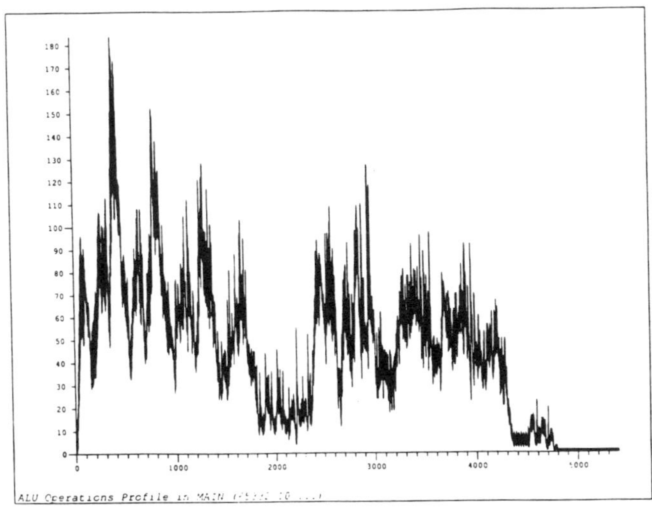

Fig. 11. The parallelism profile.

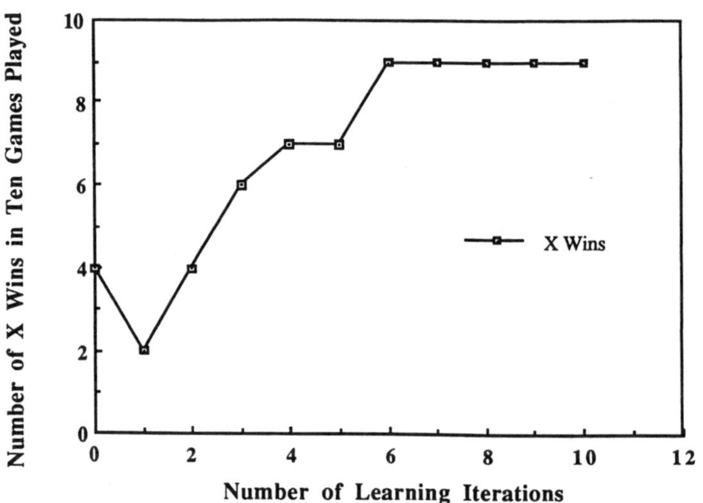

Fig. 12. The learning curve.

applications can be efficiently implemented by using dataflow computers. The performance increase in parallel machines is also related to the communication patterns in application programs and the communication infrastructure. It is very important to test and experiment with alternate transformation and integration strategies.

This paper proposed a systematic approach to realize parallel machine learning. It discussed several machine learning techniques and the performance evaluation of a robotics application based on the robot/game transformation to a Tic-Tac-Toe game. A parallel machine learning algorithm for computations of a robotic problem was deveolped. A tagged token dataflow transformation was used to unravel the parallelism and map the algorithm on a dataflow architecture. The experimental results of a tic-tac-toe algorithm show that the algorithm is suited for an asynchronous parallel machine. The results also show that the algorithm could be modified to better exploit the available parallelism. The ID World simulation environment provides an effective parallel computing environment to simulate autonomous learning intelligent systems.

Acknowledgments: There are many people without whom this study would not have been possible. Particularly, we would like to gratefully acknowledge the help and assistance of the reviewers who offered very helpful suggestions. Finally we want to express our thanks to the ECE Department of Drexel University, Philadelphia.

REFERENCES

[1] Arvind, R.S. Nikhil, "Executing a Program on the MIT Tagged-Token Dataflow Architecture," *IEEE Transactions on Computers*, Vol. 39, No. 3, March 1990.

[2] Y. Yamaguchi, S. Sakai, K. Hiraki, Y. Kodama, T. Yuba, "An Architectural Design of a Highly Parallel Dataflow Machine", Information Processing 89, G. X. Ritter (ed.), Elsevier Science Publishers B.V. (North-Holland), IFIP, 1989.

[3] J. Herath, Y. Yamaguchi, N. Saito, T. Yuba, "Dataflow Computing Models, Languages, and Machines for Intelligence Computations," *IEEE Transactions on Software Engineering*, Vol. 14, No. 12, pp. 1805-1828, Dec. 1988.

[4] R. Mooney, J. Shavlik, G. Towell, and A. Gove, "An Experimental Comparison of Symbolic and Connectionist Learning Algorithms," In *Readings in Machine Learning*, J. Shavlik and T. Dietterich, Eds., Morgan Kaufmann, 1990, pp. 171-176.

[5] R.S. Nikhil, "Id reference manual," Computation Structures Group Memo 284, MIT, 1988.

[6] G. Tecuci, "A Multistrategy Learning Approach to Domain Modeling and Knowledge Acquisition," In *Lecture Notes in Artificial Intelligence*, J. Siekmann, Eds., Springer-Verlag, 1991.

[7] J.M.Carter, "Parallel Machine Learning on a Dataflow Machine," MS Thesis, Drexel Univ., 1992 January

[8] J. Levy, "Game Palying I, II, III," Springer-Verlag, 1988.

Appendix A: The Id code for the Tic-Tac-Toe Problem.

```
%***************************************************************************

def random x =
     { a = 25173 ;
       c = 13849 ;
       m = 65536 ;
       r = x / (m-1) ;
       n = round (r * 8) ;
       x1 = mod (a * x + c) m ;
     In
       n,x1 } ;

%***************************************************************************

def findrandomopenpos mark seed =
     { occupied = true ;
       randompos = 5 ;
     In
       { while occupied do
              next randompos, next seed = random seed ;
              next occupied = If (mark[next randompos] == 0) then
                                    false
                              else
                                    true ;
     finally randompos } } ;

%***************************************************************************
```

```
%*****************************************************************************

def winortie mark =
     { tie = { tie1 = true ;
             In
              { for i <- 0 to 8 do
                     next tie1 = if (mark[i] == 0) then
                                   false
                                 else
                                   tie1 ;
              finally tie1 } } ;

       xwin = If    (  (( mark[0] + mark[1] + mark[2]]) == 3 ) or
                       (( mark[0] + mark[4] + mark[8]]) == 3 ) or
                       (( mark[0] + mark[3] + mark[6]]) == 3 ) or
                       (( mark[1] + mark[4] + mark[7]]) == 3 ) or
                       (( mark[2] + mark[5] + mark[8]]) == 3 ) or
                       (( mark[2] + mark[4] + mark[6]]) == 3 ) or
                       (( mark[3] + mark[4] + mark[5]]) == 3 ) or
                       (( mark[6] + mark[7] + mark[8]]) == 3 ) ) then
                  true
               else
                  false ;

       owin = If    (  (( mark[0] + mark[1] + mark[2]]) == -3 ) or
                       (( mark[0] + mark[4] + mark[8]]) == -3 ) or
                       (( mark[0] + mark[3] + mark[6]]) == -3 ) or
                       (( mark[1] + mark[4] + mark[7]]) == -3 ) or
                       (( mark[2] + mark[5] + mark[8]]) == -3 ) or
                       (( mark[2] + mark[4] + mark[6]]) == -3 ) or
                       (( mark[3] + mark[4] + mark[5]]) == -3 ) or
                       (( mark[6] + mark[7] + mark[8]]) == -3 ) ) then
                  true
               else
                  false ;

       result = if xwin then
                      1
                else  if owin then
                             -1
                      else if tie then
                             2
                           else
                             0 ;
       In result } ;

%*****************************************************************************
```

```
%*****************************************************************************

def learn n_learn seed =
        { value = { vector (0,8) | [i] = 0 || i <- 0 to 8 } ;
        In
        { for j <- 1 to n_learn do
                mark = { vector (0,8) | [i] = 0 || i <- 0 to 8 ) ;
                _ , next seed = random seed ;
                next value = { while ((winortie mark) == 0) do
                                    _ , next seed = random seed ;
                                    mark1 = If ((winortie mark) == 0) then
                                                { newpos = findrandomopenpos mark
seed ;
                                                  temp = { vector (0,8)
                                                          | [i] = mark[i]
                                                          || i <- 0 to 8 when
i<>newpos
                                                          | [i] = 1
                                                          || i <- 0 to 8 when
i==newpos ;
                                                In temp }
                                            Else
                                                  mark ;
                                    mark2 = If ((winortie mark) == 0) then
                                                { newpos = findrandomopenpos mark
seed ;
                                                  temp = { vector (0,8)
                                                          | [i] = mark[i]
                                                          || i <- 0 to 8 when
i<>newpos
                                                          | [i] = 1
                                                          || i <- 0 to 8 when
i==newpos ;
                                                In temp }
                                            Else
                                                  mark1 ;
                                    next value = If (((winortie mark2) == 1) or
                                                    ((winortie mark2) == 2) then
                                                          { vector (0,8)
                                                          | [i] = value[i] + 1
                                                          || i <- 0 to 8 when
mark2[i]==1
                                                          | [i] = value[i]
                                                          || i <- 0 to 8 unless
mark2[i]==1 } ;
                                                  Else If (winortie mark2) == -1
then
                                                          { vector (0,8)
                                                          | [i] = value[i] + 1
                                                          || i <- 0 to 8 when
mark2[i]==1
                                                          | [i] = value[i]
                                                          || i <- 0 to 8 unless
mark2[i]==1 } ;
                                                      Else
                                                        { vector (0,8)
```

```
                                                          | [i] = value[i]
                                                          || i <- 0 to 8 } ;
                                        next mark = mark2 ;
                                  finally value }
        finally value } } ;

%*****************************************************************************
```

```
%************************************************************************

def realgame value seed =
       { mark = { vector (0,8) | [i] = 0 || i <- 0 to 8 } ;
       In
            { while ((winortie mark) == 0) do
                    _ , next seed = random seed ;
                    mark1 = If ((winortie mark) == 0) then      % (X Moves)
                                { highest = { highest1 = -1000 ;
                                In
                                       { for m <- 0 to 8 do
                                              next highest1 = if (value[m] >
highest1)
                                                                   and
(mark[m]==0) then
                                                                     value[m]
                                                                else
                                                                     highest1 ;
                                       finally highest1 } } ;
                                newpos = { randompos , seed1 = random seed ;
                                         In
                                              { while ((value[randompos] <
highest) or
                                                         (mark[randompos] <> 0 ))
do
                                                       next randompos , next
seed1 =
                                                                       random
seed1 ;
                                              finally randompos } } ;
                                temp = { vector (0,8)
                                                     | [i] = mark1[i]
                                                     || i <- 0 to 8 when i <>
newpos
                                                     | [i] = 1
                                                     || i <- 0 TO 8 when i ==
newpos };
                                In temp }
                          else
                                mark ;
                    mark2 = If ((winortie mark1) == 0) then       % (O Moves)
                              { newpos = findrandomopenpos mark1 seed ;
                                temp = { vector (0,8)
                                              | [i] = mark1[i]
                                              || i <- 0 to 8 when i <> newpos
                                              | [i] = 1
                                              || i <- 0 TO 8 when i == newpos }

                              In temp }
                          else
                              mark1 ;

                    next mark = mark2 ;
       finally mark , (winortie mark) } } ;

%************************************************************************
```

```
%*************************************************************************

def main seed n_learn n_games =
     { value = (learn n_learn seed) ;
       xwins = 0 ; ties = 0 ; owins = 0 ;
     In
       { for i <- 0 to n_games do
              _ , next seed = random seed ;
              _ , outcome = (realgame value seed) ;
              next xwins  = If (outcome == 1) then
                                   xwins + 1
                         Else
                                   xwins ;
              next ties = If (outcome == 2) then
                                   ties + 1
                        Else
                                   ties ;
              next owins = If (outcome == -1) then
                                   owins + 1
                         else
                                   owins ;
       finally value , xwins , ties , owins } } ;

%*************************************************************************
```

Appendix B: Pseudocode for the Tic-Tac-Toe problem.

```
%***************************************************************************

FUNCTION random(seed)

       n = random integer number from 0 to 8 new_seed = a new seed value

RETURN  n, new_seed

%***************************************************************************

FUNCTION findrandomopenpos(mark seed)

       r = a random position
       WHILE the r position is occupied DO
             randompos, seed = random(seed)
             IF mark[randompos] = 0 THEN
                   false
             ELSE
                   true
             ENDIF
       ENDWHILE

RETURN randompos

%***************************************************************************

FUNCTION winortie(mark)

       IF all board positions filled THEN
             tie = true
       ENDIF
       IF there are three x's in a row THEN
             xwin = true
       ENDIF
       IF there are three o's in a row THEN
             owin = true
       ENDIF
       IF xwin THEN
             result = xwin
       ELSEIF owin THEN
             result = owin
       ELSEIF tie THEN
             result = tie
       ELSE
             result = 0 ENDIF

RETURN result
%***************************************************************************
```

```
%*****************************************************************************

FUNCTION learn(n_learn,seed)

        value = array of boardsize initialized to 0

        FOR i=1 to n_learn DO
                mark = array of boardsize initialized to 0
                junk, seed = random seed
                WHILE winortie(mark)=0 DO
                        find a random open position, put x there (in mark)
                        IF winortie(mark)=0 THEN
                                find a random open position, put o there
                        ENDIF
                        IF winortie(mark)<>0 THEN
                                IF x won THEN
                                        add one to all positions in the value array
which
                                        correspond to the places where x was in the
mark array
                                ELSEIF o won THEN
                                        as above, but subtract one for each space x
occupied                                        ENDIF
                        ENDIF
                ENDWHILE
        NEXT i

RETURN value

%*****************************************************************************

FUNCTION realgame(value,seed)

        mark = array of boardsize initialized to 0

        WHILE winortie(mark)=0 THEN
                junk,seed = random seed ;
                find the open position with the highest value (based on the value
array) and
                   put x there (in mark)
                IF winortie(mark)=0 THEN
                        find any open position and put y there (in mark)
                ENDIF
        ENDWHILE

RETURN mark, winortie(mark)

%*****************************************************************************
```

```
%***********************************************************************

FUNCTION main(seed,n_learn,n_games)

       value = learn(n_learn,seed) xwins = 0 owins = 0 ties = 0

       FOR i = 1 to n_games DO
              junk, seed = random seed junk ;
              outcome = realgame(value, seed)
              CASE outcome OF
                     xwin: xwins=xwins+1
                     tie: ties=ties+1
                     owin: owins=owins+1
       NEXT i

RETURN value, xwins, ties, owins

%***********************************************************************
```

CHAPTER 16

ARCHITECTURAL SCHEMES FOR SEMANTIC NETWORKS

José G. Delgado-Frias[†] Stamatis Vassiliadis[†‡]
Jamshid Goshtasbi[†*] George Triantafyllos[†‡]

[†]Electrical Engr. Dept.
State Univ. of New York
Binghamton, NY 13902

[‡]IBM Glendale Laboratory
DSD Division
Endicott, NY 13760

[*]School of Engr. Tech.
Penn State University, WSC
Dunmore, PA 18512

ABSTRACT

Semantic networks as a means for knowledge representation and manipulation are used in many artificial intelligence applications. A number of computer architectures, that have been reported for semantic network processing, are presented in this chapter. A novel set of evaluation criteria for such semantic network architectures has been developed. Semantic network processing as well as architectural issues are considered in such evaluation criteria. A study of how the reported architectures meet the requirements of each criterion is presented. This set of evaluation criteria is useful for future designs of machines for semantic networks because of its comprehensive range of issues on semantic networks and architectures.

1 INTRODUCTION

Artificial intelligence (AI) applications and techniques have grown steadily in many fields, such as computer vision, robotics, natural language understanding, and expert systems. As a consequence AI software complexity has increased; this in turn creates a need for high performance computers that can execute AI algorithms at reasonable speed. Since the conventional numerically oriented von Neumann computers are not well suited for artificial intelligence, novel architectures for AI need be investigated and developed in order to achieve the performance required [6,26,39,40,41].

Knowledge representation and manipulation are fundamental requirements for artificial intelligence systems [33]. Knowledge representation has been studied intensively by the artificial intelligence community for an extended period of time [27,29]. The objective in knowledge representation is to allow AI programs to behave as if they know something about the problems they solve. Schemes for knowledge representation include logic programming, semantic networks, procedural interpretation, production systems and frames [1,25,36]. Knowledge representations are found in applications such as automated deduction systems, inference machines, expert systems and knowledge bases. Processing a large body of knowledge tends to require a considerable amount of time due to the non-deterministic nature of the AI problems. Conventional uni-processor architectures, which are designed mainly for sequential and deterministic numeric computations, are not able to meet these performance requirements. As the domain and complexity of AI systems grow, the performance of existing computer systems tends to degrade drastically and these systems can no longer solve AI problems on acceptable time scales. Special purpose computers are needed to manipulate large knowledge representations.

Semantic networks (SN), as a method for knowledge representation and manipulation, have played a significant role [33,34]. The semantic network approach provides a general capability for knowledge representation; it handles not only binary relations, but also unary and higher-order relations which make SN an extremely powerful tool for artificial intelligence applications. In this chapter, architectures associated with semantic network processing are studied and evaluation criteria for such architectures are proposed.

This chapter has been organized as follows. An introduction to the concepts and properties of semantic networks is provided. The semantic network architectures that have been reported are then presented. Finally, a set of evaluation criteria for semantic network architectures is discussed and it is shown how these architectures satisfy the requirements of each criterion.

2 SEMANTIC NETWORKS

The concept of semantic networks, since its introduction [32], has played a significant role in knowledge representation research. Several proposals and changes have been made since its introduction [4]. Semantic networks express knowledge in terms of concepts, their properties, and hierarchical sets/subsets of relationships between concepts. Concepts and/or objects are represented by nodes and the hierarchical relationship between them is represented by a labelled link. Figure 1 shows a semantic network. Some important issues of semantic networks such as hierarchical representation, inheritance, and implicit and explicit knowledge are briefly described below.

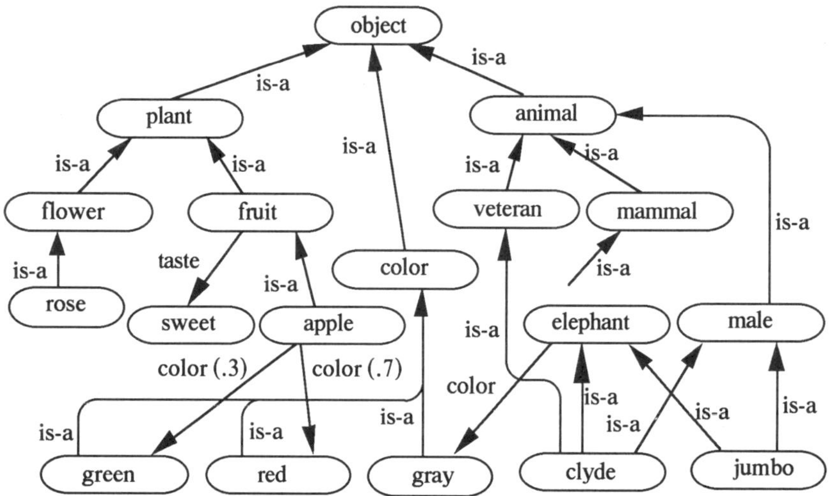

Figure 1. A semantic network.

Hierarchical representation. Knowledge in a semantic network may be represented in a hierarchical form. The knowledge of whether or not an item belongs to a set is important for answering and retrieving facts [18]. A method of providing a hierarchical representation is to use the arcs (or links) to classify the concepts represented by various nodes [3,18,43]. Nodes at the lowest level in the IS-A hierarchy denote individuals (tokens) while nodes at higher levels denote classes or categories of individuals (types). An example of this method is shown in Figure 1.

Inheritance. As soon as human beings identify something, many assumptions are made; for example, that birds fly, whales live in water, etc. A similar process can be done in semantic networks by means of inheritance. In a hierarchical representation, nodes at lower levels inherit all the properties of nodes above them. The hierarchy determines the way that inheritance is passed; properties of a node do not affect the properties of nodes at higher levels. Inheritance is a complex issue that has been formulated in a mathematical form [37]. In Figure 1 for example Jumbo is described as an elephant; however, there is no direct link that determines Jumbo's color. By using inheritance the color of Jumbo can be obtained from the elephant description. Inheritance from another branch of the semantic network tree must be disallowed in order to avoid contradictions; for instance, no node below PLANT can inherit anything that is below the ANIMAL node.

Implicit and Explicit Knowledge. A human mind can store a great quantity and variety of knowledge and can access whatever knowledge it needs very quickly and flexibly [11]. For example, if it is stated that Clyde is an elephant; a human being can tell a great deal more about Clyde than what was stated explicitly. It is possible to infer (with a high degree of certainty) the color of Clyde, the number of legs, the size of Clyde, and so on. It is impossible to believe that all the knowledge about Clyde is stored in explicit form. The most feasible alternative is that knowledge is stored in an implicit form. A semantic network must be able of handle implicit knowledge, since it would be impractical to store all facts explicitly. Figure 1, for example, shows how implicit knowledge is set in a semantic network. It can be seen that Clyde is an elephant, a mammal, an animal and a physical object by using implicit knowledge. Also, it can be observed that Clyde is a male and a veteran by using explicit knowledge representation.

3 ARCHITECURES FOR SEMANTIC NETWORKS

In this section a description of the main features of the architectures for semantic networks is presented. There are six architecures that are studied: NETL, The Connection Machine, SNAP, a Dataflow approach, the semantic network machine, and IXM.

3.1 NETL

In 1979, Fahlman proposed a system for implementing and manipulating in hardware semantic networks, this system is called NETL [13]. NETL is a massively-parallel marker-passing connectionist architecture [10,11,12]. The NETL system has two major components: a parallel network memory scheme that stores knowledge as a pattern of interconnections of very simple processing elements (similar the semantic network proposed by Quillian); and a language-like vocabulary of conventions and processing algorithms for representing various kinds of knowledge as nodes and links in the network.

Processing of the semantic network in NETL is handled by two types of simple processing elements: *node units* which store concepts and *link units* which represent relationships among concepts (nodes). Each node unit has a number of flag bits which indicate the type of the concept that it represents, a few marker bits (to mark a node) which indicate the current state of the node, and a unique serial number (address) as its identification number. Each link unit has also a serial number and a few flag bits for information about relationship type; but it has no marker bit. A central controller (host sequential computer) broadcasts commands to the node units and mark them in parallel. The link units can propagate (pass) markers, in parallel, to the related nodes (that are connected to them) through the network under the control of the host computer. The NETL elements are capable of performing simple Boolean operations on the markers. Deduction searches are performed in parallel by propagation and interaction of various marker bits.

Conceptually, the NETL architecture is capable of handling any size semantic network if the hardware can provide interconnections needed for all nodes and links. However, designing a network with all physical individual interconnections between nodes and links of a reasonably large semantic network, presents itself as a practical challenge. In addition, the network must be capable of adding and/or eliminating individual interconnections, whenever the semantic network is to be modified. A switching network, called *hashnet*, was developed by Fahlman [12] for a million-element NETL machine. This switching network is a multi-level time-shared permutation network that is able to establish one-to-one connection among NETL elements. Figure 2 illustrates the portion of a NETL hardware that corresponds to a section *Jumbo is an Elephant* of the semantic network of Figure 1.

NETL handles inheritance as well as search and inference by marker propagation. The marker-passing scheme only allows the all-or-none set operations. Thus the architecture is able to handle the recognition tasks to a limited extend. To overcome this shortcoming, The addition of a value-passing scheme has been proposed; where each connection has an associated weight [10]. In each NETL unit, the weighted sum of the incoming values is computed, resulting in passing out a single value. A simulation of the NETL architecture has been reported [13], but there is no report of its hardware implementation [10].

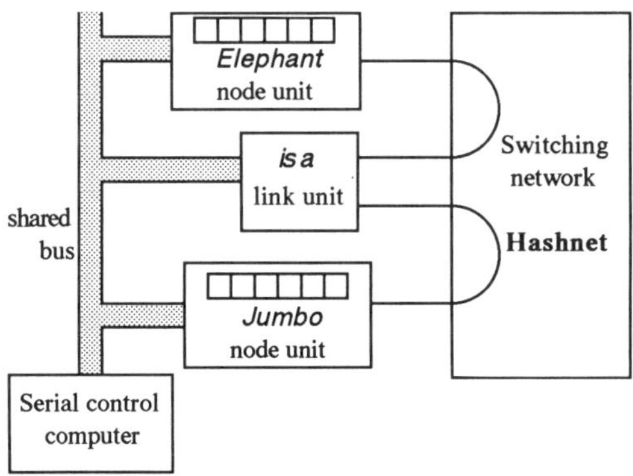

Figure 2. NETL Organization.

3.2 THE CONNECTION MACHINE

In 1984, W. D. Hillis proposed a computer architecture based on cellular automata, denoted as the connection machine (CM), that was initially developed at MIT [23,24]. While one of the primary motivations for the design of this architecture was a particular AI application, retrieving common-sense knowledge from a semantic network, the resulting machine is a more general-purpose data-parallel computing system.

The CM is a massively parallel message-passing architecture that connects together millions (conceptually) of small processing cells. Each cell is connected by physical wires to a few of its nearest neighbors and by message-passing through a packet-switched communication network to any other cell. Each processing cell consists of a few memory words, a bit-serial ALU, and a router. The communication connections can be configured to suit the specific problem being solved. For a semantic network, each node and link can be mapped onto a data processing cell. The cells are connected in the same way as the nodes and links in the semantic network; data is transferred by means of message passing scheme.

The first Connection Machine model CM-1 was built by the Thinking Machines Corporation (TMC) in 1985 [38]. In addition to some semantic network applications [16], the CM has been used for applications such as parallel free-text search [35], document retrieval, memory-based reasoning, and bulk processing of natural language [42]. Other application of the connection machine have been reported in the fields of Geophysics, VLSI design, Computer Vision, Computer Graphics, etc. [38].

The CM-1 system consists of up to 64K data processors (processing cells), partitioned in four sections. Thus, 16K, 32K, 64K processor machines may be implemented. The PEs communicate via a combination of hyper-cube and grid communication networks. The 64K PE implementation consists of a 12-cube inter-processor communication network with 16 PEs on each vertex of the hyper-cube connected on a grid. Each 16K region is controlled by a sequencer. A front-end computer interface is required for communication of the machine with the outside world. The CM-1 data processor is shown in Figure 3.

The processing element (PE) of CM-1 is a single-bit serial reduced-instruction-set-computer (RISC) processor having a 4,096 bit private bit-addressable memory, an arithmetic and logic unit, eight one-bit flag registers, a router interface, and a two-dimensional-grid interface. The ALU is capable of reading two data bits from memory and a bit from the flag register and producing two result bits; one for the memory and one for the flag registers. The instruction set consists of simple logic and arithmetic operations, communication operations with other PEs and diagnostic functions. Each ALU cycle breaks into sub-cycles that execute a nanoinstruction issued by the sequencer. Thus, and integer ADD instruction, for example, executes in three sub-cycles each currying out a nanoinstruction; LOAD first operand, LOAD second operand, STORE result. Operations on the ALU require approximately 0.75 microseconds per bit plus decode overhead. A 32-bit ADD operation can be executed in approximately 24 microseconds. For a 64K processor configuration, this yields a maximum performance of more than 2,700 millions additions per second.

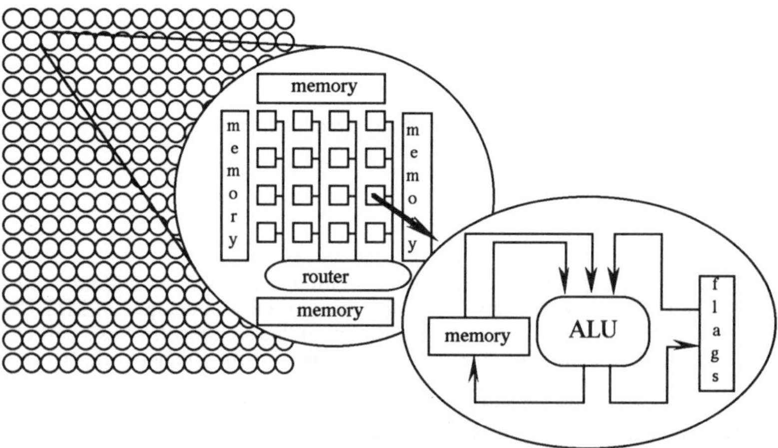

Figure 3. The Connection Machine.

Users can program the CM using conventional languages and program constructs. Programs have normal sequential flow and they don't need new synchronization structures. Algorithms that are naturally mapped onto structures like trees or graphs are programmed using these structures. Unlike other machines, however, where a data structure has to be mapped on the architecture of the particular machine, the connection machine can reconfigure the topology of its processors to match the structure of the problem [38]. Each PE is assigned a node of the structure and the communications between the PEs expresses the relations among the nodes.

To provide this flexibility, CM supports several distinct interprocessor communication mechanism that allow for fast and flexible communication. Communication among nearest neighbor data processors is through a two-dimensional-grid interface; while a router interface facilitates communication among data processors throughout the network. The parallel operation of data processors (and their associated memory) is controlled by the sequencer in a SIMD fashion.

- Broadcast allows data to be broadcasted from the host machine or the sequencer to all PEs at once.
- Global OR of the ALU curry output is used to quickly discover unusual or termination conditions.
- Hyper-cube communications is used for fast data transmission to any PE on the vertex of the 12-cube.
- The router is implemented on the PEs chips and provides overlapped pipelined message switching with routing decision. It uses the hypercube for data transmission.
- The NEWS (north east west south) grid is used to communicate between PEs on the same vertex of the cube. All PEs on a grid communicate in the same direction, thus the target addresses need not be explicitly specified and data collisions are avoided.

The CM supports a "virtual machine" parallel instruction set called paris; mostly implemented in firmware. This virtual processor mechanism provides the user with the number of virtual processors required by the size of the application problem which may exceed the size physically available processors. For applications that require more PEs that are physically available, the CM virtual machine model can split each PE into as many regions as necessary to meet the demand. Each PE is automatically time-sliced among all regions. Assuming that each PE, having M bits of memory, is split into N regions, each virtual PE, as seen by the user, has M/N bits of memory and the virtual machine runs at 1/N the speed of the physical.

The CM virtual-machine instruction set, paris, provides the user with a large number of parallel primitives such as arithmetic and logical operations, high-level APL-like reduction operators, sorting operations, etc. Paris runs on the sequencers where it receives instructions from the front-end computer and supplies nanoinstructions to PEs. Since it defines the behavior of the virtual machine, paris is used as the assembler language of the CM.

An improved version of the Connection Machine, model CM-2, was introduced in 1987 [38]. The added enhancements to the data processor include the addition of an error correction system to the memory, an improved diagnostic capability of the data paths, a larger memory, an optional floating-point accelerator, and a generalized NEWS-grid interface to support n-dimensional grids. The peek performance of the CM-2 has been shown to exceed 20 gigaflops (billions of floating-point operations per second) when no interprocessor communication is required.

3.3 The Semantic Network Array Processor

The Semantic Network Array Processor (SNAP) developed by Moldovan's group, is a VLSI architecture designed for processing knowledge represented by semantic networks [31]. The architecture consists of an array of identical processing cells which are interconnected both globally and locally, as shown in Figure 4. Each cell can communicate to its nearest neighbors via local buses; and to any other cell in the array through a chain of intermediate cells.

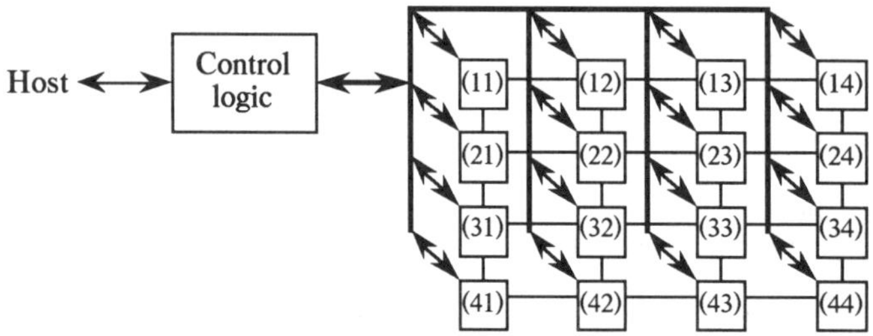

Figure 4. SNAP Organization.

Two underlying concepts of the SNAP architecture are associative processing (using associative memories for performing fast information retrieval) and cellular array processing (to process various tasks in parallel). Each processing cell consists of three main units; namely, a Content Addressable Memory (CAM), a Processing Unit (PU), and a Communication Unit (CU). The CAM is further divided in two parts: a cell memory which stores a semantic network node and a pointer memory which stores both relation names and the addresses that relate to the node. The PU controls operations of the CAM and the CU. A cell interfaces with its nearest neighbors and accesses the global bus through the CU. The PU has a reduced and simple set of microinstructions (SNAP primitives). An external controller supervises the global communication of the array and also provides the interface between SNAP and a host computer.

To process a semantic network, it is represented as a colored graph which is then mapped onto the SNAP architecture. This graph structure of a semantic network correspond to a set of three-tuple relations, (I_i R_k I_j). The ordered pair of items (I_i I_j) represent nodes of the semantic network linked by a predicate R_k, a relation which specifies the type of association between I_i and I_j. This three-tuple relation is called an atomic relation. Each node of the semantic network (represented as a collection of atomic relations) is stored in one cell memory and the links from (or to) that node are stored in the pointer memory of that cell. Thus, full information about a node and its environment is kept in a single processing cell. Several applications of the SNAP architecture have been studied using simulation programs [9,31].

Natural language understanding (NLU) has been selected as the main application domain for SNAP [30]. As a result, SNAP has become a marker propagation architecture, where a set of propagation rules control the movement of markers between processing cells. Markers are assigned to certain semantic network nodes; they are then propagated to other nodes by way of messages (marker passing).

This SNAP architecture is an array of SNAP chips interconnected by means of a modified hypercube network. The operation of the SNAP array is controlled by a central controller. A host computer, connected to the SNAP array by the controller, tasks it with jobs. Several nodes of a semantic network can be stored in the memory of a chip, where links (relations) associated with these nodes are stored as pointers. Each chip consists of four units: a microprogrammed processing unit (PU) which controls the operation of the chip, a relation memory (RM) which provides the main storage of the chip and is built around a CAM in order to provide parallelism within the chip, a marker unit (MU) which controls the marker propagation within the chip (it also contains a simple ALU), and a communication unit (CU) which interfaces the chip with the rest of the SNAP by providing for communication with other chips and the controller. The PU, CU, and MU can work simultaneously, executing instructions, sending messages, and processing messages, respectively.

SNAP-1, a prototype of this SNAP architecture, has been implemented as an array of 144 Digital Signal Processor (DSP) chips. It is organized into 32 tightly-coupled clusters of four to five processors each [8]. Clusters replace the processing chips of the SNAP architecture described above. A combination of DSPs and 4-ports memories provide each cluster with three functional elements (similar to those of the processing chips): the processing unit (PU) which decodes the SNAP instructions received from the controller and also performs arithmetic cost calculations and implements collection of results, the marker control unit (MU) which processes markers and their associated weights, and the communication unit (CU) which provides interface between clusters and can also task the MUs with jobs.

In order to be processed on this SNAP-1, a semantic network is partitioned into regions (sub-nets). Each region (concepts, relations between concepts, and markers) of the semantic network is allocated to cluster; where it is stored and processed within that cluster. Parallelism is exploited in two levels: when reasoning operations such as marker-passing and cost calculation are performed on a sub-graph within a cluster; and when multiple partitions of the semantic network are processed in parallel in different clusters.

3.4 DATAFLOW APPROACH

The use of dataflow flow architectures for processing of semantic networks was proposed by Bic [2]. In this approach, the semantic network rather than being a passive representation of knowledge (maintained in a primary memory and manipulated by an outside agent) is represented as an active dataflow graph. Each node of this graph is an active element capable of accepting, processing, and emitting value tokens (messages) which travel asynchronously along the network arcs. This dataflow graph of a semantic network has the following form

$$t_1 \underline{\qquad\qquad p \qquad\qquad} t_2$$

where two nodes and the arc connecting them are represented by constants t_1 and t_2 and label p, respectively. A query has a similar form

$$T_1 \underline{\qquad\qquad p \qquad\qquad} T_2$$

and it is assumed to be a connected graph. If a query consists of many not connected sub-graphs each of these sub-graphs may be viewed as an independent query and fed to the system independently. It is also assumed to contain at least one node that corresponds to a constant value. It is argued that queries that contain only variables correspond to finding sets via unspecified relations to unspecified sets and such queries are too general to be of any practical value. Under these assumptions a query may be transformed to a linear chain defined as a connected chain of edges containing no cycles or branches where the leftmost node of the chain is a constant and the other nodes correspond to either constants or variables.

In this dataflow approach, answering a query requires to bind a constant to each variable in the query such that the query matches a portion of the semantic network. A query, considered as a graph template, is fitted into the semantic network. The fitting of this graph template is performed by tokens propagating asynchronously along the dataflow graph of the semantic network. A query template is assumed to form a connected graph and to have at least one node that corresponds to a constant value. A template is transformed into a "tree structure" or a "linear chain". It is then placed on a token which is send to all nodes of the semantic network that matches the leftmost node of the template. These nodes send tokens along all edges that match the first template edge. If the match is successful, the process continues to the next level. Each receiving node sends responds back to the sending node, indicating a match or failure.

Each token contains sufficient information to be guided through the network independent of other tokens. There is no need for centralized control. Any existing dataflow architectures could be adopted to efficiently support the processing of semantic networks according to his proposed model [2].

3.5 SNM Architecture

The Semantic Network Machine (SNM) was proposed by J. G. Delgado-Frias and W. R. Moore [5,6]. This architecture is essentially a two-dimensional array of processing elements (PEs), as shown in Figure 5(a), that operates in a data-parallel fashion. A central controller sends micro-instructions to all PEs on the network. A message-passing communication scheme is used for PE intercommunication.

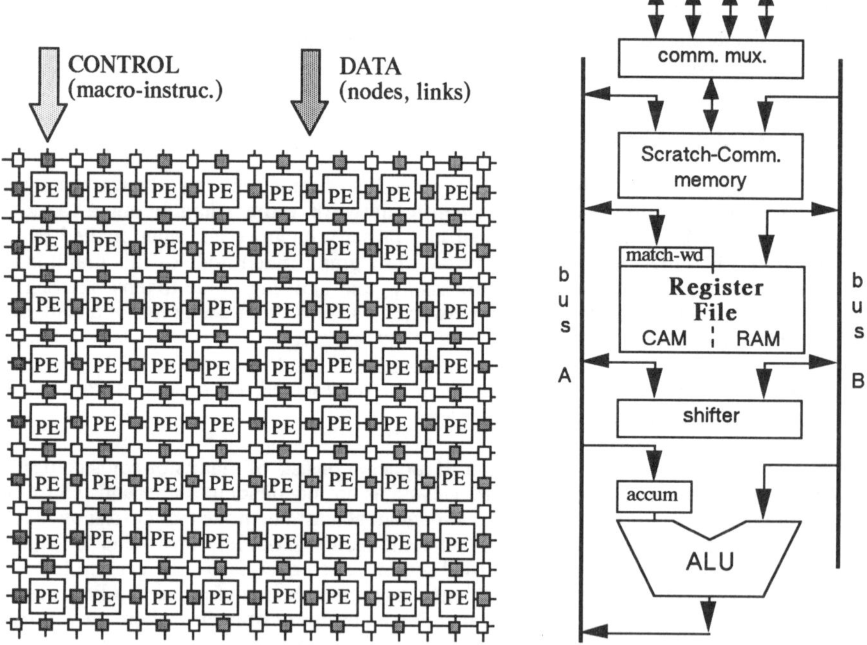

(a) SNM Organization. (b) SNM processing element.

Figure 5. Semantic network machine.

Each PE, shown in Figure 5(b), consists of a scratch-communication memory module (SCM), a register file (CAM-based file), an ALU, and an I/O controller. The PE can perform symbolic operations on a node of the semantic network, arithmetic operations, and communication tasks. The communication tasks are performed by the I/O controller, independent of the processing tasks performed by the ALU. Reading/writing messages from/to the scratch-communication memory provides synchronization of two computational tasks. The scratch-memory is also used to store temporarily results.

The register file is used to store nodes, links, and probabilities which are all part of the semantic sub-network allocated to a PE. Each node record contains the addresses of all its links which may reside in another resister on the same PE or on different PEs. When all the links of a node cannot be stored on the same resister, buffers are provided to point to all links.

The interconnection scheme provides a fast communication link to any of the PE's eight nearest neighbor as well as communication paths to any PE in the entire network. It consists of two types of links; PE-PE link and Row-Column link. The PE-PE link allow of independent bidirectional connections of a PE with its immediate neighbors while the R/C links allow for signal to travel along a row or column of the array. The traffic on the R/C links is regulated by a priority controller which permits the link to be set by only one of the four PEs that can access the link. This communication scheme allows a PE to be connected to two rows and two columns which provides two distinct paths of a PE to its nearest neighbors. Thus, alternative communication paths may be chosen by PEs when a path is busy or unused due to a fault in the array.

A semantic network is stored in the register files of the PEs. The SN is partitioned into sub-networks so that several nodes and links of the SN may be stored and manipulated by a processing element. Figure 6 shows three data types used to represent the nodes and links of a SN in the registers of a PE. The first field of the record is used to distinguish between a node and a link, the second field contains information about the size of a node/link, the third field is used during matching to compute a probability of belief which indicates how good a matching is. The pointer fields contain the addresses of nodes/links which may reside on the same or different PEs. Since nodes may contain more links than can be handled by a node record a continuation field is provided which points to a 'BUFFER' type record that holds the additional information about the node (see Figure 6).

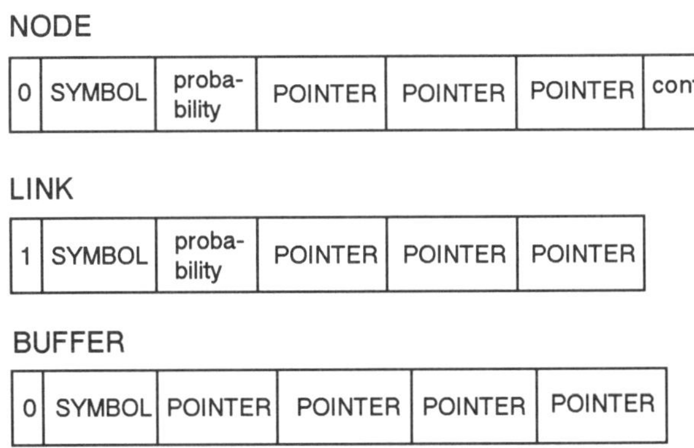

Figure 6. Formats of data types.

Operations on the semantic network are initiated by a central controller (the host computer) that sends macroinstructions to all PEs. As an example, consider a matching operation where a given semantic network is to be matched with the knowledge base (a SM already stored in the SNM). In this case the host computer sends the nodes of the network to the SNM which compares them with the entire knowledge base simultaneously. Once all node-link pairs of the node are matched, a measure of believe is computed that determines the goodness of the match. If the computed MB is above a threshold value the variable can be assigned, otherwise the node remains unassigned [99].

3.6 IXM ARCHITECTURE

The IX system has been developed [22]. It consists of a semantic network oriented language for knowledge representation, IXL, and a massively parallel hardware dedicated to semantic network processing, IXM. The IXL language is a super set of Prolog [17]; and includes special predicates for semantic network processing. A typical IXL program is interpreted on a host computer; the special predicates are passed to the IXM machine for parallel processing [15, 20, 21].

The IXM is a multiprocessor system with large associative memories (AM). The overall structure of IXM is shown in Figure 7. It operates under the control of a host computer and consists of the pyramid shaped associative network with one network processor (NP) at each node, processing elements (PEs), and a broadcast processor. Each PE consists of three main components: the semantic network AM (SNAM) which stores a sub-network of the SN, the instruction AM (IRAM) which stores the IXM instructions (subroutines) for the IXL interpreter, and the control processor (CP) which treats procedure execution (e.g., processing arithmetic operations) and controls marker propagation between nodes. Each node of the associative network consists of a network processor (NP) that includes a routing logic for message passing (among separate PEs) and an AM which provides for parallel marker propagation. The broadcast processor receives the IXL commands from the host computer and sends each one of them simultaneously to all PEs; it also accepts answers from each PE and passes them back to the host computer.

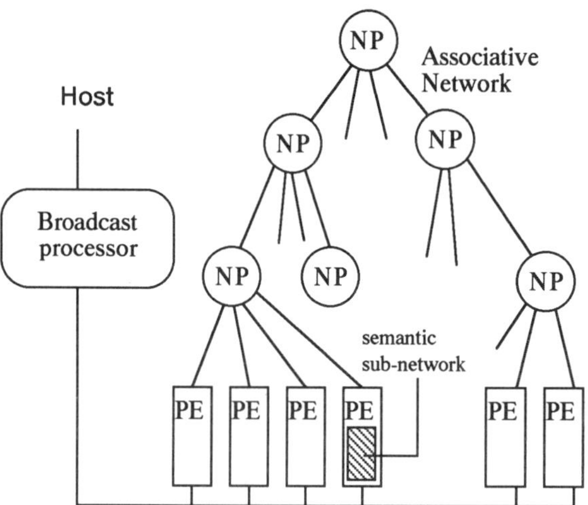

Figure 6. The IXM Architecture.

A large semantic network is decomposed into sub-networks which are mapped onto associative memories (SNAMs). One word of a SNAM stores one triple of the semantic network (source node, link, destination node). Marker propagation is the mechanism used for processing of the semantic network. Nodes with large fan-out are partitioned into nodes with smaller number of connecting links called nodes of equivalence which are distributed among the PEs. Association operations, marker propagation, and set intersection operations are performed in parallel.

A prototype of the IXM machine was developed to evaluate the architecture [20]. A newer version called IXM2, a parallel associative processor, consists of 64 associative processors (AP) and nine network processors (NP). Major decisions in IXM2 design include adoption of large associative memories, allocation of each sub-network of the semantic network to one associative processor (AP), adoption of an interconnection scheme that is based on complete connection which connects APs, and parallel marker propagation to deal with large fan-out nodes [19]. Using AM in network processors, multiple marker propagations from a node with large fan-out are done in parallel, independent of the number of fan-out. Marker propagation is performed either sequentially by message passing or in parallel within an associative processor by the use of associative memory. APs are organized into eight groups of 8 completely connected APs. The APs in each group are also connected to NP and together, they form a processing module (PM); also completely interconnected to each other and to a host computer via a NP.

4 SN ARCHITECTURE EVALUATION CRITERIA

In order to evaluate architectures for semantic network processing, a set of criteria has been established. In establishing an evaluation method, semantic network processing as well as architectural issues must be taken into account. The criteria along with a brief explanation are listed below.

- *Flexibility of communications.* Given that any PE must be able to communicate with any other PE in a semantic network architecture, it is required that the SN machine provides the capability of flexible communication in the configuration.
- *Communication network topology.* To avoid long delays in communication between PEs, it is desirable to implement a communication network that avoids long distances so that the latency of communication is small.
- *Run-time overhead.* Depending on the approach chosen for SN processing, run-time bookkeeping requirements may arise. In such circumstances it is desirable to reduce the run time overhead associated with such requirements.
- *Size of the PEs.* In a SN implementation it is desirable to implement the largest possible network which imposes a requirement of a large amount of processing elements. In order to avoid prohibitive cost for any given technology, the size of the PE should be kept small.
- *Load balancing.* In order to avoid delays associated with an overloaded PE, it is desirable to balance the work load for the entire network. An overloaded PE may create a bottleneck in the overall machine performance due to the computation and communication requirements.
- *Fault tolerant features and capabilities.* Fault tolerance is a concern when a large number of processing elements are put together. This feature is vital in large multiprocessor computers, since with a large amount of hardware the reliability of these computers may be small if no fault tolerant scheme is provided.
- *Fast Matching.* In order to process a large SN, in a number of circumstances, it is necessary to be able to identify an arbitrary node or link to initiate a pattern match process. Therefore, it is necessary to provide the capability of a fast search of the node (or link).
- *Computational speed of execution unit.* SN computation has a sequential processing part, consequently the speed of the execution unit is of importance in order to obtain a high performance SN machine.

- *Scalability.* As IC technology improves, to have a large number of PEs becomes feasible. Thus, scalability of parallel machines may be a need. Scalability should require little (or no) change in machine design.
- *Synchronization.* SN processing usually requires to compute several alternative paths; in a multiprocessor machine, these paths can be searched in parallel. When a solution is found, it may be required to abandon the other paths. Thus a synchronization mechanism should be available to cut the search with a minimum impact on the machine performance.

The evaluation is not a direct one as it reports the ways the considered architectures meet the identified criteria. The information has been compiled from available literature; a few issues are not fully addressed due to the unavailability of such information.

4.1 FLEXIBILITY OF COMMUNICATIONS

The knowledge network is built from nodes and links that are connected together to form the patterns of knowledge that are present in the knowledge base. Each element of the network is potentially connected to any other element. Each PE should be therefore able to provide communication paths with any other PE. There are three types of communication approaches that are generally used for semantic network computers: marker-passing, where the communication among processing elements is in the form of passing single-bit markers; value-passing, where continuous quantities or numbers are passed around and simple arithmetic operations are performed on them; and message-passing, where messages of arbitrary complexity are passed around and complex operations are performed on them [10].

NETL. In NETL, each link unit has a number of distinct terminals (wires) that can be connected to single terminals of various nodes in the network as shown in FIgure 2. These link-wire-nodes connections provide communications among different nodes of the network by means of marker propagation [13]. In order to provide for parallel marker propagation a switching network, which provides flexibility in communication, was proposed as a solution. However, designing the required switching network is a challenge (in terms of physical size of the network, packaging, degree of parallelism and simultaneous communication paths, and speed). A multi-level time-shared permutation network called *hashnet*(some of its internal connections are wired up in a random manner) was developed to enable the establishment of one-to-one connections among elements of a million-element NETL machine [12]. The basic concept used in the design of this communication network is a 960X960 seldom-blocking switching network which is time-shared 1024 times. This provides 983,040 virtual connections (flexibility in communication). This design would require a large number of devices (7008 chips) and a basic propagation time of about 5 milliseconds is estimated for it.

The Connection Machine. In order to overcome some of the shortcomings of the marker propagation systems, message-passing scheme was selected for the Connection Machine (CM) [24]. The CM's processing cells are connected through a connection network and can communicate with each other by sending and receiving messages. Each cell has a router and is physically connected (by wires) to few of its nearest neighbors. The routers form a packet switched communication network that allows processing cells to interact throughout the network by sending messages. The speed of the connection machine is limited by the bandwidth of the communication network.

The routers, which are the building blocks of the interconnection network, are autonomous switching elements. Due to the network topology not every router is connected to every other. Message-passing is similar to forwarding mails in a post office from one branch to another: processing cells communicate with one another through the routers, with the routers forwarding messages between processors. Choosing the topology for connecting the routers and selecting the algorithm for routing the messages are two major issues in designing such a message-passing system [23].

The CM provides 64K (four 16K units, selectable through a sequencer) physical processing elements, interconnected through reconfigurable communication networks. The CM-1 was designed with flexible interprocessor communication in mind [38]. Several distinct communication mechanisms, such as broadcast communication, global OR, hypercube communication, the router, and the NEWS grid (for nearest neighbor communication), are supported. The communication scheme in the CM-2 is basically the same as the CM-1 with two improvements. First, the router is redesigned to improve reliability, diagnostic capability, and performance. Second, the two-dimensional NEWS grid is replaced with a more general n-dimensional grid implemented on top of the Hypercube (by gray-encoding addresses) to increase flexibility and functionality.

SNAP. Each cell of the SNAP array contains its own communication logic (CU) that provides interfacing of the cell with its neighboring cells and access to the global buses. For intercell communications, signals are propagated from one cell to a neighboring cell via local buses. Global communication between a cell and any other cell in the array is possible through a chain of intermediate cells [31]. Data is transferred in packets via local connections and will be held in the n-input queue of the CU until it can be tranferred to its neighbor. The route taken by a packet to reach its destination depends on the routing algorithm and the actual traffic [9].

The control unit (CU) of each cluster in the SNAP-1 prototype [8] is dedicated to communication functions. Communication between clusters is implemented by a buffered message-passing scheme. Incoming messages from other clusters are disassembled by the CU. Messages destined for other clusters are relayed after examining a packet header; while messages that remain in the cluster constitute marker propagation jobs which are served by one of the marker control units [28].

Dataflow. A communication network must permit different PEs to communicate (passing tokens) with one another among the (logical) arcs. Each PE must able to communicate with any other PE directly or via other PEs. Although, it is suggested that a number of the existing interconnection schemes could satisfy this requirement [2], it is necessary for the switching network to be able to handle relatively complex tokens (templates).

SNM. The SNM architecture uses a message-passing communication scheme which provides paths between a PE and its eight nearest neighbors as well as row and column interconnection [5]. The nearest neighbor interconnection paths (through PE-PE link and row/column link modules) are bi-directional and provide two independent connections between two nearest neighbors. It is also possible to arrange the array into a row and column communication scheme by programming the row/column links. This provides long distance communications in a switching circuit fashion with buffers at each row/column link. The PEs perform communication and processing tasks independently; these two tasks are synchronized by writing and reading messages from a scratch and communication memory.

Nodes and links that are connected might not be in the same PE; they might be stored in any neighboring PE. Communication consists of an exchange of short messages among the processing elements. The two independently performed tasks (by a PE) are synchronized by message passing through the search and communication memory (SCM) [5].

IXM. The pyramid-shaped packet switching network is one of the main components of the IXM architecture [22]. Three communication tasks are performed by this network: packet communication between processing elements (mainly used for marker propagation), broadcasting of IXL commands, and the equivalence node functions (i.e, propagating markers in parallel for all nodes of a large fan-out node). This is an associative network which consists of connection paths and network processors at each node of the network [15]. Each network processor has a message routing logic which provides for packet communications throughout the network and an associative memory which exploits the concurrency in marker propagation.

4.2 COMMUNICATION NETWORK TOPOLOGY

The implemented communication network topology must avoid long distances to reduce the latency of communication. Different communication topologies may favor certain semantic network approaches or structures. Therefore, an interconnection network with reconfigurable communication topology is desirable.

NETL. The hashnet interconnection scheme used in NETL system is a seldom blocking, permutation circuit switching network in which elements are connected by means of a random pattern [12]. Due to the fact that the inter-layer wiring of the network is random and that fewer switches than needed for a strictly non-blocking network, there could not be a guarantee that a desired connection could be made at all times. However, it is noted that the probability of not being able to find a desired connection is extremely small [12].

The Connection Machine. In the Connection Machine the communication patterns are programmable. Each processing element can be connected to any other PE in the machine; thus, this allows to configure the topology of the machine to match the topology of the problem (semantic network) [23]. Two means of communications are available in the CM: routers and grids.

Routers are physically wired-up according to the topology of 12-cube network and are responsible for routing messages and delivering them to the destination specified by the address using an adaptive routing algorithm. Each router handles messages for all processing elements on its cluster of PEs. Each cluster consists of 16 processing cells and a router. The grid-like communication system provides support for local communication patterns. Through this grid, each processing element can communicate directly with its North, East, West, and South neighbors (NEWS grid) without involving the router.

SNAP. The interconnection topology used in the SNAP architecture is a two-dimensional array that supports irregular data communications via local and global buses and packet switching. The intercell communication is achieved by means of passing communication packets from one cell to a neighboring cell via local buses. Global intercell communications is handled through a chain of intermediate cells through the two-dimensional array. The communication unit (CU) of each cell handles the receiving, processing, and sending of communication packets. A simulation study of different interconnection schemes revealed that little could be gained in reducing the communication overhead by using eight neighbor connections instead of four [31].

In the SNAP-1 prototype, each cell of SNAP is replaced by a cluster of processors. The intra-cluster communication of processors (marker propagation) is achieved via multi-port memories. The CU of each cluster is interconnected to the CUs of other clusters by multi-port memories based on an interconnection topology similar to a spanning bus hypercube, with spanning buses being replaced by multi-port memories.

SNM. The basic interconnection topology of the SNM architecture is a two-dimensional array. However, in addition to the nearest neighbor connections the PE-PE links and the row/column links facilitate the connection of a PE to any other faraway PE in the array by means of row/column buses that are form dynamically [5, 6]. Fast communication between any nearest neighbor PEs is achieved by means of a reduced number of modules; such communication requires only one PE-PE link. The communication is based on a circuit switch network [5].

IXM. Using a reconfigurable (by software) hardware, different interconnections (such as 3-ary and 4-ary trees and hypercube) topologies for the associative network have been studied [20]. The interconnection structure adopted for the IXM2 is based on complete connection of associative processors [19]. Eight completely interconnected associative processors (APs) and one node processor form a processing module (PM). Similarly, eight PMs are completely interconnected to each other and to one NP which has connection with the host computer. The purpose of this adoption is to increase the speed of marker propagations performed between associative processors by providing direct communication between any two APs in a PM and between any two PMs.

4.3 RUN-TIME OVERHEAD

The run-time bookkeeping requirements, such as computing the address of nodes and links, may arise in the SN processing; the associated run-time overhead must be reduced.

NETL. Address matching and marker propagation (setting markers at selected nodes) are done in hardware in the NETL system. Therefore, the runtime overhead is minimal because there is no need for computing the address of links and nodes. In the one-million-element design [12], the NETL elements are implemented in a time-shared fashion such that each element exists in hardware only during its assigned time-slice. In order to create a "connection" between two NETL elements during a time-slice, the network switches must be set properly to establish a communication path from the specified input element to the output element. Setting these "connections" causes some run-time overhead.

The Connection Machine. In the CM system, the destination address of a message is specified by the sending processing cell as the relative displacement of the recipient cell. The path of the message is decided by the router that processes the message. On the basis of the relative address and local information, the router determines where the message should go next; it modifies the address and sends it to the selected neighbor. In the prototype CM-1 [23], the router of each cluster of PEs uses an adoptive algorithm to determine the path of a received message through the packet switch network. Communication among the processing elements in the same cluster is done through the two-dimensional NEWS grid.

It is clear that when communication is needed between nodes of a semantic network which reside in different processing chips, run-time overheads are unavoidable. The redesigned router of the CM-2 [38] provides heavily overlapped, pipelined message switching with routing decisions, buffering, and route combining of messages directed to the same destination all implemented in hardware. This results in less run-time overhead for some operations such as Sum, Logical Or, Max, Min, Overwrite.

SNAP. The address of a cell in the SNAP architecture is specified by row and column numbers. When a data packet is to be send from one cell to another, the CU of the sending PE determines the next immediate destination (one of the nearest neighbor PE) according to a routing algorithm and the actual traffic. This process obviously creates a run-time overhead which increases as communication is required between nodes (cells) that are far apart, since communication is done through a chain of intermediate cells.

In the SNAP-1 prototype [8] communication occurs in two levels: intra-cluster and inter-cluster. The CU of each cluster determines if the incoming message is to remain in the cluster or must be send to another cluster. Intra-cluster communications is achieved trough multi-port memories. The use semaphore and cycle stretching techniques for maintaining the integrity of data and utilize several software protocols to enable the communicating processors to coordinate their actions. To accomplish the inter-cluster communication, the CU of the requesting cluster determines the address of the cluster of the destination node and a routing path for the communication. Run-time overheads arise from both inter-cluster and inter-cluster communications.

Dataflow. In the Dataflow approach [2] procedures for token manipulation and communication are part of each node. Each token carries with it the address of its destination node. The sender PE must therefore determine the address of the PE holding the receiver node and the routing path. In addition, token coloring schemes may be used to distinguish tokens belonging to different graph templates. Such bookkeeping processes generate run-time overheads.

SNM. The register file of a PE is used to store nodes, links, and probabilities of the semantic network [5]. The format in which nodes and links are stored includes address fields that have information about the PE and register number in which the destination node or link resides. Address fields (pointers) give information about node-link connections as well as the direction of information. Nodes with large fanout are handled using buffer registers. The PE address is relative in order to have simple decoding hardware and small address words. Communication among nodes within a PE is done using pointers (address fields) while the same pointers are passed to the PE of a destination node (not residing in the current PE) through the network. Use of pointers and the communication links reduces the run-time overhead. The symbol field of the register file is implemented in CAM. This allows to match a symbol with the entire register file in parallel. The proposed architecture provides hardware support for pointer processing [5]; they are handled directly by the PEs hardware. This feature reduces the time to process the pointers; thus reducing the run-time overhead.

IXM. The destination of a packet in the PE-to-PE communication in the IXM system consists of the PE number and the displacement in its SNAM of the recipient node [21]. This information is used by the network processor to route the packet or to make copies of the packet and sending them to all members of nodes of equivalence, if needed. Therefore, within a PE, the CU controls the communication among nodes (words of the PE's SNAM) and since associative memory is used, the run-time overhead for finding the address of the destination node is small. However, communication between nodes in different PEs is performed by the network processors of the pyramid network using packet switching. This requires unavoidable run-time overhead. Marker propagations are handled in a similar manner in the IXM2 machine; while within an AP it can be either sequential (by means of passing messages) or parallel (using the associative memory), it is performed sequentially among APs by the network processors using message-passing method [19].

4.4 SIZE OF THE PE

Large semantic networks require a large number of processing elements. This might imply that the size of the PEs must be kept small to avoid prohibitive implementation costs.

NETL. The NETL elements that are used to represent nodes and links of the semantic network are very simple hardware devices [13]. Each element is capable of storing and manipulating few marker bits and does not have an ALU. However, the NETL elements must have a simple logic for simple Boolean operations and probably a decoding mechanism to understand the instructions broadcasted by the host computer. Still, the PE

(NETL element) can be very simple and small. If the NETL system is to incorporate a value-passing mechanism [10], then the NETL elements should be designed with an ALU.

The Connection Machine. The processing cells of the Connection Machine are simple [24]. The data processor of the CM-1 consists of a bit-serial ALU and associated latches, a small bit-addressable memory, single-bit flag registers, a router interface, and a two-dimensional-grid interface [23, 38]. The CM-2 data processor is enhanced by increased size of the bit-addressable memory, smaller number of one-bit flag registers, a generalized NEWS-grid interface, an optional floating-point accelerator, an I/O interface, and increased error-detection circuitry [38].

SNAP. Each processing cell of the SNAP architecture with its CAM, microprogrammed processing unit (PU), and control unit (CU) is dedicated to storing and processing of one node of the semantic network and its associated relations [31]. However, in contrast with this originally envisioned one node per one simple processing cell design, the SNAP-1 prototype is multi-microprocessor architecture that uses clusters of functionally dedicated Digital Signal Processors (TMS320C30) [8].

Dataflow. In the dataflow approach [2], each PE must be able to receive/send and process tokens (query templates). It must have interface logic (for communication network) and be capable of communicating with any other PE in the network. The PE must be able to determine the address of any destination node and to perform token coloring.

SNM. The processing element of the SNM architecture is able to match nodes and links as well as computing probabilistic measure of believes [6]. It is a small processor consisting of an I/O controller, communication multiplexer, scratch-communication memory, register file (partially implemented in CAM), a shift register (for fast multiplication and division), and an ALU.

IXM. In the IXM2 machine [19], the PE of the original IXM design is implemented as an associative processor (AP). In this multiprocessor architecture, each AP consists of an IMS T8100 transputer, associative memories (CAM), RAM, link adaptors, and associated logic. Each network processor consists of a T600, link adaptors, CAM, and static RAMs.

4.5 LOAD BALANCING

Having an overloaded PE (i.e. a PE with a large active portion of the semantic network) can create a bottleneck, while having an idle PE would be considered a waste of resources. A load balancing scheme is required to avoid delays due to bottlenecks.

The Connection Machine. Processing cells of the CM can be viewed as memory cells [23]. Thus, similar allocation issues and algorithms may applied. An important issue for semantic network processing is load balancing; i.e., mapping the semantic network onto the CM in a balanced way. A method for representing a semantic network for mapping onto the CM is representing each node of the network as a balanced binary tree of cells [23, 24]. A link is also represented by a single processing cell.

SNAP. SNAP simulation results indicated the effect of allocation algorithms on the processing time; it was improved when a spiral allocation algorithm was used [31]. A semantic can be loaded onto the SNAP-1 prototype with up to 1024 nodes per cluster using random or spiral allocation algorithms. A sequence control processor is used to broadcast the instantiated SNAP instructions to all clusters which may process them in their own rate. This keeps the clusters busy and balances the workload on the SNAP-1 array [8].

SNM. The semantic network knowledge base is mapped onto the architecture by means of a static load balancing algorithm [5]. This algorithm takes into account the following parameters: number of PEs in the architecture, hardware interconnection, PE status and KB's semantic network configuration. At the compile time each processor is assigned a collection of the nodes and links of the KB's semantic network. This static load balancing would help to reduce the SN computing time. It would provide an evenly distribution of the load and short communications paths [5].

IXM. Simulation results [15] indicated that an allocation method which utilizes the node of equivalence by distributing them to different PEs as many as possible could improve the performance of the IXM machine. The possibility of taking advantage of the interconnection structure (complete connection) of the IXM2 machine and the locality of knowledge represented in a typical semantic network is studied using a heuristic allocator [19].

4.6 FAULT TOLERANT FEATURES AND CAPABILITIES

A fault tolerant scheme is another concern when a large number of processing elements are put together. This feature is vital in large multiprocessor computers, since with such amount of hardware the reliability of these computers may be small if no fault tolerant scheme is provided. For the semantic network computers, fault tolerance should be considered in at least two levels: interconnection paths and processing elements

NETL. The NETL architecture provides fault tolerance to some extent at the interconnection setting level; i.e. at hashnet network level. When an attempt to create a new connection fails, the system simply skips over the failed attempted link and tries to set the connection using the next free one [12].

The Connection Machine. Two types of failure are considered in the design of the CM: soft failures which are errors that occur during a computation; hard failures which are defected components of the machine (such as a processing cell or communication unit) [23]. Each chip of the CM contains circuitry for checking various units and diagnosing faults within the chip (neighboring processors and associated routers). This failure detection capability and the redundancy in processor/memory and router cells provides the machine with fault tolerance capability.

SNAP. Full information about a node and its associated links of a semantic network is kept in a cell of the SNAP machine [31]. Each cell has link information about both its predecessor and successor nodes. This mapping provides the machine with recoverability and fault tolerance.

SNM. The SNM architecture has fault tolerance at several levels. The redundancy of communication paths in the PE-PE and row/column links provides fault tolerance capabilities at the communication level. Information about node-to-link and link-to-node connections as well as the direction of links of a node is kept in pointers. This feature provides enhancement in fault tolerance. The static load balancing avoids to map the SN onto faulty PEs or faulty registers [5].

4.7 FAST MATCHING

Matching is often needed in SN processing in order to find an element and/or to perform pattern matching. Fast matching capability is essential requirement for any architecture that deals with semantic network processing.

SNAP. The global bus of the SNAP architecture consists of two parts: the global data path and the global instruction path. The global data path is used in associative matching [31]. Also, the CAMs of the processing cells provide the machine with associative processing capability that is used along with cellular array processing to perform fast information retrieval and matching subgraphs and patterns.

SNM. Using a CAM as part of the register file of the SNM architecture reduces the matching time enormously. With a single instruction an input symbol can be compared with the entire knowledge base contents [5].

IXM. Associative memories are used in the processing elements of the IXM architecture to perform fast matching [22]. In a performance study of the IXM2 machine [8], the query processing time in a French wine benchmark is measured as 0.8 milliseconds.

4.8 COMPUTATIONAL SPEED OF EXECUTION UNIT

Arithmetic operations are also needed in a SN processing; therefore, the PE of the semantic network architecture must provide fast arithmetic and logic execution unit.

NETL. The NETL elements do not have any computing unit [13]. If value-passing is used in addition to marker-passing, then the speed of the execution unit (ALU) of the NETL elements (when processing values) will affect the overall processing speed of the system.

The Connection Machine. Although the data processing elements of the CM use single-bit, serial ALUs, the fact that many of these processors will be working on a same computation, results in a high computational speed [23, 24]. In CM-1, a 32-bit Add takes about 24 microseconds. With 64K processors computing in parallel, this yields an aggregate rate of 2,000 MIPS [38] (Adds per second). The CM-2 model incorporates an optional floating-point accelerator that can increase the overall computational speed of the machine.

SNAP. In the SNAP-1 prototype [8], the TMS320C30 Digital Signal Processor provides single-bit logical and multiplication is used to implement cost evaluation functions needed in some AI applications.

SNM. The PEs of the SNM architecture have word-parallel execution units that could provide fast processing of the semantic network Knowledge Base [5].

IXM. Bit-serial algorithms are used to perform arithmetic and logical operations on the contents of the associative memories of the IXM2 machine [19]. The execution time is constant and independent of the number of items. This provides fast execution time per item if the number of data stored in the associative memory is large.

4.9 SCALABILITY

In order to accommodate any large size of semantic network, as the knowledge base grows, the SN architecture must be scalable; i.e., it should be possible to add PEs without need for design change (for example, in the interconnection network).

NETL. Theoretically, the NETL system can be of any size. However, large NETL systems have the problem of physical wiring of the NETL elements. On the other hand, using packet switching interconnections can eliminate this problem; but the design of such a communication scheme is a challenge [13]. The hashnet packet switching network [12] is designed for one million NETL elements. For larger number of NETL element, changes must be made in components (their design, probably) of the interconnection network.

The Connection Machine. The CM architecture is designed to be scalable [23, 24]. The CM-1 and CM-2 use 12-cube interconnection network, which allows up to 64K processor/memory cells [38]. Therefore, the machine is incrementally scalable within this size. Although theoretically n-cube interconnection networks with larger n can be used to scale up the CM, some of its components (such as the router) must be redesigned.

SNAP. In order to increase the size of the array (to scale up the SNAP), changes in the components may be required. Specifically, since the address of a cell is determined by its row and column number, this will require modifications in parts such as the communication unit (CU), the packet register, CAM, etc. Scaling up the SNAP-1 machine (that is, increasing the number of clusters in the array) requires design modifications to accommodate changes in the number of clusters (and hence the addresses of the nodes).

SNM. The SNM machine could be scaled with no hardware redesign. The PEs as well as the inter-connection network are designed to support scalability. The SNM machine would be able to operate efficiently with a large number of PEs. Load balancing software would be able to handle a variable number of PE with minor modifications [5].

IXM. Theoretically, the pyramid network can be made of any size in order to scale up the IXM. However, to do so requires changes in the design of those components of the PEs and NPs that will be affected by changes in the size of the addresses of PEs and NPs [17]. The scalability of the IXM2 machine is prohibited due to the fact that the completely connected interconnection network [19] is designed to accommodate 64 associate processors. In order to scale up the machine, it may be needed to change the whole design of the interconnection network. Changes in APs and NPs would involve those components that use the address of the AP (nodes).

4.10 SYNCHRONIZATION

SN processing usually requires to compute several alternative paths; in a multiprocessor machine, these paths can be searched in parallel. When a solution is found, it may be required to abandon the other paths. Thus a synchronization mechanism should be available to cut the search with a minimum impact on the machine performance. The SN architecture must avoid complex mechanism for synchronization.

NETL. The NETL hardware is controlled by a central controller, the host computer [13], which could perform the synchronization tasks too.

SNAP. The SNAP-1 prototype uses aspects of both SIMD and MIMD processing [8]. While the controller sequences the SNAP instructions and broadcasts them to the array of clusters for execution in parallel, based on the portion of the semantic network assigned to each cluster they may require varying amount of time to execute each instruction. During marker propagation, each cluster executes independently and performs programmer or compiler-specified barrier synchronizations.

SNM. A PE of the SNM machine performs communication and processing tasks independently; they are synchronized by message-passing through the scratch and communication memory [5]. Once the PEs receive their macro-instructions (broadcasted to them by the host computer), they execute their tasks independently. Synchronization is achieved by the use of a central controller that allows to abandon a redundant or unnecessary computations with a minimum impact on the overall performance [5]. Once a satisfactory answer is obtained, the matching process may be abandoned.

IXM. The IXM machine uses both SIMD and MIMD aspects of parallel processing. The host computer broadcasts IXL commands PEs [20] which execute them independently and asynchronously in a MIMD manner using subroutines stored in their local memories (IRAMs). During this period, PEs require no synchronization. Answers are sent back to the host via the broadcast processor as soon as they are found. Similarly, associative processors of the IXM2 machine operate independently in MIMD manner with no synchronization during the execution of an IXL command [19].

Table 1 summarizes how some of the criteria are matched by architectures for semantic networks. In this table only the main features are shown.

Table 1. Computational and machine organization issues and architectures for SN processing.

Architecture / Issue	NETL	TCM	SNAP	Dataflow	SNM	IXM
Comm. approach	marker	message	message	message	message	marker
Comm. network	hashnet (random pattern)	12-cube and NEWS	local and global buses	N/A	2-D array row/colum n comm.	tree fully connected
PE	simple	bit-serial	micropro-grammed	N/A	micropro-grammed	Transputer
Load balancing algorithm	N/A	binary tree	spiral allocation	N/A	strengths	heuristic
Fault tolerance	at network level	checking & diagnosing of faults	software links	N/A	hardware links & mapping	N/A
Fast matching	processor per SN node	processor per SN node	CAM is used	N/A	CAM is used	CAM is used
Computational speed	N/A	bit-serial	bit-serial (implement ation)	word-parallel	word-parallel	bit-serial
Scalability	up to a million PEs (hashnet)	up to 64K PEs	physical addressing may limit scalability	N/A	relative addressing allows scalability	64 PEs
Synchronization	Central controller	Central controller	Central controller	Token	Central controller	Central controller

CONCLUSION

In this chapter, a comprehensive overview of issues that are involved in processing semantic networks on multiprocessor systems was presented. These issues are related not only to semantic network requirements but also to computer architectures. A novel set of evaluation criteria for computers that process AI semantic networks has been developed. Semantic network issues, such as matching, communication requirements, synchronization and processing, as well as architectural issues, such as communication topology, scalability and processing element organization, were considered in the evaluation criteria. Architectures that have been used or proposed for artificial intelligence semantic network processing were analyzed to determine how they meet the evaluation criteria. This study was based on the available information of each architecture.

The set of evaluation criteria is applicable to novel architectures for semantic network processing. The issues in these evaluation criteria deal with the semantic network processing on a multiprocessor environment, rather than with a particular machine.

REFERENCES

[1] A. Barr and E. A. Feigenbaum, *The Handbook of Artificial Intelligence.* Los Altos, Calif.: William Kaufmann, Inc. 1981.

[2] L. Bic, "Processing of Semantic Networks on Dataflow Architectures," *Artificial Intelligence*, Vol. 27, pp. 219- 227, 1985.

[3] R. J. Brachman, "What IS-A Is and Isn't: An Analysis of Taxonomic Links in Semantic Networks," *Computer*, vol. 16, no. 9, pp. 30-36, October 1983.

[4] R. J. Brachman, "On the Epistemological Status of Semantic Networks," in *Associative Networks.* N. V. Findler (Ed.), New York, NY: Academic Press, pp. 3-50, 1979.

[5] J. G. Delgado-Frias and W. R. Moore, "A Semantic Network Architecture for Knowledge Base Processing." in *Int. Journal for Engineering Applications of Artificial Intelligence,* vol. 3, pp. 4-10, March 1990.

[6] J. G. Delgado-Frias and W. R. Moore (Eds.), *VLSI for Artificial Intelligence.* Boston, Mass.: Kluwer Academic Publishers, 1989.

[7] J. G. Delgado-Frias and W. R. Moore, "Parallel Architectures for AI Semantic Network Processing," *Knowledge-Based Systems,* Vol. 1, No. 5, pp. 259-265, December 1988.

[8] R. F. DeMara and D. I. Moldovan, "The SNAP-1 Parallel AI Prototype," *Proc. of 18th Annual Int. Symp. on Computer Arch.,* ACM SIGARCH, pp. 2-11, May 1991.

[9] V. Dixit and D. I. Moldovan, "Semantic Network Array Processor and Its Application to Image Understanding," *IEEE Trans. on Pattern Analysis and Machine Intelligence,* Vol. PAMI-9, No. 1, pp. 153-160, January 1987.

[10] S. E. Fahlman and G. E. Hinton, "Connectionist Architectures for Artificial Intelligence," *Computer*, Vol. 20, No. 1, pp. 100-109, January 1987.

[11] S. E. Fahlman et. al., "Massively Parallel Architecture for AI: NETL, Thistle, and Boltzmann Machines," in *AAAI Proc. of the Annual Conference on Artificial Intelligence,* pp. 109-113, August 1983.

[12] S. E. Fahlman, "Design Sketch for a Million-Element Machine," in *AAAI Proc. of the Annual Conference on Artificial Intelligence,* pp. 249-252, August 1980.

[13] S. E. Fahlman, *NETL: A System for Representing and Using Real-World Knowledge.* Cambridge, Mass.: The MIT Press, 1979.

[14] K. A. Frenkel, "Evaluating Two Massively Parallel Machines," *Communications of the ACM,* Vol. 29, No. 8, pp. 752-758, August 1986.
[15] T. Furuya et al., "Architectural Evaluation of a Semantic Network Machine," in *Database Machines and Knowledge Base Machines,* M. Kitsuregawa and H. Tanaka (Eds.), Boston, Mass.: Kulwer Academic Publishers, 1988.
[16] J. Geller, "A Theoretical Foundation for Massively Parallel Knowledge Representation," *Parallel Computing News,* Northeast Parallel Architectures Center at Syracuse University, pp. 4-8, 1991.
[17] K. Handa et. al., "Flexible Semantic Networks for Knowledge Representation," *J. of Information Processing,* Vol. 10, No. 1, 1986.
[18] G. G. Hendrix, "Encoding Knowledge in Partitioned Networks," in *Associative Networks.* N. V. Findler (Ed.), New York, NY: Academic Press, pp. 51-92, 1979.
[19] Higuchi et. al., "IXM2: A Parallel Associative Processor," *Proc. of 18th Annual Int. Symp. on Computer Arch.,* ACM SIGARCH, pp. 22-32, May 1991.
[20] T. Higuchi et. al., "The Prototype of a Semantic Network Machine IXM," *IEEE Proc. of Int. Conf. on Parallel Processing,* Vol. 1, pp. 217-224, August 1989.
[21] T. Higuchi et al., "The IX Supercomputer for Knowledge Based Systems," *Fall Joint Computer Conference,* November 1986.
[22] T. Higuchi et. al., "A Semantic Network Language Machine," in *Microcomputers, Usage and Design,* K. Waldschmidt and B. Myhrhaug (Eds.), EUROMICRO, pp. 95-104, 1985.
[23] W. D. Hillis, *The Connection Machine.* Cambridge, Mass.: The MIT Press, 1985.
[24] W. D. Hillis, "The Connection Machine: A Computer Architecture Based on Cellular Automata," *Physica,* Vol. 10D, pp. 213-228, 1984.
[25] W. D. Hunt, *Artificial Intelligence and Expert Systems Sourcebook,* Chapman and Hall, 1986.
[26] K. Hwang et. al., "Computer Architectures for Artificial Intelligence Processing," *Computer,* Vol. 20, No. 1, pp. 19-27, January 1987.
[27] IEEE, Special Issue on Knowledge Representation, *Proceedings of the IEEE,* vol. 74, no. 10, October 1986.
[28] W. Lee and D. Moldovan, "The Design of a Marker-Passing Architecture for Knowledge Processing," *Proceedings of the National Conference on Artificial Intelligence,* 1990.
[29] H. C. Mishkoff, *Understanding Artificial Intelligence,* SAMS, Texas Instruments Learning Center, 1986.
[30] D. Moldovan et al., "Parallel Knowledge Processing on SNAP," *International Conf. on Parallel Processing,* August, 1990.
[31] D. L. Moldovan and Y. W. Tung, "SNAP A VLSI Architecture for Artificial Intelligence Processing," *J. Parallel and Distributed Computing,* Vol. 2, No. 2, pp. 109-131, 1985.
[32] M. R. Quillian, "Semantic Memory," in *Semantic Information Processing,* M. Minsky (Ed.), Cambridge, Mass.: The MIT Press, 1968, pp. 216-270.
[33] L. Shastri, *Semantic Networks: An Evidential Formalization and its Connectionist Realization.* Los Altos, Calif.: Morgan Kaufmann Publishers, Inc., 1988.
[34] J. F. Sowa (Ed.), *Formal Aspects of Semantic Networks.* Los Altos, Calif.: Morgan Kaufmann Publishers, Inc., 1991.
[35] G. Stanfill and B. Kahle, "Parallel Free-Text Search on the Connection Machine System," *Communications of the ACM,* Vol. 29, No. 12, December 1986.
[36] S. L. Tanimoto, *The Elements of Artificial Intelligence.* Computer Science Press, 1990.
[37] D. S. Touretsky, *The Mathematics of Inheritance Systems.* Los Altos, Calif.: Morgan Kaufmann Publishers, Inc., 1986.
[38] L. W. Tucker and G. G. Robertson, "Architecture and Applications of the Connection Machine," *Computer,* Vol. 21, No. 8, pp. 26-38, August 1988.

[39] L. Uhr, *Multi-computer Architectures for Artificial Intelligence.* John Wiley & Sons, 1987.

[40] B. Wah and C. V. Ramamoorthy, *Computers for Artificial Intelligence Processing.* John Wiley & Sons, 1990.

[41] B. W. Wah and G. J. Li, "A Survey on Special Purpose Computer Architectures for AI," *SIGART News,* Vol. 4, No. 96, pp. 28-46, April 1986.

[42] D. L. Waltz, "Applications of the Connection Machine," *Computer,* Vol. 20, No. 1, pp. 85-97, January 1987.

[43] P. H. Winston, *Artificial Intelligence,* (2nd Edition), Reading, Mass: Addison-Wesley Company, 1984.

CHAPTER 17

Artificial Neural and Neuromorphic Models

by Cris Koutsougeras and Nickolas Bourbakis

1. Introduction

Any survey of abstract tools which are fundamental to the AI objectives cannot but encounter the neural networks approach. The ideas of adaptive networks existed since the 50's. However, certain disappointments experienced with the Perceptron, the predominant and most publicized model of those times, led many researchers to desert this field. Recent developments though revived the interest in the neural networks approach. The result of the revived interest is a volume of new models and adaptive techniques. It has even become very difficult to categorize the existing knowledge in order to provide a systematic analysis of the various models and their associated adaptive mechanisms. The purpose of this chapter is to discuss the fundamentals and the objectives of the neural networks approach with the hope to contribute to the understanding of what can be expected of existing neural network models and what not. It would be impossible to include in the scope of this chapter all the variety of existing models. Instead, we discuss the general approaches implemented through some specific representative models. It is however true that there is a subjective factor involved in ranking the usability and significance of each one of various approaches which is mainly due to one's perspective and to the variability of the problem instances which each model targets. Thus, it is not the objective here to promote any opinion of which models are more important, but rather to discuss the fundamentals involved and to illustrate how the neural net approach is implemented in some variety of models.

2. The emergence of the neural networks approach

The idea of network-like parallel computational models is as old as the Von-Newman sequential model. The faster development of the sequential model may be attributed to the existence of the necessary theoretical and technological background such as the Boolean algebra, the cathodic tube and latter the transistor and the integration technology. The existence of the theoretical background enabled the understanding, analysis and synthesis of sequential models. The technology was then naturally tuned to such models. But theory of computation showed that there exist problems which sequential models cannot solve and other problems for which sequential models are impractical for. It was understood then that the approach to more powerful computing machines is not simply an issue of advancements in implementation technology, but it is also an issue of the underlying theoretical models for computing. In addition to that understanding, there was a disappointment related to the performance of sequential computers on specific categories of problems. These problems centered mostly around automatic knowledge acquisition, or learning, and the efficient manipulation of acquired knowledge. These were problems rather simple for humans but which proved very difficult for sequential computers. The computer speed and precision was no match for the human brain ability in classes of problems such as pattern recognition, associative recall, natural language, etc. Processing in the brain is known to be noisy and extremely slow as compared to that of a computer. Thus the conjecture emerged that the "intelligent" property of the brain is due to the massively parallel fashion in which computation is carried out. Research on formal models simulating the function of the brain brought up again the neural network models and various developments revived a serious interest in them.

The neural networks thus are models for computing originating from an effort to simulate the structure and, hopefully, the function of the brain. This also explains the inherited terminology. For many researchers the objective remains to be the development of formal models for the analysis and understanding of the brain's function. However, for many other researchers, especially those coming from engineering disciplines, the objective is the development of formal computational models with performance comparable with that of the brain. For the latter research direction, developments in understanding the functionality of the brain are conceptually interesting but not binding. In other words, the exploration of the brain's structure and functionality is inspiring for the development of computing models performing comparably to the brain in problem solving, but otherwise the new models do not have to look like the brain. It should thus be clear that for many researchers the interest in the brain is due to the fact that its structure and its related functionality is a source of fundamentals and concepts. The lack of such concepts today makes it difficult to built comparable artificial systems. Indeed, one could tear a little radio in pieces and see its structure, but it would be impossible to understand how it does what it does if he/she lacks the concept of electromagnetism. To that respect we still have a long way to go, so one should not expect that current neural net models provide a tool for all kinds of problems. However, the various models developed so far are elegant and quite powerful for some classes of problems and indeed their performance is remarkable. Furthermore, neural net models should not be thought of as models which must exactly preserve the structure or the conjectured functionality of the brain. The basic characteristics that they generally preserve are the massively parallel and asynchronous processing and the distributed control. These are properties which are thought of being fundamental to the intelligent properties of the brain and thus it is believed that they suggest a way to the design of intelligent machines. Otherwise the brain prototype is not dictative.

3. Types of neural net models

The conceptual target of neural net models is a mechanism which can acquire knowledge and self adapt to an environment by mere observation. The model mechanism is supposed to automatically readjust its internal structure in order to encode and incorporate that knowledge and then effectively use it to interpret states of its environment which are encountered for the first time. The output (or interpretation) to such new inputs (or states) is to be produced by some sort of extrapolation on the observations and on the basis of the similarity of the input with the observed instances. This kind of functionality can be viewed as a capability of the target mechanism to draw generalizations on the basis of the observations. Pattern recognition and associative recall provide particularly opportune application areas for such mechanisms. The development of a mechanism which can infer behavior rules or behavior (transfer) functions from the observation of example input-output instances is a key issue in these areas. Actually almost all of the widely known models are either pattern recognizers/classifiers or associative recall mechanisms. Common in all is the two phase operation: training phase, and normal operating phase. In the training phase the internal structure of a model is adjusted based on observations of example input-output instances referred to as the training set. In the normal operating phase the model can be presented with arbitrary inputs for which it produces outputs based on its internal function F as this was adjusted in the training phase.

Perhaps the easiest way to explain the conceptual target of the neural nets approach is to say that it is an approach to function approximation which lends itself well to engineering implementation. Function approximation is a quite old topic in mathematics. Various mathematicians have shown that functions can be approximated by a weighted collection of other simple but standardized functions under various restrictions. The goal of the neural nets approach is similar although a restriction is imposed on the basis of the approximation. The idea is to develop a theoretical system model whose input-output function is modifiable by changing certain system parameters. It is desired that this system function can approximate any given member of a certain class of functions. The objective however is that the adjustment of the parameters should be possible on the basis of a collection of samples of the function to be approximated. If such a system model can be mapped on hardware then it would provide the basis for designing machines which can learn to perform a function from given examples of the behavior which that function entails. Looking at it in another way, such machines would be able to draw generalizations about relations governing input objects from the mere observation of examples of related objects. Thus it would be possible to provide as examples a collection of pairs of input-output values of some function M (which is otherwise unknown to the machine), and have the machine develop a generalization or hypothesis as to which that function exactly is. Then the machine should be able to apply these hypotheses or generalizations to inputs it has never seen before and respond by some sort of extrapolation from the observations, in a manner that approximates the value of M for that same input. In an abstract way the above described goals can be formulated as follows: The system model (neural net) has a variable input-output function F which can be adjusted by certain system parameters. A collection of examples, called the training set, consists of samples of a certain function M. The samples are pairs of input-output values $(X, M(X))$. The goal of an adaptive method operating on the system model is to adjust the system parameters so that F approximates M while, as stated already, the only information available about M is the training set. The success in developing such system models is very significant not only for the field of computing science but also for a wide variety of engineering applications. The classic symbolic paradigm of algorithmic state machines provide solutions to problems which involve finitely describable functions. There are however significant engineering problems which involve functions that are not finitely describable, or at least, the involved functions are not explicitly known through some finite description. For example, the area of automatic control is rich in such kind of problems. Neural nets target exactly this kind of problems which involve functions which are only known partially (through samples) and which may or may not be explicitly describable through finite descriptions.

The adaptive techniques for a wide variety of models could be categorized in two major types : ***curve fitting*** and ***clustering***. In the following we discuss the main ideas and the fundamental problems associated with these two major approaches. There are other ways to classify the various models: (i) according to their net structure (net topology) as ***feed-forward*** or ***feedback*** and (ii) according to the type of the adaptive methods they support as ***supervised*** or ***unsupervised***. However, the focus of our interest here is the internal representation of knowledge and the approaches to adaptation.

3.1. Curve Fitting Models

With a curve fitting approach to adaptation the system function F is adjusted so that it represents a curve or surface which contains the sample points or as we say, it fits the samples of the training set. Equivalently the objective of the adaptation is the adjustment of F so that it accounts for the training set. The best way to present this approach is by means of a general ***feed-forward*** model.

In feed-forward models the network structure is such that the output of each neuron does not affect itself. That is, the output of each neuron does not contribute to that neuron's input. For such networks without feedback, the topology can be thought as representing a dependency graph. Neurons are arranged in layers so that the total input stimulus to each neuron depends only on neurons of previous layers. The output of the net is a vector consisting of the output values of the neurons in the output layer. If the inputs to the net are vectors from an n-dimensional space V and there are m neurons in the output layer then the (transfer) function F of the net is a mapping from V to R^m. Since there are no lateral interactions among neurons in any given layer, F can be assumed decomposable into m functions $F_i:V \rightarrow R$ for i=1..m. Thus without loss of generality we can restrict our discussion to nets with a single output. All observations then pertain to each of the F_i's in the case of many output neurons.

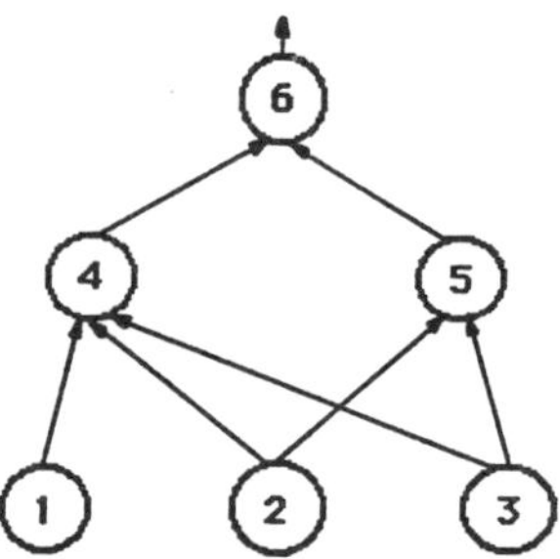

Figure 1: A feed-forward net topology

Consider now the function of the net shown in figure 1. Let F be the net's output, O_k and f_k be respectively the output and the activation or squashing function of neuron n_k, and let w_{ij} be the connection strength or weight from n_i to n_j. The total net output being the output of neuron n_6 can be expressed as :

$$F = O_6 = f_6(I_6) = f_6(W_{46}O_4, W_{56}O_5) = \\ = f_6(W_{46}f_4(W_{14}O_1, W_{24}O_2, W_{34}O_3), W_{56}f_5(W_{25}O_2, W_{35}O_3)) \quad (1)$$

The above equation shows that with such a feed-forward structure the net's function is a ***composition*** of the simple activation functions of the net's neurons. The number of layers defines the depth to which the activation functions are embedded. The above function can be generalized to general feed-forward nets with arbitrary numbers of layers and neurons per layer. The connection strengths or weights are parameters in this general function. Usually, the form of the activation functions f_i is fixed and all neurons have the same activation function. The activation function is usually a very simple function whose form varies from one model to another. In the Perceptron for example it is a linear threshold function and in Rumelhart's model it is a sigmoid function. In all models however, the weights are flexible parameters which are determined during the net's training phase. With given f_i's, by adjusting the values of the weight parameters the net's general transfer function F can be adjusted to a variety of specific well defined target functions. The set of target functions which in principle can be approximated within any desired accuracy depends on the nonlinearity available through the function (1) which in turn depends on the particular form and number of the f_i's and the way they are embedded. However, knowledge about the target functions is limited to a finite sets of point samples (training sets). Thus the objective of the adaptive mechanisms is to determine the weight parameters so that the net's function fits the samples of the training set. The important issues associated with this approach revolve around the question of how well F can approximate M. Some key issues are the following:

* The capability of the model to represent a particular function M. This capability is sometimes referred to as the capacity of the model. For many models this capability is related to the nonlinearity inherent in the model's structure. This nonlinearity determines the limits or the extend to which a given model can represent a function M of certain complexity.

* How effectively the training set reveals the essential properties of M. In other words, how well is M sampled or represented by the training set. For all models the richness or information content of the training set is essential for the goodness of the approximation of M.
* The particular characteristics of the adaptive mechanism. The function F developed by a given adaptive mechanism should approximate M but the only criterion for this approximation is the samples of the training set. On the basis of the knowledge about M which is provided by the training set only, many hypotheses as to which M could be are possible. The function F developed by the adaptive mechanism can be viewed as a generalization based on the training set or as a hypothesis about M. As long as F coincides with M on the instances of the training set, F is a legitimate generalization. However, the training set is usually assumed to point out some "rationale" or "logic" characteristic of M. Consider for example a second order polynomion which is sampled with sufficient density by a finite training set of n samples. If n is sufficiently large the shape of the sampled polynomion could be quite apparent. However, the exact same samples could have been obtained by a particular way of sampling a specific polynomion of degree n or higher which fits the given samples. Whether the intended function or some other was determined by the adaptive mechanism depends on how well the mechanism captures semantic properties exhibited by the training set as a whole.

3.2. Clustering Models

The second approach to adaptation, is based on the hypothesis that inputs which are similar should produce similar outputs. The measure for similarity is usually the Euclidean distance. An input not appearing on the training set is assumed to be mapped on an output which bears a simple relation to the outputs associated with the instances of the training set which are closest to that input. Usually this relation is an equivalence relation which implies a partition of the entire input space into a set of regions. In most models the relation between outputs of similar inputs is assumed to be equality. Thus all inputs within a given region of the above mentioned partition are mapped on the same output. The goal of the adaptive mechanism in these cases is to determine an appropriate partition of the input space, which reflects the equivalence relation. This approach to adaptation is particularly tailored to target functions M which are piecewise constant. It generally performs poorly if M is an analytic (continuous and differentiable) function. For analytic functions the curve fitting approach is better suited than clustering. However, for non-analytic functions the curve fitting techniques currently used are not well suited.

A piecewise constant function defines an equivalence relation on its input space and thus implies a partition of the space in regions corresponding to the equivalence classes. Clustering models are capable of developing internal representations identifying with the delimiting surfaces of such partitions thus they are capable of learning partitions consistent with the sample (training) sets. The building element which is popular in these models is the hard thresholding neuron. This type of neuron compares the weighted sum of its inputs $W^t X$ against a threshold value T and depending on the outcome it goes active or inactive. Its state is represented either as $\{0,1\}$ or $\{-1,1\}$. A weight vector W_i and threshold T_i is associated with each neuron n_i which thus represents some hyperplane $P_i = \{ Y \mid Y \in R^n \;\; and \;\; W_i^t Y = T_i \}$. The output of neuron n_i on input X tells on which side of hyperplane P_i the vector X lies. The delimiting surfaces of any partition can then be approximated by such hyperplane segments. Of course the partition - like the mapping function which defines it - is not known a priori and the only information about it is the training samples. So the main objective is to find a partition consistent with the samples but otherwise similar type of issues relevant to the curve fitting models apply for the clustering models as well. In some types of clustering models a slightly different approach is taken; there is no direct representation of the delimiting surfaces but instead the equivalence classes are represented by alternative methods.

In the following we discuss a few selected models. These models are chosen as representatives for illustration of the above outlined mechanisms. It is not possible to contain in this discussion detailed descriptions so the choice of models for the purposes of this discussion is partly based on the wide publicity they have received, the impact they have implied in the field, and the variability of applications they may be employed for. There are numerous models which present great interest but it is physically impossible to contain them all in this discussion.

4. Feed-Forward Nets

We discuss here some specific representative models of the feed forward type. We are not particularly interested in the details but in the general approach implemented with each of them.

4.1. The Perceptron

This is an example of a clustering type of model. In the Perceptron [26,28,29,30] the neuron's activation function is a simple threshold (step) function of the neuron's total input stimulus. The total input stimulus to a neuron n_k is the sum of the signals it receives: $\sum_i O_i W_{ik}$. The form of internal representations follow the line discussed in section 3.2. Since the output of this type of net is discrete, it can only represent functions $M : V \rightarrow Z$ where Z is a discrete set. It can be shown that any such function can be performed by this type of net if the net has a sufficient number of layers. In the descriptions of the Perceptron usually the first layer is a simple register for the input. The outputs of the neurons in the second layer provide information as to what is the position of the input vector relative to the hyperplanes represented by the neurons of the second layer. The rest of the layers essentially represent a logic function which provides the output on the basis of what region the input vector is in. Convex regions are represented as intersections (logic operation AND) of half-spaces (each hyperplane separates the entire input space in two half-spaces). General regions (non-convex) are represented as unions (logic operation OR) of convex regions. Thus with three layers (excluding the input register) the Perceptron can represent any discrete function: the first layer represents hyperplanes and their associated half-spaces, the second one represents convex hauls, and the third layer represents arbitrary regions as unions of convex hauls. However, determining the weight parameters which actually cause the net to simulate a given function M requires an adaptation mechanism which essentially boils down to a discrete search. Considering the dimensionality of this search, adaptation becomes extremely difficult. However, if M is a linearly separable one then M is a two valued function and a simple net with two layers is sufficient for representing M because really all that is needed is one neuron representing the separating hyperplane. An efficient algorithm is known for the adjustment of the weights in the linearly separable case but no efficient algorithm is known for the general case.

4.2. Back Propagation

In this model [33] the neuron activation function is a sigmoid approximation of the step function and the total input stimulus is the same as that of the Perceptron. With the f_i's being analytic functions, the net's total transfer function (1) becomes an analytic one. Thus it is possible to express the differentials of the net's output as a function of the differentials of the weight parameters. In other words the changes of the net's function F can be expressed in closed form in terms of changes on the weights.

The goodness of fit of F to the training set is measured by the total square error E. The fact that F is analytic permits us to determine exactly how changes in each specific weight affect changes in that error. The adaptive mechanism thus effects stepwise changes in the weights which cause the output error E to decrease to a minimum value. Thus this mechanism simulates a gradient descent according to the rule: $\Delta W = -\alpha \frac{\partial E}{\partial W}$ known as the Delta rule.

The adaptive process terminates when E cannot be reduced further. There is of course the question of the gradient descent getting stuck in local minima of E but various heuristics deal with that problem quite effectively. Such heuristics include the addition of momentum terms in the Delta rule and the simulated annealing method [19]. What is a real problem though is determining the net's topology which is chosen a priori. One must virtually guess the necessary number of layers and neurons per layer which would facilitate proper approximation of a target function $\boldsymbol{M}$. The adaptation mechanism operates on a net of predefined topology and it is not easy to determine whether the nonlinearity of a given net is sufficient for a certain target function $\boldsymbol{M}$. The problem with the number of layers is not very serious because it has been shown that three layers (two hidden) are sufficient for a wide variety of target functions [13]. However, the number of neurons to be used in each layer is a serious problem for which no good answer is known. So using this model with a given $\boldsymbol{M}$ often requires experimentation with various topologies. But even that practice does not provide a reliable topology choice either. Assume that with a given net the error E cannot decrease down to 0. Then it is obvious that the net does not contain enough nonlinearity. On the other hand assume that a 0 for E can be attained. This means that the net's F coincides with the target $\boldsymbol{M}$ at least at the points of the training set, but there is no guarantee that $\boldsymbol{M}$ is approximated properly in other points. In other words, a 0 for E may mean the possibility that the net may contain more nonlinearity than is exactly necessary. The excessive nonlinearity may induce an unfavorable net behavior (sometimes random) outside the specific instances of the training set.

The inability to determine a net topology appropriate for a given $\boldsymbol{M}$ is the major difficulty with this model. Other models allow an incremental formation of their corresponding net structures but with this type of net this is not an efficient technique. The Delta rule explicitly connects a weight parameter to layers which follow the one directly affected by that weight. Thus the entire net structure must be known in advance and further changes in the topology cannot be allowed. Another problem is that with a given net structure it may be possible to represent many different functions all of which fit exactly the training set. Which is the one to be identified by the adaptive mechanism is random and it is heavily dependent on various parameters of the adaptation mechanism such as initial weight values, step size (reflected by the learning rate α), momentum etc. Thus there is a strong potential to obtain various functions F with the same training set depending on the particular choice of initial random parameters such as the initial weights. There is a lot of ongoing research targeting various improvements on the basic Back Propagation algorithm in order to counter its sensitivity to initial parameters and the problem of topology choice.

4.3. The Coulomb Net

In this model [31] the network and the activation functions are the same as those of the Rumelhart model. However, this is a model for unsupervised learning and the adaptive mechanism is not based on curve fitting. This model is useful for pattern classification and essentially performs a recoding of its inputs. Inputs are classified into a finite set of disjoint classes. The objective of the adaptive mechanism here is to adjust the function (1) to one which has the following property : inputs which are of the same class should be mapped to the same output value and inputs of different classes should be mapped to different output values. The important variance here is that no particular output value is specified for each input of the training set. The net is at freedom to determine the values to which inputs are mapped.

Since the adaptive mechanism is not constrained by the explicit relation of weights to the output value, it is possible to determine the net's structure incrementally. The adaptation thus starts with a single layer of neurons in which all weights are fixed and then additional layers are recursively added with all weights of each layer determined before the next layer addition. Consider a specific layer L_k of neurons in a general feed-forward net. The vector of output values of the neurons in the preceding layer L_{k-1} is the input to the layer L_k and it belongs to a multidimensional real space which we call input space of L_k. The output space of L_k is defined by the output vector of L_k. This is also the input space of L_{k+1}. Now the function of the entire L_k can be seen as transforming its input space to its output space which is in turn transformed by L_{k+1} etc. When the adaptive mechanism is applied on the layer L_k, its objective is to obtain a transformation which contributes as much as possible to the overall objective of the net's function as it was stated above. Thus the transformation at this layer should map inputs of L_k which have been produced from net inputs of the same class to outputs which are as similar as possible (and at the same time, as dissimilar as possible for inputs of different classes). The measure for similarity of the output vectors is the Eucledian distance. The adaptive mechanism therefore attempts to maximize the harmonic mean of the Euclidean distances of output vectors produced by all inputs of the same class while minimizing the harmonic mean of the interclass means. It turns out that this can be achieved in a very elegant way by drawing an analogy with the electrostatic field where the output vectors can be viewed as the position vectors of electrostatic charges which attract or repel each other. Due to this similarity the mathematical formulation for the study of the electrostatic field can be used and the objective of the adaptive mechanism as applied on a single layer is to optimize a function corresponding to the potential of the electrostatic field. Since there is an explicit relation between the weights incident with the layer and the potential function, a gradient descent is employed to determine the weights.

Of course using one layer only with an a priori chosen number of neurons it may not be possible to map all inputs of the same class to the same output vector. This however can be achieved by the addition of successive layers. This allows a relative independence from the choices of topology since the choice of number of neurons at each layer is not critical. If the nonlinearity of the net as this has been developed to a point is not enough, further additions of layers can compensate for it. Termination of the net's expansion depends on the required accuracy of discrimination among the output vectors.

As was mentioned earlier, this network performs a recoding of its inputs. The recoding however is not known a priori. All that is provided to the adaptive mechanism which forms the net is the set of inputs along with their classification identifiers. Since the measure of similarity used for adaptation is the Eucledian distance, inputs which do not appear on the training set are expected to produce an output similar to the one corresponding to the input's closest vector (again in terms of Euclidean distance) of those in the training set. Thus this model is expected to perform well when vectors of the same class cluster well together. This model is of further interest since it can be combined with other models. Indeed, it discovers input recodings which can be employed for filtering or reduction of the dimensionality of the input space. Thus in many cases it can be used as a preprocessor to other neural net models or to other recognition techniques.

4.4. Kohonen's feature maps

This model [20] is an example of an unsupervised learning approach where the learned object classes are not represented by their corresponding delimiting surfaces within the input space. Instead, each object class is represented by a few representative objects chosen appropriately from that class. Membership of an input to a class is decided on the basis of greatest similarity to one of the objects which have been chosen to represent classes. Assume for example a partition of the input space in a number of object classes. The selection of vectors to represent each class is made with the following objective: given a certain measure of similarity, any member X of a class C_i should present a stronger similarity to one of the representative objects corresponding to C_i than to any other of the representative objects for any other class. Another characteristic of this model is that it is an ***unsupervised learning*** model. No a-priori classification characterization is provided along with the samples. Instead, the various object classes are dynamically determined through the learning (adaptive) process and the samples are partitioned in disjoint groups of highly correlated samples. This process identifies clusters of input objects with a high degree of similarity, and these clusters constitute the various classes.

The measure of similarity used in this model is the scalar product of two vectors which reflects the correlation between the two vectors. Objects are represented as vectors. The model consists of a set of neurons each of which is associated with a weight vector. An input is fed to all the neurons which then compute the scalar products with their corresponding weight vectors. The weight vectors correspond to the objects representing the various classes as discussed above. The open question is how many neurons are needed given a training set, because it is not known a priori how many sets of highly correlated input objects can be distinguished upon. The higher the number of neurons the better the granularity of the partition which however may end up in trivial sets of one object each if a large enough number of neurons is used.

The neurons are assumed to form an array and their initial weights are random. We will assume a two dimensional array here. In repeated presentations of the training set, each neuron computes the scalar product $W^t X$ for each presented object (vector) X. Then the neuron which computes the highest value is determined. The weight vectors of this neuron and its physically nearest neighbors on the array are updated. The updates are such that the measures of the weight vectors remain always normalized to unity while their directions become closer to the currently presented object X according to the update rule:

$$W' = \frac{W + a\,X}{|W + a\,X|} \tag{2}$$

where W' and W are the new and old values for a neuron being updated.

4.5. The Athena model

This model [22,23] is an alternative to the Perceptron. It has the same expressive power as that of a multilayer Perceptron with hard thresholding neurons. However, Athena's structure is restricted to a tree-like one which, as will be explained in the following, alleviates the training problems arising with the Perceptron. Objects are again represented in terms of vectors of values corresponding to a collection of properties or attributes. Thus the object space is an n-dimensional vector space V. The domain knowledge is some mapping M from the vector space V onto a finite set of elements $Z = \{z_1, z_2, z_3, \ldots z_m\}$. The set of objects (elements of V) which map on a given value z_i constitute an object class C_i.

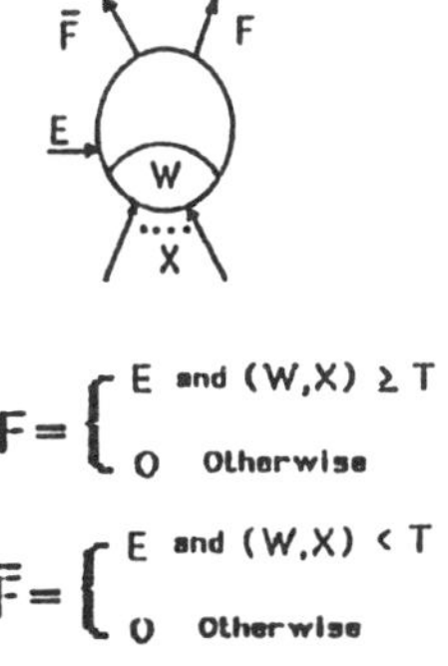

Figure 2: The neuron type of Athena

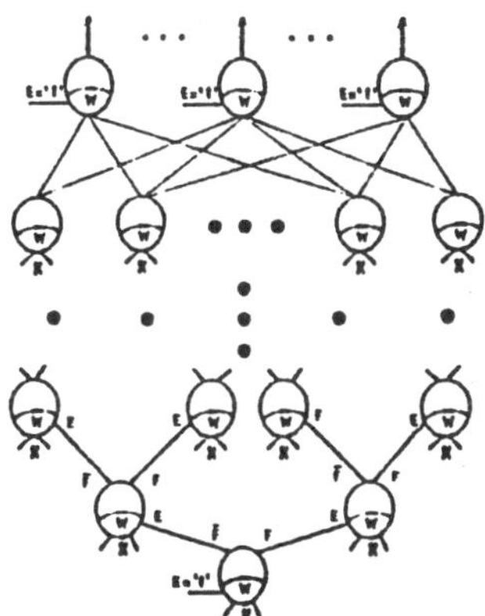

Figure 3: The structure of Athena

The internal representations for this model aim the approximation of delimiting surfaces separating the various object classes according to the general approach outlined in section 3.2 for clustering models. The building element of this model is also a hard thresholding neuron as illustrated in Figure 2. Each neuron n_i has an associated weight vector W_i and threshold T_i and represents a hyperplane P_i. An input X to the net is fed to all the neurons. The arrangement of neurons in this model forms a decision tree as shown in Figure 3, thus the model's structure is based on a standard interconnection pattern. Neurons pass on to their children neurons an enable signal which activates a single path of neurons in the tree structure. If the threshold test at neuron n_i succeeds then its F_i output is activated enabling n_i's right child neuron otherwise $\hat{F}_i$ is activated enabling the left child neuron. This operation takes place if n_i has itself been activated, otherwise both its outputs remain inactive. The neuron at the root is always active.

The (active) output of a neuron indicates the position of the input X relative to that neuron's hyperplane. For each input vector at most one chain (path) of neurons is activated and the leaf activated node represents a specific convex set whose boundaries are the hyperplanes of the activated neurons and in which the input lies. In fact the activation of any neuron u_k (not necessarily a leaf) provides the information that the input lies in a specific convex set bounded by the hyperplanes of the ancestors of u_k in the tree. This convex set which is associated with neuron u_k will be referred to as the space of activity of u_k. The hyperplane associated with u_k divides u_k's space of activity in two parts which then become the corresponding spaces of activity of u_k's children neurons. In this way the input space is successively subdivided until each one of the convex sets of the leaf neurons contains vectors (objects) of a single class. This way of partitioning the input space is illustrated in figure 4. Thus each object class can be represented as a collection of convex sets. This is the common representation basis with decision trees. The problem however is how does one go about discovering the necessary hyperplanes and thus how the model is trained given a finite number of samples (classified vectors).

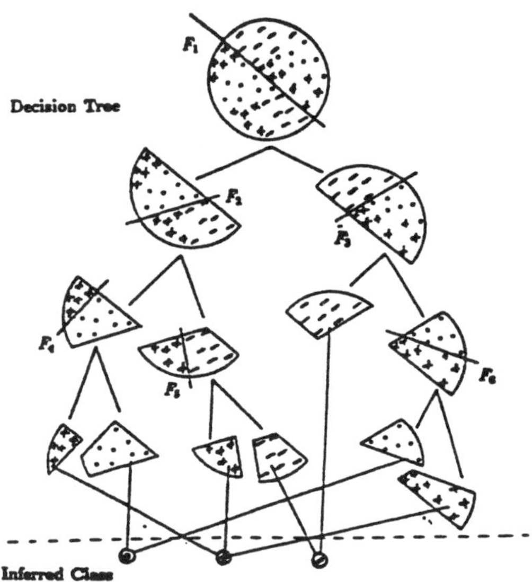

Figure 4: Partitioning the input space into object classes with Athena

It is evident that one could proceed with random selections of hyperplanes and terminate when no convex set of the developed partition contains samples of more than one class. However, the objective is to use as few hyperplanes as possible which is a difficult problem. The basis of this optimization can be formulated in terms of an entropy measure as follows. If neuron u_k is activated while an input X is being presented then X belongs to u_k's activity space. On the basis of only the fact that the input vector belongs to the activity space of u_k the overall classification decision is restricted among the limited subset of classes which intersect with u_k's activity space. The decision of u_k then further restricts the region in which X lies and reduces further the uncertainty about the overall classification decision for the input vector. The information enhancement, or expected ***information gain***, which is due to u_k's output decision (F or $\hat{F}$) is then proportional to:

$$[\frac{N_r}{N_r+N_l}]\sum_i \frac{p_{ir}}{N_r}\log(\frac{p_{ir}}{N_r}) + [\frac{N_l}{N_r+N_l}]\sum_i \frac{p_{il}}{N_l}\log(\frac{p_{il}}{N_l}). \tag{3}$$

where p_{iu} and p_{il} are the corresponding numbers of example vectors of class C_i in the activity spaces of the left (subscript "l") and right (subscript "r") children of u_k, and $N_u = \sum_i p_{ir}$ and $N_l = \sum_i p_{il}$. The ideal selection of hyperplane P_k (corresponding to u_k) is the one which maximizes the above expression (3). This optimization aims in developing a decision tree of minimal expected height.

Given all the possible orientations of a hyperplane and its possible positions with respect to the origin, this optimization is a difficult problem. Therefore a heuristic method is used here to reduce the dimensionality of the problem. The heuristic method is used to identify the orientation of the target hyperplane. The orientation determined in this way yields the weight vector. Then the hyperplane is allowed to sweep the space while its orientation is kept constant (parallel movement) and a position is determined which corresponds to an optimal value for the expression (3). This determines the threshold value and thus the target hyperplane is obtained.

The value of the measure of equation (3) for a chosen P_k is unchanged if equation (3) is written for the projections of the sample vectors on the direction of the weight vector which is normal to P_k. Then for the vector W_k defining the orientation of P_k, it is required that the projections of the example vectors are separated as best as possible. Thus a measure of the goodness of a given projection direction W_k is needed and Fisher's approach of discriminant vectors [18] lends itself well for this task. Assume that there are totally r classes associated with the input space. The goodness of a given discriminant vector W can be heuristicly measured by :

$$J(W) = \frac{\textit{Sum of squared distances of the mean projections of all classes from the projection of the overall mean}}{\textit{Variance of all sample projections}} \tag{4}$$

where projections are understood to be in the direction of W. If M is the mean of the entire sample set and m_i is the mean of class C_i, then the above measure can be expressed as:

$$J(W) = \frac{W^t B\, W}{W^t S\, W} \tag{5}$$

where S is the lumped covariance matrix $S = \sum_{i=1}^{r} \sum_{X_j \in C_i} (X_j - m_i)(X_j - m_i)^t$, and $B = \sum_i (m_i - M)(m_i - M)^t$. The vector W which maximizes $J(W)$ is the eigenvector which corresponds to the largest eigenvalue of $S^{-1}B$ as shown in [18].

The S matrix may be singular in some cases where the training set presents certain peculiarities. This case occurs when all the instances of the training set are linearly dependent, i.e. they all happen to lie in a single hyperplane, or when the instances of the training set lie in a set of parallel hyperplanes so that the instances of each class are in a single hyperplane. In the latter of the above cases the solution W vector is an eigenvector corresponding to a 0 eigenvalue of S (scaling is not important). Otherwise, i.e. the singularity is not due to that specific case, the approach suggested in [18] is followed, which virtually leads to a transformation of the input space V. Then the above method involving the ratio (5) is applied in the transformed space V' whose corresponding matrix S' is always non-singular.

The transformation is defined by a matrix Φ whose rows are the eigenvectors of S which correspond to the non-zero eigenvalues of S. The transformed space V' consists of the vectors ΦX, where X is a vector of the original input space V. This technique transforms the entire input space (and thus the training set) to another one which does not present the peculiarities of the original space. For example, as a result of the transformation certain dimensions of the original space may be rejected as unimportant to the classification decision. It should be noted that if such a transformation must be used then it is employed only locally at the neuron under consideration and not necessarily at the successor neurons also. Each neuron receives only an enable/disable signal from its parent thus simply being called to produce a decision. This decision is local and concerns only the space of activity of this neuron. Each neuron need only receive the decision of its parent and otherwise it does not matter how the parent's decision was obtained.

5. Models with feedback: The Hopfield Net

This is another curve fitting model but with feedback [15,16]. The neuron activation function in this model is the same linear threshold function used in the Perceptron. However, unlike in the Perceptron in this model there is feedback which is essential to its function. Originally, this model was developed in an effort to explain how a massively connected network of simple processing units can display abilities similar to those of the brain. So in essence it was developed as an effort to model the brain and explain how with such a structure some functions of the brain, such as memory and associative recall, are possible. Beyond that however, this model was shown to be a computational tool which can in principle handle optimization problems which are hard for sequential computers.

The net in this model consists of bistable neurons with bidirectional connections among them. In principle, a connection may exist between every pair of neurons. The term ***state of activation*** has been adopted to refer to a collective state of the network in which every neuron has assumed one of its two states usually referred to as "on" or "off". The net's state of activation at a given time also represents the output of the net at that time. Thus the net output is a vector of the (binary) values produced by the neurons. In this model all the neurons check their total stimulus (linear sum of all inputs received from other neurons) against their corresponding threshold values and readjust their states (outputs) accordingly. This operation takes place in a parallel, continuous and asynchronous fashion. If some neuron n_k is connected to another neuron n_m with a positive connection strength (or weight) then n_k provides a positive stimulus to n_m thus favoring n_m's "on" state. If the weight is negative then n_k favors n_m's "off" state. It is thus apparent that given an initial state of activation, a given neuron n_k may change states continuously as a result of variations of its total input stimulus which is induced by changes of the states of other neurons. But changes of n_k's state also induce changes in the total input stimulus of other neurons and so possibly to their corresponding states.

The effect of this massive interaction is a chaotic transition of the net's states. However, it can be shown that if the connections are symmetric, i.e. $W_{ij} = W_{ji}$ then this transition will eventually terminate with the net ending up in a dynamically stable state. The way that stability is attained is to show that a Lyapunov function for this net (as a system) exists. This function is called ***energy function*** and it is always positive. It can be shown that if the net's connections are symmetric and the neurons assume their states according to the threshold activation function then the energy function is monotone decreasing. Given the fact that it is always positive, a state has to be assumed during the transition which must be stable, otherwise the energy would be decremented indefinitely.

This model can be seen as a computational structure used in the following way : Feeding an input to the net is done by forcing the net's state of activation to the one dictated by the input (vector). Then the net is let to go through state transitions to equilibrium. The state of activation at equilibrium represents the output which the net produces in response to the original input. This point of view of a computation basically redefines the notion of an effective procedure or algorithm. Under this point of view the effective procedure is no more a stepwise process which terminates but rather a continuous process which converges.

Hopfield has shown that this model can in principle be used to solve the classic Traveling Salesman Problem [17]. He has shown this by showing how a path among the nodes of a given graph can be represented by an appropriate structure of this type of net. The connection weights of the net can be chosen in such a way that the energy function is equivalent to the cost function of the Traveling Salesman Problem.

Since the net's operation is such that it naturally optimizes the energy function, the stable state which the net assumes represents a path with optimal cost thus representing a solution. This point of view is very significant since the Traveling Salesman Problem is NP-hard. It is known that all NP-hard problems can be effectively transformed to this problem, and thus the same principle use of this net is significant for them too. In fact other researchers have shown that a variety of other NP-hard problems can be directly mapped on the Hopfield net. The significance however is broader. This model can be used as a natural optimizer of its energy function. Given a general optimization problem, if the problem can be mapped on the Hopfield net so that the net's energy function becomes equivalent to the cost function to be optimized, then the net can in principle identify a solution. Thus an optimization problem can be solved with this net, simply by virtue of its ability to be mapped on the net.

6. Neuromorphic systems and implementation considerations

Learning (from the perspective of function approximation/adaptation) is currently the most intense focus of neural nets research. The discussion of the previous sections aimed in illustrating in the technical level some approaches to learning (in the context of automatic function approximation) and to knowledge representation as they are implemented in certain neural net models. We expand here the discussion to neuromorphic systems, that is, systems based on connectionist principles and where the distribution of processing is essential for their efficient operation. Often it is difficult to classify a certain model on the basis of its processing structure or its functional target. We could say that the original term "neural net" identifies a distributed system where distribution of processing is ***fundamental*** for its operation rather than simply a matter of design choice. A pure neural net thus would be thought of as a model employing distributed representations, processing, and control, and constituting of a massive set of processing elements which exchange simple signals and perform very simple operations on a local level. The response of the system is collectively influenced by the local decisions or responses of the constituent processing elements. After all, the development of neural systems was motivated by the brain structure whose neurons seem to perform very simple functions and whose processing capability seems to be due to the massive interaction of the neurons. Neuromorphic systems on the other hand are based on designs which adopt only certain characteristics of the pure neural net principles and mainly the distributed processing and the connectionist structure. Processing elements are usually much more powerful than neurons typically are and the exchange of information among them is more structured (it may consist of both data and control information) and it is usually synchronized. Such a neuromorphic system is discussed in the next section. Neuromorphic systems are the result of the effort to employ the current VLSI technology and design concepts which are well understood in order to implement neural net principles. Indeed there is some difficulty in developing with current VLSI technology the hardware which would be perfectly compatible with pure neural net principles. The massive interconnectivity which is generaly required is a serious limitation for VLSI designs. New technology is sought by many researchers in the neural nets field for the implementation purposes. Optical technology is a promising candidate and many serious efforts have surfaced which employ experimental optical processing structures. In the following the implementation considerations are illustrated for two systems.

6.1. Hermes: a neuromorphic system for vision

Hermes [2,3,4] is an example of a neuromorphic system in which processing and control is distributed over a structure of identical processing elements which exchange information and control signals on the basis of local decisions. The system has been developed for vision and thus its input are two-dimensional arrays (grids) representing images. The structure of Hermes is a pseudo-quadtree of processing elements (PE's) where control flows top-down (root element to leaf elements) and processing proceeds bottom-up. An input image is divided in sets of adjacent pixels (quartets) and each set feeds a PE which is responsible for local decisions in that region of the image. The structure and the distribution of inputs are shown in figure 5. The hardware organization of the HERMES processor nodes for 16 nodes is shown in figure 6. Each element of the lower layer (leaf) receives as inputs pixel values only. All other elements (inner nodes) receive as inputs both pixel values and information from their children elements. Additionally, each element receives input from its parent PE. This input represents hypotheses which must be checked against the image and it also implies some sort of control to the receiving element since the testing of these hypotheses determines the further actions of the receiving element. To produce a response (or to perform the testing of the hypothesis received from its parent) each element, while accounting for its own pixel inputs, produces requests or other hypotheses which must be checked at lower levels and submits them to its children elements. On the basis of the pieces of information returning to the element considered, a response is synthesized and submitted to the parent PE. This response constitutes an abstraction on the total information arriving at the PE. Thus, the overall processing involves a top-down flow of requests and hypotheses and a bottom-up flow of information which is abstracted more and more as it reaches higher layers. These abstractions are made locally at each PE on the basis of combined local information and lower level abstractions. The root node initiates the processing and produces the overall response.

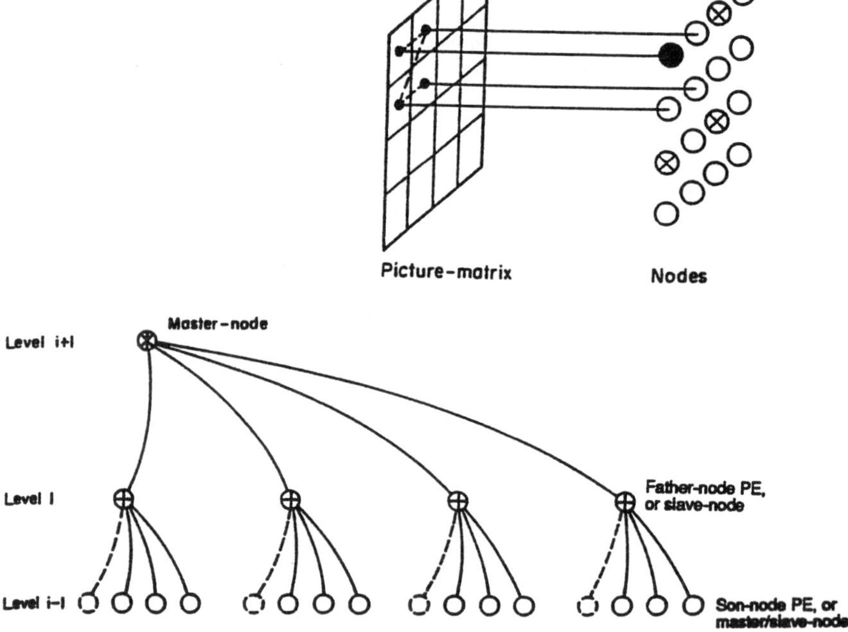

Figure 5: The structure and distribution of inputs in Hermes

Hermes is an autonomous system and thus its operation includes three phases: training, pattern recognition, and image interpretation [4,5,6]. The training phase pattern classes are formed on the basis of unsupervised learning schemes. In particular, at the lower level of the HERMES structure, the only available information is the correlation of the input pixel values. Thus each lower level node is expected to create several clusters (see Table 1) from these correlations by producing output signals and values related to the input pixel

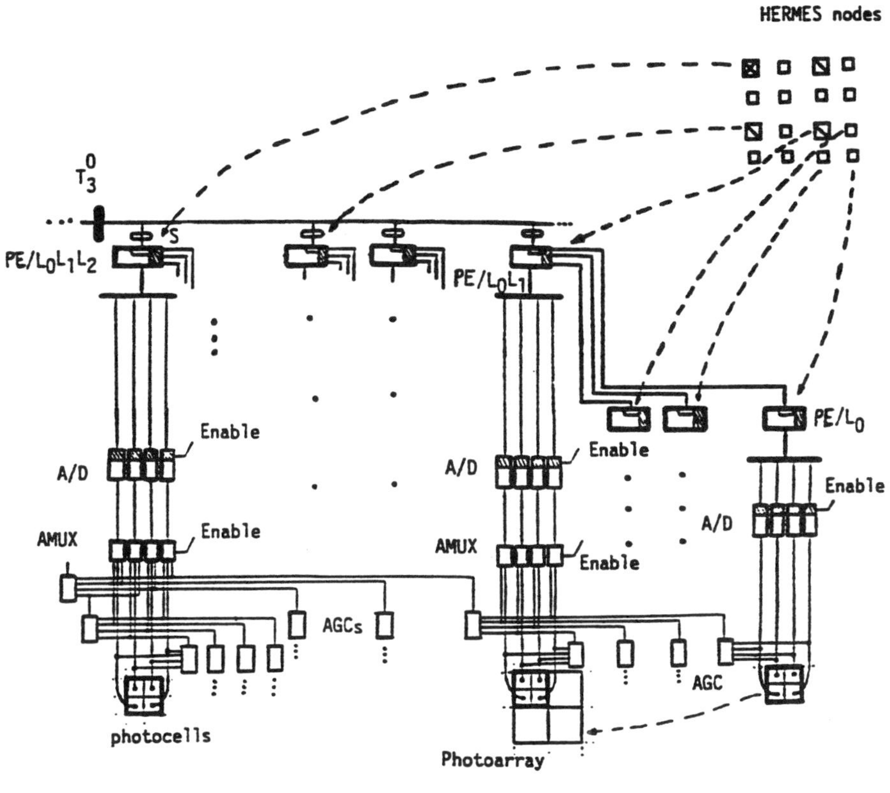

Figure 6: The vertical hardware organization of the HERMES processor nodes for 16 nodes. $PE/L_0L_1 \cdots L_k$ represents a PE which functions at $k+1$ consecutive levels.

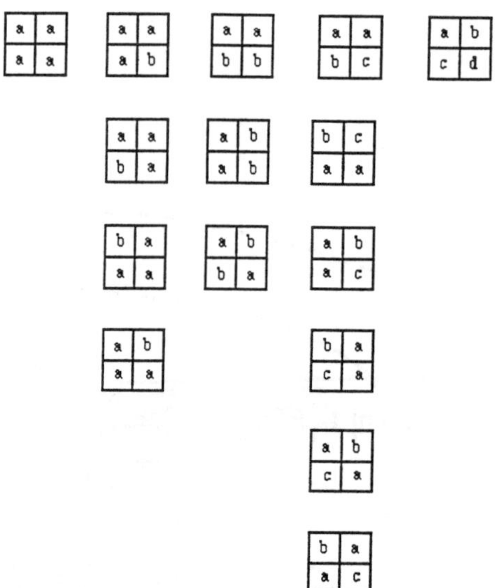

Table 1: Clustering of the input pixel values (learned)

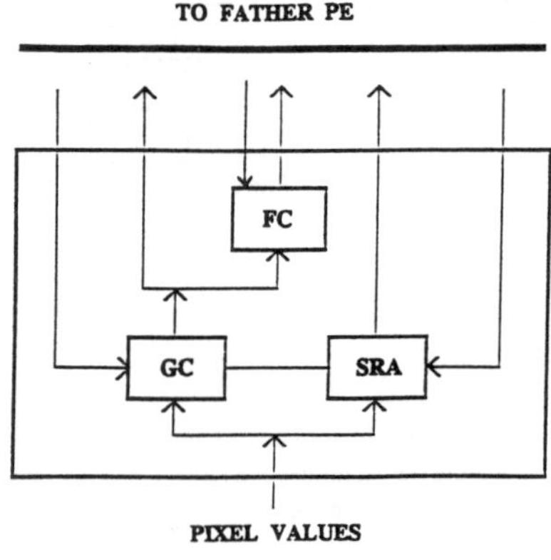

Figure 7: The global design of a PE at the lowest level (L_0)

values. At the higher levels, the HERMES nodes form high level abstracted pattern classes by using synthesis, deduction, and induction mechanisms. In the recognition phase objects are recognized on the basis of attributed graph representations of a form similar to that of semantic nets. In the interpretation phase, the overall scene is interpreted on the basis of (i) distance measures computed in a hierarchical manner, and (ii) learned information which is represented as semantic nets.

Effective VLSI implementation is possible for HERMES because it has a standardized array-tree structure with more than 75% of the PEs lying at the lower level. Also, the tasks to be performed by the PEs at the lower level (see figure 7) are well defined. Thus the emphasis for the VLSI design is focused on the PEs at the lower levels. The basic tasks that a PE performs are as follows: (i) General Coding (GC), (ii) Segmentation Region Analysis (SRA), (iii) Freeman Coding (FC), and (iv) Simple Transfer (ST). Thus each PE can be designed as four interconnected hardware units each dedicated to one process.

GC unit

A block diagram for the hardware architectural representation of the GC unit is given in figure 8. As mentioned earlier, the input image is segmented into photoarray regions and each segment (four pixels) is fed to a corresponding PE. Within a PE pixels are received by the GC unit and, by means of an A/D converter, they are encoded in 8-bit grey-level binary values (GLV's). Since each PE receives only four adjacent pixels, there are a total of 15 possible generic combinations of GLV values. Thus, the output of GC is a code identifying the GLV combination which characterizes the photoarray region of the PE. For most precision two

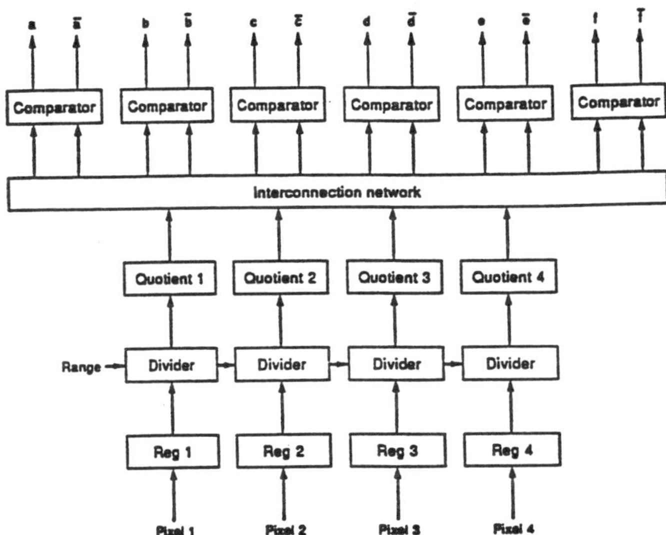

Figure 8: Block diagram of the GC unit

pixels are considered different when their GLVs differ by only one bit. In general however the entire range of the 2^8 GLVs can be segmented into blocks of range values. The number of these blocks is determined by either the grand master node (the PE at the root of the tree) or the local father node. The local father node is the upper left node in each quartet of PEs (see figure 5). Each local father PE receives signals and values from its own three successor PEs at the lower level of the HERMES structure. The global internal design of a father PE is shown in figure 9. In essence, the number of the encoding bits is variable and set by the master node although this has to be done indirectly since the D/A converter has a fixed number of output encoding bits. The function of the GC unit is thus as follows:

1. Receive the GLV of the four pixels, where each pixel has its own id.
2. Divide each pixel's GLV with the range of the sub-blocks and find the quotient of each division. For each quotient an id is assigned. This assignment follows the same pattern as that of the pixels.
3. Instead of comparing the GLV of the pixels the corresponding quotients are compared:
   * Quotients are separated in six pairs of combinations (Q_1,Q_2), (Q_1,Q_3), (Q_1,Q_4), (Q_2,Q_3), (Q_2,Q_4), (Q_3,Q_4). If the two quotients in a pair are different then the corresponding pixels are also considered to be different.
   * 12 signals are produced (six positive and six complementary logic) which indicate the relation between the GLVs of the pixels which correspond to each of the above six pairs.
4. The AND-block (which will be defined later) uses these 12 signals to produce an encoding corresponding to one of the 15 combinations which characterizes the input.

As shown in figure 8, the first network structure provides the appropriate paths for the production of the six previously introduced pairs. The second interconnection network provides the interface between the output of the comparator and the inputs of the AND-block. The GLVs of the four pixels are stored in the four registers R_1,R_2,R_3,R_4. The four dividers are circuits that divide an input A by a input B and produce a quotient through the output C which is stored in one of the registers Q_1,Q_2,Q_3,Q_4. The block R_i and Q_i, i=1,2,3,4, are 8-bit registers. The blocks called "comparators" have two inputs A and B and two outputs C and C'. The output C equals 1 when $A=B$ $(C'=0)$ and $C=0$ when A/B $(C'=1)$. The divider is a block that performs an integer division.

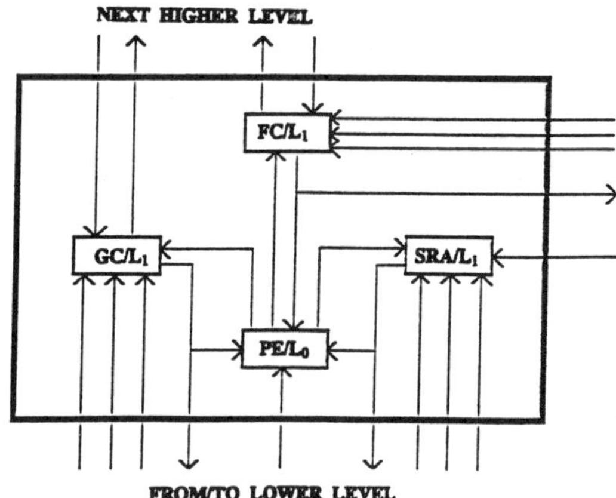

Figure 9: The global internal design of a father PE

The first network mentioned above, consists of the paths that form the required six pairs of quotients. To find these paths the Deutsch dogleg algorithm [10] is used. The output that this algorithm provides is shown in figure 10. According to Deutsch algorithm doglegs would be introduced at terminal positions of the net only.

The comparator circuit is implemented using a five device EXCLUSIVE-NOR gate, as shown in figure 11. When the activation transistor, the one at the bottom of each five devices block, is ON the comparator is operational. When it is OFF, the comparator is disabled and the compare output indicates a match irrespective of the comparator's inputs. Note that the match state is a logical ONE, hence when several EXCLUSIVE-NOR gates are connected in a parallel to construct a comparator, only one not-compare element is necessary to pull the compare line down to the low state. The maximum operating speed of the comparator is set by the compare line capacitance and its associate pick-up device resistance. A single not-compare bit must be able to pull the compare line down in one block cycle.

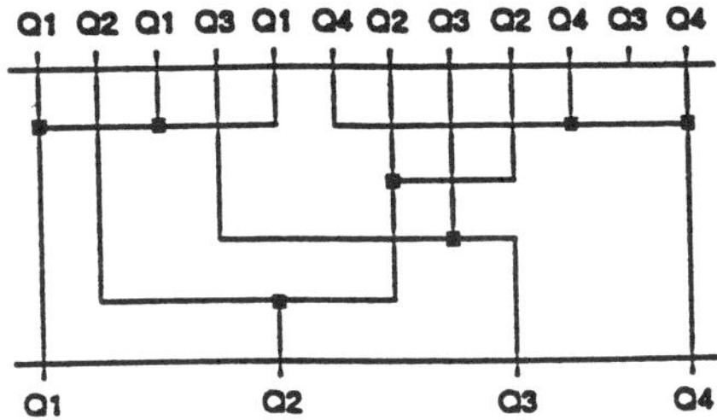

Figure 10: Output of the Deutsch dogleg algorithm for 4 lines

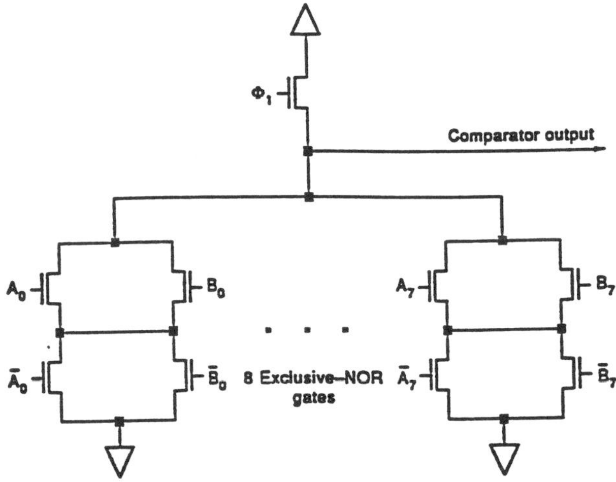

Figure 11: Implementation of one stage of the comparator circuit

The second interconnection network is produced by using the Deutsch algorithm again. The solution is not shown here since it is too complex to be displayed. The design of the AND block is straightforward with 15 sections one for each of the 15 combinations of the input pixel GLVs.

SRA unit

The SRA's output provides the upper level nodes with the pixel's id and its value, if the later is within a range defined by the father node. A possible block diagram is shown in figure 12. The comparator block in figure 12, is different from the comparator of GC. The purpose of this comparator is to compare the pixel's GLV with the lower and upper bound of the range. If the pixel's GLV is within the range, its id and GLV will be transferred to the father node. To achieve this operation the comparator rises the signal E_i to high when a successful comparison is accomplished and passes the GLV of the pixel. Signal E_i feeds the enable input of the register P_i, which holds the id of the specific pixel. The merging network needs further research and its design is beyond the scope of this article. The purpose of the merging network is to receive in parallel the pixels ***id***'s and their GLVs coming from the comparators and produce a serial output of ***id***'s and GLVs which is sent to the father node.

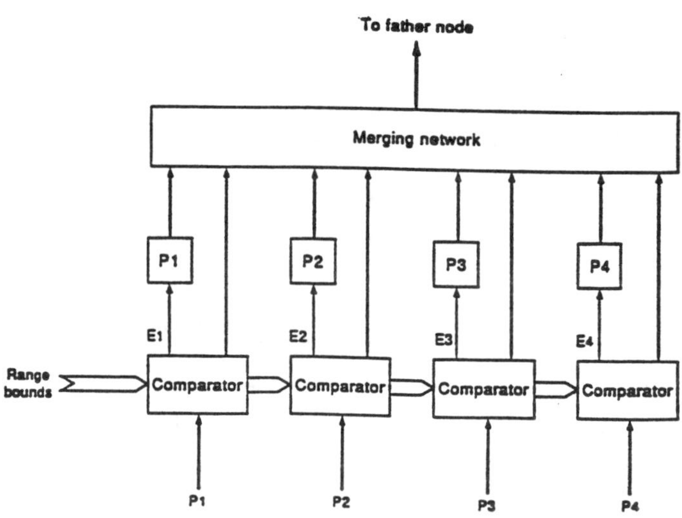

Figure 12: Block diagram of the SRA unit

The P_i blocks are simple registers which hold pixels ***id***'s, therefore they don't need any further attention. On the contrary, the attention is focused on the comparator block. It is divided into two sub-comparators. One compares the GLV of the pixel against the lower bound (LB) of the range, while the other one against the upper bound (UB). If both comparisons are successful, which means that $LB \leq GLV \leq UB$, the pixel's GLV is passed through the circuit. A possible block diagram of the comparator is shown in figure 13. The transistor level schematic of the sub-comparator for only one bit section is shown in figure 14.

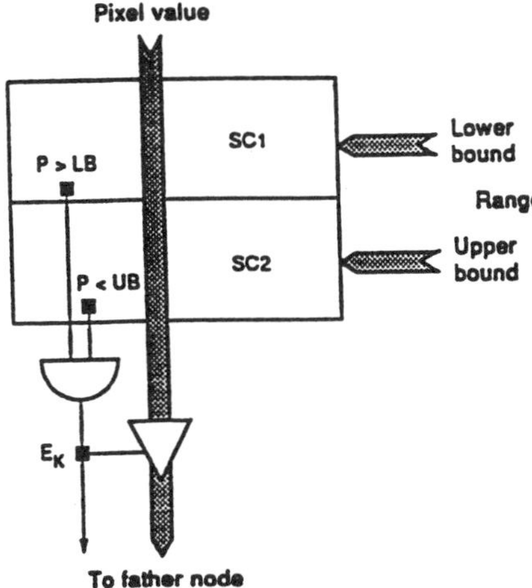

Figure 13: Comparator for the SRA unit

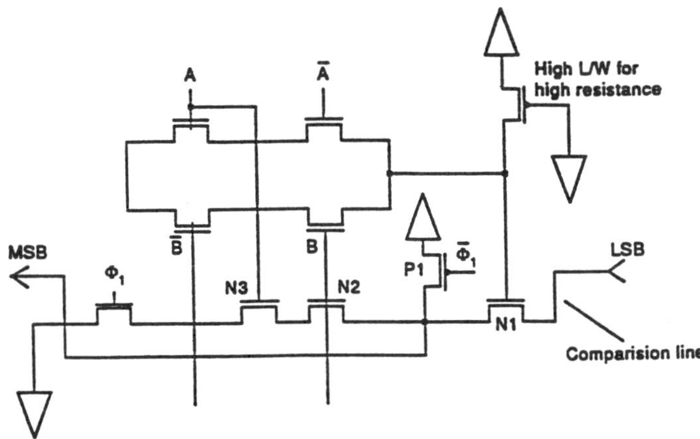

Figure 14: Transistor level schematic of the SRA sub-comparator for a 1- bit section

Both the positive and the complemented logic of the two values are needed for the comparison to be carried out. The comparison is done in parallel for all the bits. Dynamic logic is used for the implementation of the circuit and only one clock pulse is needed. The circuit's operation is as follows:

1. During the low phase of the clock 0, the transistor(s) P_1 is ON, therefore the whole comparison line, as well as the output of the circuit, are high.
2. The comparison is performed when 0 rises to high.
   * If the corresponding bits of A and B are different then transistor N_1 is OFF and the current state is isolated from the previous one. In this case transistors N_2 and N_3 determine the current ratio ('<' or '>') between A and B bits. If $A_i > B_i$ ($A_i = 1$ and $B_i = 0$) then $C_{out} = 1$, otherwise $C_{out} = 0$.
   * If the corresponding bits of A and B are equal then the transistor N_1 is ON at least one of N_2 and N_3 will be OFF. In this case the status of the previous state is transferred to the next one.

FC unit

Describing pixel locations as a sequence of points represented by their x-y coordinates is a rather inefficient method for purposes of feature extraction and normalization. An efficient representation scheme has been introduced by Freeman which takes advantage of the fact that pixels are located on a grid structure. Directions of orientation (see figure 15) are encoded by a symbol each and a sequence of pixels is represented by a sequence of symbols which represent the sequence of directional steps by which the sequence of pixels can be traversed. Each PE develops the Freeman Code for its own pixel array. The function of FCA is as follows:

* The position or geographic location of the pixel which is the head of a chain of pixels with similar GLVs.
* A chain of directions, based on figure 15, connecting one pixel to another with similar GLVs with the starting one.
* If the chain has a break and does not cover the whole region, pick another pixel not covered from the previous chain, based on the priority level scheme shown in figure 16, and develop a new chain directions.
* Perform the steps above until the whole region is covered.

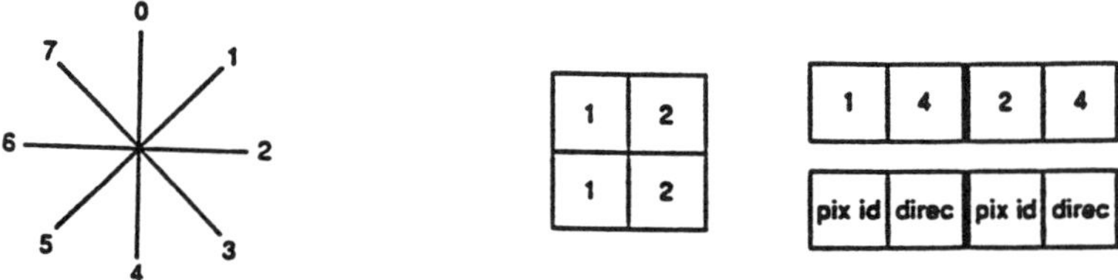

Figure 15: Freeman coding directions

Figure 16: GLVs of a region and its Freeman Coded information

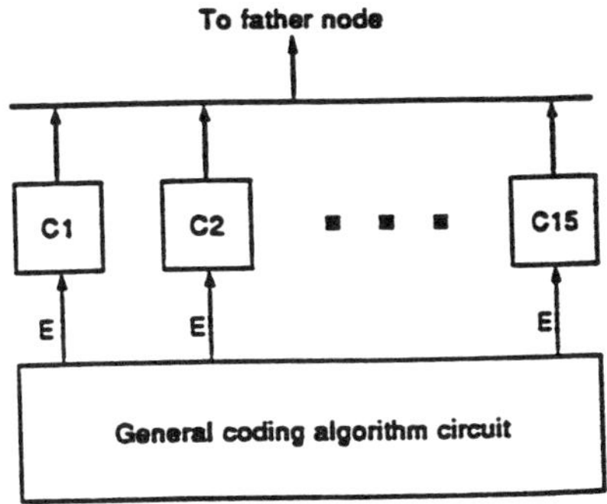

Figure 17: Block diagram of the FC hardware

The block diagram of the FC hardware is shown in figure 17. A slightly extended GC hardware circuit serves the purposes of FC. The blocks $C_1, ..., C_{15}$ are composed of registers. Each one of them holds the FC information which corresponds to the combination in which the four pixels belong to. Only one of these blocks of registers is enabled at a time.

ST unit

There are cases where the father node requires a simple transmission of the data from its son nodes, i.e., correlation. In this case the PE must simply pass the pixels ***id***'s and their GLVs to the father node. No extra circuit overhead is needed for the implementation of the ST transfer. The SRA circuit is sufficient to support this transmission. In this case the range input of SRA should cover the whole domain GLVs.

6.2. Hybrid machine architecture for Athena

One more machine architecture is discussed in this section. This architecture is based on the Data Flow model [34,35] and can easily employ optical processing structures. It is thus a good example for illustrating the use of optical technology. The architecture has been proposed for the Athena model and thus its design objective is to achieve high throughput for the normal processing phase of the model. The training phase is performed only once, while in the normal processing phase streams of inputs must be processed. The machine architecture supports the simulation of many different instances of the model (i.e. many trees for various applications) and processes streams of inputs for all the trees simulated on it.

The global architecture is shown in figure 18. It consists of a set of Data Flow clusters interconnected by a ring communication network and a host processor. The host processor is used for input-output and for the performance of matrix computations required during the training phase, while the computations required in the normal processing phase are carried out in the Data Flow clusters. The frequency of training phase computations is very low and they also require powerful hardware, so this hardware is allocated to the host only and it is shared. The structure of a Data Flow cluster is shown in figure 19.

Athena's tree is mapped onto the architecture like a normal Data Flow graph stored in the local memory (node store) of one or more clusters. A graph is simulated as templates corresponding to nodes and residing in the node store. Templates are linked with pointers representing directed arcs. A template contains the weight vector and threshold, pointers to the templates corresponding to children nodes, and two additional fields used for labeling and timestamping. The label is used as an identifier of the tree to which a template belongs.

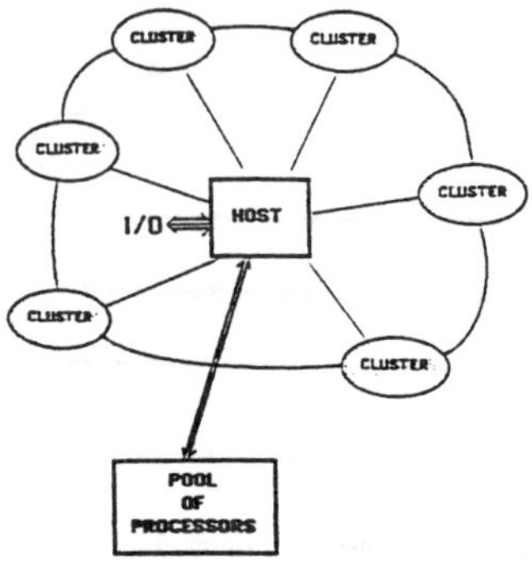

Figure 18: The global architecture for Athena

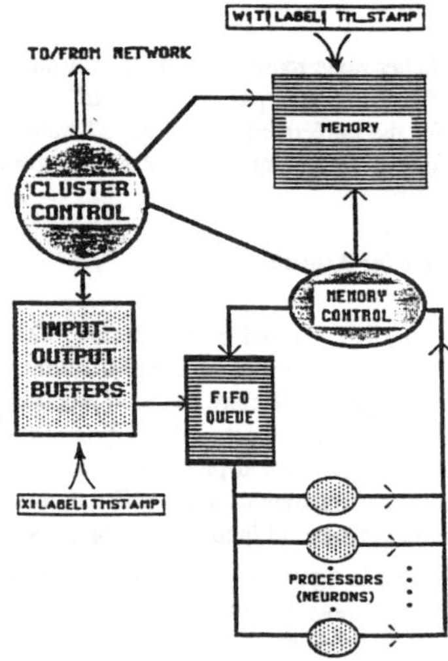

Figure 19: The structure of a single cluster

Inputs are entered from the host and are also represented by packets. When an input is entered, the host forms a packet containing the input, a timestamp, and a label identifying the decision tree for which it is intended. The timestamp is used to distinguish this input from others intended for the same tree. The input packet is then broadcasted to the clusters. Each cluster containing a tree with the same label retains a copy of the input packet in its input buffer.

The processing phase is carried out as follows: Consider a template corresponding to a neuron (tree node of Athena) which gets activated. Then the template is "fired", that is, a packet copying the info of that template is formed and sent to the processing queue. It is then augmented with the value of the input which resides in the input buffer and which matches its label and timestamp. Subsequently, it is assigned to a free processing element (PE) for execution. At that PE the threshold test is performed and an output packet is produced. The output packet contains the same label and timestamp values and a pointer to the node (template) which is to be activated next. This output packet is sent back to the activity store whose controller creates the new packet to be sent for processing. This new packet carries the same label and timestamp as the output packet which triggered its creation and the weight vector and threshold of the template referenced by the same output packet.

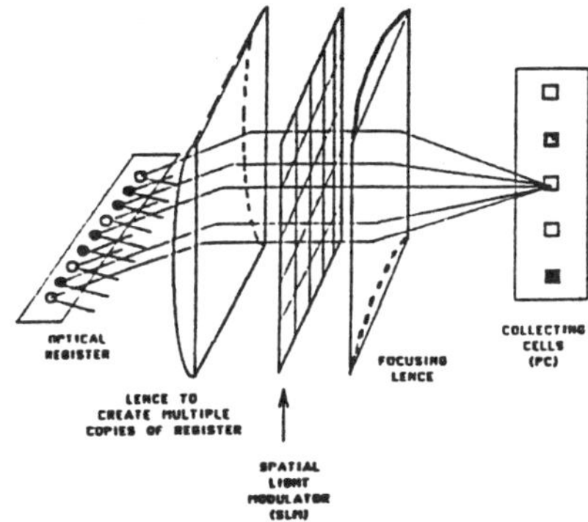

Figure 20: Optical processor for computation of scalar products of vectors

Although the PEs can be implemented by VLSI technology, it is more advantageous to utilize optical technology for their implementation as it is explained in the following. The structure of figure 20 has been proposed by Cassasent in [8] for the optical computation of the scalar products $X^t Y_1$, $X^t Y_2$,... $X^t Y_k$, between a vector X and a set of vectors Y_i, i=1..k. The vector X is held in an optical register of LED's and its component values are encoded by the emitted light intensities. The values of the vectors Y_i are encoded by the electronically controlled transparencies of the spatial light modulator (SLM). The electronic outputs of the photosensitive array of elements encode the scalar products, all in parallel. Thus a total of k node computations can be performed optically in parallel. Rather than firing a single packet at a time a whole subtree of packets can be fired at once. When the node store receives a signal (activation packet from the PEs) to activate a template, it activates that template and $k-1$ of its successors in a Breadth First manner, where k is the capacity of the SLM in any of the (optical) PEs. The weight vectors of these packets are eventually loaded in the SLM of a PE while the input vector X is loaded into the LED register and the corresponding thresholds are used as biases on the PC cells. The outputs of the PC register represent the outputs that each node in the subtree would produce if activated with input X. A simple search through these outputs determines the correct output which the decision subtree produces when processing X. Although this implies processing of nodes which would not actually be activated, it saves circulation time in the cluster, and determines the path to be activated on the tree by a given input in $log(k)$ segments.

The advantages offered by optical processing are remarkable. Other significant efforts been made by various researchers to implement neural net models by use of optical technology. For example the Hopfield model has been implemented with optical structures which quite resemble the one of figure 20 since it also requires the computation of a large number of scalar products of vectors. For the Hopfield model alternative implementations have been proposed with SLM's [14] and with holograms [36]. In this model there is feedback and dense interconnectivity, since each neuron is virtually connected to every other, which makes it very difficult to employ VLSI technology. With very dense interconnectivity the circuit graphs cannot always be planar and the crosstalk problem becomes severe. Optical technology on the other hand offers advantageous alternatives but it is still in an experimental stage. The use of light beams allows much greater bandwidth than electrical signals do and light beams can cross without interference. The difficulty is that optical structures cannot yet be manufactured to packages analogous to VLSI density and the miniaturization stumbles on quantum phenomena. The VLSI design concepts cannot easily be applied in optical processing structures because there are fundamental differences in the two approaches. In VLSI data are represented by voltage whereas in optical processing they are represented by energy. Also for electrical signals there are amplifying elements and cascading is easy whereas for optical signals the dissipation makes cascadability hard. Today it is possible to design electro-optical structures which present many advantages, but it is not easy to design pure optical structures because it is not easy to control light signals with other light signals. However, one of the focuses of the optical technology research is new materials which have already found their way to market products. There is still way to go but the new technology seems to offer interesting grounds for the implementation of the new and demanding computational models. As important as these theoretical computational models are, so is the technology which will eventually make it possible to implement them efficiently.

7. Conclusion

In conclusion of this chapter a note is due about the impact introduced with the neural nets approach. The impact reaches beyond the AI field. Neural nets have promoted the fundamental theoretical basis of AI. Many other AI approaches were based on heuristics, depended on efficient programming techniques, and were tuned to specific applications and their peculiarities. It was not easy to formulate the relevant mechanisms in abstract analytical terms and abstract mathematical tools were of limited use. The neural nets approach however, starts of with a mathematical/analytical formulation and makes it possible to study the related problems on an analytic/theoretical basis. This is partly the reason that neural nets has been the research object of many scientists from many areas - and not only from computer science - and it is also the reason that the neural nets approach has allowed the transport of concepts and methods from various disciplines into the computing field. Concepts from physics (spin glasses, coulomb field, etc.), from thermodynamics (annealing methods, Boltzmann machine, etc.), from signal processing (Kalman filters, approximation techniques, etc.), from control systems (stability, convergence, etc.), from mathematics and so on have been used for computing related problems which before the neural net models did not seem to have any connection to computing methodology. But it is not only the shift in methodology that is associated with the neural nets approach. This approach, being based on concepts which are formulated theoretically/analytically, has provided new grounds for many other computer science areas such as theory of computation, knowledge representation, learnability, etc. Last but not least there is an impact on technology trends. Optical processing as an alternative to electronic processing has received an increased attention and promotion partly due to the technological demands of neural nets which VLSI technology has difficulty to meet. However, above all and ultimately, what is interesting and useful about the neural nets approach is that it targets directly and on theoretical grounds the design of autonomous machines. Many other approaches have not managed to detach themselves from the need of a programmer who organizes the knowledge base and encodes it for the system. The neural nets approach assumes changing, noisy, and uncertain environments and it operates on raw observation of examples from which it automatically extrapolates. This independence from the need of a programmer who processes/organizes the knowledge and transfers it to the net is obvious in many neural net models: after training, it is usually difficult for the user to comprehend the reasoning by which the net produces its output.

The neural networks approach emphasize a new paradigm for AI: the dynamic systems paradigm. At the current point of AI history a lot of people wonder whether this dynamic systems paradigm will eventually prove more powerful than the classic symbolic paradigm of algorithmic state machines. Considering the current underlying premises of each paradigm there is very little ground for comparison. The classes of problems which are targeted by each paradigm present some fundamental differences. The symbolic paradigm is better suited when dealing with functions which are finitely describable whereas neural nets are better suited when dealing with functions for which finite descriptions are not known. In addition, the neural nets approach has currently some limitations, such as dealing with structured inputs, which the symbolic paradigm does not have. It is difficult with current neural net models to process sequences (structure on the basis of a time parameter) or to process syntactic structures. The reason is that neural nets in the internal level essentially perform functional composition whereas the operation of the symbolic paradigm is based on syntactic compositionality. It thus appears more likely that in the near future hybrid systems will be targeted as more promising, that is, systems which constitute of subsystems from both paradigms.

References

[1] R.B. Banerji "Artificial Intelligence: A Theoretical Approach", Elsevier/North Holland Scientific Publishers, 1980

[2] N.G. Bourbakis, "Design of Real-Time Supercomputing Vision Systems", Proc. IEEE Conf. on Supercomputing, Vol. 1, pp 392-398, CA, 1987.

[3] N.G. Bourbakis and F. Barlos, "Hardware Design of the Lower Level Nodes of the HERMES Heterogeneous Neural Network", Intl. Journal on EAAI, vol. 5, No. 1, 1992

[4] N. Bourbakis, "Symbolic Learning on a Connectionist Structure", TR-1990.

[5] N. Bourbakis and D. Tabak, "Working Mechanisms and their Petri-net Modeling for the HERMES Multiprocessor Vision System", Intl. Journal on EAAI, vol. 1, No. 1, pp. 102-110, 1988.

[6] T. R. Gowrshakar and N. Bourbakis, "Specifications for the Development of Knowledge-Based Image Understanding System", Intl. Journal on EAAI, vol. 3, No. 2, pp. 79-90, 1990.

[7] G.A. Carpender and S. Grossberg, "Neural Dynamics of Category Learning and Recognition in Brain Structure, Learning, and Memory", AAAS Symposium Series, 1986.

[8] D. Casassent and E. Baranoski, "Directed graph for adaptive organization and learning of a knowledge base", in Applied Optics Vol.27, No. 3, February 1988

[9] W.S. McCulloch and W.H. Pitts "A Logical Calculus of Ideas imminent in Nervous Activity", Bulletin Math. Biophysics, 5, 115 1943

[10] D. Deutsch, "A Dogleg Channel Router", Proc. 13th DAC, pp 425-33, 1976.

[11] R. Duda and P. Hart "Pattern Recognition and Scene Analysis", John Wiley & Sons 1973

[12] R. A. Fisher "The use of multiple measurements in taxonomic problems", Ann.Eugenics, 7, Part II, 179-188 (1936); also in Contributions to Mathematical Statistics (John Wiley, New York, 1950)

[13] K.I. Funahashi, "On the Approximate Realization of Continuous Mappings by Neural Networks", Neural Networks, Vol.2, 1989

[14] G.R. Gindi, A.F. Gmitro, and K. Parthasarathy, "Hopfield model associative memory with nonzero-diagonal terms in memory matrix", Applied Optics, Vol. 27, No. 1, 1988

[15] J.J. Hopfield, "Neural Networks and Physical Systems With Emergent Collective Computational Abilities", Proc. NAS, Vol. 79, pp 3088-3092, May 1984.

[16] J.J. Hopfield, "Computing With Neural Circuits: A Model, Science", Vol. 233, pp 625-633, Aug 1986.

[17] J.J. Hopfield adn D.W. Tank, "Neural Computation of Decisions in Optimization Problems", Biological Cybernetics, 52, 141-152, 1985

[18] R.A. Johnson and D.W. Wichern, "Applied Multivariate Statistical Analysis" 2nd ed. Englewood Cliffs, N.J. : Prentice Hall, 1988.

[19] Kirkpatrick, S., C.D. Gellat Jr. and M.P. Vecchi, "Optimization by Simulated Annealing," Science, Vol. 220, No. 4598, May 13, 1983.

[20] T. Kohonen, "Representation of sensory information in self-organizing feature maps, and relation of these maps to distributed memory networks" SPIE Vol. 634 Optical and Hybrid Computing(1986), pp. 248-259.

[21] Kolen, J.F., and J.B. Pollack, "Backpropagation is Sensitive to Initial Conditions", Complex Systems, V.4, 1990

[22] C. Koutsougeras and C.A. Papachristou, "Training of a Neural Network Model for Pattern Classification Based on an Entropy Measure", in Proc. IEEE Internat. Conf. on Neural Networks (ICNN '88), New York: IEEE, July 1988.

[23] C. Koutsougeras and C.A. Papachristou, "A Neural Network Model for Discrete Mappings", in Proc. IEEE Internat. Conf. on Languages for Automation (LFA '88), New York: IEEE, October 1988.

[24] C. Koutsougeras C., H. Barad and A. Martinez, "Neural Networks in Scene Analysis", Invited paper, SPIE conference, Orlando FL. April 1990.

[25] R.P. Lippman, B. Gold and M.L. Malpass, "A Comparison of Hamming and Hopfield Neural Nets for Pattern Classification", MIT, TR-769.

[26] M. Minsky and S. Papert "Perceptrons - An Introduction to Computational Geometry", MIT Press 1969 (1987, 2nd edition)

[27] J.R. Quinlan, "Learning Efficient Classification Procedures and their Application to Chess End Games", in Machine Learning, Vol1. R.S. Michalski, J.G Carbonell and T.M. Mitchell (editors), Tioga Pub. Co. CA (1983)

[28] F. Rosenblatt, "Principles of Neurodynamics: Perceptrons and the theory of brain mechanisms", Spartan Books, Washington, D.C. 1961

[29] F. Rosenblatt, "The Perceptron: a Probabilistic Model for Information Storage and Organization in the Brain", Psych. Review 65 386-408 Nov. 1958

[30] F. Rosenblatt, "A Comparison of Several Perceptron Models", in Self-Organizing Systems 1962 ed.

[31] C.L. Scofield "Learning Internal Representations in the Coulomb Energy Network", in Proc. IEEE Internat. Conf. on Neural Networks (ICNN '88), New York: IEEE, July 1988.

[32] M.C. Yovits, G.T. Jacobi, and G.D. Goldstein, Spartan Books , Washington, D.C. (1962)

[33] D.E. Rumelhart, G.E. Hinton and R.J. Williams "Learning Internal Representations by Error Propagation", in Parallel Distributed Processing: Explorations in the Microstructure of Cognition. Vol1: Foundations, D.E. Rumelhart and J.L. McClelland (editors), MIT Press, Cambridge, MA (1986)

[34] I. Watson and J. Gurd, "A Prototype Data Flow Computer with Token Labeling", in AFIPS Conf. Proc. Nat'l Comput. Conf. June 1979

[35] I. Watson and J. Gurd, "A practical Data Flow Computer", in Computer, Vol.15, No.2, Feb. 1982

[36] H.J. White and W.A. Wright, "Holographic implementation of a Hopfield model with discrete weightings", Applied Optics, Vol. 27, No. 2, 1988

SECTION 7

AI APPLICATIONS

CHAPTER 18

Specifications for the Development of a Knowledge-Based Image Understanding System

T. R. Gowrishankar
The University of Chicago, Chicago, IL

and

N. G. Bourbakis
State University of New York, Binghamton, NY

Abstract

This chapter presents the structure and design criteria of a knowledge-based system to classify an image, based on its constituent entities. A knowledge base is used to store the structural and spatial information which form part of a frame-based expert system. A frame data structure is used to represent the knowledge of image entities from different points of view, and a semantic net representation is used to reflect the relative positions of these entities within an image. The search through the knowledge base utilizes a heuristic, data-driven approach over an entity-space tree whose nodes are labeled with apriori goodness measures [1]. The entity-space tree describes various complex patterns in terms of a hierarchical composition of simpler subpatterns (entities). The knowledge base is augmented by including data pertaining to identified images, and modifying the weights on the corresponding nodes of the entity-space tree accordingly. A set of knowledge rules is used to determine the system path strategy. This chapter discusses the structure of the knowledge-based system mentioned above, along with the search technique suggested for the proposed system.

1. Introduction

In contemporary computer-vision applications, images encountered in practice are usually complex and the number of features required to describe them is often very large. Thus, it is impractical to contemplate the description of every image in the application domain for classification purposes. Consequently, segmentation of images into meaningful entities presents an attractive alternative for image recognition [2]. Constraints based on contextual information, called the *world model*, are used to obtain a consistent and unambiguous valid assignment of entities [3]. This amounts to two stages of processing, a low-level stage concerned with segmentation, and a high-level stage corresponding to the understanding of the segmented image. Segmentation of images should result in regions which correspond to objects, parts of objects, or groups of objects which appear in the image. The features of these entities, along with their positions relative to the entire image, help us in making a meaningful analysis.

One of the early attempts at addressing the issue of representing spatial relations between image entities using predicates like left(x,y), right(x,y), above(x,y), etc. was made by Barrow and Popplestone [4]. These predicates were used to formulate rules defining the elements of an image. The VISIONS system [4], on the other hand, interprets the elements of an image by combining low-level output with computed attributes, viz., *color, texture, orientation*, etc. This type of knowledge is highly sensor- and scene-dependent and is often viewed as being shallow. For image-processing applications, the characteristics of components of interest are usually best described by resorting to *structural* relationships. The properties of these *structural* classes are best exploited by the systematic recognition methods [5].

Most image-segmentation applications provide a '*knowledge-rich*' environment, with functional relationships between image constructs and spatial constraints. In addition, the presence of a body of literature pertaining to segmentation heuristics enables easy acquisition of the knowledge essential for an expert system. It is logical, therefore, to use these sources of apriori knowledge in designing a segmentation system.

The primary motivation for the use of an expert system or a knowledge-based system is the need for an explicit scheme for representing the knowledge embodied by a large number of segmentation heuristics. Earlier expert systems suggested for the low-level segmentation of images were constructed on a rule-based design [6]. In ANGY, an expert system for a medical application, knowledge was represented in the form of a relational model, including both geometrical and procedural knowledge [7]. Knowledge, when expressed as a set of rules, is not always as easily understood as it would be if it were expressed in some other form [8]. This is due to the fact that all necessary contextual knowledge must be stated explicitly in the condition part of each rule. Unless the rule-based system is built on well-defined semantics, it can result in unjustifiable and unpredictable inferences.

One of the important objectives in the design of this knowledge-based system was to use the information related to various segmentation heuristics efficiently in understanding the contents of an image. The image understanding system blends the knowledge describing different primitive entities and sub-images and also enables the interaction of this entity knowledge. Meaningful information extracted from images in the application domain constitute the knowledge base and also helps in formulating the knowledge rules [9]. These knowledge rules are used to decide the type of processing required for purposeful analysis. Both class-specific and image-specific knowledge, and interaction between these knowledge sources are utilized in the analysis of images. The instances of these knowledge types are used in determining the path through a search tree. In essence, knowledge corresponding to a world model helps in determining the *goodness* measure associated with each node of the search tree. This in turn drives the search procedure towards a meaningful inference.

For a general image understanding system, spatial analysis based on semantics of the form *above, below, left-of, right-of*, etc. are not adequate [10]. Hence, knowledge about key entities or key attributes related to one or more objects in an image is used to supplement the spatial relations between different structures. This helps in relating the world model to an image under analysis.

The knowledge base that forms part of an overall system is constructed using various types of knowledge. This includes knowledge concerning definition of domain entities, knowledge of spatial relationships and constraints between these entities, knowledge of various possible collections of entities forming sub-images, knowledge about combinations of these sub-images to form the complete image and knowledge of methods used in resolving conflicts between competing inferences.

The proposed system uses frames to represent the knowledge characteristic of different entities. This facilitates the implementation of a heuristic-based search through the knowledge base. Frame structures accommodate a taxonomy of knowledge with default values and generic properties. This type of data structure is particularly suitable for the current application, as it enables clustering of all properties related to an entity or a set of entities. Frames also facilitate analogical reasoning of both procedural and declarative knowledge [8].

In addition, semantic net representation is adapted for reflecting relations between various entities in different classes of images. This form of representation makes it convenient to test the validity of logical inferences of relational properties in image-understanding applications. Semantic networks can be implemented with ease using languages employed in conventional knowledge-based systems. A semantic network is highly suitable for extracting potential search areas in an image, and for partial matching of entities in an image of high complexity.

This chapter discusses the representation of above knowledge sources and the implementation of a knowledge-based system in understanding an image. In the following section, we present an overview of the image understanding system. Next, we discuss the representation of knowledge using frame and semantic nets. In the subsequent section, the search techniques used in accessing the knowledge base, and the functional aspects of the system are detailed. An example of the use of an expert system in the field of biomedical imaging is also illustrated. Aspects of possible improvements are analyzed in the last section of this chapter.

2. Overview of the System

One of the important objectives of expert systems used in image processing is to develop efficient image-analysis procedures for each image in the application domain by composing primitive image-processing operators. Thus, an expert system not only requires image-domain knowledge, but also needs knowledge about various image processing techniques for proper implementation. These sources of knowledge establish correspondence between object models and features extracted from an image. The knowledge sources also enable the introduction of certain measure of flexibility in selecting the type of process needed to analyze any fragment of an image.

The system is built around a knowledge base consisting of two banks of data, pertaining to low-level structural description of entities and high-level spatial relations between them. The preprocessing stage converts an input image into a form suitable for processing by the system. Analysis of an image from primitives obtained by segmentation is done using the spatial and structural information contained in the knowledge base. An inference-engine module is incorporated into the expert system to achieve this task using the contents of the knowledge base. Each stage of segmentation and inference process has access to the knowledge base, as shown in Figure 1. In addition, the outputs of different stages invoke necessary modifications in the knowledge base [11].

The knowledge base that is proposed for use in this understanding system contains knowledge pertaining to both low-level and high-level stages of processing. This includes knowledge about characteristic properties of entities, and knowledge about the spatial relationships between these entities. As mentioned in the last section, frames are used to store descriptions of different entities that form a world model. However, semantic net representation is found to be the appropriate form for storage of relational knowledge. Also, a measure of goodness is associated with each attribute of a frame, proportional to the relevance of the

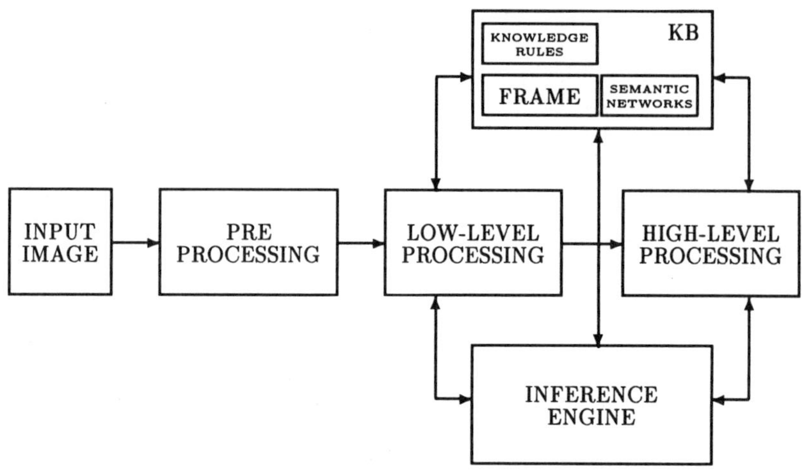

Figure 1: Block Diagram of the Image Understanding System

represented feature to the corresponding object class. This allows incorporation of *'analogical reasoning'* in the understanding process. The control knowledge needed to determine the order of processing and resolution of conflicts is also embedded in the knowledge base.

As noted in the previous section, low-level processing corresponds to identification of image entities based on primitive elements present in the image. The main advantage of analyzing an image in terms of a set of primitive elements is that a recursive method of processing can be employed [12]. For example, an object *'house'* can be recognized on the basis of its attributes, '*presence of a triangle and a rectangle*', '*rectangle containing a square within it*', '*area(square)* $\leq$ *area(triangle)*', *etc.* Also, in the above example, the first attribute is assigned a higher goodness measure relative to other attributes as it is the most relevant of all attributes that describe the object under consideration. In addition, positional constraints relating different fragments are also used in making a meaningful inference.

The design of a segmentation system should ensure that it be driven by data, and yet be responsive to the needs of the world model. The segmentation system should extract the dominant regions or objects first, and use these to structure further search for a final segmentation. In addition, the system must be capable of generating partial, or less-detailed, segmentations of the image for initial processing, and also be capable of producing detailed segmentations of the same image. Thus the main criterion for designing a segmentation method is the possibility of its implementation using recursive execution of the same simple procedure [13]. Complete segmentation of an image into its entities is considered the basic process in image analysis. The mathematical modeling for segmentation as developed by Pavlidis is [14]:

For an image function $\mathcal{F}(x,y)$ defined on an image domain D, a logical predicate P is defined on the subsets S_i of D, such that $P(S_i)$ denotes a similarity measure *between the image elements in D belonging to S_i. A segmentation of D is a partition of D into subsets or regions S_i, $i = 1, 2, ..., m$ such that:*

$$
\begin{array}{ll}
(i) & D = \cup_{i=1}^{m} S_i \\
(ii) & S_i \cap_{\forall i \neq j} S_j = \phi \ (emptyset) \\
(iii) & P(S_i) = TRUE \ \forall i \\
(iv) & P(S_i \cup S_j) = FALSE \ \forall i, j
\end{array}
$$

where S_i and S_j are adjacent in D.

Region selection is one of the important steps in the image-segmentation process. There exist a number of criteria to split an image into several regions and further into subregions. This limits the total area of the image which is analyzed at each step. Initially, the entire image is selected as the working region. One of the well-known methods of region-splitting is based on histograms. A set of histograms is computed for all features within a selected region of the image, and are smoothed to eliminate small peaks. The best peak in the histogram determines the choice of a subregion and the segmentation process is repeated to zoom-in on an elementary area of interest. The unsegmented area is considered for selection at a later time of processing.

The other criterion commonly used to determine the area to be processed next is based on the position and size of various regions. The selected portion of an image may correspond to a line, a region, or a group of lines and/or regions. The selection of a process domain is performed by a set of knowledge rules in the knowledge base. These rules are successively applied to the selected region till the segmentation procedure results in the identification of a primitive element or a set of primitive elements.

Among the other commonly used methods for selecting a sub-image from an image is to threshold the input image. Thus, a variety of sub-images can be selected by varying the threshold value. Another approach to extracting the subimages is *boundary following and tracking*. This amounts to searching the image systematically until a pair of adjacent image elements having different values are found [12].

Once a region is selected for further processing, it is partitioned by low-level segmentation. This process results in the identification of the image components contained in the region under consideration. These components are identified based on characteristic features of primitive elements extracted from processed regions and their spatial relationships. The features mentioned above are related to instances in the knowledge base in order to interpret the process output. In other words, information pertaining to the world model depicted in the contents of the knowledge base is used in comparing the characteristics of primitive elements to obtain meaningful inferences. The presence of a large number of features may indicate a need for partitioning the current region of attention into subregions in order to understand the contents of the selected area in an efficient manner. On the other hand, if no primitive elements are identified in the current area of focus, the current region can be merged with one of its yet-unprocessed neighboring regions to form a new area of interest [15].

High-level segmentation follows the low-level process mentioned in the last paragraph. This stage of processing utilizes the spatial relationships of the image entities extracted during the low-level segmentation process. As mentioned in the previous section, the knowledge base stores spatial relationships of image entities corresponding to world models. This form of knowledge constitutes the principal source of the high-level image understanding process. It is apparent that the higher the correspondence between regions in the segmentation output and objects in the scene, the easier the task of the high-level process.

However, it is found that high-level processing often helps in identifying the contents of an image in cases where the results of low-level segmentation correspond to points in an overlapped region of more than one decision domain (corresponding to different classes of images). In other words, high-level segmentation of images helps in partitioning the decision surface into non-overlapping regions. Also, spatial relationships of image entities enable proper analysis of the image in the event of a misinterpretation in the low-level processing, provided sufficient key relations hold in the high-level analysis.

The image understanding stage of this expert system essentially translates the outputs of low-level and high-level stages into a meaningful result. Applying the appropriate knowledge implies that the required knowledge was either located as existing knowledge in the knowledge base or was inferred from existing knowledge. The process of searching for appropriate knowledge, and inferring new knowledge from it, is a key element of expert-system processing [16]. This function is performed in an expert system by an *inference engine*. The *inference engine* is the software system that locates knowledge and infers new knowledge from the base knowledge. The engine's *inference paradigm* is the search strategy that is used to develop the required knowledge.

A deductive inference is made by the inference engine, depending on the existence and characteristics of an entity or a set of entities. When a sufficient match is made (in comparison with a world model), it is inferred that an entity represented by the instantiation has the generic values. If a match is made between the values known for the properties of an entity and the values corresponding to features extracted by the segmentation process, then a corresponding entity is assumed to exist in the image. The relative weights of characteristic features of entities and of the entities themselves, enable the use of *'analogical reasoning'* in arriving at an inference. The inference stage can also be used to check the body of knowledge that forms the core of the system for inconsistencies and omissions.

This section provided a description of the overall organization of the proposed image-understanding system. Functions of different processing stages of the system were also briefly described in this section. The next section presents the representation schemes used in organizing the body of knowledge used in the proposed system.

3. Knowledge Representation

Various types of knowledge used in the proposed system were described in previous sections. This section is devoted to the discussion of the properties of the data structures used to represent the above-mentioned knowledge. As mentioned in above, while frame-based storage is found to be appropriate for representing properties describing various entities, semantic-net representation is considered suitable to represent the spatial relationships between them.

A frame is a data structure which represents an entity type [7]. It consists of a collection of named '*slots*', each of which can be '*filled*' by values or by pointers to other frames. When the slots of a frame are filled, the frame is said to be '*instantiated*' and it represents a particular entity of the type represented by the unfilled frame. Frames can be used to represent an entity from different points of view. Frame representation also permits the incorporation of default values corresponding to one or more slots. In addition, integrity constraints on the values assumed by various slots can be included in this representation scheme.

Vehicle

Automobile

Car *(Side View)*

Entity	*Primitive*	*Attributes*	Goodness Measure
Roof	*Line*	$l \leq 2 \times l(window)$	*8*
Wheel	*Ellipse*	*color=black,no.=2*	*10*
Wheel Arches	*Semi-circle*	$r > r(wheel)$	*4*
Window	*Rectangle*	$no. = 2, a < a(door)$	*10*
Door	*Rectangle*	$l > l(window)$	*10*

Figure 2: Frame Representation of side view of a car

In the present application, frames are used to represent various image entities that form a world model. The slots of a frame are attributes that correspond to properties describing the particular entity. Since clustering of properties relating to an entity or a set of entities enables efficient traversal through the search tree, frame-based representation is chosen. This form of representation enables the description of an entity with a high order of detail.

Frame systems are highly suited for representing general description of an image in terms of its low-level structural components. Thus, a real image can be compared with different object models to identify the class to which an object belongs. As an example, a description of the general side view of a car is given below [17].

> *"A car usually has a roof. A car always has wheels. Wheels are black. They are sort-of shaped like ellipses. Each wheel is placed at a position near the bottom corners of the car. Sometimes only the bottom half of the wheels are visible. A car sometimes has wheel arches. These are concave regions in the body of the car. The wheel arches are roughly semicircular shapes near the bottom of the vehicle. The wheel arches sometimes mask the wheels. A car usually has doors. A door incorporates a window. The door extends from the top of the car to near the bottom of the car body. A car always has windows. These are closed shapes that have four sides. The windows are near the top of the car body".*

The above description can be represented as a frame system as in Figure 2. Numbers accompanying the attribute names indicate the '*measure of goodness*' associated with a corresponding feature, relative to the entity represented by the particular frame. For example, in the above description, all features with the qualifier, '*always*' are assigned very high goodness measures, whereas, those features categorized as '*sometimes*', '*usually*', etc. are assigned relatively lower values. The weighing criterion determines an efficient path through the nodes of the search tree for each set of extracted features. Thus, the presence of a predetermined number of features with high goodness measures can be considered sufficient to suggest a valid inference.

Another major advantage of using a frame structure to represent an entity is that the same entity can be represented from different points of view. This property of frame representation is extremely useful in image processing applications. As shown in Figure 3, an object '*car*' described in the previous paragraph can be represented from different points of view. This feature of the frame data structure enables those regions of an object occluded in one view to be described by a second frame for the same object, describing it from an-

Vehicle

Automobile

Car (Front View)

Entity	*Primitive*	*Attributes*	Goodness Measure
Roof	*Line*	$l = l(dashboard)$	*8*
Wheel	*Rectangle*	*color=black,no.=2*	*10*
Dashboard	*Rectangle*	$a > 2 * r(window)$	*10*
Steering Wheel	*Semi-circle*	$r < l(roof)$	*10*
Headlight	*Circle*	$no. = 2, r < l(dashboard)$	*10*

Figure 3: Frame Representation of front view of a car

other point of reference. Multiple descriptions of this type helps in recognizing images with features having low measures of goodness. In such cases, different views of an object can be matched for possible understanding.

The main application of frames in the proposed system is to cluster properties relating to an entity or a set of entities. The logical method of representing and manipulating knowledge using a frame structure is given below [7]:

- A frame with slot relationships $R_1, \ldots.., R_n$ representing the properties of an image entity set E can be described using a predicate logic formula such as:

$$\forall\ x\ \in (x, E) \rightarrow \quad \exists y_1, \ldots.., \exists y_n \quad (R_1(x, y_1) \wedge \ldots.. \wedge R_n(x, y_n))$$

- Generic properties in which default values are specified may be represented as, for example:

$$\forall\ x\ \in (x, TRIANGLE) \rightarrow number\_of\_sides(x, 3)$$

- A commonly encountered construct is the *part_of* relationship which can be represented as, for example:

$$part\_of(automobile, vehicle)$$
$$part\_of(car, automobile)$$
$$\forall\ x, y, z\ \in (x, y)\ \wedge part\_of(y, z)\ \rightarrow \in (x, z)$$
$$i.e.,\ x \in \{y\},\ y \subset z \rightarrow x \in \{z\}, \forall\ x, y, z.$$

  This enables an individual entity to inherit all generic properties of all its ancestors.

- Constraints on values assumed by various attributes of a frame can be expressed as, for example:

$$\forall\ x, y \quad included\_angle(x, y) \wedge \in (x, TRIANGLE) \rightarrow (> (y, 0)) \wedge (< (y, 180)).$$

- Using the above form of representation, matching can be performed as, for example:

$$\begin{aligned} \forall x \quad & number\_of\_sides(x, four) \wedge \\ & opposite\_angles(x, EQUAL) \wedge \\ & opposite\_sides(x, EQUAL) \wedge \\ & adjacent\_angles(x, EQUAL) \wedge \\ & adjacent\_sides(x, EQUAL) \\ \rightarrow \quad & \in (x, SQUARE). \end{aligned}$$

It is clear from the points mentioned above that the use of frames requires the user to view the universe (or the world model) as consisting of entity sets and entities.

The frame data structure enables clustering of properties relating to an entity or a set of entities. This characteristic feature of a frame is highly suitable for describing the entities of a world model; this form of description helps in implementing efficient search procedures to find matching objects. This form of storage can be viewed as an object-oriented data base, and implemented as one, thus enabling the use of a database-management system to manage the proposed knowledge base.

As observed in the previous sections, the proposed understanding system utilizes knowledge from various sources. We now discuss the representation of spatial knowledge concerning positional relations between entities. The use of semantic networks to represent this knowledge is discussed in this section.

A semantic network is a directed graph in which nodes represent entities and arcs represent binary relationships between entities. Arcs are labeled with the names of relationship types, i.e., the binary relation to which the relationship belongs. Graph-matching serves as an efficient tool for locating instances in a knowledge base. Hence, semantic net representation is particularly suited to the high-level segmentation process.

A collection of knowledge facts is represented by logical predicates, which form the elements of a corresponding semantic network. An entity in the world model is represented by a single node in a semantic network, irrespective of the number of relations in which it participates. The semantic net representation uses an object-oriented approach, so that all the facts about a certain object are grouped together.

Even ternary (or n-ary) relations can be represented in a semantic net using equivalent multiple binary relations. This enables the description of positional relations involving more than two entities. This apart, semantic networks can also be used to represent multiple occurrences of objects belonging to the same class. This is particularly useful in describing relational constraints pertaining to different world models.

In this application, the class of each object is represented in the semantic net by a *'part_of'* arc. For example, an object *'car'* corresponding to a node in the semantic net may be associated with a *part_of* arc connected to another node *'vehicle'*. In other words, spatial relations described by the above semantic net correspond to an object *'car'* of type *'vehicle'*. It may be noted that all properties characteristic to the class *'vehicle'* can be stored as a frame pointed to by a corresponding node in the semantic network.

The features of the semantic net representation mentioned above may be illustrated as follows. Consider an image featuring a microcomputer with its peripheral devices. The representation of the spatial aspects of this image, represented using a semantic network is shown in Figure 4.

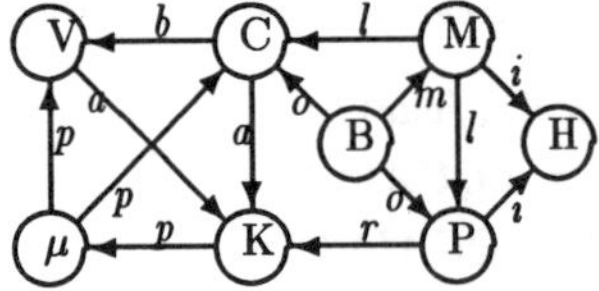

Legend:

Node	Object Class
V	Video Unit
μ	μsystem
C	CPU
K	Keyboard
B	Between
M	Mouse
P	Printer
H	Peripheral

Arc	Relation Type
a	*above*
p	*part_of*
b	*below*
l	*left_of*
r	*right_of*
o	*one_end*
m	*middle*
i	*is_a*

Figure 4: Semantic Net Representation of a microcomputer system

As shown in Figure 4, the given image is represented in terms of the relative positions of its constituent entities. The semantic net represents only the primary relations between entity locations. The secondary relations can be derived using the transitive properties of different relational operators. The ternary relation *'between'* is represented using a transitive node B1 of type *between* having three arcs (each representing a binary relation) connecting the three entities participating in the relation.

Since a semantic net is essentially a labeled directed graph, it is easy to implement in practice. This form of knowledge description enables the structural representation of parts of the universe. As the proposed system employs knowledge concerning world models, this form of representation is considered highly suitable.

The characteristic properties of the frame data structure and the semantic net representation of knowledge sources were described in this section. The inherent advantages of using these forms of representation in a knowledge-based system were also presented. The search techniques and the matching procedure for the proposed system are discussed in the following section.

4. System Implementation

Different schemes of knowledge representation selected for the proposed knowledge-based system were presented in the preceding section. The access methods used in retrieving information stored in the knowledge base are described here. The search techniques used in implementing this task fully utilize the advantages offered by the data structures described earlier. This section describes the procedures involved in meaningfully understanding a segmented image.

Frame systems are often used as components of pattern-recognition systems, involving the matching of visual patterns or abstract components. A frame system is used to *'recognize'* the existence of a particular type of entity from a given input. When an entity is recognized as being of a particular entity type, all generic properties associated with that type are inherited by the entity. The frame system in this case is said to be performing in a *'pattern recognition and inference mode'* [7].

In the image understanding system under consideration, frames are employed to store the knowledge concerning objects that form a world model. In a frame system, recognition of an image entity essentially involves *'matching'* a set of values corresponding to a set of extracted features. If the values concerned with an image entity under analysis correlate with all the slot values of a frame F relating to some entity E, then the corresponding entity can be categorized as being of type E [7].

However if F represents a *'general'* entity set, then we may want to find a more specific match. In this case, we must traverse down the *'type'* hierarchy to see if a specialization of F can be instantiated. For example, we might find that values related to a processed entity match those which fill the slots of a frame G representing an object *'high chair'*. Matching this input entity against G is more informative in this case than matching against F which may represent an object, say *'chair'*. It is clear that frame G represents an object which is an element of a subset of the class of objects represented by frame F.

In cases where an exact match could not be found, it may be sufficient to find a *'best'* match. This becomes necessary when certain values are hard to measure or when a value or a set of values falls outside the allowed range. Image processing applications encounter this situation due to occluded portions of an input image. However, since frames facilitate the description of images from different points of reference, the frequency of occurrence of this type of problem is greatly reduced [7].

The search procedure suggested for the proposed segmentation system is described in detail here. As described earlier, the frames that describe different objects are distributed as nodes in an object space tree. Neither the depth-first nor the breadth-first search techniques commonly employed to determine the path of traversal through this tree utilize the problem-specific information that may be available. These types of strategy are unsuitable for the problem under consideration where we have a considerable level of knowledge about world models. This is incorporated in the expert system using the *'measures of goodness'* described earlier. Thus a knowledge rule is formulated which states that if a choice exists, the node with the highest score should be chosen. Such a search is commonly referred to as a *'heuristic'* search. In order to keep track of nodes which are *'open'*, i.e., nodes which can be developed, such nodes are generally kept on a list called an *'agenda'*. The next node to be developed is always the one associated with the heighest weighting [7].

The system uses values of the various properties of the object under consideration, to select a *'candidate domain'*. Now, starting at the top of the tree hierarchy corresponding to this domain, the frame with the best *measure of goodness* is selected. The system then partially matches the frame by comparing the values of different slots. If required, the system may request additional knowledge in an attempt to make a proper comparison.

A *'match value'* is then computed as the sum of the *'goodness measure'* for each slot which indicates the *'goodness'* of the match. Depending on the application, the match value will signify the degree of success. If the match value is high enough, and the frame is specific enough for the application in hand, then the system need not look at other frames. However, if the match value is not high enough or the frame is not specific enough, then the system will consider other frames.

The system utilizes the frame structure to identify the frames that can be considered for processing at a later stage from the list of open frames in the agenda. The system moves up the hierarchy in the object space tree until it finds a perfect match. It then searches the subtree below the perfectly matched frame in an attempt to find a more specific match. In an alternative approach the system looks at frames related to the current one by the *'sibling'* relation (i.e., nodes at the same level in the hierarchy) [7].

The search procedure can be further improved by choosing only those slots necessary for comparison. The following set of heuristics serves to implement this [7]:

- Select values which are relatively high or relatively low compared with normal values for the slot.
- Select slots which contribute critically to match values, i.e., the key attributes of the frame.
- Select slots which no close relative of the frame under consideration possesses. In other words, select slots which do not occur in frames which are related to the current frame by the *sibling* relation.
- Select values which no close relative of the current frame possesses. Relatives of the current frame may not possess the same value for the particular slot.
- Use all the values of the current frame.

Each property describing a set of entities is stored in the highest level (of the overall frame structure) to which it applies. This requires a smaller amount of storage in comparison with the storage of this property with each individual instance. All properties of a superset can also hold for the instances of that superset, unless otherwise indicated. In the case of an exception, the fact that the property does not apply is stated with the unit itself [18].

As mentioned above, heuristic-based search of the object space tree can be performed using a frame data structure. This technique incorporates analogical reasoning to arrive at a meaningful inference. The knowledge of sub images thus identified are related to recognize the entire image. This requires use of spatial knowledge concerning entities, which (as described above) are represented using semantic networks. The technique employed in matching the knowledge of entities with that represented by a semantic network is described below.

Semantic networks are chosen to represent spatial relations between entities because they are easy to implement. A semantic network can be represented by two arrays V and A. Array V stores the vertex names and array A stores the starting vertex, ending vertex and names of arcs, where V and A are defined as follows [20]:

$$\begin{aligned} V &: N \rightarrow S \\ A &: N \times N \rightarrow S \cup \{e\} \end{aligned}$$

where

$N = \{1, ..., n_{obj}\}$ is the index set for the vertices

S is a finite nonempty set of names and

e is a special symbol not in S, indicating *'no arc'*.

At every stage relational constraints derived from the segmentation process are matched with spatial knowledge represented by a semantic network. This can be viewed as matching a graph G' representing the extracted features at that stage with a subgraph of G. The subgraph-matching problem for a semantic network can be formally stated as follows [20]:

Let $G'(V, A)$ and $G(V, A)$ be two labeled directed graphs defined as follows:

$$\begin{aligned} V' &: N' \rightarrow S \cup X \\ A' &: N' \times N' \rightarrow S \cup X \cup \{e\} \\ V &: N \rightarrow S \\ A &: N \times N \rightarrow S \cup \{e\} \end{aligned}$$

where

$N' = \{1, ..., n'_{obj}\}$ is the vertex index set

S is the arc name set

X is the variable name set

e is a special symbol indicating *'no arc'*

The subgraph-matching problem is to find a one-to-one mapping into T such that

- $V'[i] = V[T(i)], \forall\, i \in N'$
  (corresponding vertices have identical names)
- $A'[i,j] \ni \{e\}, A'[i,j] = A[T(i), T(j)], \forall\, i, j \in N'$
  (corresponding arcs have identical names)

For nonexact matching, the equality sign in each of the above expressions should be interpreted more liberally. A similarity measure can be assigned for S so that two sufficiently similar elements are considered to be correlated.

Subgraph matching can be accomplished using a backtracking search technique [20]. Suppose it is required to match a graph G' to a graph G (described above). To start with, all non variable names in V' are matched with names in V. Since all vertex names are unique in a semantic network, the non-variables in V' should match corresponding non-variables in V. This leaves us with only the variables in V', denoted by $V' - S$. Names are then substituted for variables one by one, and the second expression above is checked for consistency to confirm the matching of arc names. In the event of an inconsistency, an alternative variable substitution is attempted. If vertex names are not unique, all combinations are tried.

The subgraph-matching problem can be modified to accommodate non-exact matching where nonidentical node names and nonidentical arc names can be matched. In addition, some of the nodes need not have matching nodes. This necessitates a measure for the *'goodness of matching'* defined as follows [20]:

$$\begin{aligned} MC = & \sum_{i \in N', \exists T(i)} C_N(V'[i], V[T(i)]) + \\ & \sum_{i \in N', \nexists\, T(i)} C_{M'}(V'[i]) + \end{aligned}$$

$$\sum_{i,j \in N', \exists T(i), \exists T(j)} C_A(A'[i,j], A[T(i), T(j)]) \; + \\ \sum_{j \in N, i \ni N', T(i)=j} C_M(V[j])$$

where

C_N is the cost of matching two similar nodes (*'template cost'*)

C_A is the cost of matching two similar arcs (*'spring cost'*)

$C_{M'}$ is the cost of a missing node in the input graph

C_M is the cost of a missing node in the reference graph

MC is the total missing cost for the particular matching

There may be some nodes in G' which cannot be matched to nodes in G (*i.e.,* T(i) undefined). There may also be some nodes in G which cannot be matched to nodes in G' (*i.e.,* no T(i) equal to j).

Making C_N and C_A infinite translates into exact arc and exact node matching allowing for missing nodes. The *'best match'* in this case is the one which minimizes the cost of missing nodes or, equivalently, the one which maximizes the number of exact matches. No missing nodes can be allowed in G and G' by making $C_{M'}$ and C_M infinite which redefines the subgraph matching problem into a graph matching problem. If $C_{M'}$ is made infinite, the matching extracts a subgraph G' totally embedded in G, which conforms to the original subgraph matching problem. In a general relational matching problem, all the cost functions, *viz.,* C_N, C_A, C_M, *and* $C_{M'}$ are finite.

Graph matching, on the other hand, can be done by constructing an auxiliary data structure called an *association graph.* Consider two graphs G and G'. The association graph $G'' = (V'', A'')$ is then defined as [20]

$$\begin{aligned} V'' &= \{(i,j) : i \in N, j \in N', V[i] = V'[j]\} \\ A'' &= \{(i_1, j_1), (i_2, j_2) : (i_1, j_1), (i_2, j_2) \in V'', \\ &\quad A[i_1, i2] = A'[j_1, j_2]\}. \end{aligned}$$

In other words, V'' is the set of all possible matching among nodes and A'' is the set of all compatible node matchings. For the case of infinite C_N and C_A, the *'best match'* problem is reduced to finding the largest set of compatible node matchings. This is equivalent to finding the *maximal clique* in the association graph. A *clique* is a fully connected subgraph of G'' and a *'maximal clique'* is a clique whose node set is not a proper subset of the node set of another clique. For a general relational matching problem in an association graph, the clique with minimal cost is chosen to be the *'best match'*.

The search procedures described thus far are used to retrieve structural and spatial knowledge of objects that form the world model. As mentioned earlier, the structural knowledge of entities is considered as the primary source of knowledge for image understanding. The spatial information is utilized in cases where frame-represented structural knowledge is considered inadequate. The relational knowledge also finds a use in cases where knowledge concerning entity description fails to yield an unambiguous inference.

As described in an earlier section, various segmentation heuristics are employed to direct the system in processing an input image [5]. The sources of knowledge concerning these heuristics determine the regions of input image to be processed next, and the type of processing to be applied on the selected region. This ordering is implemented using a set of strategy and ordering knowledge rules embedded in the expert system.

The selected region is processed to generate characteristic features by a technique determined by various segmentation heuristics . These features are compared with the slots of various frames, following the procedure described earlier. This results in the recognition of the type of object represented by the current region. The failure to make an unambiguous inference may necessitate suitable modification in the chosen area of attention. This may require either the enlargement of the current area of processing, or the selection of an alternate region for further processing. The class of object represented by the current region, if recognized, is stored along with its location (with respect to the entire image) for further reference during the traversal of the object-space tree. In addition to the apriori knowledge of various objects that form a world mode, their frequency of occurrence must be taken into account in determining an unbiased goodness measure [20]. Thus, the measures of goodness of the frame instantiated by the recognition procedure is updated to record the occurrence of a particular entity.

If an entity recognized in the preceding step, along with previously recognized entities, corresponds to a leaf node in the object-space tree, then a meaningful inference can be realized. On the other hand, if the resulting node is a non-leaf node, the image is processed further to find an entity corresponding to the node with the heighest measure of goodness in a subtree with the current node as its root. Finally, the spatial knowledge concerning all the recognized entities is used to match a subgraph in the semantic network representing the world model. This process generates a meaningful understanding relating an input image to the world model.

The set of knowledge rules that form part of the expert system determines a defined path strategy and specifies how an image should be segmented. These rules serve to select a region for processing and also determine the type of process to be applied on the selected region. The choice of type of processing needed next is determined by the node in the object-space tree having the highest measure of goodness.

This section describes different search and matching techniques employed in the image understanding system. Details of the overall inference process are also presented, and the advantages of frame and semantic net representation in accessing information from the knowledge base are highlighted.

5. Application in Medical Diagnostic Imaging

Several knowledge based expert systems have been developed in the field of diagnostic imaging. The criteria outlined in this chapter can be used to develop an expert system for analyzing medical images. We provide an example of the functional block of a image understanding system employing the design procedures described thus far.

Various nuclear medicine techniques such as magnetic resonance imaging (MRI), computed tomography (CT), single photon emission computed tomography (SPECT) and positron emission tomography (PET) are widely used in diagnostic radiology. These methods provide a way to visualize the three-dimensional structures of organs by means of an array of two-dimensional tomographic slies. Thus, wide and detailed knowledge about anatomy, 3-D morphology, and functional and anatomical relationships among organs can be obtained using these modalities [21]. However, these images are characterized by low contrast between organs, blurred edges, and slight variations in grey levels and texture. Small changes in the acquisition parameters and in the tomographic planes, or differences in the anatomy of human beings can produce variations in the image content. Thus, these images require extensive preprocessing before it could be interpreted. The preprocessing operations include noise reduction, contrast enhancement, iterative edge-preserving smoothing, correction for nonuniformities in the detector, etc.

An expert system for understanding nuclear medicine images can be designed with a lowlevel image processing and feature extraction stage and a highlevel production system comprising of a rule interpreter and submodules for various organs to be detected in the image. Each submodule may contain knowledge specific to an organ and some relational properties with respect to other organs in the immediate neighborhood. Semantic network is appropriate for representing anatomical knowledge and for the representation of relational aspects and for hierarchical organization. Production rules can be used in both high and low level systems for guiding the search paths and for conflict resolution.

Frames are appropriate for representing the organs that are normally seen in images from MRI/CT/SPECT/PET systems. The frame representation shown in Figure 3 can be used for the description of these organs. The entity of each instance in the frame corresponds to an organ, the primitives correspond to the shape parameters that best describe the organs and the attributes correspond to the ratio of pixel intensity values to the background value of the image (as a measure of relative contrast). The spatial details of the anatomy can be described using semantic networks with the different organs as the nodes and their spatial relationships using links of the type { *IN_FRONT, BEHIND, TO_LEFT, TO_RIGHT, ABOVE, BELOW, PART_OF*}. The ABOVE and BELOW relationships pertain to the three-dimensional image formed by a number of two-dimensional slices. In addition, in the case of three-dimensional imaging, the degree of concavity or convexity can be used as a descriptor of an organ.

Production rules are used both in lowlevel processing and in highlevel region understanding. In lowlevel manipulation, the production rules are used to segment the image into several regions of interest and subsequently to merge these regions to identify entities for further processing. In the intermediate stage, knowledge rules are used to identify these entities from the list of organs in the anatomical dictionary of the knowledge base. The identification of organs employs the spatial relationships between the various organs represented by semantic networks. The production rules are formulated using a world model that describe the features of a normal anatomy as obtained by the particular nuclear medicine technique.

The knowledge base for this application may initially contain the details of various organs, their anatomical positions and the image parameters, viz., contrast, pixel intensity, shape parameters, etc. The image parameters are then updated as realtime knowledge about the application domain is gathered. The image understanding system described here can be logically extended to help in diagnosing common abnormalities that could be identified from these functional and anatomical images. The knowledge base in the latter case should contain sufficient knowledge about the characteristics of the abnormal features as seen in the image to provide a diagnosis of acceptable confidence. The learning capability of the expert system will help in improving the diagnostic aspect of the image understanding system.

6. Conclusions

In the previous sections, we describe the overall design aspects of a knowledge-based system for image understanding. The system utilizes knowledge concerning both structural and spatial descriptions of various entities that form a world model. Unlike most other systems, this source of knowledge is neither scene-dependent nor sensor-dependent. Descriptive features of images are represented in terms of the knowledge of their constituent entities. This facilitates the recognition of a number of images described by one or more of these entities.

Data representation using frames is found to be appropriate in various knowledge-based systems. However, most image understanding systems do not employ this form of representation. In this chapter, we describe the use of frames to represent structural knowledge of entities. Frames are particularly suited for representing a world model, as the entities can be described from different views. This feature of frame representation finds application in identifying objects partially occluded from one or more points of reference. In addition, integrity constraints and default values can be easily implemented in any slot of a frame.

Use of semantic nets to represent spatial knowledge of image entities is widely encountered in image processing systems. Use of semantic networks in conjunction with frames enables the description of both structural and spatial properties of a world model. Semantic net representation helps in easy extraction of potential search areas in an image, and in partial matching of entities in an image of high complexity. These properties of semantic networks are particularly useful in segmentation of an image into meaningful entities.

The different frames employed in the image understanding system are distributed as nodes of an object-space tree. In addition, every frame in the expert system and each of its slots is assigned a *measure of goodness*. This heuristic measure is based on apriori knowledge of a world model and denotes the relevance of the particular attributes to the class under consideration. These parameters help in performing a heuristic-driven search through the object-space tree to elicit meaningful information regarding an input image. The measures of goodness also define the order in which an image is processed.

Correlation between the world model used in the expert system, and the underlying environment, is improved by updating goodness measures of different nodes after every successful recognition. Thus, the process of knowledge updating is greatly simplified in the proposed system. Also, representation of knowledge sources involves only the creation of new frames and the assignment of suitable measures of goodness to each attribute of the newly-created frame.

The proposed system can be improved by using attributed hypergraphs to represent spatial relations between entities of the world model. The system can also be improved by selecting a proper form of representation to incorporate various heuristics concerning different image processing techniques. This feature provides greater flexibility in analyzing an input image.

References

[1] Gowrishankar, T. R., N. G., Bourbakis, "Specifications for the development of a knowledge-based image interpretation system", *Int. J. of Engineering Applications of Artificial Intelligence*, vol. 3, pp. 79-90, June 1990.

[2] Fu, K.S., *Syntactic Methods in Pattern Recognition*. New York: Academic Press, 1974.

[3] Bhanu, Bir, "Shape Matching of Two-Dimensional Objects", *IEEE Transactions on Pattern Analysis and Machine Intelligence*, vol. PAMI-6, No. 2, pp. 137-156, Mar. 1984.

[4] McKeown, D.M. Jr., W.A. Harvey and L.E. Wixson, "Automating Knowledge Acquisition for Aerial Image Interpretation", *Computer Vision, Graphics, and Image Processing*, vol. 46, pp. 37-81, 1989.

[5] Gonzalez, R.C. and M.G. Thomason, *Syntactic Pattern Recognition: An introduction*. Reading, Massachusetts: Addison-Wesley Publishing Company, 1978.

[6] Nazif, A.M. and M.D. Levine, "Low Level Image Segmentation: An Expert System", *IEEE Transactions on Pattern Analysis and Machine Intelligence*, vol. PAMI-6, No. 5, pp. 555-577, Sept. 1984.

[7] Stansfield, Sharon A., "ANGY: A Rule-Based Expert System for Automatic Segmentation of Coronary Vessels From Digital Subtracted Angiograms", *IEEE Transactions on Pattern Analysis and Machine Intelligence*, vol. PAMI-8, No. 2, pp. 188-199, 1986.

[8] Frost, Richard, *Introduction to Knowledge Base Systems*. New York: Macmillan Publishing Company, 1986.

[9] Levine, M.D. and A.M. Nazif, "Rule-Based Image Segmentation: A Dynamic Control Strategy Approach", *Computer Vision, Graphics, and Image Processing*, vol. 32, pp. 104-126, 1985.

[10] Bourbakis, Nikolais G., "A Rule Based Scheme for Synthesis of Textured Images", in *Proc. IEEE Conference on Systems, Man and Cybernetics*, George Mason University, Fairfax, VA, vol. 3, pp. 999-1003, Oct. 1987.

[11] Matsuyama, Takashi, "Expert Systems for Image Processing: Knowledge-Based Composition of Image Analysis Processes", *Computer Vision, Graphics, and Image Processing*, vol. 48, pp. 22-49, 1989.

[12] Fu, K.S., "Syntactic (Linguistic) Pattern Recognition" in *Digital Pattern Recognition*, K.S. Fu, Ed. New York: Springer-Verlag, 1980.

[13] Ohlander, Ron, K. Price and D. Raj Reddy, "Picture Segmentation Using A Recursive Region Splitting Method", *Computer Graphics and Image Processing*, vol. 8, pp. 313-333, 1978.

[14] Pavlidis, T., *Algorithms for Graphics and Image Processing*.Computer Science Press, 1982.

[15] Cappellini, V., M.T. Pareschi and C. Raspollini, "A technique for object recognition based on subpart classification", in *Image Analysis and Processing*, V. Cantoni, *et al.*, Eds. New York: Plenum Press, 1986.

[16] Rolston, David W., *Principles of Artificial Intelligence and Expert Systems Development.* New York: McGraw-Hill Book Company, 1988.

[17] Fretwell, P. and P.J. Goillau, "Linguistic Definition of Generic Models in Computer Vision".

[18] Ringland, G.A., *Approaches to Knowledge Representation: An Introduction*, G.A. Ringland, D.A. Duce, Eds. New York: John Wiley and Sons Inc., 1988.

[19] Chang, S.K., *Principles of Pictorial Information System Design.* Prentice-Hall Inc., 1989.

[20] Good, I.J., *The Estimation of Probabilities–An Essay in Modern Bayesian Methods.* Research Monograph No. 38. Cambridge, Massachusetts: The M.I.T. Press.

[21] Vernazza, G. L., S. B. Serpico, and S. G. Dellepiane, "A Knowledge-Based System for Biomedical Image Processing and Recognition", *IEEE Transactions of Circuits and Systems*, vol. CAS-34, pp. 1399-1416, 1987.

CHAPTER 19

Document Image Analysis and Recognition

Sargur N. Srihari, Stephen W. Lam, Peter B. Cullen and Tin K. Ho

Center of Excellence for Document Analysis and Recognition
226 Bell Hall
State University of New York at Buffalo
Buffalo, New York 14260, USA

Abstract

Reading is the process of mapping an image containing text into a meaningful symbolic representation. Primary subtasks in reading are: extraction of textual regions of interest, recognition of symbols (characters, words, etc), and the interpretation of the recognized symbols using contextual knowledge. We describe the architecture of a reading machine to achieve a high rate of correct interpretation of text.

The refinement of the architecture for a specialized reading machine, to find and interpret addresses on a stream of postal letters, is described. Here, the primary subtasks correspond to finding the block of text corresponding to the destination address, recognizing characters and words within the address, and interpreting the text using postal directories.

The task of interpreting machine-printed addresses is discussed. Words in an address block are first segmented and parsed to assign probable semantic categories (city, state, ZIP code, etc). Word images are then recognized by a combination of digit, character and word recognition algorithms. The control structure uses a constraint satisfaction problem solving approach to match the recognition results to an entry in the ZIP+4 file and assigns a ZIP+4 Code to the mailpiece.

1 Introduction

The development of machines that can read printed and handwritten text, with a performance level similar to that of humans, has long been a goal with scientific and economic importance.

The scientific challenge arises from the artificial intelligence goal of developing machines to perform tasks that when done by humans are said to require intelligence. As a human skill, reading is learnt. It has long been a topic of study by cognitive and educational psychologists, whose studies can be useful for those interested in developing reading machines. The reading of text on paper encompasses both perception and language (and is thus said to involve both the left and right parts of the brain). Both perception and language have long been frontiers for artificial intelligence research. Reading poses the challenge of naturally integrating methods from both domains.

There are many goals in human reading. Some examples are: reading to relieve boredom, searching for a telephone number in a directory, reading an address on an envelope to determine its destination, reading poetry, reading as an editor (primarily concerned with style and punctuation, not content), reading a newspaper article, and reading a textbook for content. According to Singer[1], "In reading along a particular sentence, a reader must retrieve and mobilize systems for recognizing words and phrases, next link the recognized words or phrases to their corresponding meanings, and subsequently utilize various cognitive processes for inferring, interpreting, and inductively, or deductively arriving at conclusions or solutions to problems".

Its economic importance arises from numerous applications such as automatic sorting of postal mail pieces, reading machines for the blind, data entry from bank checks, processing manually filled-out tax forms, etc.

In today's offices, there exist two types of documents: (i) documents on paper, and (2) documents in electronic devices. However, only the second type can easily be accessible to various media such as word processing, data transfer, and information retrieval. Office automation is one focal point in recent information processing research. However, the original goal of creating a *paperless office* has been revised to a *less paper office* due to the fact that documents will not exist or be distributed exclusively by electronic media. Instead, paper will still remain one of the dominant media for documentation and communication in foreseeable future[2].

The development of recognition systems to transfer documents from paper to electronics has become an area of intensive research in the last decade. The goal of research is to realize system(s) capable of transforming everyday office documents into equivalent representations in electronic storages, e.g., texts are represented by ASCII codes and pictures are represented by bit maps. Another significance of this transformation is the reduction of storage space for documents. A letter-size document of text requires 8 MB of disk space if it is scanned at 300 ppi and stored in imagery format while it only needs about 5 KB(0.005 MB) if the iconic representations of text are coded as ASCII characters. The time to transfer or retrieve coded information will obviously be shortened accordingly.

For the purpose of developing reading machines, we will define the process of reading as the process of mapping a visual field containing iconic representations of text (handwriting or machine printing) into an appropriate symbolic representation. The mapping is realized by the following algorithmic approaches: (i) extracting regions of interest (ROIs) in a document image, which is an optically scanned and digitized representation of a paper document; and (ii) recognizing and interpreting content of the ROIs. A high-performance system performs these tasks with a high degree of accuracy and at high speed.

2 An Architecture for Reading Machines

The major steps in reading text in a given visual field are image acquisition, layout analysis and reading and understanding the text (Fig. 1).

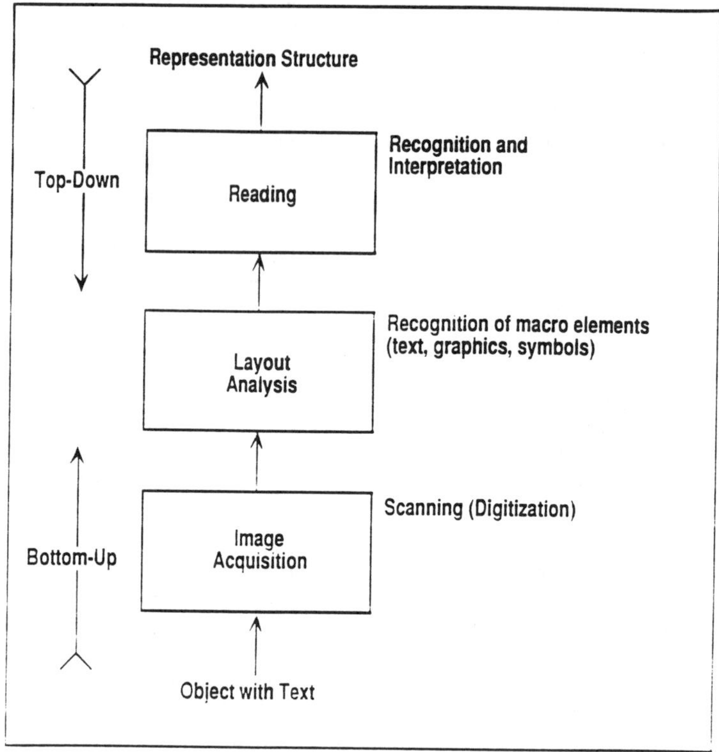

Figure 1: A general architecture for reading machines.

2.1 Image Acquisition

Image acquisition is the process of scanning a document so as to represent its image as a grey-scale array. Four basic building blocks form functional image scanners: a detector (and associated electronics), an illumination source, a scan lens, and a document transport[3]. To capture an image, the object is placed in the scanning field, a light source floods the object with illumination, and the lens forms an image on the detector. The detector consists of an array of elements each of which converts incident light into a charge, or analog signal. These analog signals are then converted into a digital image. Scanning is performed by the detector and the motion of the text object with respect to the detector.

Three types of integrated circuits are said to dominate the scanner market today: photodiode arrays, charge-coupled device (CCD) arrays, and charge-coupled photodiode device (CCPD arrays). They differ in how light is converted into analog signals and how signals are transferred off chip. Time delay integration (TDI) CCDs operate under low illumination levels since they collect photons over a larger temporal space. TDI arrays are also preferable for high-speed scanning applications.

The image acquisition module is expected to scan and digitize the image at a single resolution and with a fixed quantization level (number of grey-levels). A resolution of 300 pixels per inch (ppi), 8 bit grey scale, is sufficient for recognizing 8-point printed text and thin strokes in handwriting. In many cases, however, image resolution needed to perform layout analysis is much lower than that for recognizing characters and words. In order to speed up the reading task, a down-sampled image (around 100 ppi) may be used as input to the layout analysis subsystem to locate the ROIs. The higher resolution subimage of the ROIs will be used in the reading subsystem.

Since text is printed as dark points on light backgrounds (or vice versa) binary images are generally considered to be sufficient both for layout analysis and document reading. However, grey-scale images can enhance recognition rate, particularly for poor quality images, at an increase in processing expense. The scanned grey-scale image can be converted to binary using thresholding algorithms. For documents with high contrast, such as those with printing or handwriting on a white background, a global threshold obtained from a grey-scale histogram is sufficient[4]. For other documents it may be necessary to adapt to local contrast[5].

2.2 Layout Analysis

The task of locating textual regions of interest is the primary function of layout analysis. The task of reading involves recognizing shapes (of characters, words, etc.), i.e., mapping icons to symbols, and interpreting the symbols, i.e., mapping low-level symbols to higher-level symbols. The location task is often separable from the recognition/reading task; for example, it is possible to tell where the text is present even if it is unreadable. However, a system interactive with recognition is needed for nonstandard text structures such as handwritten documents.

Layout analysis involves both segmentation of the document into textual, graphical and other regions as well as labeling certain textual regions according to their logical role in the document. Recognition is performed on the resulting components so as to hypothesize the logical role of textual regions.

Tang[6] defines a document is composition of two classes of objects: *geometric (layout) objects* and *logical objects*. Layout object formation is the result of partitioning the content of a document into increasingly smaller regions based on *physical appearance* of the object. Layout objects, such as characters, line segments, boxes, photographs, are the building blocks of documents.

Logical object formation is the result of partitioning the content of a document into increasingly smaller regions based on *contextual interpretation* of the object. Logical objects are specific to different document types, e.g., addressee and sender on the mail pieces, and title and author on the front pages of technical publication. Knowledge about a document type is needed to locate logical objects.

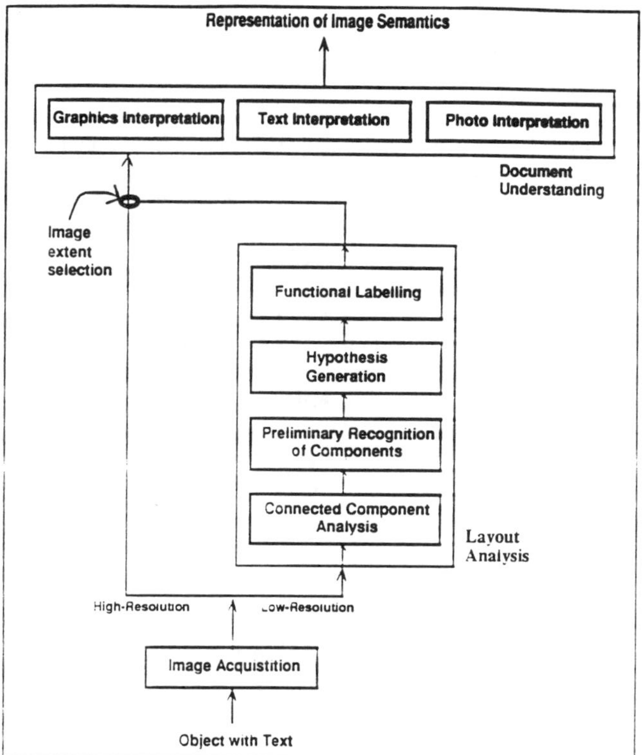

Figure 2: An architecture for reading and understanding document.

2.3 Reading and Understanding

The task of recognizing textual symbols and interpreting the symbols using knowledge is referred to as reading. When the reading task involves the interpretation of text as well as accompanying photographs and graphics (e.g., drawings and graphs), the task may be more appropriately referred to as document understanding[7].

A general architecture for reading and interpretation of a document is given in Fig. 2. This is a refinement of the process illustrated in Fig. 1. The flow of data is from the point-of-view of a efficient implementation. It shows a recognition-based approach to layout analysis. Preliminary recognition of connected components allows hypothesization of the nature of the document region. Final assignment of region labels is based on a more global analysis.

A complex document, e.g., a page of a daily newspaper, consists of text, photographs and graphics. The understanding task is to begin with the image of a page, extract a story of interest and map the textual and accompanying graphical information into a symbolic representation (such as a semantic network). For a specialization of the architecture to newspaper images, the reader is referred to Govindaraju[8]. The text location task for newspaper images, which can exploit the regular layout usually employed, is discussed in Wang[9]. The reading of degraded text encountered in newsprint is discussed in Lam[10], and the integration of information from textual and photographic information in newspapers is the topic of Srihari[11].

3 Application to Postal Mail Sorting

Postal mail sorting is a goal-oriented reading task, where the objective is to determine the destination of a mailpiece from an image of its face. Mailpieces are usually divided into different classes, such as letters (e.g., envelopes and postcards), flats (e.g., magazines) and parcels. Postal address reading differs from most other document reading tasks due to the wide variability of fonts and printing quality encountered, the presence of either machine-printing or handwriting, the variability of document layout, etc.

There exists a natural representation for the semantics of an address within the United States. The goal of the U.S. Postal Service is to encode each mail piece by a string of digits, the first five of which are referred to as the ZIP Code, and together with the next four as the ZIP+4. The first five digits usually encode the state, city and major post-office information, the next four digits encode the street address information (down to a block face). The goal of the address interpretation task is to assign to each mail piece its destination encoding. The destination encoding can be a five-digit ZIP Code or nine-digit ZIP+4 Code or even an advanced eleven-digit code (ZIP+4 plus an additional two digits corresponding to the last two digits of the street address). Once the destination encoding has been determined, it is then sprayed as a bar code on the face of the mail piece.

In the mail sorting application, the three major components specialize to: (i) capturing high resolution images of incoming mail stream, (ii) finding a block of text corresponding to the destination address, and (iii) reading and interpreting the address (Fig. 3). The tasks of interpreting machine-printed addresses and handwritten addresses are divided into different streams, due to the fact that the techniques involve several differences: handwriting consists of elongated strokes whereas machine print consists of regular blocks, the shapes of characters in handwritten words are dependent on word context, handwriting reading requires greater contextual interaction whereas machine print reading can be separated into character recognition and contextual analysis, etc.

The need to process large numbers of letters in short time-spans translates to a stringent requirement on the throughput. The letter mail sorting system needs to process between 5 and 12 mail pieces per second. The economics of postal mail sorting requires that the error rate be kept low (roughly 0.5% overall).

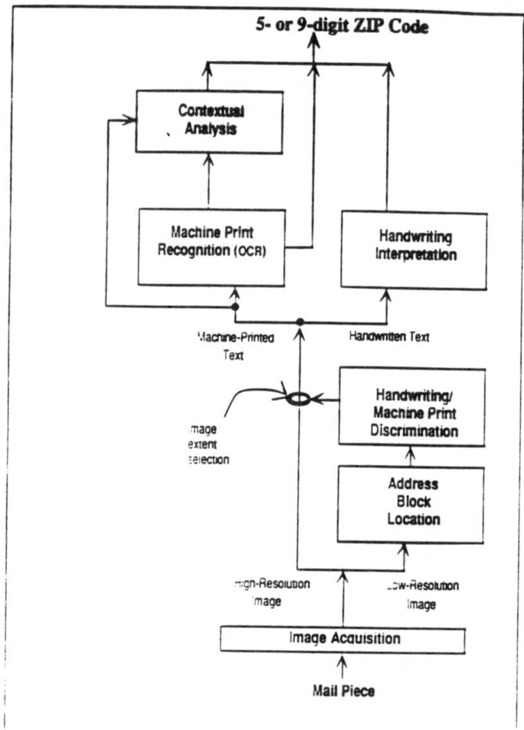

Figure 3: An architecture specialized for mail destinating encoding.

3.1 Image Acquisition

The image acquisition subsystem needs to scan approximately 13 mailpieces per second. An entire mail piece is scanned and digitized at 300 ppi and with 256 grey levels.

The image lift subsystem contains three basic components: (i) mailpiece transport, (ii) video camera, and (iii) image capture processor. The transport moves the mail past a stationed, illuminated zone that is visible to the video camera. The image of the mailpiece is read out of the camera by the image capture processor and written into memory. The image is the input to the address block location and the address interpretation subsystems.

3.2 Address Block Location

In goal-oriented document layout analysis, the document is analyzed only to the extent that it is necessary to find one or more fields of interest. Address block location (ABL), is such a goal-oriented task where the input is an image of the face of an arbitrary mail piece. The objective is to extract one or more rectangular subregions of the image as candidates for the destination address block (DAB).

A typical mail piece has several regions or blocks that are meaningful to mail processing, e.g., address blocks (destination and return), postage (meter mark or stamp) as well as extraneous blocks such as advertising text, logos and graphics. The significant blocks have certain characteristic properties and spatial relationships that can be derived from images and used to assist in the task.

The task is one of finding regions of interest in either a structured or cluttered environment. The regions of interest are blocks of machineprinted or handwritten text. The complexity of the task depends on whether the mail piece is a letter (which usually has structure), flat (where the address block may be randomly placed) or parcel. The handwriting/machine print discrimination function is a byproduct of this operation.

The approach taken was to first develop a set of tools to segment the image and to detect characteristic properties that are relevant to assigning appropriate labels to the segmented regions. The design was arrived at by examining a large data-base of characteristics of mail pieces relevant to ABL. The design uses several specialized functional tools[12]. The tools are divided into two categories: image analysis tools and block analysis tools (see Table 1). The basic system consists of three image analysis tools and eleven block analysis tools. The image analysis tools take down-sampled images as input, and produce other images or symbolic information, e.g., grey-scale to binary, extraction of extent of sub-images. The block analysis tools take symbolic descriptions as input, e.g., extents of different blocks, confidences associated with blocks for different labels, and produce other symbolic descriptions.

Segmentation is the process of generating candidate regions by analyzing the binary image. Due to the fact that addresses have several different visual structures, several segmentation tools are used. One specializes in handwriting (which consists of elongated thin strokes) and another specializes in machine print (which consists of regularly spaced blobs). Segmentation is performed by labeling all connected components and then determining a region-adjacency graph. Components having similar sizes and near each other are connected together in this graph. Clusters of connected regions in this graph represent blocks of text. Different size parameters are used for handwriting and machine-print.

Performance

Examples of images with handwritten and machine-printed address blocks located by ABLS are shown in Fig. 4. ABLS was tested on 2,046 MLOCR (multi-line postal OCR) binary images, all from the letter mail class. The images were not destination encoded by the postal OCR. The images were processed in the form of down-averaged 100 ppi binary images. The resulting performance was as follows: success (correct top choice) = 88.3%, partial success (city, state, ZIP included) = 1%, correct reject (top candidate was not DAB) = 0.4%, wrong reject (top candidate was DAB) = 1.3%, type 1 error (something other return address chosen) = 7.7%, and type 2 error (return address chosen) = 1.2%.

Category	Tool	Description
Image Analysis Tools	DIGI	Produces digitized images of the original document
	ADTH	Adaptive thresholding to convert a gray-scale image into a binary image using local contrast.
	MSEG	Segmenter to locate connected components corresponding to machine-print and group them into blocks using a region adjacency graph. Consists of MSEG1 and MSEG2.
	HSEG	Segmenter to locate handwritten blocks by first filtering blobs using HSEGF and then using HSEG1 and HSEG2 (analogous to MSEG1 and MSEG2).
	LSEG	A segmenter that groups blobs into lines and lines into blocks. Uses output of MSEG1.
Block Analysis Tools	ZIPM	Merges ZIP code block in lower right of a destination address candidate.
	BLCS	Splits a too high or too wide machine-generated text block into several smaller text blocks.
	BLCM	Merges machine-generated text blocks which are parallel and close in proximity.
	SIZE	Uses block features, *e.g.*, aspect ratio, length, height, number of text lines, and number of components, etc., to classify how likely a block is a destination address, return address, or advertising text.
	LAYO	Examines the layout of text lines in a block.
	LOCA	Uses the location of a block to determine the likelihood of this block being the destination address, return address, or postage.
	HEUR	Uses spatial heuristics or rule-of-thumb to guess the destination address from a list of candidates.
	COVF	Verifies the consistency of labeling hypotheses among neighboring blocks.
	UNIF	Unifies the block features between blocks generated by different tools.
	EVHP	Pools together the evidence generated by various tools and generates labeling hypotheses.
	STOP	Decides whether to halt processing or not.

Table 1: Functional Descriptions of Tools in basic ABL system.

Window Detection

The performance of ABLS can be aided by a hardware system that can detect the presence of windows on envelopes. Glassine windows on envelopes can be detected from the reflective properties of the material. By placing sensor pairs at a critical angle, the amount of reflectance can be measured. The output of the sensors is processed by a high-speed digital signal processor (DSP). This processor calculates the coordinates of the window that is present on the mail piece. The result of window detection can be used as additional segmentation

The volume of machine-printed addresses is much higher than handwriting (85% versus 15%). Also, machine-printed addresses are often destined to businesses which have more complex address structures. The following section is devoted to the process of reading machine-printed addresses.

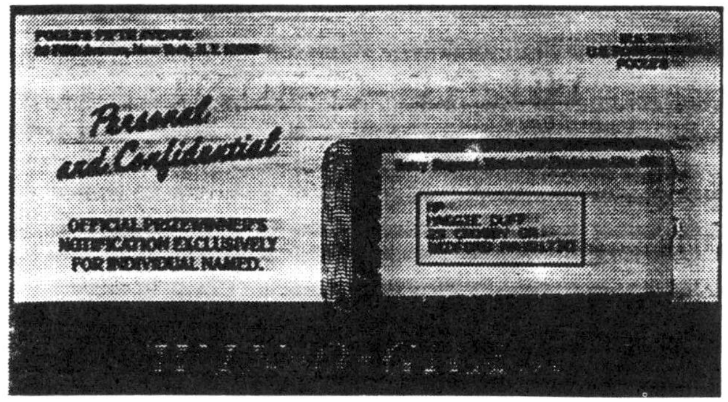

Figure 4: Examples of handwritten and machine-printed address blocks located by ABLS.

---

4 Address Reading and Interpretation

The goal of machine-printed address interpretation is to assign nine-digit ZIP Codes to mailpieces. Most addresses contain only a five-digit ZIP Code. This information can only specify a single city or a large portion of a city. However, the ZIP+4 Code specifies a small portion of a street. Thus, the goal of address reading and interpretation is to find ZIP+4 Codes for those mailpieces that don't contain them. This can be done by recognizing other information on the mailpiece and then using this information to look up the ZIP+4 Code in the ZIP+4 file.

For example, the address block shown in Fig. 5 does not contain a ZIP+4 Code[a]. However, recognizing that the city word is "DALLAS", the ZIP Code is "75240", the street address is

[a]Portions of addresses in this paper have been modified or blocked out to preserve confidentiality.

"5000 QUORUM DR", and the suite number is "310", we can look in the ZIP+4 file for a single entry that matches this address. In this case there is an entry that matches all of this information and the ZIP+4 code is 75240-7035.

SUITE 310
5000 QUORUM DR
DALLAS TX 75240

Figure 5: Sample Machine Printed Address Block.

The range of addresses that correspond to each ZIP+4 code are described by a single record in the national ZIP+4 file. The United States Postal Service (USPS) designed the ZIP+4 Code so that mail can be automatically sorted by an Optical Character Reader (OCR) down to the level of individual carriers and sections of their routes. A further desire of USPS automation efforts is to sort the mail into carrier walk sequence. This is the order that a carrier visits the customers on his/her route. It should be noted that both of these goals depend on the ability of OCRs to read and assign ZIP+4 Codes.

Current postal OCRs can, to a certain degree, read ZIP+4 Codes if they appear on a mailpiece. However, the ZIP+4 Code has not been fully accepted by the American public and only a small amount of mail bears the ZIP+4 Code. To counter this problem, USPS has been deploying OCRs that can read several lines of text in an address and lookup the proper ZIP+4 Code. However, this strategy has met with limited success because of processing speed requirements for the OCRs (about ten pieces per second) and the limits that this placed on the recognition techniques that could be designed into the system.

This section describes the research effort that seeks to improve the ability of OCRs to assign ZIP+4 Codes to addresses that may only contain a five-digit ZIP Code or no ZIP Code at all. This is done by applying advanced word recognition techniques that avoid various recognition problems[13] as well as a control structure based on the constraint satisfaction paradigm[14] which exploits the contextual information found in the address block.

An additional goal of this system is to overcome various uncertainties that can be found when interpreting an image. Only half of the address block images tested by our system can be assigned a ZIP+4 Code just by matching the address information to the ZIP+4 file, assuming we have perfect word recognition. The other half require extra processing to find the ZIP+4 Code. This extra processing is designed to overcome three kinds of uncertainties. First, an incomplete image may be input. For example, in the case of an address block, the street suffix may be left out. Second, errors may be present in the image, such as misspellings or an incorrect street number. Finally, recognition errors may have occurred.

Each of these uncertainties are illustrated in Fig. 6. The city name has been obscured during image acquisition, the patron has actually made an error in the ZIP Code, and word recognition was unable to perform correctly on the suffix due to poor image quality.

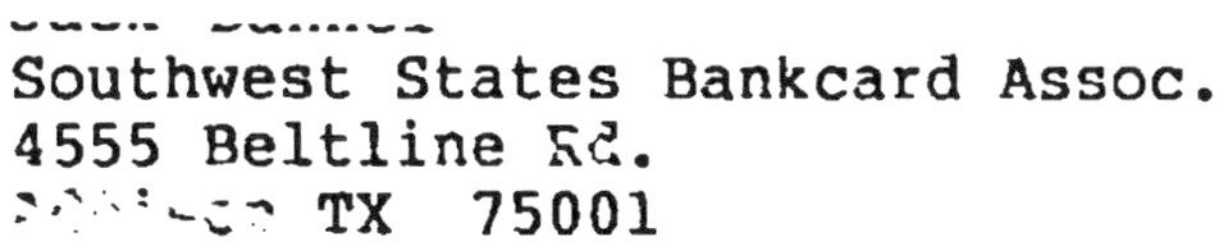

Southwest States Bankcard Assoc.
4555 Beltline Rd.
TX 75001

Figure 6: Address Block Image Containing Uncertainties.

The system attempts to overcome these types of uncertainties using the constraints provided by the ZIP+4 file. In addition to providing the ZIP+4 Code for a given address, we are able to query this database and ask whether certain pieces of information are compatible. The control structure for our system is then able to overcome these types of uncertainties by using only information from the address block that is compatible.

4.1 System Overview

The flow of control in the contextual analysis system is shown in Fig. 7. The digital image of an address block is input to the system.

Segmentation/Parsing

The first step is segmentation/parsing. This step segments the image into lines of text and then breaks up each line into individual word images. The parser assigns semantic categories to each word. The assignment for a given word is based on structural characteristics of the address block, including the number of lines in the address block, the number of words in the given word's line, and the number of characters in the given words. This information is then used to look up the most probable category for the given word. Additional processing by the parser compensates for redundant words on the same line and redundant configurations of lines in the same address block.

Word Recognition

The next step in the system is recognition. Depending on the semantic category assigned by the parser, either digit recognition or word recognition is used. Digit recognition is used for ZIP Codes, street numbers, box numbers and so on. The digit recognizer assigns one or more

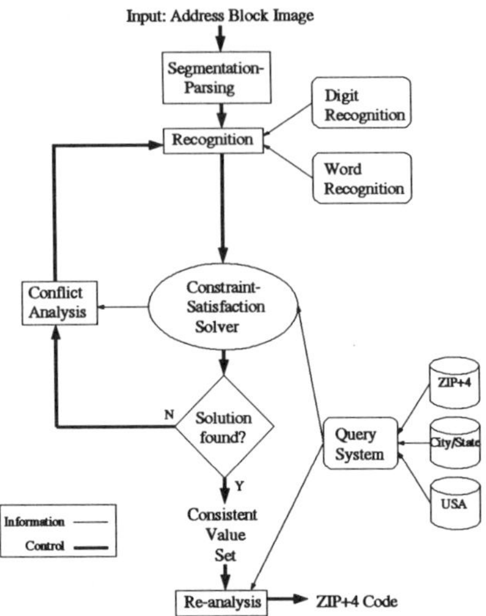

Figure 7: Control Flow Diagram.

---

choices (0...9) to each image. Word recognition is used for city words, street name words, street suffixes, etc. The word recognizer is less constrained. It uses the semantic category to choose a lexicon of possible words. That is, there are separate lexicons for city words, street words, suffixes and so on. The word recognizer then ranks the lexicon in descending order in terms of what it thinks is the correct word. Due to processing limitations, the system only uses the top twenty choices.

Constraint Satisfaction

The parsing and recognition results are then sent to the constraint satisfaction solver. This part of the system attempts to assign a single recognition choice to each word in the address block such that all assigned choices, when taken together, match an entry in the ZIP+4 file. Since each word may have more than one recognition choice this part of the system must use some "intelligence" to select choices that are most compatible. A blind, brute force approach would be to try all possible combinations of assignments for all the words. This would be too time consuming though. Instead, the constraint satisfaction solver initially uses the top recognition choice for each word. Then it compares two words at a time to see if they are compatible. If the choices assigned to each of the words are compatible then a solution has been found. Otherwise the most incompatible word has another recognition choice assigned and the process repeats.

If a solution cannot be found, the system proceeds to the section labeled conflict analysis. This part of the system either modifies the recognition results of a word or removes it from consideration altogether. This word is chosen as the most likely candidate that is preventing the system from finding a solution. This step is possible because many addresses contain redundant information. So parts of the address can be removed without affecting the chance that the correct interpretation can be found. Once the modification or removal has taken place the system returns to the constraint satisfaction solver to once again try and find a solution.

Once a solution has been found, the system proceeds to the re-analysis step. This is where the ZIP+4 Code is assigned. Each address block might match several ZIP+4 Codes. The most general corresponds to a record that matches a range of houses or buildings on a given street. A finer ZIP+4 Code corresponds to an actual building on a street. Getting even more specific, there could be a ZIP+4 Code for all suites or apartments on a single floor in the building or there could even be a unique ZIP+4 Code for a given office in the building. The reanalysis section attempts to find the most specific ZIP+4 Code using the solution found in the constraint satisfaction solver.

ZIP+4 access

An extremely important part of the context system is querying the ZIP+4 database. This is accessed from the constraint-satisfaction solver and the reanalysis step. This is a multi-access database system that supports of variety of queries. A given query may consist of all the information given in an address block or may be as simple as whether a given city and ZIP Code are compatible. Most of the queries only require a yes/no answer. Others expect a list of ZIP+4 Codes to be returned. The query system accesses the city/state file, the USA (Universal System of Addressing) file as well as the ZIP+4 file. The city/state file relates ZIP Codes to city and state names. The USA file contains the carrier walk sequence information. Due to the enormity of this information (the national ZIP+4 file contains over 28 million records), this data must be compressed. Thus, an additional effort in developing this system has been the compression and access of this data.

4.2 Parsing

The parser uses a bottom-up algorithm to classify the lines and words in the address block. There are three major steps in the algorithm that use progressively more contextual information[15].

4.2.1 Individual Word Parsing

The first step is to classify the type of each word in the address block individually. In this step, the information used is the position of the word in the address block (line and word number), its length, whether it contains letters or digits and more global characteristics of the address block such as the number of lines and the number words on the line of the word being parsed. Discrimination between words that contain only letters and words that contain digits is performed with an algorithm based on template matching character recognition. Such an algorithm uses a large set of templates whose meaning is known. Then the meaning of the template that most closely matches the input is assigned. In this case, all we are concerned about is whether the template that matched was a digit or a letter.

The above information is used to access a database of frequencies of words of different types occurring at various locations in a set of sample address blocks. For example, the system may be given an address block with three lines, the bottom line containing three words and the last word consisting of 5 digits. To assign a category to the last word on the bottom line, the above information would be used to lookup the most probable category for that word, in this case, the ZIP Code.

4.2.2 Horizontal Parsing

The second (horizontal) step uses the context of words within a line to choose a configuration of word types for a whole line, given a list of choices for each word from the first step. This step is accomplished by using frequencies of occurrence of various configurations of words on various lines together with the confidences of word types computed in the first step. This step of the algorithm works by considering all possible configurations of words in the given line. This promotes more likely category assignments based on the context of the given line.

4.2.3 Vertical Parsing

The third (vertical) step uses the context between the lines of the address block in order to choose the best combination of line types for the address block. In this step the results of the horizontal parser for each line are collected and each choice is labeled by the kind of information it contains. If a line contains any street words the line is labeled a street line; a line with city, state, ZIP Code is labeled city-state-ZIP line. These labelings are referred to as line classifications. The purpose of this step is to select from each line all choices that have the same line classification and in this way to select the best configuration of line classifications in the address block.

4.2.4 Keyword Recognition

After the vertical step of the algorithm is performed, keyword recognition is applied to all the word images. Keyword recognition is simply a recognition procedure that looks for words in the address block which are contained in a small lexicon of keywords. Example keywords are: PO, BOX, RURAL, APT, etc. The keyword recognition procedure makes use of the template matching algorithm. If any keywords are recognized in the address block, then the output of the vertical step is re-ranked to reflect the identified keywords.

4.2.5 Parsing Results

The result of these steps is a ranked list of vertical configurations for the words in the address block. Each vertical configuration may have a ranked list of horizontal configurations for each line. This way, the system can attempt to process the address block using several different configurations from the parser. Fig. 8 shows an example address block and the top two vertical configurations as output by the parser. Each configuration contains the line number, the line classification and the individual category assignments for each word. For example, in the top configuration, the first choice for the street line incorrectly assigns the street suffix category (ss) to the last word. It should in fact be the category for secondary number (cn). This is the case in the second choice for the street line. By using more than a single choice from the parser the system is much more likely to develop a correct interpretation for the address block.

4.3 Word Recognition

Words extracted by the segmentation algorithm may or may not be valid postal words, due to errors in segmentation or in the part of the patron who composes the address. Outputs from word segmentation include several types:

1. numeral strings, such as '2307', '74260', etc.;
2. mixed alphanumeric strings, such as '123E', 'W24-01', etc.;
3. postal words, such as 'Main','Street','Buffalo','New','York', etc.;
4. aliases and misspelled words, such as 'Carrolltn' for 'Carrollton', 'Philadelephia' for 'Philadelphia', etc.;
5. merged words by patron, such as 'FORESTSPRINGS', 'SAINTCHRISTOPHER', etc;
6. split words by patron, such as 'Stony' and 'Brook' for 'Stonybrook';
7. missegmented words, such as 'Dal' and 'las' for 'Dallas', '10Rural' etc.

Most of the extracted words are in types 1 and 3. These words are contained in a lexicon obtainable from postal databases, such as all valid street numbers in a region, or the collection of all city names in the nation. Contextual constraints embedded in a lexicon can be used to facilitate recognition. Section 4.3.1 is devoted to lexicon based word recognition methods.

Words of other types are not contained in any lexicon and have to be recognized as character strings. Empirical statistical knowledge including letter distribution and transition

1325 N. NURSERY #115D
IRVING, TX 75061

```
1 city-state-zip cw sw z5
1 city-state-zip cw sw z9
2 street sn sp st ss
2 street sn sp st cn
2 street sn sp st st
2 street sn st st ss
3 recipient nn nn nn
3 recipient nn nn ow

1 city-state-zip cw sw z5
1 city-state-zip cw sw z9
2 po-box pw pw pi pn
3 recipient nn nn nn
3 recipient nn nn ow
```

Figure 8: Address Block and Parse Results.

probabilities derived from a sample set can be used to postprocess the decisions. Methods for character string postprocessing are discussed in Section 4.3.2.

Unfortunately in practice it is difficult to predict whether an extracted word is or is not contained in a lexicon, especially in the presense of segmentation errors. The address syntax parser assumes correct segmentation and outputs a list of guesses of the syntactic category of each word. Recognition of a word is then based on each of the guesses which is accompanied by a predefined lexicon. Ideally, the recognition decisions are qualified by confidence measures. If none of the decisions is reliable, the word is recognized as an unconstrained character string.

4.3.1 Lexicon Based Word Recognition

Given a word image and a lexicon, the recognition algorithm produces a ranking of the words in the lexicon with respect to their similarities to the image. Difficulty in recognition arises from variations in the shape of a word as well as from the size of the lexicon. The shape of a word varies because of differences in font types and patterns of image degradation. Confusions between similar words are more likely if a large lexicon is given.

Recognition of a word from its image is based on visual features extracted from the image. Visual features may be extracted from the word as a whole object. Alternatively, a word may be segmented, or separated, into individual characters, each of which is recognized in isolation. The word's identity is then derived from the decisions made on individual characters.

Methods to use shape information in a word image and context information from a lexicon can be divided into three major classes: *character recognition based* methods, *segmentation-based* methods, and *word-shape analysis* methods. A robust solution is constructed that uses all three simultaneously[16]. The final decision about a word's identity is made by combining the results of the individual methods. This is an example of a *multiple classifier system*[17].

In character-based word recognition algorithms, the individual characters in a word are first isolated and recognized[18]. The character decisions are then *postprocessed* with a lexicon to correct recognition errors[19] (See Fig. 9). These methods are suitable for cases where a reliable segmentation can be obtained and the segmented characters are not deformed by normalization. It is also an appropriate strategy for shorter words which are easier to segment and where little word-level context can be utilized.

An alternative to the character based techniques is to defer decisions about character identity and to perform *segmentation-based word recognition* (Fig. 10). This is suitable for images where the characters can be easily extracted but are difficult to recognize in isolation. In this approach, feature descriptions of the extracted characters are assembled and matched to a similar representation of the words in a lexicon. These techniques effectively focus word-level knowledge on the recognition process and are suitable for situations where characters can be segmented and better recognized together with other characters in the word.

A third type of word recognition algorithm determines features from the whole *word shape* and uses this description to calculate a group of words in a lexicon that match the input (Fig. 11). Useful features for word shape description include local stroke directions[20] and template defined features detected by convolution[21]. Such methods are especially suitable for images that are difficult to segment into characters, or where the characters are distorted when they are extracted and normalized.

Each of these three methods uses contextual information at a different level. In the character recognition approach, contextual constraints are used only in the last stage, that is, the postprocessing stage after the character classes are decided. In the segmentation-based word recognition approach, contextual information is used before the class decisions are made, but after feature extraction. In the word shape analysis approach, word context information is used directly in feature computation and matching.

Most previous solutions to word recognition have used only one of the three methods

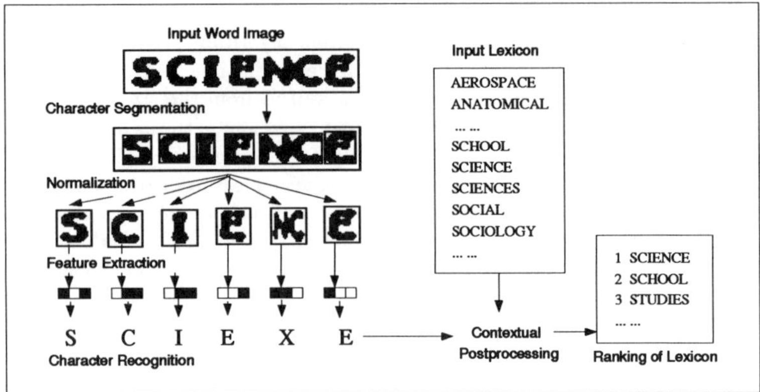

Figure 9: The character recognition approach.

---

outlined above. Since each of them excels for a limited type of image, their performance and generality have been restricted. To achieve maximum reliability, the three approaches are integrated into a multiple classifier system, such that the weakness of one method may be complemented by the strength of another method.

The three approaches are integrated in a computational model which consists of an activation control mechanism, a set of parallel classifiers, and a decision combination mechanism. The control mechanism uses information from the input image and the input lexicon. It activates suitable words in the lexicon based on a set of global features computed from the image, and then selectively applies appropriate classifiers to the image. The parallel classifiers take three different approaches (character recognition based, segmentation-based, and word-shape based) to recognize the word. Each computes a ranking of the activated words in the lexicon according to their similarities to the image in shape. These rankings are combined in the decision combination mechanism which produces a consensus ranking (Fig. 12).

To derive the consensus ranking, a confidence score is computed for each word in a lexicon which is a weighted sum of the rank scores computed by the independent classifiers. The weight for each classifier is estimated using a regression analysis that uses a log-odds transformation[22]. A consensus ranking is then derived by sorting the words by the computed confidence scores. This ranking is to be used by the control structure in further contextual analysis.

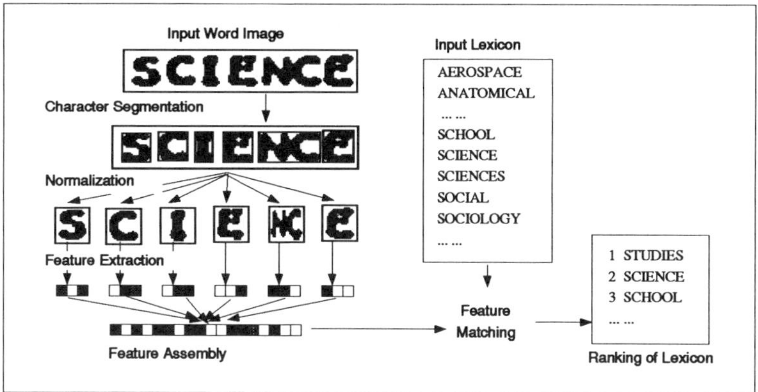

Figure 10: The segmentation-based word recognition approach.

4.3.2 Word Recognition without a Lexicon

When results from lexicon based recognition are determined to be unreliable, the word is recognized as a character string. The word is segmented into isolated characters which are recognized independently. A string is formed by concatenating the character decisions. Alternative strings can be constructed by different combinations of several decisions for each character, and ordered by the joint likelihood computed by a postprocessing algorithm.

Empirical and a priori statistical knowledge can be used to postprocess such character strings. These include knowledge from the recognizer such as confidence measures associated with the decisions and letter or letter group confusion probabilities, and knowledge of the word sources such as character n-gram frequencies representing constraints of case consistency and spelling rules[23,24]. The statistics are typically derived using a training set. Some adjustments according to a priori expectations can be made to overcome the problem of undertraining. For instance, binary n-grams[25,26] can be used to remove letter combinations that are forbidden by spelling rules. Whether some or all of these constraints are applicable depends on the syntactic category of the word indicated by the parser.

Assuming independence between all sources of errors, the statistical knowledge can be represented by a Bayesian model, implemented by tree searching[23] or relaxation techniques[27]. Other useful methods include Markov models implemented by a Viterbi algorithm[28] or its variants[29], and string editing methods implemented by dynamic programming algorithms[30].

Certain character strings are variants of words contained in a lexicon, though the strings are not exhaustively listed. These include alternative spellings of the same word, words

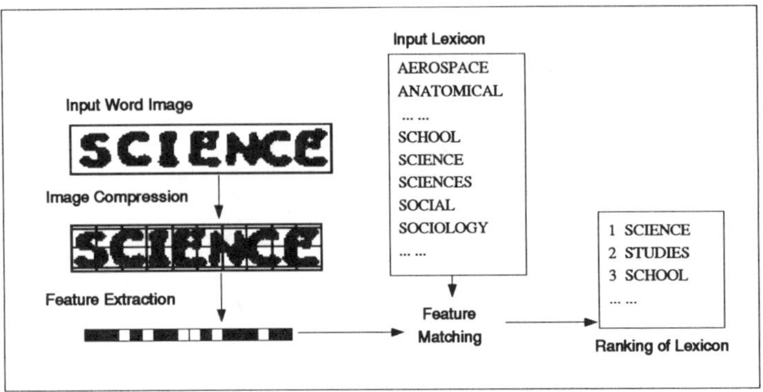

Figure 11: Word-shape analysis approach.

---

of a common root in various grammatical forms and abbreviated forms, and expansions of abbreviations. In case that no possible ambiguity will be introduced, these strings can be translated to their standard forms by rules listed in a translation table[24]. A postprocessed string can also be marked at positions corresponding to individual phonemes to provide possible separation points if it is guessed by the control structure as a merged word.

4.4 Constraint Satisfaction

The constraint satisfaction solver in our system is based on the constraint satisfaction paradigm. This paradigm is used to solve what are called constraint satisfaction problems (CSPs). A constraint satisfaction problem consists of n variables, X1...Xn, each having an associated domain of possible values. Each variable can be assigned any value in its domain but *constraints* are imposed on the legal combinations of values that two or more variables can assume. A solution to the CSP consists of a set of values, one for each variable, such that the constraints over all variables are satisfied.

A classic example of a CSP is the N-Queens problem. The goal is to place N Queens on an N by N chess board such that no two queens are attacking each other horizontally, vertically or diagonally. Fig. 13 shows a solution to the 4-Queens problem. In terms of a CSP, the N variables are the positions of the N queens on the chess board and the constraints are all pairwise: no two queens are attacking each other. By placing only one queen in each column the vertical constraint is removed. A brute-force solution, called backtracking, is to start each queen in the first row. Then, starting with the second column, for each queen that is in conflict with another, move it to a lower row. If a row can't be found for some

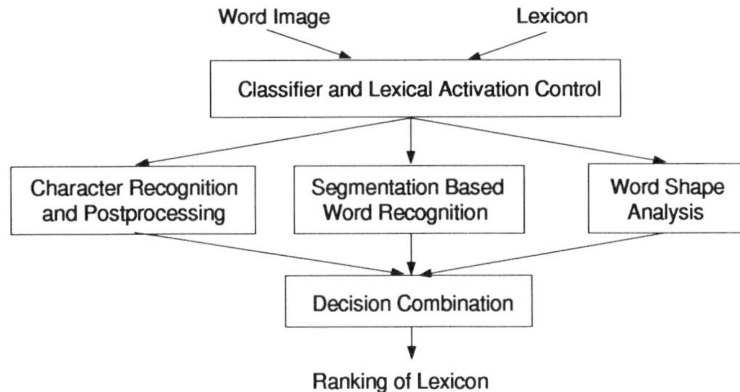

Figure 12: A computational model for word recognition using multiple approaches.

queen where it is not in conflict then backtrack to one of the previous queens and move it to a lower row. This is where the algorithm gets its name. This search is brute-force because it doesn't consider how good or bad a given assignment is, only whether it is in conflict or not.

Informed backtracking[31] is a more intelligent backtracking algorithm. It differs from backtracking in that it looks ahead when a variable must be repaired. When a variable is in conflict and must be assigned a new value, instead of simply choosing the next value in the domain, informed backtracking considers all values in the domain. It determines which one would have the fewest conflicts with the current values of the other variables that have not previously been repaired. This value is then assigned and the process continues forward until a solution is found or the algorithm backtracks. In the latter case, the value with the next fewest conflicts is tried. This algorithm is much less likely to backtrack which is a major problem with the ordinary backtracking algorithm. This type of algorithm is easily applied to interpreting postal images as well as other image interpretation problems that are similarly constrained.

4.4.1 Constraint Satisfaction Solver

The constraint satisfaction paradigm maps very easily to postal image interpretation. Each word in the address block image is considered to be a variable in the CSP. The domains for each variable are provided by the recognition routines. Finally the constraints are imposed by the ZIP + 4 database. In the N-Queens problem, it is easy to visualize the constraints;

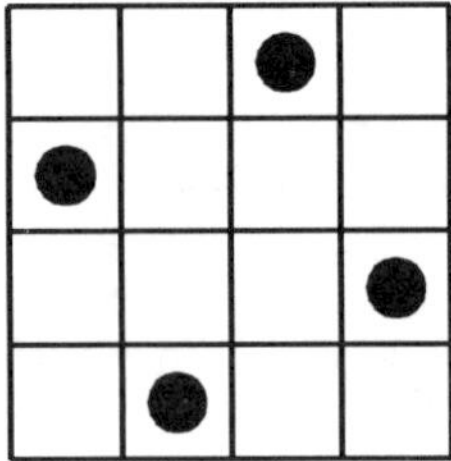

Figure 13: Solution to the 4-Queens problem.

however, it may not be so easy to visualize the constraints used to process a mail piece. The constraints between two or more pieces of information from a mail piece are satisfied if there is at least one record in the ZIP + 4 database that contains all the specified information. This process is carried out by a query system[32] built around the ZIP + 4 database which allows access to the data in a fast and efficient method. Fig. 14 illustrates a graph of the various fields in the ZIP + 4 database that can be used in queries. Notice that every field is linked to every other field. Thus, every piece of information provides a constraint on every other piece of information. For example, we may be interested in the constraints between the ZIP Code (z5) and the first street word (st1). A query in this case might take the form of the ZIP Code being "75248" and the street word being "HIDDEN". If this were a legal combination of values, the query would return "yes". That is, these two values would satisfy the constraints imposed by the ZIP + 4 database.

The constraint satisfaction solver uses the informed backtracking algorithm to assign a value (recognition choice) to each variable (word) in the address block. An initial assignment for each variable is made using the top recognition choice. If all these values, taken together, do not satisfy the constraints of the ZIP + 4 database, the variable whose value has the most conflicts with the other assigned values is repaired. As described in the previous section, this repair process does not blindly choose the next choice from the recognition routine, but considers all choices. Each is compared to the values of the other variables and the one with the fewest conflicts (not necessarily zero) is assigned. This process repeats until a solution is found, or the algorithm backtracks to where it was first called. In the latter case, conflict analysis is used to try to loosen or remove some of the constraints.

4.4.2 Conflict Analysis

This section is closely tied to the constraint satisfaction solver in that it uses information about which variables have been repaired in selecting a variable to be removed or modified, also known as the *culprit*. This section uses a heuristic that says the most likely candidate

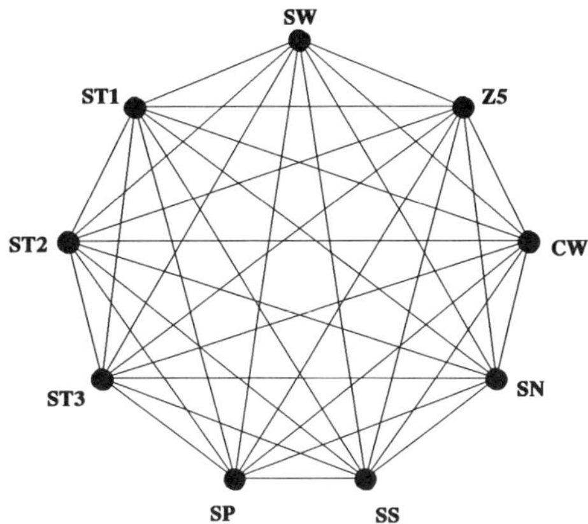

Figure 14: Constraints from the ZIP + 4 File.

to be the culprit is the variable that was repaired first. This will be the variable that, using the top recognition choices, had the most conflicts. Depending on the category of the selected culprit, various methods may be tried to improve or modify the recognition results. An example of this is when the culprit is a PO box number. Sometimes this is written as "#248". The "#" is often misrecognized as a "4" due to low resolution and poor image quality. Thus a recognition choice for this number could be "4248". A simple modification to the recognition results in this case would be to drop the choices for the first digit from the recognition results. The constraint satisfaction solver will be called again, but this time "248" will be used instead of "4248". If nothing can be done to modify the recognition results of the culprit, then the culprit will be removed from further processing.

In some cases information should be removed not because of misrecognition but because it is written incorrectly. For example, if a person addressing an envelope accidentally writes the wrong ZIP Code, conflict analysis would want to identify the ZIP Code as being incorrect and remove it from further consideration. In this way our system is able to overcome errors on the address block itself, as well as correct the occasional recognition error.

4.4.3 Reanalysis

The reanalysis section is also closely tied to the constraint satisfaction solver. It uses the solution found by informed backtracking to retrieve all ZIP + 4 records that match the address believed to be on the mail piece. If only one record is found, then the ZIP + 4 Code for that record is assigned to that mail piece. Otherwise, reanalysis looks for differences between the records. Unused information from the address block is used to distinguish between two or more records. This process continues until a single record is isolated or there is no more usable information on the address block.

The kinds of information used in this part of the system are not necessarily needed to find the correct ZIP + 4 record, but may be of use to choose between similar ones. For example, most street addresses can be fully specified without using the suffix (street, drive, road, etc.), but sometimes the suffix is the only difference between two records. In such a case, if the suffix was printed on the address block, it can be recognized and used to decide which record is correct. Similarly, the apartment or suite number is not needed to find the correct street address, but can be used to choose between multiple ZIP + 4 records for a single apartment building.

4.5 Experiments and Results

The system was tested on 1013 address block images which had not been previously seen. The output was a sortation assignment for each address block. In some cases the system was not able to resolve the address down to a nine-digit ZIP+4 Code. In such cases the system would output only the five-digit ZIP Code or possibly reject the image altogether.

In the test, the system was able to encode 462 (45.61%) to nine-digits. This compares to the encode rate of a current postal OCR of 165 (16.29%). Both the system and the OCR made errors in about 10% of the nine-digit assignments. An important point to note is that these 1013 images are divided up based on the sortation performance of a current postal OCR. USPS is most interested in developing technology that can correctly process the rejects of a current OCR. With that in mind, the test contains many more images that were rejected by the current OCR. Thus, if our system were to be tested on a more representative mailstream, the projected encode rate for our system would be 73%, while the encode of the OCR would be only 45%.

5 Summary

As an area of computation research, machine reading continues to be of great scientific and economic importance. Among the basic literate skills of humans (reading, arithmetic, reasoning and writing), a significant amount of success has been achieved in arithmetic (the *raison d'être* for early computers), in computational reasoning (e.g., expert systems), and in computational aids for writing (e.g., text processing, natural language synthesis). Computational reading, which spans the spectrum of signal processing to symbol processing, continues to be a challenging frontier.

A general architecture for machine reading and its specialization to postal mail sorting had been presented. Three subsystems are developed in accordance with the architecture to: (i) capturing image of a mailpiece, (ii) locating destination address in the image, and (iii) interpreting the address to determine the destination code.

Locating destination address block is a special case in document layout analysis. It is goal-oriented which only needs to find one or more subregions of a mailpiece image as candidates for the address block. It is different from other document layout analysis tasks, e.g., extracting headlines and stories on newspaper pages, due to the uncertainty and variability of address block location.

The task of interpreting machine-printed address is realized by a constraint satisfaction approach. The system uses various levels of contextual knowledge in processing the address block. Words from the address are recognized and then matched to the ZIP+4 file using an intelligent backtracking algorithm. Experimental results demonstrate that such approach attains an encode rate of 73% while the current postal OCR attains 45% only.

References

[1] H. Singer, A developmental model of speed reading in grades three through six, in *Theoretical Models and Processes of Reading*, H. Singer and R.R.Ruddell (eds), International Reading Association, Newark, DE, 1970.

[2] W. Doster, Different States of a Document's Content on its Way from the Gutenbergian World to the Electronic World, *Proceedings of the Seventh International Conference on Pattern Recognition*, 1984, 872-874.

[3] R. Fenrich, S.W. Lam, S.N. Srihari, Optical Character Readers, in *Encyclopedia of Computer Science and Engineering*, A. Ralston (ed.), Second Edition, Van Nostrand-Reinhold, New York, 1991, in press.

[4] N. Otsu, A threshold selection method from gray-level histograms, *IEEE Transactions on Systems, Man and Cybernetics*, **9**, 1, 1979, 63-66.

[5] P.W. Palumbo, P. Swaminathan, S.N. Srihari, Document image binarization: evaluation of algorithms, *SPIE Vol. 697, Applications of Digital Image Processing IX*, 1986, 278-285.

[6] Y.Y. Tang, C.Y. Suen, C.D. Yan, M. Cheriet, Document Analysis and Understanding: A Brief Survey, *Proceedings of the First International Conference on Document Analysis and Recognition*, Saint-Malo, France, 1991, 17-31.

[7] S.N. Srihari, Document image understanding, *Proceedings ACM-IEEE Fall Joint Computer Conference*, Dallas, TX, 1986, 87-96.

[8] V. Govindaraju, S.W. Lam, D. Niyogi, D.B. Sher, R. Srihari, S.N. Srihari, and D. Wang, Newspaper image understanding, in *Knowledge Based Computer Systems*, S. Ramani, R. Chandrasekhar, K.S.R. Anjaneyulu (eds.), Lecture Notes in Artificial Intelligence, Springer-Verlag, 1990.

[9] D. Wang, S.N. Srihari, Classification of newspaper image blocks using texture analysis, *Computer Vision, Graphics and Image Processing*, 47, 1989, 327-352.

[10] S.W. Lam, D. Wang, S.N. Srihari, Reading newspaper text, *Proceedings of Tenth International Conference on Pattern Recognition*, Atlantic City, New Jersey, 1990, 703-705.

[11] R.K. Srihari, *Extracting Visual Information from Text: Using Captions to Label Human Faces in Newspaper Photographs*, Ph.D. Thesis, Department of Computer Science, SUNY at Buffalo, 1991.

[12] C.H. Wang, S.N. Srihari, A framework for object recognition in a visually complex environment and its application to locating address blocks on mail pieces, *International Journal of Computer Vision*, **2**, 2, 1988, 125-152.

[13] J.J. Hull, S.N. Srihari, A Computational Approach to Visual Word Recognition: Hypothesis generation and Test, *IEEE Computer Society Conference on Computer Vision and Pattern Recognition*, Miami Beach, Florida, 1986, 156-161.

[14] A.K. Mackworth, Constraint Satisfaction, in *Encyclopedia of Artificial Intelligence*, **1**, John Wiley and Sons, 1987, 205-210.

[15] M. Prussak, J.J. Hull, A Multi-level Pattern Matching Method for Text Image Parsing, *Proceedings of the Seventh IEEE Conference on Artificial Intelligence Applications*, Miami, Florida, 1991.

[16] T.K. Ho, J.J. Hull, S.N. Srihari, Word Recognition with Multi-Level Contextual Knowledge, *Proceedings of the First International Conference on Document Analysis and Recognition*, Saint-Malo, France, 1991, 905-915.

[17] T.K. Ho, J.J. Hull, S.N. Srihari, Combination of Structural Classifiers, *Pre-Proceedings of the IAPR Syntactic and Structural Pattern Recognition Workshop*, Murray Hill, New Jersey, 1990, 123-136.

[18] J. Schuermann, A Multifont Word Recognition System for Postal Address Reading, *IEEE Transactions on Computers*, **C-27**, 8, August 1978, 721-732.

[19] D.G. Elliman, I.T. Lancaster, A Review of Segmentation and Contextual Analysis Techniques for Text Recognition, *Pattern Recognition*, **23**, 3/4, 1990, 337-346.

[20] S. Mori, K. Yamamoto, M. Yasuda, Research on Machine Recognition of Handprinted Characters, *IEEE Transactions on Pattern Analysis and Machine Intelligence*, **PAMI-6**, 4, July 1984, 386-405.

[21] H.S. Baird, H.P. Graf, L.D. Jackel, W.E. Hubbard, A VLSI Architecture For Binary Image Classification, in *From Pixels to Features* , J.C. Simon (ed.), North Holland, 1989, 275-286.

[22] A. Agresti, *Categorical Data Analysis*, John Wiley and Sons, 1990.

[23] M.A. Jones, G.A. Story, B.W. Ballard, Integrating Multiple Knowledge Sources in a Bayesian OCR Post-Processor, *Proceedings of the First International Conference on Document Analysis and Recognition*, Saint-Malo, France, 1991, 925-933.

[24] P.A.V. Hall, G.R. Dowling, Approximate String Matching, *ACM Computing Surveys*, **12**, December 1980, 17-38.

[25] E.M. Riseman, R.W. Ehrich, Contextual Word Recognition Using Binary Diagrams, *IEEE Transactions on Computers*, **C-20**, 4, April 1971, 397-403.

[26] C.Y. Suen, N-Gram Statistics for Natural Language Understanding and Text Processing, *IEEE Transactions on Pattern Analysis and Machine Intelligence*, **PAMI-1**, 2, April 1979, 164-172.

[27] A. Goshtasby, R.W. Ehrich, Contextual Word Recognition Using Probabilistic Relaxation Labeling, *Pattern Recognition*, **21**, 5, 1988, 455-462.

[28] G.D. Forney, Jr., The Viterbi Algorithm, *Proceedings of the IEEE*, **61**, March 1973, 268-278.

[29] J.J. Hull, S.N. Srihari, Experiments in Text Recognition with Binary n-Gram and Viterbi Algorithms, *IEEE Transactions on Pattern Analysis and Machine Intelligence*, **PAMI-4**, 5, September 1982, 520-530.

[30] R.A. Wagner, M.J. Fischer, The String to String Correction Problem, *Journal of ACM*, **21**, 1, 1974, 168-173.

[31] S. Minton, M.D. Johnston, A.B. Philips, P. Laird, Solving Large-Scale Constraint Satisfaction and Scheduling Problems Using a Heuristic Repair Method, *Proceedings of the Eighth National Conference on Artificial Intelligence*, Boston, Massachusetts, 1990, 17-24.

[32] P. Filipski, C.S. Bharathi, J.J. Hull, S.N. Srihari, Compression for fast read-only access of a large memory resident structured database, *Proceedings of the Second Data Compression Conference*, Snowbird, Utah, 1992, to appear.

CHAPTER 20

INCREMENTAL LEARNING MECHANISMS FOR SPEECH UNDERSTANDING

WILLIAM LEE MAHOOD
E-Systems, Inc., Melpar Division
7700 Arlington Blvd.
Falls Church, VA 22046

ABSTRACT

This study investigated the feasibility of using machine-learning techniques to support the development of a speech understanding system. The research studies the behavior of Hidden Markov Models as an incremental learning mechanism. The approach is to train whole-word recognizers using a minimal set of training tokens and then incrementally train them as new examples of the words are recognized and added to the training set. The results show that it is practical to generate "seed" recognizers from a small training set made up of word tokens composed from segmental fragments. This yields better results than a model formed by chaining hidden Markov models. A "seed" recognizer may be used to locate additional tokens. One iteration of the Baum-Welch training algorithm is sufficient to incrementally train the hidden Markov model. There is a rapid improvement in the performance of the hidden Markov model with each new token added.

1. Introduction

There are many applications for machine learning in speech understanding systems. This is especially true of large-vocabulary, continuous-speech recognition systems. It is easy to see how machine learning might apply in the higher level understanding processes such as context tracking, user modeling, grammar adaptation, vocabulary expansion, etc. But machine learning techniques are also useful for the low-level speech recognition processes to provide rapid training, speaker adaptation, bootstrapping recognition capability, phonological adaptation, etc. This study focused upon applying machine learning to the lower level speech recognition processes: those that perform the primary utterance recognition, facilitate the segmentation of continuous speech and guide lexical access.

The primary application for this learning mechanism is to serve as a tool for developing a large-vocabulary speech understanding system. Such a system might be used in a dialog-based, man-machine interface. The proposed speech understanding system will use a hybrid of utterance recognizers at different levels of segmentation: phonetic, syllabic and whole-word models. In the early stages of development, the tools will be used to "bootstrap" the training of the basic phoneme-level utterance recognizers and to build whole-word recognizers for high-frequency-of-occurrence function words. If the speech understanding system has the appropriate learning mechanisms in place, the method can provide for ongoing adaptation and self-modification once it becomes operational.

In a speech understanding system, it is anticipated that the higher level speech-recognition and speech understanding processes will control and guide the low-level training of the basic utterance recognizers. The higher level processes will provide an estimate of the credibility of parsed speech input and thus pick out good examples of phonemes or primary utterances for inclusion in the incremental training process. Such a mechanism might be used in the initial stages to "bootstrap" the system by building up the training database. In later stages, the process might replace older tokens or less credible tokens and thus provide for ongoing adaptation.

Another application for this learning mechanism is for constructing speaker-dependent, key-word spotters. Such a key-word spotter is useful for screening large volumes of recorded speech material to locate important information: occasions where a speaker has discussed a particular subject or topic. Training a key-word spotter may be difficult because of a limited amount of speech samples from the desired speaker and few or no examples of the desired key words. A key-word spotter can be primed with as few as six training tokens. The results of this research suggest that it is feasible to prime a key-word spotter using the available training tokens supplemented with training tokens that have been composed out of subunits of other words collected from the desired speaker. The primed key-word spotter can then be used in an interactive system to locate occurrences of the key word. The operator will review probable occurrences of the key word. Each confirmed occurrence will be extracted, added to the training set, and used to incrementally train the key-word spotter. As the system is used, the probability of detection should improve and the false-alarm rate should diminish.

The project investigates the use of first-order hidden Markov models (HMM) as the modifiable element of a machine learning mechanism (figure 1). It is an exploratory project in that it examines the behavior of the hidden Markov model in very simple learning paradigms. This preliminary work provides insight into the behavior of the hidden Markov model and into the performance of a basic learning mechanism. The results of this study serve as a basis for future work on learning mechanisms at the utterance recognition level.

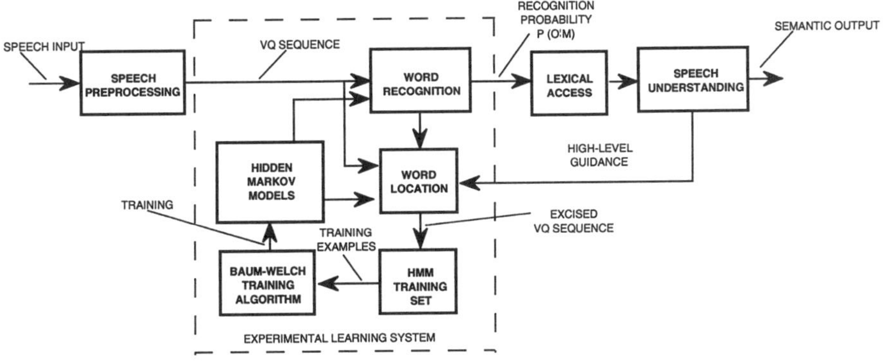

Figure 1. The Hidden Markov Model is the Modifiable Element of this Experimental Learning System for Speech Understanding.

The objective of this research is to develop tools that will allow a speech understanding system to be developed using a minimal amount of training effort. The strategy is to create an utterance recognizer that is trained on a minimal set of training tokens and then progressively train the recognizer as new examples of the target utterance are recognized and added to the set of training tokens. Using this strategy, the performance of the recognizer will be "bootstrapped" as it performs the recognition task.

Two tasks are accomplished. The first task explores methods of initiating a "seed" hidden Markov model. The second task investigates the feasibility of incrementally training the speech recognizer.

2. Hidden Markov Models

The technique of hidden Markov models is an information theoretic method of recognizing a pattern sequence that has a statistical variability in both the symbol sequence and in the temporal distribution of the sequence.[1] It is currently the most advanced method used to perform discrete utterance recognition in speech applications.

In the following discussion of hidden Markov models attention appears to be focused upon whole-word recognition. The term "word" is used loosely here since the hidden Markov modeling technique may be applied at any level of phonological segmentation: phonemes, diphones, syllables, whole words, connected words, phonological words, etc. In the discussion that follows, the term "word" will be used to refer to the specific segmentation of speech that the hidden Markov models are trained to recognize.

To understand how hidden Markov models function, it is necessary to realize that a given hidden Markov model is a statistical model of a speaker uttering the "word" that the model represents. In a speech recognition system, at least one hidden Markov model is required for each "word" that is to be recognized. A speech recognizer is implemented as a Viterbi style decoder with a bank of hidden Markov models acting to analyze a sequence of symbols received from a speech preprocessing system. In operation, each model is used to ascertain the probability of that model generating the received sequence of symbols. Presumably, the hidden Markov model having the greatest probability of generating the sequence of symbols represents the "word" intended. In practice, the hidden Markov models are not able to make fine distinctions between similar sounding "words" and the decision is prone to error. It is necessary to use higher level phonological, syntactic, semantic and pragmatic knowledge to thread among the stream of candidate "words" and synthesize a plausible sentence or meaning representation.

The operation of a hidden Markov model decoder can be explained by taking an analogy to a simple communications system. The sender wishes to send a message, one that is taken from a finite set of possible messages. The sender has a unique code for each possible message that consists of sending a sequence of symbols taken from a finite size alphabet. The receiver needs to perceive the sequence of symbols at the receiving end and look up the sequence in a code book to ascertain the message that it represents. Unfortunately, the communication channel is noisy. The perceived sequence has both added noise and temporal corruption: there are symbol insertions and deletions as well as symbol replacement. The task of the receiver is to look at the perceived symbol sequence, compare it with the set of legal symbol sequences in his code book, attempt to choose the most likely matching sequence, and select the message received on that basis. A hidden Markov model recognizer does the receiver's job of finding the most likely code book sequence that matches the perceived symbol sequence.

Underlying the hidden Markov model is a state graph.[2] In a general model, the state of the model may transition from any node of the graph to any node of the graph with a finite probability. A node may transition to itself. A hidden Markov model may take on any number for forms. Most speech recognition work is done using first-order, left-to-right models consisting of about four nodes (figure 2). The initial state is presumed to be the left-most node of the model. Successive state transitions will either remain in the same node or move to the right along a linear chain. In a first-order model, the state may remain at the same node or move to the right either one or two nodes. The state will most likely end up in the right-most node at the completion of the modeled sequence. The state transition probabilities of a first-order, left-to-right hidden Markov model are typically represented as a square matrix with only the center diagonal and two adjoining upper right diagonals filled with non-zero probability values. This Markov state graph models the temporal pattern of the generated symbol sequence.

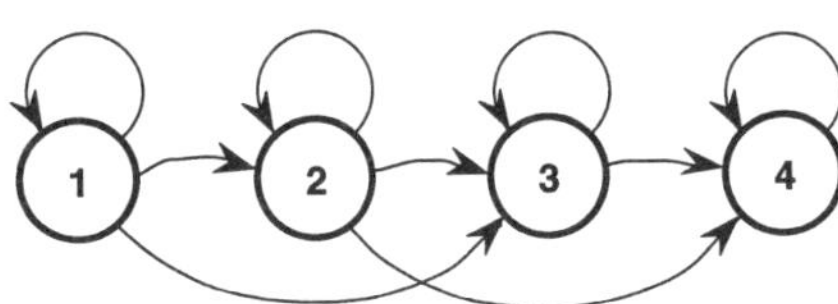

Figure 2. State Diagram of a First-Order Hidden Markov Model.

For each state of the hidden Markov model, there is a statistical distribution of the probability of a given symbol of the alphabet being issued. When the model is in a given state, the most likely symbol apt to be generated will be the received analog of the symbol sent. The most likely symbols will include the most likely substitutions that may occur as a result of noise, speaker variability, mispronunciation, dialect, stress, etc. In the course of modeling an utterance the probability distribution of generated symbols will change as state transitions occur. The symbol generation probability distribution is typically represented by a rectangular matrix with a row for each node of the underlying hidden Markov model and a column for each symbol of the code alphabet. The probability of a model producing a given symbol sequence is a function of this and the underlying state probabilities.

The hidden Markov models are implemented such that the model evaluates the perceived sequence of symbols and yields an estimate of the likelihood of that model generating the perceived sequence. The probability of a hidden Markov model producing a given symbol stream can be computed using the Baum-Welch "forward-backward" algorithm.[3] For a given state; i, it is possible to compute partial forward probabilities using a recursive function: The partial forward probability of being in state; i, and producing the symbol sequence up to and including the current symbol is estimated by multiplying the probability of state; i, producing the current symbol by a summation over the states of their partial forward probabilities of generating the predecessor symbol stream times their transition probability to state; i. This recursive function terminates when it reaches the first symbol of the stream where the probability of generating that symbol is the probability of the left-most state generating that symbol. The overall probability of a given model producing the received symbol stream is a summation over all the nodes of the partial forward probabilities of generating the entire sequence.

A similar computation may be made by summing over partial backward probabilities. The partial backward probability is a recursively defined function that estimates the probability of all successor states of state; i, producing the remaining sequence of the symbol stream excluding the current symbol. The recursion terminates with the probability of any state producing the terminal symbol being unity.

The forward and backward probabilities can be used to estimate the parameters of the hidden Markov model for a given set of training sequences. Training is accomplished by an iterative re-estimation of model parameters over an arbitrary starting model. By using a set of training sequences for a given utterance, it is possible to use the forward-backward algorithm to calculate the expected number of transitions from one given state to another. It is also possible to estimate the expected number of transitions out of a given state. The ratio of these expected values may then be used as new estimates of the state transition probabilities for a new iteration over the training set. The frequency of occurrence of a given symbol by a state can be estimated relative to the occurrence of any symbol by that state. This then serves as a new estimate of the symbol generation probability distribution.

The input to the experimental system consists of vector quantizer (VQ) code sequences derived from "live" speech. The method of vector quantization is a means of compressing the information content of speech to a discrete form that is compatible with the use of hidden Markov models. The VQ code sequences are derived from speech as follows: Analog speech from a microphone is sampled at 10 kHz and digitized with a resolution of 12 bits. Next the sequence of digital words is blocked into a window of 300 samples weighted by a Hamming window. Linear predictive coding (LPC) coefficients are computed for each window using the autocorrelation method. A vector of the first 10 LPC coefficients is vector-quantized into a code book of 256 prototype vectors representing the minimum-mean-error set of natural speech LPC vectors. This process is repeated sliding the 300 sample window by 100 samples along the sequence of digital words. This process results in the generation of an 8-bit VQ code word every centisecond (10 ms). Thus, VQ code sequences are generated at the rate of 100 bytes per second of speech. The output is a sequence of VQ symbols that represent the incoming speech.

In this experimental work, VQ sequences are used in the training sets of hidden Markov models and serve as test tokens analyzed by the models. Thus, VQ sequences are the primary input to the system. First-order hidden Markov models are used as utterance recognizers. All models have the form shown in figure 2.

3. Generating "Seed" Hidden Markov Models

The traditional method of generating hidden Markov models is to collect a set of examples of the word to be recognized. This set of training tokens is then used to train the hidden Markov model using several iterations of the Baum-Welch algorithm. The training is done in a batch mode using a moderate size set (20-100) of training tokens. These examples of the word or tokens are manually excised from speech input to the system during training. In almost all cases, hidden Markov models are trained in the process of implementing a speech recognition system, and little or no training takes place once the system becomes operational.

The objective of this research is to find a better method that minimizes the manual effort and allows the speech understanding system to assume a role in the training process. If the task of locating and collecting training tokens is assumed by the speech understanding system, then the system will be capable of creating word recognizers on the fly. There are several methods that may be used to automate target word recognition and training token collection:

1. The system may rely upon the existing recognition capability and higher level speech understanding to deduce the identification of the target word and thus collect training tokens. In this case, the system relies upon syntax, semantics, context and pragmatics to recognize the word.

2. A whole-word recognizer could be created by chaining together several phonetic or segmental hidden Markov models. The chained hidden Markov model would then serve as the initial recognizer to collect additional training tokens.

3. An initial training set could be generated by composing training tokens from a library of phoneme tokens and syllabic tokens. Vector quantizer sequences would be taken from the training sets of the respective subsegment recognizers and composed to form larger training tokens. Once a "seed" hidden Markov model is synthesized, it serves to bootstrap the learning process by collecting additional training sequences as the system is used.

The first phase of this research investigates the feasibility of the latter two methods: models generated from composed-token training sets and chained hidden Markov models. Experiments were conducted to compare the recognition performance of hidden Markov models created by the two methods and to compare them with hidden Markov models trained upon actual examples of the target word.

Composed-token hidden Markov models were generated using training sets containing six composed tokens. The composed tokens were created by concatenating vector-quantizer sequences from a library of phoneme, diphone, and syllabic training tokens. As an example, the six training tokens for the word "speech" were synthesized as follows: One training token was created concatenating a VQ sequence for phoneme -sp- with one representing the rhyme -eech-. In this case, the rhyme came from the word "teach." Two more tokens were formed by composing an example of -spee-, derived from words like "speed," and examples of -ch-, extracted from the words "church" and "reach." The remaining three tokens were composed from individual phoneme libraries -sp-ee-ch-. This example shows that there is an inherent flexibility in composing the training tokens. The tokens may be composed from a mixture of segmental fragments: phonemes, diphones, syllables, or any combination available.

Chained hidden Markov models were formed by linking hidden Markov models representing appropriate fragments of the target word. For example, a recognizer for the word "lisp" was formed by chaining a hidden Markov model trained for the sound li- with a hidden Markov model for the sound -sp-. This approach follows the method suggested by Frederick Jelinek.[4,5] The chained models were formed from well-trained hidden Markov models that were generated using large training sets. This method tends to produce relatively long chain models. For example, six-state hidden Markov models are formed by chaining two three-state models. Thus, this method is not amenable to the formation of short-chain models.

To serve as a comparison reference, whole-word hidden Markov models were generated using training sets made up of six tokens of the actual word. These tokens were manually extracted from live speech. These models represent the conventional method of training hidden Markov models. Six token training sets were used so that the performance of "seed" recognizers might be compared.

All of the target words used in these experiments were short, monosyllabic words. Thus, it was practical to conduct the experiment using relatively short-chain hidden Markov models. Three- and four-state hidden Markov models were used for composed-token and whole-word recognizers. Four- and five-state, chained recognizers were created by linking two- and three-state utterance recognizers.

In all cases, the resulting "seed" recognizers were tested against a set of ten test tokens that were manually extracted from real speech. The tokens used in the test set were distinct from any word used to train the whole-word models and were not used as a source of training material for any of the models.

The Baum-Welch algorithm was used to measure the recognition probability for each test token. This is the probability of the model generating the test VQ sequence: P(O¦M). In order to make comparisons between words of different length, the test results were normalized to an average symbol recognition basis: p(O¦M). This was done by taking the Nth root of the recognition probability where N is the number of VQ symbols in the test sequence. The results of these experiments are summarized in table 1.

Table 1. A Comparison of "Seed" Hidden Markov Models.

Average Symbol Recognition p(O¦M)

Type of HMM	Number of HMM states		
	3	4	5
Whole Word	4.29×10^{-2}	7.59×10^{-3}	
Composed Token	4.85×10^{-2}	4.27×10^{-2}	
Chained		8.60×10^{-3}	9.61×10^{-3}

The composed-token hidden Markov models performed as well as the whole-word models. The average symbol recognition performance of the composed-token hidden Markov models averaged over the different experimental words is commensurate with that of whole-word hidden Markov models. The chained hidden Markov model method did not perform as well as expected and tended to yield an average symbol recognition performance about one-fourth that of either the whole-word or composed-token models.

The composed-token and whole-word methods make it easier to generate the smaller three- and four-state hidden Markov models. The chained model method results in a long-chain model even when linking relatively short-chain phoneme models. Chaining phoneme models to form polysyllabic word models will result in an excessively long-chain model. The resulting model will be significantly less efficient than a short-chain model created by either of the other methods. Long-chain models carry a significant computational burden. This is probably the chief disadvantage of the chained hidden Markov model method.

These results demonstrate that the composed-token method is a practical method for generating "seed" hidden Markov models. Part of the success of the composed-token method is believed to come from the ability to use a variety of word fragments to compose the training set. This was illustrated by the example where the training set for the word "speech" was composed of a mixture of phoneme and diphone fragments. Although not quantified in these tests, recognizers generated in this way seemed to yield better results than composed-token models made from a more uniform selection of phonetic fragments. It is suspected that the introduction of diphone and triphone fragments in the training set helps account for coarticulation effects that occur in the target word better than fragments that originate from words selected at random.

4. Incremental Learning using Hidden Markov Models

There is a potential for using the Baum-Welch training algorithm to incrementally train hidden Markov models. In this mode, a speech recognition system is "bootstrapped" from "seed" hidden Markov models that have been trained on relatively few (6) training tokens. Subsequent training of the hidden Markov models occurs as respective words are recognized and the corresponding VQ symbol sequence is excised and added to the training set of the hidden Markov model. Each successive retraining of the hidden Markov model should progressively improve the performance of the model in terms of yielding a better probabilistic estimate for subsequent recognitions of the target "word" and greater breadth of recognition in terms of the ability to recognize different enunciations of the target "word."

This "bootstrapping" method is potentially useful in a newly installed speech understanding system as a method of having the basic recognition processes adapt to the intended user(s). In this case, the delivered system would contain seed hidden Markov models that have been trained to "generic" voices. After delivery, the "bootstrap" mechanism would gradually incorporate examples of the user's voice into the training sets, ultimately supplanting the "generic" examples of the original training set.

This phase of the research models a speech understanding system where the system autonomously creates whole-word models of high-frequency-of-occurrence function words. The word "the" is the most common function word in the English language. Thus, this experiment demonstrates the incremental training of a hidden Markov model to recognize the word "the". In the experiment, an initial hidden Markov model is trained on relatively few (6) examples of the word "the." In operation, this model is used to locate and excise additional tokens for the training set from simple trial sentences presented to the program. The hidden Markov model is incrementally trained as new tokens are added to the training set. With each trial, the retrained model is tested against a reserved set of examples of the word "the" to test the overall performance of the incrementally trained hidden Markov model.

A data base of 39 sentences was collected and transformed into VQ sequences. Each sentence consisted of three words: a verb, the word "the" and an object (e.g., "Feed the bear", "Cross the street", "Sail the boat", etc.). All sentences were spoken by a single male speaker. Examples of the word "the" were collected in sentence form to assure a more natural enunciation. In almost all cases, the word "the" is separated from the preceding verb by a distinct pause. On the other hand, the word "the" is frequently run together with the succeeding object. Thus, the beginning of the word "the" is quite uniform, and coarticulation effects are more noticeable at the end of the word.

Of these 39 sentences, six were used for initial training of a hidden Markov model, fifteen were used to generate a set of test examples of the word "the" and the remaining eighteen were used as trial sentences in the experiment. VQ sequence of the word "the" were extracted manually from some of the sentences. Six of these manually extracted tokens were used for the initial training of a hidden Markov model for the experiment. Manually extracted tokens were used for the fifteen test examples. Full sentence VQ sequences were used as input to the experimental learning program.

The experiment was started with a "seed" hidden Markov model trained using six tokens of the word "the." A training set of six tokens probably represents the minimal training set that can be used successfully. A larger training set should yield better recognition results in the early stages of learning, but is less likely to show a high rate of improvement in performance that occurs using the smaller initial training set.

When the program is run, an example (VQ sequence) of the word "the" is extracted from each of the trial sentences and added to the training set used to retrain the model. During the course of the experiment, the size of the training set grows from six tokens to twenty-four tokens.

The current instance of the hidden Markov model is used to recognize and locate the word "the" within a trial sentence. Recognition is based upon finding the highest recognition-probability result sliding a window along the VQ code sequence of the trial sentence. It proved necessary to constrain the recognition search artificially to the region of the sentence where the target word is actually located. Obviously, in a speech understanding system, higher level knowledge will participate in the recognition and location of words within the speech sequence.

One of the objectives of the project was to assess the feasibility of using the hidden Markov model to find the precise location and sequence duration of the modeled word within a trial sentence. The experiment showed that there are problems in using the hidden Markov model for this purpose. High-level speech understanding constraints are needed to assure reliable recognition of the target word. It is difficult to get the hidden Markov model to align correctly with the VQ sequence in the trial sentence. VQ symbols appearing at the ends of the utterance tend to have a greater variability and make it difficult to determine the end points reliably. Without high-level constraints, this had the effect of shortening the length of the VQ sequence excised from the trial sentence and gradually reducing the time dimension of the resulting hidden Markov model. Both of these problems can be alleviated through the use of prosodic information (energy contours, zero crossing rate, etc.) and higher level knowledge that would exist in a fully implemented speech understanding system.

Once the basic position of the target word is recognized, a search is made in the immediate vicinity to locate the best match between a sequence excised from the trial sentence and the current instance of the hidden Markov model. Initially, it was thought that it would be sufficient to pick the highest average symbol recognition probability in the search to find an optimum sequence position and sequence length representing the target word. In practice, this method truncated the excised VQ sequence much shorter than expected. A strategy was adopted of looking at the distribution of average symbol recognition probabilities as a function of position and sequence length. The centroid of the data in an area immediately surrounding the initial recognition point was used to locate the VQ sequence to be excised.

After the target word was located, the VQ segment selected by the centroid method was appended to the training set of the hidden Markov model. Each trial sentence analyzed contributes another example of the target word "the." Each token added to the training set tends to increase the diversity of VQ symbol sequences accepted by the hidden Markov model.

The final step of the process is to retrain the hidden Markov model using the appended training set. The Baum-Welch "forward-backward" training algorithm is used to re-estimate new state-transition probabilities for the underlying Markov model and to re-estimate a new symbol generation probability distribution for each state.

Early trial runs of the program used several iterations of the training algorithm in an effort to achieve convergence of the training with each new token. It turned out that new tokens are rapidly assimilated into the hidden Markov model and it is not necessary to perform more than one training iteration.

The results demonstrate a progressive refinement of the hidden Markov model with each trial sentence presented to the program (figure 3). There is a gradual improvement in the breadth of the hidden Markov model; i.e., the ability to accept different enunciations of the target word.

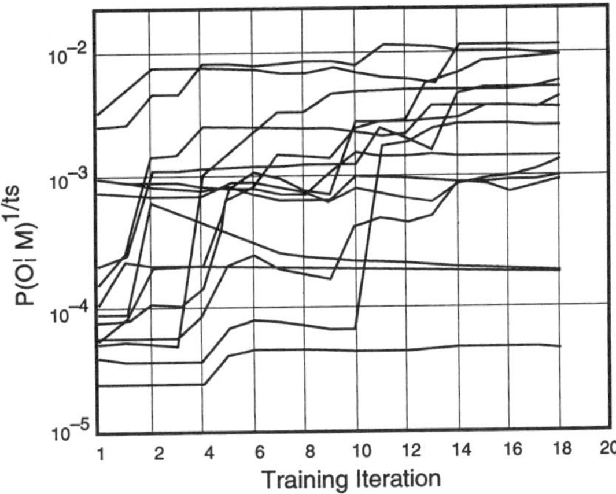

Figure 3. Average Symbol Recognition Improves with Training.

5. Summary

The results of these experiments show that it is feasible to automate the process of generating hidden Markov model recognizers. It is practical to generate "seed" hidden Markov models either by using whole-word training tokens or by composing training tokens from phonological fragments: phonemes, diphones, syllables, etc. Both methods yield comparable results. A "seed" model needs at least six training tokens for satisfactory initial performance.

These "seed" hidden Markov models may then be used to help locate additional training tokens in the process of parsing speech. Higher level knowledge is needed to support this process and constrain the search. New training tokens are rapidly assimilated by the hidden Markov model using one iteration of the Baum-Welch training algorithm. There is a rapid improvement in the performance of the recognizer with each added token.

The initial application for these speech recognition training tools is to aid in developing a large-vocabulary speech-understanding system. In this system, basic recognition is performed using a hybrid of utterance recognizers at different levels of phonological segmentation: phonetic, syllabic and whole-word recognition. This incremental training method will be used to develop whole-word recognizers for high-frequency-of-occurrence words.

This method is suggested as a tool for creating key-word recognizers for screening large volumes of speech. This approach is especially useful for generating key-word recognizers where few or no training tokens of the key word exist and there is a limited sample of the speaker's voice available for training.

Acknowledgements

Credit is given to Dr. Ryszard Michalski for inspiring this research through his teachings at George Mason University. I am indebted to Dr's. Kenneth DeJong, Henry Hamburger, Anna Baraniecki and Andrew Sage for encouraging my work on speech understanding. For their understanding and support while doing this research, I owe a special thanks to my family: Charlotte, Shannon, Debra and Rachel.

References

1. L. R. Rabiner, "A Tutorial on Hidden Markov Models and Selected Applications in Speech Recognition," *Proceedings IEEE*, **v77**, #2, pp 257-286, Feb. 1989.
2. L. R. Rabiner, S. E. Levinson and M. M. Sondhi, "On the Application of Vector Quantization and Hidden Markov Models to Speaker-Independent, Isolated Word Recognition," *Bell System Technical Journal,* **v62**, #4, April 1983.
3. S. E. Levinson, L. R. Rabiner & M. M. Sondhi, "An Introduction to the Application of Probabilistic Functions of a Markov Process to Automatic Speech Recognition," *Bell System Technical Journal*, **v62**, #4, April 1983.
4. Frederick Jelinek, Lalit R. Bahl & Robert L. Mercer, "Design of a Linguistic Statistical Decoder for the Recognition of Continuous Speech," *IEEE Trans. on Information Theory*, **IT-21**, #3, May 1975.
5. Frederick Jelinek, "Continuous Speech Recognition by Statistical Methods," *Proceedings IEEE*, **v64**, #4, April 1976.

CHAPTER 21

SIGNAL UNDERSTANDING: AN ARTIFICIAL INTELLIGENCE APPROACH TO MODULATION CLASSIFICATION

J.E. WHELCHEL, D.L. MCNEILL, R.D. HUGHES, and M.M. LOOS
E-Systems, Melpar Division
7700 Arlington Boulevard
Falls Church, Virginia 22046

ABSTRACT

The results of the study presented in this paper indicate the feasibility of recognizing a variety of signal modulations in the radio spectrum. A new demodulation technique is proposed, and a comparative evaluation of neural network as opposed to maximum likelihood recognition is presented.

1. Introduction

A typical communication system receives and demodulates specific signals whose parameters are known beforehand. For example, a 90 Mbit/s digital microwave radio is carefully tailored to the spectral characteristics, baud rate, carrier center frequency, and bandwidth of QPSK. For radio spectrum surveillance applications, however, a system must be designed to receive and recognize signals with a variety of modulations and signal parameters.[1,2] In response to these requirements, a "signal understanding" system is being developed and evaluated by means of simulation. The system consists of a new type of generalized demodulation/feature extraction section followed by statistical moment generator, then by a pattern classifier. The classifier is based on neural network topology. An algorithmic Maximum-Likelihood (ML) pattern classifier was also used to evaluate the performance of the neural network. Signal generation, feature extraction, and the ML classifier were implemented using VAX/VMS FORTRAN. The neural network was implemented on a PC-based Hecht-Neilson (HNC) ANZA Neurocomputer.

2. Feature Extraction

We selected a small, high information content subset of possible signal features. The most direct and intuitive way to find out the modulation type is to examine "activity" on candidate demodulator outputs. This is the approach we have taken, as shown in figure 1. Feature vectors composed of statistical variance, skew, and kurtosis of demodulated amplitude, phase, and frequency were assembled. For the signal classification system, precise carrier frequency estimation is essential to eliminate linear trends in the phase demodulated outputs. Precise carrier phase lock and tracking are not necessary, since we are interested in activity on the outputs of a generalized demodulator, that is, delta changes or second and higher-order moments, all of which are independent of absolute initial carrier phase. Therefore, we chose a sliding-block Forward-Backward Linear Predictor (FBLP) with median filtering and averaging for carrier frequency estimation driving a standard complex demodulator. This algorithm exploits the high resolution, rapid frequency, lock capabilities of autoregressive estimation to provide frequency, phase, and amplitude demodulated outputs to subsequent feature extraction and classifier algorithms. Accurate carrier frequency and relative phase estimation are thus obtained without the use of a Costas-type estimator designed specifically for particular data signals such as 16-QAM. Median filtering is effective in eliminating the transients occurring out of an FM demodulator whenever a phase transition occurs in a signal containing discrete phase shifts. The primary requirement is that the estimator window size be less than half the number of samples per baud. This allows the stable frequency estimates to retain a majority over a symbol duration interval. Data communication systems are, in some cases, oversampled to facilitate optimal detection algorithms (matched filtering, etc.). For radio surveillance applications, eight or sixteen samples per baud are not uncommon. Therefore, oversampling should not present a severe constraint.

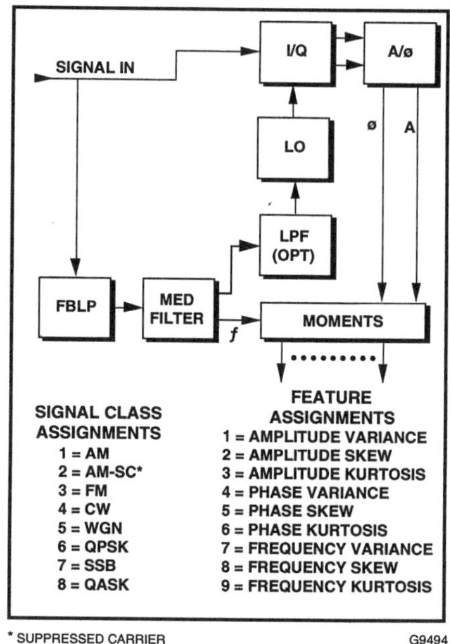

Figure 1. Generalized Demodulator.

A lowpass filtered version of the median filtered frequency estimate time series is used as a control signal to drive the local oscillator of a standard quadrature I/Q demodulator. This yields demodulated amplitude and phase. As an example, figure 2 shows demodulated phase of a CCITT standard V.29 16-OASK data signal centered at fc = .256, initial phase = 130 degrees. The signal to noise ratio was 24 dB. A block length 8 FBLP was used with length 16 median filtering for center frequency estimation. A sliding-block FBLP was implemented, with the average of the overall median filtered time series used to drive the LO of the I/Q demodulator. Length 5 median filtering was applied to smooth the amplitude and phase demodulator outputs.

Examples of two-dimensional feature space representations for nine signal classes are shown in figure 3. The figure illustrates variance histograms of AM plotted versus FM variance using a logarithmic variance scale.

3. Classifier Selection and Training

Once feature vectors were computed as previously discussed, a neural network pattern classifier was trained and used to identify unknown signals. For comparison purposes, we

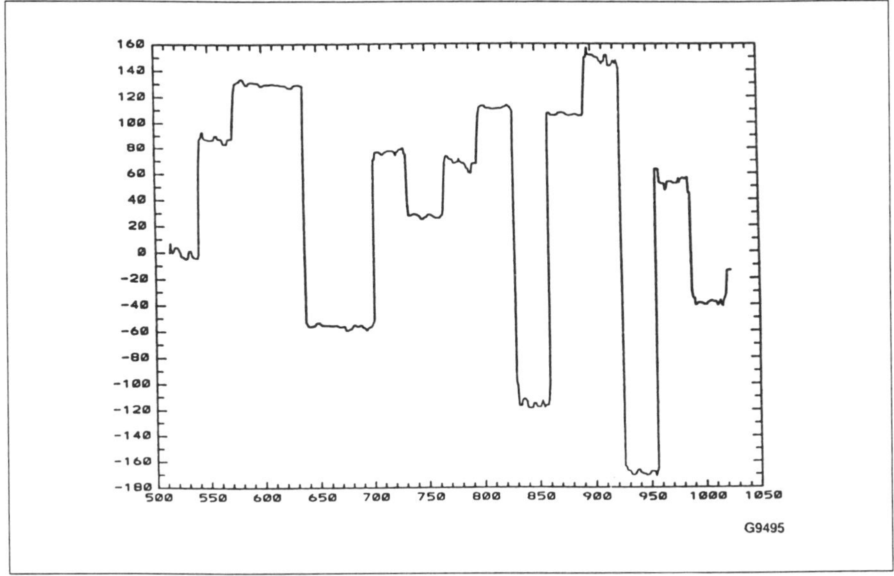

Figure 2. Demodulated Phase of 16QASK.

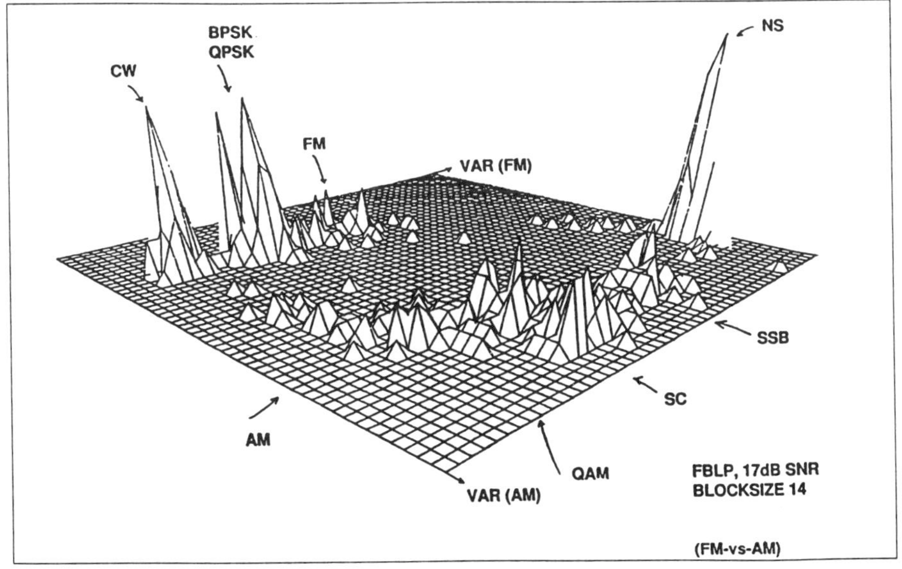

Figure 3. FM vs. AM Variance Feature Space.

implemented a classical Maximum- Likelihood algorithmic pattern classifier based on means and covariances of the feature vectors/feature clusters in multidimensional space.

3.1 Neural Network Classifier

Two neural network paradigms were used in this application: the Counter Propagation Network (CPN) and Back Propagation Network (BPN). The purpose of the CPN is to create a competitive, supervised, self-programming, optimal look-up table where each element has an equal probability of being chosen. The network functions by activating the processing element (PE) or node in the center layer whose weights are closest to the input vector. This excited PE sends its weights to the output layer as the network's actual output. The CPN is composed of three layers: the input, Kohonen (middle), and Grossberg (output) layers. The middle Kohonen layer contains PEs with a given weight vector. The number of Kohonen nodes in the network corresponds to the number of elements in the look-up table or the number of partitions in the input space if allowing only one winner. For the application of interest here, the number of PEs in the Kohonen layer can be anywhere between M, the number of signal classes, and M*K, where K is the number of feature vectors per class. After the input is introduced to the network, the winner in the Kohonen layer is determined by measuring the proximity of the input vector to the weight vector using the dot product. The competition layer node determines which weight vector best matches the input vector and declares a winning PE. Only the winning vector can adjust its weight toward the input vector.

The BPN uses associative learning to create a mapping from the input vectors to their corresponding outputs by training through examples. The network's name is derived from having the error, or the difference between the desired and actual output, propagated back through the network to modify the connections. The network is composed of three layers: the input, hidden (middle), and output layers. The hidden layer is composed of N nodes. There is no set standard or theory on how to choose the number of PEs in this layer. It is known, however, that the lesser the amount of hidden units, the more the network generalizes; the greater the number of hidden units, the more the network will learn special cases. We have chosen the number of PEs between M and M*K, as discussed before. When the network is in the training mode, all of the weights will be adjusted to decrease the total mean square error over the training data. If there is no difference between the actual and desired output, no learning takes place. Otherwise, the weights are changed to reduce the difference.

3.2 Maximum-Likelihood Classifier

A Maximum-Likelihood Bayes pattern classifier was used in both training and operational modes. Here we are assuming a multivariate Gaussian model and that we have used a feature extraction technique that yields an r-dimensional feature vector for each training set entry consisting of a signal from each class. The training set data is then used to estimate the conditional probability density or likelihood function for each class. The required mean vector and covariance matrix representing each class are estimated from the feature vectors using 64 training signals for each class. Decisions are made in favor of the class that has the greatest likelihood. In the training phase, prototype feature vectors for each class are first passed through a length 3 median filter to remove outliers occurring across the training set. Then, axis normalization scaling factors are computed prior to covariance and mean estimation.

4. System Performance

Preliminary evaluation to select networks were conducted using both five and six signal classes. Using six signal classes, the BPN performance on increasing complex signal environments was evaluated. The degree of environment complexity is a function of the extent to which statistical variations are imposed on signal parameters. Different BPN architectures were evaluated using eight signal classes. For each signal class, 64 feature vectors were generated as a training data set and 64, using the same signal variations, were generated as a testing data set.

In early experiments five signal classes (AM, AM- SC, FM, CW, and WGN) were used to establish network learning parameters and the hidden layer size. For these data sets with little variation, the CPN with 41 or more and BPN with 10 or more hidden nodes would converge to zero training error. As a result of these initial experiments, a 45 hidden node CPN and 30 hidden node BPN network were selected for subsequent experiments.

In the next set of experiments, six signal classes (AM, AM-SC, FM, CW, WGN, and QPSK) representing a simple environment, were used to compare the performance of a CPN with 45 hidden nodes, two BPNs with hidden nodes (one BPN having the input nodes connected and the other without the input nodes connected to the output nodes), an ML classifier, and a minimum distance (MD) classifier. Again, dual sets of 64 input feature vectors per signal class were used for training and testing. As shown in figure 4, the ML and both BPNs performed substantially better than the CPN or MD classifier. Limited experimentation with different numbers of hidden nodes confirmed that the choice of 45 for the CPN and 30 for the BPN was reasonable.

CLASSIFIER	CPN	BPN CONNECTED	BPN UNCONNECTED	MD	ML
ERRORS	5.2%	2.0%	2.5%	13.8%	2.8%

G9497

Figure 4. Classifier Performance in a Simple Signal Environment.

As a consequence of the previous experiment, further experimentation emphasized the BPN approach and used both connected and unconnected 30 hidden node BPN networks. Both network and the ML classifier were trained and tested on dual data sets of 64 feature vectors per signal class of increasing variations. The BPN used all nine features. For the ML method, only the three standard deviations were used. Figure 5 shows the data variation parameters for the simplest and most complex data sets. For the simple data set, the ML classifier trained to zero errors, while both BPNs missed one sample out of 384. For the complex data set, the training errors were six for the ML, five for the connected BPN, and seven for the unconnected BPN. In all cases, the training was considerably better than using a parse tree, figure 6, which loses relationships between features. The confusion matrices are given in figure 7 for the simple and complex testing data sets. In some of the data sets of intermediate complexity the three feature ML classifier performed better than either BPN, and the unconnected BPN performed better than the connected BPN.

Using dual test and training data sets (64 feature vector per signal class) consisting of eight signal classes (AM, AM-SC, FM, CW, WGN, QPSK, SSB, and QASK), the performance of different size BPN networks was evaluated. Figure 8 summarizes these results along with the ML classifier using only the three standard deviation input features.

Training of the BPN networks was halted when there had not been any improvement in learning after numerous (on the order of 15,000) trials. In some cases, it was noticed that as training improved the testing errors increased. To substantiate this, an unconnected BPN network with 30 hidden

PARAMETER	TEST CASE #1 VALUE	TEST CASE #2 VALUE	UNITS
SNR	30	23	dB
CARRIER FREQUENCY	.25	.25 + − .025	Hz*
CARRIER PHASE	0	0 + − 180	DEGREES
AM/FM BASEBAND BANDWIDTH	.1	.1 + − .05	Hz*
AM MODULATION INDEX	.85	.7 + − .25	- -
FM MODULATION INDEX	.4	.4 + − .2	- -
DATA SIGNAL SAMPLES/ SYMBOL	32	32 + − 4	- -

DATA SETS WERE 512 SAMPLES PER TEST SIGNAL IN EACH OF 64 TRIALS PER CLASS PER TEST CASE.

THE SIX CLASSES WERE AM-LC, AM-SC, FM, CW, WGN, QPSK.

* NORMALIZED TO 1 Hz SAMPLE RATE

G9498

Figure 5. Training/Test Set Characteristics for Two Data Sets.

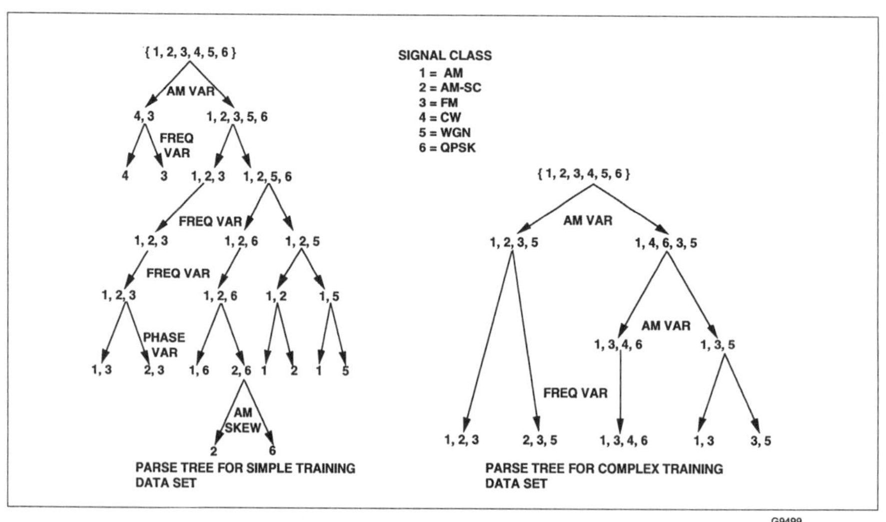

Figure 6. Parse Trees Constructed from Individual Features.

MAXIMUM LIKELIHOOD CLASSIFIER

2.8% ERROR

CLASS	1	2	3	4	5	6
1	98	0	0	1	0	0
2	0	98	0	0	1	0
3	0	0	90	0	9	0
4	0	0	3	96	0	0
5	0	0	0	0	100	0
6	0	3	0	0	0	96

11.2% ERROR

CLASS	1	2	3	4	5	6
1	85	9	4	0	0	0
2	0	93	0	0	6	0
3	1	6	89	0	3	0
4	7	0	10	78	0	3
5	0	6	0	0	93	0
6	12	0	0	0	0	87

BPN CONNECTED NETWORK

2.0% ERROR

CLASS	1	2	3	4	5	6
1	98	0	0	1	0	0
2	1	98	0	0	0	0
3	1	0	90	0	0	9
4	0	0	0	100	0	0
5	0	0	0	0	100	0
6	0	0	1	0	0	98

8.7% ERROR

CLASS	1	2	3	4	5	6
1	78	10	0	9	1	0
2	1	90	0	0	6	1
3	1	0	89	9	0	0
4	0	0	4	92	1	1
5	1	0	1	0	96	0
6	6	0	0	0	0	93

BPN UNCONNECTED NETWORK

2.5% ERROR

CLASS	1	2	3	4	5	6
1	98	0	0	1	0	0
2	0	96	3	0	0	0
3	1	0	89	0	0	9
4	0	0	0	100	0	0
5	0	0	0	0	100	0
6	0	0	1	0	0	98

10.3% ERROR

CLASS	1	2	3	4	5	6
1	82	1	0	15	0	0
2	4	84	1	3	6	0
3	3	0	84	9	1	1
4	9	0	3	85	0	1
5	0	0	0	0	100	0
6	4	1	0	0	0	93

SIMPLE DATA SET
TEST CASE - 1

COMPLEX DATA SET
TEST CASE - 2

G9500

Figure 7. Confusion Matrices for Six Signal Classes.

CLASSIFIER	UNCONNECTED BPN 20 NODES	CONNECTED BPN 20 NODES	UNCONNECTED BPN 30 NODES	UNCONNECTED BPN 40 NODES	ML
ERRORS	15.4%	14.3%	15.3%	14.9%	16.5%

G9502

Figure 8. Classifier Performance with Eight Signal Classes.

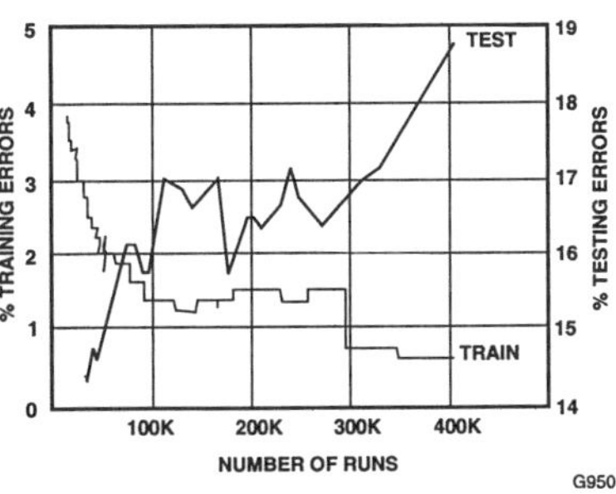

Figure 9. Results of Extended Training.

nodes was trained and tested with eight signal classes. As shown in figure 9, the training errors dropped from 4.0 to 0.6 percent while the testing errors increased from 14.4 to 18.8 percent.

5. Conclusions

By taking advantage of research in signal understanding and capabilities developed to generate realistic signal data, the signal classifying performance of neural networks was evaluated. Without optimization, the BPN performed comparably to the ML classifier, both of which performed considerably better than the CPN or MD classifiers. For complex signal environments, the BPN classifier could be overtrained on a fixed data set resulting in a degeneration of performance on a fixed test data set.

References

1. F. Jondral, "Automatic Classification of High Frequency Signals," *Signal Processing Journal*, **vol. 9**, 1985, p. 177.

2. J. Aisbett, "Automatic Modulation Recognition Using Time Domain Parameters," *Signal Processing Journal,* **vol. 13**, 1987, p. 323.

CHAPTER 22

A KNOWLEDGE BASED ENVIRONMENT FOR INTEGRATED CIRCUIT TESTING

Apostolos Dollas Grant L. Castrodale*

Digital Systems Laboratory,
Dept. of Electrical Engineering, Duke University,
Durham, NC 27706, U.S.A.

Abstract

The testing of very large scale integrated circuits (VLSI) has been a difficult and cumbersome task. The reasons are the physical separation of the testing equipment from the design environment, and the intrinsic difficulty of making a physical piece of equipment operate within a computer aided design (CAD) environment. By using knowledge base technology, a system which makes the physical testing equipment appear as virtual testing equipment to the CAD environment was developed. The new system includes an integrated circuit device description language, a test vector language, a tester description language, and a knowledge based system to facilitate full integration of the testing equipment with the VLSI design environment. As a consequence, the simulations performed during the design of an integrated circuit can be applied as test vectors against the actual device. The user does not need to be concerned with vector conversions or the operational details of the target test equipment. Except for the most rudimentary tasks of powering the tester up, connecting the device under test to the tester, and providing power to it, all other testing related tasks are done by the new knowledge based system from within the computer aided VLSI design environment. The system has been in operation since 1988 and demonstrates how artificial intelligence can be applied as a tool to address previously unsolved problems.

1 Introduction

The testing of very large-scale integrated circuits (VLSI) is a major aspect of the design cycle. Recent progress in the area includes many software tools which lead to testable VLSI designs. Typical examples are the Test Engineers' Assistant,[1] and the Automatic Test Pattern Generation tool.[2] Additional techniques such as built-in self-test[3] aim at field testing of designs without the need of a tester. Virtually all designs to date, however, are exercised externally with some tester in order to verify correct operation.

*Now with IBM Corporation, Charlotte, NC.

Despite this major progress in making VLSI circuits testable and generating test patterns automatically, there has been little progress in integrating the actual process of testing with the computer-aided design (CAD) environment. The reason is that the design environment is generally virtual, since most VLSI design tools run transparently and with identical results on a variety of hosts, whereas the physical testing environment is dependent on the capabilities of the testing equipment as well as the software which is used.

A new environment was developed at Duke University to integrate the design and test of integrated circuits. This environment employs knowledge base technology[4] to achieve its operational requirements. Knowledge base technology has been employed in a large range of applications[5] including some aspects of VLSI design.[6] Existing publications, theses, reports, and manuals provide both documentation and descriptions of various aspects of the environment. In particular, existing publications include a system-level operational description,[7] how integrated circuit testing is done in the new environment,[8] the user interface which links the testing environment with the computer aided design (CAD) environment,[9,10] a technical description of the system,[11] and experiences from its use.[12] The purpose of this book chapter is to demonstrate how knowledge base methodology was used to achieve the desired goals, to describe the technical issues of implementing the knowledge based system, and to show how the artificial intelligence components of the system are completely transparent to the user, yet they provide essential functions in the operation of the environment. Some material from the above references has been included in this chapter to make it self contained. We have avoided duplication of material unless there was a need to present some topics in more detail than has been published before, or to make this chapter more complete.

1.1 Motivation

Traditional "stuck-at" faults are typically detected using static tests which apply vectors using the scan path[13] of the circuit under test. The use of functional simulation data for testing purposes[14] has become a popular testing methodology for two reasons: the circuit output is known from the simulations and the test generation time is reduced since the vectors are already available. Functional simulation based tests provide the additional advantage of detecting dynamic or timing related faults.

Once the chip is fabricated, a typical testing cycle commences. First the tester must be programmed to supply the same voltage levels and timing parameters that were used during the simulations. Next the vectors, as determined by the simulations, are converted to an appropriate format for the testing equipment. This may involve netlist translation (e.g. with AUNT[15]), manual editing, and data transfer between a variety of machines. Ultimately the test data is loaded in the tester and the chip is tested. This step is most often followed by an inverse procedure of data transfer, translation and comparison to simulation outputs for the determination of correct chip operation.

Clearly, it is desirable for the testing equipment to be a part of the CAD environment for VLSI design, and furthermore, for the physical testing of chips to be done in a way transparent of the characteristics of the specific equipment. This necessitates the existence of a test vector format which is tester-independent, the capability for automatic translation to this format from a variety of simulators, and the capability to exercise a variety of testers from a unified design and test environment.

1.2 Previous Work

Previous work by Middleton,[16] Teisher,[17] and Boggs[18] has lead in the above described direction, but with very limited scope. Tester-independent vectors in a uniform system have been proposed by Falkenstrom and others.[19] Intent capture concepts[20] address the conflicts that arise when simulation waveforms are modified to meet tester requirements. Havlicsek[21] has proposed the use of knowledge-based systems for testing purposes, but mainly in the derivation of the test patterns, as opposed to the transparent use of various testers. Existing systems lack either flexibility or environment integration. Various environments have been developed to integrate a specific set of simulators to specific test equipment. The interactive use of arbitrary simulators and testers, and their transparent use in a single, open environment has not been addressed until now.

1.3 Aspects of Logical and Physical Testing

The expression "logical testing" is used throughout this chapter interchangeably with "simulation" in order to highlight the qualitative affinity of simulation and testing, despite the difference in the environments in which they are typically performed.

Simulations can be performed at the behavioral level, functional level, switch-level, and circuit level.[22] Many simulation packages allow mixed-mode simulation, e.g. the simulation of certain portions of a circuit at the switch-level, with other portions simulated at the functional or behavioral level.

One convenience of the logical testing of circuits is that nodes can be labeled and exercised with test vectors without the need of any physical connections or maps. Therefore, a desired bitstream can be applied directly to a circuit node (either a pad or an internal node) by simply naming the node and specifying the bitstream. In contrast, physical testing necessitates the specification of the tester input and output channels which correspond to the probed parts of the circuit. This map is one of the differences between logical and physical testing.

Different testers have significantly different capabilities. For example, a typical configuration of a Hewlett-Packard 8180A data generator with a Hewlett-Packard 8182A data analyzer provides 16-32 channels of stimulus with 16 channels of acquisition, a maximum frequency of 50MHz, and a depth of 1K vectors for generation and storage. A typical Tektronix DAS 9200 data acquisition system has some 32 channels of stimulus and 60 channels of data collection, with various frequency vs. channel configurations, and 32K depth of vector and response storage. The Mega-One tester has 160 pins (and can be expanded up to 256 pins) configurable as inputs or outputs operating at 40MHz and a 1M word deep storage for vectors. It is clear that the task of driving each of the above testers *transparently* from a common interface is not trivial. Many more testers, including industrial models, may have over 1000 channels at frequencies in excess of 80MHz.

Another difference between logical and physical testing is in the process itself. In physical testing the device under test (DUT) has to be placed on a board which is mounted on the tester. The board itself needs to be prepared in order to connect the circuit I/O pins to the tester channels. The circuit must be powered-up and, in the case of testing multiple chips, dismounted so that others can be tested. Simulation, on the other hand, requires only that the CAD packages run on the same environment; simulation of various circuits necessitates that the appropriate circuit netlists and vector files are used with the simulation package of choice. Generally no physical preparation is necessary. It is possible, however, that in an environment where the tools change daily, the obsolescence of some tools may require some format translation in order to use their replacements. The proposed EDIF[23] standard may provide a common language and format for CAD tool transparent circuit descriptions. Other differences exist also, but the ones mentioned in this section are most important in the development of a common simulation and testing environment.

1.4 Scope of Work and Chapter Overview

This book chapter describes an integrated environment for the simulation and testing of VLSI circuits that was developed at Duke University. The environment consists of a knowledge based common tester interface and a tester-specific module for each of the supported testers. The knowledge based common tester interface was developed with extensive use of compiler technology[24] and includes a device specification file parser, a vector file parser, a tester specification file parser, a pin map parser, device-to-tester functionality checking routines, and a vector translator. The device specification files are written in a subset of the Omnitest device description language[25] and the vector files are written in the Omnitest vector language. The Omnitest language was developed at MCNC. The tester description language, representation of knowledge, all of the parsers, data structures, and software were developed at Duke University. The grammar rules portion of the Omnitest device specification parser complies with the MCNC developed language but a new parser was developed. Finally, a user interface which integrates the simulation and testing software and all the other VLSI design tools into a common environment was implemented.

The design and test of VLSI circuits is inherently a complex task, requiring the proper use of large numbers of CAD tools, and many steps. Some of the steps are the layout of the integrated circuit, the simulation of its operation from a netlist extracted from the layout, various connectivity checks to ensure that the final design is the same as the simulated one, and finally the testing of the fabricated chip to verify its operation against the original specifications. The newly developed environment is by no means a simple computer program. It is therefore possible to question whether such a complex system was worth developing. In fact, it was. The process of testing VLSI circuits took days or weeks, and can now be done in a matter of hours. The evaluation of actual device response and its comparison to the simulated data had to be done either by hand or by looking at computer files, whereas now is done automatically. The most significant effect of the system was a change in attitude of the designers, who can now test their fabricated chips more thoroughly in less time, and as a result they run more proper and comprehensive tests.

Section 2 presents an overview of the simulation and testing environment and its user interface. Section 3 motivates the use of knowledge base technology for the system and describes the implementation tradeoffs for the system. Section 4 describes how the system appears to its user and its programmer. Section 5 presents the implementation of the environment and its major components, the knowledge based common tester interface, and the tester-specific module. Section 6 provides an example session of simulation and testing of an actual device using the integrated environment. The chapter is concluded with a summary, acknowledgements, and references. In a work of this nature, citations to manuals and technical references are included by necessity. The technical references can be obtained from the originating departments and organizations. Other references have been included (e.g. those for Lex and Yacc) for proper citation of the source of these tools, but any UNIX™ manual has sufficient information on their use. Should any reader have difficulty in finding some of the cited references, the primary author may be contacted for help.

2 The Integrated Simulation and Testing Environment

The design and test environment addresses the needs of the community of the Microelectronics Center of North Carolina. In this community, which includes several universities (Duke, UNC-Chapel Hill, UNC-Charlotte, NC State, NC A&T) and the Research Triangle Institute, VLSI designers often work on the community-wide set of computers and testers. As a result, chip designs are developed on university as well as MCNC computers. The wide availability of simulation tools, such as the CAzM circuit simulator,[26] the HILO digital circuit simulator,[27] and various switch-level simulators, has made the logical testing on different computers trivial. Physical testing on the other hand is non-trivial. The MegaOne tester, located at MCNC, has been used for high-performance and high-pinout devices, whereas various lower performance testers are located at the participating institutions and RTI. The main goal of the integrated simulation and testing environment is to allow for the transparent use of all of these resources.

2.1 System Requirements

In addition to integrating the simulation and testing tools, the system satisfies the following requirements:

- The system makes physical testing as easy as the simulation of the circuit.
- It allows for the use of various testers without user expertise in any specific one.
- It is interactive so that the tester is configured, the vectors applied, and results displayed in real-time under control of the user.
- Finally, the system is modular in its addition of simulation tools and test equipment.

2.2 Testing System Overview

Throughout the chapter, the term "user" is defined to be the person performing the simulations and physical testing, and "test programmer" to be the person responsible for integrating new test equipment into the system. The test programmer has to be familiar with the detailed operation of the tester hardware and software and the user does not. The system block diagram is shown in Figure 1. In addition to the three simulators shown at the top of Figure 1, a variety of other CAD tools are used in VLSI design, such as the Magic layout editor, the Espresso logic minimization package, the VPNR placement and routing tool, and more. The UNIX operating system has been assumed as a common platform, since all of the existing tools run under UNIX. Even though UNIX itself could provide the user interface, it was decided that the large number and the interdependency of the different tools warranted the development of a unified environment to run them. This is the Duke Applications Environment (DAE),[10] which is a menu-driven shell management program. The same user interface is used to run the testing environment, thus making VLSI design and test accessible from the same computational platform for the users. The integrated testing system is comprised of two components: the common tester interface and the tester specific modules. The common tester interface receives chip specifications, tester descriptions, tester address to DUT pin translations, and simulation vectors and creates tester programming data and test vectors which are used by the tester-specific modules to drive the testers. Outputs from each of the simulators are converted into an intermediate vector format either directly or through a simple filter program. The MCNC-developed Omnitest vector language[25] is used for that purpose.

Driving the testers *directly from the user workstations* has several requirements: the physical proximity of the user to the tester in order to load the DUT board to

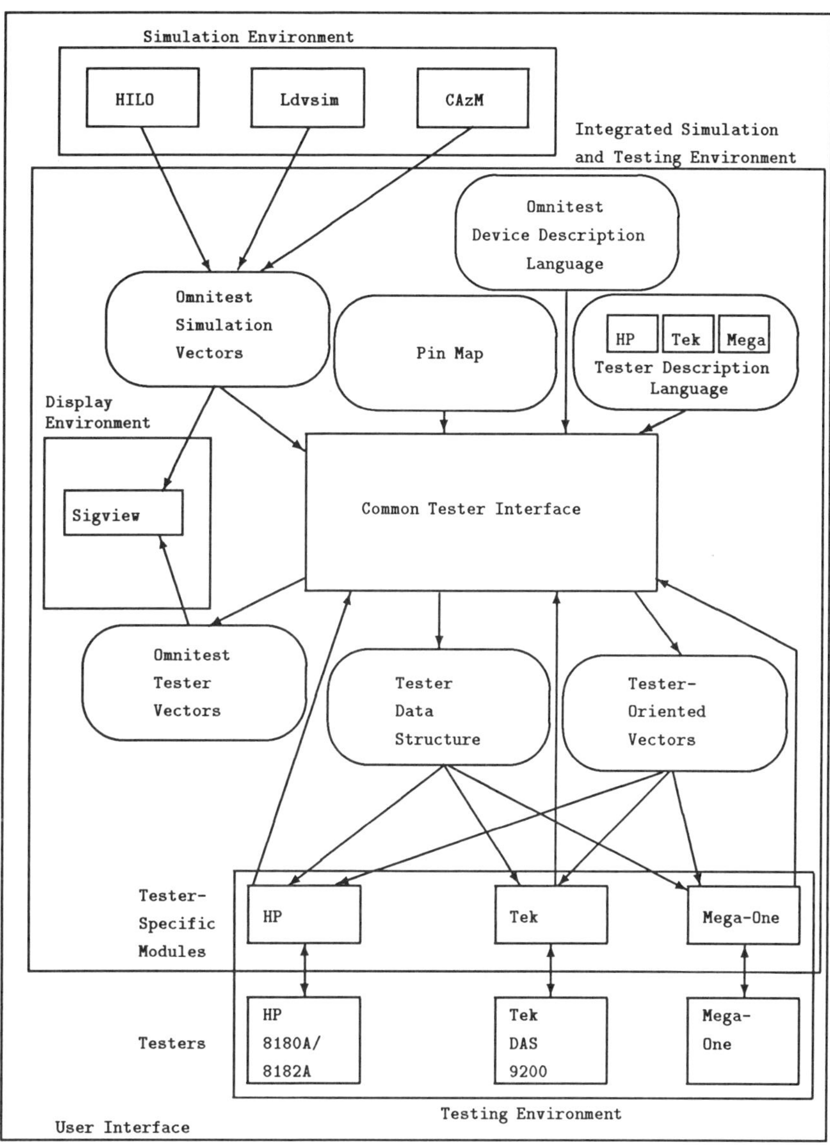

Figure 1: The integrated simulation and testing environment

the tester, and tester choice specification by the user together with signal-to-channel map and device parameters. The tester channel to circuit pin map is written in a tester-independent format and the device specifications are written in a subset of the Omnitest device description language. The language is used to describe the timings, voltages, and waveforms of the DUT. The modularity of the system is addressed by the tester description language. The language was developed to specify the characteristics of any arbitrary tester. The test programmer derives a tester specification file directly from the tester manuals. The file describes the vector depth, frequency, and capabilities of the individual channels. A file exists for each one of the testers in the system and is completely transparent to the user. In order to add new test equipment the test programmer creates a new tester specification file and tester-specific module.

The simulation vectors, pin map, device specification file, and appropriate tester specification file are parsed by the common tester interface and the functions in the device specification are compared by the knowledge based system with the limitations of the target tester. Based on the type of problems encountered, warning or error messages are passed to the user. For example, if the user has specified some test sequence to run at a 10 MHz clock, the testing can proceed on either the HP or Tektronix test system. The same sequence at 60 MHz, however, would lead to an error indication if it were attempted on the HP tester because it is limited to 50 MHz. If an error occurs, the user is given an opportunity to update the device specification so that it specifies supported test features. If no errors are detected, the common tester interface produces tester programming data and a tester-specific vector file. The vector file contains vectors which have been rearranged so they may be directly applied to the target tester. Each one of the supported testers is driven by a tester-specific module. The module configures the tester according to the tester programming data and applies the translated simulation vectors to the DUT. The module also interacts with the user to prompt whether the tester is powered, whether the circuit is connected and so forth.

One of the primary advantages of the system is that the user does not have to be familiar with the details of the low-level tester operation. The user just simulates his or her chip and specifies its voltage and timing parameters. The knowledge based testing system configures the tester appropriately based on the tester specifications. The test programmer can utilize the sophisticated features of the test system by incorporating complexities into the tester module. The decoupling of the "desired set of tests" from an actual tester could have its drawbacks too: for a completely transparent run on all testers, the set of all commonly available features would have to be used. Thus, completely identical testing on all platforms with absolutely no user intervention would reduce the operation to the set of features which all testers support, and not take advantage of the more powerful models. This was not the purpose of the system. Rather, the migration of tests from one tester to another, with no vector editing from the user and with no extensive tester-specific descriptions, was the goal. For example, a user could perform a variety of tests on an HP tester at

10MHz, and then continue on the Mega-One at higher frequencies, having to change only the desired test frequency specification and the pin map.

The final aspect of system operation is the need to post-process data from physical testing runs and from simulations, determine correct or incorrect operation, and prompt the user with varying levels of diagnostic messages, such as graphical presentations of simulated vs. physical data for some signal. In Figure 1, the arrows from the tester-specific modules toward the common tester interface indicate translations of the tester-oriented responses back into the Omnitest vector format. These translations are reverse in order and function from the previous conversions from Omnitest vectors to tester-specific vectors. The unified format allows for the comparison not only of simulated to actual data, but also of data between different types of simulators and testers. The present version of the system does not translate the physical testing results back into the Omnitest format but performs the comparisons directly between the actual responses and the tester-oriented vectors. The comparisons are performed by a small C program similar to the UNIX diff utility. The program has additional features such as the ability to ignore masked outputs.

2.3 User Interface

The user interface to the VLSI design and test software is provided by the Duke Applications Environment (DAE) which was developed as part of the same project. DAE is a user-definable, menu-driven package that runs under the X Window System™.

The VLSI design and test environment consists of a number of tools which were not specifically designed to interface to one another. For example, a designer may want to perform simulations on circuits designed with tools that have different netlist descriptions. A separate set of translations is necessary to convert each design tool's netlist into each simulator's expected input format. The designer should not have to be concerned with the specific file transformations. The tools should be integrated into a common environment that contains the steps that are necessary and automatically performs them. Several existing environments integrate VLSI tools but support only tools which conform to the their specification. For example, the SDA SKILL environment language[28,29] and the Berkeley VEM environment approach with the OCT database[30] both necessitate the porting of the tools to the environment database before they can be used. Since no environment could integrate arbitrary VLSI design and test tools *without modifications*, the Duke Applications Environment was developed. DAE conforms to the tools rather than forcing the tools to conform to the environment. Any tools that run under UNIX and X can be integrated within DAE.

2.3.1 User Interface Requirements

In addition to integrating tools without requiring modifications, DAE was designed to have the following properties:

Easy to use. Typically, the translation of one tool's output netlist to another tool's expected input netlist consists of invoking a number of preprocessors. The environment should enable the user to bind these translation steps to a single event so the tools appear to run seamlessly. Furthermore, the user should not have to suspend the operation of one tool in order to perform the translations to another.

Portable. The environment should be portable across all workstations in the VLSI design and test environment.

Versatile. The addition and deletion of tools should be easy and advanced users should be able to customize the environment to their needs.

Benign. The environment should run concurrently with window managers and the graphical interfaces of the integrated tools.

Small. The environment should be small in executable code size and CPU requirements.

Fast. The speed of the integrated tools should not be affected by the environment.

2.3.2 Operation and Customization of DAE

DAE is an environment that interactively manages VLSI design and test tools through its own menu system. The menus are cascadable to an arbitrary level so the tools may be organized in a hierarchical fashion. The operation of the menu system is controlled by a configuration file which is parsed as the environment starts up.

While the environment is running, a button labeled *DAE* appears on the user's workstation display along with the X terminal window that invoked DAE (the term button refers to a small window that appears on the workstation screen that simulates the behavior of an ordinary push button). A prompt appears in the window to indicate that DAE is in its main processing loop. Like other applications windows, the DAE button may be moved around on the screen using the window manager. When the left mouse button is pressed while the pointer is in the DAE window, the primary DAE menu pane pops up and none of the other applications are affected (a menu pane is a window that contains a title and a list of options that the user may select from). A user may execute a function by pressing the right mouse button over the desired item or may pop up a sub-menu pane by moving the pointer over the entries which indicate with arrows that they have sub-menus. The functions may include executing UNIX shell commands, opening DAE text windows or changing the working directory of the environment. During the execution of the shell commands, all prompting of the user occurs in the associated X terminal emulator window.

The environment is customized by writing UNIX shell scripts to perform the format translations that are necessary to integrate the tools. The shell scripts also obtain input from the user and invoke the tools with the appropriate options. The text windows may be included to display information about the translations and options. The configuration file maps the shell scripts and text windows to menu selections which may occur at any level of hierarchy. As a result, complex sequences of commands and sets of options may be constructed and customized as desired. In a typical setup, an expert user could configure a default environment to integrate a certain set of tools. Since the configuration file is parsed every time DAE is invoked, tools may easily be added or removed without re-compiling the environment. Each user could choose to run the default environment or customize it to his or her preference by editing the configuration file.

2.3.3 Use and Implementation of DAE

A typical VLSI environment consists of a set of design tools and simulation tools which have different circuit description languages. For example, at Duke University, the netlist of the Magic VLSI layout editor has a different format than that of Lnetlist network description program. Duke simulation tools consist of CAzM, HILO, and Ldvsim. During the course of a design, a user may want to run different simulators on the same circuit. For instance, he or she may run Ldvsim to verify the logical operation of a circuit, then run CAzM to check timings and power dissipation. The environment can be customized so that all possible paths from design to simulation and subsequently test are included. By binding shell scripts to mouse buttons and providing hierarchical nesting of mouse controlled menus, DAE makes CAD tool operation appear seamless to the user, without the need to modify the tools themselves. The interoperability is achieved with the use of filters and conversions which are hidden from the user through shell scripts. For more information on the use of DAE see reference,[9] or the manual of the tool.[10]

For reasons of portability, DAE was developed using the C language, with extensive use of Lex[31] and Yacc.[32] Detailed information on the implementation of the environment can be found in reference.[11] The source code consists of about 100 lines of Lex, 100 lines of Yacc, and 1200 lines of C. The DAE environment was written originally for X Window System Version 10, and rewritten in its entirety for X Version 11, Release 3. The latter version of the tool can also be compiled with no modifications under X Version 11, Release 4. The environment runs on a variety of computers, including Digital Equipment Corporation VAXstations and DECstations, Hewlett Packard HP 9000, and Sun SPARCstation computers.

3 Development of the Knowledge Based System

The integrated simulation and testing environment has led to easier VLSI testing but its implementation created a host of problems. In this section some of the issues involved in the system design will be presented. The use of knowledge base technology to address these issues will be motivated and the use of techniques common to compiler design to build the system will be described.

3.1 Motivation for Use of Knowledge Base Technology

The main problem in solving the general case of the transition from simulation to testing is the existence of a large number of simulators and testers, each with its own data representation, capabilities, and peculiarities. If there was a single simulator and a single tester the problem would be relatively simple. A translator could be made for vector format conversion, and the capabilities of the tester could be rigidly coded in a specifically designed driver program. Existing commercial applications are in fact collections of translation programs. This approach was undesirable for the new system as expansion would necessitate re-development of code. The use of knowledge based methodology was a natural solution to the problem. Specifically, by developing a tester independent tester description language, the specifications and capabilities of any tester in the market could be described. The development of such a language was not trivial because characteristics and limitations of testers vary widely. Shared resource testers[33] are based on a central resource (or set of resources) that is shared among the channels. An example of a shared resource is a timing generator. If two channels share a timing generator, even though each channel may strobe data at any time during a tester cycle, if a certain device has pins connected to both channels, the data must be strobed at the same time on both pins. As a further complication, the range and placement of waveform edges is typically a function of the tester cycle period. The language is powerful enough to describe these dependencies.

The knowledge based system reads the descriptions of various testers and builds a knowledge base regarding capabilities, limitations, and formats of each tester class. This type of knowledge is developed once for each tester type. When a user wants to perform some tests, a list of desired tests is made and a target tester is chosen. The knowledge on tester capabilities can be used to either execute the tests or flag errors to the user. An integral component of the process is the internal knowledge of input data formats for simulation vectors and tester formats. By incorporating knowledge in the system both error checking and the vector translation process can be handled easily. For example, a signal is referenced in a simulation by a node name. The same signal ultimately may appear in a physical channel pin of a tester, determined by a bit position of the vector word. The user provides a map that specifies what logical signal name is mapped to what tester channel *name* (rather than tester channel pin). The knowledge based system has the map of tester channel name to bit position in the tester memory word from the tester description file. Thus there is enough information to track and convert the signal throughout the testing process, from the user supplied simulation data down to the derivation of the bit pattern for any target tester. Unlike previous approaches, no filters or translators need to be supplied externally, even though multiple translation processes need to take place (i.e. mapping of logical signal names to the appropriate data in the simulation file, mapping of simulation data to tester channel names, mapping of data corresponding to tester channel names to data for the tester). The inverse path needs to be accounted also, so that tester responses can be interpreted according to functional requirements.

An even more complex task, unsuitable for direct coding but suitable for a knowledge based system is that of error checking. By building a knowledge representation of the tester capabilities as described above, error checking including subtle features or limitations of the tester can be accomplished. The main idea is that the user can specify what he or she wants to do, and the knowledge based system can check the desired tests against the tester capabilities. If the desired tests are valid they are performed and if they are not, appropriate errors are flagged. The error discovery mechanism of the system is described in Section 5.

3.2 Implementation Technology

The incorporation of knowledge in the system, the derivation of errors and the modular system upgrade was a major issue. The language of choice for the knowledge-based system was PROLOG.[34] The intrinsic capabilities of PROLOG for tree searching, pattern matching and backtracking could be used to match the desired set of tests to the PROLOG described capabilities of a testing system, and thus PROLOG itself could have been used for tester description. This approach, however, would have lead to major problems of portability and limit the usefulness of the system. Only a few interpreters and one compiler for PROLOG were available at that time in the local community. A necessary compromise was the use of the C language for the implementation. As a result, the description language and the system itself were implemented with procedural methods. Therefore, knowledge was represented with conventional data structures, and the knowledge based system was built with procedural methods. A combination of knowledge representation data structures including linked lists and hashing tables, and, the use of the recursive descent methodologies common in compiler design to do the equivalent of tree search were employed in the implementation of the system to offer the same capabilities as a PROLOG based implementation. A new language was developed to describe the capabilities of each tester to be supported under the new system.

Because of the language restrictions discussed above, two powerful methodologies were combined to build the system: formal languages, and compiler technology. Specifically, by developing a formal language for each aspect of the system, both error checking and system actions are performed using parsing. For example, the building of the knowledge base for the tester capabilities is accomplished by parsing the tester description which is expressed in the tester description language. If there are any representation errors (e.g. improper keywords) appropriate errors are flagged. The knowledge base itself, once developed, is parsed whenever tests are requested by the user. If the tests are valid, the terminal reached in the knowledge base indicates that the option is valid, whereas if no terminal exists an error is flagged.

In building the system, Lex and Yacc were used extensively, mostly due to their widespread use which makes software support easier. Changes might be needed only if the tester description language itself needs to be modified. The incorporation of testers, on the other hand, does *not* require recompilation of the tester description language. This task is accomplished by a header file which the environment reads, which in turn has a pointer to the appropriate tester specification file and tester specific module. As a result the expandability of the system comes in the least tedious way.

One of the primary advantages of the system is that the user does not have to be aware of low level tester operation details. The user just needs to simulate his or her chip and specify its voltage and timing parameters. The integrated testing system configures the tester appropriately, based on the specifications. The test programmer can support the sophisticated features as needed. Subsequent sections describe the implementation of the system in sufficient detail to give the reader an indication of the power of the system as well as how it was developed. This way similar methodology will be accessible for other fields of applications too.

4 The Common Tester Interface

The knowledge-based common tester interface coordinates the process of parsing the device-oriented input, cross-checking for unsupported features on the desired tester, and invoking the appropriate tester module. The inputs to the common tester interface are the user-generated device specification and pin map, the vector file from the simulation data, and the tester specification file provided by the test programmer. The interface parses the inputs, generates a tester data structure and a set of tester-oriented vectors, and calls the tester-specific module. This section describes the appearance of the interface to the user and test programmer, and the implementation of the interface.

4.1 Appearance to the User

The user is responsible for supplying a vector file in the Omnitest vector language, a device specification file written in a subset of the Omnitest device description language, and a pin map. The formal syntax of each of the languages and the format of the pin map are given in reference.[11]

4.1.1 Device Specification

The device specification file is created by the user and requires no knowledge of the detailed operation of the target tester. The format of the file is such, that it can be derived directly from the chip specification. A sample device specification file is given in Figure 2. The file consists of a `device` statement, a `definitions` section, and an `assignments` section. The `device` statement enables the user to declare a name for the DUT.

The `definitions` section sets the default technology, and defines voltages, stimulus and strobe timings, and waveforms based on the timings. Keywords begin every statement and user-defined names appear on the left of the equal sign. The `tech` keyword causes default values to be used for unspecified voltage definitions. Power and signal voltages are defined. Signals may be inputs, outputs, or bidirectional (`in_out` keyword). The `wavefm` statement defines waveforms based on the timings from the `timing` statement. The user specifies the format of the waveform and the timings for all edges. The `vector` statement designates the name of the Omnitest vector file.

The `assignments` section associates DUT pins to the values specified in the definitions section. Each DUT pin is assigned a name, a number, and a voltage. In addition, signal pins are assigned waveforms. An input requires one waveform for driving and an output requires one waveform for strobing and an optional waveform for high impedance strobing. The high impedance waveform is applied when there is a `Z` in the vectors for a certain cycle. Bidirectional pins are handled differently. A control signal must be included in the `assignments` section and vector file to control whether the pin is an input or an output at a certain tester cycle. The waveforms portion of the bidirectional pin assignment must have four fields: the control signal name, the drive waveform, the strobe waveform, and the high impedance waveform. Sets of pins are grouped together by their representation (either decimal, binary, octal, or hexadecimal). The ordering of the signals and their representation are reflected in the Omnitest vector file.

4.1.2 Pin Map

The pin map is written by the user in a tester-independent format. It specifies the connections of DUT pins to tester channels. An example is provided in Figure 3.

4.1.3 Vectors

The vector file contains vectors from the DUT simulation which are translated into the Omnitest vector language. Outputs from a variety of simulators can be converted directly into Omnitest vectors. A sample vector file is given in Figure 4. The sample is just for illustration purposes; actual vector files from simulations are much larger. The ordering of signals and their representation is provided in the `assignments` section of the device specification file discussed earlier. For example, the `F` in the first vector field refers to the hexadecimal group of pins `in3` through `in0` since they are listed first in the device specification file in Figure 2. The second field (`00`) corresponds to the binary group of pins `Out1` and `Out0` and the last field (`5`) corresponds to the octal group of pins `in6`, `in5`, `in4`. The language includes provisions for repetition factors,

```
/* device specification file */

device sample;
definitions {
   tech                         CMOS;
   ground                       GND;
   power                        Vdd = {vnom=5.0v};
   input                        DIn = {vil=600mv, vih=2.4v};
   output                       DOut = {vol=0.8v, voh=2.0v};
   period                       P1 = {pnom=500ns};
   timing                       T0 = 0ns,
                                T100 = 100ns,
                                T300 = 300ns;
   wavefm                       WF1 = NR(T0),
                                WF2 = ES(T300),
                                WF3 = RTZ(T0, T100);
   vector                       sample.omni;
}
assignments {
hex;
   in3 = {1, DIn, WF1};
   in2 = {2, DIn, WF1};
   in1 = {3, DIn, WF1};
   in0 = {4, DIn, WF1};
   gnd = {14, GND};
bin;
   out1 = {18, DOut, WF2};
   out0 = {19, DOut, WF2};
oct;
   in6 = {21, DIn, WF3};
   in5 = {22, DIn, WF3};
   in4 = {23, DIn, WF3};
   vdd = {28, Vdd};
}
end
```

Figure 2: A sample device specification file

```
/* HP pin map
 *
 *    device pin        tester channel
 *    ----------        --------------
 */
           1                 g02
           2                 gc1
           3                 g00
           4                 gc2
           18                a03
           19                a01
           21                g01
           22                g10
           23                g03
```

Figure 3: A sample pin map for the HP test system

```
/* Omnitest vector file */

      F, 00, 5;
20 {  A, 01, 7;
      6, 10, 2; }
      C, 01, 3;
      4, XX, 0;
      8, 00, 4;
end
```

Figure 4: A sample Omnitest vector file

output masking (X), and high impedance (Z). Note that the vectors include inputs intermixed with outputs. Only inputs (and bidirectional pins used as inputs) are used to drive the tester. The outputs are stored for later comparison with physical testing results.

4.2 Appearance to the Test Programmer

The test programmer creates the tester specification file. The common tester interface checks for functions required by the device that the target tester cannot provide and, if no errors are found, generates a tester knowledge data structure and tester-oriented vectors. The user does not have to be aware of the details on the tester specific data and vectors; these are read by the tester-specific module developed by the test programmer.

4.2.1 Tester Specification

The tester specification file is created by the test programmer and never directly accessed by the user. The file is written in the tester description language. The language was developed to describe the characteristics and limitations of any tester that can be integrated into the system. The formal syntax of the language is provided in reference.[11] A portion of the specification file for the HP tester is given in Figure 5. The file consists of a `declarations` section, a `channels` section, and a `conditions` section.

The `declarations` section specifies the vector depth of the tester and declares the period, timings, and voltages used in the other sections. The `channels` section describes the functionality of each tester channel. Each channel is assigned a name, a signal type, a voltage range, and a list of waveforms it supports. The type of channel may be either `input`, `output`, or `in_out` for bidirectional. The voltage range is declared in the `declarations` section and bounded in the `conditions` section. The ordering of channels is significant. The tester-oriented vectors and the channel linked list portion of the tester data structure are arranged in the same order to ease development of the tester-specific modules.

The `conditions` section describes timing and voltage ranges and dependencies between channels that arise with shared resource testers. The `timeRange` and `voltRange` keywords specify the lower and upper bounds for timings and voltages respectively. The timing ranges may be functions of the period. The `timeDiff` keyword is used to define the minimum and maximum pulse width between edges of a waveform. The `maxTimeSet` and `maxVoltSet` statements are used to limit the number of values a certain set may contain. For example, on the HP test system, a voltage level can be assigned to any generator pin (pins having names that begin with the letter `g`) *but* only a total of four different levels can be set up. This restriction is specified using `maxVoltSet (V2, 4)`.

```
/* HP tester specification file */

declarations {
    vectDepth               1024;
    period                  P;
    timings                 T1, T2, T3, T4, T5;
    powerSupplies           PSV1;
    voltages                V1, V2;
}
channels {
    gc1 = [input, V2, RTZ(T3, T4)];
    gc2 = [input, V2, RTZ(T3, T4)];
    g33 = [input, V2, NR(T2)];
    g32 = [input, V2, NR(T2)];
       "                 "
       "                 "
    a03 = [output, V1, ES(T5)];
    a02 = [output, V1, ES(T5)];
    a01 = [output, V1, ES(T5)];
    a00 = [output, V1, ES(T5)];
}
conditions {
    timeRange               [P] = (20ns, 950ms),
                            [T1] = (0ns, 0.9*P - 18ns),
                            [T2] = (0ns, 0ns),
                            [T3] = (0ns, 0.9*P - 18ns),
                            [T4] = (0ns, P),
                            [T5] = (0ns, 0.95*P - 1ns);
    timeDiff                [T3, T4] = (0ns, 0.9*P - 8ns);
    maxTimeSet              (T5, 1);
    voltRange               [PSV1] = (5.0v, 5.0v),
                            [V1] = (-10v, 10v),
                            [V2] = (-1.5v, 10v);
    maxVoltSet              (V1, 6),
                            (V2, 4);
}
end
```

Figure 5: A portion of a tester specification file for the HP test system

4.2.2 Tester Knowledge Data Structure

The tester knowledge data structure completely defines the setup of the target tester. The structure contains the number of vectors for the device, the period of the test to be performed, a linked list of power supply structures, and a linked list of channel structures. The power supply linked list has an entry for all of the target tester's supplies. The entry contains the voltage required of a particular supply by the DUT. The channel structures are arranged in the same order as the tester specification file. Each structure includes the name, signal type, voltage and timing definitions, and waveforms of a particular channel of the target tester.

4.2.3 Tester-oriented Vectors

The tester-oriented vectors are the rearranged simulation data. The file contains a column for each channel in the same order as the tester specification file. There is also a column for each bidirectional control signal. Each row in the vector file corresponds to a tester cycle.

5 System Implementation

The common tester interface is comprised of a main program, parsers for the device specification file, pin map, tester specification file, and vector file, and a vector translator routine. These collective parts comprise the knowledge based system and incorporate both the representation and the processing of knowledge information. As described in Section 3, parsers were used to do both the error checking and the derivation and use of knowledge in the system.

5.1 The Main Program

The purpose of the main program is to

- process command line arguments
- call the parsers
- call the vector translator
- invoke the tester-specific module

The command line arguments contain the pin map file name, device specification file name, and the name of the tester to be driven. The program calls the device specification parser, the pin map parser, the tester specification parser and the vector file parser. The name of the vector file is obtained from the device specification. After the parsing and error-checking is complete, the vector translator is called and the appropriate tester-specific module is determined and invoked. One of the goals of the design was to enable the addition of new testers without the need to add source code to the main program. The objective was accomplished using C's ability to handle *pointers to functions.* The test programmer who is incorporating a new tester just adds three lines to the header file to associate the new tester's name with the name of its specification file and a pointer to its module and re-compiles. The main program is comprised of about 600 lines of C code.

5.2 Device Knowledge Representation and Parser

The device specification file parser:

- checks for syntax errors in the input
- stores device specifications into the device knowledge data structure

The device specifications knowledge data structure contains the device name, technology type, period, name of the vector file, and a linked list of device pin structures. The device knowledge representation data structure is shown in Figure 6. The pin linked lists contain both signal and power pins (a signal pin is pictured). Before the parser begins, a hash table is initialized to store user-defined names and the associated values. The name is used as a key to generate a pointer into the hash table. The value stored in the table is a pointer to a structure which holds the device data. The data can be a power supply voltage, an input pin voltage, an output pin voltage, a bidirectional pin voltage, a timing, a driving waveform, or a strobing waveform.

As the `definitions` section is parsed, the knowledge is stored in the hash table. Voltage values are assigned defaults for unspecified levels based on the technology statement. Parsing errors correspond to improper descriptions. The appropriate error is flagged if the `definitions` section does not contain a `tech`, a `ground`, a `power`, a `period`, and a `vector` statement. The `wavefm` statement utilizes the hash table differently than the other definitions statements. A `wavefm` definition assigns a waveform to a user-defined name. The waveform consists of a format type and a set of names for timings. The names must have been defined using the `timing` keyword. The names serve as keys to search the hash table. The timing values are retrieved and placed in the waveform structure. A pointer to the structure is then stored in the hash table using the waveform name as a key. This way dynamic knowledge is built and maintained in the system.

When the `assignments` section is parsed, the linked list of device pins is created. The pins are grouped together by their representation. Every time a `dec`, `bin`, `oct`, or `hex` keyword is encountered, a new group is initiated. The linked list includes power and signal pins. When a voltage or waveform is referenced in a pin assignment, the hash table is searched and the values are extracted and placed in the device pin linked list. Error checking for signal mismatches and inappropriate waveform definitions is

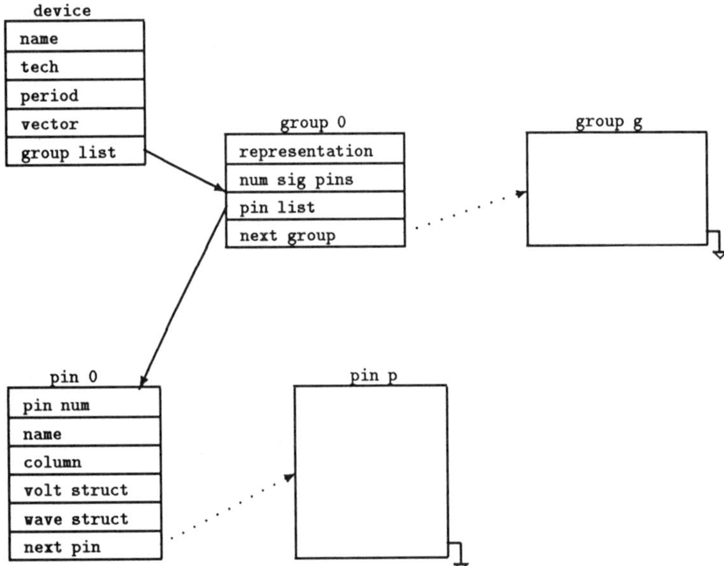

Figure 6: The device knowledge representation

performed. For example, an input pin must have only one waveform defined and it must be a driving waveform. Parsing continues until all device pins are assigned. The device specification lexical analyzer is generated from 200 lines of Lex and the parser from 1700 lines of Yacc. Most of the lexical analyzer and the grammar rules portion (about 400 lines of Yacc) of the parser was provided by Wayne Dettloff of MCNC.

5.3 Pin Map Parser

The pin map parser:

- checks for syntax errors in the input
- creates two hash tables

One hash table uses the device pin number as the key and holds the corresponding channel and the other uses the channel name as the key and stores the corresponding device pin. These hash tables are used by other routines to obtain a channel name from a pin number or a pin number from a channel name. The pin map parser is written directly in C so it is responsible for handling the low-level lexical analysis details. The parser ignores blanks, tabs, and comments as do the other parsers. When a device pin and tester channel pair is located, the data is stored in the pin-based hash table and the channel-based hash table. Duplicate channels or pins are flagged as errors. The parser consists of about 200 lines of C code.

5.4 Tester Knowledge Representation and Parser

The most important portion of the knowledge based system for the common tester interface is the tester specification parser. It responsible for:

- checking for syntax errors in the input
- determining whether functions desired in the device specification are supported on the target tester
- creating the tester knowledge data structure which is read by tester-specific modules

The data structure for tester knowledge representation is shown in Figure 7. As in the device specification file parser, a hash table is created to contain user-defined names and values. In the tester specification parser, the value stored in the table is just a pointer to the declaration type of the name. A name can be a period, a timing, a power supply voltage, or a signal voltage. Similarly to the constructs for device knowledge representation, this structure facilitates the addition of knowledge to the system. By supporting primitives like a period or a voltage and building the

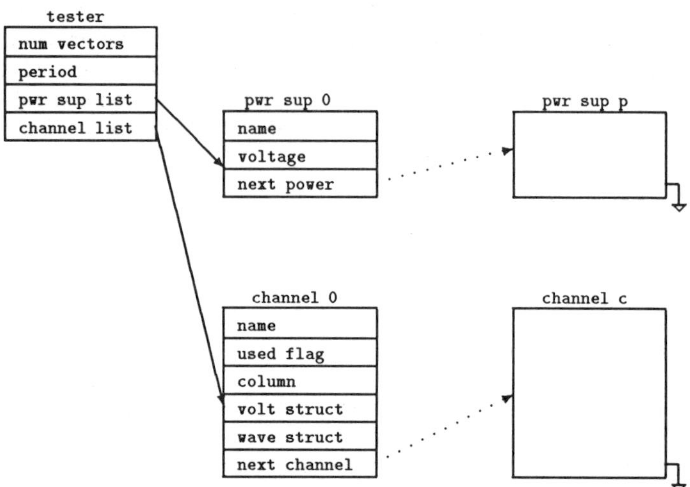

Figure 7: The tester knowledge representation

knowledge base, arbitrarily complex systems and interactions can be modeled through the nesting and linking of knowledge representation data structures.

As the `declarations` section is parsed, the vector depth of the tester is stored in the tester knowledge data structure and the user-defined names are entered into the hash table. The vector depth will later be checked against and replaced with the actual number of vectors. This approach allows for consistent knowledge in cases where the type of knowledge is known *a priori* but the actual value cannot be bound until the user request is processed, yet error checking of the user request is still maintained. The names of the power supplies are placed in the power supply linked list. While processing the `channels` section, the linked list of channel structures is created by retrieving values from the device specification knowledge data structure. The signal type, voltages and waveforms of each device pin are copied into the appropriate channel structure by referencing the channel-based hash table. Signal and waveform type checking is performed on channels which are connected to the device. For instance, a device input cannot be connected to a channel that can only receive data and an `RTZ` waveform cannot be defined on a channel that is capable of supplying only the `NR` format. As the channels are parsed, another knowledge data structure is generated to hold user-defined names instead of actual values. The structure is a linked list of channels which is used exclusively for error checking while parsing the `conditions` section. The channel name, voltage name, and a linked list of supported waveforms with timing names are stored for each channel. As an example, for channel gc1, the string V2 is stored as the voltage and the strings T3 and T4 are stored as edges of the RTZ waveform. The voltage and timing names must have entries of the correct type in the hash table.

Finally, the **conditions** section is parsed to check for the remaining tester limitations that interfere with device requirements. Every instance of the five possible different condition statements are evaluated and checked for compliance on all applicable channels. The ranges and differences may be arithmetic expressions. The expressions are evaluated and the conditions checked as the statements are parsed. For the **timeRange** keyword, the name for which the range is specified must be a period or timing. If the name is a period, the period stored in the device specification knowledge data structure is compared against the endpoints. If the name is a timing, the time corresponding to every waveform edge using the name is checked against the endpoints. As an example, consider the statement `timeRange [T3] = (0ns, 0.9*P - 18ns)`. First, the right endpoint is computed based on the period in the device structure. Next, the waveforms of every channel are searched for the name T3. This is accomplished by traversing the error-checking structure which was built while the **channels** section was parsed. From Figure 5, T3 is used as the first edge of the RTZ waveform for channel gc1. The channel-based hash table is consulted to obtain the device pin which is connected to gc1. If no pin is connected or if the RTZ format is not used by the device pin which is connected, the other waveform edges and the rest of the channels are processed. If the device pin connected to gc1 is using the RTZ format, however, the timing value of its first edge is compared against the left and right endpoints. If the value is out of range, an error message is printed and parsing is aborted. When the edges of all waveforms of every channel are checked, the next statement (or portion of statement) is parsed.

For the **voltRange** statement, the user-defined name must be a power supply voltage or a signal voltage. If it is a power supply voltage, the endpoint voltages are stored in a temporary structure which is used later when voltage pins are assigned to power supplies. If the name is a signal voltage, actual voltage values corresponding to every channel using the name are checked against the endpoints. For input pins, **vil** and **vih** are verified and for output pins, **vol** and **voh** are verified. All four possible levels are verified for bidirectional pins.

The **timeDiff** statement is handled similarly to **timeRange**. Only waveforms in the error-checking data structure which have multiple edges are considered. If both timing names match waveform edge names and a device pin is connected to the channel and the same waveform format is used by the device, the difference between the actual edge values are checked to be within range.

For the **maxTimeSet** and **maxVoltSet** keywords, the number of distinct time and voltage values are counted and compared against the maximum. For example, while processing `maxVoltSet (V2, 4)`, the voltage values of all channels with the name V2 defined are stored in a linked list. Duplicate voltages are ignored. When all channels are examined, the number of distinct voltages must be less than or equal to **4**. After all **conditions** statements have been parsed, all the power supply ranges are known. The linked list of pins in the device structure is searched for all power pins. Voltage requirements are checked against existing power supply ranges until all power pins have been matched with a power supply. The voltage values are placed with the corresponding power supply name in the linked list of supplies contained in the tester knowledge data structure. The lexical analyzer was generated from 100 lines of Lex and the parser from 2200 lines of Yacc.

5.5 Vector File Parser

The vector file parser:

- checks for syntax errors in the input
- reads Omnitest vectors and expands them to eliminate repetition factors
- converts vectors to binary and stores them in an array

When the vectors are expanded, the device specification knowledge data structure is consulted to find the representation of the various fields and the number of pins in each group. An improper number of vector fields in relation to the number of groups in the device specification knowledge data structure is flagged as an error. A column is output for every device pin. Parsing is complete when all Omnitest vectors have been converted to binary and placed in the device-oriented array. The lexical analyzer and parser are produced from 100 lines of Lex and 300 lines of Yacc respectively.

5.6 Vector Translator

The vector translator:

- converts vectors from device specification ordering to tester specification ordering

The vectors are read from the device-oriented array, translated, and output to a file. A bit is output in every cycle for each channel in the tester specification file. At the end of each column, extra entries are inserted for the values of the bidirectional control signals. The translator is composed of about 100 lines of C code.

5.7 The Tester-Specific Modules

The tester specific modules are not a part of the knowledge based system. Nonetheless, they are required in order to drive the testing equipment and will be described briefly so that the entire system description will be complete. The tester specific modules are linked with the common tester interface to drive the individual testers. The HP test system will be used in this chapter to demonstrate a typical module's design and operation.

5.7.1 Generic Module Requirements

The tester-specific module is a software package that controls a tester from a remote workstation. The workstation and tester communicate with one another through an interface network, in this case the HP-IB bus. The workstation itself is networked with the other CAD workstations, which makes the testing equipment fully accessible from any CAD workstation. The common tester interface produces a tester data structure and a tester-oriented vector file that the module uses to drive the tester. The module sets up the interface, configures the tester, extracts the necessary input vectors from the vector file, downloads the vectors, prompts the user to plug in the device and power it on, applies the vectors, and uploads the response. A detailed discussion of the development of tester-specific modules is given in reference.[11] The complexity of the module is reduced by two factors: it does not need to check for unsupported tester features (because that is done in the common tester interface) and the tester configuration data is conveniently organized. The arrangement of the tester data structure and tester-oriented vector file is controlled by the tester specification file.

5.7.2 Operation of The HP Module

When the HP module is called by the common tester interface, it prompts the user to power on the generator and analyzer and verify that the synchronization wire is patched on the DUT board. The module verifies that the generator and analyzer are on and begins programming the generator. The generator is configured based on information in the generator portion of the tester data structure. HP-IB commands are sent to set the clock source to be internal and to initialize the first and last vector addresses, the period, and the channel and clock voltages, timings, and waveform formats. Similarly, HP-IB commands are sent to set up the analyzer. The commands establish the voltages and strobe timing of the channels.

After the generator and analyzer are configured, the input vectors are downloaded to the generator from the tester-oriented vector file created by the common tester interface. Data is extracted from all columns of the vector file which correspond to generator pins. Next, the user is prompted to plug in the device and apply power to it. When the user has finished, the generator outputs are turned on and the vectors are applied. After the generator applies the vectors, the module turns off the generator outputs. The response is uploaded by reading data stored in the analyzer and placing it in a file. The comparison between simulation and testing results is performed externally. An example session using the HP module is given in Section 6. The entire HP module is written in about 600 lines of C code.

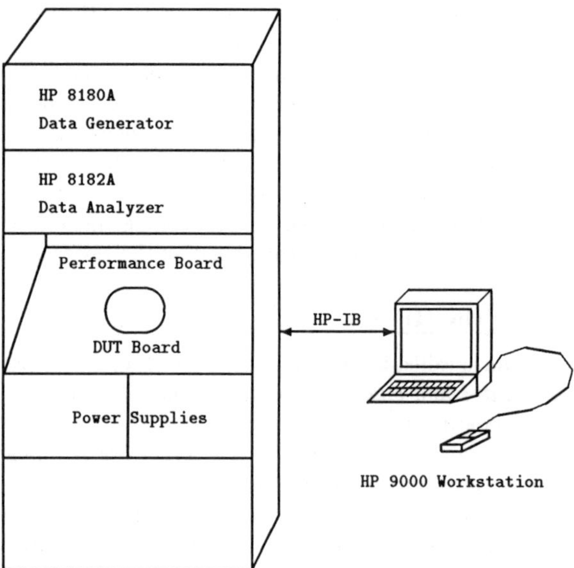

Figure 8: The HP test system

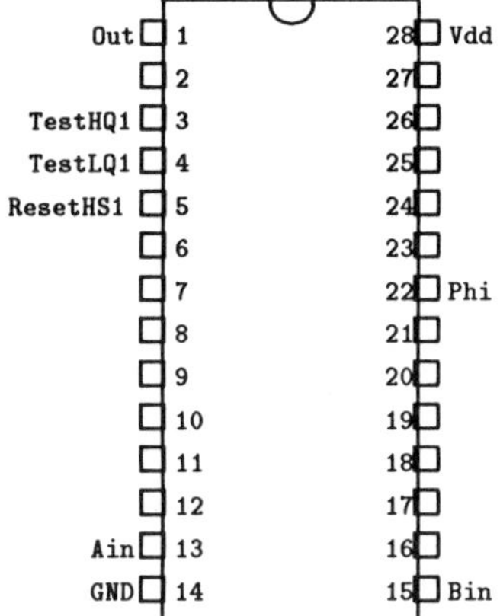

Figure 9: The pin assignment for the 8-bit serial multiplier

6 An Example Session

This section provides an example to illustrate the operation of the integrated VLSI simulation and testing environment. The example utilizes the Ldvsim logic simulator and the HP testing system. The DUT is an 8-bit serial multiplier developed at Duke University.

6.1 The Multiplier

The multiplier contains about 2000 devices and was fabricated in 3μm CMOS technology by the MOSIS Service™. The pin assignment for the multiplier is given in Figure 9. `Ain` and `Bin` are the serial multiplier and multiplicand and `Out` is the serial output. The inputs are applied and the output is available least significant bit (LSB) first. `Phi` is the clock input, `TestHQ1` and `TestLQ1` are the test inputs and, `ResetHS1` is the reset input. The multiplier operates at a clock frequency of up to 5 MHz.

6.2 The Simulation and Testing Session

In the VLSI environment, simulations are performed to verify the functionality of a design. After the design is fully simulated, a device is fabricated. With the new integrated environment, test vectors are generated as the design is simulated and the same vectors are used in the subsequent physical testing of the device. The session described in this section includes the simulation and the physical testing of the multiplier.

At the beginning of the session, assume DAE is running concurrently with a Magic edit session of the multiplier layout. From DAE, the user selects Ldvsim simulation from a Magic circuit description. DAE executes a shell script which performs the necessary preprocessing and opens an X window for the user to create an Ldvsim command file. A portion of the command file for the multiplier is given in Figure 10. The `stepsize` sets the simulation step size in tenths of ns. The period of the basic clock is twice the step size so a step size of 1000 corresponds to a period of 200 ns. The `setclock` command sets the order of the signals within the simulation vector file. To begin the simulation, the test inputs are disabled and the multiplier is reset using the `ResetHS1` signal. After the reset signal is asserted for several clock cycles, a set of multiplications is performed. The first simulation vectors multiply decimal `ain` = 13 by `bin` = 3. The least significant bits are applied at the beginning of one period, the clock is toggled, and the LSB of the result is sampled at the beginning of the following period. The remainder of the command file consists of the multiplication of some judiciously chosen operands such as `ain` = `bin` = 0 and `ain` = `bin` = 255. After the command file is complete, Ldvsim produces the simulation log file and test vector file *mult.ldv*.

After the multiplier device is fabricated, it is tested on the HP test system. In addition to having the simulation vectors, the user creates a device specification file (*mult.dev*) and a pin map (*mult.map*). The device specification for the multiplier is given in Figure 11. Within the device specification, the period is set to 200 ns, default CMOS values are used for the input and output voltages, and three waveforms are defined. The clock is configured to go high at 50 ns and return low at 150 ns. The other inputs drive data and the output strobes data at 0 ns. Within a tester cycle, the bits of `Ain` and `Bin` are applied at the beginning of the cycle, the multiplier is clocked, and the output is strobed at the beginning of the following cycle. The assignments section lists the pins in the same order as the `setclock` command to the Ldvsim command file. The pin map of the multiplier is given in Figure 12.

From DAE, the user selects the HP tester from Ldvsim. This step executes a shell script that prompts the user for the prefix of the files (typically the device name) and calls a program to convert the vectors from the Ldvsim format (*mult.ldv*) to the Omnitest vector format (*mult.omni*). The shell script invokes the knowledge based common testing interface to check for errors and drive the HP tester. The HP-specific module controls the programming of the HP 8180 data generator and the 8182 data analyzer, the application of the test vectors from the Ldvsim simulation, and the retrieval of the tester response. The user powers on the generator and analyzer, patches the generator strobe to the analyzer clock on the DUT board, plugs the multiplier into the DUT board, and applies power to it. Vectors converted from the Ldvsim simulation are then applied to the multiplier and the results uploaded to the host workstation. Finally, the shell script calls a program to compare the

```
| Ldvsim command file for multiplier

stepsize 1000
vector inputs Ain Bin TestHQ1 TestLQ1
vector outputs Out
t inputs
t outputs
setclock -P Phi -C ResetHS1 -I inputs -O outputs -V mult.ldv -Z
logfile mult.log
l Ain
l Bin
h ResetHS1
l TestHQ1
h TestLQ1
cclock 2
l ResetHS1
h Ain
h Bin
cclock
l Ain
h Bin
cclock
h Ain
l Bin
cclock
h Ain
l Bin
cclock
l Ain
l Bin
cclock 5
   "
   "
```

Figure 10: A portion of the Ldvsim command file

```
/* Device specification for multiplier */

device mult;
definitions {
   tech                       CMOS;
   ground                     GND;
   power                      Vdd = {vnom = 5.00v};
   input                      Vin;
   output                     Vout;
   period                     P1 = {pnom = 200ns};
   timing                     T0 = 0ns,
                              T50 = 50ns,
                              T150 = 150ns;
   wavefm                     WF1 = RTZ(T50, T150),
                              WF2 = NR(T0),
                              WF3 = ES(T0);
   vector                     mult.omni;
}
assignments {
bin;
   Phi = {22, Vin, WF1};
   ResetHS1 = {5, Vin, WF2};
   Ain = {13, Vin, WF2};
   Bin = {15, Vin, WF2};
   TestHQ1 = {3, Vin, WF2};
   TestLQ1 = {4, Vin, WF2};
   Out = {1, Vout, WF3};
   GND = {14, GND};
   Vdd = {28, Vdd};
}
end
```

Figure 11: The device specification file for the multiplier

```
/* HP pin map for multiplier
 *
 *    device pin        tester channel
 *    ----------        --------------
 */
        1                   a00
        3                   g10
        4                   g03
        5                   g02
        13                  g01
        15                  g00
        22                  gc1
```

Figure 12: The pin map for the multiplier

actual response of the multiplier to the expected response obtained from the Ldvsim simulation. Differences are listed and the user is given an opportunity to either test another multiplier or modify one of the parameters in the device specification and retest the original multiplier. A trace of the testing portion of the session is given in Figure 13.

Errors are handled interactively by the environment. The environment prints the line number of any syntax error it detects and opens an edit session on the file automatically. The environment performs extensive checking for device functions which are not supported on the target tester. If such functions are requested, an error message is printed and an X terminal emulator window is opened for the user to edit the device specification file. For example, if the user specifies a period of `2ns`, the environment prints a message stating that `A period of 2000ps is out of range for the tester`.

The entire session described above including Ldvsim simulation and test generation, creation of the device specification and pin map, and verification of the multiplier using the HP tester took about one hour. The same task without the new environment would take as little as two days or as much as two weeks, depending on how many of the tasks would need to be done manually.

7 Summary

This chapter has presented an integrated simulation and testing environment which receives simulation data and a device specification and transparently drives a number

```
Enter the prefix of the files > mult
...  Convert vectors from Ldvsim to Omnitest format ...

THE COMMON TESTER INTERFACE

...  Parse the device specification file (mult.dev) ...
...  Read the pin map (mult.map) ...
...  Parse the tester specification file (hp.spec) and
      check desired functions vs. HP features ...
...  Parse the vector file (mult.omni) and expand vectors ...
...  Translate vectors from device to tester order ...

THE HP MODULE

## Make sure generator and analyzer are on and
## generator strobe is patched to analyzer clock
## Hit RETURN when ready to proceed >
...  Set up generator ...
...  Set up analyzer ...
...  Download input vectors to generator ...
## Make sure device is plugged in and powered on
## Hit RETURN when ready to proceed >
...  Turn on generator outputs ...
...  Arm analyzer ...
...  Run generator and wait for vectors to be applied ...
...  Turn off generator outputs ...
...  Upload captured response from analyzer ...

COMPARE SIMULATION TO TESTING

***** No errors found *****

Would you like to test another device?  [n] > n
Would you like to modify the device spec and re-test?  [n] > n
```

Figure 13: A trace of the testing session

of different testers which have significantly different features. The environment and all of the other VLSI design tools run under the DAE user interface. A key feature of the environment is the ease with which new testers can be incorporated. The modularity is accomplished using a knowledge based system which maintains knowledge about tester capabilities and user requests, checks for consistency, and performs the tests. The use of compiler methodology to build and maintain the knowledge base was described in detail in this chapter.

The system is complete and has been in operation since 1989. All VLSI design courses at Duke University have used the new environment, and user response has been very favorable. Future extensions of the system will involve the support of additional testers, as they become available in the community.

8 Acknowledgements

We would like to express our appreciation to the Department of Electrical Engineering at Duke University, the Microelectronics Center of North Carolina (MCNC), the General Electric Company, and the Hewlett-Packard Company for supporting this work. The HP testing station was purchased through a grant from General Electric and the workstation which is used to drive the testing station was donated by Hewlett-Packard.

We would like to thank Mr. Wayne Dettloff of MCNC for development of the Omnitest language, Mr. Barry Schmitt of Duke University for the development of the software which enables manual configuration of the the Hewlett-Packard test system from a remote workstation, Dr. Ricardo Pantazis of Duke University for supporting the extraction of vectors from the Ldvsim simulator, Mr. Dimitris Pantzartzis of Duke University for supplying the 8-bit serial multiplier netlist and fabricated devices, and Mr. Darwin Thielman of Duke University for maintaining the integrated environment in VLSI design and test courses. We would also like to thank Dr. David Overhauser who developed a new course on VLSI testing, leading to extensive use and enhancement of the new testing system.

References

[1] J. J. Hallenbeck, J. R. Cybrinski, et al. The Test Engineer's Assistant: A Support Environment for Hardware Design for Testability. *IEEE Computer*, pages 59–68, April 1989.

[2] J. Calhoun, D. Bryan, and F. Brglez. Automatic Test Pattern Generation (ATPG) for Scan-Based Digital Logic: Version 1.0. Technical Report 17, Microelectronics Center of North Carolina, 1987.

[3] P. H. Bardell, W. H. McAnney, and J. Savir. *Built-In Test for VLSI: Pseudo-random Techniques.* Wiley-Interscience, 1987.

[4] J. D. Ullman. *Principles of Database and Knowledge-Base Systems*, volume 1. Computer Science Press, 1988.

[5] J. S. Kowalik, editor. *Knowledge-Based Problem Solving.* Prentice-Hall, 1986.

[6] M. A. Jabri. BREL-A PROLOG Knowledge-Based System Shell for VLSI CAD. In *Proceedings, 1990 Design Automation Conference (DAC)*, pages 271–277. IEEE Computer Society Press, 1990.

[7] A. Dollas, G. L. Castrodale, and W. T. Krakow. A Knowledge-Based Environment for the Integration of Logical and Physical Testing of VLSI Circuits. In *Proceedings, TAI '89, IEEE International Workshop on Tools for Artificial Intelligence*, pages 259–265. Computer Society Press, 1989.

[8] G. L. Castrodale, A. Dollas, and W. T. Krakow. An Interactive Environment for the Transparent Logic Simulation and Testing of Integrated Circuits. In *ITC '90 International Test Conference Proceedings*, pages 394–403. IEEE Computer Society Press, 1990.

[9] G. L. Castrodale, A. Dollas, D. V. Overhauser, and V. L. Gibbs. An Environment to Integrate CAD Tools Used in Education. In *Proceedings, 1991 Microelectronic System Education Conference and Exposition*, pages 39–49, 1991.

[10] G. L. Castrodale and A. Dollas. The Duke Applications Environment (DAE) User's Guide. Technical Report DU-EE/CEG-88-04, Computer Engineering Group, Dept. of Electrical Engineering, Duke University, 1988.

[11] G. L. Castrodale. An Integrated Environment for the Simulation and Testing of VLSI Circuits. Master's thesis, Duke University, 1989.

[12] A. Dollas. Knowledge Based Systems at Work: Experiences from a Knowledge Based Integrated Circuit Testing System. In *Proceedings, COMPSAC 90, The Fourteenth Annual International Computer Software and Applications Conference*, page 29. Computer Society Press, 1990.

[13] M. J. Y. Williams and J. B. Angel. Enhancing Testability of Large Scale Integrated Circuits via Test Points and Additional Logic. *IEEE Transactions on Computers*, C-22(1):46–60, January 1973.

[14] G. Prokter. The Logic Simulator-Tester Link: It's a Two-Way Street. In *ITC '87 International Test Conference Proceedings*, pages 254–260. IEEE Computer Society Press, 1987.

[15] P. B. Reintjes. AUNT: A Universal Netlist Translator. In *Proceedings of the 1987 Symposium on Logic Programming*, pages 508–515. IEEE Computer Society Press, 1987.

[16] T. Middleton. Recycling Functional Test Vectors: Techniques and Tools for Pattern Conversion. In *ITC '85 International Test Conference Proceedings*, pages 291–301. IEEE Computer Society Press, 1985.

[17] J. Teisher. Improved Workstation/Tester Interface is the Key to the Quality of Test-Program Generation. In *ITC '86 International Test Conference Proceedings*, pages 626–630. IEEE Computer Society Press, 1986.

[18] W. Boggs. Integration into the CAD Environment. In *ITC '83 International Test Conference Proceedings*, page 150. IEEE Computer Society Press, 1983.

[19] L. J. Falkenstrom, D. Keezer, et al. Tester-Independent Support Software System (TISSS). In *ITC '85 International Test Conference Proceedings*, pages 685–690. IEEE Computer Society Press, 1985.

[20] W. E. Den Beste. Intent Capture Concepts for Simplifying Device Simulation and Test. In *ITC '87 International Test Conference Proceedings*, pages 261–266. IEEE Computer Society Press, 1987.

[21] B. L. Havlicsek. A Knowledge-Based Diagnostic System for Automatic Test Equipment. In *ITC '86 International Test Conference Proceedings*, pages 930–938. IEEE Computer Society Press, 1986.

[22] N. Weste and K. Eshraghian. *Principles of CMOS VLSI Design: A Systems Perspective.* Addison-Wesley, 1985.

[23] A. Etherington. Interfacing Design to Test Using the Electronic Design Interchange Format (EDIF). In *ITC '87 International Test Conference Proceedings*, pages 378–383. IEEE Computer Society Press, 1987.

[24] A. V. Aho, R. Sethi, and J. D. Ullman. *Compilers: Principles, Techniques and Tools* . Addison-Wesley, 1986.

[25] W. D. Dettloff and M. D. Tebbs. The Omnitest System: A No-Generate, No-Compile, Interactive Test Methodology. In *ITC '89 International Test Conference Proceedings.* IEEE Computer Society Press, 1989.

[26] D. J. Erdman, D. J. Rose, G. B. Nifong, et al. *CAzM: Circuit Analyzer with Macromodeling.* Microelectronics Center of North Carolina and Duke University, July 1989.

[27] GenRad Fareham Ltd. *HILO-3 User Manual*, June 1987.

[28] SDA Systems, Inc. *SDA Language Reference Manual, Version 2.0*, 1988.

[29] T. J. Barnes. SKILL™: A CAD System Extension Language. In *Proceedings, 1990 Design Automation Conference (DAC)*, pages 266–271. IEEE Computer Society Press, 1990.

[30] R. K. Brayton, A. R. Newton, et al. *OCT Tools Distribution 2.1*. Electronics Research Laboratory, University of California at Berkeley, 1988.

[31] M. E. Lesk and E. Schmidt. Lex - A Lexical Analyzer Generator. Technical Report 39, Bell Laboratories, Murray Hill, NJ, 1975.

[32] S. C. Johnson. Yacc: Yet Another Compiler-Compiler. Technical Report 39, Bell Laboratories, Murray Hill, NJ, 1972.

[33] S. Bisset. The Development of a Tester-per-Pin VLSI Test System Architecture. In *ITC '83 International Test Conference Proceedings*, pages 151–155. IEEE Computer Society Press, 1983.

[34] L. Sterling and E. Shapiro. *The Art of Prolog: Advanced Programming Techniques*. MIT Press, 1986.

BIBLIOGRAPHY

Adams, D., "A model for parallel computations", *Parallel Processor Systems, Technologies and Applications* (Spartan Books, New York, 1970) pp. 311-334.

Agerwala, T., "Some applications of Petri Nets", *Proc. 1978 Nat. Electronics Conf.* **23** (1978) 149-154.

Agerwala, T. and Flynn, M., "Comments on capabilities, limitations and 'correctness' of Petri nets", *Proc. 1st Annual Symp. on Computer Architecture* (ACM, New York, 1973) pp. 81-86.

Agresti, A., *Categorical Data Analysis* (John Wiley and Sons, 1990).

Aho, A.V., Sethi, R. and Ullman, J.D., *Compilers: Principles, Techniques and Tools* (Addison-Wesley, 1986).

Aho, A.V. and Ullman, J.D., *The Theory of Parsing, Translation and Compiling* (Prentice-Hall, Inc. Englewood Cliffs, NJ, 1972).

Aho, A.V. *et al.*, *Data Structures and Algorithms* (Addison-Wesley, Reading, 1983).

Aisbett, J., "Automatic modulation recognition using time domain parameters", *Signal Process.* **13** (1987) 323.

Aleshinsky, S.Y. and Zatsiorsky, V.M., "Human locomotion in space analyzed biomechanically through a multilink chain model", *J. Biomech.* **11** (1978) 101-108.

Aletan, S., "The influence of algorithms and languages versus programmers experience on programs execution efficiency", *Modelling and Simulation Conf.* May 1988, pp. 1131-1135.

Aletan, S., "Current and future trends in artificial intelligence architectures and programming languages", *Tools for Artificial Intelligence*, 1989 pp. 215-221.

Almasi, G.S. and Goltlieb, A., *Highly Parallel Computing* (Benjamin/Cummings Pub. Co., 1989).

Alshawi, H., Boguraev, B. and Briscoe, T., "Towards a dictionary support environment for real time parsing", *Proc. 2nd Conf. European Chapter of the ACL*, Geneva, Switzerland, Mar. 1985, pp. 27-29.

Anderson, J.A., "Cognitive and psychological computation with neural models", *IEEE Trans. Syst. Man Cybern.* **13** (1983) 799-815.

Anderson, J.M. *et al.*, "The architecture of FAIM-1", *IEEE Computer* **20** (1987) 55-65.

Ankenbrandt, C.A., Buckles, B.P. and Petry, F.E., "Scene recognition using genetic algorithms with semantic nets", *Pattern Recogn. Lett.* **11** (1990) 285-293.

Araki, T. and Kasami, T., "Some decision problems related to the reachability problem for Petri nets", *Theoret. Comput. Sci.* **3** (1976) 85-104.

Arvind and Nikhil, R.S., "Executing a program on the MIT tagged-token dataflow architecture", *IEEE Trans. Comput.* **39** (1990).

Aso, H. and Kimura, M., "Absolute expediency of learning automata", *Inf. Sci.* **17** (1979) 91-112.

Azema, P., Valette, R. and Diaz, M., "Petri nets as a common tool for design verification and hardware simulation", *IEEE Proc. 13th Design Automation Conf.*, New York, June 1976, pp. 109-116.

Bachmair, L., "Proof by consistency in equational theories", *Proc. 3rd IEEE Symp. on Logic in Computer Science (LISC)*, Edinburgh, 1988.

Bachmair, L. and Dershowitz, N., "Equational inference, canonical proofs, and proofs ordering", *JACM* (1991, to appear).

Bachmair, L., Dershowitz, N. and Plaisted, D., "Completion without failure", *Proc. Colloquium on Resolution of Equations in Algebraic Structures*, Lakeway, Texas, 1987.

Bachmair, L. and Ganzinger, H., "Completion of first-order clauses with equality", *Proc. 2nd CTRS*, Montréal, 1990(a).

Bachmair, L. and Ganzinger, H., "On restriction of ordered paramodulation with simplification", *Proc. 10th CADE*, 1990(b).

Backus, J.W., "The syntax and semantics of the proposed international algebraic language of the Zurich ACM-GAMM Conference", *Proc. Int. Conf. on Information Processing*, 1959, pp. 125-132.

Baffes, P. and Wang, L., "Mobile transporter path planning", *Proc. SOAR '89*, Houston, TX, 1988, pp. 51-59.

Baird, H.S., Graf, H.P., Jackel, L.D. and Hubbard, W.E., "A VLSI architecture for binary image classification", *From Pixels to Features*, J.C. Simon, ed. (North Holland, 1989) pp. 275-286.

Baker, H. Jr., "Petri nets and languages", Computation Structures Group Memo 68, Project MAC, MIT, Cambridge, MA, May 1972.

Baker, J.E., "Reducing bias and inefficiency in the selection algorithm", *Proc. 2nd Int. Conf. on Genetic Algorithms and Their Applications* (Lawrence Erlbaum, 1987) pp. 14-21.

Banerji, R.B., *Artificial Intelligence: A Theoretical Approach* (Elsevier/North Holland Scientific Pub., 1980).

Bardell, P.H., McAnney, W.H. and Savir, J., *Built-In Test for VLSI: Pseudo-Random Techniques* (Wiley-Interscience, 1987).

Barnes, J., Private Communication, Arlington, VA, Mar. 1988.

Barnes, T.J., "SKILL^{TM}: A CAD system extension language", *Proc. 1990 Design Automation Conf. (DAC)*, IEEE Computer Society Press, 1990, pp. 266-271.

Barr, A. and Feigenbaum, E.A., *The Handbook of Artificial Intelligence* (William Kaufmann, Inc., Los Altos, CA, 1981).

Becker, J.D., "The Phrasal Lexicon", Bolt, Beranek and Newman Tech. Rep. 3081, 1975.

Bernold, T. and Gunter A., eds. *Artificial Intelligence: Towards Practical Application* (Elsevier Science Pub. B.V., North-Holland, 1985).

Bernstein, P. and Tsichritzis, D., "Models for description of computer systems", *Proc. 8th Annual Princeton Conf. on Information Sciences and Systems*, Princeton University, Princeton, NJ, 1974, pp. 340-343.

Berthelot, G., "Checking liveness of Petri-nets", *Parallel Computers – Parallel Mathematics* (North-Holland, Amsterdam, 1977) pp. 217-220.

Berthelot, G. and Roucairol, G., "Reduction of Petri nets", *Proc. 5th Symp. on Mathematical Foundations of Computer Science*, Lecture Notes in Computer Science, Vol. 45, (Springer-Verlag, Berlin, 1976) pp. 202-209.

Bertling, H., "Knuth-Bendix completion of horn clause programs for restricted linear resolution and paramodulation", *Proc. 2nd CTRS*, Montréal, 1990.

Best, E., "On liveness problem of Petri net theory", ASM/6, Computing Lab., University of Newcastle upon Tyne, Newcastle upon Tyne, England, June 1976.

Best, E., "Path programs", Lecture Notes in Computer Science (Springer-Verlag, Berlin, 1980).

Bhanu, B., "Shape matching of two-dimensional objects", *IEEE Trans. Pattern Anal. Mach. Intell.* **6** (1984) 137-156.

Bic, L., "Processing of semantic networks on dataflow architectures", *Artif. Intell.* **27** (1985) 219-227.

Biggerstaff, T. and Richter, C., "Reusability framework, assessment, and directions", *IEEE Software* **4** (1987).

Birkhoff, G., "On the structure of abstract algebras", *Proc. Cambridge Phil. Soc.* **31** (1935) 433-545.

Bisiani, R., Anantharaman, T. and Butcher, L., "BEAM: An Accelerator for Speech Recognition", CMU-CS-89-102, 1989.

Bisset, S., "The development of a tester-per-pin VLSI test system architecture", *ITC '83 Int. Test Conf. Proc.*, IEEE Computer Society Press, 1983, pp. 151-155.

Blelloch, G.E., "CIS: A massively parallel concurrent rule-based system", *Proc. AAAI-86*, 1986.

Bobrow, D.G., Kaplan, R.M., Kay, M., Norman, D.A., Thompson, H. and Winograd, T., "GUS, a frame-driven dialog system", *Artif. Intell.* **8** (1977) 155-173.

Bobrow, D.G. and Winograd, T., "An overview of KRL: A knowledge representation language", *Cognitive Sci.* **1** (1977).

Boehm, B., Brown, J., Kaspar, J. and Lipow, M., *Characteristics of Software Quality* (North Holland, 1978).

Boggs, W., "Integration into the CAD environment", *ITC '83 Int. Test Conf. Proc.*, IEEE Computer Society Press, 1983, p. 150.

Bond, A.H. and Gasser, L., *Readings in Distributed Artificial Intelligence*, (Morgan Kaufmann Pub. Inc., 1988).

Booker, L.B., "Triggered rule discovery in classifier systems", *Proc. 3rd Int. Conf. on Genetic Algorithms and Their Applications* (Morgan Kaufmann, 1989) pp. 265-274.

Booker, L.B., "Intelligent behavior as an adaptation to the task environment", Doctoral Thesis, CCS Dept., University of Michigan, 1982.

Bouhoula, A., Kounalis, E. and Rusinowitch M., "A mechanization of inductive reasoning", (1991, submitted).

Bourbakis, N.G., "Design of real-time supercomputing vision systems", *Proc. IEEE Conf. on Supercomputing* **1** (1987) 392-398.

Bourbakis, N.G., "A rule based scheme for synthesis of textured images", *Proc. IEEE Conf. on Systems, Man, and Cybernetics*, Vol. 3, Oct. 1987, pp. 999-1003.

Bourbakis, N.G., "A heuristic, real-time path planning for collision-free navigation in a dynamic multiple robots unknown environment", *Proc. Int. Conf. on Tools for Artificial Intelligence*, Virginia, Oct. 1989.

Bourbakis, N., "Symbolic learning on a connectionist structure", TR-1990.

Bourbakis, N.G., "ARTEMIS – An automated software environment for analysis, design and simulation of computing systems", *Int. J. Softw. Eng. Knowl. Eng.*, (1992) (forthcoming).

Bourbakis, N.G. and Barlos, F., "Hardware design of the lower level nodes of the HERMES heterogeneous neural network", *Int. J. EAAI* **5** (1992).

Bourbakis, N. and Tabak, D., "Working mechanism and their Petri net modeling for the HERMES multiprocessor vision system", *Int. J. EAAI* **1** (1988) 102-110.

Bourbakis, N.G. *et al.*, "An RISC-bit sliced design of the HERMES multilevel vision system", *J. Microcomput. Appl.* **11** (1988) 155-167.

Bourbakis, N.G. *et al.*, "Multiprocessors and microprocessor vision system", *Int. J. Microprocess. Microsyst.* **11** (1990) 155-167.

Boyer, R.S. and Moore, J.S., *A Computational Logic* (Academic Press, New York, 1979).

Brachman, R.J., "What IS-A is and and isn't: An analysis of taxonomic links in semantic networks", *Computer* **16** (1983) 30-36.

Brachman, R.J., "On the epistemological status of semantic networks", *Associative Networks*, N.V. Findler, ed. (Academic Press, New York, 1979) pp. 3-50.

Brachman, R. and Schmoltz, J., "An overview of the KL-ONE knowledge representation system", *Cognitive Sci.* **9** (1985) 171-216.

Brand, "Proving theorems with the modification methods", *SIAM J. Comput.* **4** (1975) 412-430.

Brayton, R.K., Newton, A.R. *et al.*, *OCT Tools Distribution 2.1.*, Electronics Research Lab., University of California at Berkeley, 1988.

Bredt, T., "Analysis of parallel systems", Tech. Rep. 7, Digital Systems Lab., Stanford University, Stanford, CA, Aug. 1970; also *IEEE Trans. Comput.* **20** (1971) 1403-1407.

Brennan, S., Friedman, M. and Pollard, C., "A centering approach to pronouns", *Proc. ACL-86*, 1986.

Bresnan, J., "Control and complementation", *The Mental Representation of Grammatical Relations* (MIT Press, 1982).

Brinsfield, W. and Miller, R., "On the composition of parallel programs schemata", *IEEE 12th Annual Symp. on Switching and Automata Theory*, New York, Oct. 1971, pp. 20-23.

Brooks, R.A., "Solving the find-path problem by good representation of free space", *IEEE Trans. Syst. Man. Cybern.* **13** (1983) 190-197.

Brown, T.C. Jr., "A structured design-method for specialized proof procedures", Ph.D. Thesis, California Institute of Technology, Pasadena, CA, 1975.

Bruce, B., "Case systems for natural language", *Artif. Intell.* **6** (1975).

Buckles, B.P., Petry, F.E. and Kuester, R.L., "Schema survival rates and heuristic search in genetic algorithms", *Proc. 2nd Int. Conf. on Tools for A.I.*, Nov. 1990, Washington D.C., pp. 322-327.

Buntine, W., "Generalized subsumption and its applications to induction and redundancy", *Artif. Intell.* **36** (1988) 149-176.

Burstall, R.M., "Proving properties of programs by structural induction", *Comput. J.* **12** (1969) 41-48.

Burstall, R. and Darlington, J., "A transformation system for developing recursive programs", *JACM* **24** (1977).

Cĕrny, V., "A thermodynamical approach to the travelling salesman problem: An efficient simulation algorithm", Tech. Rep. Institute of Physics and Biophysics, Comenius University, Bratislava, 1982.

Calhoun, J., Bryan, D. and Brglez, F., "Automatic test pattern generation (ATPG) for scan-based digital logic: Version 1.0", Tech. Rep. 17, Microelectronics Center of North Carolina, 1987.

Cappellini, V., Pareschi, M.T. and Raspollini, C., "A technique for object recognition based on subpart classification", *Image Analysis and Processing*, V. Cantoni, *et al.* eds. (Plenum Press, New York, 1986).

Carberry, M., "Pragmatic modeling in information system interfaces", Ph.D. thesis, Dept. of Computer and Information Science, University of Delaware, Newark, DE, 1985.

Carpender, G.A. and Grossberg, S., "Neural dynamics of category learning and recognition in brain structure, learning, and memory", *AAAS Symp. Series*, 1986.

Carter, J.M., "Parallel machine learning on a dataflow machine", M.S. Thesis, Drexel University, Jan. 1992.

Casasent, D. and Baranoski, E., "Directed graph for adaptive organization and learning of a knowledge base", *Appl. Opt.* **27** 1988.

Castrodale, G.L., "An integrated environment for the simulation and testing of VLSI circuits", Master's Thesis, Duke University, 1989.

Castrodale, G.L. and Dollas, A., "The Duke Applications Environment (DAE) user's guide", Tech. Rep. DU-EE/CEG-88-04, Computer Engineering Group, Dept. of Electrical Engineering, Duke University, 1988.

Castrodale, G.L., Dollas, A. and Krakow, W.T., "An interactive environment for the transparent logic simulation and testing of integrated circuits", *ITC '90 Int. Test Conf. Proc.* IEEE Computer Society Press, 1990, pp. 394-403.

Castrodale, G.L., Dollas, A., Overhauser, D.V. and Gibbs, V.L., "An environment to integrate CAD tools used in education", *Proc. 1991 Microelectronics System Education Conf. and Expo.*, 1991, pp. 39-49.

Cercone, N. and McCalla, G., "AI: Underlying assumptions and basic objectives", *Computers for Artificial Intelligence Applications* (IEEE Computer Society Press, 1986) pp. 12-22.

Chang, C.L. and Lee, R.C.T., *Symbolic Logic and Mechanical Theorem Proving* (Academic Press, New York, 1971).

Chang, S.K., *Principles of Pictorial Information System Design* (Prentice-Hall Inc., 1989).

Chapman, D., "Planning for conjuctive goals", *Artif. Intell.* **32** (1987) 333-377.

Charniak, E., "Passing markers: A theory of contextual influence in language comprehension", *Cognitive Sci.* **7** (1975) 171-190.

Charniak, E., "A neat theory of marker-passing", *Proc. AAAI-88*, 1988.

Chatila, R., "Path planning and environmental learning in a mobile robot system", *Proc. European Conf. on Artificial Intelligence*, Orsay, France, 1982.

Chernoff, H., "A measure of asymptotic efficiency for tests of a hypotheses based on the sum of observations", *Ann. Math. Stat.* **23** (1952) 493-509.

Chomsky, N., "Three models for the description of language", *IRE Trans. Inf. Theory* **2** (1956) 113-124.

Chomsky, N., "On certain formal properties of grammars", *Inf. Control* **2** (1959) 137-167.

Chung, K., "Efficient AI nonlinear planning based on resource reasoning", Ph.D. thesis, University of Southern California, 1990.

Clark, P. and Niblett, T., "The CN2 induction algorithm", *Mach. Learn.* **3** (1989).

Cleghorn, T., Baffes, P. and Wang, L., "Robot path planning using a genetic algorithm", *Proc. SOAR '88*, Houston TX, 1988, pp. 81-87.

Cleveland, F.A. and Smith, S.F., "Using genetic algorithms to schedule flow shop releases", *Proc. 3rd Int. Conf. on Genetic Algorithms*, Fairfax, VA, 1989, pp. 160-169.

Cohen, P. and Fertig, S., "Discourse structure and the modality of communication", *Symp. on Prospects and Problems of Interpreting Telephony*, 1986.

Commoner, F., Holt, A., Even, S. and Pnueli, A., "Marked directed graphs", *J. Comput. Syst. Sci.* **5** (1971) 511-523.

Condon, J.H. and Thompson, K., "Belle chess hardware", *Advances in Computer Chess* (Pergamon Press, 1982).

Console, L. and Torasso, P., "Integrating models of correct behavior into abductive diagnosis", *Proc. 9th European Conf. on Artificial Intelligence (ECAI)*, Stockholm, 1990, pp. 160-166.

Cook, S.A., "The complexity of theorem-proving procedures", *Proc. 3rd ACM Symp. on Theory of Computing*, 1971, pp. 151-158.

Corkill, D.D., "Hierarchical planning in a distributed environment", Proc. Int. Joint Conf. on Artificial Intelligence, 1979, pp. 168-175.

Cormen, T.H., Leiserson, C.E. and Rivest, R.L., *Introduction to Algorithms* (MIT Press, Cambridge, 1990).

Cottrell, G., "A model of lexical access of ambiguous words", *Lexical Ambiguity Resolution*, S. Small *et al.*, eds. (Morgan Kaufmann Pub., 1988).

Cox, L. Jr., "Predicting concurrent computer system performance using Petri net models", *Proc. 1978 ACM Nat. Conf.*, New York, Dec. 1978, pp. 901-913.

Cox, P.T. and Pietrzykowski, T., "General diagnosis by abductive inference", *Proc. Symp. on Logic programming*, San Francisco, California, 1990, pp. 183-189.

Crain, S. and Steedman, M., "On not being led up the garden path: The use of context by the psychological syntax processor", *Natural Language Parsing* (1985).

Crespi-Reghizzi, S. and Mandrioli, D., "Petri nets and Szilard languages", *Inf. Control* **33** (1977) 177-192.

Cullingford, R., "SAM", *Inside Computer Understanding*, R.C. Schank and C.K. Riesback, eds. (Erlbaum, Hillsdale, NJ, 1981).

Cummins, F.A., Bejcek, W.E., Ibrahim, M.H., O'Leary, D.J. and Woyak, S.W., "OWL 3.0 reference manual", Internal Tech. Rep. #AAI-87007 , EDS Research and Development, Troy, MI, Aug. 1987.

Darlington, J., "An experimental program transformation and synthesis system", *Artif. Intell.* **16** (1981).

Darlington, J. and Reeve, M., *ALICE and the Parallel Evaluation of Logic Programs* (IEEE Computer Society Press, 1985).

Davis, L., ed., *Handbook of Genetic Algorithms* (Van Nostrand Reinhold, New York, 1991).

Davis, M., *Computability and Unsolvability* (McGraw-Hill, NY, 1958).

Davis, M. and Putnam, H., "A computing procedure for quantification theory", *J. ACM* (1960) 201-215.

De Jong, K.A., "An analysis of the behavior of a class of genetic adaptive systems", Doctoral Thesis, Dept. of Computer and Communications Science, University of Michigan, Ann Arbor, 1975.

De Jong, K.A., "Genetic algorithms: A 10 year perspective", *Proc. 1st Int. Conf. on Genetic Algorithms and Their Applications* (Lawrence Erlbaum, 1985) pp. 169-177.

De Jong, K.A., "Using genetic algorithms to search program spaces", *Proc. 2nd Int. Conf. on Genetic Algorithms and Their Applications* (Lawrence Erlbaum, 1987) pp. 210-216.

De Jong, K.A. and Spears, W.M., "Learning concept classification rules using genetic algorithms", *Proc. 12th Int. Joint. Conf. on Artificial Intelligence* (Morgan Kaufmann, 1991) pp. 651-656.

De Kleer, J., "Diagnosing multiple faults", *Artif. Intell.* **32** (1987) 97-130.

De Kleer, J., Mackworth, A.K. and Reiter, R., "Characterizing diagnoses", *Proc. Int. Workshop on Expert Systems in Engineering*, Vienna, LNAI 462, Springer-Verlag, (1990) pp. 1-15.

De Smedt, K., "Distributed unification in parallel incremental syntactic tree formation", *Proc. European Workshop on Natural Language Generation*, 1989.

Dechter, R. and Pearl, J., "Network-based heuristics for constraint-satisfaction problems", *Artif. Intell.* **34** (1988) 1-38.

Delahaye, J.P., *Formal Methods in Artificial Intelligence* (John Wiley & Sons, 1987).

Delgado-Frias, J.G. and Moore, W.R., "Parallel architectures for AI semantic network processing", *Knowl.-Based Syst.* **1** (1988) 259-265.

Delgado-Frias, J.G. and Moore, W.R., eds., *VLSI for Artificial Intelligence* (Kluwer Academic Pub., Boston, MA, 1989).

Delgado-Frias, J.G. and Moore, W.R., "A semantic network architecture for knowledge base processing", *Int. J. Engin. Appl. Artif. Intell.* **3** (1990) 4-10.

DeMara, R. and Moldovan, D., "The SNAP-1 parallel AI prototype", Tech. Rep. PKPL 90-15, University of Southern California, Dept. of EE-Systems, 1990.

DeMara, R.F. and Moldovan, D.I., "The SNAP-1 parallel AI prototype", *Proc. 18th Annual Int. Symp. on Computer Architecture, ACM SIGARCH*, May 1991, pp. 2-11.

Den Beste, W.E., "Intent capture concepts for simplifying device imulation and test", *ITC '87 Int. Test Conf. Proc.*, IEEE Computer Society Press, 1987, pp. 261-266.

Dershowitz, N., "Applications of the Knuth-Bendix completion procedure", *Proc. Séminaire d'Informatique Théorique*, Paris, 1982, pp. 95-111 (Revised version in 1987).

Dershowitz, N., "Computing with rewrite systems", *Inf. Control* **65** (1985) 122-157.

Dershowitz, N., "Synthesis by completion", *Proc. 9th Int. Joint Conf. on Artificial Intelligence (IJCAI)*, Los Angeles, U.S.A. 1985.

Dershowitz, N., "Termination of rewriting", *J. Symbolic Comput.* **3** (1987).

Dershowitz, N., "Canonical sets of horn clauses", *Proc. 2nd CTRS*, Montréal, 1990, pp. 267-278.

Dershowitz, N., Hsiang, J., Josephson, N. and Plaisted, D., "Associative-commutative rewriting", *Proc. IJCAI* (1983) 940-944.

Dershowitz, N. and Jouannaud, J.P., "Rewrite systems", *Handbook of Theoretical Computer Science*, J. Van Leeuwen, ed. (North-Holland, 1991) pp. 243-320.

Dershowitz, N. and Manna, Z., "Proving termination with multiset orderings", *CACM* **22** (1979) 465-476.

Dershowitz, N. and Okada, M., "A rationale for conditional equational programming", *Theoret. Comput. Sci.* **75** (1990) 111-138.

Dershowitz, N. and Pinchover, E., "Inductive synthesis of equational programs", *Proc. 8th Nat. Conf. on Artificial Intelligence (AAAI-90)*, 1990, Boston, U.S.A.

Despain, A.M. and Patt, Y.N., *Aquarius – A High Performance Computing System for Symbolic/ Numeric Applications* (IEEE Computer Society Press, 1986).

Dettloff, W.D. and Tebbs, M.D., "The omnitest system: A no-generate no-compile, interactive test methodology", *ITC '89 Int. Test Conf. Proc.*, IEEE Computer Society Press, 1989.

Deutsch, D., "A dogleg channel router", *Proc. 13th DAC* 1976, pp. 425-433.

Dietterich, G.T. and Michalski, R.S., "Inductive learning of structural descriptions: Evaluation criteria and comparative review of selected methods", *Artif. Intell.* **16** (1981) 257-294.

Digital Equipment Corporation, *VAX Architecture Handbook.*

Dixit, V. and Moldovan, D.I., "Semantic network array processor and its applications to image understanding", *IEEE Trans. Pattern Anal. Mach. Intell.* **9** (1987) 153-160.

Dollas, A., "Knowledge based systems at work: Experiences from a knowledge based integrated circuit testing system", *Proc. COMPSAC 90, 14th Annual Int. Computer Software and Applications Conf.*, Computer Society Press, 1990, p. 29.

Dollas, A., Castrodale, G.L. and Krakow, W.T., "A knowledge-based environment for the integration of logical and physical testing of VLSI circuits", *Proc. TAI '89 IEEE Int. Workshop on Tools for Artificial Intelligence,* IEEE Computer Society Press, 1989, pp. 259-265.

Doster, W., "Different states of a document's content on its way from the Gutenbergian world of the electronic world", *Proc. 7th Int. Conf. on Pattern Recognition,* 1984, pp. 872-874.

Duda, R. and Hart, P., *Pattern Recognition and Scene Analysis* (John Wiley & Sons, 1973).

Dym, C.L., "Issues in the design and implementation of expert system", *AI EDAM,* **1** (1987) 37-46.

Earley, J., "An efficient context-free parsing algorithm", Ph.D. Thesis, Computer Science Dept., Carnegie Mellon University, Pittsburgh, PA, 1968.

Ebeling, C., *All the Right Moves* (The MIT Press, Cambridge, 1987).

Eisenstadt, T.O.M., *Artificial Intelligence: Tools, Techniques, and Applications* (Harper & Row Pub., 1984).

El Ayeb, B., Marquis, P. and Rusinowitch, M., "A new diagnosis approach by deduction and abduction", *Proc. Int. Workshop on Expert Systems in Engineering,* Vienna, LNAI 462 (Springer-Verlag, 1990) pp. 32-46.

Elliman, D.G. and Lancaster, I.T., "A review of segmentation and contextual analysis techniques for text recognition", *Pattern Recogn.* **23** (1990) 337-346.

Elliot, L.B. and Holliday, F.L., "Automating conversion: FORTRAN to Ada via Ada", *Comput. Lang.* **4** (1987) 63-70.

Erdman, D.J., Rose, D.J., Nifong, G.B. *et al., CAzM: Circuit Analyzer with Macromodeling* (Microelectronics Center of North Carolina and Duke University, Jul. 1989).

Erdös, P. and Spencer, I., *Probabilistic Method in Combinatorics* (Academic Press, New York, 1974).

Ernst, G.W. and Newell, A., *GPS: A Case Study in Generality and Problem Solving* (Academic Press, New York, NY, 1969).

Esteva, J.C. and Reynolds, R.G., "Learning to recognize reusable software by induction", *Int. J. Softw. Eng. Knowl. Eng.* **2** (1991).

Etherington, A., "Interfacing design to test using the electronic design interchange format (EDIF)", *ITC '87 Int. Test Conf. Proc.*, IEEE Computer Society Press, 1987, pp. 378-383.

Fahlman, S.E., *NETL: A System for Representing and Using Real-World Knowledge* (MIT Press, Cambridge, MA, 1979).

Fahlman, S.E., "Design for a million-element machine", *AAAI Proc. Annual Conf. on Artificial Intelligence* Aug. 1980, pp. 249-252.

Fahlman, S., "Computing facilities for AI: A survey of present and near-future options", *AI Mag.* (1980-1981) 16-23.

Fahlman, S.E. and Hinton, G.E., "Connectionist architectures for artificial intelligence", *Computer* **20** (1987) 100-109.

Fahlman, S.E. *et al.*, "Massively parallel architectures for AI: NETL, THISTLE, and BOLTZMANN Machines", *Proc. Annual Nat. Conf. on Artificial Intelligence*, Aug. 1983, pp. 109-113.

Falkenstrom, L.J., Keezer, D. *et al.*, "Tester-independent support software system (TISSS)", *ITC '85 Int. Test Conf. Proc.*, IEEE Computer Society Press, 1985, pp. 685-690.

Faverjon, B., "Obstacle avoidance using an octree in the configuration space of a manipulator", *IEEE Int. Conf. on Robotics*, 1984, pp. 504-512.

Feldman, J.L. and Cowman, J.D., "Large-scale activity of neural nets II: A model for the brainstem respiratory oscillator", *Biol. Cybern.* **17** (1975) 39-51.

Fenrich, R., Lam, S.W. and Srihari, S.N., "Optical character readers", *Encyclopedia of Computer Science and Engineering*, A. Ralston, ed., 2nd edn. (Van Nostrand Reinhold, New York, 1991) in press.

Fenton, N.E., *Software Metrics: A Rigorous Approach* (Chapman and Hall Press, 1991).

Fields, S., "Surveying AI languages", *PC AI* **1** (1987) 28-35.

Fikes, R. and Nilsson, N., "STRIPS: A new approach to the application of theorem proving to problem solving", *Artif. Intell.* **2** (1971) 189-208.

Filipski, P., Bharathi, C.S., Hull, J.J. and Srihari, S.N., "Compression for fast read-only access of a large memory resident structured database", *Proc. 2nd Data Compression Conf.*, Snowbird, UT, 1992, to appear.

Filmore, C., "The case for case", in *Universals in Linguistic Theory*, E. Bach and R.T. Harms, eds. (Holt, New York, 1968).

Firebaugh, M.W., *Artificial Intelligence, A Knowledge-Based Approach* (Boyd & Fraser Pub. Co., 1988).

Fisher, R.A., "The use of multiple measurements in taxonomic problems", *Ann. Eugenics* **7**, Part II (1936) 179-188; also in *Contributions to Mathematical Statistics* (John Wiley, New York, 1950).

Flynn, M.J., "A canonic interpretive program form for measuring 'ideal' HLL architectures", *Comput. Architecture News* **6**, 8 (1978).

Ford, M., Bresnan, J. and Kaplan, R., "A competence-based theory of syntactic closure", *The Mental Representation of Grammatical Relations*, J. Bresnan, ed. (MIT Press, 1981).

Forgy, C.L., "The OPS5 user's manual", TR CMU-CS-81-135, Computer Science Dept., Carnegie Mellon University, Pittsburgh, PA, 1981.

Forney, G.D. Jr., "The Viterbi algorithm", *Proc. IEEE* **61** (1973) 268-278.

Frenkel, K.A., "Evaluating two massively parallel machines", *Commun. ACM* **29** (1986) 752-758.

Fretwell, P. and Goillau, P.J., "Linguistic definition of generic models in computer vision".

Freuder, E.C., "A sufficient condition for backtrack-free search", *J. ACM* **29** (1982) 24-32.

Fribourg, L., "A strong restriction of the inductive completion procedure", *Proc. 13th ICALP*, Rennes, 1986.

Frost, R., *Introduction to Knowledge Base Systems* (Macmillan Pub. Co., New York, 1986).

Fu, K.S., *Syntactic Methods in Pattern Recognition* (Academic Press, New York, 1974).

Fu, K.S., "Syntactic (linguistic) pattern recognition", *Digital Pattern Recognition*, K.S. Fu, ed. (Springer-Verlag, New York, 1980).

Fukushima, K., Miyake, S. and Ito, T., "Neurocognitron: A neural network model for mechanism of visual pattern recognition", *IEEE Trans. Syst. Man Cybern.* **13** (1983) 826-834.

Fukushima, K., "A model of associative memory in the brain", *Kybernetik* **12** (1973) 58-63.

Funahashi, K.I., "On the approximate realization of continuous mappings by neural networks", *Neural Networks* 2 (1989).

Furuse, O., Sumita, E. and Iida, H., "A method for realizing transfer-driven machine translation", *Workshop on Natural Language Processing,* IPSJ, 1990 (in Japanese).

Furuya, T. *et al.*, "Architectural evaluation of a semantic network machine", *Database Machines and Knowledge Base Machines*, M. Kitsuregawa and H. Tanaka, eds. (Kluwer Academic Pub., Boston, MA, 1988).

Gabriel, R.P., *Performance and Evaluation of LISP Systems*, 2nd edn. (MIT Press, Cambridge, MA, 1986).

Ganzinger, H., "Ground term confluence in parametric conditional equational specifications", *Proc. 4th Symp. on Theoretical Aspects of Computer Science*, Passau, RFA, 1987.

Ganzinger, H., "A completion procedure of conditional equations", *J. Symbolic Comput.* (1991).

Garey, M.R. and Johnson, D.S., *Computers and Intractability: A Guide to the Theory of NP-Completeness* (W.H. Freeman and Co., San Francisco, 1979).

Gaschnig, J., "Performance measurements and analysis of certain search algorithms", Ph.D. Thesis, Carnegie-Mellon University, Dept. of Computer Science, May 1979.

Geller, J., "A theoretical foundation for massively parallel knowledge representation", *Parallel Comput. News*, Northeast Parallel Architectures Center, Syracuse University 1991, pp. 4-8.

GenRad Fareham Ltd., *HILO-3 User manual* Jun. 1987.

Genrich, H. and Lautenbach, K., "Facts in place/transition-nets", *Proc. 7th Symp. on Mathematical Foundations of Computer Science*, Lecture Notes in Computer Science, vol. 64 (Springer-Verlag, Berlin, 1978) pp. 213-231.

Genrich, H. and Stankiewicz-Wiechno, E., *A Dictionary of Some Basic Notions of Net Theory,* Lecture Notes in Computer Science (Springer-Verlag, Berlin, 1980).

Gevarter, W.B., *Intelligent Machines: An Introductory Perspective of Artificial Intelligence and Robotics* (Prentice Hall, 1985).

Ghosh, S., "Some comments on timed Petri nets", *AFCET Journees sur les Reseaux de Petri (AFCET Workshop on Petri Nets)*, Paris, France, Mar. 1977, pp. 213-226.

Gimarc, C.E. and Milutinovic, V.M., "A survey of RISC processors and computers of the mid-1980s", *Computer* **20** (1987) 59-69.

Gindi, G.R., Gmitro, A.F. and Parthasarathy, K., "Hopfield model associative memory with nonzero-diagonal terms in memory matrix", *Appl. Opt.* **27** (1988).

Ginsburg, S. and Ullian, J.S., "Preservation of unambiguity and inherent ambiguity in context-free languages", *J. ACM* **13** (1966) 364-368.

Goldberg, A., Purdom, P.W. and Brown C. A., "Average time analysis of simplified Davis-Putnam procedures", *Inf. Process. Lett.* **15** (1982) 72-75.

Goldberg, D.E., "Sizing populations for serial and parallel genetic algorithms", *Proc. 3rd Int. Conf. on Genetic Algorithms*, Fairfax, VA, 1989, pp. 70-79.

Goldberg, D.E., *Genetic Algorithms in Search, Optimization, and Machine Learning* (Addison-Wesley, Reading, 1989).

Gonzalez, R.C. and Thomason, M.G., *Syntactic Pattern Recognition: An Introduction* (Addison-Wesley, Reading, MA, 1978).

Goodman, S.E. and Hedetniemi, S.T., *Introduction to the Design and Analysis of Algorithms* (McGraw-Hill Book Co., New York, 1977).

Good, I.J., *The Estimation of Probabilities - An Essay in Modern Bayesian Methods*, Research Monograph No. 38 (MIT Press Cambridge, MA).

Goshtasby, A. and Ehrich, R.W., "Contextual word recognition using probabilistic relaxation labeling", *Pattern Recogn.* **21** (1988) 455-462.

Gostelow, K., "Computation modules and Petri nets", *Proc. 3rd IEEE-ACM Milwaukee Symp. on Automatic Computation and Control*, New York, Apr. 1975, pp. 345-353.

Gouzenes, L., "Strategies for solving collision-free trajectories problems for mobile and manipulator robots", *Int. J. Robot. Res.* **3** (1984) 51-65.

Govindaraju, V., Lam, S.W., Niyogi, D., Sher, D.B., Srihari, R., Srihari, S.N. and Wang, D., "Newspaper image understanding", *Knowledge Based Computers Systems*, S. Ramani, R. Chadrasekhar and K.S.R. Anjaneyulu, eds., Lecture Notes in Artificial Intelligence (Springer-Verlag, 1990).

Gowrishankar, T.R. *et al.* "Specification for the development of a knowledge-based image-interpretation system" *Eng. Appl. Artif. Intell.* **3** (1990) 79-90.

Graham, S.L., Harrison, M.A. and Ruzzo, W.L., "An improved context-free recognizer", *ACM Trans. Program. Lang. Syst.* **2**, 3 (1980) 415-462.

Green, C.C., "Application of theorem-proving to problem solving", *Proc. 1st Int. Joint Conf. on Artificial Intelligence (IJCAI)*, Washington, DC, 1969, pp. 219-239.

Greene, D. and Smith, S., "A genetic consumer system for learning models of consumer choice", *Proc. 2nd Int. Conf. on Genetic Algorithms*, 1987, pp. 217-223.

Grefenstette, J.J., "Incorporating problem specific information in genetic algorithms", in *Genetic Algorithms and Simulated Annealing*, L. Davis, ed. (Morgan Kaufmann, San Mateo, CA, 1987) pp. 42-60.

Grefenstette, J.J., Gopal, R., Rosmaita, B. and Van Gucht, D., "Genetic algorithms for the traveling salesman problem", *Proc. 1st Int. Conf. on Genetic Algorithms*, Boston, 1985, pp. 160-165.

Greiner, R. and Genesereth, M., "What's new? A semantic definition of novelty", *Proc Int. Joint Conf. on Artificial Intelligence (IJCAI)*, 1983, Karlsruhe, pp. 450-454.

Grossberg, S., "Neural network research: From a personal perspective", *Electronic Engineering Times*, Mar. (1988) A12-A40.

Grosz, B. and Sidner, C., "The structure of discourse structure", CSLI Rep. No. CSLI-85-39, 1985.

Grosz, B. and Sidner, C., "Plans for discourse", *Intentions in Communication*, Cohen, Morgan and Pollack, eds. (MIT Press, Cambridge, MA, 1990).

Grosz, B.J., Jones, K.S. and Webber, B.L., *Readings in Natural Language Processing* (Morgan Kaufmann, Los Altos, California, 1986).

Gu, J., "Parallel algorithms and architectures for very fast search", Tech. Rep. UCCS-TR-88-005, Jul. 1988.

Gu, J., "How to solve very large-scale satisfiability (VLSS) problems", 1988; (Present in part in, J. Gu, "Benchmarking SAT algorithms", Tech. Rep. UCECE-TR-90-002, Oct. 1990).

Gu, J., "Efficient local search for very large-scale satisfiability problem", *SIGART Bull.* **3** (1992) 8-12.

Gu, J., *Constraint-Based Search: Algorithms and Architectures* (Cambridge University Press, New York, 1992).

Gu, J. and Gu, Q.P., "Average time complexities of several quantitative local search algorithms for the satisfiability problem", submitted for publication, Nov. 1991.

Gu, J. and Huang, X., "Implementation and performance of the SAT14 algorithm", submitted for publication, Feb. 1991.

Gu, J. and Wang, W., "DRA VLSI architectures", 1986; (Present in part in: J. Gu, W. Wang and T. C. Henderson, "A parallel architecture for discrete relaxation algorithm", *IEEE Trans. Pattern Anal. Mach. Intell.* **9** (1987) 816-831.

Gu, J. and Wang, W., "A novel discrete relaxation architecture", *IEEE Trans. Pattern Anal. Mach. Intell.* **14** (1992).

Gu, Q.P. and Maruoka, A., "Learning monotone boolean functions by uniformly distributed examples", accepted in *SIAM J. Comput.* to appear in 1992. Haralick, R.M. and Elliot, G., "Increasing tree search efficiency for constraint satisfaction problems", *Artif. Intell.* **14** (1980) 263-313.

Hall, P.A.V. and Dowling, G.R., "Approximate string matching", *ACM Comput. Surv.* **12** (1980) 17-38.

Hallenbeck, J.J., Cybrinski, J.R. *et al.*, "The test engineer's assistant: A support environment for hardware design for testability", *IEEE Comput.* (1989) 59-68.

Halstead, M.H., *Elements of Software Science* (Elsevier-North Holland, New York, 1977).

Hampson, S. and Kibler, D., "A boolean complete neural model of adaptive behavior", *Biol. Cybern.* **49** (1983) 9-19.

Handa, K. *et al.*, "Flexible semantic networks for knowledge representation", *J. Inf. Process* **10** (1986).

Hart, T.P. and Edwards, D.J., "The alpha-beta heuristic", MIT AI Project Memo, MIT, 1963.

Hart, T.P., Nilsson, N.J. and Raphael, B., "A formal basis for the heuristic determination of minimum cost paths", *IEEE Trans. Syst. Man Cybern.* **4** (1968) 100-107.

Haugeland, J., *Mind Design* (MIT Press, 1987).

Havlicsek, B.L., "A knowledge-based diagnostic system for automatic test equipment", *ITC '86 Int. Test Conf. Proc.*, IEEE Computer Society Press, 1986, pp. 930-938.

Hecht-Nielson, R., "Neurocomputing: Picking the human brain", *Spectrum* Mar. (1988) 36-41.

Hendrix, G.G., "Encoding knowledge in partition networks", *Associative Networks*, N.V. Findler, ed. (Academic Press, New York, 1979) pp. 51-92.

Hendrix, G.G., Sacerdoti, E.D., Sagalowicz, D. and Slocum, J., "Developing a natural language interface to complex data", *ACM Trans. Database Syst.* **3**, 2 (1978) 105-147.

Herath, J., Yamaguchi, Y., Saito, N. and Yuba, T., "Dataflow computing models, languages, and machines for intelligence computations", *IEEE Trans. Software Engin.* **14** (1988) 1805-1828.

Hewitt, C., "PLANNER: A language for proving theorems in robots", *Proc. 2nd IJCAL*, 1971.

Higuchi, T., Kitano, H., Handa, K., Furuya, T., Takahashi, H. and Kokubu, A., "IXM2: A parallel associative processor for knowledge processing", *Proc. AAAI-91*, 1991.

Higuchi, T. *et al.*, "A semantic network language machine", *Microcomputers, Usage and Design*, K. Waldschmidt and B. Myhrhaug, eds. (EUROMICRO, 1985) pp. 95-104.

Higuchi, T. *et al.*, "The IX supercomputer for knowledge based systems", *Fall Joint Computer Conf.*, Nov. 1986.

Higuchi, T. *et al.*, "The prototype of a semantic network machine IXM", *IEEE Proc. Int. Conf. on Parallel Processing*, Vol. 1, Aug. 1989, pp. 217-224.

Higuchi, T. *et al.*, "IXM2: A parallel associative processor", *Proc. 18th Annual Int. Symp. on Computer Architecture* ACM SIGARCH, May 1991, pp. 22-32.

Hill, M. *et al.*, "Design decisions in SPUR", *Computer* **19** (1986) 8–22.

Hillis, D.W., "The connection machine: A computer architecture based on cellular automata", *Physica* **10D** (1984) 213-228.

Hillis, D.W., *The Connection Machine* (MIT Press, Cambridge, MA, 1985).

Hillis, D.W., "The connection machine: A computer architecture based on cellular automata", *Tutorial: Computer for Artificial Intelligence Applications* (IEEE Computer Society Press, 1985) pp. 491-506.

Hillis, D., "The connection machine", *Scientific American* June (1987) 108-115.

Ho, T.K., Hull, J.J. and Srihari, S.N., "Combination of structural classifiers", *Pre-Proc. IAPR Syntactic and Structural Pattern Recognition Workshop*, Murray Hill, NJ, 1990, pp. 123-136.

Ho, T.K., Hull, J.J. and Srihari, S.N., "Word recognition with multilevel contextual knowledge", *Proc. 1st. Conf. on Document Analysis and Recognition*, Saint-Malo, France, 1991, pp. 905-915.

Hogger, C.L., "Derivation of logic programs", *JACM* (1982) **28**.

Holland, J.H., *Adaption in Natural and Artificial Systems* (University of Michigan Press, Ann. Arbor, MI, 1975).

Holland, J.H., "Escaping brittleness: The possibilities of general-purpose learning algorithms applied to parallel rule-based systems", *Machine Learning: An Artificial Intelligence Approach*, R. Michalski, J. Carbonell, and T. Mitchell, eds., vol. 2 (Morgan Kaufmann, 1986).

Hooker, J.N., "Resolution versus cutting plane solution of inference problems: Some computational experience", *Operat. Res. Lett.* **7** (1988) 1-7.

Hopcroft, J. and Ullman, J., *Formal Languages and Their Relations to Automata* (Addison-Wesley, Reading, MA, 1969).

Hopcroft, J. and Ullman, J., *Introduction to Automata Theory, Languages and Computation* (Addison-Wesley, Reading, 1979).

Hopfield, J.J., "Collective processing and neural states", *Modeling and Analysis in Biomedicine* (World Scientific, Singapore, 1984).

Hopfield, J.J., "Neural networks and physical systems with emergent collective computational abilities", *Proc. NAS* **79** (1984) 3088-3092.

Hopfield, J.J., "Computing with neural circuits: A model science", **233** (1986) 625-633.

Hopfield, J.J. and Tank, D.W., "Neural computation of decisions in optimization problems", *Biol. Cybern.* **52** (1985) 141-152.

Hovy, E.H., *Generating Natural Language Under Pragmatic Constraints* (Lawrence Erlbaum Associates, 1988).

Hsiang, J., "Refutational theorem proving using term-rewriting systems", *Artif. Intell.* (1985) 255-300.

Hsiang, J. and Rusinowitch, M., "A new method for establishing refutational completeness in theorem proving", *Proc. 8th CADE*, Oxford, LNCS 230 (Springer-Verlag, 1986) pp. 141-152.

Hsiang, J. and Rusinowitch, M., "On word problems in equational theories", *Proc. 14th Int. Colloquium on Automata, Languages and Programming*, Karlsruhe, RFA, LNCS 267 (Springer-Verlag, 1987) pp. 57-71.

Huang, X. and Gu, J., " A quantitative solution for constraint satisfaction", submitted for publication, Mar. 1991.

Huet, G., "Résolution d'équations dans des langages d'ordre 1, 2, ..., ω", Thèse d'Etat, Université de Paris 7, 1976.

Huet, G., "Confluent reductions: Abstract properties and applications to term rewriting systems", *JACM* **27** (1980) 797-821.

Huet, G. and Hullot, J.M., "Proofs by induction in equational theories with constructors", *J. Comput. Syst. Sci.* **25** (1982).

Huet, G. and Oppen, D.C., "Equations and rewrite rules: A survey", *Formal Language Theory: Perspectives and Open Problems*, R.V. Book, ed., (Academic Press, 1980).

Hull, J.J. and Srihari, S.N., "Experiments in text recognition with binary n-gram and Viterbi algorithms", *IEEE Trans. Pattern Anal. Mach. Intell.* **4** (1982) 520-530.

Hull, J.J. and Srihari, S.N., "A computational approach to visual word recognition: Hypothesis generating and test", *IEEE Computer Society Conf. on Computer Vision and Pattern Recognition*, Miami Beach, FL, 1986, pp. 156-161.

Hunt, W.D., *Artificial Intelligence and Expert Systems Sourcebook* (Chapman and Hall, 1986).

Huston, R.L. and Passerello, C.E., "On the dynamics of a human body model", *J. Biomech.* **4** (1971) 369-378.

Hwang, K. *et al.*, "Computer architectures for artificial intelligence processing", *Computer* **20** (1987) 19-27.

Hwang, Y.K. and Ahuja, N., "Path planning using a potential field representation", *Proc. IEEE Int. Conf. on Robotics and Automation*, April 1988, pp. 648-649.

Ibrahim, M.H. and Cummins, F.A., "KSL: A reflective object-oriented programming language", *Proc. Int. Conf. on Computer Languages*, Miami, FL, 1988, pp. 186-193.

IEEE, Special Issue on Knowledge Representation, *Proc. IEEE* **74**, Oct. (1986).

Ingria, R., "The limit of unification", *Proc. ACL-90*, 1990.

Inmos, *IMS T800 Transputer*, 1987.

Irons, E.T., "Syntax graphs and fast context-free parsing", Res. Rep. 71-1, Dept. of Computer Science, Yale University, New Haven, CT, 1971.

Jabri, M.A., "BREL-A PROLOG knowledge-based system shell for VLSI CAD", *Proc., 1990 Design Automation Conf. (DAC)*, IEEE Computer Society Press, 1990, pp. 271-277.

Jackson, P.C. Jr., "Heuristic search algorithms for the satisfiability problem", submitted to 3rd *IEEE TAI Conf.* Jul. 1991.

Janikow, C.C., "Inductive learning of decision rules from attribute-based examples: A knowledge intensive genetic algorithm approach", TR91-030, Doctoral Thesis, Dept. of Computer Science, University of Chapel Hill, North Carolina, 1991.

Jantzen, M., "On the hierarchy of Petri net languages", *RAIRO Theoretical Inf.* **13** (1979) 19-30.

Jelinek, F., "Continuous speech recognition by statistical methods", *Proc. IEEE* **64** (1976).

Jelinek, F., Bahl, L.R. and Mercer, R.L., "Design of a linguistic statistical decoder for the recognition of continuous speech", *IEEE Trans. Inf. Theory* **21** (1975).

Jog, P., Suh, J.Y. and Gucht, D.V., "The effects of population size, heuristic crossover and local improvement on a genetic algorithm for the traveling salesman problem", *Proc. 3rd Int. Conf. on Genetic Algorithms*, Fairfax, VA, 1989, pp. 110-115.

Johnson, D.S., "Local optimization and the traveling salesman problem", *Automata, Languages and Programming*, LNCS, vol. 443, M.S. Paterson, ed., (Springer-Verlag, Berlin, 1990) pp. 446-461.

Johnson, R.A. and Wichern, D.W., *Applied Multivariate Statistical Analysis*, 2nd edn. (Prentice Hall, Englewood Cliffs, NJ, 1988).

Johnson, R.C., "Gated dipoles may be flip-flop of nervous system", *Electronic Engineering Times* Nov. (1987) 49-50.

Johnson, R.C., "Lockhead targets neural nets", *Electronic Engineering Times* Dec. (1987) 51.

Johnson, R.C., "Optics and neural nets: Marriage of convenience", *Electronic Engineering Times* Jan. (1988) 41.

Johnson, S.C., "Yacc: Yet another compiler-compiler", Tech. Rep. 39, Bell Labs., Murray Hill, NJ, 1972.

Johnson, S.C., "YACC - Yet another compiler compiler", CSTR 32, Bell Labs., Murray Hill, NJ, 1975.

Jondral, F., "Automatic classification of high frequency signals", *Signal Process.* **9** (1985) 177.

Jones, M.A., Story, G.A. and Ballard, B.W., "Integrating multiple knowledge sources in a Bayesian OCR Post-Processor", *Proc. 1st Int. Conf. on Document Analysis and Recognition*, Saint-Malo, France, 1991, pp. 925-933.

Jouanaud, J.P. and Kounalis, E., "Automatic proofs by induction in equational theories without constructors", *1986 Proc. 1st IEEE Symp. on Logic in Computer Science*, Full paper in *Informat. Control* **82** (1989) 1-33.

Kaplan, R. and Bresnan, J., "Lexical-functional grammar: A formal system for grammatical representation", *The Mental Representation of Grammatical Relations*, J. Bresnan, ed. (MIT Press, 1982).

Kaplan, R. and Zaenen, A., "Long-distance dependencies, constituent structure, and function uncertainty", 1989.

Kaplan, S., "Simplifying conditional term rewriting systems: Unification, termination, confluence", *J. Symbolic Comput.* 4 (1987) 295-334.

Kapur, D. Narendran, P. and Zhang, H., "On sufficient completeness and related properties of term rewriting systems", *Acta Inf.* **24** (1987) 395-415.

Kapur, D. and Zhang, H., "Mechanizing induction for equational specifications", *Proc. 9th CADE*, Argone, USA, LNCS 310, Springer-Verlag, 1988.

Karp, R. and Miller, R., "Parallel program schemata", RC-2053, IBM T.J. Watson Res. Ctr., Yorktown Heights, New York, Apr. 1968; also, *J. Comput. Syst. Sci.* **3** (1969) 167-195; preliminary draft, *IEEE Conf. 1967 8th Annual Symp. on Switching and Automata Theory*, New York, Oct. 1967, pp. 55-61.

Kasper, R., "Unification and classification: An experiment in information-based parsing", *Proc. Int. Workshop on Parsing Technologies*, Pittsburgh, 1989.

Kay, M., "Algorithm schemata and data structures in syntactic processing", *Proc. Symp. Text Processing*, Nobel Academy, 1980.

Keller, R., "Generalized Petri nets as models for system verification", Tech. Rep. 202, Dept. of Electrical Engineering, Princeton University, Princeton, NJ, Aug. 1975.

Kempen, G. and Hoenkamp, E., "An incremental procedural grammar for sentence formulation", *Cognitive Sci.* **11** (1987) 201-258.

Kent, E.W., Shneier, M.O. and Lumia, R., "PIPE (Pipelined Image-Processing Engine)", *J. Parallel Distributed Comput.* (1985).

Kim, J. and Moldovan, D., "Parallel classification for knowledge representation on SNAP", *Proc. 1990 Int. Conf. on Parallel Processing*, 1990.

Kipps, J.R., "A table-driven approach to fast context-free parsing", RAND Note N-2841-DARPA, RAND Corp., 1988.

Kipps, J.R., "Analysis of Tomita's algorithm for general context-free parsing", *Proc. Int. Workshop on Parsing Technologies*, Pittsburgh, PA, 1989, pp. 193-202.

Kipps, J.R., "RACK: A parser generator for AI languages", *Proc. IEEE Int. Conf. on Tools for AI*, 1990, pp. 430-435.

Kipps, J.R., "The RAND compiler kit (RACK): Reference manual and users guide", RAND Note N-3100-RC, RAND Corp., 1991.

Kipps, J.R., Florman, B. and Sowizral, H.A., "The new ROSIE reference manual and user's guide", RAND Rep. R-3448-DARPA/RC, RAND Corp., 1987.

Kipps, J.R. and Gajski, D.D., "Automating technology adaptation in design synthesis", *Applications of Learning and Planning Methods*, N. G. Bourbakis, ed. (World Scientific, Singapore, 1991).

Kipps, J.R. and Marti, J., "Extracting data from operation orders", RAND Note N-3300-A, RAND Corp., 1991.

Kirkpatrick, S., Gelat, C.D. and Vecchi, M.P., "Optimization by simulated annealing", *Science* **220** (1983) 671-680.

Kita, K., Kwabata, T. and Saito, H., "HMM continuous speech recognition using predictive LR parsing", *Proc. ICASSP – IEEE Int. Conf. on Acoustic, Speech, and Signal Processing*, 1989.

Kitano, H., "Hybrid parallelism: A case of speech-to-speech dialog translation", *Proc. IJCAI-89 Workshop on Parallel Algorithms for Machine Intelligence*, 1989(c).

Kitano, H., "Φ DMDIALOG: An experimental speech-to-speech dialogue translation system", *IEEE Comput.* June 1991(a).

Kitano, H., "Unification algorithm for massively parallel computers", *Proc. Int. Workshop on Parsing Technologies*, Cancun, 1991(b).

Kitano, H., Tomabechi, H. and Kevin, L., "Ambiguity resolution in DMTRANS PLUS", *Proc. 4th Conf. European Chapter of the Association for Computational Linguistics*, 1989.

Klein, C.A. and Kittivacharapong, S., "Optimal force distribution for the legs of a walking machine with friction constraints", *IEEE Trans. Robot. Autom.* **6** (1990) 73-85.

Knuth, D.E., "On the translation of languages from left to right", *Inf. Control* **8** (1965) 607-639.

Knuth, D. and Bendix, P., "Simple word problems in universal algebras", in *Computational Problems in Abstract Algebra*, 1970, pp. 263-297.

Kodratoff, Y., "Generalizing and particularizing as techniques learning", *Comput. Artif. Intell.* **2** (1983) 417-441.

Kodratoff, Y. and Ganascia, J.G., "Improving the generalization step in learning", *Machine Learning: An Artificial Intelligence Approach*, vol. 2 (Morgan Kaufmann, 1986) pp. 215-244.

Kodratoff, Y., *Introduction to Machine Learning* (Pitman, 1988).

Kodratoff, Y. and Ganascia, J.G., "Careful generalization for concept learning", *Proc. 6th European Conf. on Artificial Intelligence*, 1984, pp. 483-492.

Kohonen, T., "Representation of sensory information in self-organizing feature maps, and relation of these maps to distributed memory networks", *SPIE, Opt. Hybrid Comput.* **634** (1986) 248-259.

Kolen, J.F. and Pollack, J.B., "Backpropagation is sensitive to initial conditions", *Complex Syst.* **4** (1990).

Korf, R.E., "A weak method for learning", *Artif. Intell.* **26** (1985) 35-77.

Korf, R.E., "Depth-first iterative deepening: An optimal admissible tree search", *Artif. Intell.* **27** (1985) 97-109.

Korf, R.E., "Planning as search: A quantitative approach", *Artif. Intell.* **27** (1987) 97-109.

Korf, R.E., *Search: A Survey of Recent Results*, *Exploring Artificial Intelligence*, H.E. Shrobe, ed., chap. 6 (Morgan Kaufmann Pub. Inc., San Mateo, 1988).

Kotov, V., "An algebra for parallelism based on Petri nets", *Proc. 7th Symp. on Mathematical Foundations of Computer Science*, Lecture Notes in Computer Science, Vol. 64 (Springer-Verlag, Berlin, 1978) pp. 39-55.

Kounalis, E., "Completeness in data type specifications", *Proc European Conf. in Computer Algebra (EUROCAL)*, Linz, Austria, LNCS 204 (Springer-Verlag, 1985) pp. 348-362.

Kounalis, E., "A calculus of systems with equality", Mémoire d'Habilitation á Diringer des Recherches en Informatique, Université de Nancy I, 1990(a).

Kounalis, E., "Learning from examples and counter examples with equational background knowledge", *Proc. 2nd IEEE Int. Conf. on Tools for Artificial Intelligence*, Herndon, VA, USA, 1990(b), pp. 254-260.

Kounalis, E., "Pumping lemmas for tree languages generated by rewrite systems", *Proc. 15th Conf. on Mathematical Foundations of Computer Science (MFCS 90)*, Banska Bystrica, LNCS 452 (Springer-Verlag, 1990(c)) pp. 369-378.

Kounalis, E., "Testing for inductive-(Co)-Reducibility in Rewrite Systems", *Proc. 15th Colloquium on Trees in Algebra and Programming (CAAP 90)*, Copenhagen, LNCS 431 (Springer-Verlag, 1990(d)) pp. 221-238.

Kounalis, E. and Rusinowitch, M., "Operational semantics of horn clauses", *Ist CTRS*, Paris, 1987.

Kounalis, E. and Rusinowitch, M., "On the word problem in horn theories", *Proc. 9th CADE*, Argone, USA, LNCS 310, Springer-Verlag, 1988, pp. 347-357.

Kounalis, E. and Rusinowitch, M., "A mechanization of conditional reasoning", *Proc. Ist Int. Symp. on Mathematics and Artificial Intelligence*, Fort Lauderdale, Florida, 1990(a).

Kounalis, E. and Rusinowitch, M., "Mechanizing inductive reasoning", *Proc. 8th Nat. Conf. on Artificial Intelligence (AAAI-90)*, Boston, USA, pp. 240-245; also in the *Bulletin of the European Association of Theoretical Computer Science (EATCS)*, **41**, June 1990(b), pp. 216-226.

Kounalis, E. and Rusinowitch, M., "Discovering new facts in first-order knowledge-based theories", *Proc. 4th Int. Symp. on Knowledge Engineering*, Barcelona, 1990(c), pp. 186-199.

Kounalis, E. and Rusinowitch, M., "A logical basis for learning in robots' worlds", *Proc. 5th Int. Conf. on Applications of Artificial Intelligence in Engineering*, Manufacture and Planning, vol. 2, Boston, USA, 1990(d), pp. 275-288.

Kounalis, E. and Rusinowitch, M., "On word problems in horn theories", *J. Symbolic Comput.* 1991(a).

Kounalis, E. and Rusinowitch, M., "Studies on the ground convergent property of conditional theories", *Proc. 2nd Int. Conf. on Algebraic Methodology of Software Technology*, Iowa City, USA, May 1991(b).

Koutsougeras, C., Barad, H. and Martinez, A., "Neural networks in scene analysis", invited paper, *SPIE Conf.*, Orlando, FL, Apr. 1990.

Koutsougeras, C. and Papachristou, C.A., "Training of a neural network model for pattern classification based on an entropy measure", *Proc. IEEE Int. Conf. on Neural Networks (ICNN '88)*, New York, Jul. 1988.

Koutsougeras, C. and Papachristou, C.A., "A neural network model for discrete mappings", *Proc. IEEE Int. Conf. on Languages for Automation (LFA '88)*, New York, Oct. 1988.

Kowalik, J.S., ed. *Knowledge-Based Problem Solving* (Prentice-Hall, 1986).

Kreutzer, W. and McKenzie B., *Programming for Artificial Intelligence – Methods, Tools and Applications* (Addison-Wesley, New York, 1991).

Kucera, H., "Uses of on-line Lexicons", *Information in Data, 1st Conf. University of Waterloo Center for the New Oxford English Dictionary*, Waterloo, Canada, Nov. 1985, pp. 11-24.

Kumar, V., "Algorithms for constraint satisfaction problems: A survey", Tech. Rep. TR-91-28, Dept. of Computer Science, Univ. of Minnesota, 1991.

Lakshmivarahan, S., *Learning Algorithms Theory and Applications* (Springer-Verlag, New York, 1981).

Lam, S.W., Wang, D. and Srihari, S.N., "Reading newspaper text", *Proc. 10th Int. Conf. on Pattern Recognition*, Atlantic City, NJ, 1990. pp. 703-705.

Lankford, D.S., "Canonical inference", Tech. Rep. ATP-32, University of Texas at Austin, 1975.

Lassez, J.L. Maher, M. and Marriott, K., "Elimination of negation in term algebras", *Proc. 16th Conf. on Mathematical Foundations of Computer Science (MFSCS 91)*, Poland, 1991.

Lassez, J.L. and Mariott, K., "Explicit representation of term defined by counter examples", *J. Autom. Reasoning* **3** (1987) 301-317.

Laur, P. and Campbell, R., "A description of path expression by Petri nets", Tech. Rep. 64, Computing Lab., University of Newcastle upon Tyne, England, May 1974.

Layer, K.D. and Richardson, C., "LISP systems in the 1990s", *Commun. ACM*, Sept. (1991) 48-57.

Lee, C.T., "Critical configuration path planning and knowledge-based task planning for robot systems", Ph.D. Thesis, Purdue University, May 1990.

Lee, K.F., "Large-vocabulary speaker-independent continuous speech recognition: The SPHINX system", Ph.D. Thesis, Carnegie Mellon University, 1988.

Lee, W. and Moldovan, D., "The design of a marker passing architecture for knowledge processing", *Proc. Nat. Conf. on Artificial Intelligence, AAAI-90*, 1990.

Lesk, M.E., "LEX – A lexical analyzer generator", CSTR 39, Bell Labs., Murray Hill, NJ 1975.

Lesk, M.E. and Schmidt, E., "Lex – A lexical analyzer generator", Tech. Rep. 39, Bell Labs., Murray Hill, NJ, 1975.

Levine, D.S., "Neural population modeling and psychology: A review", *Math. Biosci.* **66** (1983) 1-86.

Levine, M.D. and Nazif, A.M., "Rule-based image segmentation: A dynamic control strategy approach", *Comput. Vision Graph. Image Process.* **32** (1985) 104-126.

Levinson, S.E., Rabiner, L.R. and Sondhi, M.M., "An introduction to the application of probabilistic functions of a Markov process to automatic speech recognition", *Bell. Syst. Tech. J.* **62** (1983).

Levy, J., *Game Playing I, II, III* (Springer-Verlag, 1988).

Lin, C. and Moldovan, D., "SNAP: Simulator results", Tech. Rep. PKPL 90-5, University of Southern California, Dept. of EE-Systems, 1990.

Lin, S., "Computer solutions of the traveling salesman problem", *Bell Syst. Tech. J.* **44** (1965) 2245-2269.

Lin, S. and Kernighan, B.W., "An efficient heuristic algorithm for the traveling salesman problem", *Operations Res.* **21** (1973) 498-516.

Lippman, R.P., Gold, B. and Malpass, M.L., "A comparison of hamming and Hopfield neural nets for pattern classification", MIT, TR-769.

Litman, D. and Allen, J., "A plan recognition model for subdialogues in conversation", *Cognitive sci.* **11** (1987) 163-200.

Little, W.A. and Shaw, G.L., "Analytic study of the memory storage capacity of a neural network", *Math. Biosci.* **39** (1978) 281-290.

Lloyd, W., *Foundations of Logic Programming* (Springer-Verlag, 1984).

Loveland, D.W., *Automated Theorem Proving. A Logical Basis* (North-Holland, 1978).

Lovins, J.B., "Development of a stemming algorithm", *Mechan. Translat. Comput. Linguist.* **11** (1968) 11-31.

Lozano-Perez, T., "Spatial planning: A configuration space approach", *IEEE Trans. Comput.* **32** (1983).

Luger, G.F., *Artificial Intelligence and the Design of Expert Systems* (Benjamin/Cummings Pub. Co., 1989).

Mackworth, A.K., "Consistency in networks of relations", *Artif. Intell.* **8** (1977) 99-119.

Mackworth, A.K., "Constraint satisfaction", *Encyclopedia of Artificial Intelligence*, vol. 1 (John Wiley and Sons, 1987) pp. 205-210.

Maher, M., "Complete axiomatizations of the algebras, rational and infinite trees", *Proc. 3rd IEEE Symp. on Logic in Computer Science*, 1988, pp. 348-357.

Manna, Z., "Fixed point induction of programs", in *CACM*, 1970.

Manna, Z. and Deshowitz, M., "Proving termination with multiset ordering", *Commun. ACM* **22** (1979) 465-476.

Manna, Z. and Waldinger, R., "A deductive approach to program synthesis", *ACM Trans. Program. Lang.* **2** (1990).

Manuel, T., "LISP and prolog machines are proliferating", *Electron.* Nov. (1983) 266-271.

Marcus, M.P., *A Theory of Syntactic Recognition for Natural Language* (MIT Press, Cambridge, MA, 1980).

Marquis, P., "Contribution á l'étude des méthodes de construction d'hypothéses en intelligence artificielle", Thèse d'Université de Nancy 1, 1991(a).

Marquis, P., "Extending abduction from propositional to first-order logic", *Proc. Fundamentals of Artificial Intelligence Research (FAIR)*, Bratislava, LNAI 535, Springer-Verlag, 1991(b).

Matsuyama, T., "Expert systems for image processing: Knowledge-based composition of Image analysis processes", *Comput. Vision Graph. Image Process.* **48** (1989) 22-49.

McCarthy, J., "Recursive functions of symbolic expressions and their computation by machine", *Commun. ACM* **7** (1960) 184-195.

McCarthy, J., "History of LISP", *SIGPLAN Not.* **13** (1987) 217-222.

McClelland, J., Rumelhart D. and the PDP Research Group, *Parallel Distributed Processing: Explorations in the Microstructure of Cognition*, Vols. 1 & 2 (MIT Press, 1986).

McClulloch, W. and Pitts, W., "A logical calculus of the ideas immanent in nervous activity", *Bull. Math. Biophys.* **5** (1943) 115-137.

McClulloch, W. and Pitts, W., "How we know universals", *Bull. Math. Biophys.* **9** (1947) 127-147.

McKeown, D.M. Jr., Harvey, W.A. and Wixson, L.E., "Automating knowledge acquisition for aerial image interpretation", *Comput. Vision Graph. Image Process.* **46** (1989) 37-81.

McLean, C.R. and Dyer, C.R., "An analog relaxation processor", *Proc. 5th Int. Conf. on Pattern Recognition*, 1980, pp. 58-60.

Michalski, R.S., "A theory and methodology of inductive learning", *Artif. Intell.* **20** (1983) 111-161.

Michalski, R., "A theory and methodology of inductive learning", *Machine Learning: An Artificial Intelligence Approach*, R. Michalski, J. Carbonell, and Mitchell, T., eds., vol. 1 (Tioga Publishing, 1983).

Michalski, R.S., *Machine Learning: An Artificial intelligence Approach*, vols. 1 & 2 (Springer-Verlag, 1984 & 1986).

Michalski, R., Mozetic, I., Hong, J. and Lavrac, N., "The AQ15 inductive learning system: An overview and experiments", University of Illinois Rep. No. UICDCS-R-86-1260, 1986.

Middleton, T., "Recycling functional test vectors: Techniques and tools for pattern conversion", *ITC '85 Int. Test Conf. Proc.*, IEEE Computer Society Press, 1985, pp. 291-301.

Miller, G., "The magical number seven, plus or minus two: Some limits on our capacity for processing information", *Psychol. Rev.* **63** (1956).

Miller, R., "A comparison of some theoretical models of parallel computation", Rep. RC-4230, IBM T.J. Watson Res. Ctr., Yorktown Heights, New York; also, *IEEE Trans. Comput.* **22** (1973) 710-717.

Minsky, M., "A frame for representing knowledge", *The Psychology of Computer Vision*, P. Winston, ed. (McGraw-Hill, New York, 1975).

Minsky, M., "Artificial intelligence", *Electronic Engineering Times Anniversary Issue* Nov. (1987) A65-A69.

Minsky, M. and Papert, S. *Perceptrons – An Introduction to Computational Geometry*, 2nd edn. (MIT Press, 1969; 1987, 2nd edn.).

Minsky, M. and Papert, S., *Perceptron*, Expanded Edition (MIT Press, 1988).

Minton, S., Johnston, M.D., Philips, A.B. and Laird, P., "Solving large-scale constraint satisfaction and scheduling problems using a heuristic repair method", *Proc. 8th Nat. Conf. on Artificial Intelligence*, Boston, MA, 1990, pp. 17-24.

Mishkoff, H.C., *Understanding Artificial Intelligence*, SAMS, Texas Instruments Learning Center, 1986.

Mitchell, T.M., "Version spaces: An approach to concept learning", Ph.D. Thesis, STAN-CS-78-711, Stanford University, 1978.

Moldovan, D., Lee, W. and Lin C., "SNAP: A Marker-Passing Architecture for Knowledge Processing", Tech. Rep. PKPL 90-1, Dept. of Electrical Engineering Systems, University of Southern California, 1990.

Moldovan, D.L. and Tung, Y.W., "SNAP: A VLSI architecture for artificial intelligence processing", *J. Parallel Distributed Comput.* **2** (1985) 109-131.

Moldovan, D. *et al.*, "Parallel knowledge processing on SNAP", *Int. Conf. on Parallel Processing*, Aug. 1990.

Montana, D.J. and Davis, L., "Training feedforward neural networks using genetic algorithms", *Proc. Int. Joint Conf. on Artificial Intelligence*, 1989, pp. 762-767.

Moon, D.A., "Symbolics architecture", *Computer* **20** (1987) 43-52.

Mooney, R., Shavlik, J., Towell, G. and Gove, A., "An experimental comparison of symbolic and connectionist learning algorithms", *Readings in Machine Learning*, J. Shavlik and T. Dietterich, eds. (Morgan Kaufmann, 1990) pp. 171-176.

Moore, R.C., "Reasoning about knowledge and action", Tech. Rep. 191, SRI International, 1980.

Mori, S., Yamamoto, K. and Yasuda, M., "Research on machine recognition of handprinted characters", *IEEE Trans. Pattern Anal. Mach. Intell.* **6** (1984) 386-405.

Morii, S., Niyada, K., Fujii, S. and Hoshimi, M., "Large vocabulary speaker-independent Japanese speech recognition system", *Proc. ICSSP – IEEE Int. Conf. on Acoustics, Speech, and Signal Processing*, 1985.

Morimoto, T., Iida, H., Kurematsu, A., Shikano, K. and Aizawa, T., "Spoken language translation: Toward realizing an automatic telephone interpretation system", *Proc. InfoJapan – 90*, Tokyo, 1990.

Musser, D.R., "On proving inductive properties of abstract data types", *Proc. 7th POPL Conf.*, Las Vegas, 1980.

Nagao, M., "A framework of a mechanical translation between Japanese and English by analogy principle", *Artificial and Human Intelligence*, A. Elithorn and R. Banerji, eds. (Elsevier Science Pub. B.V., 1984).

Nagao, M., *Machine Translation: How Far Can It Go?* (Oxford, 1989).

Naps, T.L. and Singh, B., *Introduction to Data Structures with PASCAL* (West Pub. Co., St. Paul, 1986).

Nau, D.S. and Reggia, J.A., "Relationship between deductive and abductive inference in knowledge-based diagnostic problem solving", *Proc. 1st Int. Workshop on Expert Database Systems*, San Diego, California, 1986, pp. 549-558.

Nazif, A.M. and Levine, M.D., "Low level image segmentation: An expert system", *IEEE Trans. Pattern Anal. Mach. Intell.* **6** (1984) 555-577.

Newquist III, H., "Will the real AI language please stand up?", *Comput. Lang.* **4** (1987) 58-59.

Nikhil, R.S., "Id reference manual", Computation Structures Group Memo 284, MIT, 1988.

Nirenberg, S., ed., "Knowledge-Based Machine Translation", Center for Machine Translation Project Rep., Carnegie Mellon University, 1989(a).

Ogura, K., Sakano, T., Hosaka, J. and Morimoto, T., "Spoken Language Japanese-English Translation Experimental Systems (SL-TRANS)", TR-I-0102, ATR Interpreting Telephony Research Labs. 1989.

Ogura, T., Yamada, J., Yamada S. and Tanno, M., "A 20-K bit associative memory LSI for artificial intelligence machines", *IEEE J. Solid-State Circuits* **24** (1989).

Ohlander, R., Price, K. and Reddy, D.R., "Picture segmentation using a recursive region splitting method", *Comput. Graph Image Process.* **8** (1978) 313-333.

Oliver, I.M., Smith, D.J. and Holland, J.R.C., "A study of permutation crossover operators on the traveling salesman problem", *Proc. 2nd Int. Conf. on Genetic Algorithms*, Hillsdale, NJ, 1987, pp. 224-230.

Oommen, B.J., "Ergodic learning automata capable of incorporating a priori information", *IEEE Trans. Syst. Man Cybern.* **17**.

Oommen, B.J., Iyengar, S.S., Rao, S.V.N. and Kashyap, R.L., "Robot navigation in unknown terrains using learned visibility graph. Part I: The disjoint convex obstacle case", *Proc. Nat. Conf. on Artificial Intelligence*, Philadelphia, 1986.

Oonuki, M., "Firing probability of neural networks: First-order differential equation", *J. Theor. Biol.* **58** (1976) 59-81.

Otsu, N., "A threshold selection method from gray-level histograms", *IEEE Trans. Syst. Man Cybern.* **9** (1979) 63-66.

Padawitz, P., *Computing in Horn Clause Theories* (Springer-Verlag, 1988).

Palumbo, P.W., Swaminathan, P. and Srihari, S.N., "Document image binarization: Evaluation of algorithms", SPIE Vol. 697, *Applications of Digital Image Processing IX*, 1986, pp. 278-285.

Papadimitriou, C.H. and Steiglitz, K., "On the complexity of local search for the traveling salesman problem", *SIAM J. Comput.* **6** (1977) 76-83.

Papadimitriou, C.H. and Steiglitz, K., *Combinatorial Optimization* (Prentice-Hall, Englewood Cliffs, NJ, 1982).

Pavlidis, T., *Algorithms for Graphics and Image Processing* (Computer Science Press, 1982).

Pearl, J., *Heuristics* (Addison-Wesley, Reading, 1984).

Pereira, F.C.N. and Warren, D.H.D., "Definite clause grammars for language analysis – A survey of the formalism and a comparison with augmented transition networks", *Artif. Intel.* **13** (1980) 231-278.

Peretto, P., "Collective properties of neural networks, a statistical physics approach", *Biol. Cybern.* **50** (1984) 51-62.

Peretto, P. and Niez, J.J., "Stochastic dynamics of neural networks", *IEEE Trans. Syst. Man Cybern.* **16** (1986).

Peterson, G.E., "A technique for establishing completeness results in theorem proving with equality", *SIAM J. Comput.* **12** (1983) 82-100.

Peterson, J., *Petri Net Theory and the Modeling of Systems* (Prentice Hall, 1981).

Petri, C., "General net theory", *Proc. Joint IBM/University of Newcastle upon Tyne Seminar on Computing System Design*, Computing Laboratory, University of Newcastle upon Tyne, Newcastle upon Tyne, England, Sept. 1976, pp. 131-169.

Plaisted, D., "Semantic confluence tests and completion methods", *Inf. Control* **65** (1985) 182-215.

Pleskun, A.R. and Thashuthaveetil, M.J., "The architecture of LISP machines", *Computer* **20** (1987) 35-44.

Plotkin, G.D., "A note on inductive generalization", *Mach. Intell.* **5** (1970) 153-163.

Plotkin, G.D., "A further note on inductive generalization", *Mach. Intell.* **6** (1971) 101-124.

Pohl, I., *Bi-directional Search – Machine Intelligence*, B. Meltzer and D. Michie, eds. (Elsevier, New York, 1971) pp. 127-140.

Pollard, C. and Sag, I., *Information-Based Syntax and Semantics*, Vol. 1, CSLI Lecture Notes, 13, 1987.

Polya, G., *How to Solve It* (Princeton University Press, Princeton, 1945).

Poole, D., "Representing knowledge for logic-based diagnosis", *Proc. 5th Generation Computer Systems Conf.* Tokyo, 1988, pp. 1282-1290.

Poole, D., "Normality and Faults in Logic-Based Diagnosis", *Proc. 11th Int. Joint Conf. on Artificial Intelligence (IJCAI)*, Detroit, Michigan, 1989, pp. 1304-1310.

Pople, H.E. Jr., "On the mechanization of abductive logic", *Proc. 3rd Int. Joint Conf. on Artificial Intelligence (IJCAI)*, Stanford, California, 1973, pp. 147-152.

Prather, P. and Swinney, D., "Lexical processing and ambiguity resolution: An autonomous processing in an interactive box", *Lexical Ambiguity Resolution*, S. Small *et al.* eds. (Morgan Kaufmann, 1988).

Prieto-Diaz, R., "A software classification scheme", Ph.D. Thesis, Dept. ICS, University of California, Irvine, 1985.

Prokter, G., "The logic simulator-tester link: It's a two-way street", *ITC '87 Int. Test Conf. Proc.*, IEEE Computer Society Press, 1987, pp. 254-260.

Prussak, M. and Hull, J.J., "A multilevel pattern matching method for text image parsing", *Proc. 7th IEEE Conf. on Artificial Intelligence Applications*, Miami, FL, 1991.

Przymusinski, T., "On the declarative semantics of stratified deductive databases and logic programs", 1987.

Purdom, P.W., "Search rearrangement backtracking and polynomial average time", *Artif. Intell.* **21** (1983) 117-133.

Purdom, P.W. and Brown, C.A., "An analysis of backtracking with search rearrangement", *SIAM J. Comput.* **12** (1983) 717-733.

Pylyshyn, Z., *Computing and Cognition* (MIT Press, 1986).

Quillian, M.R., "Semantic memory", *Semantic Information Processing*, M. Minsky, ed. (MIT Press, Cambridge, MA, 1968) pp. 216-270.

Quinlan, J.R., "Learning efficient classification procedures and their application to chess end games", *Machine Learning*, Vol. 1., R.S. Michalski, J.G. Carbonell and T.M. Mitchell, eds. (Tioga Pub. Co., CA, 1983).

Quinlan, J.R., "Induction of decision trees", *Machine Learning* **1** (1986) 1.

Quinlan, J.R., "Documentation and User's Guide for C4.5", unpublished, 1989.

Rémy, J.L., "Etude des Systèmes de Réécriture conditionnels et application aux types abstraits algébriques", Thèse d'Etat, Institut National Polytechnique de Lorraine, 1982.

Rémy J.L. and Zhang, H., "Contextual rewriting", *Proc. Rewriting techniques and Applications*, LNCS 202 (Springer-Verlag, 1985) pp. 46-62.

Rabiner, L.R., "A tutorial on hidden Markov models and selected applications in speech recognition", *Proc. IEEE* **77** (1989) 257-286.

Rabiner, L.R., Levinson, S.E. and Sondhi, M.M., "On the application of vector quantization and hidden Markov models to speaker-independent, isolated word recognition", *Bell Syst. Tech. J.* **62**, 4 (1983).

Raiman, O., "Diagnosis as a trial: The alibi principle", *Proc. IBM Workshop on Model-Based Diagnosis*, Paris, 1989, pp. 1-10.

Raiman, O., "A circumscribed diagnosis engine", *Proc. Int. Workshop on Expert Systems in Engineering*, Vienna, LNAI 462, Springer-Verlag, 1990, pp. 90-101.

Raphael, B., "A computer program for semantic information retrieval", *Semantic Information Processing*, M. Minsky, ed. (MIT Press, Cambridge, MA, 1968).

Reddy, U., "Rewriting techniques for program synthesis", *Proc. 3rd Int. Conf. on Rewriting Techniques and Applications*, Chapel Hill, USA, LNCS 355 (Springer-Verlag, 1989).

Reddy, U., "Term rewriting induction", *Proc. 10th CADE*, 1990.

Reggia, J.A., Nau, D.S. and Wang, P.Y., "A formal model of diagnostic inference", *Inf. Sci.* **37** (1985) 227-285.

Reintjes, P.B., "AUNT: A universal netlist translator", *Proc. 1987 Symp. on Logic Programming*, IEEE Computer Society Press, 1987, pp. 508-515.

Reiter, R., "A theory of diagnosis from first-principles", *Artif. Intell.* **32** (1987) 57-95.

Rendell, L., "Genetic plans and the probabilistic learning system: Synthesis and results", *Proc. 1st Int. Conf. on Genetic Algorithms and their Applications*, 1985, pp. 60-73.

Rendell, L., Cho, H. and Seshu, R., "Improving the design of similarity-based rule-learning systems", *Int. J. Expert Syst.* **2** (1989) 1.

Requicha, A.A.G., "Representations for rigid solid: Theory, methods, and systems", *ACM Comput. Surv.* **12** (1980) 437-463.

Reynolds, R.G., Maletic, J.L. and Porvin, S., "PM: A system to support acquisition of programming knowledge", *IEEE Trans. Knowl. Eng. Data Eng.* Sept (1990).

Rich, E., *Artificial Intelligence* (McGraw-Hill Book Co., New York, 1983).

Riddle, W., "The equivalence of Petri nets and message transmission models", SRM/97, Computing Lab., University of Newcastle upon Tyne, England, Aug. 1974.

Rieger, C. and Small, S., "Word expert parsing", Proc. 6th Int. Joint. Conf. on Artificial Intelligence, 1979, pp. 723-728.

Riesbeck, C. and Martin, C., "Direct memory access parsing", Yale University Rep. 354, 1985.

Riesbeck, C. and Martin, C., "Direct memory access parsing", *Experience, Memory, and Reasoning* (Lawrence Erlbaum Associates, 1986).

Riesbeck, C. and Schank, R., *Inside Case-Based Reasoning* (Lawrence Erlbaum Associates, 1989).

Ringland, G.A., *Approaches to Knowledge Representation: An Introduction*, G.A. Ringland and Duce, D.A., eds. (John Wiley and Sons Inc., New York, 1988).

Riseman, E.M. and Ehrich, R.W., "Contextual word recognition using binary diagrams", *IEEE Trans. Comput.* **20** (1971) 397-403.

Robinson, J.A., "A machine-oriented logic based on the resolution principle", *JACM* **12** (1965) 23-41.

Rolston, D.W., *Principles of Artificial Intelligence and Expert Systems Development* (McGraw-Hill Book Co., New York, 1988).

Rosenblatt, F., "The Perceptron: A probabilistic model for information storage and organization in the brain", *Psych. Rev.* **65** (1958) 386-408.

Rosenblatt, F., *Principles of Neurodynamics: Perceptrons and the Theory of Brain Mechanism* (Spartan Books, Washington DC, 1961).

Rosenblatt, F., *Principles of Neurodynamics* (Spartan Books, New York, 1962).

Rosenblatt, F., "A comparison of several perceptron models", *Self-Organizing Systems* (1962 edn).

Rosenfeld, A., Hummel, R.A., and Zucker, S.W., "Scene labeling by relaxation operations", *IEEE Trans. Syst. Man Cybern.* **SMC-6** (1976) 420-433.

Rumelhart, D.E., Hinton, G.E. and Williams, R.J., "Learning internal representations by error propagation", *Parallel Distributed Processing: Explorations in the Microstructure of Cognition Foundations*, Vol. 1, D.E. Rumelhart and J.L. McClelland, eds. (MIT Press, Cambridge, MA, 1986).

Rusinowitch, M., *Démonstration automatique – Techniques de réécriture* (InterEditions, 1989).

Rusinowitch, M., "Theorem proving with resolution and superposition", *J. Symbolic Comput.* **11** (1990) 21-49.

Saab, Y.G. and Rao, V.B., "Combinatorial optimization by stochastic evolution", *IEEE Trans. CAD* **10** (1991) 525-535.

Sacerdoti, E.D., "Planning in a hierarchy of abstraction spaces", *Artif. Intell.* **5** (1974) 115-135.

Sacerdoti, E.D., *A Structure for Plans and Behavior* (Elsevier, NY, 1977).

Sacerdoti, E.D., "The Copernican view of artificial intelligence", *Sun Technol.* **2** (1989) 46-52.

Saito, H. and Tomita, M., "Parsing noisy sentences", *Proc. COLING-88*, 1988. Sato, S. and Nagao, M., "Toward memory-based translation", *Proc. COLING-90*, 1990.

Salomaa, A., *Formal Languages* (Academic Press, New York, 1973).

Samuel, A., "Some studies in machine learning using the game of checkers", *IBM J. Res. Develop.* **3** (1959) 210-223.

Schank, R.C., *Conceptual Information Processing* (North Holland, Amsterdam, 1975).

Schank, R., *Dynamic Memory: A Theory of Learning in Computer and People* (Cambridge University Press, 1982).

Schank, R.C. and Abelson, R.P., *Scripts, Plans, Goals, and Understanding* (Erlbaum, Hillsdale, NJ, 1977).

Schuermann, J., "A multifont word recognition system for postal address reading", *IEEE Trans. Comput.* **27** (1978) 721-732.

Schutzer, D., *Artificial Intelligence: An Applications-Oriented Approach* (Van Nostrand Reinhold Co. Inc., New York, 1987).

Schwartz, D.C., "The LISP machine architecture", *GDI Technology Assessment and Management of Artificial Intelligences Towards Practical Applications*, T. Bernold and A. Gunter, eds. (Elsevier Science Pub., 1985).

Schwartz, J.T. and Sharir, M., "On the piano movers' problem: I. The special case of a rigid polygonal body moving amidst polygonal barriers", *Commun. Pure Appl. Math.* **36** (1983) 345-398.

Schwartz, J.T. and Sharir, M., "On the piano movers' problem: III. Coordinating the motion of several independent bodies: The special case of circular bodies moving amidst polygonal barriers", *Int. J. Robot. Res.* **2** (1983) 46-75.

Schwartz, J.T. and Yap, C.K., *Advances in Robotics* (Lawrence Erlbaum Associates, Hillsdale, New Jersey, 1987).

Schwartzschild, B.M., "Statistical mechanics algorithm for Monte Carlo optimization", *Physics Today* **35** (1982) 17-19.

Scofield, C.L., "Learning internal representations in the Coulomb energy network", *Proc. IEEE Int. Conf. on Neural Networks (ICNN '88)*, New York, Jul. 1988.

SDA Systems, Inc., *SDA Language Reference Manual, Version 2.0*, 1988.

Selman, A., "Completeness of calculi for axiomatically defined classes of algebra", *Algebra Universalis* **2** (1971) 20-32.

Shannon, C.E., "Programming a computer for playing chess", *Philos. Mag.* **41** (1950) 256-275.

Shapiro, E., *Algorithmic Program Debugging* (MIT Press, Cambridge, 1983).

Shastri, L., *Semantic Networks: An Evidential Formalization and its Connectionist Realization* (Morgan Kaufmann Pub. Inc., Los Altos, CA, 1988).

Shensa, M.J., "A computational structure for the propositional calculus", *Proc. IJCAI*, 1989, pp. 384-388.

Sidner, C., "Towards a computational theory of definite anaphora comprehension in English discourse", Ph.D. Thesis, Artificial Intelligence Lab. MIT, 1979.

Siedlecki, W. and Sklansky, J., "A note on genetic algorithms for largescale feature selection", *Pattern Recogn. Lett.* **10** (1989) 335-347.

Siegel, P., "Representation et utilization de la connaissances en calcul propositionel", Ph.D. Thesis, University Aix-Marseille II, 1987.

Sifakis, J., "Homomorphisms of Petri nets: Application to the realization of fault-tolerant systems", Tech. Rep. 90, Institute of Applied Mathematics and Computer Science, Grenoble, France, Nov. 1977.

Simmons, R.F., "Semantic networks: Their computation and use for understanding English sentences", *Computer Models of Thought and Language*, R.C. Schank and K.M. Colby, eds. (Freeman, San Francisco, 1973).

Simon, H., *The Science of the Artificial* (MIT Press, Cambridge, MA, 1967).

Singer, H., "A developmental model of speed reading in grades three through six", *Theoretical Models and Processes of Reading*, H. Singer and R. R. Ruddell, eds. (International Reading Association, Newark, DE, 1970).

Singh, J.S. and Wagh, M.D., "Robot path planning using intersecting convex shapes: Analysis and simulation", *IEEE J. Robot. Autom.* **3** (1987) 101-108.

Slate, D.J. and Atkin, L.R., "CHESS 4.5 – The Northwestern University Chess Program", *Chess Skill in Man and Machine*, P.W. Frey, ed. (Springer-Verlag, New York, 1977).

Small, S., "Viewing word expert parsing as linguistic theory", *Proc. Int. Joint. Conf. on Artificial Intelligence*, 1981, pp. 70-76.

Small, S. *et al.* eds., *Lexical Ambiguity Resolution* (Morgan Kaufmann, 1988).

Smith, D., "A survey of synthesis of LISP programs from examples", *Proc. Int. Workshop on Program Construction*, Bonas, 1980.

Smith, D., "Derived preconditions and their uses in program synthesis", *Proc. 6th CADE*, New York, 1982.

Smith, K., "New computer breed uses transputers for parallel processing", *Electron.*, Feb. (1983).

Smith, S.F., "Flexible learning of problem solving heuristics through adaptive search", *Proc. 8th Int. Joint Conf. on Artificial Intelligence*, 1983, pp. 422-425.

Sosič, R. and Gu, J., "How to search for million queens", Tech. Rep. UUCS-Tr-88-008, Dept. of Computer Science, University of Utah, Feb. 1988.

Sosič, R. and Gu, J., "A polynomial time algorithm for the n-queens problem", *SIGART Bull.* **1** (1990) 7-11.

Sosič, R. and Gu, J., "3,000,000 queens in less than one minute", *SIGART Bull.* **2** (1991) 22-24.

Sosič, R. and Gu, J., "Fast search algorithms fir the n-queens problem", *IEEE Trans. Syst. Man Cybern.* **21** (1991).

Sosič, R. and Gu. J., "Efficient local search with conflict minimization", *IEEE Trans. Knowl. Data Engin.* (1992).

Sowa, J.F., ed., *Formal Aspects of Semantic Networks* (Morgan Kaufmann Publishers, Inc., Los Altos, CA, 1991).

Spears, W.M., "Using neural networks and genetic algorithms as heuristics for NP-complete problems", Master's Thesis, Computer Science Dept., George Mason University, 1990.

Spears, W.M. and Gordon, D.F., "Adaptive strategy selection for concept learning", *Multistrategy Learning (MSL-91) Workshop*, 1991, pp. 231-246.

Srihari, R.K., "Extracting visual information from text: Using captions to label human faces in newspaper photographs", Ph.D. Thesis, Dept. of Computer Science, SUNY at Buffalo, 1990.

Srihari, S.N., "Document image understanding", *Proc. ACM- IEEE Fall Joint Computer Conf.* Dallas, TX, 1986, pp. 87-96.

Stanfill, C., "Memory-based reasoning: Reasoning applied to English pronunciation", *Proc. AAAI-88*, 1988.

Stanfill, C. and Waltz, D., "Toward memory-based reasoning", *Commun. ACM*, 1986.

Stanfill, C. and Waltz, D., "The memory-based reasoning paradigm", *Proc. Case-Based Reasoning Workshop*, DARPA, 1988.

Stanfill, G. and Kahle, B., "Parallel free-text search on the connection machine system", *Commun. ACM* **29** (1986).

Stansfield, S.A., "ANGY: A rule-based expert system for automatic segmentation of coronary vessels from digital subtracted angiograms", *IEEE Trans. Pattern Anal. Mach. Intell.* **8** (1986) 188-199.

Steenkiste, P. and Hennessy, J., "Lisp on a reduced-instruction-set processor: characterization and optimization", *Computer* **21** (1988) 34-45.

Sterling, L. and Shapiro, E., *The Art of Prolog: Advanced Programming Techniques* (MIT Press, 1986).

Stockwell, R.P., Schachter, P. and Partee, B.H., *The Major Syntactic Structures of English* (Holt, Rinehart and Winston, New York, 1973).

Stone, H.S. and Stone, J.M., "Efficient search techniques – An empirical study of the *n*-queens problem", *IBM J. Res. Develop.* **31** (1987) 464-474.

Suen, C.Y., "*N*-gram statistics for natural language understanding and text processing", *IEEE Trans. Pattern Anal. Mach. Intell.* **1** (1979) 164-172.

Suh, S.H. and Shin, K.G., "A variational dynamic programming approach to robot-path planning with a distance-safety criterion", *IEEE J. Robot. Autom.* **4** (1988).

Sumita, E., Iida, H. and Kohyama, H., "Example-based approach in machine translation", *Proc. InfoJapan-90*, 1990.

Tanaka, H. and Numazaki, H., "Parallel generalization LR parsing based on logic programming", *Proc. 1st Int. Workshop on Parsing Technologies*, Pittsburgh, 1989.

Tang, Y.Y., Suen, C.Y. and Cheriet, M., "Document analysis and understanding: A brief survey", *Proc. 1st Conf. on Document Analysis and Recognition*, Saint-Malo, France, 1991, pp. 17-31.

Tanimoto, S.L., *The Elements of Artificial Intelligence* (Computer Science Press, 1990).

Tank, D. and Hopfield, J., "Collective computation in neuronlike circuits", *Scientific American* Dec. (1987) 104-114.

Tarski, A., "Equational logic and equational theories of algebras", *Contribution to Mathematical Logic*, K. Schutte, ed. (North-Holland, 1968).

Tate, A., "Generating project network", *Proc. Int. Joint Conf. on Artificial Intelligence*, 1977, pp. 888-893.

Taylor, "Equational logic", *Universal Algebra*, G. Grätzer, ed., 1979, pp. 378-400.

Taylor, D., "Languages past, present and future", *Comput. Lang.* **4** (1987) 57-62.

Tecuci, G., "A multistrategy learning approach to domain modeling and knowledge acquisition", *Lecture Notes in Artificial Intelligence*, J. Siekmann, ed. (Springer-Verlag, 1991).

Teisher, J., "Improved workstation/tester interface is the key to the quality of test-program generation", *ITC '86 Int. Test Conf. Proc.*, IEEE Computer Society Press, 1986, pp. 626-630.

Thinking Machine Corporation, "Model CM-2 Technical Summary", Tech. Rep. TR89-1, 1989.

Tomabechi, H., "Direct memory access translation", *Proc. Int. Joint. Conf. on Artificial Intelligence (IJCAI-87)*, 1987.

Tomabechi, H., Saito, H. and Tomita, M., "SpeechTrans: An experimental real-time speech-to-speech translation", *Proc. 1989 Spring Symp. of the American Association for Artificial Intelligence*, 1989.

Tomita, M., "An efficient context-free parsing algorithm for natural languages and its applications", Ph.D. Thesis, Computer Science Dept., Carnegie Mellon University, Pittsburgh, PA, 1985.

Tomita, M., "An efficient context-free parsing algorithm for natural languages", *Proc. 9th Int. Conf. on Artificial Intelligence*, 1985, pp. 756-763.

Tomita, M., *Efficient Parsing for Natural Language* (Kluwer Academic Publishers, 1986).

Tomita, M. and Carbonell, J.G., "The universal parser architecture for knowledge-based machine translation", *Proc. Int. Joint Conf. on Artificial Intelligence (IJCAI-87)*, 1987.

Torrero, E., *Next Generation Computers* (IEEE Press, 1985) pp. 94-99.

Toulousi, G., "Neural networks", *Nature* **327**, June (1987) 662.

Touretsky, D.S., *The Mathematics of Inheritance Systems* (Morgan Kaufmann Pub. Inc., Los Altos, CA, 1986).

Tournassoud, P., "A strategy for obstacle avoidance and its application to multi-robot systems", *Proc. IEEE Int. Conf. on Robotics and Automation*, San Francisco, CA, 1986, pp. 1124-1229.

Treleaven, P.C., "The new generation of computer architecture", *Proc. 10th Annual Int. Symp. on Computer Architecture*, June 1983, pp. 402-409.

Tremblay, J.P. and Sorenson, P.G., *An Introduction to Data Structures with Applications* (McGraw-Hill Book Co., New York, 1984).

Tsujii, J., "The roles of dictionaries in machine translation", *Jouhou-syori* (*Information Processing*), Information Processing Society of Japan, **26** (1985) (in Japanese).

Tsypkin, Y.Z. and Poznyak, A.S., "Finite learning automata", *Eng. Cybern.* **10** (1972) 478-490.

Tucker, L.W. and Robertson, G.G., "Architecture and applications of the connection machine", *Computer* **21** (1988) 26-38.

Uhr, L., *Multicomputer Architectures for Artificial Intelligence* (John Wiley & Sons, 1987).

Ullman, J.D., *Principles of Database and Knowledge-Base Systems*, Vol. 1 (Computer Science Press, 1988).

Ungar, D. *et al.*, "Architecture of SOAR: Smalltalk on a RISC", *IEEE/ACM Conf. Procs. 11th Annual Int. Symp. on Computer Architecture*, June 1984, pp. 188-197.

Utgoff, P.E., "Improved training via incremental learning", *Proc. 6th Int. Workshop on Machine Learning*, 1989, pp. 62-65.

Valiant, L.G., "A theory of learnable", *Commun. ACM* (1984) 1134-1142.

van Melle, W., Shortliffe, E.H. and Buchanan, B.G., "EMYCIN: A domain-independent system that aids in constructing knowledge-based consultation programs", *Mach. Intell.: Infotech State-of-the-Art* **9** (1981).

Vere, S.A., "Multilevel counterfactuals for generalization of relational concepts and productions", *Artif. Intell.* **14** (1980) 139-164.

Vere, S.A., "Planning in Time: Windows and Patterns for Activities and Goals", *IEEE Trans. Patt. Anal. Mach. Intell.* May (1983) 246-267. Wilkins, D.E., "Domain-independent planning: Representation and plan generation", *Artif. Intell.* **22** (1984) 269-301.

Vernazza, G.L., Serpico, S.B. and Dellepiane, S.G., "A knowledge-based system for biomedical image processing and recognition", *IEEE Trans. Circuits Syst.* **34** (1987) 1399-1416.

Viterbi, A.J., "Error bounds for convolutional codes and an asymptotically optimum decoding algorithm", *IEEE Trans. Inf. Theory* **13** (1967) 260-269.

Von Neumann, J., *Collected Works*, Vol. 5 (Pergamon, New York, 1963) p. 304.

Von Neumann, J., "Programmable synaptic arrays for electronic neural network", NASA Tech. Briefs, Jan. 1988.

Von Neuman, J. and Morgensterm, O., *Theory of Games and Economic Behavior* (Princeton University Press, Princeton, 1944). Nilsson, N.J., *Principles of Artificial Intelligence* (Tioga Pub. Co. Palo Alto, California, 1980).

Wagner, R.A. and Fischer, M.J., "The string to string correction problem", *J. ACM* **21** (1974) 168-173.

Wah, B. and Li, G.-J., eds., *Artificial Intelligence Languages and Programming* (IEEE Computer Society Press, 1985) pp. 57-61.

Wah, B.W. and Li, G.J., "A survey on special purpose computer architectures for AI", *SIGART News* **4** (1986) 28-46.

Wah, B. and Ramamoorthy, C.V., *Computers for Artificial Intelligence Processing* (John Wiley & Sons, 1990).

Waibel, A., Hanazawa, T., Hinton, G., Shikano, K. and Lang, K., "Phoneme recognition using time-delay neural networks", *IEEE Trans. Acoustic, Speech Signal Process.* (1989).

Waldmann, B., "Reductive conditional term rewriting systems", Rapport de DEA, CRIN, Nancy, 1986.

Waltz, D., *Generating Semantic Descriptions from Drawings with Shadows*, Ph.D. Thesis, AI Lab. MIT, 1975.

Waltz, D.L., "Applications of the connection machine", *Computer* **20** (1987) 85-97.

Waltz, D., "Massively parallel AI", *Proc. AAAI-90*, 1990.

Waltz, D.L., and Pollack, J.B., "Massively parallel parsing: A strongly interactive model of natural language interpretation", *Cognitive Sci.* **9** (1985) 51-74.

Wang, C.H. and Srihari, S.N., "A framework for object recognition in a visually complex environment and its application to locating address blocks on mail pieces", *Int. J. Comput. Vision* **2** (1988) 125-152.

Wang, D. and Srihari, S.N., "Classification of newspaper image blocks using texture analysis", *Comput. Vision Graph. Image Process.* **47** (1987) 327-352.

Wang, F., "Cognitive models of software reuse: Extracting procedural knowledge in a multiple pass knowledge compiler", Master's Thesis, Wayne State University, Oct. 1991.

Warren, D.H.D. and Pereira, L.M., "Prolog – the language and its implementation compared to Lisp", *Proc. Symp. on Artificial Intelligence and Programming Languages, SIGPLAN Not.* **12** and *SIGART Newslett.* **64** (1977).

Watson, I. and Gurd, J., "A prototype data flow computer with token labeling", *AFIPS Conf. Proc. Nat. Comput. Conf.*, Jun. 1979.

Watson, I. and Gurd, J., "A practical data flow computer", *Computer* **15** (1982).

Webber, B., "So what can we talk about now?" *Computational Models of Discourse*, M. Brady and R. Berwick, eds. (MIT Press, 1983).

Weiser, M. *et al.*, "Status and performance of the zmob parallel processing system", *Tutorial: Computers for Artificial Intelligence Applications* (IEEE Computer Society Press, 1985) pp. 423-426.

Weste, N. and Eshraghian, K., *Principles of CMOS VLSI Design: A Systems Perspective* (Addison-Wesley, 1985).

White, H.J. and Wright, W.A., "Holographic implementation of a Hopfield model with discrete weightings", *Appl. Opt.* **27** (1988).

Whitley, D., Starkweather, T. and Fuquay, D., "Scheduling problems and traveling salesman: The genetic edge recombination operator", *Proc. 3rd Int. Conf. on Genetic Algorithms*, Fairfax, VA, 1989, pp. 133-140.

Wilensky, R., *Planning and Understanding: A Computational Approach to Human Reasoning* (Addison-Wesley, Reading, MA, 1983).

Williams, M.J.Y. and Angel, J.B., "Enhancing testability of large scale integrated circuits via test points and additional logic", *IEEE Trans. Computers* **22** (1973) 46-60.

Wilson, S.W., "Classifier systems and the animation problem", *Machine Learning* **2** (1987) 4.

Winograd, T., *Understanding Natural Languages* (Academic Press, New York, 1972).

Winograd, T., *Language as a Cognitive Process: Syntax* (Addison-Wesley, Reading, MA, 1983).

Winston, P.H., *Artificial Intelligence* (Addison-Wesley, Reading, MA, 1977).

Winston, P.H., *Artificial Intelligence*, 2nd Ed. (Addison-Wesley, Reading, MA, 1984).

Woods, W.A., "Transition network grammars for natural language analysis", *Commun. ACM* **13** (1970) 591-606.

Wos, L.T. and Robinson, G.A., "Paramodulation and theorem proving in first-order theories with equality", *Mach. Intell.* **4** (1969) 135-150.

Wos, L.T., Robinson, G.A., Carso, D.F. and Shalla, L., "The concept of demodulation in theorem proving", *JACM* **14** (1967).

Wu, D., "A probabilistic approach to marker propagation", *Proc. Int. Joint. Conf. on Artificial Intelligence (IJCAI-89)*, 1989.

Yamaguchi, Y., Sakai, S., Hiraki, K., Kodama, Y. and Yuba, T., "An architectural design of a highly parallel dataflow machine", *Information Processing 89*, G.X. Ritter, ed. (Elsevier Science Publishers B.V., North-Holland, IFIP, 1989).

Yap, C.K., "Coordinating the motion of several discs", Tech. Rep. No. 105, New York University, Computer Science Dept., Courant Institute of Mathematical Sciences, 1984.

Young, S., Ward, W. and Hauptmann, A., "Layering predictions: flexible use of dialog expectation in speech recognition", *Proc. Int. Joint Conf. on Artificial Intelligence (IJCAI-89)*, 1989.

Younger, D.H., "Recognition and parsing of context-free languages in time n^3", *Inf. Control* **10** (1967) 189-208.

Yovits, M.C., Jacobi, G.T. and Goldstein, G.D. (Spartan Books, Washington, DC 1962).

__________, "Stimulus context and absolute magnitude estimation: A study of individual difference", *Perception and psychophysics* **50** (1991).

__________, *Scientific American* **256**, Mar. (1987) pp. 88-95.